Mystics, Philosophers, and Politicians

.

Mystics, Philosophers, and Politicians

Essays in Jewish Intellectual History
in Honor of Alexander Altmann

Edited by Jehuda Reinharz *and* Daniel
Swetschinski, *with the collaboration*
of Kalman P. Bland

Duke Monographs in Medieval and Renaissance Studies number 5
DUKE UNIVERSITY PRESS   Durham, North Carolina 1982

© 1982, Duke University Press
Printed in the United States
of America

Published with the assistance of the Louis and Minna
Epstein Fund of the American Academy for Jewish Research

Library of Congress Cataloging in Publication Data

Main entry under title:

Mystics, philosophers and politicians.

(Duke monographs in medieval and
Renaissance studies; no. 5)
"Bibliography of Alexander Altmann's
writings": p. 343
Includes bibliographical references and
index.
1. Philosophy, Jewish—Addresses, essays,
lectures.   2. Philosophy, Medieval—Addresses, essays, lectures.   3. Mysticism—
Judaism—Addresses, essays, lectures.
4. Jews—France—Identity—Addresses, essays,
lectures.   5. Herzl, Theodor, 1860-1904—Addresses, essays, lectures.   6. Altmann,
Alexander, 1906-   —Addresses, essays,
lectures.   I. Altmann, Alexander, 1906-
II. Reinharz, Jehuda.   III. Swetschinski,
Daniel, 1944-   .   IV. Bland, Kalman P.,
1942-   .   V. Series.
B755.M95   296   81-5540
ISBN 0-8223-0446-5   AACR2

Contents

Acknowledgments

We would like to thank the following individuals for their encouragement and assistance in locating funding for this book: Professor Edward Mahoney, Duke University; Professor Eric Meyers, Duke University; David R. Pokross, Esq., Boston; Dr. Abram L. Sachar, Chancellor Emeritus, Brandeis University; Mr. Harry Starr, President, The Lucius N. Littauer Foundation; Professor David J. Steinberg, Vice President and University Secretary, Brandeis University.

The following scholarly organizations and foundations have contributed generously toward the publication of this volume: the American Academy for Jewish Research; The Cooperative Program in Judaic Studies of Duke University and the University of North Carolina at Chapel Hill; the Leo Wasserman Foundation; and The Lucius N. Littauer Foundation. We are grateful for their support.

Festschriften are notoriously long "in press," and this one is no exception. We thank the authors for updating their footnotes during the galley stage and for their cooperation throughout this joint endeavor. We would also like to thank Amy-Jill Levine for the preparation of the indexes.

Jehuda Reinharz
Daniel Swetschinski

Contributors

Phyllis Cohen Albert, Ph.D. (Brandeis University). Her publications include: *The Modernization of French Jewry: Consistory and Community in the Nineteenth Century* (Hanover, N.H., 1977); *Essays in Modern Jewish History: A Tribute to Ben Halpern* (East Brunswick, N.J. in press); "Le rôle des consistoires israélites au milieu du 19ᵉ siècle," in *Revue des Études Juives*, CXXX (1971); "Non-Orthodox Attitudes in Nineteenth Century French Judaism" (in press). She is a Research Associate of the Center for European Studies, Harvard University, and her current scholarly projects include studies of antisemitism in nineteenth-century France before Dreyfus, French-Jewish responses to antisemitism, and the contemporary French-Jewish community.

Kalman P. Bland, Ph.D. (Brandeis University). Associate Professor of Religion, Duke University. His publications include: *The Epistle on Conjunction with the Active Intellect by Ibn Rushd with the Commentary of Moses Narboni*, a critical edition and annotated translation (New York, 1981); "The Rabbinic Method and Literary Criticism," in K.R.R. Gros Louis (ed.), *Literary Interpretations of Biblical Narratives* (Nashville, 1974); "Neo-Platonic and Gnostic Themes in R. Moses Cordovero's Doctrine of Evil," *Bulletin of the Institute for Jewish Studies*, III (1975).

Lawrence Fine, Ph.D. (Brandeis University). Assistant Professor, Department of Religious Studies, Indiana University. He has published articles and reviews in *Judaism, Midstream, Religious Studies Review* and *Revue des Études Juives*. His translation of sixteenth century mystical texts from Safed will be published by Paulist Press.

Arthur Green, Ph.D. (Brandeis University). Associate Professor of Religious Studies, University of Pennsylvania. His book *Tormented Master: A Life of Rabbi Nahman of Bratslav*, based on his Brandeis doctoral dissertation, was published by University of Alabama Press in 1980 and reissued by Schocken Books in 1981. He has also edited two volumes of Hasidic sources in translation and has written several articles in the history of Jewish mysticism and theology.

Alfred L. Ivry, Ph.D. (Brandeis), D. Phil. (Oxon). Professor of Islamic and Jewish Philosophy, Walter S. Hilborn Professor of Near Eastern and Judaic Studies, Department of Near Eastern and Judaic Studies, Brandeis University. His publications include: *Al-Kindi's Metaphysics* (Albany, 1974); *Moses of Narbonne: Treatise on the Perfection of the Soul* (Jerusalem, 1976). His current scholarly projects are concerned with Averroes's epistemology and its influence upon late medieval Jewish philosophers.

Daniel J. Lasker, Ph.D. (Brandeis University). Lecturer in Jewish Thought, Department of History, Ben Gurion University of the Negev. He has published *Jewish Philosophical Polemics Against Christianity in the Middle Ages* (New York, 1977), and other studies in medieval Jewish philosophy. He is currently working on the philosophy of the Karaites and various aspects of the Jewish prayer for rain.

Allan Lazaroff, Ph.D. (Brandeis University). Associate Professor of Religion, Boston University. Author of "Bahya's Asceticism Against Its Rabbinic and Islamic Background," *Journal of Jewish Studies*, XXI (1970), 11–38, and *The Theology of Abraham Bibago* (University, Ala., 1981). Main scholarly interest is in late medieval Jewish religious philosophy.

Frances Malino, Ph.D. (Brandeis University). Associate Professor, University of Massachusetts (Boston). Her publications include "Mémoires d'un Patriote Proscrit," *Michael IV* (Tel Aviv, 1976); *The Sephardic Jews of Bordeaux: Assimilation and Emancipation in Revolutionary and Napoleonic France* (University, Ala., 1978). She is the coeditor of *Essays in Modern Jewish History: A Tribute to Ben Halpern* (East Brunswick, N.J., in press) and is working on *Jewish Autonomy and Citizenship in Eighteenth-Century France* to be published by SUNY Press.

Paul R. Mendes-Flohr, Ph.D. (Brandeis University). Leeds Lecturer in Comparative Religion and Modern Jewish Thought and director of S. H. Bergman Center for Philosophical Studies, Hebrew University of Jerusalem. He is the author of *Von der Mystik zum Dialog: Martin Bubers geistige Entwicklung bis hin 'Ich und Du'* (Königstein/Ts., 1978) and with Jehuda Reinharz, *The Jew in the Modern World: A Documentary History* (New York, 1980); editor of *A Land of Two Peoples: Martin Buber on Jews and Arabs* (forthcoming), and *The Philosophy of Franz Rosenzweig: Proceedings of the Fourth Jerusalem Philosophical Encounter* (forthcoming).

Barry Mesch, Ph.D. (Brandeis University). Associate Professor of Religion and Director of the Center for Jewish Studies, University of Florida. He has published *Studies in Joseph ibn Caspi* (Leiden, 1975), in *Études sur le Judaisme Medievale*. He is presently working on approaches of medieval Jewish exegesis to the biblical narrative.

Benjamin C. I. Ravid, Ph.D. (Harvard University). Jennie and Mayer Weisman Associate Professor of Jewish History, Department of Near Eastern and Judaic Studies, Brandeis University. Author of *Economics and Toleration in Seventeenth-Century Venice: The Background and Context of the Discorso of Simone Luzzatto* (Jerusalem, 1978). Author of several articles on the Jews of Venice. Editor of *Iyyunim Bemahashevet Yisrael: Hebrew Studies in Jewish Thought by Simon Rawidowicz*, 2 vols. (Jerusalem, 1969–71). He is presently engaged in research on the institution of the ghetto and the history of the Jewish merchants of Venice.

Jehuda Reinharz, Ph.D. (Brandeis University). Professor of History, University of Michigan. Author of *Fatherland or Promised Land; The Dilemma of the German Jew 1893–1914* (Ann Arbor, 1975); Editor of *The Letters and Papers of Chaim Weizmann, 1918–1920* (Oxford and Jerusalem, 1977, and in Hebrew in 1978). Editor of *Dokumente zur Geschichte des Deutschen Zionismus* (Tübingen, 1979); Coeditor with Paul R. Mendes-Flohr of *The Jew in the Modern World: A Documentary History* (New York, 1980). Author of scholarly articles in *Leo Baeck Institute Year Book, Jewish Social Studies, Encyclopaedia Judaica*, and others. He is currently working on a biography of Chaim Weizmann.

Shulamit T. Reinharz, Ph.D. (Brandeis, Sociology). Assistant Professor of Psychology, University of Michigan. Author of *On Becoming a Social Scientist: From Survey Research and Participant Observation to Experiential Analysis* (San Francisco, 1979). Her publications are concerned with community mental health problems in contemporary Israel and the United States, and with innovative strategies of education, work, and research. Her current scholarly project is a study of the quality of life of elderly kibbutz members.

Lawrence H. Schiffman, Ph.D. (Brandeis University). Associate Professor of Hebrew and Judaic Studies, Department of Near Eastern Languages and Literatures, New York University. His publications include: *The Halakhah at Qumran*, Studies in Judaism in Late Antiquity 16 (Leiden, 1975); "A Forty-Two Letter Divine Name in the Aramaic Magic Bowls," *Bulletin of the Institute of Jewish Studies*, I (London, 1973); "The Qumran Law of Testimony," *Revue de Qumran*, VIII, no. 32 (1975); and "The Recall of Rabbi Nehuniah ben Ha-Qanah from Ecstasy in the *Hekhalot Rabbati*," *AJS Review*, I (1976). He is currently working on a book tentatively entitled "Law and Community in the Dead Sea Scrolls: Aspects of the Qumran Legal Tradition," as well as a critical edition of Targum Neofiti to Genesis to be published with a commentary by Bernard Grossfeld.

Daniel Swetschinski, Ph.D. (Brandeis University). Assistant Professor of Jewish History, Department of Oriental Studies, University of Arizona. Specializes in the history of seventeenth-century Sephardic Jewry. Dissertation: "The Portuguese Jewish Merchants of Seventeenth-Century Amsterdam: A Social Profile."

Abbreviations

AJSreview	Association for Jewish Studies Review
DJD	Discoveries in the Judaean Desert
EB	Encyclopaedia Britannica
EI	Ha-Encyclopedia ha-Ivrit
EJ	Encyclopaedia Judaica (1972)
EM	Encyclopedia Miqra'it
HTR	Harvard Theological Review
HUCA	Hebrew Union College Annual
JANES	Journal of Ancient Near Eastern Studies
JBL	Journal of Biblical Literature
JJS	Journal of Jewish Studies
JQR	Jewish Quarterly Review
JSS	Jewish Social Studies
KS	Kiryat Sefer
LBIYB	Leo Baeck Institute Year Book
MGWJ	Monatschrift für Geschichte und Wissenschaft des Judentums
PAAJR	Proceedings of the American Academy for Jewish Research
RB	Revue Biblique
REJ	Revue des Etudes Juives
RMI	Rassegna Mensile di Israel
RQ	Revue de Qumran
VT	Vetus Testamentum

A Note on Transliteration

Since personal style plays an important role in scholarship, the editors retained authors' preferences wherever possible, e.g., A.D. or C.E., *ashkenazi* or *ashkenazic*. Hebrew words commonly used in English, however, are always spelled in their most familiar form: Zaddik, Israel, etc. On the other hand, *antisemitism* was not hyphenated, for it is a coinage *sui generis* and does not denote the *anti* of a separately existing *semitism*.

The editors standardized all Hebrew transliterations, according to the clearest and most economic system, as follows:

'alef	'	*lamed*	*l*
bet, vet	*b, v*	*mem*	*m*
gimmel	*g*	*nun*	*n*
dalet	*d*	*samekh*	*s*
he'	*h*	*'ayin*	*c*
waw	*w*	*pe', fe'*	*p, f*
zayin	*z*	*tzadi*	*tz*
het	*h*	*qof*	*q*
tet	*t*	*resh*	*r*
yod	*y**	*shin, sin*	*sh, s*
kaf, khaf	*k, kh*	*taw*	*t*

*Except at the end of a word.

No distinction was allowed for longer and shorter vowels. Only on few occasions involving highly technical philological discussions, e.g., in the article by Lawrence Schiffman, was it necessary to distinguish between *tet* and *taw*, and *he* and *het*. In these half dozen instances, the editors resorted to the unusual practice of reserving *t* for *taw* and *h* for *he*, and transcribing *h*et for *het* and T*et* for *tet*. Where it was important to transliterate the Hebrew consonontal roots, small caps were used, e.g., T*et*HRM.

The few Arabic transliterations are standard except that diacritical marks were omitted. Long vowels were indicated with a circumflex (^).

Mystics, Philosophers, and Politicians

Alexander Altmann: A Portrait

Daniel Swetschinski

Obviously more than miles separates Kassa, Hungary, from Newton, Massachusetts, and much of what characterizes the great distances between them has formed a part of the man's life that connects them.

This connection cannot be fully explained as the result of a concatenation of accidents or a steadily pursued design. Yet both accident and design, contingencies as well as commitment, are facts of Alexander Altmann's life. They are parts of a multidimensional reality in which fortune spurred the will as often as human resolve discovered new opportunities for itself. To view his life is to enter such a multidimensional reality, whose boundaries stretch from the Austro-Hungarian Empire to a cosmopolitan Germany, to a provincial England, to a suburban America, from a rabbinical student, one engaged in modern philosophy, to a rabbi, a theologian, a scholar, and a professor. We become acquainted (if we have not yet been introduced) with Max Scheler, Moses ben Maimon, Saadya, Franz Rosenzweig, Isaac Israeli, Azriel of Gerona and Eleazar of Worms, Leopold Zunz, Hermann Cohen, Moses Mendelssohn, Moses Narboni, Isaac Aboab da Fonseca, Moses de Leon, and Levi ben Gerson. Alexander Altmann lived in these landscapes, with these philosophers and mystics. He is honored here by his students as a man deeply appreciated by all who have read his work.

However much may have changed over the past seventy years of Altmann's life, one central commitment was there, always and everywhere—his commitment to Judaism. His mother, Malwine, née Weisz, and father, Adolf, a reflective, scholarly rabbi and devoted early Zionist, nurtured him in an intensely religious home. His commitment gained greater depth at the yeshivot of Cologne and Pressburg—the latter the *alma* yeshivah of his father—and ultimately received its final, proud and complex form at the Berlin Rabbiner-Seminar. There he found not a "rabbi factory" (the term is Ezriel Hildesheimer's) but a happily modern, typically German-Jewish environment of learning and devotion; a Rabbiner-Seminar no longer in the process of implementing *Torah-im-Derekh-Eretz*, but solidly established, expressing the twin-reality of Torah-loyal Judaism and modern *Bildung*. Altmann was so much at home in this environment that we are almost inclined to think that he would have wanted to create it had it not existed already. For if he followed the path of so many German scholar-rabbis, he was motivated to do so as much by personal disposition as by educational opportunity. The Friedrich-Wilhelms-Universität of Berlin—where students of the Rabbiner-Seminar simultaneously studied towards an academic degree—was as congenial an environment to the graduate of the Cologne gymnasium as was the rabbinical school. The reflectiveness of his father and the intellectual reverberations of the First World War had left him groping for critical reason, just as personal experience had endeared him to the value of tradition.

During five happy years spent at the Rabbiner-Seminar and the Friederich-Wilhelms Universität (from 1926 to 1931), Joseph Wohlgemuth's sympathetic understanding of modern man's religious perplexity, Jakob Jehiel Weinberg's sensitive approach to the living texture of the Halakhah, Heinrich Maier's logical acuity in dealing with epistemology, and Max Dessoir's insights into contemporary aesthetics and psychology, furnished Altmann with impressive examples of men restlessly at home in the past and in the present. With the roots of familial piety and a classical education firmly embedded within him and with the intellectual provisions of critical reason and contemporary involvement, Altmann embarked on his career.

In rapid succession he became rabbi of the Passauerstrasse Synagogue and of the Jüdische Gemeinde in Berlin; he married Judith Frank, a daughter of a respected physician and Zionist leader and president of the Jewish community of Altona; and was appointed *Dozent* in religious philosophy and homiletics at the Rabbiner-Seminar, as successor to Joseph Wohlgemuth who had fallen seriously ill in 1932.

Altmann's writings of this period are little known today. They are not only in a different language from his later works, they also deal with subjects not immediately related to his subsequent scholarly pursuits. Yet they provide insights into continuous concerns as well as examples of changing foci and styles.

His doctoral dissertation entitled *Die Grundlagen der Wertethik: Wesen, Wert, Person: Max Schelers Erkenntnis- und Seinslehre in kritischer Analyse*—written under the direction of Max Dessoir and honored with a "summa cum laude" and a government subsidy for its publication—seems least related to his later publications. Nonetheless, even though the dissertations of the period mostly follow the routine exigencies of academic tradition, Altmann's dissertation goes beyond that pattern. It did not merely set as its goal an analytical reconstruction of Scheler's doctrine of values, i.e., explicate the premises underlying Scheler's ethics. It also provided an epistemological critique of Scheler's basic concepts, a twofold approach that remained with him throughout his later research. Again and again, Altmann will reconstruct the ideas of a thinker and subtly suggest the criticisms to which they might be subjected in the light of their context and tradition. The history of philosophy is for him not the unfolding of the pure *Geist*. It is creative individuals confronting tradition and reality, whose works surrender their meaning only when viewed in their total context.

More closely related to his later research, Altmann's earliest creative efforts were in the field of modern Jewish theology. Prior to his first *Wissenschaft* article, between 1930 and 1935, he published four interrelated reflections, viz. "Metaphysik und Religion," *Was ist jüdische Theologie?*, "Religion und Wirklichkeit," and "Zur Auseinandersetzung mit der dialektischen Theologie," contributions to a reorientation of Jews towards Judaism (as one of them was subtitled). The first draws a firm line between theology and metaphysics, as to their objects and their intentions. The relativity of metaphysical knowledge is contrasted with the intent of the religious act that is directed towards the Absolute. The second defines the central concepts of Judaism—peoplehood and revelation—and reestablishes the centrality of the Halakhah and ponders the existential possibilities of redirecting secularized Jews to the religious domain of Jewish theological thought. The third—written shortly after the Nazis seized power—restates the relationship between religion and reality: "Religion and reality will not be experienced so much as two opposed areas of being but as two potencies in dynamic tension with each other."[1] And the fourth delineates Jewish from Christian theology. It demonstrates the irreconcilability of the theses of Karl Barth's dialectical theology with the basic concepts of Judaism. There exist affinities between the positions of all theologies, but essential, structural differences thwart the possibility of a common theological language.

These reflections—in continuous dialogue with Scheler, Heidegger, Cohen, Barth, and others—squarely face the need for a reformulation of Torah-anchored Jewish theology. Modern philosophy—especially that of Heidegger—constituted its dynamic counterpoint and modern Christian theology —whether that of Karl Barth or of Erich Przywara—served as a reminder of the possibility of such a reformulation from within, even though in essence and meaning quite distinct. Altmann's essays describe a need, point to a possibility, and furnish the basic concepts. They do not proffer a full-fledged

---

1. All quotations, unless otherwise indicated, are from the writings of Alexander Altmann. They have not been identified individually, as their original context has very little bearing on their context in this essay.

Jewish theology. We may guess that under different circumstances he might have continued in that direction, inspired as he was by the "profoundly mystical attitude" of Franz Rosenzweig's *Stern der Erlösung*. For on the eve of his departure from Germany he wrote: "The solution [i.e., the transformation of Jewish theology] depends on the strength of persistence, of not giving up too soon; it depends on the degree of responsibility and attachment felt towards the old inheritance"; qualities he possessed to an eminent degree.

Already prior to his emigration in 1938, Altmann changed the focus of his concern and began to turn his attention to Jewish scholarship, to an explication—a re-creation—of the inner structure of Judaism as it had evolved in history. *Wissenschaft*, i.e., the retrieval of Judaism as a living and expanding organism, not in need of transformation but crying for positive and creative understanding, and teaching grounded in profound and thorough knowledge of that living reality became and remained his main preoccupations. Neither his commitment nor his critical stance had altered, but the perplexities had changed. The brutally enforced confusion of his fellow Jews demanded not excursions into speculative uncertainties but teaching based on solid scholarship.

No less than three institutions of Jewish learning, two series of scholarly monographs, a journal devoted to Jewish studies, and a great many publications which earned him renown in the three fields of Judeo-Arabic philosophy, Jewish mysticism, and the German Enlightenment testify to the power of his conviction and the efficacy of his constructive efforts. Like works of art they are to be seen, not to be described. I may just point to the genesis of some of these works, highlight their style, and suggest their setting, for they are simultaneously as diverse, yet akin as the sentiments and commitments that Altmann brings to bear on everything he touches.

As a scholar-rabbi in Berlin, a rabbi and scholar at large in Manchester, and a teacher-scholar at one of the finest new universities in America, Altmann remained essentially himself. Notwithstanding the differences in culture, the dissimilarities in social fabric, and the varying wants of the respective Jewish communities, Altmann found or devised ways to fit his personal commitments and demands into the public needs and trends. Thus, the Rambam-Lehrhaus in Berlin (1934–38), the Institute of Jewish Studies in Manchester (1953–59), and the Philip W. Lown Institute of Advanced Judaic Studies at Brandeis University (1960–65) bore not only different names reflecting their respective surroundings, they also addressed diverse audiences—interested adults in Berlin, advanced students in Manchester, and the university community at Brandeis. Yet their methods and approaches were strikingly similar because of the unwavering commitment of their founder and director. In founding the Rambam-Lehrhaus, amidst the hostility of Nazi Germany, in an act of spiritual resistance, Altmann defined the function of a *Lehrhaus* in this way:

> The *Lehrhaus* will have to insist that notwithstanding its genuine historical orientation it not be guided by destructive criticism, but by sympathetic analysis of the totality of meaning. We do not wish to give our people stones instead of bread, but intend to transmit to them an understanding of Judaism as it exists in all its greatness and self-reliance.

The conveyance of this ideal with its unmistakably central European roots succeeded, to no small degree, because of the intimate link between the needs of the community and the type of service these institutes rendered.

In England and in America, Altmann gave generously of his editorial talents and inspired many others to transmit their understanding of the Jewish past, "its currents and crosscurrents, its rational and irrational tendencies, its ethical and mythical trends, its sublime and sometimes less sublime aspects" (as he formulated the scope of Jewish historical studies in 1957). The first six years of the expanded *Journal of Jewish Studies* (1954–59), the five volumes of the "Scripta Judaica" (published by Oxford University Press), and the four volumes of "Studies and Texts" (published by Harvard University Press) contain, without exaggeration, some of the most important publications in Jewish studies of the postwar period; works of truly first-rate scholarship in a generally publication-happy age.

But Altmann brought more than skills from Germany. He also retained the memory of what it means to live and labor in community, community not in the sense of a mere aggregate of people but, in a more profoundly philosophical sense, as distinguished from society. According to Max Scheler, the distinction between community and society ultimately lies in the immediacy of the experiencing of the other, in the sharing of basic concepts and values.

> In community, the other with his inner life is *himself observably present* and given in gesture and expression; all his actions and manifestations are comprehended directly [as stemming] from the familiar stance (*Gesinnung*). . . . In society, the other is, first and foremost, *seen from outside*, is a changing body "harboring" thoughts, feelings, and resolutions most difficult of access.[2]

2. Max Scheler, "Der Bourgeois," *Gesammelte Werke*, Vol. III, *Vom Umsturz der Werte. Abhandlungen und Aufsätze* (Berne, 1955), p. 349.

Did Altmann find such a "community" in England? Manchester provided a much appreciated haven of refuge and a sympathetic environment to the rabbi, but the different traditions of Anglo-Jewry were not especially hospitable, at first, to his scholarly commitments nor to his theological concerns. The natural affinity between the scholar and the community that had existed in Berlin was largely missing. In Manchester's John Rylands Library Altmann recaptured, almost stealthily, the atmosphere he cherished, spending many lonely hours in research. But, fortunately, a visiting professorship at the Hebrew University in 1951 fortified him in his resolve to carry his dream of a publicly supported center of Jewish learning into effect. Single-handedly Altmann created the Institute of Jewish Studies; not an ivory tower in industrial Manchester but a bridge spanning the gap between those barely "connected with their past," hardly "at home in their literature," and often unfortunately little "in sympathy with themselves" as Jews, on the one hand, and that world-wide community of scholars concerned with the formation of "a more or less unified vision of Jewish reality in all its ramifications and with all its defeats as well as its triumphs," on the other. At Brandeis another gap needed a somewhat different bridge. Between the loyalty to individual universities and a narrowly conceived professionalism, American scholars lacked a congenial place to meet, that ground where "all their actions and manifestations" can stand on their own unapologetically, outside the argumentative framework of disinterest or ulterior motive with which American scholarship is often plagued. These institutions were creations in Altmann's image but, therefore, all the more effective, for they derived from a reality experienced, not from a past imagined or a future craved.

Stimulated rather than hampered by his administrative duties, Altmann steadily pursued his labors in the field of Jewish studies. *Wissenschaft des Judentums*, the *Lehrhaus* quotation clearly reveals, was defined in Diltheyan terms. From Wilhelm Dilthey he learned "a more refined art of 're-living' and sympathetically understanding the literary expressions of the past" and "the necessity of seeing historical phenomena in terms of total configurations (*Gestalt*) rather than isolated elements." Whatever the form of his publications, sympathy for creative minds and a grasp of the totality of their expressions are their most pervasive characteristics.

I do not wish to "unfold the latent processes" of Altmann's research. Scholarly work should be judged by its finished contributions to the common stock of knowledge and by its expository qualities. Neither do I mean to enumerate the lacunae that his work has filled. One merely has to read

Georges Vajda's bibliographical essays on Jewish philosophy and mysticism to gain a sense of the significance of Altmann's contributions. This is not an introduction to Judeo-Arabic philosophy nor to Jewish mysticism, nor to the German Enlightenment, but to the man who applied his mind to these three fields of our tradition.

Nobody is as acutely aware of the "tension between the historical and the theological approach" as is Altmann. His theological and historical writings should never be confused. The relation between the two is not a simple dialectic to be resolved in a readily apparent synthesis. It derives rather from an acceptance of the tension itself, a refusal to short-circuit a multidialectical reality by manipulative simplification. The examples of so historically conscious a theologian as Franz Rosenzweig and of so theologically sensitive a historian as Harry Austryn Wolfson reveal, as they did to Altmann, the sparks that such a tension is capable of producing. The unity of Altmann's theological and historical writings lies in Altmann himself, in his primary stance (*Gesinnung*) not in his afterthoughts (*Hintergedanken*), a stance all the more difficult to explicate as Altmann simultaneously moved from one sociocultural context to another.

A few examples may serve to illustrate the way his research developed. In the very first of his theological reflections, "Metaphysik und Religion," Altmann distinguished the metaphysical from the religious meaning of transcendence. He writes: "The meaning of the absolute transcendence of the Divine is only retained, with complete trenchancy, in that religious-philosophical tradition which, taking its departure from Plotinus, leads to the Jewish and Arabic scholastics. . . ." Many of us will immediately think of his first *magnum opus*, "The Philosophy of Isaac Israeli." In that work Altmann, in collaboration with S. M. Stern, provided the most important missing link in the history of Jewish Neoplatonism. Fewer of us, however, are aware that the *Isaac Israeli* book owed its genesis to a felicitous suggestion of Gershom Scholem to the effect that a certain Mantua Fragment might be the work of Isaac Israeli. Altmann, subsequently, was able to demonstrate the veracity of Scholem's assumption but also showed a pseudo-Aristotelian, Neoplatonic passage contained in the Mantua Fragment to underlie other works of Isaac Israeli as well. On this basis, S. M. Stern, renaming the source "Ibn Hasday's Neoplatonist," elaborated further. And finally, the two scholars joined forces and produced a study which in the words of one reviewer "placed neoplatonic research on a new basis." The historical sensitivity evidenced already in the young theologian, Scholem's felicitous suggestion, the disposition to view fragments in their total configuration, the keen response of another scholar, and the readiness to collaborate merged to create a masterly work which still serves as a model of historical investigation.

A somewhat different mixture of personal predilection, commitment to Jewish tradition, and certain contingencies engendered in Altmann an interest in Jewish mysticism at a time when hardly any rabbi-scholar in Germany—with the exception of Leo Baeck—paid any serious attention to this discipline. The decisive inspiration grew out of a reading of the early works of Gershom Scholem on Jewish mysticism, and of Hans Jonas's then brand-new book on Gnosticism; an inspiration momentous indeed, but in and of itself insufficient to explain Altmann's concomitant change of focus. For subsequently—and in view of his education rather surprisingly—the very first of Altmann's *Wissenschaft* articles (viz. "Das Verhältnis Maimunis zur jüdischen Mystik," "Olam und Aion," "Gnostische Motive im rabbinischen Schrifttum," and "Gnostic Themes in Rabbinic Cosmology") plunged into this newly discovered current in the Jewish tradition.

It would be a mistake to regard Altmann's interest as at all related to the mythical propensities of some of his German contemporaries. His interest stems, it seems to me, more immediately from his own theological reflections, whose direction had lately been influenced by the 'mystical' Franz Rosenzweig, as well as from his personal experiences of alienation produced by Nazi atrocities. "The relation of the subject to the phenomenon of 'evil'" (or *"das Erlebnis der Dämonie des Daseins"*) was tellingly singled out as the basic principle of divergence between mysticism and philosophy.

Prior to the first article, Altmann had chosen to introduce Jewish mysticism to a wider audience in his first public lecture at the Rambam-Lehrhaus on 18 June 1935. The lecture, enthusiastically reported in the Jewish newspapers, reveals the enthusiasm of the young rabbi-*Dozent* for the "positive, creative assimilation" characteristic of the spiritual history of the Jews—positive owning to "the astonishingly tenacious orientation towards the Bible" and creative in that "the mystic plunges himself with all his being into the revelation." "Mysticism is nothing but the ultimate, bold thinking-through of the biblical word rooted in religious experience." And guided by the biblical word, Jewish mysticism, he believed then, had successfully steered clear of the Scylla and Charybdis of myth and magic, an allusion whose meaning could hardly have escaped the attentive listeners, as they were being watched by the Nazi police. Tenacity and boldness focused upon the Bible were also the foundation upon which Altmann envisaged the contemporary, positive, and creative reformulation of Judaism.

The first article, "Das Verhältnis Maimunis zur jüdischen Mystik," exhibits boldness—if not a certain degree of youthful exuberance—in its revealing second part which is devoted to an explication of "the difference between the basic existential attitudes" of philosophy and mysticism. Not unexpectedly, Altmann added in a footnote that one and the same person may oscillate between these two attitudes. It is as if in these last seven pages of striking generalizations—conspicuous by their absence from his later studies—Altmann crossed the threshold, reformulating his past reflections in terms of a scheme he was to belabor in greater detail subsequently. "For the philosopher God *is*, for the mystic God *lives*" reads the most quoted sentence of the Rambam-Lehrhaus address. And the *Monatschrift* article concludes: "[In philosophy] the direction of causality descends from above to below [from the Divine to man], while the more extensive principle of causality of mysticism enables one to attribute efficacy (*Wirkung*) also to the acts of man."

The relationship between man and the Divine, as well as the interweaving of philosophical and mystical ideas, are developed in Altmann's most successful and most characteristic studies in the history of such motifs as "The Delphic Maxim," "The Ladder of Ascension," and the anthropomorphism of *Shiʿur Qoma*. But these studies reveal more than the dominant method of most of his work. The penchant for *Motivgeschichte* suited not only an intellectual preoccupation, but also satisfied an aesthetic sensibility. To borrow a comparison from an art particularly close to Altmann's heart, these *motivgeschichtliche* studies read like sonatas in which a sympathetic performer recreates the creative moment in which the theme was born. I, for one, will never forget the applause following Altmann's luncheon address at a 1974 conference when he spoke of "the somewhat bizarre simile describing emanation in terms of a 'radiance that goes forth from mirrors of glass set in the windows of baths and palaces when the radiance and the splendour of the sun fall upon them'" (as he described his first encounter with this simile in the Mantua Fragment). It was the kind of explosive applause usually elicited only by exciting artistic performances.

Simultaneously, from the Rambam-Lehrhaus lecture to the present, the term *boldness* is a characteristic Altmann has continued to preserve, with telling consistence, for the mystics. *Incisive* is the epithet used most frequently with reference to the philosophers. Thus, faintly but perceptibly, two innocent adjectives—*bold* reflecting a mode of behavior, *incisive* an intellectual quality—echo his earlier assessments of the 1930s. In a recent article, "Eternality of Punishment," the concept of boldness has inadvertently come into greater relief. The article, an edition of a text he had chanced to discover at the John Rylands Library in Manchester, stands out in the midst of a veritable avalanche of articles on Moses Mendelssohn. Here, the approach of the Amsterdam rabbi Isaac Aboab da Fonseca, a Kabbalist, to the existentially significant issue of eternal punishment is "characterized by the dialectical pattern of 'Yes, but.'" This candid "Yes, but" offers a key to Altmann's understanding of boldness. *Yes* refers to tradition and establishes the commitment; the comma images the dialectical moment presented by reality, a suspended moment of reflection; and *but* launches the response. The same "Yes, but" configuration of commitment, reflection, and response also unlocks—hence the inadvertence at that opportune moment—the mystery of Altmann's approach in his latest *magna opera*, the two books on Moses Mendelssohn.

In certain respects the two books differ markedly from anything Altmann has ever published. They delve into an area formerly outside the scope of his already extensive erudition. Moreover, *Moses Mendelssohns Frühschriften zur Metaphysik* is the first larger study he has written in German since his departure from Germany in 1938. *Moses Mendelssohn: A Biographical Study*, on the other hand, is the only real life story he has ever ventured to examine and describe. Many, therefore, feel justified to regard the two volumes as highly personal digressions—aside from their obvious, substantial scholarly merit— to the point of assuming a virtual identification of the biographer with the enlightened philosopher. Though undoubtedly highly personal works, this should not obscure the fact that in them Altmann maintains the consistent approach that epitomizes his entire creative life.

The excursus into the Enlightenment was initially inspired by an invitation from the Leo Baeck Institute—which on various previous occasions had served to reconnect Altmann with his own immediate past—to collaborate in a collective work on "German Jewry and the Idea of Europe," made possible by Martin Buber's gift of part of the Erasmus prize money to the Institute. Altmann accepted the challenge and with unexpected boldness approached his task, straying in the process beyond what the initiators had in mind.

In his study of Moses Mendelssohn, Altmann was confronted with a modern tradition that had always been, to say the least, ambivalent towards Mendelssohn, an ambivalence resulting from the sorrow over the disintegration of modern Jewry that followed in Moses Mendelssohn's wake. Altmann shares this grief. Yet at the same time he retains the conviction that modern philosophical inquiry need not be incompatible with profound religious commitment. Nothing less than the historical facts of Altmann's and Mendelssohn's lives prove the point. But this similarity is in situation only, the actual forms of religious commitment and philosophical inquiry being centuries apart. This analogous dissimilarity (or this disparate correspondence) allowed the biographer to bring his entire personality, his own experiences and his intellectual commitments to bear upon his subject, creating a multiplicity of dialectical moments which he approached with the by now familiar boldness of a 'Yes, but.'

Altmann accepted the tradition of post-Mendelssohnian Judaism, "its sublime and sometimes less sublime aspects." He had shown himself committed to that tradition in everything he ever published, whether theology or *Wissenschaft*. Unlike those who responded with "a blind type of orthodoxy unable to face the challenge of the modern age or a platitudinous kind of progressiveness out of touch with the realities of Jewish history," he refused to suspend his reflection and close the chapter on either religion or history. He retained the dialectical moment and urged his contemporaries—then in Germany as a theologian and now in the United States as a historian—to do the same. Once he had become conscious of his own open-ended acceptance of both tradition and history, Altmann created the space for the figure of Moses Mendelssohn to emerge. And there he met Moses Mendelssohn with *Sympathie*. "Authentic sympathy," to quote the *Encyclopedia of Philosophy*'s summary of Max Scheler's famous work, "is not the experience of fusion: it recognizes, meets, and respects unequivocally the subjectivity of another human existence in a genuine encounter." Hence the seeming overabundance of biographical details. In the eyes of the "sympathetic" biographer who allows his subject to present himself "with all his defeats as well as his triumphs," there are no insignificant minutiae. Two centuries of distance and obfuscation forced Altmann to strain his eyes to perceive more than the mere silhouette of his subject. Yes, he saw Moses Mendelssohn, but he looked somewhat different from the man past observers had painted.

Altmann's commitment, reflection, and response, rooted in tradition and experience, enlightened and revamped our understanding of Jewish history. The placement of a mere comma turned reflection into method and vice versa, just as it had promised to do in the 1930s. Altmann has come full circle. The incisive German volume on the intellectual subtleties of one of Europe's most cherished *Aufklärer* and the bold and "sympathetic" English sequel on the life of one of the most controversial Jews of the modern era symbolize the positive and creative career of Alexander Altmann. His "cultural migration" fused the analytical keenness of the New with the *Sympathie* of the Old World. The boldness has always been his.

I do not wish to preempt the prerogatives of others by trying to formulate what Alexander Altmann has meant and still means to his students. Such sentiments are the private domain of each and every one of the contributors to this volume—whose diversity can speak for itself. But some of the feelings we all share resound in the observations of another student regarding his relationship with Abraham Geiger: "The attraction for me was respect for his great scholarship, his appreciation of the poets, which relieved his personality of the suspicion of narrowness, and his treatment of the younger man as one who had a career before him, and might take up the torch. The young are particularly grateful to an older person of superior standing who perceives possibilities in them before they have made good. The honor paid to the young by the old is the source of the greatest attraction."[3]

3. Quoted in Benny Kraut, "Felix Adler's Emergence out of Judaism" (Ph.D. diss., Brandeis University, 1975), p. 85.

Merkavah *Speculation* at *Qumran:* The 4Q Serekh Shirot ʿOlat ha-Shabbat

Lawrence H. Schiffman

Since the discovery of the Dead Sea Scrolls a quarter century ago, there have been many attempts to show that Gnostic influence could be discerned in the writings of the Qumran sect.[1] While some similarities of expression and language may exist, evidence has not supported any historical connections. Much more important is the suggestion that links can be shown between Qumran and the traditions of what Professor Gershom Scholem has called "Jewish Gnosticism,"[2] traditions embodied in a series of texts called *hekhalot* or *merkavah* literature.

In 1957, Professor Scholem delivered a series of lectures at the Jewish Theological Seminary. These were published in 1960 under the title *Jewish Gnosticism, Merkabah Mysticism, and the Talmudic Tradition*. In the introductory chapter, Scholem mentions the Qumran scrolls briefly. He notes that there are "several similarities in phraseology and possibly also in technical terminology"[3] between the Qumran and *hekhalot* corpora. Some scholars had suggested that the Dead Sea texts were of a Gnostic or pre-Gnostic character. Scholem took issue with this conclusion. He also observed that there had been insufficient discussion by scholars of the connection between the Dead Sea Scrolls and later Jewish esotericism.[4] Further on,[5] he alluded to a summary report[6] on the text that forms the basis of this study, the 4Q *Serekh Shirot*

Professors Yigael Yadin (Hebrew University) and John Strugnell (Harvard Divinity School) were kind enough to supply the author with information regarding the still unpublished fragments of the 4Q *Serekh Shirot ʿOlat ha-Shabbat.*

1. For a survey, see H. Ringgren, *The Faith of Qumran*, trans. E. T. Sander (Philadelphia, 1963), pp. 250 f., and the literature in his n. 18; and R. Marcus, "The Qumran Scrolls and Early Judaism," *Biblical Research*, I (1957), 31–40.

2. Cf. K. Schubert, "Der gegenwärtige Stand der Erforschung der in Palästina neugefundenen hebräischen Handschriften, 25. Der Sektenkanon von En Feschcha und die Anfänge der jüdischen Gnosis," *Theologische Literaturzeitung*, LXXVIII (1953), 496–506.

3. *Gnosticism*, p. 3.

4. Ibid., p. 4. Cf. I. Gruenwald, "Knowledge and Vision," *Israel Oriental Studies*, III (1973), 67–107; and his "Qetaʿim Hadashim mi-Sifrut Hakkarat Panim we-Sidre Shirtutim," *Tarbiz*, XL (1970–71), 304 f. See now his *Apocalyptic and Merkavah Mysticism* (Leiden, 1979), which appeared while this study was in press.

5. Ibid., p. 29.

6. J. Strugnell, "Le travail d'édition des manuscrits de Qumran," *RB*, LXIII (1956), 65: "un type de liturgie angélique (qui peut être associé à un ouvrage plus ample, forme ancienne de la vision de la *merkabah* qui a des points de contact avec la littérature d'Hénoch). . . ."

ᶜOlat ha-Shabbat, and stated that, if the preliminary report were accurate, it would show a connection between the angelic hymnology of the hekhalot literature and the Dead Sea Scrolls.

By the time Scholem's book appeared in a second edition (1965), J. Strugnell, to whom the Qumran text had been entrusted for publication, had issued a more complete description of the material, including publication of two selected fragments.[7] In the "Addenda" to the second edition of his book, Scholem wrote of the recently published fragments: "These fragments leave no doubt that there is a connection between the oldest Hebrew Merkabah texts preserved in Qumran and the subsequent development of the Merkabah mysticism as preserved in the Hekhaloth texts. The solemn and pompous language of the new fragments has already many ingredients of the particular style of the Hekhaloth hymns."[8]

Strugnell noted, in introducing these fragments,[9] that various linguistic affinities indicated this was surely a sectarian composition. Further, he stated that the work survives in four manuscripts, the earliest being dated palaeographically (with the help of F. M. Cross) to about 60 B.C. Strugnell observed that linguistic parallels are found with a still unpublished text entitled 4Q Ber(akot) and a "damaged work from cave VI," 6Q 18, a Composition hymnique.[10] A glance at what is preserved of this text shows that the whole composition would certainly be important for our understanding of the angelology of the Dead Sea sect.

Strugnell has described the text of the 4Q Serekh Shirot ᶜOlat ha-Shabbat as follows: "The first line of a typical section runs 'By a sage.[11] The song of the Sabbath sacrifice for the seventh Sabbath on the 16th of the 2nd month. Praise God all ye angels . . .' and then the Maskil exhorts the angels, under various names, to various forms of praise."[12] Strugnell understands the material to be elements of the "liturgy of the Sabbath offering, composed by a

7. "The Angelic Liturgy at Qumran—4Q Serek Sirot ᶜOlat Hassabbat," Suppl. to VT, VII (1959), 318–45, and Plate. We are still awaiting publication of the entire text. Our text is included in K. G. Kuhn, "Nachträge zur 'Konkordanz zu den Qumrantexten,'" RQ, IV (1963), 163–234.

8. Gnosticism, p. 128; cf. his Major Trends in Jewish Mysticism (New York, 1961), pp. 57–63; and "Kabbalah," EJ, X, 499, 502.

9. Strugnell, "Angelic Liturgy," p. 318.

10. Strugnell (ibid., p. 319) only spoke of a "damaged work from cave VI" which was to be published by M. Baillet in Discoveries in the Judaean Desert III. From Strugnell's citation of 6Q 18 on p. 332 it is certain that he was referring to this Composition hymnique published in M. Baillet, J. T. Milik, R. de Vaux, DJD III, Les 'Petites Grottes' de Qumran (Oxford, 1962), pp. 133–36.

11. Heb. maskil. On this term, see N. Wieder, The Judean Scrolls and Karaism (London, 1962), pp. 104–20; and H. Kosmala, "Maskil," in The Gaster Festschrift, JANES, V (1973), 235–41. In Dan. 11:33 and 12:3 the verb yavinu is applied to the activity of the maskilim. This verb must be taken in the sense of giving instruction, as in Neh. 8:7. The maskil is thus both a "wise man" and an "instructor" who shares his wisdom with others.

12. Strugnell, "Angelic Liturgy," p. 320.

Maskil for every Sabbath of the year according to the Essene calendar. . . ."[13]
Aware of the scholarly debate as to whether sacrifices took place at Qumran,[14] Strugnell notes that some will consider these to be songs accom-
panying the sacrifices "schismatically" performed at Qumran, while others
will consider the songs a liturgy which replaced the cult in which the sectarians did not participate. Strugnell observes that "this is no angelic liturgy, no
visionary work where a seer hears the praise of the angels, but a *Maskil's*
composition for an earthly liturgy in which the presence of the angels is in a
sense invoked and in which . . . the Heavenly Temple is portrayed on the
model of the earthly one and in some way its service is considered the pattern of what is being done below."[15]

We cannot judge to what extent the material preserved in this text was
used in liturgical context in actual worship by the sect. We must grant the
truth of Strugnell's statement as long as we cannot see the entire text. Two
things should be noted, however. First, the second excerpt published by
Strugnell[16] appears to be no more than a speculative description of the
heavenly chariot-throne based on an exegesis of the relevant material in
Ezekiel and other biblical traditions. Second, the descriptions of angelic
praise found in pseudepigraphic literature[17] are not linked in any way
to earthly liturgies. Only in the later *hekhalot* tradition do we encounter the
notion that the angels recite such prayers as the *shema*ᶜ and *qedushah*.[18] It is
clear that the earthly pattern of the twice-daily recitation of the *shema*ᶜ is being
ascribed to the angels.

In the case of the *qedushah*, the matter is more complex. Scholars are
divided on the question of whether the *qedushah de-yotzer*[19] or the *qedushah
de-ᶜamidah*[20] was developed first. The former is a description of the angelic
praise of God that takes place in the heavens. The latter is an opportunity for
man to utter the same praise formula ascribed by Is. 6:3 to angels. Professor
A. Altmann has argued that the *qedushah de-yotzer* is earlier and that it forms

13. Ibid.
14. See F. M. Cross, *The Ancient Library of Qumran* (Garden City, 1961), pp. 100–103; Ringgren,
The Faith of Qumran, pp. 214–17; and J. M. Baumgarten, "Sacrifice and Worship Among the
Jewish Sectarians of the Dead Sea (Qumran) Scrolls," *HTR*, XLVI (1953), 141–59.
15. Strugnell, "Angelic Liturgy," p. 320.
16. Ibid., pp. 336 f.; below, pp. 34–35.
17. Test. Levi 3:7 f.; 2 En. 17 and 18.
18. See H. Odeberg, *3 Enoch or the Hebrew Book of Enoch*, with Prolegomenon by J. Greenfield
(New York, 1973), pp. 183–87; and V. Aptowitzer, "Bet ha-Miqdash shel Maᶜalah ᶜal pi ha-'Ag-
gadah," *Tarbiz*, II (1930–31), 262 f.
19. Recited as part of the first blessing before the *shema*ᶜ in the morning service. See I. Elbogen,
Ha-Tefillah be-Yisra'el, ed. J. Heinemann (Tel Aviv, 1972), pp. 13–15.
20. Recited as part of the third blessing of the repetition of the ᶜ*amidah* in the morning and
afternoon services; see Elbogen, *Ha-Tefillah*, pp. 47–52.

the basis of the *qedushah* hymns in the *hekhalot* texts.[21] If so, the heavenly pattern of recitation of the *qedushah* is being imitated on earth. If the reverse were the case, and the *qedushah de-camidah* were earlier as some scholars maintain,[22] then the notion of the angels reciting the *qedushah* on high would seem to be an imposition of the synagogue liturgy upon the angelic hosts.

In any case, the earliest traditions embody speculation about the chariot-throne and the praise of God sung by the angels. But there is no evidence until the tannaitic period for any link between the celestial and earthly liturgies or for the notion that man should imitate the angelic praise of God.[23] One might wonder, then, if the text at hand does not simply describe the angelic praise in heaven on the particular Sabbath. From later sources we know of the belief in a heavenly sanctuary.[24] If we accept V. Aptowitzer's view that this idea reaches back even into the biblical period, it might be that the sacrifices described in our text were believed to occur in heaven.[25] Hence, the 4Q *Serekh Shirot cOlat ha-Shabbat*, like its pseudepigraphal counterparts, would be a speculative description of what went on in heaven.[26]

Strugnell raises the question of whether the many phrases descriptive of the angels found in this and other Qumran texts represent different classes of angels or are simply multiple names for the same angels. He is certainly correct in pointing out that these titles are not "merely decorative."[27] At Qumran, as in the pseudepigrapha and the later *hekhalot* literature, there were complicated angelologies in which the angels were divided in respect to class (nature) and function. Besides the seven chief princes and seven words found in Strugnell's excerpt, there are also in unpublished sections (according to Strugnell) "seven princes of the second rank" and "seven tongues each of which is more powerful than the one which was speaking before."[28]

21. "Shire Qedushah be-Sifrut ha-Hekhalot ha-Qedumah," *Melilah*, II (1946), 8–10. See now E. Fleischer, "Li-Tefutzatan shel Qedushot ha-cAmidah we-ha-Yotzer be-Minhagot ha-Tefillah shel Bene 'Eretz Yisra'el," *Tarbiz*, XXXVIII (1968–69), 255–84. Cf. his "cIyyunim be-Vacayot Tafqidam ha-Liturgi shel Suge ha-Piyyut ha-Qadum," *Tarbiz*, XL (1970–71), 48. Fleischer's conclusion is that both *qedushot* are already assumed in the earliest Palestinian Payyetanic tradition, even if differences in custom regarding when they were to be recited are found. Note that M. Weinfeld, "cIqbot shel Qedushat Yotzer u-Fesuqe de-Zimrah bi-Megillot Qumran u-ve-Sefer Ben Sira'," *Tarbiz*, XLV (1975–76), 15–26, finds evidence for the *qedushah de-yotzer* preceded by the reading of Psalms (*pesuqe de-zimra'*) in 11Q Ps^a 36:9–12.
22. To the sources cited in Altmann, ibid., p. 8, add those surveyed in Elbogen, *Ha-Tefillah*, pp. 52 f.
23. Cf. Strugnell, "Angelic Liturgy," p. 335; and Aptowitzer, "Bet ha-Miqdash," p. 266.
24. Ibid., pp. 137–53, 257–87.
25. Heavenly sacrifices are discussed in Aptowitzer, "Bet ha-Miqdash," pp. 257–66. The earliest source cited there appears to be Test. of Levi 3, roughly contemporary with our text. See below, n. 33.
26. Note the phrase *be-mishkan 'ele dacat*, "in the tabernacle of the angels of knowledge," in our text B, line 2, which seems to confirm this notion.
27. Strugnell, "Angelic Liturgy," p. 321; cf. pp. 330 f.
28. Ibid., p. 328.

It is not certain that a seven-heaven concept was part of the author's cosmology.[29] If not, the seven archangels are to be found in one heaven. If the author did believe in the seven heavens, we are still unsure if he placed each archangel in one heaven (as commander of its angelic hosts)[30] or if all the archangels were to be located in one of the seven heavens.[31] Both of these possibilities are observable in the pseudepigrapha and early Hebrew mystical texts. The absence of any mention of the seven heavens in a work of this type may indicate that the author did not have such a belief.[32] On the other hand, this concept is found in the Greek text and one Armenian recension of the Testament of Levi, chapter 3.[33] The Testament of Levi has been found at Qumran in an Aramaic version[34] and the *Zadokite Fragments* appear to cite it.[35]

Strugnell notes that the description found here of the chariot-throne is not of the "guided tour" type. The visionary is not taken to see the heavens.[36] This may be because the visions are the result of intellectual endeavor in interpreting the biblical material rather than of a mystical experience.

Strugnell has commented on the style of the second passage. He notes that there is frequent use of participles, startling paucity of verbs, and chains of

29. Ibid., p. 329. 2 En. contains a description of Enoch's journey through the seven heavens. This text, however, must be dated later than the Qumran corpus. We may note, incidentally, that the so-called "similitudes of Enoch" (1 En. 37–71) were not part of the Qumran Enoch literature. They likewise should be dated later. For a survey of the current state of the Enoch question at Qumran, see J. Greenfield, "Prolegomenon," in H. Odeberg, *3 Enoch*, pp. xvi–xx.

30. This is the pattern in some later *hekhalot* literature. See Odeberg, *3 Enoch*, note to 3 En. 17:3.

31. Test. of Levi 3 groups them all in one heaven.

32. Strugnell, "Angelic Liturgy," p. 329.

33. Strugnell (in ibid., n. 1) has taken the view that Test. of Levi 3 cannot be considered for methodological reasons since the fragments of Test. of Levi which have been found at Qumran have not yet been published. While it is certainly true that we would like to know what the text of chapter 3 contained in the Qumran recension, it does not mean that other recensions were not in circulation. It has been amply demonstrated that biblical materials circulated in differing recensions at Qumran. There is no reason why this might not have been so for the Test. of Levi. M. de Jonge, *The Testaments of the Twelve Patriarchs* (Assen, 1953), pp. 46–50, has discussed Test. of Levi in detail. His observation that "a reasonable sweet-smelling savour and a bloodless sacrifice" in verse 6 must be a Christian interpolation need not be accepted in light of the talmudic evidence which he himself cites. See below, our note to Text A, line 22, s.v. *la-tamid*. For the Armenian text, see M. E. Stone, *The Testament of Levi* (Jerusalem, 1969), pp. 61–67, 135. Recension β describes seven heavens, the angels, the holy of holies, and the heavenly cult. There is also mention of what Stone translates as "thrones and dominions." Recension α is missing some of the heavens and the cult, but does have a holy of holies. We can therefore assume that the cult must have been mentioned in the original text. In his note to 3:3–8, Stone comments that "the text is much reworked at this point." He prefers recension β.

34. D. Barthélemy, J. T. Milik, et al., *DJD* I, *Qumran Cave I* (Oxford, 1955), pp. 87–91; J. T. Milik, "Le Testament de Lévi en araméen," *RB*, LXII (1955), 398–406; P. Grelot, "Le Testament araméen de Lévi est-il traduit de l'hébreu?" *REJ*, CXIV (1955), 91–99.

35. CDC 4:15. So S. Schechter, *Documents of Jewish Sectaries* (reprinted, New York, 1970), I, 43, 67; but cf. the note of C. Rabin, *The Zadokite Documents* (Oxford, 1954), p. 16, to the effect that the text attributed to Levi is "not in the extant T. Levi." When we have the opportunity to examine the Qumran fragments of Test. of Levi, we will be able to see if the passage in question is found there. But see above, n. 33.

36. Strugnell, "Angelic Liturgy," pp. 335 f.

nouns that frequently leave one in doubt as to how to divide the phrases.[37] The strange impression created by the syntax of these texts can best be understood in light of later *hekhalot* literature. The latter also lack a structured syntax and clear division of phrases and clauses. It is apparent that there is a long tradition behind the *hekhalot* which reaches back to material like that preserved in our text. The awesome nature of the throne being described and the effusive praise and grandiose descriptions lent themselves to this syntactic character. To a certain extent the intoxicating nature of the *hekhalot* texts results from the constant flow of praise.[38]

Subsequent to the discovery of the 4Q *Serekh Shirot ʿOlat ha-Shabbat* at Qumran, parts of the same text were also unearthed at Masada. Y. Yadin[39] reports that the Masada fragments should be dated somewhat later than the Qumran material in the hands of Strugnell. Yadin's fragment contains a beginning formula similar to that of Strugnell's. It reads: [*La-maskil shir*]*at ʿolat ha-shabbat ha-shishit be-tishʿah le-hodesh* [*ha-sheni*], "To a sage. The song of the Sabbath sacrifice for the sixth Sabbath on the ninth of the second month." Yadin notes that his fragment contains the end of the fifth Sabbath and the beginning of the sixth. (The latter takes up the whole length of the left column of his text.) Yadin agrees with Strugnell's judgment that linguistically the text must be placed within the Qumran corpus, and he states that this conclusion is confirmed by the dating of the Sabbaths based on the special calendar of the sect.[40]

According to Yadin, "The scroll contains songs devoted to Sabbath sacrifices—each Sabbath with its special sacrifice. The Thanksgivings, Psalms and Rejoicings are recited by the seven *nesiʾe rosh* ('chief princes')—each prince in his turn."[41] Yadin cites examples of names used for these songs: *zemer ʿet le-ʾelohe qodesh, tehille rum, hodot nifleʾotaw, zemirot qodsho.* He correctly observes the sectarian character of these phrases. He also notes that the sectarian view of predestination is evidenced in the introduction to the song for the fifth Sabbath.[42] Yadin also considers the chief princes to be identical with the seven archangels. He believes that the scroll deals with the sacrifices performed in the heavenly temple.[43]

He finds it significant that this "Qumran" text was found at Masada. To

---

37. Ibid., pp. 342 f.
38. Cf. Altmann, "Shire Qedushah," pp. 3 f.; Scholem, *Major Trends*, pp. 57–63.
39. "The Excavation of Masada—1963/4, Preliminary Report," *Israel Exploration Journal*, XV (1965), p. 106.
40. Ibid., pp. 106 f., and Plate 19B.
41. Ibid., p. 107.
42. Ibid.
43. Ibid., p. 107, n. 84.

him it shows that the Dead Sea sect (identified by Yadin as the Essenes) took part in the revolt.[44] While this is certainly an important conclusion, there is another lesson to be learned from this discovery. Qumran texts, we know now, were read outside the sectarian settlement. One cannot be sure who read this text at Masada. But if, in the first century A.D., texts of the sect were allowed to circulate outside of the confines of the sectarian settlement, some of the ideas contained in these texts may have been preserved in later traditions.

Behind our text lies the notion that Sabbaths are counted sequentially. J. M. Baumgarten suggests that the "exegetical source" for this system was the phrase *ʿolat shabbat be-shabbato* in Num. 28:10.[45] The Tannaim learned from this phrase, among other things, that if the offering of one Sabbath were omitted, it could not be made up the following week.[46] The sect, according to Baumgarten, went further and assumed that each Sabbath of the year possessed a "unique ritual character as highlighted by its specific angelic liturgy."[47] The individual Sabbaths were "looked upon as part of the sequence of holy days which occur throughout the year."[48]

The *Psalms Scroll* from Qumran cave 11 may provide an idea as to who the sect thought had composed the songs (*shirot*) contained in our text. In a passage entitled by the editor "David's Compositions," the author states that besides 3,600 psalms (*tehillim*) and 4 songs (*shir*) of uncertain purpose, David composed ". . . songs to sing (*shir le-shorer*) before the altar over the whole-burnt *tamid* offering every day, for all the days of the year, 364; and for the *qorban* of the Sabbaths, 52 songs; and for the *qorban* of the New Moons and for all the Solemn Assemblies (*ha-moʿadot*) and for the Day of Atonement, 30 songs. And all the songs that he spoke were 446 . . ." (11 Psª 27:5–9).[49] The 52 songs for the Sabbath may be identical to the material in the 4Q *Serekh Shirot ʿOlat ha-Shabbat*. It has already been shown conclusively that the numbers of songs described by the *Psalms Scroll* fit well with the sectarian calendar in use

44. Ibid., p. 108. Yadin's view is accepted by R. de Vaux, *Archaeology and the Dead Sea Scrolls* (London, 1973), pp. 121 f. De Vaux rejects the argument of C. Roth, "Qumran and Masadah: A Final Clarification Regarding the Dead Sea Sect," *RQ*, V (1964–66), 81–87, that the finding of our text at Qumran and Masada indicates that both communities were "Zealots/Sicarii."

45. "The Counting of the Sabbath in Ancient Sources," *VT*, XVI (1966), pp. 277 f.

46. *Sifre Num.* 144. For other rabbinic interpretations, see B. Epstein, *Torah Temimah* to Num. 28:10.

47. Baumgarten, "Counting of the Sabbath," p. 278.

48. Ibid.

49. The translation is that of J. A. Sanders, *DJD* IV, *The Psalms Scroll of Qumran Cave 11* (Oxford, 1965), p. 92. Cf. his textual notes on p. 93. The transliterations in parentheses are added by me. CDC 11:17 f. indicates that the sect permitted only the *ʿolah* on the Sabbath. This is presumably what the *Psalms Scroll* refers to as *qorban ha-shabbatot*. For analysis of this *halakhah*, see my study, *The Halakhah at Qumran* (Leiden, 1975), pp. 128–31.

at Qumran.[50] A similar observation has been made by Strugnell and Yadin in regard to the 4Q *Serekh Shirot ʿOlat ha-Shabbat*.[51] The sect, then, may have believed that David composed the angelic liturgy.

One of the most important revelations provided by the *Psalms Scroll* and by the many Psalms fragments unearthed at Qumran is that the canon of Psalms was still in a fluid state at Qumran. (Indeed, this same conclusion can be drawn for the Daniel literature.) The Qumran *Psalms Scroll* includes several clearly "apocryphal" compositions like the five noncanonical psalms.[52] Even if we accept S. Talmon's suggestion that this scroll was essentially a liturgy,[53] it is still certain that the Psalms were not finally canonized.[54] So the sect may have easily ascribed to David the composition of the material found in the 4Q *Serekh Shirot ʿOlat ha-Shabbat*.

In view of the scant attention this text has received, a thorough study is in order. To that end, the text, translation, and detailed commentary are presented here. The commentary strives to make this difficult material understandable by providing thorough philological notes and tries to show how this text fits into the Qumran corpus linguistically and theosophically. Further, we investigate parallels from biblical, apocryphal, rabbinic, and *hekhalot* literatures. These parallels are invaluable for an understanding of the text and for reaching conclusions on its historical relevance.

Text A: 4Q S1 39 I1 16 ff.[55]

16–17 [הרביעי]/ בנש[י]אי רו[ש
יברך בש[ם] הו[ד המ]לך
לכ[ו]ל [הולנ]כי י[ ]שר
ב[ ]שב[ע]ה דברי ה[ ]וד]

ו]ב[ר]ך ליוסד]י הוד]
18 ב[שב]עה]/ דבר]י פלא
ו] ברך לכול אל[ו]ים מרו]מ[ים דעת אמ]תו
בשבע]ה דברי צדק לרחמי [כ]ב[ו]דו]

50. W. H. Brownlee, "The Significance of 'David's Compositions,'" *RQ*, V (1964–66), 569–71; and S. Talmon, "Mizmorim Hitzoniyim ba-Lashon ha-ʿIvrit mi-Qumran," *Tarbiz*, XXXV (1965–66), p. 215, n. 9. On the solar calendar of the Dead Sea sect, see S. Talmon, "The Calendar Reckoning of the Sect from the Judean Desert," *Aspects of the Dead Sea Scrolls (Scripta Hierosolymitana*, IV), ed. C. Rabin, Y. Yadin (Jerusalem, 1958), pp. 162–99; and M. D. Herr, "Calendar," *The Jewish People in the First Century*, Vol. II, ed. S. Safrai and M. Stern (Assen-Amsterdam, 1976), 839–43.

51. Strugnell, "Angelic Liturgy," p. 320; and Yadin, "Excavation," pp. 106 f.

52. See *DJD* IV, pp. 53–95, for the noncanonical material in 11Q Psᵃ.

53. Talmon, "Mizmorim," pp. 215 f.

54. See J. A. Sanders, "Cave 11 Surprises and the Question of Canon," in *New Directions in Biblical Archaeology*, ed. D. Freedman and J. Greenfield (Garden City, N.Y., 1971), pp. 113–30.

55. For palaeography and additional manuscripts, see Strugnell, "Angelic Liturgy," p. 321. We cite 4Q Sl 38 and 4Q Sl 40 as mss. 38 and 40 respectively. 4Q Sl 39, our main text, appears in

19 הֿחמיש[ין]/ בנש[יאי רוש]
יברך בשם נפ[ל]ל[אותיו]
ל[כו]ל[ן] יודעי רזי טהור[]ֿ טוהר
20 בשבעה ד[ברי]רֿום / אמת]ו

וברך] לכול נמהרי רצונו
בֿשבעה [דברי פלא
וב]רֿ[ך] לכול מודי לו
21 בשבעה[ן] דב]רי הוד/ [ל]הוד[ֿ [פלא]

הששי בנשיאי רוש
יברך בשמֿ [גבורות] אלים
לכול גבֿורי שכל
22 בֿשֿבעה / [ד]בֿ̇רֿי גבורות פלאו

וברך לכול תמימי דרך
23 ב[ש]בעה דֿבֿרי פלא ל[ת]מֿיד עם כול הווי / [עול]מֿ[י]ֿם
וברך לכול חוכי לו
בשבעה דברי[ן] פלא ל[מ]שֿוב ר[חמי] חסדיו

[השב]ֿ[י]עי בנשיאי רוש /
24 יברך בשם קודשו
לכול קדושים ממיסדי ד[עת]
בשב[ן]עה] דֿברי קודש פלא]ו

25 וברך[לֿכול מרומי / משפטיו
בשב[ן]עה דב[ך]ֿ̇רֿי פלא למגני עוז
וברך לכול נו[ת]עדי[ן] צֿד[ק מה]ֿללי מלכות כבודו [.......] נצח/
26 בשבעה ד]ברי פלא ל[שלום עולמים

וכול נשיאי [רוש
פלא יברכ[]ֿ ל[א]ל[וֹהֿ̇י אלים
ב[שם.....ו]כול

Plate Ia opposite ibid., p. 336. The text given differs only occasionally with ibid., p. 322. All references to mss. 38 and 40 are taken directly from his transcription as no photographs are provided. The text and translation have been arranged to indicate the poetic structure of the document. (See Kuhn, "Nachträge," pp. 184 f.) Slash marks indicate the beginning of each line in the manuscript. Commentary is keyed to the line numbers of the text. In accordance with the practice followed in the series *Discoveries in the Judaean Desert*, Strugnell placed a small circle above a letter the reading of which was uncertain and a dot over a letter if the reading was probable. For technical reasons we follow Yadin in using a horizontal line above uncertain letters. In the commentary, these indications have been dispensed with except in regard to quotation of the variant readings supplied by Strugnell. Vocalizations are mine.

16–17   The fourth / of the chief princes
Shall invoke blessing in the name of the majesty of the King
Upon all those who live uprightly
With seven majestic words.

And bless those who recite majesty
18   With seven / wondrous words,
And bless all the angels who exalt in His true knowledge
With seven righteous words for those who cherish His glory.

19   The fifth / of the chief princes
Shall invoke blessing in the name of His wonders
Upon all who know the secrets of the most pure
20   With seven words of His true / exaltation.

And bless all who hasten to do His will
With seven wondrous words,
And bless all who acknowledge Him
21   With seven majestic words / for those who acknowledge (His)
wondrousness.

The sixth of the chief princes
Shall invoke blessing in the name of (God's) mighty deeds
through the angels
Upon all those distinguished for (their) knowledge
22   With seven / words of His mighty wondrousness.

And bless all of perfect path
23   With seven wondrous words as a daily offering with the
eternal / beings,
And bless all who wait for Him
With seven wondrous words for the restoration of His mercies.

The seventh of the chief princes /
24   Shall invoke blessing in His holy name
Upon all the Holy ones who recite His knowledge
With seven words of His holy wondrousness.

25   And bless all who exalt / His laws
With seven wondrous words as impregnable shields,
And bless all who have banded together for righteousness who
praise His glorious kingdom . . . eternity /
26   With seven wondrous words for eternal well-being.

And all the wondrous chief princes
Shall wondrously bless the God of the angels
In the name of . . . and all. . . .

Commentary

17. *nes[i'e ro]sh*. The restoration of RWSH is in accord with the usual Qumran orthography and is confirmed by ms. 40.[56] Strugnell points to Ezek. 38:2 f., 39:1 where the phrase occurs. It is clear that the sect did not accept the interpretation of the LXX that *rosh* was to be taken as a place name.[57] The sectarian view is shared by the Targum and Kimchi. It is probable that the language of Ezekiel is here dependent on the phrase *nesi'e yisra'el rashe vet 'avotam* in Num. 7:2. Both titles are in military context (note the use of PQD in Num. 7:2 and Ezek. 38:8). It is also possible that the heavenly aspect of the Qumran term *nesi'e rosh* may be connected with the use of *nesi'im*, "clouds," in Jer. 10:13(= 51:16), Ps. 135:7 and Pr. 25:14.[58] The Jer. and Pss. passages contain reference to lightning and wind, frequently associated with the *merkavah* (cf. Ezek. 1:4, 13). Note the text of 1QSb 5:20f. as restored by Licht, *nesi' ha-cedah 'asher [yacamod be-'aharit ha-yamin be-rosh kol cada]to*, "the prince of the congregation who [will stand in the end of days at the head of his entire congrega]tion." If Licht is correct, it would show that the archangels and the earthly rulers were to share the same title, *nesi' rosh*, "chief (lit. head) prince." That the sect envisaged *nesi'im* as tribal military leaders is shown from DSD 3:14 f., 4:1.[59] The sect called the Davidic king of the end of days the *nasi'* in accord with Ezek. 37–48. Cf. M. Horayot 3:3. Note also the common phrase NS' *rosh*, to "elevate" to a higher rank, or take a census. The *nesi' rosh* may simply be the "elevated one." In *Sefer ha-Razim* 5:11[60] *nesi'e ha-kavod* is applied to the twelve angels appointed over the fifth heaven (*raqiac*), each for one month. Indeed, in certain magical texts, angels are also apportioned to the seven days of the week.[61]

56. Cf. J. Licht, *Megillat ha-Serakhim* (Jerusalem, 1965), p. 47; and E. Y. Kutscher, *Ha-Lashon we-ha-Reqac ha-Leshoni shel Megillat Yishacyahu ha-Shelemah mi-Megillot Yam ha-Melah* (Jerusalem, 1959), pp. 125–28, 132 f.

57. Cf. G. A. Cooke, *A Critical and Exegetical Commentary on the Book of Ezekiel* (Edinburgh, 1936), pp. 409 f., 415, for evidence pro and con.

58. Cf. 11Q Psa 26:15, for *nesi'im* as "clouds."

59. Cf. Y. Yadin, *The Scroll of the War of the Sons of Light against the Sons of Darkness* (Oxford, 1962), p. 48.

60. M. Margaliot, *Sefer ha-Razim* (Jerusalem, 1966), p. 101.

61. Ibid., pp. 31 f., 35. For the connections between the *Sefer ha-Razim*, the Aramaic magic bowls, and the *hekhalot* tradition, see B. Levine, "The Language of the Magical Bowls," in J.

yevarekh be-shem. Reading with Strugnell. For BRK in the *pi'el* followed by *be-shem,* see Deut. 21:5, 2 Sam. 6:18, Ps. 129:8, 1 Chron. 16:2, and 11Q Ber. lines 1–3.[62] The phrase means "to pronounce blessing in the name of the Lord"[63] or "to invoke the Lord's blessing upon." Ms. 40 makes the restoration of *be-she[m]* certain. The *l* of *le-khol* denotes the object of the blessing. The use of *l* to signify the direct object is common in Aramaic and is attested for biblical Hebrew.[64] It occurs with BRK in late books (Neh. 11:2 and 1 Chron. 29:20 where BRK *'et* is parallel to BRK *l-*) (Strugnell). This usage contrasts with that of the *Rule of Benedictions* (1QSb) which uses BRK *'et* consistently.

h[od ha-me]lekh. Strugnell's restoration is conjectural, though his reasoning seems sound. Cf. the phrase *hod malkhut* in Dan. 11:21 and 1 Chron. 29: 25 which, however, refers to earthly kings. I am unable to locate the word *hod* in the Qumran sectarian writings (11 Ps^a 21:15 is from Ben Sira).

hole[khe yo]sher. The phrase occurs in 4Q 184:15. Cf. Pr. 14:2 (Strugnell), Mal. 2:6 and DSH 3:20 for the connection of the roots HLK and YShR.

u-varekh. Strugnell's reading is in accordance with the poetic structure whereby after the number of each chief prince, there follows the verb BRK in the imperfect, and then in the infinitive absolute. Lines 21–23 (with no restorations) exhibit this pattern: *yevarekh . . . u-varekh . . . u-varekh . . . .*

Le-yosed[e hod]. Ms. 40 reads *le-yesode h[o]d,* confirming the restoration and exhibiting the familiar Qumran interchange of *qotel* and *qetol* forms.[65] The parallels under each prince show clearly that we require the participial form. Either *yesod* or *yosed* could have served this purpose at Qumran. Strugnell compares Ps. 8:3, *yissadeta 'oz,* "you have founded strength."[66] Note the use of *hodekha,* "your splendor" in v. 2 of the Psalm. That *hod* and *'oz* are synonymous can be seen from the parallelism in Ps. 96:7 and 1 Chron. 16:27. The use of the *pi'el* of YSD in Ps. 8 and the *qal* in our text is not surprising in light of similar fluctuations attested in the scrolls.[67] Note the medieval use of YSD meaning "to compose a liturgical poem."[68]

be-shiv['ah]. Ms. 40, *be-shiv'a[h].*

Neusner, *A History of the Jews in Babylonia* (Leiden, 1970), pp. 343–73; J. Greenfield, "Prolegomenon," in Odeberg, *3 Enoch;* and idem, "Notes on Some Aramaic and Mandaic Magic Bowls," in *The Gaster Festschrift, JANES,* V (1973), pp. 150, 155 f.

62. A. S. van der Woude, "Ein neuer Segensspruch aus Qumran (11Q Ber)," *Bibel und Qumran* (*Festschrift H. Bardke*), ed. S. Wagner (Berlin, 1968), pp. 253 f.

63. New JPS to Deut. 21:5.

64. Gesenius, sec. 117 n.

65. Strugnell; and Licht, *Serakhim,* pp. 45 f.

66. So new JPS.

67. Kutscher, *Lashon,* pp. 274, 276.

68. Even-Shoshan lists Rashi to Is. 24:22 as a *qal.* (I. Maarsen [ed.], *Parshan-data', we-Hu Perush*

18. *divre pele'*. Strugnell notes that this phrase is found in the second colon under each prince. Note the *nifᶜal* of ᴘʟ' with *davar* in Gen. 18:14, Deut. 17:8, Jer. 32:17, 27, and Ben Sira 48:13 meaning "to be too wonderous, difficult or baffling for someone." The Targumim and medieval commentators consistently take ᴘʟ' in this expression to mean "hidden, secret."[69] *Divre pele'* might then be "secret words" (?). Cf. *pela'ot* parallel to *mekhusseh* in Ben Sira 3:21. This verse is cited in B. Hagigah 13a, P. Hagigah 2:1 (77c), and Bereshit Rabba' 8:2 in connection with mystical speculation.[70]

'el[im]. Strugnell translates "godly ones" meaning "angels." Yadin has collected the evidence for this usage at Qumran.[71] It is developed beyond that of the Bible where only *bene 'elim* carries this meaning.

[mero]mim. The ms. shows a dot over the final *mem* to indicate its omission. This reading is confirmed by the parallel in ll. 24 f., *merome mishpataw*. Strugnell suggests that *merome* = *meromeme* by syncope. That there was a tendency for syncope in such forms is confirmed by the vocalization with *hataf-patah* in some texts of the Hebrew Bible.[72] Carmignac disputes Strugnell here, reading *'i[sh] mi(n)* followed by a short participle ending in the pl. termination *im*. Accordingly, he translates the line, "[Et] il bénira tout hom[me parmi ceux qui -------]nt la connaissance de [Sa] véri[té]." While Carmignac maintains that Strugnell's reading is impossible, he admits that his own is only "très hypothétique."[73] Comparison with parallel cola certainly supports Strugnell's reading.

daᶜat 'ami[tto]. "His true knowledge." The phrase *daᶜat 'amittekhah* occurs in DST 10:29.[74] *Ruaḥ 'emunah we-daᶜat* occurs in 11Q Psᵃ 19:14 ("Plea for Deliverance"). *'Emet* is a covenant term and carries with it the implication of God's revealed Law.

[be-shivᶜa]h. The restoration is confirmed by ms. 40.

le-raḥame [ke]v[odo]. *Raḥamin* and *kavod* are parallel in DST 16:9. In DSH 16:3 there appears an adaptation of Is. 6:3[75] where *kavod* is replaced by *koah*

Rashi ᶜal Nakh [reprinted Jerusalem, 1971–72], p. 64.) The appearance of a *piᶜel* in the same usage in Rashi to Gen. 30:22 (A. Berliner [ed.], *Rashi ᶜal ha-Torah* [Jerusalem, New York, 1969–70], p. 61) suggests that it is also a *piᶜel* in Rashi to Is. The *piᶜel* also occurs in S. Buber (ed.), *Siddur Rashi* (Berlin, 1911), sec. 306, p. 147.

69. Aram. ᴋsʏ.

70. Quoted by three different amoraim. Cf. M. H. Segal, *Sefer Ben Sira' ha-Shalem* (Jerusalem, 1971–72), p. 17 (to 3:21); and J. Theodor and Ch. Albeck (eds.), *Midrash Bereshit Rabba'* (Jerusalem, 1965), I, 58, n. 1, for later citations.

71. *War Scroll*, p. 230.

72. See Ex. 15:2 in the Koren edition and Gesenius, sec. 10g.

73. J. Carmignac, "'Règle des chants pour l'holocauste du Sabbat.' Quelques details de lecture," *RQ*, IV (1964), pp. 563 f.

74. Cf. DSD 1:12, and 4:6.

75. For the addition of *ha-shamayim*, cf. Targum and Licht's note to the text cited.

gevurotekhah. This certainly represents an exegesis of the *kavod* as the *dynamis* of God. This same equivalence was part of the *hekhalot* tradition and may underlie certain Rabbinic traditions.[76] Gk. *doxa*, however, was usually used to translate *kavod*.[77] The Qumranites believed that a future revelation would be accompanied by *mar'ot kav[o]d* ("visions of the Glory" (1Q34[bis]).[78] This is in consonance with tannaitic traditions regarding the splitting of the Sea of Reeds and the theophany at Sinai.[79]

19. *nif[le]'otaw*. The lamed is supplied in accord with ms. 40. While the suffix in ms. 39 is spelled *yw*, ms. 40 shows the defective spelling *w*.[80] It may be that *kol raze* should be inserted in the space before *nifle'otaw* as Strugnell has suggested, but the use of one word in this position in l. 24 and comparison with the other cola indicate that it is not required. The space may be the result of a defect in the parchment as Strugnell has also suggested. The *nifla'ot* of God are also identical with his *gevurah* (*dynamis*).[81]

le-[kho]l [yode'e raze]. So ms. 40. For the combination of YD‘ and *raz*, see Dan. 2:29, DST 1:21, 4:27, 11:16, fragment 1:3 f., DSD 4:6, and the 1Q27 Book of Mysteries 1 I 3.[82] *Raze nifle'otekhah* occurs in DSW 14:14. We cannot examine here the manifold uses of *raz* in the scrolls.[83] It is enough to point to Scholem's remark[84] that the use of *raz* in the Dead Sea Scrolls and the *hekhalot* literature is the same.[85]

[tehor]e tohar. Ms. 40 preserves traces of the first *tet*. Strugnell suggests that *tohar* may be a name for heaven based on Exodus 24:10 and compares Ben Sira 43:1. Segal suggests that *tohar* in Ben Sira can mean noon. It would then

---

76. See Scholem, *Gnosticism*, pp. 67–69; *Major Trends*, p. 358, n. 16; S. Lieberman, *Tosefta ki-Fshutah* (New York, 1962), V, 1288, n. 10; and I. Gruenwald, "Re'uyot Yehezqel," *Temirin*, I (1972), p. 110.

77. H. Liddell and R. Scott, *A Greek-English Lexicon*, ed. H. Jones and R. McKenzie (Oxford, 1968), p. 444; and Scholem, *Gnosticism*, p. 68. Cf. *TDNT*, II, 233–53.

78. *DJD*, I, 154; cf. Is. 40:5.

79. See S. Lieberman, "Mishnat Shir ha-Shirim," in Scholem, *Gnosticism*, pp. 118–26. Cf. also J. van der Ploeg, "kabod-ame," *VT*, III (1953), 192.

80. See Licht, *Serakhim*, pp. 47 f.; Kutscher, *Lashon*, p. 38; and Gesenius, sec. 91k.

81. Cf. 11Q Targ. Job 29:5, 7 to Job 37:14, 16, and DSD 11:19 f. which represents the same exegesis of *nifla'ot* in Job as well as DST 9:27 (*gevurat pele'*) and 14:23 (*koah* parallel to *nifla'ot*). For the use of *gevurah* and its Greek equivalent *dynamis* in apocalyptic, New Testament, and *hekhalot* traditions, see Scholem, *Gnosticism*, pp. 67 f. Scholem suggests that Gen. Apoc. 2:4, *mareh ravuta'*, "Great Lord" (J. A. Fitzmyer, *The Genesis Apocryphon of Qumran Cave 1* [Rome, 1971], pp. 51, 83 f.), is also a representation of the *gevurah*. Cf. *TDNT*, II, 284–317.

82. Cf. J. Licht, *Megillat ha-Hodayot* (Jerusalem, 1957), p. 42.

83. See R. E. Brown, *The Semitic Background of the Term "Mystery" in the New Testament* (Philadelphia, 1968), pp. 22–30. For biblical, apocryphal, and pseudepigraphal references, see ibid., pp. 1–22.

84. *Gnosticism*, p. 3, n. 3.

85. The sect used *nistar* for esoteric legal traditions. Cf. my *Halakhah at Qumran*, pp. 50–59, and the phrase [*ni*]*stare toratekha* in 4Q S1 11b (unpublished, cited by Brown, *Semitic Background*, p. 27, n. 88, "with the kind permission of Prof. John Strugnell").

be the equivalent of Heb. *tzohar* which does appear with a *tet* in Aramaic. Note also the Ugaritic ᵀᵉᵗHRM "gems."[86] For *tehorim* as angels, cf. the variant text of the *qedushah de-yotzer* cited by S. Baer.[87]

rum. Alternately *tom* (Strugnell). *Rum* seems to fit well as an epithet of God or His angels. Verbal use of this root occurs in Ezek. 10:16 in regard to the *keruvim.* Professor Yigael Yadin kindly informs me of the phrases *yosheve merome rumim* and *sheva͑ tehille rum malkhuto* in the unpublished Masada texts of the *Serekh Shirot ͑Olat Ha-Shabbat.*[88] Note the phrases *rum kavod* (DSD 10:12), *rum godelo* (DSW 1:8), and *rum ͑olam* (DST 3:20,[89] 1QSb 5:23). *Rum ͑olam* is the place in which the angels stand while uttering the celestial *qedushah* as described in the *qedushah de-yotzer.*[90] In *Sifre Deut.* 199 *dare rum* designates the angels.[91] In *Ma͑aseh Merkavah,* sec. 32[92] God's throne is located *be-rume shamayim,* "in the heights of heaven." The reading *tom* fits less well with the parallels in the other cola. The simplicity or integrity of the angels seems far-fetched. *Tom* is used of men in the phrase *tom derekh* in DSD 1:13, 5:24, 11:2, 11 and 1QSa 1:17.

20. *nimhare retzono.* This represents an exegesis of Is. 35:4 (not 32:4, cf. Targum) *nimhare lev.* New JPS translates "anxious of heart." Licht[93] notes that *nimharim* and *nimhare lev* were names for the sect based on the sectarian exegesis. The variation *nimhare tzedeq* occurs in DST 5:21 f., immediately after Licht's restoration of *retzonkhah.* The *nif͑al* of MHR also occurs in Ben Sira 50:17 where Segal explains it as equivalent of the *pi͑el.* *Retzono* represents an exegesis of *lev* in Is. 35:4.[94]

[*divre pele' u-va*]*re*[*kh*] *le-khol.* Restoration confirmed by ms. 38 which reads [*di*]*vre pele' u-varekh le-khol.*

mode lo. Strugnell suggests that our text takes *mode* as a verbal form of the noun *hod* rather than from YDH as it appears in the lexica. His suggestion is

---

86. C. H. Gordon, *Ugaritic Textbook* (Rome, 1965), glossary, no. 1032.

87. *Siddur ͑Avodat Yisra'el* (Tel Aviv, 1956–57), p. 78; cf. A. Gordon, "Tiqqun Tefillah," in *Siddur 'Otzar ha-Tefillot* (New York, 1966), I, 130a. Elbogen, *Tefillah,* p. 14, suggests that this may be a late expansion. The angels are described as *tahor u-metohar* in "Pereq mi-Pirqe Hekhalot," in A. Jellinek, *Bet ha-Midrash,* III, 162.

88. Letter of January 4, 1975. For *merome rumim,* cf. *govhe meromim* in the *͑Alenu* (*͑Avodat Yisra'el,* p. 131; Scholem, *Gnosticism,* p. 105; *Seder Rav ͑Amram,* p. 141; and *Siddur Rav Sa͑adyah,* p. 221).

89. Cf. Licht, *Hodayot,* on the text cited; and J. van der Ploeg, "rum ͑olam," *VT,* III (1953), 191 f.

90. Found as early as D. Goldschmidt (ed.), *Seder Rav ͑Amram Ga'on* (Jerusalem, 1971), p. 13 (Heb. numerals). Cf. *͑Avodat Yisra'el,* p. 77. Cf. also B. Hagigah 14a.

91. Ed. L. Finkelstein (New York, 1969), p. 237. The statement is attributed to R. Hananiah Segan ha-Kohanim (1st generation tanna) in *Sifre Num.* 42 (ed. Horovitz, p. 47). Note the equivalent expressions in Horovitz's apparatus: *dare ma͑alah, ͑elyonim.*

92. Altmann, "Shire Qedushah," p. 14; and Scholem, *Gnosticism,* p. 115. A parallel passage in sec. 33 has *bi-merome shamayim* (Altmann, "Shire Qedushah," p. 16; and Scholem, *Gnosticism,* p. 116).

93. *Hodayot,* p. 48.

94. Cf. J. Licht, "Lev, Levav," *EM* (1962), IV, 414.

unlikely in light of the regular use of *'odekha(h)* as an introductory formula in the *Hodayot Scroll*.[95] When our text refers to *mode lo* it may designate those who recite these poems of "acknowledgment." The problem is that the liturgical use of the *Hodayot* has still not been definitely established.

21. [*le-*]*hode* [*pele'*]. Restoration according to ms. 40.

be-shem [*gevurot*] *'elim*. Ms. 40 reads *be-shem gevuro*[*t*] *'el*[. . . . Strugnell rightly notes that the *be-shem* clauses refer to attributes of God. He therefore takes *gevurot 'elim* to refer to "God's mighty acts towards or through the angels." Note the phrase *gi*]*bbore 'elim*, "mi]ghty angels,"[96] in DSW 15:14. For other uses of *gibborim* for angels, cf. DSW 12:7, DST 3:35 f., 5:21, 8:11, and the *qedushah de-yotzer*.[97]

gibbore sekhel. *Sekhel* can be shown to be a term for the sectarian legal traditions derived through *midrash halakhah*.[98] The *gibbore sekhel* must be the men of the sect who have distinguished themselves for their knowledge of the Law.[99]

divre. The letters DB are preserved in ms. 40.

gevurat pil'o. The singular *gevurat pele'* occurs in DST 9:27. The reading *nifla'ot gevurotaw* behind the Syriac of Ben Sira 42:16(17) (cited by Strugnell) appears to be a conflation of synonymous variants.[100]

temime derekh. Strugnell cites Ps. 119:1 and Pr. 11:20 where the phrase refers to men. In Ps. 119:1 *temime darekh* (pausal) is parallel to *ha-holekhim be-torat 'adonay*. Cf. also 2 Sam. 22:31, 33, Ezekiel 28:15, Ps. 18:31, 33, 101:2, 6, Pr. 10:29, 11:5 for the combination of TMM and *derekh*. Numerous Qumran texts contain this combination, e.g. DST 10:30–32, DSD 2:2, 3:9 f., 8:10, 18, 21, 9:2, 19. The *temime derekh* are the full-fledged, upright members of the sect.

be-[*shi*]*v'ah*. Restoration confirmed by ms. 38.

la-tamid. The verbal use of the root TMD is medieval and a derivative of the adverb *tamid*. In fact, BDB lists *tamid* s.v. MWD. In the Bible, Ben Sira, Qumran, and (as far as I can tell) Rabbinic literatures the adverb *tamid* does not occur with prepositions. It is certain, then, that our text represents the use of *tamid* to refer to the daily offering. While in First Temple times this was generally called *'olat tamid*, Dan. 8:11–13, 11:31, and 12:11 use *ha-tamid*.[101] The *tamid* is mentioned in DSW 2:1 f. and 11 QPs[a] 27:6. From CDC 11:17 f. it may

---

95. Cf. Licht, *Hodayot*, p. 84.

96. Yadin's translation.

97. *Seder Rav 'Amram*, p. 13; *'Avodat Yisra'el*, p. 78. Strugnell, "Angelic Liturgy," p. 333, notes the use of *gibborim* in an unpublished section of our text.

98. See my *Halakhah at Qumran*, p. 54.

99. Perhaps identical with the *maskilim*. Cf. *Halakhah at Qumran*, p. 122, n. 24.

100. Cf. *Sefer Ben Sira'* (Jerusalem, 1973), p. 49.

101. For this term in the Bible, see B. Levine, "He'arot le-Mispar Munahim shel ha-Pulhan ha-Tanakhi," *Leshonenu*, XXX (1965–66), 5–11.

be deduced that the Sabbath burnt offering (*olah*) was regarded as a substitute for the *tamid*.[102] The angels bless the members of the sect (*temime
derekh*) and the blessing constituted a daily offering (*tamid*). Cf. the notion
that Michael makes offerings on the altar of heaven. It should be noted that
this tradition is amoraic.[103]

22–23. *howe ʿolamim*. For the participle *howe*, cf. Eccl. 2:22, Neh. 6:6, and
M. Shabbat 6:6.[104] Strugnell's suggestion that the *howe ʿolamim* are a class of
angels[105] fits the context. This phrase occurs in CDC 2:10 where it has been
translated by Rabin as "them that come into being in eternity."[106] Perhaps it
refers there to angelic beings. The *hawayah* or *howeh* is "that which is" in DSD
3:15 and DSW 17:5.[107] Perhaps, then, *howe ʿolamim* means "that which has
been from eternity." Then we would have to take *tamid* as a noun meaning
"continuity" (cf. BDB) and translate "for the continuity (continuation) of that
which has been from eternity."

23. *hokhe lo*. The phrase occurs in Is. 30:18. Cf. Is. 8:17, 64:3, Zeph. 3:8.
Strugnell also cites Dan. 12:12. There the *tamid* is mentioned in v. 11. It may
be, therefore, that the antecedent of *lo* in our passage is (the restoration of) the
tamid. *Hokhe lo* would refer to the sect regardless of how we interpret *lo*. From
Hab. 2:3 it is also possible that *lo* refers to a Messianic figure. But we must
remember that the sect expected two Messiahs, one of Aaronide and one of
Davidic descent. We can learn the sectarian exegesis of Hab. 2:3 from DSH
7:10–14. There it seems to refer to waiting for the *qetz*, the end of days. But
how can we be sure that the sect did not accept multiple interpretations of
biblical passages?

le-[ma]shov ra[hame] hasadaw. Restoration of *rahame* is confirmed by ms. 40.
Further support for *le-mashov* comes from the appearance of nominal forms in
the other cola (Strugnell). *Mashov* is an Aramaic infinitival form[108] and occurs
in DSD 3:1 and numerous times in DSW (where it refers to "withdrawal").
DSW 3:6, *mashov hasadim*, cited by Strugnell, cannot be relevant. Yadin is
correct that *hesed* there must be understood as "disgrace." *Rahame hasadaw* is

102. My *Halakhah at Qumran*, p. 335.

103. B. Hagigah 12b, B. Menahot 110a, B. Zevahim 62a. Note the discussion of the nature of
the offering in *Tosafot* to B. Menahot 110a, s.v. *u-mikhaʾel*. Cf. Gruenwald, "Reʾuyot Yehezqel,"
p. 128.

104. So M. H. Segal, *Diqduq Leshon ha-Mishnah* (Tel Aviv, 1935–36), p. 154. Other examples in
J. Levy, *Wörterbuch über die Talmudim und Midraschim* (reprinted Darmstadt, 1963), I, 457 f., who,
however, vocalizes *howah*.

105. Cf. 1 En. 15:4, 6, for their eternal life.

106. *Zadokite Documents*, p. 6.

107. Cf. the respective comments of Licht and Yadin.

108. See Licht, *Serakhim*, p. 44.

an example of the common Qumran syntax of two synonyms in construct with one another. This combination appears in this and the reverse order in DSD 1:22 and 2:1. Cf. DST 4:36 f., 6:9, 10:13, 11:29–32.

[ha-shev]i⁽i. The letters нSh appear in ms. 40.

24. *shem qodsho.* The *qametz qatan* is indicated by *waw*. This is common at Qumran.[109] The same phenomenon is attested in Mishnaic Hebrew.[110] The phrase occurs in Ps. 105:3 = 1 Chron. 16:10 (Strugnell), as well as Ps. 33:21, 103:1, 145:21. *Shem* followed by *qodesh* with a possessive suffix is extremely common in the Bible. *Qodesh* here functions adjectivally. The phrase also occurs in CDC 20:34, DSW 11:3, and the marginal reading of Ben Sira 39:35.

qedoshim. Yadin has discussed the use of this term for angels at Qumran.[111] Its biblical roots are clear (cf. Ps. 89:6–8, Dan. 8:13). But biblical usage also allows *qedoshim* to refer to holy people.[112] In Ben Sira 42:17 the *qedoshe 'el* are certainly angels. This same usage is found in the magical treatise *Harba' de-Mosheh* (*Sword of Moses*),[113] in 3 Enoch 39:2,[114] and in the *qedushah de-yotzer.*[115]

mi-meyassede da[⁽at]. Restoration confirmed by ms. 40. Strugnell is correct in comparing *yosede hod* in l. 16 and understanding *meyassede da⁽at* as "those who establish knowledge." The preposition *mi-* appears superfluous in comparison with other cola. Perhaps it arose through dittography. *Da⁽at* refers to sectarian knowledge and often appears in connection with *raz*. The angels are called *tzeva' da⁽at* in DST 18:23. Cf. 3:22. Note the phrase *'azamerah be-da⁽at* in DSD 10:9. The root ysд may mean "to compose a liturgical hymn." See the commentary to l. 17.

109. Kutscher, *Lashon*, p. 110.
110. Segal, *Diqduq*, p. 32.
111. *War Scroll*, p. 231. Cf. Charles, *APOT* II, 189, for 1 En. in which "Holy Ones" and "Holy Angels" are regular. Aramaic *qadishin* is a regular term for angels in the recently published Aramaic fragments of 1 En. from Qumran. See J. T. Milik (ed.), *The Books of Enoch: Aramaic Fragments of Qumran Cave 4* (Oxford, 1976), Aramaic-Greek-Ethiopic glossary, p. 390.
112. BDB, s.v. See J. J. Collins, "The Son of Man and the Saints of the Most High in the Book of Daniel," *JBL*, XCIII (1974), 50–66.
113. M. Gaster, *Studies and Texts* (New York, 1971), III, 70 (Heb. text), and I, 314 (translation).
114. Odeberg's translation "the holy princes" (*3 Enoch*, p. 125) must be corrected to "the princes of the holy ones (angels)." His translation would require *sare qodesh*, whereas the text reads *sare qedoshim*.
115. *Seder Rav ⁽Amram*, p. 13; *Siddur Rav Sa⁽adyah Ga'on*, ed. I. Davidson, S. Assaf, B. Joel (Jerusalem, 1970), p. 36; and *⁽Avodat Yisra'el*, p. 77. The occurrence of *qedoshim* a second time (*kulam gibborim, kulam qedoshim . . .*) in Hasidic texts of the Sephardic rite (*Seder Tefillah Yesharah we-Kheter Nehora' ha-Shalem* [Przemysl, 1928–29], p. 33b) is probably a late addition as it breaks the partial acrostic. Altmann, "Shire Qedushah," p. 12, identifies this usage in the *Ma⁽aseh Merkavah*, sec. 5 (cf. Scholem, *Gnosticism*, p. 106). While the passage in question is quite difficult, Altmann compares the third blessing of the *⁽amidah* to support his view. For the text, see *Siddur Rav Sa⁽adyah*, p. 18; *⁽Avodat Yisra'el*, p. 89, and note. Indeed, *Zohar*, II, 261b interprets *qedoshim* here as angels.

be-shiv[ʿah]. Restored according to ms. 40.

qodesh pil'[o]. Cf. DST fragment 5:3.

[u-varekh] le-khol. Restored from ms. 38.

24–25. *merome mishpataw.* Cf. *meromim* in l. 18 and our comments. The phrase means "those who exalt His regulations," not "judgments" as Strugnell takes it.[116]

25. *magine ʿoz.* The blessing is to serve as a protective shield. Shields played an important part in the military equipment of the *War Scroll.*[117] *Magen* and *ʿoz* appear together in Ps. 28:7, undoubtedly the source of our phrase.

no[ʿade] tzede[q]. The *qof* is partially visible in ms. 38. *Noʿadim* followed by *yahad* in DST 4:24 and 1QSa 2:2 means those who have "banded together," the members of the sect. *Tzedeq* is frequently used in designations of the sect.[118]

[meha]llale malkhut kevodo. Restored according to ms. 38. *Malkhut kevodo* is probably identical in meaning to *kevod malkhuto* in Est. 1:4 (cf. Ps. 145:11 f.). Note also the Second Temple doxology *barukh shem kevod malkhuto le-ʿolam wa-ʿed* (M. Yoma' 6:2, T. Taʿanit 1:12, B. Taʿanit 16b, Eccl. Rab. 3:11).[119] This doxology is included in the *Maʿaseh Merkavah.*[120] Strugnell offers several admittedly speculative restorations for the gap following *kevodo.*

26. di[vre pele']. Restored according to ms. 40.

[li-]shelom ʿolamim. Restored according to ms. 40. The phrase occurs in DSD 2:4 in the expanded Priestly Blessing. *Shelom ʿolam* occurs in DST 11:27 f., 13: 17 f. and is restored in 1QSb 3:5 by Milik.[121] Cf. Testament of Dan. 5:11. The association of *shelom ʿolam* with *'orekh yamim* in DST 13:17 f. may indicate that our phrase means eternal life.[122] For the combination of *shalom* and *ʿolam,* see Numbers 25:12 f. and 1 Kings 2:33.

[rosh pele']. Strugnell suggests alternately *mishneh pele'* or either without *pele'* ("on grounds of length"). Note that *rosh* and *mishneh* are used of priests in DSW 2:1.[123] *Pele',* however, should be taken with what follows (*yevarekhu*) in

---

116. See *Halakhah at Qumran,* pp. 73–79.

117. Yadin, *War Scroll,* pp. 115–22.

118. Cf. P. Wernberg-Møller, "Sedeq, Sadiq and Sedaqah in the Zadokite Fragments, the Manual of Discipline and the Habbakuk Commentary," *VT,* III (1953), 310–15.

119. See Elbogen, *Tefillah,* pp. 19 f., 386 f., n. 19; and J. Heinemann, *Ha-Tefillah bi-Tequfat ha-Tanna'im we-ha-'Amora'im* (Jerusalem, 1966), pp. 70, 79 f., 84 ff., 92.

120. Sec. 18; Scholem, *Gnosticism,* p. 111.

121. *DJD* I, 123.

122. Cf. G. W. Nickelsburg, *Resurrection, Immortality, and Eternal Life in Intertestamental Judaism,* Harvard Theological Studies, XXVI (Cambridge, Mass., 1972), pp. 144–67.

123. For biblical precedent, see Yadin, *War Scroll,* p. 207, n. 6.

line with the frequent occurrence of "And bless . . . with seven wondrous words."

le-['e]lohe 'elim. For *'elim* see the commentary to l. 18. The sect apparently interpreted the biblical passages cited by Strugnell (Deut. 10:17, Ps. 136:2, Dan. 2:47, 11:36) to mean "God of the Angels." This is the meaning of *'el 'elim* in DSW 14:16, and 18:6 (restored with certainty).[124] Cf. Azariah 68, 1 En. 9:4, Jub. 8:20 and 23:1, which are probably dependent on the biblical traditions and need not agree with the sectarian exegesis.

be-[shem]. The restoration is speculative as is Strugnell's discussion of what might follow.

Text B: 4Q S1 40 24 2 ff.[125]

2   ... מֹשׁר]חֹי פָּנֵי הכבוֹד במשכָּן אלי] דְעת יפוֹלוֹ] לפנוֹ ה[כרו]בִֿים וֹבָֿר]כֹו בהרומם

3   קול דממת אלוֹהים / למעלה]וֹהמוֹן רנה ברום כנפיהם קול [דממ]תֿ אלוֹהים תבנית כסא

4   מרכבה מברכים ממעל לרקיע הכרובים / וֹהו]ֿד רקיע האור ירננו (מ)מתחת מוֹשׁב כֹבוֹדו

5   ובלכת האוֹפנים ישוֹבוֿ מלאכי קוֹדש יצאוֹ] (ו)מבין / [ג]לגלי כבודו כמראֿי אש

6   רוֹחוֹ]ת] קוֹדש קדשים סֹבִיב מראי שבִֿילֹי אש בדמות חשמל ומעשׂי / [נ]וֹגה בריֿקמֿת כבוֹד
    צבעי פלא ממולח טוֹהֹר]

7   רוֹחוֹת [א]לוהים חיים מתהלכים תמיד עם כבוד מרכבוֹת / [ה]פלא וקול דממת ברכ

8   בהמון לכתם והללוֹ קוֹדש בהֿשיב דרכיהם בהרומם ירוממו פלא ובשוכן / [יעמ]דֿו קול

9   גילות רנה השקיט ודמֹמֹ]ת] בֹרֹךֿ [א]לוהים בכול מחני אלוהיֿם [ו]קֿול תשב]חוֹת[... /
    ומבין כול דגליה]ֿם] בעב] יֿ]רֿננו כול פקודיהם אחד אֿ[ח]ֿד במעמֿד

2   . . . those who serve before the glory in the tabernacle of the angels of knowledge.

The *keruvim* fall before Him and utter blessing. When they rise up, the

3   gentle voice of the angels (is heard)/on high. And there is much song when their wings lift up, the gentle voice of the angels, blessing the figure of the

4   chariot-throne above the firmament of the *keruvim*./ Then they sing the praise of the firmament of light from beneath His glorious throne.

124. It is interesting that the manuscripts which form the basis of S. Lieberman's *Tosefta'* (New York, 1955–) use *'elim* and its forms where the Masoretic tradition uses *'elohim*. These manuscripts clearly represent early Palestinian traditions, and a linguistic study of them is a desideratum.

125. For manuscript and palaeography, see Strugnell, "Angelic Liturgy," p. 336. Kuhn ("Nachträge," pp. 165 f.) has disputed Strugnell's reconstruction of the line length, suggesting that the column was wider on both ends. He is certainly right that only publication of all fragments of the text can confirm Strugnell's reconstruction. However, our analysis, according to which the text makes sense as a description of the *merkavah*, supports Strugnell.

And when the wheels ('*ofanim*) move back and forth, the holy angels go
5   forth. And from between/ His (its) glorious wheels (*galgalim*), like the
appearance of fire, are the spirits of the holy ones (angels). All around are
the appearances of paths of fire in the likeness of the electrum (*hashmal*)
6   and shining/creatures (dressed) in glorious embroidery of wondrously
refined pure colors.

Spirits of the living God move to and fro continuously with the won-
7   drous glory of the chariot-/thrones, and the gentle voice of blessing (is
heard) with the sound of their going. And they praise the Holy One when
they return. When these rise up, those (also) rise up. When these stand
8   still,/those (also) stand still. The quiet voice of songs of joy and the gentle
9   blessing of God (are heard) in all the camps of the angels . . ./And the voice
of praises . . . and from among all their cohorts . . . All their troops, singing
one after another in position.

Commentary

2. [*meshare*]*te pene ha-kavod*.[126] For *mesharet pene* see 1 Sam. 2:18 and Est. 1:10.
Note that the root ShRT in the Bible usually refers to cultic or royal service. It
is used of heavenly beings in Ps. 104:4 (parallel to *mal'akhaw*). Perhaps DSW
13:2 f. uses *mesharetaw* for angels. The glory (*kavod*) is a surrogate for the
divine name in 1 En. 14:20, 102:3, and Test. Levi 3:4. *Kavod* in the scrolls is
both an attribute of God and a reward for men.[127] Even though the sectarians
avoided the Tetragrammaton, I know of no use of *kavod* as a substitute.
Mesharete kavod appears in 3 En. 6.[128] A close parallel to our text comes from
the *qedushah de-ʿamidah*. Maimonides (followed by the Yemenite rite) follows
the recitation of Is. 6:3 *each morning* with *kevodo we-godelo male' ʿolam u-mesha-
retaw sho'alim 'ayeh meqom kevodo le-haʿaritzo le-ʿumatam meshabbehim we-'omerim*.
This is the earliest source we have for this liturgical formula. Perhaps it was
derived from the ancient Palestinian ritual.[129] Here the *mesharetim* are clearly
angels. Note the Rabbinic *mal'akhe ha-sharet*, "Angels of Service" or "Minis-
tering Angels" appearing also in *Maʿaseh Merkavah*.[130] The verbal use of ShRT

126. Kuhn ("Nachträge," p. 166) disputes Strugnell's reading of this line, but offers no
alternative.
127. Cf. DSD 4:23.
128. Quoted in *Tziyyoni* 13d f.; A. Jellinek, *Bet ha-Midrash* (reprinted Jerusalem, 1967), II, xvi.
129. Cf. Elbogen, *Tefillah*, p. 50. In *Maʿaseh Merkavah*, sec. 4, there occurs *kevodekha male ʿolam*)
Scholem, *Gnosticism*, p. 104. In sec. 29, ʿolam seems to have been accidentally omitted from some
Vorlage; Altmann, *Shire Qedushah*, p. 22; and Scholem, *Gnosticism*, p. 114.
130. Sec. 3; Scholem, *Gnosticism*, p. 103.

occurs frequently in 3 En.[131] *Mesharetim* is also used for angels in *Hekhalot Rabbati*.[132]

be-mishkan. *Mishkan* in the Bible usually designates the "tent of meeting." In some passages, *mishkan* can be a synonym for *miqdash*, the Temple (e.g., Ezek. 37:27). This second usage continued into the postbiblical period.[133] The *Shicur Qomah*,[134] a text very much a part of the *hekhalot* literature, makes use of *mishkan* for the heavenly sanctuary.[135] This is exactly the usage found in our text.

[*'ele*] *dacat*. See notes to text A, lines 18 and 24. Carmignac[136] disputes this restoration on the grounds that the large space would better accommodate *ruhot* or *mal'akhe*. In any case, the text would refer to angels.

yippol[*u*] *lefanaw ha-*[*keru*]*vim. Yippolu* is a "pausal" used in medial position, a characteristic feature of Qumran Hebrew.[137] The next word may be *lifne* or *lefanaw* as Qumran manuscripts do not distinguish between *waw* and *yod*. Further, the *yod* of the third singular pronominal suffix on plural nouns and certain prepositions need not be written.[138] H. Yalon points out that this phenomenon is attested in the MT.[139] I do not believe that the *keruvim* are mentioned in any other Qumran text. In reading *lefanaw* we accept Strugnell's analysis which regards *keruvim* as the subject of the sentence. Cf. Rev. 4:10. 3 En. 18, however, describes prostration of one angel to another.

be-heromam. *Nifcal* (of toleration) of RMM, a bi-form of RWM, infinitive absolute with preposition *b* and third person plural masculine pronominal suffix. The usage is drawn from Ezek. 10:15-19. Carmignac, however, reads *be-hiddomem* (BHDWMM) which he takes as the *hitpolel* of DMM with regular assimilation of the *taw*. He translates, ". . . quand se met au silence la voix silencieuse du Dieu. . . ."[140] But Carmignac ignores the fact that this selection tends to be a patchwork based primarily on Ezekiel's *merkavah* vision. This last point would favor the reading proposed by Strugnell.

qol demamat 'elohim. This phrase is derived from 1 Kings 19:12 (cf. Job 4:16)

131. See Odeberg, *3 Enoch*, index.
132. E.g., Jellinek, *Bet ha-Midrash*, III, 84, 89 f.; S. Wertheimer, *Bate Midrashot* (Jerusalem, 1967-68), I, 69 f., 84.
133. *Sifra, Be-Huqotay* 3:2; and the amoraic tradition in B. cEruvin 2a and B. Shevucot 16b.
134. Talmon, "Mizcmorim," p. 224, finds the first occurrence of this phrase in 11Q Ps^a 28:9 f.
135. S. Musajoff, *Sefer Merkavah Shelemah* (Jerusalem, 1920-21), p. 40a. Cf. the later *Be-Midbar Rabba'* 12:12 (Scholem, *Gnosticism*, p. 49, whose reference in n. 20 probably should be corrected accordingly).
136. "Règle des chants," p. 564.
137. Licht, *Serakhim*, p. 46; Kutscher, *Lashon*, pp. 254 ff.
138. Licht, *Serakhim*, pp. 47 f.; Kutscher, *Lashon*, p. 38.
139. *Megillot Midbar Yehudah* (Jerusalem, 1967), p. 61 f. Cf. Gesenius, sec. 91k.
140. "Règle des chants," pp. 564 f.

where the "still small voice" may have been thought by the sect to be that of God. While Kings used the Tetragrammaton, the sect may have substituted *'elohim*.[141] More likely, the sect may have meant *'elohim* here as the angels. The "gentle" song of the angels is mentioned in 2 En. 21:1. In *Midrash Konen*[142] the *qol demamah daqqah* is praise uttered by the angels. In *Ma'aseh Merkavah* sec. 33[143] angels are described as *te'unim demamah daqqah*.[144] In section 32 they stand silent (*demumin*) before the throne of glory.[145] This motif also occurs in the *Hekhalot Rabbati*.[146] God is pictured as sitting in a *hekhal demamah*, a "chamber of silence."[147] The ruler of the sixth hall (*hekhal*) is Dumiel.[148] The holy beasts standing before God are *demamah daqqah*.[149] *Sefer ha-Razim* places a Damimiel among the angels of the second heaven.[150] The *mal'akhe demamah* in this work have become angels who silence others.[151] Silence is very much part of the new *hekhalot* fragments from the Cairo *genizah* published by I. Gruenwald.[152] In B. Hagigah 12b the angelic bands (*kittot*) are silent (*hashot*) by day in honor of Israel who praise God by day.[153] A variant reading is *domemot*.[154]

[*le-ma'alah*]. An alternate restoration of *la-rum* is mentioned by Strugnell. Cf. Ezek. 10:16.

141. The avoidance of the Tetragrammaton at Qumran is regular in nonbiblical texts. Cf. S. Lieberman, "Light on the Cave Scrolls from Rabbinic Sources," *PAAJR*, XX (1951), 400–402; and J. P. Siegel, "The Employment of Palaeo-Hebrew Characters for the Divine Names at Qumran in the Light of Tannaitic Sources," *HUCA*, XLII (1971), 159–72, esp. 172.

142. Jellinek, *Bet ha-Midrash*, II, 33 f. This *midrash* has elements from Second Temple sources, according to M. D. Herr, "Midrashim, Smaller," *EJ*, XVI, 1517.

143. Altmann, "Shire Qedushah," p. 17; Scholem, *Gnosticism*, p. 116.

144. Altmann explains that the holy beasts carry the throne and recite praises as they go. For *te'unim*, Altmann compares *Hekhalot Rabbati* in Jellinek, *Bet ha-Midrash*, III, 91; and Wertheimer, *Bate Midrashot*, I, 87.

145. Altmann, "Shire Qedushah," p. 14; Scholem, *Gnosticism*, p. 115.

146. Jellinek, *Bet ha-Midrash*, III, 104; Wertheimer, *Bate Medrashot*, I, 111; and Altmann, "Shire Qedushah," p. 17, n. 7.

147. Jellinek, *Bet ha-Midrash*, III, 85, 89; Wertheimer, *Bate Midrashot*, I, 71. Cf. *melekh shoqet* in Wertheimer, *Bate Midrashot*, I, 104.

148. Jellinek, *Bet ha-Midrash*, II, 98; Wertheimer, *Bate Midrashot*, I, 99. He was also ruler of the elements; Scholem, *Gnosticism*, p. 33; and H. Lewy, "Seride Mishpatim we-Shemot Yewaniyyim be-Sefer Hekhalot Rabbati," *Tarbiz*, XII (1940–41), 165.

149. Jellinek, *Bet ha-Midrash*, II, 104; Wertheimer, *Bate Midrashot*, I, 111.

150. 2:15, p. 82.

151. 2:21, p. 82.

152. "Qeta'im Hadashim mi-Sifrut ha-Hekhalot," *Tarbiz*, XXXVIII (1968–69), 357, l. 12; 360, l. 48; 362, l. 10. This text is extremely unclear, however.

153. So Rashi. The statement is attributed to R. Simeon b. Laqish, a third-century Palestinian amora.

154. R. N. Rabbinovicz, *Diqduqe Soferim*, ad B. Hag. 12b. Cf. also B. Megillah 18a. For silence as a divine attribute in the Hellenistic world, see E. R. Goodenough, *Jewish Symbols in the Greco-Roman Period* (New York, 1953), II, 270 f. See also *'Alfa' Beta' de-Ven Sira'*, ed. D. Friedmann and S. Loewinger, *Ha-Tzofeh le-Hokhmat Yisra'el*, X (1926), 258.

3. *we-hamon rinah.* Cf. Ps. 42:5.

be-rum kanfehem. Strugnell prefers *ba-rim* (= *be-harim*).[155] But comparison with Ezek. 10:16 (which Strugnell cites) seems to support *be-rum*. Perhaps vocalize *be-rom* following Ezek. 10:15. Strugnell supports his reading by alluding to the syntactic problems of the text. Comparison with the *hekhalot* texts shows that hymns of this type exhibit flexible syntax.

Carmignac[156] ignores Ezek. 10:16 and proposes reading *be-dom kanfehem qol[am yofi]a^c*. He translates, "Quand leurs ailes cessent [leur] bruit (littéralement: taisent leur voix), Dieu [fait apparaî] tre la forme du siège du char." The causative usage of YF^c in the *hif^cil* is not as common as the intransitive, yet it is attested for biblical and rabbinic literature. Carmignac also notes that reading *ba-rim* (with Strugnell), the rest might still be restored as he suggested. According to this last interpretation, the *merkavah* vision comes as a result of the praise uttered by the celestial beings. In *Hekhalot Rabbati* 1:1 the songs of the adept are seen as helping to bring him the vision.[157]

tavnit kise' ha-merkavah. The phrase *tavnit ha-merkavah* is found in 1 Chron. 28:18 where the *merkavah* is part of the earthly sanctuary. *Merkavah* is already used in connection with Ezekiel's vision in Ben Sira 49:8. *Tavnit* is used to guard against anthropomorphism in the phrase *be-tzelem demut tavnito* in the marriage blessings first found in B. Ketubot 8a.[158] Note that *tavnit* appears in Ezek. 10:8 and that in Ezek. 1:28 the supreme vision is of the *mar'eh demut kevod 'adonay.* This phrase exhibits the same tendency to guard against anthropomorphism.[159] *Kise'* here means "throne" and may serve to explain *merkavah.* Cf. Is. 6:1; Ezek. 1:26, 10:1.

mi-ma^cal li-reqia^c. The phrase is taken from Ezek. 1:25 f. (Strugnell).

4. *[we-ho]d.* Alternately *[u-khevo]d* (Strugnell).

reqia^c ha-'or. Based on Gen. 1:14 f. where *me'orot* is used, however.

mi-tahat. Omitting a superfluous *mem* before the word which was, no doubt, caused by dittography.

moshav kevodo. Moshav kavod occurs in Ben Sira 7:4 where it is apparently the seat of an officer of the king (cf. 1 Sam. 2:8). In our text, the *moshav kavod* is the divine throne or *merkavah.*[160] Note the phrase *moshav yeqaro* in the *^cAlenu*

---

155. Cf. Licht, *Serakhim*, p. 40, for the form.

156. "Règle des chants," p. 565.

157. M. Smith, "Observations on Hekhalot Rabbati," in A. Altmann (ed.), *Biblical and Other Studies* (Cambridge, Mass., 1963), p. 142.

158. For variant readings, see M. Herschler, *Massekhet Ketubot* (Jerusalem, 1972), p. 41 Cf. Gen. 1:26.

159. This tendency is probably behind *tavnit 'esh* in *Sefer ha-Razim* 3:3, p. 92.

160. For this use of *moshav*, see *Ma^caseh Merkavah*, sec. 10 (Scholem, *Gnosticism*, p. 108); sec. 30 (Altmann, "Shire Qedushah," p. 22; Scholem, *Gnosticism*, p. 114); sec. 31 (Altmann, "Shire Qedushah," p. 24; Scholem, *Gnosticism*, p. 115); and Scholem, *Gnosticism*, p. 28, n. 18.

hymn. Variant readings are *moshav kevodo* and *kise' kevodo*.[161] This prayer was part of the *Ma'aseh Merkavah*, yet the phrase is absent from the published texts.[162] *Moshav yeqaro* is widely attested in the *hekhalot* literature.[163]

u-ve-lekhet ha-'ofanim yashuvu. Strugnell compares Ezek. 1:19 and 10:16 according to which the *'ofanim* move with the *keruvim* (*hayyot*). For the use of sнwв, cf. Ezek. 1:14. Strugnell further observes that in our text the *'ofanim* and *keruvim* have not yet become angelic bands.[164] Our account is completely in accord with that of Ezekiel.

mal'akhe qodesh. This term occurs in DST 1:11 (partly restored), DSW 7:6, 1QSa 2:9 f., 1QSb 3:6 (partly restored) and 11Q Ber lines 5 and 13 f. (the latter partly restored). From the context in DSW and 1QSa it appears that *qodesh* in this epithet stresses the angels' state of ritual purity (cf. Deut. 23:15). The phrase has also been found in an Aramaic inscription[165] which Scholem analyzes in the context of the *hekhalot* literature.[166]

yatz'[u]. Strugnell adds the *waw* in light of LXX to Ezekiel 1:14. The plural is certainly preferable, but it would be possible to read *yatzo'*, an infinitive absolute. Strugnell's transcription is confusing. The scribe had accidentally added this *waw* to the next word. Cf. Ezek. 1:13.

4–5. *mi-ben [ga]lgale kevodo ke-mar'eh 'esh*. Dependent upon Ezek. 10:6 (Strugnell).[167] But note the addition of *kevodo*, probably as a precaution against anthropomorphism. *Ke-mar'eh* has also been added from Ezek. 1:27 where its purpose probably is to combat anthropomorphism. Strugnell also compares Rev. 4:5. *Galgale 'esh* occurs in *Ma'aseh Merkavah* sec. 3.[168] Association of the angels with fire is a common motif in the *hekhalot* literature and the *Sefer ha-Razim*.

5. *ruho[t]*. The *taw* is supplied by Strugnell. We may also read *ruhe*.[169] The

---

161. *Seder Rav 'Amram*, p. 141; D. Goldschmidt (ed.), *Mahazor la-Yamim ha-Nora'im* (Jerusalem, 1970), I, 150, n. 5; A. Gordon, "'Iyyun Tefillah," in *'Otzar ha-Tefillot*, I, 217b; *Tur 'Orah Hayyim* 133; J. Epstein, *'Arukh ha-Shulhan* 133:1.

162. Sec. 5 (Scholem, *Gnosticism*, p. 105). Altmann ("Shire Qedushah," p. 12) does not transcribe the entire hymn.

163. See the sources cited in Scholem, *Gnosticism*, p. 28, n. 18.

164. Contrast Odeberg, *3 Enoch*, pp. 148 f., 166, 170.

165. First published by M. A. Dupont-Sommer, "Deux lamelles d'argent à inscription hebréo-araméenne trouvées à Agabeyli (Turquie)," *Jahrbuch für kleinasiatische Forschung*, I (Heidelberg, 1950–51), 201–17.

166. *Gnosticism*, pp. 84–93, esp. pp. 87 f., and 134 (addendum to p. 87). For the relation of the inscription to the magic bowls, see Levine, "Language," pp. 360 f.

167. Cf. Ex. 25:22 and Num. 7:89, for the form *mi-ben* with *keruvim*.

168. Scholem, *Gnosticism*, p. 103. Cf. *galgale merkavah* in secs. 30 (Altmann, "Shire Qedushah," p. 23; Scholem, *Gnosticism*, p. 114) and 32 (Altmann, "Shire Qedushah," p. 14; Scholem, *Gnosticism*, p. 115).

169. This form is attested elsewhere in the text. Cf. Strugnell, "Angelic Liturgy," pp. 332 f.

use of this term for angels is widespread in the Apocrypha and pseudepigrapha, as well as at Qumran.[170] Especially interesting in light of our text is its
use with *mal'akhe qodesh* in DST 1:10 f. This is, no doubt, based on Ps. 104:4.
Whereas in 3 En. the *ruhot* are basically the "winds," they appear to be angels
in the *Sefer ha-Razim*.[171] According to *Pirqe Rabbi 'Eli'ezer* 4, the angels take
the form of *ruhot* when sent on a mission. The plural in Talmudic literature
invariably refers to "demons," usually evil, but on occasion benevolent.[172]

qodesh qodashim. This is no doubt to be read *qedoshim*, "angels" (see commentary to Text A, line 24). At some point in the textual history a scribe
accidentally wrote QWDSh and neglected to indicate its erasure before continuing with the correct form.

ruhot qedoshim saviv. This represents the sect's exegesis of *we-'esh mitlaqahat
we-nogah lo saviv* in Ezek. 1:4. This is confirmed by the soon to follow exegesis
of *hashmal*.[173]

shevile 'esh. We must prefer *shevile* to *shibbole*, "rivers," as we would expect
the fem. construct *shibbolot*. The biblical *shibbole* is used only with the meaning
"grains." *Mar'eh shevile 'esh* represents an exegesis of *hashmal*. Cf. Ezek. 1:27
and 8:2. Strugnell cites the parallel *shevive 'esh* and *shevile mayim*[174] in a
qedushta' of Yannai.[175] Note the *shevile shamayim* mentioned in *Ma'aseh
Merkavah*.[176] Cf. *shevilin d[i nur]* in an Aramaic Enoch fragment from Qumran
(4Q En^c 1 VII 1) as restored by J. T. Milik.[177]

bi-demut. As in Ezekiel's visions of the throne,[178] *demut* serves here to guard
against anthropomorphism. Apparently, the *hashmal* was considered close
enough to God that such protection was necessary. The danger of correctly
understanding the *hashmal* is illustrated in the story of the youth who was
"burned," recorded in tannaitic and amoraic formulations in B. Hagigah 13a.
In *Ma'aseh Merkavah* sec. 23 *demut* appears before the name of the angel
ZHRRY'L, immediately below the divine throne.[179] See also the marriage
benediction discussed in our commentary to Text B, line 3. *Demut* and *mar'eh*
serve this purpose in 3 En. 35 and 44 for large numbers of angels.

170. Yadin, *War Scroll*, pp. 231 f.
171. 2:2, p. 81; 6:1, p. 104.
172. On the benevolent *ruah pasqanit*, see the sources cited in R. Margaliot, *Mal'akhe 'Elyon*
(Jerusalem, 1964), pp. 178 f.
173. Kuhn, "Nachträge," p. 166, did not understand this exegesis. His reading of *sheviv* cannot
be accepted.
174. Cf. *darkekha u-shevilkha ba-mayim konanta* in *Ma'aseh Merkavah* sec. 4 (Altmann, "Shire
Qedushah," p. 11; Scholem, *Gnosticism*, p. 104).
175. A. Murtonen, *Materials for a Non-Masoretic Hebrew Grammar* (Helsinki, 1958), p. 99, l. 97.
176. Secs. 2 and 3 (Scholem, *Gnosticism*, p. 103).
177. Milik, *Enoch*, p. 199, and Plate XIII.
178. E.g., Ezek. 1:26, 28; 8:2; and 10:1. Cf. Gen. 1:26.
179. Scholem, *Gnosticism*, p. 112. Cf. *Sefer ha-Razim* 2:14, p. 82.

nogah. This word serves to link Ezek. 1:4 (which our text has just explained) to Ezek. 10:4 where the phrase *nogah kevod 'adonay* appears. This is the source of *kavod* in the next line of our text. This is a common literary technique in Qumran texts. The *nogah* appears often in the *hekhalot* literature.[180]

6. *be-riqmat kavod*. Strugnell read ʀᴡǪᴍᴛ but why grasp at an unattested form when *riqmah*, "variegated stuff, embroidery," is regular?[181] The confusion of *waw* and *yod* in the Dead Sea Scrolls is well known. *Reqem* appears in the "Song of the Kine" and in other *merkavah* hymns.[182] Strugnell points out that the angelic garments are being described in priestly terms. Cf. Ex. 39:29. This same priestly usage occurs in DSW 7:10[183] and a military usage is found in DSW 5:6 and 9.[184] Strugnell observes that the language of our text is dependent on Jud. 5:30. Cf. also Ps. 45:15.[185]

tzevaʿe peleʾ. For the root ᴛᴁʙᶜ referring to the angels, see *Maʿaseh Merkavah* sec. 33.[186]

memullah toha[r]. Strugnell correctly supplies the *resh* based on Ex. 30:35. The "metaphorical" use of *memullah* is presumed in the Targum Onkelos and Jonathan to Ex. 30:35 (*meʿarev*), followed by Rashi, Rashbam, Luzzatto (who gives added support), and Cassuto. New JPS translates, "refined." The word also describes Josiah in Ben Sira 49:1. This usage appears in a *baraitaʾ* in B. Qiddushin 29b[187] where the rule of *lectio difficilior* makes the reading of the Vilna edition preferable to that of the marginal note.[188] This root in Arabic can convey the sense of "to be beautiful, handsome, pretty, comely, nice, elegant."[189] *Hekhalot Rabbati* uses *roqeah memullah* in a list of praises uttered

180. See, e.g., *Maʿaseh Merkavah* 33 (Altmann, "Shire Qedushah," p. 17; Scholem, *Gnosticism*, p. 117).
181. So Kuhn, "Nachträge," p. 166. J. M. Allegro, *Qumran Cave 4 DJD* V (Oxford, 1968), I, 14 (originally published in his "Further Messianic References in Qumran Literature," *JBL*, LXXV. [1956], 181), reads *bigde roqmo[t*, referring to the garments of the Messiah of David. While the traces (Plate V) might support his reading, we suggest *bigde riqma[h*.
182. Scholem, *Gnosticism*, pp. 25 f., and n. 16, and 128 (addendum to p. 26); 3 En. 22.
183. Cf. Yadin, *War Scroll*, p. 220, n. 3.
184. Cf. Yadin's note. Kutscher (*Lashon*, p. 496) suggests reading ʀᴡǪᴍʜ in DSW 5:6, 9. On this form, see above, n. 171.
185. Allegro, "Messianic References," p. 181, n. 44.
186. Scholem, *Gnosticism*, p. 117. Altmann ("Shire Qedushah," p. 17) reads ɴᴡʙᶜ (*noveaᶜ*). Context, however, seems to support Scholem here.
187. In the words of R. Judah (bar Ilai), a pupil of Akiva; H. Strack, *Introduction to the Talmud and Midrash* (New York, 1965), p. 115.
188. The Vilna edition reads *memullah*. The note appears based on Alfasi who reads *memullaʾ*. For both readings, see A. Kohut, ʿ*Arukh ha-Shalem*, III, 322, n. 4; and R. Hananel in B. M. Lewin (ed.), ʿ*Otzar ha-Geʾonim* (Jerusalem, 1939), IX, 23. Maimonides (*Hilkhot Talmud Torah* 1:4) paraphrases *navon u-maskil le-havin*. A confusion of the roots ᴍʟʜᵉᵗ and ᴍʟʾ occurs in the variant readings of B. Bavaʾ Qammaʾ 117b. See Rabbinovicz, *Diqduqe Soferim*, on BQ 117b, n. *tzade*. This is a phonological phenomenon.
189. H. Wehr, *A Dictionary of Modern Written Arabic*, ed. J. M. Cowan (Ithaca, 1966), p. 920. Cf. E. W. Lane, *An Arabic-English Lexicon* (London, 1885), Bk. I, Pt. 7, p. 2731.

by the throne of glory each day.[190] This text ignores the Masoretic accents of Ex. 30:35 which divide the verse between these two words.

ruhot ['e-]lohim hayyim. Cf. the phrase 'elohe ha-ruhot in Num. 16:22 and 27:16 as well as 1 En. 62:2 ("Lord of Spirits"). 'Elohim hayyim occurs in Deut. 5:23, 1 Sam. 17:26, 36, Jer. 10:10, 23:36. The phrase also appears in the *qedushah de-yotzer*,[191] the *Harba' de-Mosheh*,[192] and, quite prominently, in the *Sefer Yetzirah*.[193] A Greek epithet of God 'εν οὐρανῷζων," who lives in heaven," has been found in the *Hekhalot Rabbati* by H. Lewy.[194] He points out that the phrase "living God" is frequent in Greek Jewish literature.[195] *Divre 'elohim hayyim* appears in halakhic context in a *baraita'* in B. Yoma' 35b and amoraic statements in B. ʿEruvin 13b and B. Gittin 6b.

mithallekhim. Strugnell calls attention to *mithallekhet* in Ezek. 1:13. Gen. 3:8 ('elohim mithallekh) supplies the connection to the phrase 'elohim hayyim. This method of linking verses is common at Qumran.

merkavot. The concept of a multiplicity of chariot-thrones is familiar from the *hekhalot* literature. *Maʿaseh Merkavah* section 6 places increasing numbers of "chariot-thrones of fire" in each of the seven heavens.[196] 3 En. 24 contains a scheme of many *merkavot* based on the assumption that wherever God appears, He appears on a chariot-throne.[197] According to Odeberg, chapter 37 uses the term *merkavot* for the four holy beasts. *Massekhet Hekhalot* 5 and 6 locate the *merkavot* in the seventh heaven.[198] The *Re'uyot Yehezqel*[199] sees one *merkavah* in each of the seven heavens. According to one tradition in *Pesiqta' de-Rav Kahana'*,[200] 22,000 chariot-thrones, each like that seen by Ezekiel, descended to Sinai and were seen by Israel. Infinite *merkavot* are mentioned in the *qedushah* hymn for the additional service on high holydays.[201] Gruenwald

190. Jellinek, Bet ha-Midrash, III, 101; Wertheimer, Bate Midrashot, I, 105.

191. Seder Rav ʿAmram, p. 13; Siddur Rav Saʿadyah, p. 36; ʿAvodat Yisra'el, p. 77. Jer. 10:10 is the source of this prayer as can be seen from the continuation, u-melekh ʿolam.

192. Gaster, Studies and Texts, III, 70.

193. 1:1, 9, 14; 5:4. G. Scholem ("Yezirah, Sefer," EJ, XVI, 786) postulates that the text was written between the third and sixth centuries, "apparently in Palestine."

194. "Seride Mishpatim," p. 166.

195. Lewy cites 2 Macc. 15:4. For equivalent terms in the Aramaic magic bowls and hekhalot literature, see Levine, "Language of the Magical Bowls," p. 358.

196. Scholem, Gnosticism, p. 106. Cf. sec. 25 (Altmann, "Shire Qedushah," p. 20; Scholem, Gnosticism, p. 113). And Sefer ha-Razim 2:133, p. 88.

197. Odeberg, 3 Enoch, p. 84.

198. Jellinek, Bet ha-Midrash, II, 43 f.

199. Gruenwald, "Re'uyot Yehezqel," p. 119. Cf. his commentary, p. 115. The attribution of this tradition to R. Meir accepted by Scholem (Gnosticism, p. 47) must be rejected with E. Urbach, Hazal, Pirqe 'Emunot we-Deʿot (Jerusalem, 1971), p. 211, n. 80.

200. Ed. S. Buber (Lyck, 1868), p. 107b; ed. B. Mandelbaum (New York, 1962), I, 220. See Lieberman in Scholem, Gnosticism, pp. 121 f., and the parallel in Pesiqta' Rabbati, ed. M. Friedmann (Vienna, 1880), p. 102b, and n. 49.

201. Goldschmidt, Mahazor, I, 172.

is probably correct that the multiple chariot traditions must all be based on Is. 66:15.[202]

7. *berekh*. Strugnell calls attention to the peculiar forms developed by this literature. The present form is simply a masculine equivalent of *berakhah*. Kuhn and Carmignac both reject this reading.[203] Carmignac notes that a parallel in l. 2 suggests that "un equivalent du nom de Dieu" should appear here. Neither author realized how typical such bi-forms are of the later *hekhalot* literature. This tendency was carried on by the paytanic tradition. The possibility of a form *berekh* is raised by Rashi to Num. 23:20. Rashi argues against taking *berekh* in that verse as a noun. It is also possible to assume that the sect read *berekh* as a noun and that this is the source of the form in our text. The use of medial *kaf* in final position is not unusual in Qumran manuscripts.

lekhtam. Cf. Ezek. 1:17, 21, 24; 10:11.[204] This entire sentence is taken differently by Carmignac[205] who translates, "Les esprits (= les anges) de Dieu Vivant se déplacent continuellement avec la gloire merveilleuse du Char et (avec) la voix silencieuse de [   ] dans le bruissement de leur déplacement." This translation is, however, based on his rejection of Strugnell's reading of *berekh* which we have accepted.

qodesh. Strugnell notes two possibilities. Either we have here an equivalent of *qadosh* (the form being familiar from Qumran),[206] i.e., God, or *qodesh* refers to the sanctuary, which might be the object of veneration as is the chariot.

be-hashiv darkhehem. The *hif*^{c}*il* of sHWB with *derekh* occurs in 1 Kings 13:26, 2 Kings 19:28, Is. 37:29.

be-heromam yeromamu. Cf. the commentary to Text A, line 18. Our forms can be explained as attempts to accommodate the phrase in Ezek. 10:17 to our context. Carmignac[207] has identified *be-heromam* as a regular *nif*^{c}*al* with suffix and *yeromamu* as a *polal* imperfect. He says that the author intentionally modified the wording of Ezek. 10:17. For Ezekiel, the wheels raise themselves after the *keruvim*. For our author the chariots elevate themselves, drawing along the "spirits."

bi-shokhen. Strugnell is correct that this is an equivalent at Qumran to

---

202. "Re'uyot Yehezqel," p. 115. On the *thronoi* in Test. Levi 3:8 and 2 En. 20:1, see Odeberg, *3 Enoch*, p. 142.

203. Kuhn, "Nachträge," p. 166; Carmignac, "Règle des chants," p. 566.

204. The latter passage has been partially read in the 11Q Ezekiel Scroll; W. H. Brownlee, "The Scroll of Ezekiel from the Eleventh Qumran Cave," *RQ*, IV (1963–64), 16. It is a pity that this scroll could not be unrolled. We would have known how Ezekiel's *merkavah* visions appeared in a sectarian biblical manuscript.

205. "Règle des chants," p. 566.

206. See Licht, *Serakhim*, pp. 45 f.

207. Ibid., p. 566.

bi-shekhon. But *bi-shekhon* is an infinitive construction lacking its object. Who settled or abided? Perhaps we should read *be-shokhnam,* supplying a *mem.* This would accord with *be-ʿomdam yaʾamodu* (Ezek. 10:17) to which our phrase is equivalent.

8. *gilot.* Apparently the plural of *gilah.* The same form occurs in DSW 3:11.[208]

mahane ʾelohim. Strugnell cites Ezek. 1:24. This and *diglehem* indicate that the angels, as Strugnell notes, were divided into military units like Israel in the wilderness and the sect in the *War Scroll.* Cf. *mahane ʾel* in DSW 4:9. The notion that the angels were divided into camps is a basic motif in 3 En., *Sefer ha-Razim,* the Aramaic magic bowls,[209] *Pirqe Rabbi ʾEliʿezer* 4, and *Harbaʾ de-Mosheh.*[210]

tishba[hot]. The word is used in Ben Sira 51:12, the Hallel of Ben Sira, in the phrase *hodu le-ʾel ha-tishbahot.* It is used with *shirot* in a *baraitaʾ* in B. Pesahim 117a and in an amoraic statement in B. Berakhot 3b.[211] Strugnell reads TShBWH[et], and Kuhn[212] restores *tishbohah.* Note the Aramaic form TShBH[et]H in the Aramaic Enoch fragments from Qumran (4Q En[a] 1 ii:10 and 4Q En[c] 1 i:29, 1 En. 5:1). The equivalent in the Greek text of Enoch is *doxa* which was, as mentioned above, an equivalent of *kavod, gevurah,* and Gk. *dynamis.*[213]

9. *diglehem.* The *degalim* are military units in the *War Scroll* as in the Bible and Rabbinic literature. The *degel* was the largest permanent tactical-organizational unit.[214] Yadin identifies the *degel* with the Roman *cohors.*[215] The angels are pictured as arranged in *degalim* in later midrashic literature, each *degel* headed by an archangel.[216] Clearly, this term again shows that the sect

208. Yadin compares *gilat* in Is. 35:2.

209. See Odeberg, *3 Enoch,* "Index and Vocabulary," p. 20; and Levine, "Language of the Magical Bowls," pp. 361–64. Levine has gathered much material on the magical warrior motif.

210. Gaster, *Studies and Texts,* III, 75. *Merkavot* in this text seems to have deteriorated to "angels."

211. The words of Rav Ashi, a sixth generation Babylonian amora who died in 427 c.e. (Strack, *Introduction,* p. 132). This phrase was taken over into the last morning benediction before the *shemaʿ* (*Seder Rav ʿAmram,* p. 20; *Siddur Rav Saʿadyah,* p. 16; *ʿAvodat Yisraʾel,* p. 85) and the *birkat ha-shir* recited after the morning psalms on Sabbaths and festivals (*Seder Rav ʿAmram,* p. 70; some versions in *Siddur Rav Saʿadyah,* p. 120; Baer's textual notes in *ʿAvodat Yisraʾel,* p. 209).

212. "Nachträge," p. 166.

213. Milik, *Enoch,* pp. 146, 149, and Plate II, 185, and Plate IX. Cf. also 4Q En[g] 1 ii:15 (1 En. 91:10); ibid., p. 260, and Plate XXI. Note the occurence of *shir tushbahot* (twice) in a Chicago Oriental Institute magic bowl, Text N–IV; C. D. Isbell, "Two New Aramaic Incantation Bowls," *BASOR,* 223 (1976), 23. *Be-tishb(o)hotʿolamin* appears in a hymnic passage, 6Q18 (*DJD* III, p. 133) in which the first *waw* is suspended above the line.

214. Yadin, *War Scroll,* pp. 39, n. 1, 50. For rabbinic references, cf. ibid., p. 62, n. 2.

215. Ibid., p. 171.

216. Examples in M. Jastrow, *A Dictionary of the Targumim, the Talmud Babli and Yerushalmi and the Midrashic Literature* (New York, 1950), I, 280. See also the use of *degel* in 4 Q En[a] 1 ii, and 4Q Enastr[b] (Milik, Plates II, XXX).

conceived the angelic hosts as organized like the armies of Israel in the desert and DSW.[217]

pequdehem. Yadin, to DSW 2:4, translates "subordinates." The passages he cites, however, from CDC 15:5 f. and 1QSa 1:8 f. indicate that the *pequdim* are those who have passed muster. They are not "noncommissioned" officers.

be-macam[ad]. Note the probable use of final *mem* in medial position.[218] Yadin states that the *macamad* denotes the position assumed by the soldiers when arrayed for combat. The term applies to the angelic hosts in DST 3:21 f. and 11:13.[219] Note that the former passage uses *qedoshim* and the latter, *ruhot.* *Be-macamad* also has cultic meaning for the sect.[220]

Conclusions

The commentary has shown that the 4Q *Serekh Shirot cOlat ha-Shabbat* is replete with expressions and motifs met also in the later *hekhalot* traditions. Among the most prominent are: the notion of seven archangels, the idea that the angelic hosts praise God regularly, the notion of the *gevurah, kavod,* or *dynamis,* the heavenly sanctuary and cult, the "gentle voice," association of fire with the angels, the variegated colors, the "living God," the multiple chariot-thrones, and the military organization of the heavenly hosts. Further, the language, terminology, and style of our text are very similar to what we encounter in the later *hekhalot* literature.

The Dead Sea Scrolls often reflect our earliest exemplars of elements found in tannaitic Judaism. It is therefore necessary to inquire about the relevance of our text to the history of *merkavah* speculation.

The material studied here reflects some significant differences from later *hekhalot* literature. We have a description of the goings on in heaven. There is no ascent or guided tour. The sect simply describes what can be known from its vantage point. This information comes primarily from an exegesis of the *merkavah* visions of Ezekiel and related biblical texts. Therefore, there is no incubation or preparation for a mystical "journey." The songs of praise in our text are those uttered on high. They are not intended, like the later materials, as means to bring about ecstasy or mystical experience. Further, the angels

217. Cf. S. Talmon, "The 'Desert Motif' in the Bible and in Qumran Literature," in A. Altmann (ed.), *Biblical Motifs* (Cambridge, Mass., 1966), pp. 55–63.

218. See J. P. Siegel, "Final *mem* in Medial Position and Medial *mem* in Final Position in 11 Q Ps a, Some Observations," *RQ,* VII (1969–71), 125–30. Our example does not fit into his system.

219. *War Scroll,* p. 146.

220. Ibid., pp. 206 f.

are known in our text by epithets.[221] These are to be distinguished from the numerous and often incomprehensible names developed in the later mystical tradition. One of the prime stimuli for the development of a multitude of names is their magical use, either to bring about the vision or for other purposes.[222] Such elements are entirely lacking at Qumran.

There is a historical problem which must be taken into consideration in evaluating the results of this study. The sectarian scrolls from Qumran are considerably earlier than the tannaitic materials or *hekhalot* texts available to us. Rabbinic tradition asserts that it is a continuation of Pharisaic Judaism. Yet our sources for the understanding of the Pharisaic tradition are all post-Pharisaic in formulation. We have no sources regarding the Pharisees at the time the Dead Sea texts were being authored and copied. We must be very careful, therefore, in drawing conclusions from the Dead Sea Scrolls about the origin of elements found in tannaitic or amoraic traditions.

The text we have examined was composed at Qumran by at least the second half of the first century B.C. It is certainly the earliest known post-biblical Hebrew text containing mystical speculation regarding the divine throne (*merkavah*) and the associated retinue of angelic beings. The text shows clearly that the beginnings of the *merkavah* tradition lie in the exegesis of Ezekiel in light of other relevant texts, a form of early *midrash*.[223] This *midrash* was supplemented with angelic songs. Only later, perhaps under foreign influence, did magical and incubation elements and angelic names become part of the speculation and did it become esoteric. It is not until the tannaitic period that we encounter these developments. They probably occurred after the 4Q *Serekh Shirot 'Olat ha-Shabbat* was composed, perhaps even after the extinction of the Qumran sect in the wake of the unsuccessful Jewish revolt against Rome in 66–73 A.D.[224]

In light of our study, it is possible to conclude that *merkavah* mysticism had its origin at Qumran or in related sectarian circles. From there it somehow penetrated and was absorbed by Pharisaic and then tannaitic tradition. It would be through these channels that this speculation entered into the mainstream of Judaism.

The view still persists in certain circles that the Scrolls are the product of Karaite authorship.[225] The early Karaites castigated the Rabbinites for their

221. See the list in Strugnell, "Angelic Liturgy," pp. 331–34.

222. See Scholem, *Gnosticism*, pp. 75–83.

223. On *midrash* exegesis at Qumran, see my *Halakhah at Qumran*, pp. 54–60.

224. R. de Vaux (*Archaeology*, p. 41) concludes, basing himself primarily on numismatic evidence, that Qumran was destroyed by the Romans in June 68 A.D.

225. There are indeed many interesting parallels between the Qumran and Karaite literatures. N. Wieder, *The Judean Scrolls and Karaism* (London, 1962), has shown that many of these can be useful for understanding Qumran texts.

belief in angels and spirits.[226] How, then, could our text, replete with designations of angels associated with the divine chariot-throne, have been authored by a Karaite? This is just one more proof that the Karaites cannot have been the authors of the scrolls from the Judean desert.

The Dead Sea sect must now be considered a possible source for *merkavah* mysticism as it developed in tannaitic Judaism. After all, there is no evidence for such mysticism in proto-Pharisaism. Our text may tell us quite a bit about the history of throne speculation. Finally, this study strongly confirms the importance of the Dead Sea Scrolls for an understanding of the milieu from which come tannaitic Judaism and *merkavah* mysticism.

---

226. See Margaliot, *Sefer ha-Razim*, pp. 36 f.; L. Nemoy, *Karaite Anthology* (New Haven, 1952), pp. 30 f., 335 f. The view of Benjamin al-Nahawandi regarding an angel-creator of the world was not accepted by his Karaite brethren; see Nemoy, *Karaite Anthology*, pp. 21, 333.

Moses and the Law According to Maimonides

Kalman P. Bland

I

As a counterpoint to the theme of prophecy developed in Book II:32–48 of the *Guide of the Perplexed*, Maimonides repeatedly underscores the unprecedented singularity of the unique and the never again attainable station of Moses.[1] Chapters 32 and 33 assert that Moses occupied the "highest rank"[2] among those present at Sinai and that the rank of those who heard the created voice there "was not equal to the rank of Moses our Master."[3] Chapters 34, 36, and 45 sound the "fundamental principle" Maimonides "never ceased explaining, namely that to every prophet except Moses our Master prophetic revelation comes through an angel,"[4] by which he means that "the imaginative faculty did not enter into his prophecy."[5] Chapter 35 begins with a reference to his Commentary to the *Mishnah* (*Pereq Heleq*) and to his *Mishneh Torah*, where he had already formulated the "four differences by which the prophecy of Moses our Master is distinguished from the prophecy of the other prophets,"[6] namely that Moses, unlike all other prophets, received his revelation without an intermediary, while fully awake, without physical or emotional derangement, and whenever he so willed it.

Chapter 35 continues with the following admonition: "I will let you know

1. Invaluable studies of Maimonides' theory of prophecy are: Z. Diesendruck, "Maimonides' Lehre von der Prophetie," *Jewish Studies in Memory of Israel Abrahams* (New York, 1927), pp. 74–134; Leo Strauss, "Die philosophische Begründung des Gesetzes," in his *Philosophie und Gesetz* (Berlin, 1935), pp. 87–122; H. A. Wolfson, "Hallevi and Maimonides on Prophecy," *JQR*, XXXII (1941–42), 345–70, and XXXIII (1942–43), 49–81; S. Pines, "Translator's Introduction," in *The Guide of the Perplexed* (Chicago, 1963), pp. lxxxvi–xcii, xcviii–cii, cxx–cxxiii; and Julius Guttmann, *Philosophies of Judaism*, trans. David W. Silverman (Garden City, 1964) pp. 194–202. For the classical and Islamic background, see F. Rahman, *Prophecy in Islam* (London, 1957), pp. 7–91. Cf. A. Reines, "Maimonides' Concept of Mosaic Prophecy," *HUCA*, XL–XLI (1969–70), 325–62. All translations and references to the *Guide* are from Pines's edition cited above. Throughout the preparation of this study the Arabic text of the *Guide* established by S. Munk, *Dalâlat al-Hâ'irîn*, ed. I. Joel (Jerusalem, 1931) as well as S. Munk's French translation, *Le Guide des Egarés* (Paris, 1960; reprint), were constantly consulted.

2. II:32, p. 363.

3. II:33, p. 365.

4. II:34, p. 367.

5. II:36, p. 373; cf. II:45, p. 403.

6. II:35, p. 367. For the Arabic text of the introduction to *Pereq Heleq*, see J. Holzer, *Zur Geschichte der Dogmenlehre* (Berlin, 1901), pp. 23–26. The passage in the *Mishneh Torah* is *Hilkhot Yesode ha-Torah* VII:6.

that everything I say on prophecy in the chapters of this Treatise refers only to the form of prophecy of all the prophets who were before Moses and who will come after him. As for the prophecy of Moses our Master, I shall not touch upon it in these chapters with even a single word or in a flash. For to my mind the term prophet used with reference to Moses and to the others is amphibolous."[7] As Maimonides explains elsewhere, amphibolous terms are those which are "predicated of two things between which there is a likeness in respect to some notion, which notion is an accident attached to both of them and not a constituent element of the essence of each one of them."[8] Since the definition of prophecy given in II:36 provides that prophecy is an overflow from the Active Intellect reaching the imaginative faculty after first being received by the rational faculty, Moses, for whose apprehension the imaginative faculty is not essential, cannot be said to be a prophet in the strict sense of the term. What alone justifies the use of this term for him are those noncognitive aspects of the Mosaic mission, to be discussed shortly, which are shared by Moses and the other prophets.

Chapter 35 reiterates a motif found throughout Maimonides' writings —the absolute superiority of Moses' knowledge. Or as it is phrased in I:54, "what has been apprehended by [Moses], peace be upon him, has not been apprehended by anyone before him nor will it be apprehended by anyone after him."[9] In the Neoplatonic epistemology adopted by Maimonides, such knowledge presupposes overcoming the interference of corporeality in the acquisition of metaphysical truth and therefore explains why Maimonides denies the imaginative faculty of Moses any role in this revelation. In the *Guide* III:9, we are told that

> matter is a strong veil preventing the apprehension of that which is separate from matter as it truly is. It does this even if it is the noblest and purest matter, I mean to say even if it is the matter of the heavenly spheres. All the more is this true for the dark and turbid matter that is ours. Hence whenever our intellect aspires to apprehend the deity or one of the intellects, there subsists this great veil interposed between the two.[10]

7. II:36, p. 373.

8. I:56, p. 131. Cf. *Maimonides' Treatise on Logic*, trans and ed. Israel Efros, *PAAJR*, VIII (1938), 60. For the historical background of this term, see H. A. Wolfson, "The Amphibolous Terms in Aristotle, Arabic Philosophy, and Maimonides," *HTR*, XXXI (1938), 151–73.

9. I:54, p. 123; II:35, pp. 357–68. See also *Hilkhot Yesode ha-Torah* I:10; Munk's comments to *Guide*, I:54; and W. Bacher, *Die Bibelexegese Moses Maimunis* (Budapest, 1896), p. 78.

10. III:9, pp. 436–37. Guttmann has called our attention to the Neoplatonic moment in Maimonides' epistemology in his *Philosophies of Judaism*, pp. 177–78, 199–201. A superb overview of the ascetic tendency in Neoplatonic epistemology is given by A. Altmann, *Isaac Israeli* (Oxford, 1958), pp. 185–95.

To say then that Moses attained a knowledge of God that exceeds any humanly possible knowledge implies that Moses surpassed the rest of mankind in neutralizing the bodily and moral impediments to the acquisition of truth.[11] The seventh of Maimonides' well-known and controversial Thirteen Fundamental Principles states that "there was no veil which he [Moses] did not pierce. No material hindrance stood in his way, and no defect whether great or small mingled itself with him. The imaginative and sensual powers of his soul were stripped from him. His appetitive faculty was stilled and there remained pure intellect only."[12]

When we recall that, for Maimonides, prophecy represents "the highest degree of man and the ultimate term of perfection for his species,"[13] and that the rank of even the highest degree of prophecy is nonetheless lower than the rank of Moses, we are forced to conclude that the difference between Moses and the other prophets is one of category, rather than one of quality or intensity within the same species.[14] Citing again the language of the seventh principle, we find Maimonides unrestrained in his description of Moses' transformation: "His exaltedness reached beyond the sphere of humanity, so that he attained to the angelic rank and became included in the order of the angels."[15] As a writer, Maimonides scrupulously avoided the casual use of language, so that his choice of the term angel is no lyricism devoid of philosophic content. Angel, as he teaches in II:7, is an equivocal term applied to the separate intellects, their bodily spheres, and the sublunar elements which ultimately derive from first matter. Of these three, it is the separate intellects which, like Moses, are characterized by incorporeality and a supernal apprehension of God. Since what the philosophers call separate intellects, the Torah calls angels,[16] describing Moses as an angel conveys Maimonides' view that Moses was something like a separate intellect, located among them in the translunar realm.

This startling conclusion may be corroborated by Maimonides' critique of

11. See the so-called "Eight Chapters," chap. 7. A critical edition of this text has been published by J. Gorfinkel. Cf. *Guide* I:35, esp. pp. 76–79.

12. See Holzer's text cited above, n. 6. The latest and perhaps most valuable discussion of the Thirteen Fundamental Principles is Arthur Hyman, "Maimonides' Thirteen Principles," in A. Altmann, ed., *Jewish Medieval and Renaissance Studies* (Cambridge, Mass., 1967), pp. 119–44, esp. pp. 142–43. Cf. J. Abelson, "Maimonides on the Jewish Creed," *JQR*, XIX (1906–7), 51. A more popular survey is L. Jacobs, *Principles of the Jewish Faith* (New York, 1964), pp. 1–32.

13. II:36, p. 369.

14. This has already been forcefully emphasized by Julius Guttmann in his *Philosophies of Judaism*, pp. 195–96, and in his essay "The Religious Motifs in the Philosophy of Maimonides," in his *Dat u-Maddaᶜ*, trans. S. Esh and ed. S. H. Bergman and N. Rotenstreich (Jerusalem, 1955), pp. 86–102. The categorical singularity is also stressed by Eliezer Schweid, *Taᶜam we-Haqashah* (Ramat Gan, 1970), pp. 135–38.

15. Holzer, *Dogmenlehre*, p. 24; and Abelson, "Maimonides on the Jewish Creed," p. 51.

16. II:2, p. 253; II:6, p. 262.

astronomical science found in II:24. Assuming a transformation into existence as a separate intellect, we should expect that Moses had direct access to metaphysical truths beyond the reach of ordinary, earth-bound minds. Maimonides acknowledges that man may succeed in apprehending the sublunar realm, for "that is his world and his dwelling-place in which he has been placed and of which he himself is a part." By contrast, the heavens "are too far away from us and too high in rank" to allow more than "a small measure of . . . mathematical" knowledge pertaining to the translunar realm. Hence, "all that Aristotle states about that which is beneath the sphere of the moon is in accordance with reasoning," but "let us give over the things that cannot be grasped by reasoning to him who was reached by the mighty divine overflow so that it could be fittingly said of him: 'With him do I speak mouth to mouth' (*Num.* 12:8)"[17] The reference, of course, is to Moses, for whom the realm of separate intellects became "his world and his dwelling place in which he has been placed and of which he himself is a part."

Maimonides, however, does not claim that Moses' knowledge—on which he relies in deciding the question of the world's creation in time or its eternity—is absolutely unrestricted. Only God can know "the true reality, the nature, the substance, the form, the motions, and the causes of the heavens."[18] Moses could never have attained the ultimate in metaphysical knowledge, for only God can know Himself "in the true reality of His immutable essence."[19] Moses is no exception to the rule "that God, may He be exalted, cannot be apprehended by the intellects, and that none but He Himself can comprehend what He is."[20] Since both Moses and the separate intellects are related to a corporeal substrate, their apprehension must be limited.[21] And Moses, unlike the separate intellects, is linked to a sublunar, human body subject to generation and corruption, rendering his apprehension inferior to that of the separate intellects. This implies that Moses suffered affection. Maimonides did not shrink from emphasizing the bodily reality of Moses. Indeed, he highlights it in II:36 during his discussion of the bodily causes for the interruption of prophetic revelation. Contrasting Moses with Jacob, who ceased entirely from prophecy during his mourning for Joseph, Maimonides admits "that prophetic revelation did not come to Moses, peace be upon him, after the incident of the spies and until the whole

17. II:24, pp. 326–27.
18. II:24, p. 327.
19. III:21, p. 485; cf. I:54, p. 123.
20. I:59, p. 139.
21. II:4, p. 258; III:9, p. 436; and cf. I:72, p. 193. See *Hilkhot Yesode ha-Torah* II:5–8. For a grand review of Maimonides' Avicennian orientation to this issue as contrasted with that of Averroes, see H. A. Wolfson, *Crescas' Critique of Aristotle* (Cambridge, Mass., 1929), pp. 605–11.

generation of the desert perished, in the way that revelation used to come before, because—seeing the enormity of their crime—he suffered greatly because of this matter."[22]

From the texts we have examined, the Mosaic phenomenon emerges *sui generis*: Moses was neither altogether human nor totally divine. Because of his relative incorporeality, his apprehension of metaphysical truth surpassed the limited knowledge accessible to the greatest of prophets and philosopher/scientists alike. His was a knowledge that resembles the knowledge properly belonging to and only associated with the separate intellects, from which we may infer that Maimonides considered Moses to have become a metaphysical entity himself. There is no indication, however, that Maimonides entertained docetist-type notions concerning Moses, for as the texts clearly show, the limitations on Moses' knowledge were the direct result of the mundane bodily substrate to which his intellect was attached. To sppreciate fully how Maimonides understood this two-fold nature of Moses, we must focus our attention on the noncognitive features of the Mosaic mission.

II

Surveying Book II:32–48 of the *Guide* for references to Moses' actions as opposed to his apprehension, we discover that Maimonides attributes to Moses the following: he is the intermediary at Sinai; communicating God's word to the people (32–33); he performs miracles (35); he possessed the qualities of courage and divination (38); he issued a call to the Law (39); he governed the people (43); and he was endowed with the motivation to confer benefits on numerous people (45). Taken as a group, these actions described by Maimonides raise two problems: one literary, the other doctrinal. How could he reconcile the apparent contradiction generated by his avowed refusal to discuss the prophecy of Moses in "the chapters of this Treatise" and these numerous references to his actions? And how could he reconcile his description of a Moses preoccupied with the demands of his leadership while

22. I:36, pp. 272–73; cf. III:51, pp. 620–21, and the *Shemonah Peraqim*, chap. 7. Because of his faulty translation of the passage in II:36 (". . . Jacob did not receive any revelation. . . . The same was the case with Moses . . ."), M. Friedländer was misled into asserting that Moses did not "receive a Divine Message during the years which the Israelites, under Divine punishment, spent in the desert" (*The Guide for the Perplexed*, trans. M. Friedländer, 2nd rev. ed. [New York, 1956], pp. liii, 227). A Reines's study of this topic, cited above in n. 1, perpetuates this misunderstanding (p. 340, n. 48), undoubtedly as a result of his reliance upon Friedländer and his failure to take the advice he himself offers in n. 47. Ephodi's commentary on *Guide* II:36 is guilty of the same misunderstanding.

being located among the separate intellects engaged in receiving the divine overflow?

By prophecy, we may recall, Maimonides means "an overflow overflowing from God, may He be cherished and honored, through the intermediation of the Active Intellect, toward the rational faculty in the first place and there-after toward the imaginative faculty."[23] Prophecy, therefore, is identical with the revealed apprehension received by a properly prepared man and the internal senses[24] involved in the act of reception. Whatever a prophet may say or do following his revelation is merely the consequence of, but not a constituent element of, the essence of prophecy. Apprehension is the essence of prophecy, actions proceeding from it are attributes or accidents attaching themselves to it. Since Moses too received an apprehension, he would be termed equivocally a prophet owing to the absence of the imaginative faculty in his reception and the categorical superiority of the content of his revela-tion. His apprehension, like that of the prophets, constitutes the essence of his prophecy. His actions, whether similar to or superior to those of ordinary prophets, are, like the actions of ordinary prophets, merely accidents at-taching themselves to the essence of his reception. Insofar as he possessed a mundane body and shared in certain actions with other prophets, Moses is termed amphibolously a prophet. True to his word, Maimonides did not speak explicitly about the modality of Moses' apprehension or 'prophecy' when he spoke about Moses' miracles, his governing others, or his traits of courage. These do not constitute prophecy *per se*, but merely name the attributes of any leader. Ascribing such actions to Moses within the literary context of his discussion of prophecy does not contradict Maimonides' promise to avoid mentioning Moses' prophecy.

As for the second problem of reconciling Moses' simultaneity of earthly and celestial existence, the most we can say is that it is consistent with what Maimonides taught elsewhere in the *Guide*. In III:51, which Maimonides considered to be a "kind of conclusion" to the *Guide*, Maimonides describes that individual

> who, through his apprehension of the true realities and his joy in what he has apprehended, achieves a state in which he talks to people and is occupied with his bodily necessities while his intellect is wholly turned

23. II:36, p. 369. For a different solution to the problem, see L. Strauss, "How to Begin to Study *The Guide of the Perplexed*," in Pines's translation, pp. xxxvi–xliv. Maimonides does not admit to using this kind of contradiction in the *Guide*. It would follow, therefore, from Strauss's argu-ments that Maimonides is not only an enigmatic writer, but a mendacious one as well.

24. See H. A. Wolfson, "The Internal Senses in Latin, Arabic, and Hebrew Philosophical Texts," *HTR*, XXVIII (1935), pp. 69–133.

to Him, may He be exalted, while outwardly he is with people. . . . I do not say that this rank is that of all the prophets, but I do say that this is the rank of Moses our Master. . . . This was also the rank of the Patriarchs. . . . They performed these actions with the limbs only, while their intellects were constantly in His presence, may He be exalted.[25]

Though this passage neatly resolves the difficulty inherent in Maimonides' notion of Moses' sublunar and translunar simultaneity, it also raises two more serious questions. Why does Maimonides fail to differentiate between the status and actions of Moses and the patriarchs in the same way as he emphatically distinguished the apprehension of Moses from that of all other men? How are we to understand the correlation, if any, between Moses' apprehension and the actions he performs? These two questions apply to the passage in III:51, as well as to those numerous references to Moses scattered throughout the section of the *Guide* devoted to prophecy. What complicates matters even further are Maimonides' comments concerning Moses' miracles and his call to the Law which do differentiate these actions from those of others and which do correlate them with Moses' apprehension.

Concerning his miracles, Maimonides argues in II:35 that just as Moses' apprehension is categorically unlike that of the others, so too do his "miracles not belong to the class of miracles of the other prophets."[26] But nowhere does Maimonides assert that a causal relationship obtains between the two. In fact, the similarity between his apprehension and his miracles is restricted to their being different from the apprehension and miracles of others. Even this difference is clearly defined, for while the apprehension *per se* obtained by Moses is categorically superior, his miracles owe their singularity to the audience before whom they were performed. Whereas the miracles of others are "made known to a few people only," Moses' miracles were performed before those "who were unfavorably disposed to him" and in the public "presence of all Israel." Since the "connection and tie"[27] between Moses' apprehension and this action amounts to little more than a superficial similarity, we must explain why Maimonides bothered to raise the matter at all when he could have ignored it as he did in III:51. First, it tends to reinforce Maimonides' claim for the absolute uniqueness of Moses' apprehension, for no matter how great his actions might be, his apprehension remains still

25. III:51, pp. 623–24. See G. Vajda, *L'Amour de Dieu dans la théologie juive du moyen âge* (Paris, 1957), pp. 133–37, who calls attention to the echoes of Bahya ibn Paquda; and I. Tishby, *Mishnat ha-Zohar*, 2 vols. (Jerusalem, 1959), II, 284–87, who cites this passage in the context of the Kabbalistic doctrine of *devequt*.
26. II:35, p. 367.
27. II:35, p. 368.

greater. Second, it tends to discount the importance one might attach to miracles by depriving them of any intrinsic value apart from the circumstances in which they are performed. Such a devaluation of miracles is thoroughly consonant with Maimonides' views concerning them,[28] his relegation of prophetic miracles to a status dependent on Moses' miracles, and his insistence that miracles do not constitute in themselves credentials for prophetic status.[29] Finally, lest he inadvertently support popular tendencies toward assigning magical power to one's knowledge of matters divine, Maimonides formulated the correlation of apprehension and miracles in a very precise way.

The same desire to preclude false conclusions while buttressing his own opinions seems to be at work in II:39 where Maimonides distinguishes the call to the Law issued by Moses from the call of other prophets and where he precisely and explicitly formulates the correlation between apprehension and the call. Unlike the argument of II:35, however, Maimonides does posit a causal relationship, for the call "followed necessarily from that apprehension alone."[30] And in language echoing that used for Moses' apprehension, Maimonides states that "nothing similar to the call addressed to us by Moses has been made before him . . . nor was a call similar to that one made by one of our prophets after him."[31] By affirming the priority of the apprehension, Maimonides once again conveys his view that no matter how great Moses' actions might be, his apprehension remains still greater. Moreover, by articulating a causal relationship here, he reinforces the implicit argument of II:35 which denied that miracles necessarily belong to or characterize prophecy. Finally, by unequivocally associating the "fundamental principle" of the eternity of the Law with his call, but not his apprehension, he establishes the authority of the Law independently of Moses' apprehension and, more importantly, independently of the content of the Law.[32] Lest he inadvertently support ad hominem attacks on Moses or his revelation as a means for abrogating the Law, Maimonides very carefully formulated the correlation of his apprehension and his action so as to preclude any such arguments. In short, he distinguishes Moses' actions in a way similar to the way he distinguishes Moses' apprehension, then formulates a correlation between these two noncognitive features of the Mosaic phenomenon.

28. See, for example, III:32, p. 529; I:64, p. 156; and Guttmann's comments in his "Religious Motifs," p. 92.

29. Hilkhot Yesode ha-Torah VIII:1–3.

30. II:39, p. 378.

31. II:39, pp. 378–79.

32. See Guttmann, Philosophies of Judaism, p. 195, for a more conventional interpretation of Maimonides which seeks to emphasize the supernatural dimension of Moses' apprehension and mission as opposed to Maimonides' attempts at naturalizing the phenomenon of prophecy.

Yet, significantly, in not every reference to Moses' actions does Maimonides enforce such distinctions. Book II:38 begins with a discussion of courage and divination. Though all men possess them, "these two faculties must necessarily be very strong in prophets."[33] When we remember how assiduously Maimonides stresses the dissimilarity of the Mosaic phenomenon from ordinary prophecy in the other passages, it is startling to find Maimonides using an episode from Moses' career to exemplify the role of courage and divination in prophecy. Introducing him with a poetic circumlocution instead of by name, Maimonides states the following: "The lone individual, having only his staff, went boldly to the great king in order to save a religious community from the burden of slavery, and had no fear or dread, because it was said to him—'I will be with thee'" (Ex. 3:12).[34] Motivation to perform such actions, as Maimonides explains unapologetically in II:45, is something Moses shares in common with some of the judges and kings.[35] Ascribing these things to Moses without qualification seems to suggest that Maimonides was eager to voice his disagreement with any tendency to overspiritualize Moses. Perhaps there were docetist notions circulating in certain Jewish groups that he wished to oppose. Or perhaps he may have had in mind Christian or Islamic theological notions against which he was reacting. What may be said with certainty, however, is that Maimonides exerted special efforts to defend the physical reality of Moses while at the same time arguing for the categorical singularity of his apprehension, an apprehension which in no way interfered with his bodily existence; for which reason, he did not correlate these traits and actions with Moses' apprehension.

It is to the last of the noncognitive features of the Mosaic phenomenon that we are now prepared to turn—to Moses' governance.

III

In Book II:43, Maimonides mentions Moses together with other prophets without noting the difference between their actions and without correlating Moses' apprehension with his deeds. There Maimonides interprets Zech. 11:7 as a parable whose intention is "to show that in its beginnings the religious community subsisted in the grace of the Lord, who was the one who led and consolidated it. . . . Moses was the one who governed and directed

---

33. II:38, p. 376.
34. II:38, pp. 376–77.
35. II:45, p. 397.

this community at that time, and after him some of the prophets."[36] Now the term governance (*tadbîr, hanhagah*) names a major concept used by Maimonides in a variety of contexts. For our immediate purposes, however, it suffices to note that governance, like the call addressed by some of the prophets to the people, is the result of the measure of the overflow reaching an individual. Sometimes the overflow only perfects him

> but has no other effect. Sometimes, on the other hand, the measure of what comes to an individual overflows from rendering him perfect toward rendering others perfect. This is what happens to all beings: some of them achieve perfection to an extent that enables them to govern others, whereas others achieve perfection only in a measure that allows them to be governed by others.[37]

Governance, therefore, is not restricted to Moses, but is, like the performance of miracles, the calling of a people to a law, the motivation to perfect others, the delivering of a religious community from a wicked one, and the faculties of courage and divination, a quality of leadership potentially belonging to any man. Indeed, Moses shares in this power "with the class of those who govern cities, while being the legislators, the soothsayers, the augurs, and the dreamers of veridical dreams,"[38] in whom the rational faculty is defective and toward whom the overflow reaches the imaginative faculty only. But neither is governance restricted to Moses and other men, for as Maimonides explicitly asserts in several important passages of the *Guide*, governance also pertains to God,[39] celestial spheres,[40] and nature.[41] Given this ambiguity in the term governance, it is puzzling that Maimonides fails to clarify its association with Moses and especially with Moses' apprehension. Surely the implications of his governance are no less important than those suggested by his miracles or his call, that Maimonides should remain silent here. And having sufficiently noted the bodily reality of Moses, we may ask what Maimonides thought to gain by refusing to offer direct comments on

36. II:43, p. 393.
37. II:37, pp. 373–74.
38. II:37, p. 374.
39. See, for example, I:35, p. 80; I:54, p. 124; I:72, p. 193; and III:23, pp. 496–97.
40. See, for example, II:6, pp. 260–61; II:7, p. 266; II:10, pp. 269–70.
41. II:10, pp. 272–73. Though a full analysis of the matter is called for, it must suffice to note within this context that Maimonides here too reveals his debt to Ibn Bajja, especailly to his *Tadbîr al-Mutawahhid* (The Governance of the Solitary). See Lawrence Berman's partial translation in *Medieval Political Philosophy*, ed. R. Lerner and M. Mahdi (Glencoe, Ill., 1963), pp. 122–33; and the Arabic text established by D. M. Dunlop in *The Journal of the Royal Asiatic Society of Great Britain and Ireland* (1945), pp. 63–73; or the complete text published by M. Asin Palacios, *Tadbîr al-Mutawahhid* (Madrid, 1946). Ibn Bajja begins his discussion with a display of the manifold, equivocal nature of the term *tadbîr*.

his governance. The silence concerning governance in II:43 seems to be a missed opportunity. Yet it is a silence matched by the absolute absence of references to Moses in II:37 and II:40, chapters with a decidedly political theme. Perhaps Maimonides is signaling the careful reader of the *Guide* that what is left unsaid in an explicit way is being said in scattered hints to be gathered up and connected to form a coherent explication of some truth. A truth which the Law forbids him to communicate openly to those people who are unfit to receive it.[42] This would be the truth concerning Moses' governance.

Assuming that Maimonides would have been willing to correlate apprehension and governance in II:43, what formula might he have used? Had he used the kind of "connection and tie" between apprehension and miracles as the paradigm for relating them, he would not have done justice to the unique relationship of apprehension and Moses' governance. Unlike its effect on governance, metaphysical knowledge need not issue in the performance of miracles. In his phenomenology of miracles, therefore, Maimonides does not recognize one miracle as being truer or qualitatively better than another. His phenomenology of laws, by contrast, generates a hierarchy of laws graded by their final goal; the worthiness of the "opinions, moral qualities, and political civic actions"[43] they teach; their suitability to man's nature;[44] the extent to which they imitate God's governance of nature;[45] and their origin in the various faculties of man's soul as a result, accidental though it might be, of the overflow they receive from the Active Intellect.[46] While miracles *per se* cannot be differentiated, laws can be distinguished in terms of the apprehension underlying them and without which there could be no true Law.

The second possible model for formulating the correlation of Moses' apprehension with his governance is the one Maimonides used for linking apprehension and Moses' call to the Law. But this would have far-reaching implications leading to a conclusion contrary to Maimonides' understanding of Law. To have argued in II:43, paraphrasing the statement in II:39, that Moses' governance "followed necessarily from that apprehension alone," implies that the particulars of the Mosaic Law are supplied and determined by a knowledge of the laws governing nature. The laws that constitute Mosaic polity would therefore be natural laws. Maimonides, however, soundly rejected such a view. Though he would be willing to admit that a

---

42. I:34, pp. 72–79. Strauss makes much of this in his "The Literary Character of the Guide," in his *Persecution and the Art of Writing* (Glencoe, Ill., 1952), pp. 60–78.
43. III:31, p. 524.
44. II:39, pp. 380–81; and III:32, pp. 525–26.
45. I:54, pp. 125–27.
46. II:36, p. 372; II:37, pp. 373–75; and II:40, pp. 382–84.

political governance "follows necessarily" from apprehending God and the separate intellects and their spheres, Maimonides does not believe that a particular, historical law ever "follows necessarily" from apprehension. As others have recently shown, Maimonides' political philosophy denies that the particulars of the Mosaic Law are discoverable by exclusively rational means in the investigation of the laws governing sublunar generation and corruption.[47]

Though Maimonides denies that the Mosaic Law is genetically natural in the same sense as the laws of generation and corruption are natural, it is abundantly clear that he considers it to be natural in the utilitarian or teleological and formal senses of the term.[48] Decisive passages expressing the teleological aspect of the Law abound in the *Guide*: "The Law as a whole aims at two things: the welfare of the soul and the welfare of the body";[49] or, " . . . the first intention of the Law as a whole is to put an end to idolatry";[50] or, "the commandments and prohibitions of the Law are only intended to quell all the impulses of matter";[51] or as Maimonides states with respect to Moses and the Patriarchs, "the end of all their efforts was to spread the doctrine of the unity of the Name in the world and to guide people to love Him, may He be exalted."[52] Maimonides considers the Law to be natural in the formal or cosmological sense[53] by virtue of the fact that "many things in our Law are due to something similar to this governance on the part of Him who governs, may He be glorified and exalted,"[54] which means the employment of "wily graciousness and wisdom"[55] in the formulation of particular laws in the Torah best exemplified by the laws concerning the Temple cult. Or as Maimonides states in III:49: "Marvel at the wisdom of His commandments . . . just as you should marvel at the wisdom manifested in the things He made . . . just as the things made by Him are consummately perfect, so are His commandments consummately just."[56]

---

47. See L. Strauss, "The Law of Reason in the *Kuzari*," in his *Persecution and the Art of Writing*, pp. 95–98, 112–41; Steven S. Schwarzchild, "Do Noachites Have to Believe in Revelation," *JQR*, LII (1961–62), 296–308; LIII (1962–63), 30–65; Jose Faur, "La Doctrina de la ley natural en el pensamiento judío del medioevo," *Sefarad*, XXVIII (1967), esp. 258–65; idem, "Meqor Hiyyuvan shel ha-Mitzwot lefi Daʿat ha-Rambam," *Tarbiz*, XXXVIII (1969), 43 ff.; and Marvin Fox, "Maimonides and Aquinas on Natural Law," *Dine Israel*, III (1972), 5–36.

48. See H. A. Wolfson, *Philo*, 2 vols. (Cambridge, Mass., 1948), II, 165–200, 310–12.

49. III:27, p. 510.

50. II:29, pp. 517, 521; III:30, p. 523; and III:37, p. 542.

51. III:8, p. 433.

52. III:51, p. 624.

53. See I. Heinemann, *Taʿame ha-Mitzwot* (Jerusalem, 1959), pp. 90–91.

54. III:32, pp. 525–26.

55. See Pines's comments in his Introduction, pp. lxxii–lxxiv; and A. Funkenstein, "Gesetz und Geschichte: Zur historisierenden Hermeneutik bei Moses Maimonides und Thomas Aquinas," *Viator*, I (1970), esp. 155–57.

56. III:49, p. 605. Cf. Ibn Bajja in Lerner and Mahdi, eds., *Medieval Political Philosophy*, p. 124.

The teleological and formal dimensions of the Law presuppose the kind of apprehension Maimonides ascribes to Moses, but apprehension is only the necessary, not the sufficient cause for the Law. Maimonides, therefore, goes no farther when he formulates the relationship between the Mosaic Law and nature than to say that "the Law always tends to assimilate itself to nature, perfecting the natural matters in a certain sense."[57] This is not the same as asserting that the Law "follows necessarily" from apprehension as he asserted concerning Moses' call.

By eliminating as possible paradigms for correlating Moses' apprehension with his governance Maimonides' formulations concerning the miracles and the call, we have still not satisfactorily explained why Maimonides did not articulate an appropriate correlation in II:43 concerning governance. He does suggest such a correlation in III:51 and we have seen that it justifies the logic implicit in the careful formulations of II:35 and II:39. Indeed, in an early passage of the *Guide*,[58] using language reminiscent of Plato's cave allegory, Maimonides interprets the phrase—ascending and descending—from Jacob's dream in *Genesis* 28:12 to mean that "after the ascent and the attaining of certain rungs of the ladder that may be known comes the descent with whatever decree the prophet has been informed of—with a view to governing and teaching the people of the earth."[59] Moreover the whole of I:54 is a discussion of Moses' apprehension as it relates to his governance. We are left, therefore, with the same question: Is there a doctrine concerning Moses' governance that forced Maimonides to remain silent in II:43?

Having denied that the particular laws of Moses derive necessarily from his apprehension and willing to say only that the Law "always tends to assimilate itself to nature," how did Maimonides fully account for the origin and the actual content of the Mosaic Law? To reply that he ascribes it all to God using Moses as an intermediary fully accords with his language, but misses the subtlety of his intention. Nowhere in II:40 are we admonished to exclude the Mosaic Law from the kind of considerations discussed there concerning political law in general. Not having been warned to exempt Moses from the description offered of rulers in general, we find that Moses, like all rulers, is one who "gauges the actions of individuals, perfecting that which is deficient and reducing that which is excessive, and who prescribes actions and moral habits . . . so that the natural diversity is hidden through the multiple points on conventional accord and so that the community becomes well ordered. Therefore . . . the Law, although it is not natural, enters into

---

57. III:43, p. 571.
58. Instructions for reading an "early" passage are provided by Maimonides himself in his "Instruction with Respect to This Treatise," pp. 15–17.
59. I:15, p. 41.

what is natural."[60] The crucial difference between the Mosaic Law and any other given law is strictly one of hierarchic quality. While laws in general merely "enter into what is natural," the Mosaic Law "always tends to assimilate itself to nature, perfecting the natural matters in a certain respect." As for their basic nature, however, the Mosaic Law and other laws are conventional or positive laws. The only exceptions to this rule are the first two of the Ten Commandments. "As for the other commandments," Maimonides states in II:33, "they belong to the class of generally accepted opinions and those adopted in virtue of tradition, not to the class of intellecta."[61]

Since the laws are conventional, they cannot be ascribed to God unequivocally. To do so would openly contradict and fatally compromise the God described by Maimonides throughout the *Guide* and epitomized in I:68: "He is the intellect as well as the intellectually cognizing subject and the intellectually cognized object . . . in which there is no multiplicity."[62] Political laws which are conventional in origin cannot exist as such in the mind of God. Political laws are the products of the political faculty *par excellence*, the imaginative faculty which is a bodily function. Moreover, were the Mosaic Laws somehow integrated in God's being without implying a multiplicity in His knowledge, it would follow that the Law would be natural in the genetic sense. The passage in III:21 is decisive in stating that, "through knowing the true reality of His own immutable essence, He also knows the totality of what necessarily derives from all His acts."[63] We have already seen that Maimonides denies that the Mosaic Law is natural law, and therefore may deduce that Maimonides did not think that it existed as such in God's mind.

Finally, it is obvious from Maimonides' philosophic posture that the Law which does derive necessarily from God is only the law of nature which is categorically different from political law. The "divine governance of, the divine providence for, and the divine purpose with regard to, those natural matters differ from our human government of, providence for, and purpose with regard to, the things we govern, we provide for, and we purpose."[64] The closest our governance comes to God's governance, therefore, is the Law of Moses which "always tends to assimilate itself to nature," but which fails to be equal to it, for "there is nothing in common between the two except in name only."[65] Even God's special governance of man, what Maimonides describes as providence, is totally unlike the Mosaic Law.[66]

60. II:40, p. 382.
61. II:33, p. 364.
62. I:68, p. 163.
63. III:21, p. 485; and see above, n. 19.
64. III:23, p. 497.
65. III:23, p. 496.
66. Even though the difference between providence and the Mosaic Law is obvious and this is

Even if one were to assume that despite the theoretical impossibility of the Law's origin in God, the conventions of the Mosaic Law were transmitted to Moses from God in exactly the form they have in the Torah, Maimonides' description of Moses does not allow for his reception of these laws. Without an imaginative faculty to function during revelation, Moses was like Adam, who before the sin, "had no faculty that was engaged in any way in the consideration of generally accepted things, and he did not apprehend them."[67] Moreover, Maimonides believes that prophets "only apprehend God and His angels and will only be aware and achieve knowledge of matters that constitute true opinions and general directives for the well-being of men in their relations with one another."[68] It follows, therefore, that even ordinary prophets do not receive particular laws. Maimonides, therefore, does not believe that Moses ever received the particulars of his Law in revelation. To sum up, according to the logic of his arguments, Maimonides does not believe that God could have transmitted the particulars of the Law to Moses who was not equipped to receive what would have amounted to an inferior revelation.

Provided that our exegesis faithfully describes the premises and dialectics of Maimonides' views, the following process of elimination leads us to the discovery that Maimonides considered Moses to have been the direct author of the Law and that the correlation between his apprehension and his governance may be expressed in classical Platonic terms. Since the Law of Moses is replete with wisdom in all its parts, it cannot be said to have originated in the class of those morally degenerate men whose deficient intellects are unable to inform their *nomoi* with virtuous content. And since it is a law that most closely assimilates itself to the governance of the natural world, it cannot be said to have originated in the class of ordinary prophets whose apprehension of nature was too fragmentary and incomplete. And since it is a law, it cannot be said to have originated in the class of philosopher/scientists which lacks the faculty of imagination necessary to produce

---

not the appropriate context for a detailed analysis of the Guide III:17–25 where Maimonides discusses providence, the following comments are in order. In III:18, p. 475 Maimonides states that "providence . . . is consequent upon the intellect. Accordingly divine providence does not watch in an equal manner over all the individúals of the human species, but providence is graded as their human perfection is graded." In III:34, he concludes that if the Law "were made to fit individuals, the whole would be corrupted. . . . " Maimonides also signals the difference in notions with a shift in terminology—as shown by Strauss and kindly called to my attention by Professor Altmann. See "Der Ort der Vorsehungslehre nach der Ansicht Maimunis," *MGWJ*, n.s. XLV (1937), 93–105. Especially interesting are Strauss's comments concerning *tadbîr* in the *Guide*, p. 95, n. 9. Cf. above, nn. 39–41.

67. II:2, p. 25.
68. II:36, p. 372; cf. II:45, p. 403.

it. And since the Law of Moses brings man to his final perfection after first having established political order, it cannot be said to have originated in nature or in the separate intellects whose governance is restricted to guiding the process of sublunar generation and corruption. Finally, because it is couched in the language of actual speech and consists of conventions, it cannot be said to have originated in God in the way that the laws of nature or special providence for those whose intellects are near to Him necessarily derive from Him. Only a being who simultaneously belonged to the trans- and sublunar realms with a consummate understanding of both could have produced the Law in its particularized form. In the history of mankind, according to Maimonides, only one such individual ever existed or ever will exist, namely Moses.

This does not imply, however, that the Law is not divine. As Maimonides stipulates: "If you find a Law all of whose ordinances are due to attention being paid . . . to the soundness of the circumstances pertaining to the body and also to the soundness of belief . . . and that desires to make man wise . . . you must know that this guidance comes from Him, may He be exalted, and that this Law is divine."[69] In the final analysis, not origin, but content bespeaks of a law whether or not it is divine. The author of this Law was Moses, who, having received the divine overflow, was led to create a governance whose particular forms were determined by certain truths concerning human nature and after careful consideration of the historical context into which the Law must fit.[70] It is theoretically possible, according to Maimonides' thought, that the Law of Moses might have had different particulars if the religious institutions contemporary with Moses had been other than what they were. Though the final aim of the Law is invariable, its particulars are not. But once promulgated these historical factors are only meaningful in the attempt to uncover the rationale for many of the particulars found in the Torah. The Law retains eternal authority, despite its origin, if only because permitting permanent revision and constant updating of the Law would undermine the integrity of the Law as a whole in much the same way as a disorderly universe without immutable laws would endanger the belief in the unity of God.[71]

We have already seen that Maimonides also establishes the eternity of the Law on altogether different grounds. Though it is divine by virtue of its content, it is immutable by virtue of the call to it issued by Moses. The

69. II:40, p. 384.
70. III:32, p. 526; and see Funkenstein, "Gesetz und Geschichte."
71. III:41, pp. 562–63; and II:29, pp. 344–46. The Law, like the world, is eternal *a parte post*; II:28, pp. 335–36. The eternity of the Law is also correlated with Israel's perdurance in history; see II:29, esp. p. 342.

binding authority of its commandments is not correlated with nor justified by the wisdom embodied in it. In so doing, Maimonides protects the Law from subjective abrogation at the hand of those who might argue, mistakenly, that they apprehend God more fully than Moses and are therefore required to issue a different governance. The Law is also protected from being undermined at the hand of those who might exploit Maimonides' own historicizing interpretation of it and claim that different circumstances call for different laws. That Maimonides clearly separated the content of the Law from its authority is reflected literarily in his decision to devote a discrete principle to both in his Thirteen Fundamental Principles and doctrinally in his views of reward for obedience to the Law.[72]

IV

Radical though these seemingly heterodox opinions may appear, they are nonetheless perfectly consistent with what Maimonides teaches in the dogmatic formulation of the Thirteen Principles. Despite the obvious efforts to find language that emphasizes the divine origin of the Law while minimizing the creative role of Moses in its promulgation, there is nothing in the eighth principle that contradicts Maimonides' claim in the *Guide* that a law is divine if it is replete with wisdom in all its parts. That it is the content and not the actual origin of the Law which most interests Maimonides may be seen from the following:

> In the opinion of the Rabbis, Manasseh was a renegade and the greatest of infidels because he thought that in the Torah there was a kernel and a husk, and that these histories and anecdotes have no value and emanate from Moses.... May God be exalted far above and beyond the speech of such infidels. For truly in every letter of the Torah there reside wise maxims and admirable truths for him to whom God has given understanding. You cannot grasp the uttermost bounds of its wisdom.[73]

72. See *Hilkhot Talmud Torah* I:13; and the commentaries on that *halakhah*. Cf. *Guide* III:17, p. 470. The classical passage, however, is the one expressing his views on non-Jews who observe the Noachide laws—literature on which is found in the references cited in n. 47. The controversy rages over their being considered "wise" or not. Without entering into the arguments, we merely note that, according to Maimonides, obedience from heteronomous motivation warrants a greater reward than a deed performed from autonomous motivation.

73. Holzer, *Dogmenlehre*, pp. 26 f. The translation is that of Abelson, "Maimonides on the Jewish Creed," p. 54. See III:34, p. 534, where Maimonides describes the Law as a "divine thing" by virtue of its imitation of natural governance. Here too it is content rather than origin that is decisive.

The eighth Principle, then, is primarily directed against the charge that the Law is deficient in wisdom and that Moses independently of God invented, fabricated, and manufactured the Law. As the citations from Numbers 6:28 and *Sanhedrin* 99a incorporated by Maimonides into the eighth principle show, such heretical charges have long plagued the history of Jewish thought from biblical times through the Greco-Roman period of Talmudic Judaism.[74] The insistent tone of polemics in the eighth principle indicates that the charge of Mosaic authorship was a live issue in Maimonides' day too. In fact, in III:19 Maimonides mentions a group of "distinguished individuals of our religious community who were physicians," against whose faulty understanding of God's apprehension Maimonides fought. One of the implications of their reasoning was the view that "no command or prohibition from Him reaches the prophets."[75] And in I:46 and I:65, Maimonides justifies the pious ruse of using potentially misleading language with respect to God's speech by appealing to its aid in helping man understand that what the prophets say is not the "mere product of their thought and insight."[76] Fully aware of the implications inherent in his understanding of Moses' role in the formulation of a Law patterned after an apprehension of the divine governance, Maimonides was undoubtedly sensitive to the need for refuting this heretical view endorsed by certain intellectuals of his day. This he does by uncovering again and again the wisdom embedded in the Law.

The eternity of the Law, however, is established independently of its content. It is for this reason that Maimonides composed the ninth principle where the immutability of the Law is announced in its own terms, without reference to content or authorship. The eighth principle, however, is devoted to the Law of Moses; and the seventh, to Moses himself, the master of those who know.

74. For the non-Jewish sources, see the convenient collection of John Gager, *Moses in Greco-Roman Paganism* (Nashville, 1972). For the Jewish responses, see A. J. Heschel, *Torah min ha-Shamayyim*, 2 vols. (London-New York, 1962–65), II, chaps. 5–14, esp. pp. 102–4; and the invaluable resource of L. Ginzberg, *Legends of the Jews*, 7 vols. (Philadelphia, 1909–37), VII (Index), s.v. Moses.

75. III:19, pp. 478–80.

76. I:65, p. 158; and I:46, pp. 98–103.

Maimonides on Possibility

Alfred L. Ivry

Of the twelve premises of the Islamic theologians, the Mutakallimun, which Maimonides summarizes in the opening of chapter 73 of the first part of the *Guide of the Perplexed*, none is more puzzling than the tenth: "That the possibility of a thing should not be considered in establishing a correspondence between that which exists and mental representation." This, at least, is the way the premise is rendered by Shlomo Pines in his usually reliable and eloquent translation.[1] Clearly we have here a difficult text, and a glance at the original Arabic confirms our suspicion: *Al-muqaddamatu l-ʿâshiratu anna l-mumkina lâ yuʿtabaru bi-mutâbaqati hâdhâ l-wujûdi li-dhâlika t-tasawwur;*[2] translated by Samuel b. Tibbon into Hebrew as *ha-haqdamah ha-ʿasirit she-ha-ʾefshar loʾ yivahen be-haskim zeh ha-metziʾut la-tziyyur ha-huʾ.*[3]

Here wisdom dictates consultation with that other, earlier Solomon, who offers the following French translation: "*la Xᵉ, que le possible ne doit pas être considéré au point de vue de la conformité de l'être avec telle idée.*"[4] Munk notes, in addition, that Maimonides wishes to say the Mutakallimun regarded it sufficient, for a thing to be possible, that one be able to form an idea of it, it being unnecessary that the real existent conform to the idea.[5] This explanation is explicitly aided by Maimonides' discussion of this premise later in chapter 73, and it is this discussion that no doubt influences Munk's translation too. Pines, however, apparently sees Maimonides as making a somewhat different point here, viz., that the relationship between an existing thing and a representation of it, or as the text has it, between "this existent and that representation," should not be determined by a notion of appropriate

I wish to acknowledge with gratitude the assistance of Professor Ivan Boh, of the Department of Philosophy at The Ohio State University, who made helpful comments on an earlier draft of this paper.

1. See *The Guide of the Perplexed* (Chicago, 1963), I:73, p. 194. All future mention of the *Guide* in English refers to this translation.

2. See *Dalâlat al-Hâʾirîn*, ed. S. Munk, revised I. Joel (Jerusalem, 1929), p. 135. All future Arabic citations will be taken from this edition.

3. See *Sefer Moreh Nevukhim*, ed. I. Goldman (Warsaw, 1892; new ed.: New York, 1946), Part I, p. 116. Future Hebrew translations will be cited from this edition.

4. See *Le Guide des Egarés*, trans. S. Munk (Paris, 1860; reprint, 1959), I:376.

5. Ibid., n. 2. Cf. M. Friedländer's paraphrastic translation of this passage: "Proposition X. The test for the possibility of an imagined object does not consist in its conformity with the existing laws of nature" (*The Guide for the Perplexed* [London, 1904; reprint: New York, 1956], p. 120).

representation, i.e., by a view of what the existent may "really" become, its "true" possibility.

Put this way, Pines's translation, consistent with his understanding of the tone of this entire section, has Maimonides presenting the Kalam premise from a philosophical perspective in which the "possibility of a thing" is posited as a particular reality the relevance of which, however, if not the very existence, is here denied by the Mutakallimun. To paraphrase Munk, there-fore, the tenth premise asserts the freedom of the possible from the actual, while according to Pines it asserts the freedom of the (imaginatively) possible from the (actually) possible. In the former translation, accordingly, Mai-monides speaks from a more neutral stance, in the latter from that of a committed, if not critical, philosopher. The significance of this distinction will emerge later, after we have followed Maimonides' detailed explanation of the premise.

Maimonides' explanation begins with the concept of "admissibility" (or permissibility, at-tajwîz/ha-haʿavarah), a concept affirming (p. 206) the belief of the Mutakallimun that "everything that may be imagined as an admissible notion for the intellect,"[6] so that whatever is imaginable is possible, and all possibilities are equally real. At first sight this notion appears all-inclusive, i.e., that *anything* imagined is equally admissible. As a result, Maimonides proceeds to correct this impression, giving instances of "impossible" situa-tions that "cannot be true and cannot be admitted by the intellect." His examples might be taken to indicate that such situations are impossible to imagine and *therefore* inadmissible to the intellect. Later in this section, Mai-monides says the Mutakallimun speak of "that which may be imagined while being at the same time impossible," calling such "a fantasy and a vain imagining."[7] Although Maimonides uses this notion of "fantasy" to show that the Mutakallimun recognized a principle independent of the imagina-tion to distinguish between possible and impossible imaginings, the termin-ology alone would not force one to conclude that the intellect is this principle. It could well appear from Maimonides' rendition that the Mutakallimun may have wanted to reserve the term 'imagination' for "true" imaginings only, intellectual assent to such being seen as a necessary though merely concom-itant feature; even as such assent is never a concomitant of impossible, i.e., false imaginings.[8] Seen this way, the impossible imagination is false basically

6. Translating kullu mâ huwa mutakhayyalûn fa-huwa jâ'izûn ʿinda l-ʿaql (Munk, p. 144); rendered into Hebrew (p. 121) as kol mah she-hu' medummeh hu' ʿover 'etzel ha-sekhel.

7. So Pines, p. 211, terms rendered by Munk as "présomption et chimère" (Le Guide, p. 411), for which he also offers "erreur et imagination"; cf. Munk's note there. These represent trans-lations of the ambiguous wahm wa-khayâl of the Arabic original (p. 147).

8. Throughout this article our presentation of the Kalam view and terminology follows

on grounds other than intellectual, i.e., rational or logical, though also on those grounds.

What, however, could these extra-intellectual grounds be? Maimonides argues that the imagination *per se* possesses no critical tool by which to distinguish between true and false possibilities, since truth and falsity are a function of (demonstrable) propositions, which propositions in turn depend upon universal concepts; and the universal is the product of intellectual abstraction. The imagination, on the other hand, is tied to individual sensory impressions, which it may combine without any inherently necessary limitations.[9] Accordingly, the imagination by itself is able both to represent at times what is not the case (as a man with a horse's head and wings), as well as what cannot be the case (God as a corporeal being); and is not able to represent at times what is the case (two individuals both able to stand on opposite ends of the world with feet facing each other, and two lines extending indefinitely, so constructed that though they approach each other they never meet).

Now a Mutakallim might well respond to Maimonides that the imagination *is* able to represent those realities that Maimonides claimed imagination could not handle, the proof being that Maimonides himself referred to such things in broadly imaginative terms; and that the imagination is conversely *not* able, when true to itself, to imagine what *cannot* be the case. The Mutakallim would readily concede that the imagination does represent what is not actually the case, though this is the very heart of the doctrine of admissibility, that the limits of possibility are not to be determined by what is actually existent.

Before proceeding to investigate this central claim, it is important to notice the nature of the disagreement between Maimonides and the Kalam over the abilities, the very scope, of the imagination itself. *Prima facie*, it seems impossible to determine, as regards the absolute ability of the imagination to correctly represent things, whether or not we do truly "imagine," i.e., represent pictorially, certain scientific occurrences, even in the more abstract fields of physics, chemistry, and, of course, mathematics. It may well be held that *all* thinking is necessarily presented to the mind as "phenomena," in imaginative terms. It would not seem unreasonable to conceive of mathematical

Maimonides, and does not consider whether and how his remarks ought to be qualified in order perhaps to do full justice to the diversity and subtleties of the Mutakallimun. See, however, Pines's remarks in the Introduction to his translation, pp. cxxiv ff. Our concern is with Maimonides' understanding of the Kalam concept, and with his response.

9. *Guide*, I:73, p. 209; and cf. Aristotle, *De Anima*, III:3, 427[a]16 ff.

entities (i.e., universals) *as* individual ideas that the mind pictures to itself, in one form or another. Similarly, it is difficult if not impossible to tell, as regards the inability of the imagination to represent that which is necessarily false, if the imagination is indeed unable to offer a true representation of it.

Notice, though, that in both these cases we have been unavoidably begging the question of "true" representation. Here we need recall Maimonides' strictures concerning the necessary role of the intellect in determining truth or falsity (p. 209): "It is by means of the intellect that the universal is differentiated from the individual, and no demonstration is true except by means of universals. It is also through the intellect that essential predicates are discerned from accidental ones." Maimonides would seem here to be expressing the Aristotelian notion that the intellect, in identifying what is perceived in terms of essential and accidental properties, organizes it into categories of speech and thought which transcend the individual object but which alone enable us to communicate about it, by relating it to other similar objects. Demonstrable knowledge of *x* thus depends on our knowledge of the kind of thing *x* is, i.e., its shared or universal nature, the species and genus to which it belongs. The "truth" of *x*, therefore, is of *x qua* universal; and true—or false—propositions are accordingly concerned with defined terms, i.e., universal entities.

Be the scope of the imagination whatever it is, therefore, any claim as to true or false imaginings must be put in "intellectual," i.e., universal intelligible terms. Whatever the imagination claims, then, it must claim on rational grounds. This, however, does not disprove the contention that there is an imaginative representation to all such claims, though if there is, one must concede it will remain ever unknowable. It may accordingly seem a matter of indifference whether the Mutakallimun or Maimonides is right in relation to the capacities and incapacities of the imagination *per se*, since there is no way of establishing such claims, no way of even asserting in communicable terms what is being imagined, without using the language of the intellect. All true propositions, therefore, must be "admissible to the intellect," as the Mutakallimun say, and this regardless of their imaginative status.

To Maimonides, however, the Kalam comprehension of what the proper use of intellect entails is misconceived and, in effect, is constructed on false premises. Yet it is not immediately apparent how the Kalam use of intellectual, i.e., logical criteria, differs from the philosophers', and therefore it is worth analyzing the few examples of impossible imaginings Maimonides takes from Kalam literature. These include the logical impossibility of the "coming together of two contraries in the same substratum (literally "place," *mahâll*, as Pines recognizes) and at the same instant"; the existence of a substance (or atom, *jawhar*) apart from any accident; the transformation of a substance into an accident and vice-versa; and the penetration of one atom (literally, "body," *jism*) by another atom.[10]

The nature of these impossibilities is somewhat puzzling at first, for they do not all exhibit the Principle of Contradiction as obviously as does the first example given. Clearly each example depends upon our understanding of what is entailed by its terms, i.e., by our knowledge of their definition and the function of the substances they represent. As such, the impossibility, e.g., of an atom (or substance), existing apart from any accident follows from our understanding of the nature and functioning of the atom. Hence, to claim that an atom (i.e., that which, by definition, is not separated from accidents) can exist apart from any accident is to fall victim again to this very Principle of Contradiction. Whether immediately known or mediately, therefore, as terms or propositions used in self-contradictory ways, the Kalam impossibilities are such because they violate this law of thought.

Maimonides can have no quarrel with this use of "intellectual admissibility," the utilization of laws of thought which, when granting particular premises, correctly indicate that a specific proposition is logical or illogical. Thus, in negating the intellectual/logical aspect of Kalam notions, he must be denying the specific physical premises upon which these otherwise "intellectually admissible" examples are constructed. Clearly there must be something in these very physical premises of the Mutakallimun that violates the basic principle of thought, rendering them not merely inadequate physically but incoherent logically. It is not for Maimonides a matter of preferring one physical theory of being to another but of being forced to accept one and reject the other.

Maimonides' position is not revealed as directly as one might wish in the immediately ensuing discussion, which considers the differences between the philosopher and the Mutakallim. In the discussion each briefly presents his view of the nature of being. In essence, the philosopher affirms and the Mutakallim denies the existence of natural bodies, i.e., those possessing material and formal properties (here called "accidents," *'a'râd*). As opposed to the philosopher's view of inherent natural forms that shape matter into its various states, the Mutakallim advances an atomic theory of inherently undifferentiated being. For him all distinctions between substances are due to accidents that in themselves have no permanent nature by which they could

10. *Guide*, I:73, p. 207.

form the substantive basis, the matter, for other accidents. There is in this scheme no defined core, no substrate with properties of its own, the atom which is analogous to matter serving merely to provide a momentary physical framework for a particular accident, while being in itself completely neutral. Thus the same atom can receive any and every kind of accident, and any imaginable combination of atom and accident is theoretically possible.

Maimonides accepts the logical coherence of this view of possibility, given the premises of atoms and accidents which the Mutakallimun assert. It is thus in the basic notions of atomism, viz., the continuous yet discrete creation of atoms and accidents, that Maimonides must feel the Kalam has departed from what the intellect can tolerate. For continuous creation literally means that at each and every moment God creates (or recreates) the being of the object, its particular combination of atoms and accidents, where such creation is from absolutely nothing.[11] Hence, the assertion that atoms and accidents exist is equal to the assertion that what is has come to be from what is not, or that what is not *is* the source of what is, i.e., that in some sense what is not, is. Atomism at its core thus fails to provide an explanation of change that avoids the contradiction of employing nonbeing as though it were some kind of being.

It is thus in its refusal to accept the continuous nature of anything analogous to form and matter that the Kalam must be faulted on logical grounds. Its variety of atomism, viz., created units of being in created units of time, provides no principle of change, having no principle of identity, and none is conceivable without violating the law of contradiction. Nor could God's will be seen as an adequate philosophical substitute for the principle of change, unless one would be prepared to see the created forms as eternally preexisting in God, in which case creation can neither be said to arise from absolutely nothing, nor can God be regarded as essentially different from the philosophers' form of forms. If Maimonides sees the Kalam tenets of atomism as intellectually absurd, therefore, we must assume he is taking the Mutakallimun at their literal and more extreme sense, viz., viewing them as positing a world completely and at every moment created by God's will. This kind of world, we must conclude, does not make philosophical sense for Maimonides.

It is thus the concept of nonbeing, of nothing, which is to Maimonides the

11. Nor would that modified creationist theory, held by various Mutakallimun, which posited an accident of "duration" whereby objects remained in existence for an extended time, change the essentially dependent nature of these objects and their original—and ultimate—connection with nonbeing.

stumbling block for the Mutakallimun, even as it has been the basic challenge to philosophy ever since Parmenides. However, where the great Eleatic felt obliged, in light of the nonbeing of that which is not, to posit a monolithic sameness of Being as the ultimately real, Aristotle developed a theory of potential being meant to explain change and diversity without recourse to the logical absurdity of positing the existence of a real, absolute nonbeing. This potential being and the prior ontological state of actual being to which it is necessarily linked are viewed as aspects of that which is eternal, described in terms of form and matter which together are represented in all physical objects, i.e., in nature.

Being is thus eternal, yet multifaceted, all coming-to-be coming from prior states of being, described as either a *habitus* or privation in matter, as in III:10, pp. 438 ff. Time (and likewise motion) is on similar grounds considered as infinitely extended, viz., in that one cannot speak of a temporal period "before" or "after" the present that is void of its own nature, time; thus one cannot speak of a time devoid of (the universe's) being, of which motion time is the measure. Belief in a theoretically infinite succession of changes, of causal relations, is thus a necessary part of the Aristotelian world view, tempered only by the need to posit an actual first cause in order to avoid the awkward consequences of infinite regression. That is, it is the logical feasibility of the notion of potential infinity, together with the logical necessity of the arguments for continuous time, motion and being, that make it necessary to posit eternal principles and first causes of actual being.[12]

Now Maimonides emphasizes the impossibility of infinite magnitude, number, and causal series in the beginning of his summary of the premises used by philosophy to establish the existence of the deity, in the Introduction to the Second Part of the *Guide*, p. 235. Of the second premise he explicitly restricts the impossibility of an infinite number of magnitudes to a simultaneous, i.e., an actual, infinity; and the same restriction could be applied to an infinite causal series, viz., that there cannot be an infinite number of actual causes coexisting.[13] Maimonides does not state that it is impossible for such infinities to exist potentially, as in a succession of numbers or causes following each other to infinity, i.e., potentially to infinity, inasmuch as at any given moment there is only a finite actual number or cause. It is of course this kind of infinity that is at issue in the conflict between the Mutakallim and the

12. See Aristotle, *Physics*, VIII:1–6; and *Metaphysics*, XII:4–7. It is this logical underpinning to physics and metaphysics which provides Maimonides with the arguments that support his view of the world we experience as being an expression of God's goodness and wisdom.

13. An infinite magnitude, for its part, is also impossible to conceive only in actuality, for it is infinitely divisible.

philosopher, and it is this potential infinity that establishes the kind of eternal universe the philosopher requires.

It is thus probably not coincidental that the premises denying the possibility of an actual infinity—i.e., those that indirectly affirm the possibility of certain kinds of potential infinity—precede all other premises, those speaking of change, motion, bodies, forces, matter and form, i.e., all the components of a system that knows no vacuum, no nonbeing, and that must therefore posit a theoretical infinity of changes and causes. Maimonides is elsewhere quite explicit in accepting this notion of potential infinity, at I:73, p. 212, where he disputes the eleventh premise of the Mutakallimun which denies both actual and potential infinity; and at I:74, p. 222, where he sides with al-Farabi in rejecting the Mutakallimun's treatment of the successively or accidentally infinite, which is infinite in potentiality, as though it were infinite in actuality. It is accordingly not altogether unexpected that Maimonides should be willing to entertain the possibility of the twenty-sixth premise of the philosopher being true, viz., that time and movement, and hence the universe of which they are functions, are eternal, since this premise is based, Maimonides acknowledges, on the notion of an infinite succession of moments and movements, i.e., on the potential infinity of time and motion.[14] As Maimonides accepts the notion of potential infinity in general, it would seem likely that he accept it as regards time and motion too. Moreover, as we have seen already, Maimonides should accept the notion of an eternal universe, as it is integral to the existence of other philosophical premises he does accept.

That Maimonides is indeed basically an Aristotelian in these matters is clear also from other aspects of his summary of the premises used in the philosophical establishment of the existence of the deity, and from his specific identification with twenty-five of the twenty-six premises.[15] Thus the fourth premise affirms the four kinds of change Aristotle promulgated, substantial change being appropriately noted as generation and corruption, not creation and annihilation. The fifth premise too is crucial for our purposes, as it asserts that "every motion is a change and transition (*khurûj/yetzi'ah*, literally an "emergence") from potentiality to actuality," i.e., never an innovation from nonbeing to being. Potential existence, for its part, is categorically related to matter in the twenty-fourth premise: "Whatsoever is something in potentia is necessarily endowed with matter, for possibility is always in matter." Here possibility is clearly treated as a synonym of potentiality, and both are regarded as functions of matter. Whatever is possible, therefore, is already in matter, and when actualized emerges *from* this matter. This philosophical view of possibility is thus the complete antithesis of the Kalam notion, and Maimonides can be critical of the latter only because he sides with the former, and he does so basically for logical and not empirical reasons.

The informed reader may by now have lost patience with this presentation of Maimonides' thought because it has ignored the repeated demurrals Maimonides tenders to the notion of eternity. Creation is the opinion held by "all who believe in the law of Moses our Master," Maimonides avers repeatedly, and as opposed to the Aristotelian world which functions by necessity, he asserts unequivocally the view of a world created from absolute nonbeing by the will of God.[16]

However, asserting a view is one thing, defending it another. Particularly difficult is this for Maimonides, for in II:14, pp. 286 f., he spells out in greater detail the case for eternity as made by Aristotle and his successors, presenting a very strong case indeed for the philosopher's view. The kinds of arguments are divided into Aristotelian and post-Aristotelian, with the former emphasizing the impossibility of positing a beginning to motion, matter, and time, as contrasted with the possibility, or rather necessity, of imagining things as existing in potentiality before being actualized. Again the underlying theme is the impossibility of imagining nothing as the source of something. The post-Aristotelian arguments for eternity, for their part, take as their focus the absurdities to which God would supposedly be subject if he created the world from nothing. Thus the move from "potential" to actual creation would require a mover, as well as a reason for occurring at a particular time and not before, when nothing could have hindered God from acting before, and an agent acts when there is no impediment to his acting. Similarly, there would need be an explanation why God did not allow the world, as an expression of His perfection, to be in existence forever.

Maimonides' responses to these arguments is most disarming. It is two-pronged, like the questions. The refutation of the Aristotelian position is particularly daring, for in it Maimonides appears to concede what he earlier seemed to deny in his exposition of the Kalam notion of possibility, viz., that it is intellectually admissible to imagine a world fundamentally different

16. Ibid., II:13, pp. 281–85; III:10, p. 438; and elsewhere. At the end of II:13, p. 285, Maimonides says that it is incumbent upon an adherent of the faith not only to believe that nothing coexists eternally with God, but also "that the bringing into existence of a being out of nonexistence ('*ijâd al-mawjûd min ʿadam*) is for the deity not an impossibility (*mumtaniʿ*) but rather an obligation (*wâjib*)."

from the one we now experience, and present nature need not dictate the limits of other possible natures. True, Maimonides has prepared us for this position already in his prolonged treatment of the tenth premise of the Mutakallimun, where he concludes his discussion with the following (p. 211):

> For if the philosopher says, as he does: That which exists is my witness and by means of it we discern the necessary, the possible, and the impossible; the adherent of the Law says to him: The dispute between us is with regard to this point. For we claim that that which exists was made in virtue of will and was not a necessary consequence. Now if it was made in this fashion, it is admissible that it should be made in a different way, unless intellectual representation decides, as you think it decides, that something different from what exists at present is not admissible. This is the chapter of admissibility. And about that I have something to say, which you will learn in various passages of this Treatise. It is not something one hastens to reject in its entirety with nonchalance.

Similarly, Maimonides has foreshadowed his response to the philosophical position in II:15, p. 292, in saying that "[Aristotle's] opinion is nearer to correctness than the opinions of those who disagree with him *in so far as inferences are made from the nature of what exists*" (*bi-hasbi l-'istidlâli min tabî'ati l-wujûd; lefi leqihat ha-re'ayah mi-teva' ha-metzi'ut*). In order, then, to deny the correctness of Aristotle's position one must deny the legitimacy of inferring from the present to the past, or, for that matter, to the future. This Maimonides does explicitly in II:17, p. 297, where he says, "The essential point is ... that a being's state of perfection (*Kamâl/shelemut*) and completion (*Tamâm/Tamut*) furnishes no indication of the state of that being preceding its perfection." Maimonides' intention is to dispute inferences concerning the origin or lack of origin of the world drawn from the being of the world as we know it, i.e., in its completed or "perfect," i.e., realized, state, and he illustrates this point by elaborating upon the fact that from our knowledge of a mature or maturing creature alone we could not properly infer the nature of its being *in utero*.

Maimonides is thus prepared to grant all the Aristotelian theses that he has so ably presented, since all of them are true only insofar as they relate to the world as we know it, in its present, realized state. Hence: first matter is indeed that from which everything is generated and into which everything passes away; motion in itself, and all connected with it (time and the world in general), is indeed unimaginable as coming into being and perishing, circular motion does not have a beginning; and the possibility of everything generated necessarily precedes its actuality.[17] All this, however, is true only *after* the world has been brought into existence from nothing, and in no way discounts that possibility. In saying this Maimonides must be aware that he cannot be using the term "after" in the normal, temporal sense, since that would be obviously self-contradictory, after all he has granted.

The state of the world "before" it came to be as we know it is, therefore, something we simply cannot know with any certainty, since, as Maimonides says, "after motion has come into existence . . . *one cannot imagine* (*la yatakhayyal*) that it should come into being as a whole and perish as a whole. . . . Similarly . . . after the spherical body endowed with circular motion has been brought into being, *one cannot conceive* (*la yatasawwar*) that its motion should have a beginning"; and similarly with all the other necessary elements of our world, i.e., necessary as presently constructed and as determining our comprehension.

This view of Maimonides is not easy to accept if one wishes to regard him as a rigorous philosopher. For it is the very nature of the Aristotelian arguments for eternity, the logic of which Maimonides does accept, that they brook no limitations, and it is not clear whether Maimonides has in fact established any. That which is eternal *a parte post* only is not truly eternal, from the Aristotelian standpoint, which is that of the logically necessary entailments of "eternity." Not that Maimonides is fully prepared to grant the absolute theoretical necessity of eternity *a parte post* either, since in this same section (II:17, and cf. II:29, p. 346) he explicitly says there of first matter—and the same holds for all other "presently eternal" components of the Aristotelian system—that as the Creator brought it into existence from nothing, so may He "render it entirely and absolutely nonexistent."

The meaning of Maimonides' position is, moreover, not rendered more comprehensible by the analogy he has chosen.[18] We do in fact know the origins to which a mature creature can be traced, however improbable they may appear at first. Moreover, it would appear that there is no natural example Maimonides could give which would deny this kind of causal explanation, based on the principle of the continuity of being. Thus the notion of a past reality that cannot in principle be inferred from the present is philosophically suspect, ignorance of the causes of something not being proof for the absence of such causes. If Maimonides' example is conse-

---

17. Ibid., II:17, p. 297.
18. Cf. J. Guttmann's important study, "Das Problem der Kontingenz in der Philosophie des Maimonides," *MGWJ*, LXXXIII (1939), 414 ff.; Hebrew translation by S. Esh in Guttmann, *Dat u-Madda^c* (Jerusalem, 1955), pp. 124 ff.

quently to be rendered respectable, it must be seen merely as an analogy, of partial relevance only. This, however, should be regarded as inevitable on Maimonides' own account, for any example taken from the world as we know it will have to subscribe to the laws operating in this world, here those of causation and actualization of the potential.

Maimonides' contention regarding the creation of the world from nothing thus has no real parallel to fall back upon. Nor does he assert anything about this type of creation that renders it comprehensible to us. As he acknowledges at the end of chapter 17 (p. 298), his argument does not attempt to establish anything more than the possibility of creation. This possibility, however, is something we cannot conceive of in specific terms, any more than we can conceive of the nonexistence of first matter, form, motion, time and the world which is their expression. Maimonides is thus in the anomalous position of asserting something which he cannot really explain, and it is no wonder that through the centuries many critics have not been prepared to accept his remarks on creation at their face value.[19] Yet it seems to this reader of the *Guide* that Maimonides has a valid argument, though one which does not take him as far as he would like.

The possibilities he speaks of are something beyond our conception, and therefore indescribable. It is necessarily false for the eternal to be created, as we understand these terms, and as these terms must be understood to avoid logical absurdity. The rules of thought are a necessary part of our comprehension of this universe, and we cannot rationally understand it by any other means. Thus in advocating the possibility of what has to be regarded normally as impossible, Maimonides must know that he is being logically inconsistent. To him, though, all this is true only insofar as we stay within our spatio-temporal world of experience. This is of course inevitable for man, and thus it is inevitable that Maimonides' assertions make no literal sense. If, however, we grant that there is a spatio-temporal framework to the world, and to man's knowledge as part of the world, which framework determines our knowledge of events and the occurrences of the events themselves, then we may be prepared to grant the existence of another dimension, that "outside" of space and time. To Maimonides that possibility is a real possibility, though one necessarily divorced from anything we can experience; even, one should add, from our normal understanding of possibility. This is Maimon-

---

19. Cf. recently Y. Glicker, "The Modality Problem in the Philosophy of the Rambam" [Hebrew], *Iyyun*, X (1959), 177–91, esp. pp. 188 ff. See also A. Nuriel's acute analysis of the unexpected contexts in which Maimonides actually uses the term "Creator" (*bore'*) in the *Guide*, in "The Question of a Created or Primordial World in the Philosophy of Maimonides" [Hebrew], *Tarbiz*, XXXIII (1964), 372–87.

ides' point of difference with other philosophers,[20] in that he apparently feels it does make sense to speak of another reality, even if nothing can be said of that reality other than that there is such a one, though "is" itself cannot be understood in normal terms of existence, viz., matter and form.

Maimonides is, then, not challenging the "order of creation" or the necessary nature of the universe as are the Mutakallimun, nor is he tempted—as they are—to describe a fundamental alternative to Aristotelian physics or metaphysics. He wishes rather to pose an alternative system based on an acknowledgment of the limits of our spatio-temporal experience of the world, a world that paradoxically appears to us unlimited, in so many ways.

Maimonides' contention is unassailable in that it is totally removed from our range of experience and from the language of normal discourse based on that experience. Thus the statement that God created the world from nothing is not necessarily self-contradictory, since it is not to be taken as it would normally be construed. This is small comfort, however, for neither do we know how we should take this remark. This is the weakness of Maimonides' position, for inasmuch as his other world is totally beyond our grasp, any assertion concerning it is equally plausible and implausible. Maimonides is no more justified in asserting creation from nothing by a voluntary Creator than he is in the opposite, as he recognizes. In this other world all is indeed possible, since we know nothing about it. Hence even an assertion of some sort of $P \cdot \sim P$ could be possible, though what this means, what it could possibly stand for, is beyond our comprehension.

Maimonides, of course, does not want to posit unknowable concepts, and as it makes no literal sense to utter contradictory statements, he strictly restricts himself to the one issue, that of creation from nothing, and seeks other arguments in support of the feasibility of the notion. Here the post-Aristotelian arguments for eternity come into play, and Maimonides' refutation of them is consistent with his previous remarks. God need not have moved from potentiality to actuality in creating the world, and thus to have needed an agent to effect this change, Maimonides reasons, since only beings composed of matter and form so move and are so dependent. Nor need a pure form always act, Maimonides adds, but, on the model of the Active Intellect (the universal formal principle of our sublunar world), may act intermittently.[21]

Similarly, it is only the will which belongs to a material being, desiring

---

20. Cf., e.g., Averroes, *Tahâfut at-Tahâfut*, ed. S. Dunyah (Cairo, 1965), II:781 ff.; and S. Van Den Bergh's translation of the Bouyges edition of this work, *The Incoherence of the Incoherence* (London, 1954), I, 318 f., and 325.

21. See *Guide*, II:18, p. 299.

something external to itself, that is affected by accidents and impediments, stimulating and causing change in the will. A self-sufficient will may act as it pleases and when it pleases, and intermittent action is not a sign of change in such a will. Of such a divine agent it is, moreover, foolish to insist that the effect of His wisdom be obvious to us, and that He, being eternal, need will an eternal universe. "We are," Maimonides says (p. 302), "completely ignorant of the rule of that wisdom and of the decision made by it."

This last sentence epitomizes Maimonides' method in discussing God's nature. The arguments faulting the concept of a divine creation from nothing are all erroneous, in his view, because of the inapplicability of their language. God's wisdom, we may say, is not man's wisdom, His will not ours, nor His actions that with which we are familiar. True, there appears to be a parallel to the concept of God as actuality or pure form in the notion of the intelligences of the spheres, specifically the Active Intellect of our sphere. Maimonides is drawn to this parallel, at first, to explain how a being eternally *in actu* may yet not act always. Honesty, however, prevents him from leaving this example unqualified. The "intermittent" activity of the Active Intellect results, he concedes on p. 300, from a "material disposition" [22] of a body not prepared to receive it, not from any genuine intermittent activity on its part. The Active Intellect must always, by definition, be "in act," even if it appears and may be spoken of as though it is acting only intermittently; so too God as actual intelligence must always be expressing His being, this being the meaning of an "actual intelligence." If the transition from potentiality to actuality is, therefore, correctly regarded as inappropriately predicated of God *qua* actual intelligence, so too must the notion of such a being acting only at certain times be ruled out. God's being may presumably be realized independently of the world, but such an assumption would not help our arguments for creation, nor be something we could know with any certainty, since we do not even know what it is to be "independent of the world," i.e., independent of any relationship to form and matter. If God created the world from nothing, then, He could not have done it as the form of forms, as an intelligence comparable to any formal principle we may recognize.

This is not, admittedly, the point Maimonides is making in this chapter, but one that follows from it. Maimonides appears interested merely in establishing the fact that "action" may be predicated of separate intelligences and hence of God, even though the term is used equivocally in comparison to its normal usage, viz., as expressing the transition from potentiality to ac-

22. *At-tahayyu' al-mâddiy* (Munk, p. 209); *ha-hazmanah ha-homrit* (Hebrew, II:37); and cf. *Guide*, II:12, pp. 278–79.

tuality. We have further argued, following Maimonides' lead, that the term "action" as applicable to separate intelligences must again be used equivocally in relation to God, for whom a unique type of action is meant. It is, moreover, because of the unique nature of God's being that His action is unique.[23]

The same moral may be drawn from Maimonides' remark on p. 301 that the term "will" is used equivocally for God's will and ours. Not only does His will differ from that of any mortal creature, it also differs from that of the heavenly bodies whose "souls" possess a motive principle analogous to will, viz., their desire for perfection.[24] Of course these heavenly bodies or spheres, though "eternal," are not without their own kind of material substrate. They are, also, clearly dependent on external objects which stimulate their will/ desire. It is, in fact, the failure of these bodies to realize that state of being toward which they are attracted that keeps them in motion. Nevertheless, these bodies are regarded as being in continuous motion, and there is no impediment to the expression of their will. One can say of the heavenly bodies, therefore, that their will does not change, and this would be an instance of the type of will that Maimonides wishes to predicate of God. However, it would not be helpful to adduce this usage, for the will of the heavenly bodies, like their actions, quite literally does not change (because it cannot), whereas the will of God does not change, contrary to appearances, because there is no model of change applicable to it.

Thus God's will is *sui generis*, unrelated essentially and in every way to any factor external to Himself; as such it is totally uncaused. It is of this will that Maimonides says on p. 301, "The true reality and the quiddity of will means: to will and not to will (*haqîqatu l-'irâdati wa-mâhiyyatuhâ hâdhâ ma'nâhâ an yurîda wa-lâ yurîd; 'amitat ha-ratzon we-mahuto zeh 'inyanah she-yirtzeh we-lo' yirtzeh*). The fact that it may wish one thing now and another thing tomorrow does not constitute a change in its essence and does not call for another cause." Now, clearly the nature of such an uncaused and totally spontaneous action is beyond our ken, even as is the idea that different expressions of this will do not signify changes in it. Yet if "change" no longer has any of the normal meanings we ascribe to it, neither can such terms as "true reality" and "quiddity" of will really explicate the nature of the divine will. Far from being the quiddity of will, the divine will is the paradigmatic exception to will.[25]

---

23. This is but one instance of the inadequacy of predicating anything of God, the sort of problem which ultimately leads to the oblique kind of attribution which "negative" theology offers.

24. See *Guide*, II:4, pp. 255–56; and II:7, p. 266.

25. That is, when the divine will is considered in its unique sense. Maimonides, however, often

That which may will for no known reason, acts in response to no external stimulus, stops and starts "at will," i.e., at what must appear to be at random, is not something we can comprehend within our matrix of intelligible events. Nor can we assume that God's will is responding to His intellect and fulfilling what He wishes fulfilled, for in that case the will would again have some "external" or extraneous motivation and cause. Ultimately this will must be the same as the divine wisdom, both will and wisdom to be taken as unknowable synonyms of the divine essence.[26] The quiddity of the divine will thus transcends our understanding of will, even as the essence of God remains, for Maimonides, fundamentally beyond our understanding.

The refutation of the post-Aristotelian arguments for eternity are, then, of a piece with the refutation of the Aristotelian arguments. In both cases Maimonides consciously poses an alternative to our world of experience which is both unverifiable and putatively unintelligible (and unverifiable because unintelligible). Words are used not only out of their normal context, but out of even an extended context, and equivocation becomes a mask behind which God has nothing in common with His creation. It is thus not surprising that Maimonides' most powerful arguments against the notion of an eternal universe, as conceived in his time, are to be found in the criticism of that doctrine, which he next proceeds to offer; a criticism based on both logical and empirical observations of inconsistencies within that doctrine.[27]

Yet the problematic nature of certain aspects of the argument for eternity, which Maimonides rightly emphasizes, does not in itself establish the truth of the creationist thesis. At most it renders the idea of an alternative system attractive, even, one is tempted to say, feasible. Maimonides has tried to turn that nebulous "feasibility" into a stronger "possibility," with the results which we have discussed. His notion of possibility differs from the Kalam concept of possibility in the very strict limitations he imposes upon it,

---

treats it in a way that could be seen as assuming a univocal meaning with other wills, inasmuch as it operates within a natural framework. It should be obvious by now that Maimonides' view of the limits of meaningful discourse and comprehension obliges him to do this. To the degree that the divine will is "natural," however, it is identified with causation and necessity. Cf. in this regard A. Nuriel's philologically based examination of the two different terms for the divine will in the *Guide*, and his attempt to relate them, in his article, "The Divine Will in *Moreh Nevukhim*" [Hebrew], *Tarbiz*, XXXIX (1969), 39–61.

26. See *Guide*, I:69, p. 170. Thus, neither "will" nor "wisdom" when predicated of God can be understood in its own terms, and Maimonides' identification of one with the other, which is to be expected of (our understanding of) God in relation to the world, as discussed at III:25, p. 505, really clarifies neither.

27. Ibid., II:19, pp. 306 ff.; inconsistencies of crucial importance for the interpretation of Maimonides as advanced in N. A. Rabinovitch's recent study, "The Concept of 'Possibility' in Maimonides" [Hebrew], *Tarbiz*, XLIV (1974-75), 159-71.

rendering it in effect into a possibility we cannot comprehend, under normal circumstances. However, Maimonides does not feel, as we have said, that for that reason his notion of possibility is in itself a thoroughly impossible possibility, and he apparently does wish to hold that in some sense it is reasonable to speak of creation from nothing by the will of God. This sense cannot be based on either our intellect or imagination as normally construed, for reasons we have given; and yet what other faculties are available to us?

It is, accordingly, not unwarranted that Maimonides returns again, in chapter 15 of the third part of the *Guide* (p. 460), to the question of the legitimization of the possible, and again wonders if it is not an open question after all, which faculty determines the limits of plausibility for, in effect, those propositions beyond the normal range of the plausible.[28] We can easily say of any clearly worded, obvious impossibility that it is an impossibility, for we know what is meant and entailed by such a proposition. Similarly all our assertions and denials are founded on the certainty of our experientially based knowledge and on the limits of our rational discourse. What faculty, however, can take us beyond the limits of that discourse, and objectively interpret for us the intimation of another kind of existence? Call that faculty what we will, it is not functioning as it normally does if it is a normal faculty of the soul.[29] Yet it is this faculty Maimonides apparently feels is receptive to the lightning which may illuminate our darkness,[30] and it is ultimately this faculty that allows Maimonides in I:59, p. 137, to pen this hymn to an otherwise unknown God:

> Glory then to Him who is such that when the intellects contemplate His essence, their apprehension turns into incapacity; and when they contemplate the proceeding of His actions from His will, their knowledge turns into ignorance; and when the tongues aspire to magnify Him by means of attributive qualifications, all eloquence turns into weariness and incapacity!

I do not wish to intimate by the above that Maimonides was a mystic in any

28. This chapter has long challenged students of the *Guide*, the medieval commentators tending to disregard Maimonides' stated remarks and to assume that he naturally accepted the intellect as the reigning faculty. Cf., e.g., the remarks of Shem Tov and Crescas to this passage (in the cited Hebrew edition of the *Guide*, III:21). More recently, however, E. Fackenheim has candidly admitted to difficulties with this passage ("The Possibility of the Universe in al-Farabi, Ibn Sina and Maimonides," *PAAJR*, XVI [1947], 60, n. 61).

29. Compare the unusual role assigned to the intellect in the prophecy of Moses, mentioned briefly in the *Guide*, II:37, p. 373; II:45, p. 402; and at greater length in the *Mishneh Torah, Hilkhot Yesode ha-Torah*, VII:6.

30. *Guide*, Preface to Part I, p. 7.

formal or traditional sense.[31] The *Guide* belongs to philosophy, and Maimonides repeatedly attempts to work within that rational and scientific framework which he regards as both necessary and inevitable for man.[32] In pointing to the limits of human experience, however, and in positing a significant though necessarily vague additional dimension to being, Maimonides reached a position conducive both to a rational faith structured along medieval lines and to a philosophy vigorously modern in its insights.

31. For a definitive statement of this question, see A. Altmann, "Das Verhältnis Maimunis zur jüdischen Mystik," *MGWJ*, LXXX (1936), 305–30.

32. It is this—to return to the beginning of the article—which renders Pines's translation of Maimonides' formulation of the Kalam notion of the possible attractive, if not compelling.

Principles of Judaism in Maimonides and Joseph ibn Caspi

Barry Mesch

One of the recurring issues in Maimonidean scholarship revolves around the question of the political dimension of Maimonides' thought.[1] Few will deny that there is such a political dimension, but the questions of where it is found and how it works still remain. The famous distinction in the *Guide* between "true beliefs" and "necessary beliefs,"[2] as well as the discussion concerning the need to hide certain things from the "vulgar" reader,[3] have occasioned much controversy concerning various doctrines in the *Guide*. It is clear that Maimonides believes the Torah requires of people not only certain types of behavior but also certain beliefs about God and His relationship to man. "The Law as a whole aims at two things: the welfare of the soul and the welfare of the body."[4] This requirement concerning the welfare of the soul devolves upon the masses as well as upon the philosophical elite. What indeed are those beliefs which the Law requires of all Jews in order to provide for the welfare of the soul? Although Maimonides does not give us such a list in the *Guide*, he does enumerate Thirteen Principles in his *Introduction to Chapter 10 of Sanhedrin* called *Pereq Heleq*. The context of the discussion is the statement in the Mishnah, "All Jews have a portion in the world to come. . . . But these have no share in the world to come: one who says that the resurrection of the dead is not taught in the Torah; one who says that the Torah is not from heaven; and the atheist."[5] After Maimonides discusses the contents of the Mishnah, he makes use of this occasion to offer his Thirteen Principles. At the end of his discussion he says, "When a man believes in all these fundamental principles, and his faith is thus clarified, he is then part of that

---

1. The foremost representative of "political" interpreters of Maimonides is Leo Strauss. See *Philosophie und Gesetz* (Berlin, 1935); *Persecution and the Art of Writing* (Glencoe, Ill., 1952), pp. 7–95; "How to Begin to Study the *Guide of the Perplexed*," in Moses Maimonides, *The Guide of the Perplexed*, trans. S. Pines (Chicago, 1963), pp. xii–lvii; and numerous articles by Strauss. Representing less emphasis on the political dimension is Julius Guttmann, *Philosophies of Judaism*, trans. D. W. Silverman (Garden City, N.Y., 1966).

2. *Guide*, trans. Pines, III:28, p. 514.

3. Ibid., Introduction to Part I, pp. 5–20.

4. Ibid., III:27, p. 510.

5. *Sanhedrin*, chap. 10, as quoted in I. Twersky, ed., *A Maimonides Reader* (New York, 1972), p. 402.

"Israel" whom we are to love, pity, and treat as God commanded, with love and fellowship. . . . But if a man gives up any one of these fundamental principles, he has removed himself from the Jewish community. He is an atheist, a heretic, an unbeliever who 'cuts among the plantings.'"[6]

These Thirteen Principles have been divided into three categories or groups corresponding to the three categories of persons referred to in *Pereq Heleq* who have lost their share in the World to Come.[7] The first group includes beliefs concerning the nature of God corresponding to the *apikoros* translated as "atheist." The second group includes beliefs concerning the Torah, revelation, and prophecy corresponding to those who "say that the Torah is not from Heaven." The third group includes beliefs concerning reward and punishment corresponding to those who deny that the resurrection of the dead is taught in the Torah.

What indeed are the nature and function of these beliefs? One aspect of the problem relates to the first group concerned with beliefs about the nature of God. Many of these beliefs are rather complicated philosophical propositions which the simple pious Jew would have difficulty understanding. For example, Maimonides says concerning the second principle, "Nor is He one in the sense that a simple body is, numerically one but still infinitely divisible."[8] And the third principle: "We are to believe that He is incorporeal, that His unity is physical neither potentially nor actually. None of the attributes of matter can be predicated of Him, neither motion nor rest, for example. They cannot refer to Him accidentally or essentially."[9]

Is there any value to the mere affirmation of these beliefs without understanding them or is there a necessity to teach them in their full complexity to the uneducated masses? The view that answers affirmatively to the former question has been described as the "political interpretation" of the Thirteen Principles. The major adherents of this view include S. Pines,[10] L. V. Berman,[11] and E. Schweid.[12] The position that affirms the necessity of

6. Ibid., p. 422. See also *Introduction to Pereq Heleq* in *Haqdamot le-Perush ha-Mishnah*, ed. M. D. Rabinowitz (Jerusalem, 1960).

7. Arthur Hyman, "Maimonides' 'Thirteen Principles,'" in A. Altmann (ed.), *Jewish Medieval and Renaissance Studies* (Cambridge, Mass., 1967), pp. 127–219; E. Schweid, "The Educational and Political Justification for the Commandments of Belief in the Teachings of Maimonides" [Hebrew], in *Taʿam we-Haqashah* (Ramat Gan, 1970), pp. 93–94.

8. *A Maimonides Reader*, p. 418.

9. Ibid.

10. S. Pines, "Translator's Introduction," *Guide*, pp. cxviii–cxix.

11. L. V. Berman, "Ibn Bajja and Maimonides: A Chapter in the History of Medieval Political Philosophy" (Ph.D. diss., Hebrew University, 1959).

12. Schweid, "Educational and Political Justification."

teaching the first group of principles to the masses in all their complexity has been called the "metaphysical interpretation" and has recently been defended by A. Hyman.[13] We will look carefully at the "metaphysical interpretation" of Hyman and then the "political interpretation" of Schweid. At that point we will examine the approach of a fourteenth-century disciple of Maimonides, Joseph ibn Caspi. Caspi does not base his approach to "principles of Judaism" on Maimonides' discussion in *Pereq Heleq* but rather on the first chapters of *Hilkhot Yesode ha-Torah*. In the end his views look remarkably similar to the political interpretation of Schweid.

In his article, "Maimonides' 'Thirteen Principles,'" Arthur Hyman says, "Addressed to philosophers and masses alike, these principles [the first group] have as their function to convey true knowledge about God. This knowledge, to be sure, is set down only in the form of final conclusions and philosophers can find demonstrations for its truth, but the masses, no less than the philosophers are expected to know the content of these propositions."[14] In order to defend his contention that the masses are also intended not only to believe these propositions but also to know them, Hyman brings a number of different arguments. The major part of his proof revolves around the third fundamental principle quoted earlier concerning incorporeality. He says, "If it were the function of these principles to motivate human action, Maimonides' insistence that the masses be taught the incorporeality of God is difficult to understand. To move the masses to obedience it would have been sufficient to teach them that God exists, is one, eternal and solely to be worshipped."[15] He refers to Part 1, chapter 35 of the *Guide* where Maimonides also demands that incorporeality be taught to everyone including the masses.

In Hyman's view, the reason for this requirement is that "of the five principles concerning God, that of divine incorporeality is the only one which guarantees *conceptual* knowledge of Him for all."[16] If we remember that the whole context for this discussion was an inquiry into who has a portion of the World to Come, the solution becomes clear. Since "the World to Come" or immortality is defined by Maimonides as the actualization of the human intellect through the understanding of true opinions, primarily about God, the knowledge that the masses obtain by affirming these true propositions

13. Hyman, "Maimonides' 'Thirteen Principles'", see also Guttmann, *Philosophies of Judaism*, pp. 202–4.
14. Hyman, "Maimonides' 'Thirteen Principles,'" p. 140.
15. Ibid., pp. 140–41.
16. Ibid.

about God provides the possibility of immortality for all who so affirm. Thus they are guaranteed a portion in the World to Come along with the philosophical elite.

It seems, however, that there is a serious problem in Hyman's analysis of Maimonides' discussion of incorporeality. At the end of that discussion Maimonides says, "Accordingly there is no excuse for one who does not accept the authority of men who inquire into the truth and are engaged in speculation if he himself is incapable of engaging in such speculation. I do not consider as an infidel one who cannot demonstrate that the corporeality of God should be negated. But I do consider as an infidel one who does not believe in its negation. . . ."[17] Thus, Maimonides says that it is permissible for the masses to believe in divine incorporeality on the basis of traditional authority alone without ever coming to an independent understanding of it. Would there still be any cognitive value in that? What kind of actualization of the intellect is involved in that process? What is more, chapters 35 and 36 of Part 1 of the *Guide* are not the only places in which Maimonides discusses this topic. In chapters 5, 26, and 46 of Part 1 he seems to be taking the exact opposite position to that of chapter 35. We will see later how Caspi deals with this issue.

Eliezer Schweid formulates another approach to the problem of the first group of principles. He says, "The first group can be described as a set of pure philosophical principles. These are the same eternal truths whose comprehension is the end of man. In knowing them he truly worships his God and ascends to the level of eternity—to a point where his intellect which has become actualized does not die when he dies. Consequently, in the area of these beliefs, there is a complete identity between the philosophical viewpoint and the viewpoint of the Torah according to its literal meaning (*ke-fi peshutah*)."[18] From this it is clear that only the true philosopher is able to penetrate to the utmost meaning of the Torah and to fulfill its injunctions. What then of the nonphilosophers among the Jews and their portion in the World to Come? Obviously, most people do not really comprehend these truths and even when they are forced to affirm them there is a difference between what they say and what they understand. What is to be the relationship of the masses to these principles? Schweid suggests that for the common people these principles are to be understood not as the end of religion but rather as the means to get them to accept the *mitzwot* and the Torah, which brings them closer to perfection. The second group of principles deals with these concerns and belongs to the sphere of religion; the first

17. *Guide*, I:36, p. 85.
18. Schweid, "Educational and Political Justification," p. 94.

group of principles is purely philosophical and for the masses is subordinated to the second. "Philosophy deals first of all with eternal truth while the Torah deals first of all with political teaching. Since the Torah tried to bring all of the people, according to their ability, to the truth, there is a complete agreement between it and philosophy in terms of their goal. It is also reasonable that philosophy will try not to destroy what is a necessary condition for the existence of the exalted task of the Torah."[19] There is a perfect link here between philosophy and the Torah in the person of the prophet who himself is the complete philosopher. Thus the belief in Moses and in the Mosaic Torah is the bridge between the political, Torah-oriented principles concerned with the establishment of a society wherein the knowledge of God is the goal and the philosophical-theological principles that encompass them.

The third group of principles, which deals with "reward and punishment," is also viewed differently by the common people and the philosophers. For the common people it is seen as a means to the second group. Thus the affirmation of principles concerned with "reward and punishment" will bring one to a belief in the divine nature of the Torah which in turn will lead one to the observance of the *mitzwot*. The philosopher, on the other hand, knows that the promises of reward and punishment are means to an end, but the end is the knowledge of truth found in the first group of principles. The true reward of man is in the knowledge of these truths, which is the real "World to Come."

Schweid summarizes his approach in the following way. What the philosopher comprehends as the end, the common people imagine as a means; what the philosopher justifies as a means, the common people believe is the end.

We are still left with the question of the relative value of the masses' affirmation of these technical, philosophical theories about God. Schweid bases his discussion of this issue on the fifth fundamental principle—"Only He, blessed be He, is rightfully worshipped, magnified, obeyed."[20] Schweid connects this to the fifth chapter of the *Hilkhot Yesode ha-Torah* which is concerned with the "sanctification of the Name." He says that for Maimonides the sanctification or the desecration of God's Name is a public act that testifies either to belief or to heresy. Therefore, there is in it something of a confession either of faith or of heresy, and through this public testimony a person is judged by political institutions.

In this way Schweid interprets all of the first group of principles in a

19. Ibid., p. 95.
20. *A Maimonides Reader*, p. 418.

political manner as far as the masses are concerned. Their value for the nonphilosophical, common man is in the public acknowledgment of the truth of these statements about God. But Schweid claims that there is an educational value to them as well. By means of fulfilling all of the commandments of the Torah, particularly those concerned with the welfare of the soul, a person removes those things which might prevent him from reaching his final perfection. Thus in the performance of the commandments a person makes some progress on the road to perfection. The important thing is to be on the right path and to be going in the right direction. The acknowledgment of the truth brings one closer to it since it is a condition for the participation of the individual in the life of the perfected society and a condition for the existence of this society. In a sense, while simple affirmation of the truth is not in the realm of true faith, still "it is attached to faith."[21] A person has some part in the truth for two reasons: (1) if he has been trained in true opinions from childhood, he might eventually take the time and trouble to try to understand them; (2) the affirmation of true beliefs about God is in itself the denial of idolatry, and the denial of falsehood is considered a coming nearer to the truth. Thus the affirmation of these beliefs puts man on the right path to true understanding of these beliefs.

With this description of Schweid's views we are still left with Professor Hyman's question concerning the teaching of incorporeality. Hyman asserted that this teaching makes immortality possible for all, including the masses. In Schweid's view no specific mention is made of the third principle, and there is no attempt to show whether the masses can really attain life in the World to Come by means of a simple affirmation of belief in the Thirteen Principles. Schweid is simply not concerned with this issue and apparently we are left with a completely intellectual World to Come from which the unlettered masses are excluded.

Many of the questions that Hyman and Schweid raised concerning Maimonides' understanding of the principles of Judaism were also of concern to Joseph ibn Caspi, a fourteenth-century philosopher and exegete who considered himself a disciple of Maimonides.[22] Caspi (1280–1340), who lived in southern France and northern Spain, wrote commentaries on all the books of the Bible as well as on Maimonides' *Guide*. He also published summaries of

21. Schweid, "Educational and Political Justification," p. 101.

22. Moritz Steinschneider, "Josef Kaspi," in *Gesammelte Schriften*, ed. H. Malter and A. Marx (Berlin, 1925), I, 89–135; E. Renan and A. Neubauer, "Joseph Caspi, philosophe et exegète," in *Les Ecrivains juifs français du XIVe siècle* which is in *Histoire littéraire de la France* (Paris, 1893), XXXI, 477–548. For a recent survey of the literature on Caspi, see my *Studies in Joseph ibn Caspi* (Leiden, 1975).

some of the works of Aristotle and Plato, a Hebrew dictionary, and an ethical will. Among the major influences on Caspi besides Maimonides were Averroes, the Neoplatonist al-Batalyawsi, and Abraham ibn Ezra. Caspi does not devote any specific treatise to the topic of the principles of Judaism, but the bulk of his discussion is found in the *Sefer ha-Musar*[23] (Ethical Will) and *ʿAmmude Kesef* and *Maskiyyot Kesef*[24] (commentaries on the *Guide*). Caspi relies heavily on Maimonides and refers to him constantly; however, the references are to the *Hilkhot Yesode ha-Torah* and not to his enumeration of the Thirteen Principles as found in the *Introduction to Pereq Heleq*.[25]

Caspi says in *Sefer ha-Musar*:

> Now, the knowledge of God is the primary precept of all our 613 laws as may be seen from the texts enforcing this knowledge. It is the basis of the four precepts enumerated by Maimonides at the beginning of the Code. He specifically terms them the Foundations of the Torah. These four precepts are (1) to know that there is a first cause; (2) to recognize that He is One; (3) to love Him; (4) to fear Him. They are designated the Foundations of the Torah for they are at once the purpose and the root of all the commandments (*takhlit we-ʿiqqar le-khol ha-mitzwot*) the observance of which is the whole end of man.[26]

Caspi's understanding of the foundations of the Torah was not merely hortatory or sermonic as might appear from the *Sefer ha-Musar*. They were understood in a more technical sense to refer to those fundamental principles which define the religion of the Torah. In his commentary on the *Guide*, Caspi was disturbed by Maimonides' use of the term foundation of the Torah of Moses[27] (*yesod Torat Mosheh*) in relation to the belief in Creation. He says, "It will be understood from the opinion of Maimonides that we are not obliged to believe in Creation and his concern does not depend on that. . . . The only principles in our Torah, the Torah of God, are the first five[28] precepts that

23. Joseph ibn Caspi, *Sefer ha-Musar*, in I. Abrahams (ed.), *Hebrew Ethical Wills* (Philadelphia, 1926), Part I, pp. 127–61.

24. Joseph ibn Caspi, *ʿAmmude Kesef u-Maskiyyot Kesef*, ed. S. Werbluner (Frankfurt, 1848); reprinted in *Sheloshah Qadmone Mefarreshe ha-Moreh* (Jerusalem, 1961).

25. Caspi was aware of the Thirteen Principles and mentions them in his commentaries on the *Guide*.

26. *Sefer ha-Musar*, p. 132. See *Hilkhot Yesode ha-Torah* in *Sefer ha-Maddaʿ*, ed. M. D. Rabinowitz (Jerusalem, 1947), pp. 4–24.

27. *Guide*, II:13, p. 282.

28. Caspi interchanges the number of principles from four to five. Sometimes he even reduces the number to two (*Matzref la-Kesef*, in *Mishnah Kesef* [Cracow, 1906], II, 5). The important thing is that he is basically referring to the first four chapters of *Hilkhot Yesode ha-Torah*. There is really only one principle and that is the true knowledge of God. Cf. my *Joseph ibn Caspi*, pp. 100, 105–6.

Maimonides mentioned at the beginning of *Hilkhot Yesode ha-Torah* and he did not include there 'to believe that the world is created' and other similar statements which many of the great and small of our people have made into principles (*pinnot*)."[29] In another context Caspi even uses these principles in a negative way by terming those who would not accept them "unbelievers" (*koferim*). In arguing with those who accuse Caspi of transgressing the words of the Sages, who were very strict about keeping certain matters concealed, Caspi says, "How is it that these people who are destitute of knowledge and empty of this wisdom which is the knowledge of the mysteries of the Torah do not worry about their lives but rather worry about mine. Woe on their souls, since they do not sense that they are unbelievers not fulfilling the first five commandments which Maimonides arranged in *Hilkhot Yesode ha-Torah* in four chapters."[30]

From these and other texts[31] it is clear that the first four chapters of the *Hilkhot Yesode ha-Torah* formed for Caspi the fundamental principles of the Jewish religion. It is also clear that these chapters contain basically the same injunctions as the first group of principles in *Pereq Heleq*, those principles that both Hyman and Schweid call the "philosophical" principles. Thus for Caspi the agreement between the goal of philosophy and that of the Torah is complete. It is so complete that he eliminates consideration of principles concerning revelation, the Torah, and reward and punishment. Caspi is, at times, willing to reveal explicitly the implications of this conception. He says, "Since the Torah comes from the Fountain of Intellect and its beginning was in Moses, the Master of intellectuals, there is no doubt that all of its contents inform us about intellectual matters and look ultimately to the perfection of the intellect."[32]

Caspi is well aware of the fact that most people do not have the capacity to arrive at the level of intellectual perfection. He understands that not only are we wasting our time when we preach philosophy to the masses, but that that very activity can be quite dangerous.[33] Not only will the common man not understand the complex abstract theories of philosophy, but he might become so confused that his simple faith in God might be shaken. If this is the case, how does one teach these fundamental principles of Judaism to the common man or even more radically, does one teach them to the masses at

29. *'Ammude Kesef*, pp. 100–101.

30. Joseph ibn Caspi, *Menorat Kesef*, in *'Asarah Kele Kesef*, ed. I. Last (Pressburg, 1903), XI, 76–77.

31. See *Sefer ha-Musar*, pp. 136, 143, 153–54; *Maskiyyot Kesef*, p. 113; *Tirat Kesef*, in *Mishnah Kesef*, I, 5–6; *Commentary A on Proverbs*, in *'Asarah Kele Kesef*, I, 18–19.

32. *Tirat Kesef*, pp. 15–16.

33. Cf. *Maskiyyot Kesef*, p. 8; *Commentary A on Proverbs*, pp. 35–39; *Commentary B on Proverbs*, p. 119; *'Adne Kesef*, ed. I. Last (London, 1911), I, 174.

all? Obviously, Caspi has developed a rather elitist view of the Jewish religion. Are the masses provided for at all? In another context I have tried to show that in Caspi's view the greatness of the Torah is found in the fact that it provides both for the masses and for the philosophers.[34] He says that the Torah is more than philosophy because it contains both philosophy and teachings for the nonphilosopher. Commenting on the passage "The Torah speaks in the language of men,"[35] Caspi focuses on the term "man" (*'adam*). He uses Maimonides' interpretation in the *Guide* that one of the meanings of "man" in the Bible is a term "designating the multitude, . . . the generality as distinguished from the elite."[36] Caspi says, "Our Holy Scriptures were written to be transmitted to all of the masses [including] children and women for the improvement of the world (*tiqqun ha-ʿolam*) in general, and in particular the individual [philosopher] can become perfected [also]. The rabbis said, 'the world in its entirety was only created as a satellite for Him.'[37] Therefore the individual [philosopher] is also obligated to be concerned with the improvement of the group (*tiqqun ha-kelal*). God sent the prophets into the world from the beginning to the end for the purpose of the improvement of the world in general and in particular and for this end all of our Holy Books were written."[38] Caspi shows how the prophets were forced to use special language appropriate to the masses and even at times to say things about God Himself which were untrue in order to assure that everyone would hold a firm belief in the existence of God.

The issue becomes clarified when Caspi deals with the problem of the teaching of the incorporeality of God in the *Guide*. He points out that Maimonides contradicts himself on this issue. In Part 1, chapters 26 and 46, Maimonides says that the reason corporeal attributes have been attached to God is because "the multitude cannot at first conceive of any existence save that of a body alone; thus, that which is neither a body nor existent in a body does not exist in their opinion."[39] Consequently, ". . . the minds of the multitude were accordingly guided to the belief that He exists by imagining that He is corporeal and to the belief that He is living by imagining that He is capable of motion."[40] However, in Part 1, chapter 35, Maimonides says, "On the other hand, the negation of the doctrine of the corporeality of God and

34. My *Joseph ibn Caspi*, pp. 84 ff.
35. *Berakhot* 31b.
36. *Guide*, I:14, p. 40.
37. *Berakhot* 6b; *Shabbat* 30b.
38. *Shulhan Kesef*, ms. Turin 197, fol. 182–83. Last incorrectly named Caspi's commentaries on Job, *Shulhan Kesef*. See my *Joseph ibn Caspi* for a full discussion of this question (esp. p. 54).
39. *Guide*, I:26, p. 56.
40. Ibid., I:46, p. 98.

the denial of His having a likeness to created things and of His being subject to affections are matters that ought to be made clear and explained to everyone according to his capacity and ought to be inculcated in virtue of traditional authority upon children, women, stupid ones and those of a defective natural disposition, just as they adopt the notion that God is one, that He is eternal, and that none but He be worshipped."[41]

In his commentary to chapter 26 Caspi says that the prophets had a choice between two evils. On the one hand, they could teach that God exists but is incorporeal with the possibility that the people might come to the conclusion that God does not exist at all—which is atheism ('*apikorsut*). On the other hand, they could teach that He exists but is corporeal or a force within matter. The prophets knew that the people could not believe both that God exists and at the same time that He is incorporeal; therefore, they chose the lesser of the two evils and taught corporeality. At least the people would believe in the existence of God. Because of this "we are obliged to lie to the masses and teach corporeal attributes so that the masses will be saved from atheism, which is worse than idolatry."[42]

What then of Maimonides' statements in chapter 35? Caspi says that after we have instilled belief in the existence of God in the masses then

> we should hint little by little, at certain times, or at certain places that God is completely incorporeal and that the interpretation of corporeal attributes is thus and so or at least that they are to be understood as a parable. . . . This is what the *Guide* intended in Chapter 35. Look at all of it and compare what he said in Chapter 46 and if it appears that there is a contradiction it is not so. Chapters 26 and 46 speak about the way one must usually behave with all the masses while Chapter 36 speaks about the way one must behave with some of the masses, some times, little by little, first things first; in the way that one sprinkles the perfume of rose and myrrh on beautiful clothes.[43]

In his commentary on chapter 35, Caspi adds the point that one great advantage that Judaism has over all of the other religions is that while the Torah contains innumerable references to the corporeality of God, there are also a very small number of references to the incorporeality of God. For example, "For you saw no image."[44] All the other religions are completely

41. Ibid., I:35, p. 81.
42. *ʿAmmude Kesef*, p. 39.
43. Ibid.
44. Deuteronomy 4:15.

concerned with inculcating the belief in divine corporeality. The founders of these religions knew this to be false but they also knew that once they teach the people the truth they might lose everything, leave their religion and deny the existence of God. Our Torah, on the other hand, reveals the truth, but very rarely and in a hidden manner. Caspi goes on to say that it is for this same reason that the Torah does not reveal the true meaning of "the World to Come."[45]

Returning now to our original question, we find that while everyone has the responsibility of affirming these four or five principles concerning God, Caspi does not believe that we ought to teach the masses the real meaning of these principles because it is too dangerous. The masses need to believe in the existence of God for political reasons. They need to believe in a God who gave them the Torah and is watching over them, ready to reward or punish as their actions merit. The Torah is distinguished from other Laws in that it does provide hints for the especially sensitive reader as to what the true beliefs about God are.[46]

This approach of Caspi to the principles of Judaism appears to be identical to much of Schweid's interpretation of Maimonides' views. If we understand that for Maimonides the latter two groups of propositions reflect the belief in the Torah as the basis for the entire system of commandments, and reward and punishment as the reason for observing these commandments, then for the masses the first group of principles plays the same role for Caspi as for Maimonides. This is to say that there is no intellectual value in the masses' affirmation of these principles. Instead they form the basis for a Torah-society with a belief in God who revealed through His prophets and who rewards and punishes. The difference between Caspi and Maimonides lies in the fact that Caspi is unwilling to include purely political and religious propositions among his principles. Even though he is acutely aware of the political dimension of the Torah, he is not able to elevate statements that are not purely philosophical to the level of principles of Judaism. For Caspi the principles are not only the essence of Judaism, they are also the purpose and aim of the religion. They are the highest and most serious of the obligations that a Jew has. Caspi refers to them as "the commandments of the heart." There are three categories of *mitzwot*—commandments of the tongue, of

45. *ʿAmmude Kesef*, p. 45.
46. Cf. Pines, "Translator's Introduction," p. cxviii. Leo Strauss has suggested that for Maimonides there is a difference between the generation of the Bible and the generation of Maimonides regarding the "secret" of the incorporeality of God. Strauss says that in the days of the prophets the people could not handle the belief in incorporeality. In the days of Maimonides, however, "the time has come when even the vulgar must be taught most explicitly that God is incorporeal" (Strauss, "How to Begin to Study," p. xlvii).

action, and of the heart.[47] The philosopher knows that the commandments of the tongue and of action are basically intended for political and moral reasons but the purpose of man is found in the fulfillment of the commandments of the heart. Caspi says, "The commandments of the heart are the highest type while the two other kinds are to train and remind us. Since men are not angels, intellectual commandments are not enough. . . . Only the philosophers know that while the heart is the most important part it cannot exist without the other limbs as its servants; therefore the philosophers will be very careful in observing the commandments of the tongue and of action."[48] The masses place all of their energy on the fulfillment of the commandments of the tongue and of action and view the commandments of the heart as secondary to them. They are satisfied in observing the commandments of the heart, that is the intellectual commandments, on the basis of traditional authority alone.

Caspi shares with Maimonides an Aristotelian conception of the World to Come which is dependent on the actualization of one's intellect while one is alive. Does the nonintellectual affirmation of these principles really gain one a share in this type of World to Come? While Caspi never addresses this question directly, the answer would seem to be in the negative. Caspi does, however, give us a description and evaluation of the perfectly religious and nonphilosophical Jew. That is, according to Caspi's interpretation, the biblical figure of Job.

Caspi sees in Job a man who has fulfilled all of the commandments, but he has fulfilled the commandments of the heart by way of authoritative tradition alone. Job has come to the final point in wisdom and understanding called "the fear of God and the turning from evil."[49] However, he has not reached the other type of wisdom called "and do good."[50] This latter type of wisdom is found in the fulfillment of the commandments of the heart. "Now there is no doubt that a person is not completely righteous until he fulfills all 613 commandments, not just some of them. Therefore, Job had not arrived at the perfection of the intellectual soul, certainly not the prophetic soul."[51] Thus the friends of Job were wrong in accusing him of wrongdoing. He had not committed any transgression. Caspi imagines a dialogue between God and

47. This categorization has its origin in Abraham ibn Ezra, *Yesod Mora'* (Prague, 1833), pp. 27–32. See my *Joseph ibn Caspi*, pp. 84–88.

48. *Tirat Kesef*, p. 6.

49. This is a reference to the beginning of the Book of Job where Job is described as a man "who feared God and turned away from evil" (Job 1:1).

50. Psalms 34:15, 37:27.

51. *Longer Commentary on Job*, called *Shulhan Kesef* by Last, in *ᶜAsarah Kele Kesef*, I, 150. See above, n. 38.

Job. "Don't blame me for all of your troubles. You are still not my "lover" nor my true and absolute servant. If you had arrived at the perfection of Abraham I would have saved you from some evils and if you had reached the perfection of Moses I would have saved you from all of them. In general you are still not worthy and you are not on the level which is dearest to me as they were, peace be on them. . . . These sufferings that I brought upon you were both punishment and penalty for your deficiencies since you did not struggle to ascend to the perfection of these men, peace be on them. The good things that I brought you were reward and compensation for your perfection."[52]

According to Caspi's interpretation, Elihu is the one who truly understands Job's situation and Elihu informs Job that he needs to engage in intellectual endeavors. Job does finally fulfill the commandments of the heart truly, that is, he fully understands them and ultimately he reaches the level of prophecy.[53]

Caspi summarizes his position on the different levels of human perfection at the end of his shorter commentary on Job. He says that there are three levels of human perfection. The first level includes the completely pious Jew who, like Job, observed all the commandments but observed the commandments of the heart by way of traditional authority alone. The second level includes those who observe all the commandments and know the commandments of the heart by means of demonstrative proofs. The third and highest level include those who have reached the second level and have also reached the level of prophecy.[54] Moses represents the highest possible perfection available to a human being. While the first level is called a level of perfection, it is clear from the case of Job that this is not a rank of much stature.

This study of Caspi's conception of "principles of Judaism," which in his view are identified with the commandments of the heart, leads to the following conclusions.

1. Caspi has taken the rationalistic implications of Maimonides' system to their final conclusion and has said explicitly that the true essence and purpose of the Torah is the study of philosophy and the actualization of one's intellect. The "principles of the Torah" equal commandments of the heart which equal the obligation to strive for philosophical knowledge.

2. In order to establish a perfected society the Torah has laid down a whole system of commandments, including commandments of the tongue, of ac-

---

52. *Shorter Commentary on Job*, also called *Shulhan Kesef*, in ʿ*Asarah Kele Kesef*, I, 172.
53. Ibid., pp. 172–73.
54. Ibid., pp. 174–75.

tion, and of the heart. The masses, for the most part, should not be bothered with the intricacies of the commandments of the heart (the intellectual commandments). It is enough if they accept them on the basis of traditional authority alone.

Beliefs having to do with revelation, prophecy, creation, miracles, and reward and punishment as they are understood by the masses do not have the status of principles of Judaism and thus are not really part of the commandments of the heart. They form rather part of the political system which the prophets promulgated to the people of Israel.

3. There is no cognitive value in the masses' affirmation of the intellectual commandments, but that affirmation does at least put them in the category of those who are "God-fearing" and who "turn from evil." While they might still be technically guilty of idolatry, they are not guilty of atheism. Whether this actually gains them a real portion in the World to Come is extremely doubtful.

4. Schweid's analysis of the "commandments to believe" in Maimonides agrees almost completely with Caspi's own understanding of the nature and purpose of the Torah and of Judaism. Of course Caspi would claim that his philosophy is, after all, only an attempt at revealing the true meaning of the teachings of Maimonides.

The Jewish Philosophical Critique of Transubstantiation

Daniel J. Lasker

Medieval Jewish-Christian religious polemics focused on a number of different topics, such as the nature of God and the criteria of a true religion. One frequent subject of discussion was the relative value of two ceremonial rituals, the Jewish animal sacrifices[1] and the Christian mass. Whereas Christian criticism of animal sacrifices usually revolved around questions of efficacy and esthetics,[2] Jewish arguments against the mass were usually philosophical in nature,[3] attacking the very rationality of this Christian ceremony. The Jewish polemicists claimed that the Christian dogma of transubstantiation, which taught that the bread and wine used in the mass—the Eucharist—actually became the body and blood of Christ, was irrational. This chapter investigates the philosophical arguments used by the medieval Jewish polemicists to substantiate this assertion.

I. Jewish Knowledge of the Doctrine of Transubstantiation

The Jewish polemicists had a rather clear picture of the doctrine of transubstantiation. Profiat Duran (Efodi, 1345?–1414?), for instance, relied heavily on Peter Lombard's (d. 1165) *Sententiae* in the following account.[4]

---

1. Though the Jews no longer practiced animal sacrifice after 70 c.e., the issue was still debated, since (1) Jews prayed for the restoration of the sacrificial system, and, moreover, (2) the sacrifices were a target of the general Christian argument that the precepts of the "Old Law" (Torah) were deficient as compared with the New Law.

2. Christian polemicists argued that the mass was more efficacious than sacrifices because it brought about complete atonement for the worshipper. It was also held to be more esthetic because it did not involve burning meats and fats. Cf. Shem Tov ibn Shaprut, *'Even Bohan*, I:2, Jewish Theological Seminary of America (JTSA) ms. 2426, f. 7a. For the Jewish response to these charges, see, e.g., ibid., f. 9b; and Joseph Albo, *Sefer ha-ʿIqqarim*, III:25, ed. and trans. I. Husik (Philadelphia, 1930), III, 231.

3. For a discussion of what constitutes a philosophical argument, as contrasted with an exegetical or historical one, see my book, *Jewish Philosophical Polemics against Christianity in the Middle Ages* (New York, 1977), pp. 3–11.

4. Duran's account is given in *Kelimat ha-Goyim*, chap. 6, ed. A. Posnanski, *Ha-Tzofeh me-'Eretz Hagar* (5674/1914), III, 171–72. Lombard is quoted explicitly by Duran, and Posnanski gives appropriate references to *Sententiae*, Liber IV, Dist. 8–13 (J. P. Migne [ed.], *Patrologia Latina*, 221

One of the principles of their religion which the "misleaders"[5] established was that Jesus, in the same quantity in which he was crucified[6] will
come and apply himself to any quantity whatsoever of bread made from
wheat.[7] The bread will cast off its substantial form of bread[8] and will
receive the whole body of Jesus, while at the same time the accidents of
the bread, such as quality and quantity and others, will remain without a
subject.[9] It is he himself who, sitting in the heavens, comes to the altar
even though he remains there [in the heavens]. It is he himself who is
one in different places.[10] It is he himself who moves on the altar in
different places while he is in heaven, and no matter how the bread is
divided,[11] he still exists in the same quantity in which he was crucified,
such as a broken mirror in which the form of the person looking into it is
seen fully in each part of it.[12] Similarly, he also exists in the wine pressed

vols. [Paris, 1844–64], CXCII, 856–68). A number of Duran's statements are not found in
Lombard's work.

5. Mat'im, as distinguished from to'im, the first Christians who, though they had mistaken
beliefs, did not try to impose these beliefs on others. The former, however, were the real cause of
the spread of Christianity and its "erroneous" doctrines.

6. Christian thinkers normally stressed both the virgin birth and crucifixion aspects of the
body of Christ. Cf., for instance, the formulation found in Berengarius's confession of 1079:
"Verum Christi corpus, quod natum est de Virgine et quod pro salute mundi oblatum in cruce
pependit—It is the true body of Christ, which was born of the Virgin and which, offered for the
salvation of the world, was suspended on the Cross" (H. Denziger, Enchiridion Symbolorum
[Würzburg, 1854], no. 355; English translation: Roy J. Deferrari, The Sources of Catholic Dogma [St.
Louis, 1957], p. 144).

7. Cf. Thomas Aquinas, Summa Theologiae (ST), Q.74, A.3; Summa contra gentiles (SCG), IV, 69
(ed. Rome, 1934), p. 531.

8. ST III, Q.75,A.6: "Forma substantialis panis non manet."

9. Lombard, Sententiae, IV, Dist. 12,1, col. 864: "Potius mihi videtur fatendum existere sine
subjecto, quam esse in subjecto." This was not Thomas's view, for he held that the accidents
remained with quantitas dimensiva as subject (ST III, Q.77,A.2). Ockham, however, went back to
the view that the accidents remained without a subject and denied that quantitas remained in the
Eucharist. Cf. De corpore Christi, in The De Sacramento Altaris of William of Occam, ed. T. Bruce Birch
(Burlington, Iowa, 1930), chap. 16, pp. 240–45; and chap. 23, pp. 284–85; also G. Buescher, The
Eucharistic Teaching of William Ockham (Washington, D.C., 1950), pp. 119–40.

10. Lombard did not express it this way, but cf., e.g., Alger of Liège, De sacramentis corporis et
sanguinis Domini, chap. 14, Patrologia Latina (PL), CLXXX, 780: "Credendum est, quod eodem
tempore et vere est in sacramento suo in terris, et vere in coelo sedet ad dextram Patris—It is to be
believed, that at the same time that he is truly in his sacrament on earth, he is truly sitting at the
right side of the Father." A. J. Macdonald states that the question of Christ's location both in
heaven and on earth at the same time was a favorite problem in the first half of the twelfth
century (Berengar and the Reform of Sacramental Doctrine [London, 1930], p. 393).

11. Lombard, Sententiae, IV, Dist. 12, 5, col. 865: "Quia forma panis ibi frangitur, et in partes
dividitur, Christus vero integer manet, et totus est in singulis—Since the form of the bread is
broken there and divided into parts, Christ truly remains entire, and the whole is in each part."
Cf. also ST III, Q.76,A.3: "Utrum sit totus Christus sub qualibet parte specierum panis vel
vini—Is the whole Christ under each and every part of the species?"

12. The history of this image is not quite clear. In ST III, Q.76,A.3, Thomas quoted it as "some
say" (quidam dicunta). In his Commentary on the Sentences, IV, D.10,Q.1,A.3, Aquinas had

from grapes offered on the altar.[13] When one eats this bread and drinks this wine, the body of Jesus will unite with the body of the eater and the drinker.[14] It will remain, thus, kept inside his stomach, until the accidents of the bread, remaining after the corruption of their form, themselves become corrupted. According to them, this happens to the bread and wine after certain words are recited by the officiant priest designated for this rite, may he be old or young, wise or ignorant, righteous or evil, for the pope, Jesus' substitute on earth, has the power to confer this authority upon any priest.[15] This is so since the formula itself has the power to call down the body of Jesus from the heavenly heights[16] and to bring it through an eight thousand year journey[17] to an infinite number of altars while it remains in heaven quietly and peacefully.

Joseph Albo (d. c. 1444) summarized this doctrine much more succinctly.

For they say that the body of Jesus, which is in heaven and is of very great extension and magnitude, comes to the altar and clothes itself in the bread and the wine as soon as the priest has pronounced the word—no matter who the priest is—a good man or a bad—and the whole becomes one with the body of the Messiah, who comes down from heaven instantaneously. And after the bread and the wine have been consumed, he goes up to heaven again where he was before. This takes place at every altar.[18]

A survey of other Jewish formulations of the doctrine of transubstantiation

---

cited Augustine as the source, as did Alexander of Hales in his *Summa Theologiae*, IV, 10 (Venice, 1575), p. 195c. Augustine, however, did not use such an image. Two theologians who did employ the analogy were Innocent III (ca. 1160–1216), *De sacra altaris mysterio*, IV, 8 (*PL*, CCXVII, 861), and William of Auxerre (ca. 1150–1231), *Summa aurea* (Paris, 1500), f. 259d (quoted in Joseph Strake, *Die Sakramentenlehre des Wilhelm von Auxerre* [Paderborn, 1917], pp. 130–31, n. 2). Lombard does not mention this image at all. Thomas rejected the use of the mirror image. His reasoning was: "The multiplication of these images occurs in the broken mirror as the result of many different reflections in the different pieces, but here it is one consecration that is the sole cause of Christ's body being in the sacrament" (*ST* III, Q.76,A.3; English translation: *St. Thomas Aquinas Summa Theologiae*, Vol. LVIII, *The Eucharistic Presence*, trans. W. Barden [New York, 1965], p. 103).

13. *ST* III, Q.74,A.5; *SCG* IV, 69, p. 531. Note that the wine was of secondary importance, reflecting the custom of offering only the bread to the laity (*ST* III, Q.80,A.12).

14. Cf. John 6:56.

15. The question of the status of the wicked priest's offering of mass was a common topic. Cf. *Sententiae*, IV, Dist. 13,1, cols. 867–68; and *ST* III, Q.82,A.5,8.

16. *ST* III, Q.78,A.4.

17. This calculation was based on Jer. *Berakhot* IX:1 (13a). There are 500 years from the earth to the first firmament, each firmament (of seven) is a 500-year journey, and then there is an additional 515 years to the heavens. This adds up to approximately 8000 years. Cf. Posnanski, *Ha-Tzofeh*, III, 172–73, n. 5.

18. *Sefer ha-ʿIqqarim*, ed. Husik, III, 232.

shows a similar, if not as detailed, knowledge of Christian belief. Such descriptions were given by Hasdai Crescas (1340–1410),[19] Shem Tov Ibn Shaprut (fourteenth century),[20] Simon Duran (1361–1444)[21] Abraham Farissol (1451–1525?),[22] and Elijah Hayyim ben Benjamin of Genazzano (fifteenth century).[23]

II. *The Christian Background*

For many Christians, the sacrament of the Eucharist and the doctrine of transubstantiation were mysteries that were not amenable to rational investigation. "A mystery of the faith can be believed healthfully, but it cannot be investigated healthfully."[24] Gabriel Biel (d. 1495) suggested that one should not be too curious concerning the problems of transubstantiation, for God "who created the world out of nothing and is able to return the world to nothing when he pleases," certainly is capable of anything.[25]

The Jewish polemicists were not unaware that Christians considered the mystery of the Eucharist beyond rational proof. Duran, for instance, in *Kelimat Ha-Goyim*, stated the Christian belief that since Jesus established the Eucharistic rite, it cannot be questioned.[26] He proceeded, then, to analyze the New Testament sources to prove that, in fact, Jesus had no intention of establishing the practice of the mass.[27] Duran was followed in this method by Ibn Shaprut[28] and Farissol,[29] both of whom were largely dependent upon him.

19. *Bittul ᶜIqqare ha-Notzrim*, ed. Ephraim Deinard (Kearney, N.J., 1904), p. 8.

20. *'Even Bohan*, XII (other recension, XV):4, f. 155a.

21. *Magen 'Avot*, I:3, published in *Qeshet u-Magen* (Livorno, 5523/1763), p. 26a.

22. *Magen 'Avraham*, chap. 20, JTSA ms. 2433, ff. 24a–b.

23. *Disputation with Fra Francisco di Aquapendente*, in J. Rosenthal, *Mehqarim u-Meqorot*, I (Jerusalem, 1967), p. 451. Other Jewish polemicists referring to the doctrine of transubstantiation are Don David Nasi (1430), *Hoda'at Baᶜal Din* (Frankfurt, 1866), p. 23; Yair ben Shabbetai (sixteenth century), *Herev Pifiyyot*, ed. J. Rosenthal (Jerusalem, 1958), pp. 78–83; Issac Lupis (1695), *Kur Matzref ha-'Emunah u-Mar'eh ha'Emet* (Metz, 1847), pp. 19a–b, based on Albo's treatment; Jonah Rappa (eighteenth century), *Pilpul ᶜal Zeman Zemanim Zemanehem*, ed. George Belasco (London, 1908), p. 33; Joshua Segre (eleventh century), *'Asham Taluy Heleq Sheni*, JTSA ms. 2232, f. 26b; the authors of *Kevod 'Elohim*, Oxford-Bodleian ms. 2175, ff. 45a–47a, almost verbatim copy of Shem Tov ibn Shaprut; and *Makkot li-Khesil Me'ah*, JTSA ms. 2214, f. 4b. These later polemicists mostly copy the refutations of the earlier authors.

24. *Sententiae*, IV, Dist. 11, 3, col. 862: "Mysterium fidei credi salubriter potest, investigari salubriter non potest."

25. *Sermones de festivitatibus Christi* (Hagenau, 1510), 19C; quoted in Heiko A. Oberman, *The Harvest of Medieval Theology* (Cambridge, Mass., 1963), p. 272, n. 86.

26. P. 173. Cf. Posnanski's n. 5 for Lombard source.

27. As Duran stated, his method in his *'Iggeret* was much different.

28. *'Even Bohan*, XII:5, ff. 155a–157a.

29. *Magen 'Avraham*, chap. 20, ff. 24a–25a. Both of these authors also used rational arguments, again drawing from Duran.

Yet, the fact that mysteries were not rationally provable did not mean that Christian thinkers refrained from trying to give a philosophical underpinning to this doctrine: "Although, of course, the divine power operates with a greater sublimity and secrecy in this sacrament than a man's inquiry can search out, nonetheless, lest the teaching of the Church regarding this sacrament appear impossible to unbelievers, one must make the endeavor to exclude every impossibility."[30]

Since the Jewish polemicists knew that Christian theologians were using rational arguments to uphold transubstantiation, despite its essential mystery, it was only natural that they countered with their own philosophical contentions. And, as we shall see, the Jewish arguments were often taken from the Christian works themselves.

The orthodox Catholic doctrine of the Eucharist and transubstantiation, as first definitively established by the Fourth Lateran Council (1215),[31] and later reestablished by the Council of Trent against the reformers (1547),[32] was not uniformly accepted by all Christians. In fact, two parallel patristic traditions on the subject were kept alive in the early Middle Ages. The Neoplatonic Augustinian tradition,[33] which was finally repudiated, was carried on by John Scotus Erigena, Ratramnus, Rabanus Maurus, and the chief heresiarch Berengarius of Tours.[34] This rejected doctrine held that the presence of Christ in the Eucharist was not physically real but was only symbolic. The second tradition, that of Ambrose,[35] became dominant; it was supported by Paschasius Radbertus, Lanfranc, Guitmond of Aversa, Alger of Liege, Lombard, Thomas, and many others. These thinkers taught that the presence of Christ on the altar was real, in that the bread and the wine changed substantially into the body and blood of the Messiah. Transubstantiation, a term first used in the early twelfth century, was the process by which the bread and wine became converted into the real presence.[36]

---

30. *SCG* IV, 63, p. 526; English translation: Charles J. O'Neill, *On the Truth of the Catholic Faith,* IV (New York, 1957), 257. In fact, the use of philosophy, both realist, by Thomas and his school, and nominalist, by Ockham and his followers, was a common practice in discussions of transubstantiation.

31. Denziger, *Enchiridion,* no. 430.

32. Ibid., nos. 873a–893.

33. Cf., e.g., Macdonald, *Berengar,* pp. 258–62; and J. H. Strawley, "Eucharist (to end of Middle Ages)," in Hastings, *Encyclopedia of Religion and Ethics* (New York, 1914), V, 554. It should be remembered that both sides of the issue quoted Augustine for support.

34. He was called the first to hold this error by Thomas (*ST* III, Q.75,A.1). Cf. Berengarius, *De sacra coena,* ed. W. H. Beekenkamp (The Hague, 1941). For literature on Berengarius, see Macdonald, *Berengar,* and especially the extensive bibliography, pp. 415–30. For anti-Berengarian literature, see *PL,* CCXIX, 857–58, Index, s.v. Libri de Eucharistia tractantes.

35. For instance, in *Liber de mysteriis, PL,* XVI, 403–26, on the Eucharist, chaps. 8–9, cols. 419–26; and *De sacramentiis, PL* XVI, 435–82, esp. Bks. IV–VI, cols. 455–82.

36. The term transubstantiation was first used by Hildebert of Tours (*Sermones de diversis,* VI, "Ad sacerdotes," *PL,* CLXXI, 771–76 ["transubstantionis," col. 776]). As a verb it was first used

Despite the defeat of Berengarius in the eleventh century, and the codification of the Ambrosian, "real-presence" theory in the thirteenth, opposition in the church remained. The definition of the Fourth Lateran Council was directed against the Albigensians.[37] Transubstantiation was again upheld, in 1341, against the figurative belief of the Armenians.[38] Further objections to the interpretation of the Eucharist in terms of transubstantiation were expressed by John Wyclif (c. 1329–84), the followers of John Huss, and, of course by the Protestant reformers of the sixteenth century, Martin Luther, Ulrich Zwingli, John Calvin, and many others.[39] It might be said that internal Christian opposition to the doctrine of transubstantiation was an ongoing, though somewhat suppressed, movement in the Middle Ages. As we shall see, the Jewish polemicists were very aware of this movement and its argumentation.

The Jewish use of specifically philosophical arguments against transubstantiation, though, came surprisingly late. Whereas Berengarius (1000–88) was the first Christian to employ such methodology against the "real-presence" theory,[40] we find Jewish polemicists employing rational proofs against transubstantiation for the first time only three hundred years later.[41] This is even more surprising considering the fact that the centuries between Berengarius and Profiat Duran, the first Jew to use such arguments, were full of philosophical expositions of transubstantiation by Christians. Still, the Jewish polemicists did not use philosophical arguments until the end of the fourteenth century.

---

by Stephen of Autun, *Tractatus de sacramento altaris*, PL, CLXXII, 1273–1308, esp. col. 1293. Both these authors lived during the early twelfth century. Lombard and Hugh of St. Victoire, one of Lombard's chief sources, did not use the term (in the same century).

The description of the two traditions is obviously simplistic. The literature on the subject is extensive. See Macdonald, *Berengar*; Charles E. Sheedy, *The Eucharistic Controversy of the Eleventh Century against the Background of Pre-Scholastic Theology* (Washington, D.C., 1947); and Josef R. Geiselmann, *Die Eucharistielehre der Vorscholastik*, Forschungen zur christlichen Literatur und Dogmengeschichte XV, nos. 1–3 (Paderborn, 1926).

37. Denziger, *Enchiridion*, no. 430.

38. Ibid., no. 544.

39. The literature on this topic is enormous. See, e.g., Kilian McDonnell, *John Calvin, the Church, and the Eucharist* (Princeton, 1967), pp. 383–400 (bibliography).

40. See above, n. 37. It is the work of Berengarius that caused the church to formulate its Eucharistic doctrine explicitly.

41. Profiat Duran appears to be the first in his *'Iggeret 'Al Tehi ka-'Avotekha* (1936), Posnanski ms. offprint (Jerusalem, 5730/1970). Earlier, nonphilosophical arguments can be found. The anonymous author of *Nitzahon Yashan* (twelfth/thirteenth centuries) asked how the priest could think that the bread and wine, which he had made, could possibly be God. See David Berger, *The Jewish-Christian Debate in the High Middle Ages* (Philadelphia, 1979), pp. 220–21. Joseph ha-Meqanneh quotes scriptural objections to the mass (e.g., Hosea 9:4). See *Sefer Yosef ha-Meqanneh*,

A number of reasons can be suggested for this late appearance of philosophical anti-Eucharistic polemics. Can it be that the full implication of this doctrine was just not understood by the Jews until then, whether from lack of interest or from underestimating the importance of the mass? Was this interest in the Eucharist brought about by the growing popularity of host adoration as expressed in the exposition of the host and the Feast of the Corpus Christi?[42] Or was there a connection between Jewish arguments against transubstantiation in late fourteenth-century Spain, and the host desecration libel of Barcelona, 1367, in which Hasdai Crescas was one of those arrested and detained?[43] This question needs further research.

Whatever the reason for the late appearance of Jewish philosophical arguments against transubstantiation, it is certain that by the time of their appearance, some Jews already had a good idea of the internal Christian objections to the real presence. This fact is evident not only from the arguments themselves, but also from specific statements in the polemics. Thus, Profiat Duran, citing texts from the New Testament as proof that Jesus had no intention of establishing the Eucharist doctrine, stated that the traditional Christian interpretation was very weak, and "already some of them have realized its weakness."[44] Joseph ben Shem Tov (c. 1400–c. 1460) described the Christian doctrine and stated: "They have no doubt about this and do not interpret it figuratively;[45] rather, they believe in it literally, and he who raises rational objections to it is labeled a heretic."[46] We see, then, that Jewish cognizance of Christian opposition to transubstantiation was acknowledged.

We have now established that some of the Jewish polemicists had a very good understanding of the doctrine of transubstantiation and the internal Christian criticism of it. The Jewish critique, using the Christian arguments, began late in the fourteenth century. It is now time to turn to the specific Jewish philosophical arguments.

---

ed. J. Rosenthal (Jerusalem, 5730/1970), p. 85.

42. Solomon ibn Verga describes a celebration of such a Feast with a procession of cross and host in *Shevet Yehudah*, ed. Y. Baer and A. Shohat (Jerusalem, 5707/1947), p. 123. Isaac of Troki castigated the Christians for their "idolatry" of host worship in *Hizzuq 'Emunah*, I:2.50, ed. D. Deutsch (Breslau, 1873), pp. 39, 280. Cf. Herbert Thurston, "Exposition of the Blessed Sacrament," *The Catholic Encyclopedia*, V (New York, 1909), 713–14.

43. See Y. Baer, *A History of the Jews in Christian Spain*, 2 vols. (Philadelphia, 1961), II, 38–39. On host desecrations, see Cecil Roth, "Host, Descration of," *EJ*, VIII, 1040–44.

44. *Kelimat ha-Goyim*, p. 174.

45. Ratramnus (ninth century) was the first to distinguish between *figura* and *veritas* in the Eucharist (*De corpore et sanguine Domine*, PL, CXXI, 103–70; and ed. Van den Brink (Amsterdam, 1954).

46. *Commentary on the 'Iggeret*, Posnanski reprint, p. 88.

III. *The Jewish Arguments*

The first Jewish polemicist to offer a comprehensive, philosophical critique of the doctrine of transubstantiation was Profiat Duran in his *'Iggeret 'Al Tehi Ka-'Avotekha*.[47] Duran claimed that the whole idea of transubstantiation ran counter to the principles of the rational sciences. Thus, writing in his satirical manner to David Bonet Bonjorn, Duran stated: "Be not like your fathers who were obliged by the foundations of the intellect to accept the speculative principles, those of mathematics, physics, and metaphysics."[48] Those specific principles, which were rejected by the proponents of transubstantiation, were then enumerated, each science in turn.

Other Jewish polemicists, though relying upon Duran's arguments, used different frameworks to present their contentions. Thus, Joseph Albo divided his critique into an examination of those Christian principles that were in conflict with first principles and those in conflict with sense perception.[49] Elijah Hayyim ben Benjamin was content merely to say that this doctrine was against first principles,[50] while Elijah del Medigo said that it contradicted sense perception.[51] It is possible that these distinctions also go back to Duran, who stated in *Kelimat Ha-Goyim* that transubstantiation was based on principles which "contradict the nature of existence, refute sense perception, and contradict first principles."[52] Farissol contended that this doctrine was against reason, against that which is self-evident and commonly accepted, and against the truth.[53] Other polemicists listed the various arguments against transubstantiation in no discernible order.[54]

The philosophical arguments to be discussed here have been drawn from the various sources and will be divided into five categories: (1) the interpenetrability of bodies; (2) the concepts of number and place; (3) the concept of motion; (4) the problem of accidents, and (5) miscellaneous arguments.

47. *'Iggeret*, pp. 84–128.
48. Ibid., p. 78. Though the context here was not that of transubstantiation, this theme was picked up in the next section where the Eucharist was the topic. This categorization of the principles that were in conflict with the Eucharistic doctrine might be compared with Wyclif's statement that transubstantiation "subverts Grammar, Logic, all natural science and even (which is still worse) . . . completely destroys the sense of the Gospel" (*Trialogus*, p. 261, cited in *De Eucharistia*, ed. Johann Loserth [London, 1892], p. iii).
49. *Sefer ha-ʿIqqarim*, ed. Husik, III, 232.
50. *Wikkuah*, ed. J. Rosenthal, in *Mehqarim u-Mekorot*, I, 451.
51. *Behinat ha-Dat*, ed. I. Reggio (Vienna, 1883), pp. 12–13. Del Medigo stated that the doctrines of Trinity and Incarnation were in conflict with first principles.
52. P. 175.
53. *Magen 'Avraham*, f. 24a.
54. So Crescas and Simon Duran.

1. *The interpenetrability of bodies.*

The impossibility of one body entering another body, without the displacement of the latter, is stated by Aristotle. We know that place exists because "what now contains air formerly contained water, so that clearly the place or space into which and out of which they passed was something different from both."[55] Water and air could not exist together in the same place. Further, an argument against vacuums was based on the idea that if the void existed, one body could enter another body.[56] The impossibility of two bodies being in one place was also a consideration when trying to understand how plants grow.[57] Put succinctly, if one body could enter another, "the whole world could enter into a grain of mustard seed."[58]

The Jewish polemicists, accepting this principle, saw three basic contradictions in transubstantiation that related to the problem of the interpenetrability of bodies: (*a*) How could the body of Jesus enter into another body, that of the bread? (*b*) Assuming that Jesus could enter the bread, how could his large body fit into the smaller dimensions of the bread? (*c*) Even if one assumes the entrance into the bread, how could Jesus pass through the body of the heavens to the altars without causing damage of the heavens?

(*a*) If one body cannot enter another without the latter's displacement, how can Jesus' body enter into the sacramental bread, while the bread remains where it was? Joseph Albo stated: "They say that the flesh and the blood which comes into being at the particular moment from the substance of the bread and the wine, which is finite and limited, is the very body of the messiah, who existed from eternity, and does not thereby increase or diminish in quantity. This leads to belief in the interpenetration of bodies."[59]

(*b*) A second ramification of this principle is involved, namely the impossibility of a larger body entering into a smaller body. Duran pointed out that according to the principles of mathematics, the large and the small are different, and, as such, one cannot become the other. How, then, could the

55. *Physics*, IV:1, 208^{b}6–8; English translation: R. P. Hardie and R. K. Gaye, in *The Basic Works of Aristotle*, ed. R. McKeon (New York, 1941), pp. 269–70.

56. Ibid., IV:8, 216^{a}26–216^{b}12. Cf. H. A. Wolfson, *Crescas' Critique of Aristotle* (Cambridge, Mass., 1929), pp. 146–49, 342–43.

57. *On Generation and Corruption*, I:5, 321^{a}8–10. This reference and the one from *Physics*, IV:1, were given by Joseph ben Shem Tov, *Commentary on the 'Iggeret*, Posnanski reprint, p. 68, and Posnanski's notes.

58. *'Iggeret*, p. 84. On the use of this phrase, see Wolfson, *Crescas' Critique*, pp. 342–43.

59. *Sefer ha-ʿIqqarim*, ed. Husik, III, 233. The reference to quantity most likely was an allusion to the problem of the disparate sizes of the body of Jesus and the host.

large body of Jesus become the small wafer of bread?[60]

This argument is a paraphrase of an objection raised by Thomas: "A larger sized body cannot be completely contained under smaller dimensions. Yet the dimensions of the consecrated bread and wine are much less than the dimensions of Christ's body. Hence, it cannot be that the whole body of Christ is under this sacrament."[61] Thomas answered this objection by stating that it was the substance of Christ, not the dimensions of the body and blood, which was in the sacrament, by means of the sacramental sign. "The whole specific nature of a substance is as truly contained by small as by large dimensions."[62] Still, Duran used this same argument against transubstantiation, and Shem Tov ibn Shaprut[63] and Simon Duran[64] followed his lead.

(c) The third problem was how the body of Christ traveled from the heavens to the altars without damaging either itself or the heavens. Duran, and after him Crescas, gave two possibilities. First, one could reject the physical truth that the body of the heavens had only circular motion. This principle, claimed by Aristotle,[65] meant that the motion of the heavens was uniform and continuous, allowing no tearing or rending. But, argued Duran: "The body of the messiah, in ascending and descending perpetually every day, cannot help but have caused the body of the heavens to become full of passages and orifices.[66] Since it is now nearly thirteen hundred sixty years since Jesus' ascent to heaven, the heavens must now be like a sieve, or solely by his will or by his speech, Jesus must be able to cure them without drugs."[67] Duran's implication was that such a description of Jesus' ascent and descent was ridiculous. Crescas[68] and Albo[69] made similar arguments.

Second, belief in an alternative method of descent was founded on the belief that one body was able to penetrate another body; but this was impossible as has been shown. What Duran most probably meant by this alternative method becomes clear from a statement by Crescas. According to Crescas, the alternative to one's having to assume a rending of the heavens was the belief in a body "glorificado" that could enter the heavens without

60. 'Iggeret, p. 84.
61. ST III, Q.76,A.1; English translation: The Eucharistic Presence, p. 93. Cf. also SCG, IV, 62, p. 525.
62. The Eucharistic Presence, p. 97.
63. 'Even Bohan, f. 156b.
64. Magen 'Avot, I:3, in Qeshet u-Magen, p. 26b.
65. On the Heavens, I:2–3.
66. This phrase was borrowed from the well-known prayer 'Asher Yatzar (Authorized Daily Prayer Book, rev. ed., ed. Joseph H. Hertz [New York, 1952], p. 10). The sarcastic intent is obvious.
67. 'Iggeret, p. 94.
68. Bittul, p. 58. Joseph ben Shem Tov, the translator, also refers to "neqavim, halulim."
69. Sefer ha-ʿIqqarim, III, 232.

tearing the heavenly bodies, since it was presumed to be an ethereal body occupying no space and having no dimensions.[70] Joseph ben Shem Tov also understood Duran to be referring to a "corpo glorificado."[71]

What did a "glorified body" signify? The reference here was to the theory of transubstantiation offered by William of Auvergne (d. 1249). This thinker explained instantaneous presence in terms of the glorified body of Christ whose agility permitted this otherwise impossible feat.[72] Bonaventure also stated that the glorified body of Christ might be able to be together with the bread.[73] Albertus Magnus referred to the opinion that the body of Christ was "a glorious body capable of coexisting with another body in the same place."[74] The term "glorified body" was used also to describe the state of the body of the faithful at resurrection.[75] Joseph ben Shem Tov knew this belief, as he stated that the Christians expected that "even after their resurrection they will all merit that their bodies be after this fashion."[76]

Crescas's objection to a solution of this kind was that the glorified body was "a pure figment of the imagination that has no real existence."[77] He based this claim on his examination of the theory of the glorified body in relation to the dogma of the virgin birth.[78] Crescas argued that the glorified body must have extension, since, if it did not, it would be a body and not a body at the same time.[79] But, if it did have extension, it would not be able to pass through things that leave no space between them; hence, it could not

70. *Bittul*, p. 58: *guf glorifiq'ado*; JTSA ms. 2209, f. 16a, reads: *guf ʿilluy glorifiq'ado*. See Crescas's refutation below.

71. *Commentary on the 'Iggeret*, p. 98.

72. *Tractatus Guilhermi Parisiensis de sacramentis cur Deus homo* (1496), f. 26a: "In quo respondeo: non per motum qualis corporis, i.e., transitum continuum. . . . Et hic effectus unus est dotis corporis glorificatorum qui nominatur agilitas—To which I respond: this is not through bodily motion, i.e., continuous movement. . . . But this is one of the effects of the bodily quality which is also called the agility of glorification." Cf. also Salvatore Bonano, *The Concept of Substance and the Development of Eucharistic Theology to the Thirteenth Century* (Washington, D.C., 1960), p. 25.

73. *Commentary on Sententiae*, IV, Dist. 11, Q. 1; in the 1491 edition, paragraph 4: "Sed corpus christi cum sit gloriosum simul cum pane potest esse."

74. Cf. Banano, *The Concept of Substance*, p. 39. Albertus also referred to the *corpus gloriosum* of Christ in his *De sacramentis*, V.1, Q.1,A.2, and Q.4,A.1 (*Opera omnia*, XXVI [Aschendorff, 1958], 51, 62).

75. Cf. C. J. Corcoran, "Glorified Body," *New Catholic Encyclopedia*, VI (New York, 1967), 512–13: and A. Choller, "Corps Glorieux," *Dictionnaire de théologie catholique*, III (Paris, 1908), 1879–1906. The basic New Testament source for this belief is 1 Cor. 15. Cf. also Phil. 3:21. Cf. *ST* III, Suppl., Q.81–87.

76. *Commentary on the 'Iggeret*, p. 98.

77. *Bittul*, p. 59.

78. Ibid., pp. 55–56. The relationship between virgin birth and the Eucharist was also assumed by Christians, e.g., Hugh of St. Victoire, *Summa sententiarum*, VI, 4 (*PL*, CLXXVI, 141). Cf. A. J. Macdonald, "Berengar and the Virgin Birth," *Journal of Theological Studies*, XXX (1929), 291–94, esp. p. 293, where other references are given.

79. For Crescas's belief in the necessity of a body having extension (three-dimensionality), see Wolfson, *Crescas' Critique*, pp. 261, 590–91.

pass out of the virgin's womb. Nor could the glorified body enter into another body, because both bodies would have dimensions that would prevent their interpenetrability. If, indeed, one body could enter another body, then two cubits could be one cubit, the part could be like the whole, and the whole world could enter into a mustard seed. Joseph ben Shem Tov offered a similar argument against the doctrine of the glorified body, also stressing that if the glorified body were a body, it must have dimensions, and if it has dimensions, it cannot interpenetrate another body with dimensions.[80]

For the Jewish polemicists, then, the faith in Jesus' descent from heaven required that one accept either the rending of the heavens or a special glorified body. Duran suggested to his Christian correspondent that he take the alternative that went against reason and nature the most.[81]

2. The concepts of number and place

Two different kinds of arguments can be distinguished in this category: (a) How can there be only one Messiah if his body were found on many altars simultaneously? (b) How could one body be in more than one place at the same time?

(a) According to Aristotle, a number is a plurality of units.[82] But the Christians believed that even if the body of Christ were to be found on many altars at the same time, one could not add up all the different appearances and come up with more than one body of Christ. For Duran, this belief obviously contradicted the mathematical principle just enounced, since according to the transubstantiation doctrine, the plurality of units did not make up a number, but only a single unit, one. Accordingly, ten, one hundred, and one thousand would all be equal to each other.[83] Shem Tov ibn Shaprut presented this same argument.[84]

This argument went back to Berengarius who said that if the body of Christ were actually on the altar, there would be a million bodies of Christ at the same time.[85]

(b) Joseph ben Shem Tov related the mathematical argument just stated to a physical argument found in both Crescas and Albo, namely the impossibil-

---

80. *Commentary on the 'Iggeret*, pp. 98–100. He quoted *On the Heavens*, I:1, *Physics*, IV, and the definitions at the beginning of Euclid's *Elements*.

81. *'Iggeret*, p. 94.

82. *Metaphysics*, X:1, 1053ª31. Cf. Euclid's *Elements*, Bk. VII, Def. 2.

83. *'Iggeret*, pp. 84–86.

84. *'Even Bohan*, f. 156b.

85. *De sacra coena*, p. 109; cf. Macdonald, *Berengar*, p. 310. It is possible that the origin of this argument was Plato's *Parmenides*, 131. The question there was how the one form could participate in many objects simultaneously.

ity that one body could be in two places at the same time. This argument had two applications. Crescas saw the inconsistency in the circumstance that "at the same time as God, the Son, is in the heavens, he is also in the hand of the priest; it follows from this that he would be in many different places at the same time. Just as we see him at thousands and tens of thousands (and hundreds) of altars,[86] there either would be many gods or one body would be substantially present at many places at one time."[87]

The other aspect of the problem was the simultaneity òf existence on many altars at the same time. "It requires belief in the simultaneous presence of one body in two or more places; for the body of the messiah is present on different altars at the same time."[88] Similarly, Farissol asked how it is possible that at one time one individual substance became collected in several different substances in different places.[89]

Thomas is aware of such arguments deriving from the impossibility of one body being in more than one place at the same time, whether that body be both in heaven and on earth, or in many places on earth. Thus, he mentioned the objection: "No body can be in several places at once. Not even an angel has that power; if he had he could be everywhere. But the body of Christ is a real body and it is in heaven. Therefore, it seems that it cannot be in the sacrament of the altar in very truth, but only as in its sign."[90] Regarding the simultaneity of presence at many altars, Thomas noted the objection that: "It is further impossible that one body should exist in many places. But, manifestly, this sacrament is celebrated in many places. Therefore, it seems impossible that the body of Christ is truthfully contained in this sacrament —unless one says, perhaps, that the body is contained in one of its particles here, and in another there."[91] Thomas, of course, provided answers to these objections, but this did not prevent the Jewish polemicists from repeating them.

3. *The concept of motion*

The Jewish polemicists offered two arguments against transubstantiation using the concept of motion: (*a*) Motion in no time was impossible, and (*b*) A body could not be both in motion and at rest at the same time.

(*a*) The change in the elements of the Eucharist into the body of Christ was

---

86. This phraseology, though presumably in incorrect order, was also found in ʾ*Iggeret*, p. 84.
87. *Bittul*, p. 59.
88. *Sefer ha-ʿIqqarim*, III, 232.
89. *Magen ʾAvraham*, f. 24b.
90. *ST* III, Q.75,A.1; English translation: *The Eucharistic Presence*, p. 55.
91. *SCG*, IV, 62, p. 525; English translation: *On the Truth of the Catholic Faith*, p. 255.

held to take place instantaneously.[92] Assuming that the body of Christ descended from the heavens and entered the bread and wine at the exact moment of consecration, then it must have reached the altar in no time. But Aristotle had proved that all motion was in time.[93] Therefore, Jesus' descent from heaven, especially through a distance normally involving an eight thousand year journey, could not have been instantaneous; and so it was impossible that the body of Jesus entered the elements of the Eucharist from the outside. This argument was made by Duran,[94] Crescas,[95] and Albo.[96] Crescas also stated that the only alternative to entrance from the outside through instantaneous motion was the creation of the body of Jesus in the dimensions of the bread. "It is not possible that it be created there since that would necessitate that God is created and corrupted, along with many other impossibilities."[97]

Thomas agreed that if the body of Christ were to enter the bread by local motion, such motion would have to be instantaneous. Since, however, instantaneous motion was impossible, the change was effected by transubstantiation (conversion), not by local motion.[98]

(b) Profiat Duran twice argued that transubstantiation was impossible because one body could not be in motion and at rest at the same time. The first time that Duran suggested this argument, he phrased it as a physical proof,[99] basing himself on Aristotle's conclusion that one body could not be both in motion and at rest at the same time.[100] Turning to metaphysical proofs, Duran repeated[101] Aristotle's principle that a thing cannot at the same time be and not be.[102] Thus, a thing could not both be in motion and not be in motion, i.e., at rest. If the body of Jesus really entered into the bread as it remained in the heavens, it would follow that the body of Jesus was at rest (in the heavens) and in motion (on the altar) at the same time. Thus, transubstantiation was not possible, from both physical and metaphysical

---

92. *ST* III, Q.75,A.7.

93. *Physics*, IV:11, and VI:4; cf. *On the Heavens*, I:6, 273ª21–274ª18; and Wolfson, *Crescas' Critique*, pp. 114–47, 341–42.

94. *'Iggeret*, p. 86.

95. *Bittul*, pp. 57–58.

96. *Sefer ha-ʿIqqarim*, III, 232.

97. *Bittul*, p. 57.

98. *SCG*, IV, 63, p. 526.

99. *'Iggeret*, p. 86.

100. *Physics*, V: 5–6.

101. *'Iggeret*, p. 100.

102. *Metaphysics*, III:2, 996ᵇ29; IV:4, 1005ᵇ36. Cf. IV:4, 1007ᵇ18: contradictories cannot be predicated at the same time. In IV:2, 1004ᵇ28, rest is described as the contrary of motion.

considerations. This same argument was repeated by Ibn Shaprut[103] and Simon Duran.[104]

Thomas agreed with this argument, as he said specifically: "You cannot have something in movement and at rest at the same time; that would be to affirm contraries of the same thing. Now the body of Christ in heaven is at rest. Therefore, it is not in movement in this sacrament."[105] According to Thomas, then, the body of Christ was always at rest; when the host was moved on the altar, then the body of Christ moved only accidentally.[106]

4. *The problem of accidents*

A major problem that faced the Christian thinkers, as they sought to explain transubstantiation, was the seeming impossibility of accidents subsisting without a subject. Whereas the substances of the bread and wine were replaced by different substance, namely that of Christ, their accidents, such as color, size, weight, taste, etc., remained without a subject. This was the main issue on which Berengarius rejected the real substantial presence of Christ in the sacrament.[107] Wyclif, who also rejected transubstantiation, often referred to the problem of accidents.[108] The Christians, then, were well aware of the difficulties caused by the question of the accidents.

As the Jewish polemicists approached this problem, they divided their criticism into three recognizable categories: (*a*) How could accidents be without subjects? (*b*) The senses must not be deceived by what they perceive; (*c*) Substance could not become accident, nor accident substance.

(*a*) One of Aristotle's definitions of substance was that which was "the ultimate substratum, which cannot be further predicated of something else."[109] Accidents, however, were predicated of subjects.[110] Thus, substance came before accidents; if the substance departed, the accidents could not remain.[111] But, argued Duran, with the completion of the sacramental for-

103. *'Even Bohan*, f. 156b.

104. *Magen 'Avot*, in *Qeshet u-Magen*, p. 26b.

105. *ST* III, Q.65,A.6; English translation: *The Eucharistic Presence*, p. 113. Ockham presented this problem in the opposite manner; namely, the body of Christ was at rest on the altar and moving in the heavens to other altars (Buescher, *Eucharistic Teaching*, pp. 115–16).

106. *ST*, ibid.

107. This theme runs throughout *De sacra coena*, e.g., pp. 41–42, 110–12, 117–18, 126–27; cf. Macdonald, *Berengar*, pp. 316–20.

108. *De Eucharistia*, passim, e.g., pp. 51–52, 62–69, 132–36.

109. *Metaphysics*, V:8, 1017^{b}24.

110. *Posterior Analytics*, I:4, 73^{b}9.

111. *Metaphysics*, VII:2, 1028^{b}32; cf. *Physics*, I:4, 188^{a}6–9.

mula, the substance of bread could no longer be present at all, and, therefore, the accidents would have to remain in themselves, not in a subject.[112] This was repeated by Crescas: "It would be necessary that as he ascends to heaven; the accidents of the bread, i.e., its qualities, its color, its smell, its form, its taste, etc., subsist in themselves without a subject, which is contrary to all nature and possibility."[113] Simon Duran gave the same argument, stating that this type of belief was a *Mu'tazilite* one[114] Ibn Shaprut[115] and Albo[116] also repeated this argument.

Thomas knew of this problem, which he stated in a number of ways. First, he considered the objection that the accidents could not remain because the substance of bread no longer remained.[117] Since, however, the accidents did remain, it was necessary to find a subject for them. "For accidents to be without a subject is against the natural order of things for which God is responsible."[118] Since the subject of the accidents could not be either the body of Christ, or the surrounding air, or they themselves, and in order to be individuated they must have a subject, it appeared that the substances of the bread and wine remain.[119] Thomas solved this problem by positing the dimensive quantity of the bread and wine as the subject for the other accidents.[120] If this were so, then the substances of bread and wine would disappear after all.

(*b*) Profiat Duran stated that a principle of the science of optics was that "the sense of sight is not mistaken in that which it perceives, as long as the organ is healthy and the medium is fitting."[121] Therefore, when one sees the accidents remaining, and did not see God ascend from the host, one must conclude that nothing in the bread and wine has changed. This argument was also used by Ibn Shaprut[122] and by Albo, who cited it as proof that the Christian doctrine was in conflict with sense perception.[123] Elijah del Medigo,

---

112. *'Iggeret*, p. 100. Joseph ben Shem Tov (ibid., p. 106) quoted *Physics* I:9, concerning the impossibility that the material substratum cease to be.

113. *Bittul*, p. 59. The correct text, established by JTSA ms. 2209, f. 16a, reads: "ka-'asher ya'aleh 'el ha-shamayyim yisha'aru ha-miqrim she-hem 'ekhuyyot ha-'ugah gonah rehah te-munatah ta'mah we-zulatam 'omedim be-'etzmam be-lo' nose' we-zeh davar neged kol teva' wi-kholet."

114. *Magen 'Avot*, in *Qeshet u-Magen*, p. 26b. For the Mu'tazilite background, see Maimonides, *Guide*, I:73 (tenth premise).

115. *'Even Bohan*, f. 157a.

116. *Sefer ha-'Iqqarim*, III, 233.

117. *ST* III, Q.75,A.5.

118. Ibid., Q.77,A.1; English translation: *The Eucharistic Presence*, p. 125.

119. *SCG*, IV, 62, p. 525.

120. See above, n. 9.

121. *'Iggeret*, p. 108.

122. *'Even Bohan*, f. 157a.

123. *Sefer ha-'Iqqarim*, III, 233.

who cited this sacrament as one example of the unreasonable nature of Christianity, said that the Eucharistic belief presupposed that the senses of all people at all times were mistaken about a specific, sensible object.[124] We do not accept Christianity, he averred, because it contradicted sense perception, as one sees from their sacrifice.[125]

The Christians could hardly be unaware that the senses testified to the permanence of the appearance of bread. As Ambrose stated: "But perhaps you say: 'I do not see the appearance of blood.'"[126]Berengarius, referring to Ambrose, agreed that with one's physical eyes, one sees only bread and wine. The body and blood could be seen only with the spiritual eyes, and therefore, the body of Christ was in the sacrament only figuratively.[127] Ambrose was also quoted by Lombard, who said that the senses must be believed in this sacrament.[128] Wyclif, rejecting transubstantiation, appealed to the testimony of the senses that the body of Christ was not seen in the host.[129]

Thomas agreed that according to the judgment of the senses the bread remained after the sacramental words, and that it was not befitting a sacrament that the senses be deceived thereby. Moreover, human reason also judged that the bread remained because the accidents remained, and it was not fitting that human reason be deceived.[130] Besides, the senses were never deceived about their proper sensible objects.[131] Still, the orthodox Christian belief, which Thomas upheld, was that the substances of the bread and wine were changed into the substance of the body and blood of Christ, and the accidents remained, the dimensive quantity being their subject. There was no deception because the perceived accidents were actually there.

(c) The impossibility of substance becoming accident or accident becoming substance was based on the principle that when two things were essentially opposed, one of them never became the other.[132] Substance and accident were essentially different.[133] Therefore, substance and accident could not become each other. This conclusion had two applications to the transubstantiation polemic. First, according to Profiat Duran, before the pronounce-

---

124. *Behinat ha-Dat*, pp. 12–13.
125. Ibid. Reggio has censored the passage concerned from p. 16. Cf. Julius Guttmann, "Elia del Medigos Verhältnis zu Averroës in seinem *Bechinat ha-Dat*," in *Jewish Studies in Memory of Israel Abrahams* (New York, 1927), p. 202.
126. *De sacramentiis*, IV, 4 (20) (*PL*, XVI, 462: "Sed forte dicis: Speciem sanguinis non video").
127. *De sacra coena*, p. 95.
128. *Sententiae*, IV, Dist. 12,2, col. 865.
129. *De Eucharistia*, p. 20; cf. p. 78.
130. *ST* III, Q.75,A.5; cf. Q.77,A.1.
131. *SCG*, IV, 62, quoting *De Anima*, III:6, 430^{b}29.
132. *Physics*, I:5, 188^{a}31–188^{b}2; cf. *On Generation*, I:6.
133. *Metaphysics*, III:4.

ment of the sacramental formula, the bread was the substance of bread. After the formula was recited, all that was left of the bread were its accidents. It follows, then, that the substance had turned into accidents.[134] Second, the accidents should not become substance. But if the bread were eaten, nourished the priest, and then changed into an organ of the priest, it followed that either the substance of the bread was still in the consecrated Eucharist, or that these accidents became a substance.[135] Crescas,[136] Ibn Shaprut,[137] and Simon Duran[138] repeated this argument in the same form, but Albo changed it slightly. He said that the Christians claimed that these accidents did not nourish, but sense perception informed us that indeed they did.[139] Del Medigo also objected to the idea that accidents become substances.[140] Farissol, however, combined the two aspects of the problem as he asked: "How is it possible that the substance becomes accident and the accident becomes substance?"[141]

Thomas agreed that when two things were diverse, one never became the other. This raised the question how one substance, that of the bread, becomes another diverse substance, that of the body of Christ.[142] Though Thomas explained that such a conversion was possible, Del Medigo stated that it was impossible that one substance became another without generation and corruption.[143]

Thomas was also aware that since the sacramental species (the accidents) were not substance, they should not nourish.[144] This problem was solved by the conclusion that the sacramental species could be converted into a substance generated from them. Therefore, they could nourish.[145] In this case, as in those enumerated above, as far as the Jewish polemicists were concerned, the solutions offered by Thomas did not solve the problems that he himself had raised.

134. 'Iggeret, p. 100.
135. Ibid.
136. Bittul, p. 59. The correct text, established by JTSA ms. 2209, f. 16a, reads: "yazunu ha-miqrim ha-hem we-zeh davar yera'eh be-nissayon 'ekhol y'okhal ha-kohen ʿugah 'ahat gedolah she-yihyeh nazon we-yashuvu ha-miqrim ʿetzem rotzeh lomar ha-'avarim ke-din kol zan."
137. 'Even Bohan, f. 157a.
138. Magen 'Avot, in Qeshet u-Magen, p. 26b.
139. Sefer ha-ʿIqqarim, III, 233. Cf. Thomas, who admitted that the accidents did nourish (ST III, Q.77,A.6).
140. Behinat ha-Dat, p. 13. Reggio explained that Del Medigo was referring to nominalist philosophy.
141. Magen 'Avraham, f. 24a.
142. ST III, Q.75,A.4.
143. Behinat ha-Dat, p. 13.
144. ST III, Q.75,A.6, quoting Aristotle (De Anima, II:4, 416ᵇ12), that food gave nourishment only insofar as it was substance.
145. Ibid., and A.5.

5. *Miscellaneous arguments*

(a) According to the Christians, no matter how many times the host was divided, the whole body of Christ was still present in each and every piece. It followed, then, that the host could be divided infinitely and each little piece (*portiuncula*) would still contain the whole Christ. If this were so, then the whole bread was the whole body, and each part of the bread was also the whole body. Therefore, a part would be equal to the whole. This was logically impossible. This argument was made by Profiat[146] and Simon Duran,[147] Ibn Shaprut,[148] and Farissol.[149]

(b) According to Maimonides, "the impossible has a permanent nature."[150] If one were to admit the possibility of transubstantiation, then it followed that anything imaginable, illogical as it may be, could exist. This, indeed, was a principle of the Kalam, which Maimonides refuted.[151] It is for this reason also that Profiat Duran objected to transubstantiation.[152] Del Medigo also used this argument. "Should someone say: 'Do you, too, not say that God is omnipotent and, therefore, some of these things [incarnation, transubstantiation] are possible,' we answer that we religionists do not say that God can be predicated as having powers over contradictory and contrary matters; rather, we say, He has no desire for them at all."[153]

(c) Crescas argued that if we agreed to transubstantiation, then the son of God could be created and destroyed anywhere. Since it was part of the nature of God not to come into being or to be destroyed, transubstantiation was not possible.[154]

IV. *Conclusions*

These are the Jewish philosophical arguments against transubstantiation. We have seen that the Jewish polemicists used a large range of philosophical arguments against this doctrine, most of which were already found in

146. *'Iggeret*, p. 108. Joseph ben Shem Tov (ibid., p. 112) based this argument on Euclid's *Elements*, Bk. I, Common Notion, no. 5. It may actually go back to Plato, *Parmenides*, 145.
147. *Magen 'Avot*, in *Qeshet u-Magen*, p. 26b.
148. *'Even Bohan*, f. 156b.
149. *Magen 'Avraham*, f. 24a.
150. *Guide*, III:15.
151. Ibid., I:73 (tenth premise). Note that one of the impossible items there is the existence of accidents without a subject.
152. *'Iggeret*, pp. 114–16.
153. *Behinat ha-Dat*, pp. 16–17.
154. *Bittul*, p. 59.

Christian sources. It was Profiat Duran who put the Christian criticism into a Jewish framework, and it is from his works that later Jewish polemicists borrowed. Given the fact that most of the arguments were originally Christian, we may ask whether there is anything specifically Jewish in the Jewish critique of transubstantiation.

What distinguished the Jewish arguments from those of their Christian predecessors was their purpose. The Jewish polemicists were not interested in proving that Christ's presence in the Eucharist was figurative and not substantial, as was the heterodox Christian view. Instead, they sought to show that Christianity was irrational and in contradiction to science. Hence, they chose for criticism those doctrines that seemed to evidence this point most clearly. From the Jewish perspective, transubstantiation served as a telling example of irrationality.

For Christian believers, however, conformity with rationality was not the only criterion of truth. Certain beliefs were considered mysteries, beyond the grasp of reason. If a dogma did not conform to philosophy, there was no reason to dispense with it. The Jewish polemicists showed little evidence of appreciating this attitude. Thus, they adduced rational proof after rational proof to undermine a belief not founded on rational proofs. And so, though they were well-founded and rationally sound, from an Aristotelian viewpoint, the Jewish philosophical arguments did not address themselves to the mystery aspects of the Eucharist. On the other hand, they did show, as did the rational objections voiced by the Christians themselves, that the doctrine of transubstantiation was not in total conformity with the dictates of reason. For the Jewish philosophical polemicists, this was sufficient to invalidate it, for many of them held that while religion did not have to be demonstrated by reason, it must not be in conflict with reason.

The Absolute Freedom of the Divine Will in the Philosophy of Abraham Bibago

Allan Lazaroff

Abraham Bibago[1] flourished in the third quarter of the fifteenth century in Aragon. He was a prominent community leader and a prolific author whose works, all in Hebrew, include commentaries on treatises by Aristotle and Averroes and essays on philosophical and religious problems.[2] Although several of his writings have been preserved in manuscript form, his renown in the sixteenth century as a major philosopher apparently rested on his magnum opus, *The Way of Faith* (*Derekh 'Emunah*), which was published in Constantinople in 1521.[3]

The Way of Faith—written toward the end of Bibago's career, probably slightly more than a decade before the expulsion of the Jews from Spain[4]—is in many ways a response to the circumstances of the times in which he lived. In response to the challenges of Christianity and philosophy, Bibago argues that Judaism is the one true and rational faith bringing salvation to the believers among the Jewish people. In response to the dire straits in which his people found themselves, Bibago argues that God knows and cares for them.

The first part of the three-part book is devoted to this latter goal. Its four chapters treat consecutively of the divine will, knowledge, providence, and purpose in this world. The second part deals with man and faith, and is

1. We know only a few details about his life and there is even considerable uncertainty about the correct form of his name. The family name is variously spelled Bivagi, Bivag̃, Bivash, or even Bivatz in the earliest sources. Yitzhak Baer has identified him with a certain Abram Bivagh, and this latter spelling of the family name has recently acquired some currency in Israel. Since, however, the spelling of his name in Latin characters has been "Bibago" for the last two and a half centuries, I have retained this traditional form.

2. These works are described in Moritz Steinschneider's bibliographical essay, "Abraham Bibago's Schriften," *MGWJ*, XXXII (1883), 79–96, 125–44, 239–40. For almost ninety years this was the only article published on Bibago and so it formed the basis of the articles in the various Jewish encyclopedias. In 1972 Yosef Hakker published a short article in the *Proceedings of the Fifth World Congress of Jewish Studies*. Since then, two doctoral dissertations on Bibago have been completed, one by the author at Brandeis University and another by Avraham Nuriel at the Hebrew University in Jerusalem.

3. This edition was reproduced recently in Jerusalem and London. Joseph Rosheim, Isaac Abravanel, and Isaac Arama drew material from Bibago, and he is praised by authors such as Solomon ibn Verga, Judah Moscato, Joseph Delmedigo, and Solomon Alkabetz. His influence extended to places as diverse as Germany, North Africa, and Turkey.

4. *The Way of Faith* is most likely Bibago's last work because in it he refers, either directly or indirectly, to almost all his other known writings.

divided into the following seven chapters: (1) the nature of man; (2) the cosmic role of intellect and its importance for man's salvation; (3) the hindrances preventing man's salvation; (4) the ways in which faith overcomes these hindrances; (5) the acquisition of faith through tradition; (6) a presentation of the arguments that Moses, the first transmitter of this tradition, never sinned; and (7) the definition of faith. The third and final part of the book concerns various doctrines that form the content of faith. It discusses the basic principles of faith, miracles, the arguments for creation, the theoretical and practical commandments and the future world, and closes with a discussion of Maimonides' Thirteen Principles of Faith.

Even this brief summary of chapter headings reveals the logical construction of Bibago's argument and exposes the centrality of his first topic—the divine will or, more exactly, the absolute freedom of the divine will. It ought thus to be of considerable interest to follow Bibago's steps through the maze of Islamic, Jewish, and Christian arguments associated with this crucial problem in the history of religious philosophy.

1. God Is Not a Necessary Agent

Bibago's major source is the work of Maimonides. Like Maimonides in the *Guide* (III:13–20), Bibago prefaces his discussion of providence with analyses of the divine will and knowledge. Further, when Bibago begins his chapter on the will by asking whether the divine actions have a final end or purpose, he says that this same question was raised by Maimonides in the thirteenth chapter of the third part of the *Guide* (*DE*, 2c).[5]

The problem, says Bibago, according to those who deny any purpose in the divine acts, is that a final end implies a deficiency both in the act and in the agent himself. For the end completes and limits acts, which must therefore not be perfect in themselves. The end or purpose similarly perfects the agent who intends to achieve it and so implies a deficiency in the agent himself. Neither God nor His acts can be deficient, of course, and so the divine acts cannot be done for a final end or purpose (*DE*, 2c).

This problem of the deficiency of divine actions performed toward a final

5. The following abbreviations of philosophical works will be used in this article: *DE* = Abraham Bibago, *Derekh 'Emunah* [The Way of Faith] (Constantinople, 1521); *Guide* = Moses Maimonides, *Moreh Nevukhim* [The Guide of the Perplexed], trans. Samuel ibn Tibbon (Warsaw, 1872)—"Arabic" indicates S. Munk's Arabic text, *Dalâlat al-Hâ'irîn*, ed. I. Joel (Jerusalem, 1930–31); *OH* = Hasdai Crescas, *'Or ha-Shem* [The Light of the Lord] (Warsaw, 1859); *ST* = Thomas Aquinas, *Summa Theologica*, 16 vols. (Madrid, 1957–60); *TAF* = Abu Hamid al-Ghazali, *Tahâfut al-Falâsifah* [The Incoherence of the Philosophers] (Beirut, 1927); *TAT* = Ibn Rushd (Averroes), *Tahâfut at-Tahâfut* [The Incoherence of the Incoherence] (Beirut, 1930).

end is not mentioned by Maimonides in the chapter of the *Guide* referred to by Bibago.[6] The argument of deficiency, however, was used by the Neoplatonic and Arabic philosophers who derived the world from God by necessity. Thus Plotinus, according to whom the world is eternal and produced by necessity,[7] says that there is no desire or willingness to produce intellect that intervenes between the One and intellect, for this would imply that in the One there is the imperfection of not yet having what it wishes to have.[8] There is no previous design or craftsmanlike reflection in the production of the world.[9] The same correlation between a final end desired by God and a concomitant deficiency in Him is made by Ibn Sina (Avicenna),[10] the philosopher in Judah Halevi's *Kuzari*,[11] and Ibn Rushd (Averroes).[12] However, although Maimonides does not make this correlation and only denies, in *Guide* III:13, that the world has an ultimate end, this denial may have seemed to subsequent interpreters to place him in the camp of those philosophers who did make the correlation and who, to avoid attributing a deficiency to God, derived the world from God by necessity. Bibago's purpose in this first chapter of *The Way of Faith* is to deny that Maimonides is in the camp of the philosophers of necessity.[13]

This is not to say that the philosophers who derived the world from God by necessity, who denied a final end in the divine actions and who felt volition implied a deficiency in the agent also in fact denied a divine will. They rather asserted of God a will independent of final ends, implying no deficiency in God and consonant with the production of the world by necessity. As Ibn Rushd had said, the philosophers do not deny that God wills; they only deny that His will implies a deficiency in Him as the empirical will does in human beings.[14]

6. This is noted by Hava Fraenkel-Goldschmidt in her edition of Joseph of Rosheim, *Sefer ha-Miqnah* (Jerusalem, 1970), pp. 47–48, nn. 16, 18. Written originally in Regensburg in 1546 by the lay head of German Jewry, this work incorporates large sections of Bibago's *Derekh 'Emunah*.

7. *Enneads*, III.i.7, 9; ii.1, 2.

8. Ibid., V.iii.12; ed. P. Henry and H. Schwyzer (Paris, 1959), II, 320. MacKenna's English translation (3rd ed. rev.: London, 1962) has a slightly different rendering here, evidently reading *proumethethe* instead of *prouthumethe*. Although MacKenna's translation is based on the Volkmann text (1884), the latter has the same reading in this passage as Henry and Schwyzer. Henry and Schwyzer quote in English translation a parallel text from the *Epistola de scientia divina* also indicating that the First Agent would be defective if volition came between Him and His actions.

9. *Enneads*, V.viii.7. Also III.ii.1, and the note thereon by A. H. Armstrong in the Loeb Classical Library edition (Cambridge, Mass., 1967), pp. 44–45.

10. Ibn Sina, *Kitâb al-Shifa': Ilâhiyât* (Cairo, 1960), VIII.7, pp. 363–64, 366.

11. *Sefer ha-Kuzari*, trans. Judah ibn Tibbon, ed. A. Zifroni, I.1.

12. *TAT*, III, p. 148; XI, p. 426. Cf. *ST*, I.xix.1, obj. 2; also the appendix to Part I of Spinoza's *Ethics*, on the implication of an imperfection in God if He works to obtain an end.

13. For a presentation of the view that Maimonides agrees with the philosophers, see S. Pines's "Introduction" to his translation of *The Guide of the Perplexed* (Chicago, 1963), pp. cxxvii–cxxix.

14. *TAT*, III, p. 160; XI, pp. 438, 440, 444.

This consistency between necessity and volition may be based on the conception of a voluntary act in Greek philosophy as one which is free from external compulsion as well as involving knowledge.[15] Since "necessity" is used by Aristotle to apply to what is compelled by something external to itself as well as to what could not be otherwise,[16] it might be possible for an action to be voluntary insofar as it was free of external compulsion and yet also be necessary insofar as it was determined by the agent's own simple nature.[17]

It was in this sense that Plotinus, who said that desire would imply a deficiency in God, also explained at length that the One possesses will insofar as it is self-caused and self-determined and does not just happen to be.[18] Later philosophers also associated the divine will with a satisfaction or delight in God at the emanation of the universe.[19]

The philosophers, however, were not the only ones to assert that God wills and yet deny that His actions also have a final end. According to Shahrastani, the orthodox Islamic position is that no final cause prompted God to create the universe because He cannot profit or suffer harm.[20] Maimonides ascribes to the Ashʿariyya, an Islamic sect, the view that everything comes about through the divine will but that the divine actions have no final end.[21]

Maimonides himself, however, clearly associated will, purpose, and final ends. Thus, in citing Aristotle's opinion that the First Cause wills what is necessarily derived from Him, Maimonides immediately adds that this willing is not called purpose and that the notion of purpose is not included in it.[22] Of those who derived the divine actions from the divine will alone, and not from the divine wisdom, that is, the Ashʿariyya, Maimonides says that according to them God intends or purposes what He does, but this intention

15. Aristotle, *Nichomachean Ethics*, III:1, 1109b35–1110a2, 1111a22–24. Cf. H. A. Wolfson, *Philo*, 2 vols. (Cambridge, Mass., 1947), I, 434–35; or his "Philo on Free Will and the Historical Influence of His View," *HTR*, XXXV (1942), 135, 148–49.

16. Aristotle, *Metaphysics*, V:5, 1015a26–b3, 9–11. The Greek word is *anagkaion*.

17. This has been called the relative concept of freedom. See H. A. Wolfson, "St. Augustine and the Pelagian Controversy," reprinted in his *Religious Philosophy: A Group of Essays* (New York, 1965), pp. 159–60, 172–75.

18. *Enneads*, VI.viii.13. Plotinus uses *thelema* and *boulesis* to refer to the will. Spinoza also associates will and necessity, although not in exactly the same sense (*Ethics*, Part I, prop. xxxii).

19. This is the philosophers' opinion according to both al-Ghazali and Maimonides. See *TAF*, V, p. 157; and *Guide*, II:20, p. 46a (Arabic: p. 219). This was also the position of Isaac Albalag. See G. Vajda, *Isaac Albalag* (Paris, 1960), p. 68.

20. *Kitâb Nihâyat al-Iqdâm fi ʿIlm al-Kalâm*, ed. and trans. A. Guillaume (London, 1934), chap. 18, p. 397 (English section: pp. 126–27).

21. *Guide*, III:17, pp. 23b–24a (Arabic: pp. 336–37), the third opinion; III:23, p. 35a (Arabic: p. 358) (Zophar's opinion, attributed by Maimonides to the Ashʿariyya); III:25, p. 38a (Arabic: p. 366); III:26, p. 39b (Arabic: p. 368).

22. *Guide*, II:20, p. 46a (Arabic: p. 219). "Purpose" is used here as the English translation for the Arabic *qasd*, usually translated into Hebrew as *kawwanah*.

is still not toward any final end.[23] Maimonides' own opinion seems closer to that of the Mu'tazila, the Islamic sect that derived the divine actions from the divine wisdom[24] and upheld a final end for these divine actions.[25] Thus Maimonides not only frequently emphasizes the notion of purpose along with will;[26] he also affirms the importance of an ultimate end to existence and the divine actions in I:69 and III:25, in spite of his apparent denial of such an ultimate end in III:13.[27] Even at the beginning of III:13 he insists that every agent who acts with a purpose must necessarily have an end in view.

For Bibago as well the divine actions have a final end (*DE*, 7b) and are the result of the divine wisdom as well as will (*DE*, 5d, 7c). Thus the divine will for him also includes both the notions of purpose and a final end (*DE*, 2c), and the problem of avoiding a deficiency in the deity leads to a denial not only of final ends but also of the divine will, for one who wills an action does so for the perfection of its final end (*DE*, 2d). Bibago therefore turns now in the first chapter to an analysis and defense of the divine will.

Bibago first divides all agents truly deserving the name "agent" into two kinds, natural and voluntary (*DE*,2d). There are two characteristics which distinguish these two kinds of agents from each other. First, a natural agent such as fire acts unconsciously without knowledge of its action or its result, whereas a voluntary agent such as man is conscious of his action and acts with knowledge. Secondly, a natural agent can perform only one of two opposite actions essentially, the other being performed, if at all, only accidentally. Fire, for example, only heats essentially and cools, if at all, only accidentally. A voluntary agent, on the other hand, can perform at will either of two opposite actions essentially, both being possible for him (*DE*, 2d–3a).

According to some, Bibago continues, there is a third intermediate type of agent, an agent by necessity that is similar in the first respect to a voluntary agent and is similar in the second respect to a natural agent. Like a voluntary agent, the necessary agent is conscious of its action but, unlike a voluntary agent, the necessary agent acts without intention or change. Like the natural agent, the necessary agent performs only one of two opposite ac-

23. *Guide*, III:17, pp. 23b–24a (Arabic: pp. 336–37); III:25, p. 38b (Arabic: p. 366). Maimonides does not identify the group he is speaking about in III:25 as the Ash'ariyya, but it is clear from his description of the Ash'ariyya in III:17 that it is this sect that he has in mind in III:25.

"Final end" is used here as the English translation for the Arabic *ghâyat*, usually translated into Hebrew as *takhlit*.

24. *Guide*, III:17, p. 24a (Arabic: p. 337).

25. Shahrastani, *Nihyat al-Iqdâm*, p. 397.

26. For instance: *Guide*, II:19, p. 39a (Arabic: p. 210); II:20, p. 46a (Arabic: p. 218); II:21, p. 47b (Arabic: p. 221).

27. On the apparent contradiction between Maimonides' espousal of an ultimate end to existence in I:69 and III:25 and his denial of the same in III:13, see Z. Diesendruck, "Die Teleologie bei Maimonides," *HUCA*, V (1928), 415–534.

tions without change, but unlike the natural agent, the necessary agent is conscious and knows its action.

These philosophers further say, according to Bibago, that God is such an agent by necessity because He would be deficient if He were either a natural or a voluntary agent. For a natural agent lacks knowledge and a voluntary agent acts by intention, presumably lacking the goal he intends to achieve and so is thereby deficient. God's actions therefore, according to this opinion, proceed from Him necessarily as light proceeds from the sun, except that God knows His action and this knowledge is in fact the cause of these actions (*DE*, 3a).

Bibago agrees that God cannot be a natural agent because a natural agent is deficient (*DE*, 4d). For Bibago, however, the deficiency of the natural agent is not just its lack of knowledge. For him the deficiency is even more its inabilty to perform either of two opposite actions (*DE*, 5a–5b). An agent who can perform essentially only one of two opposite actions is a deficient agent, says Bibago, even if his one action comes about through knowledge. This deficiency then applies equally well to an agent by necessity, who in this respect is no better off than a natural agent. For of what use is his knowledge to him if he has not the power to do the opposite? If, on the other hand, he has the ability to do either of two opposite actions, he is then a voluntary agent, for the definition of will is the ability to do an action and its opposite (*DE*, 4c).

One of Bibago's major arguments against God being an agent by necessity, then, is that such an agent is as deficient as a natural agent in its inability to perform either of two opposite actions. This performance of two opposites does not imply any plurality in the deity, Bibago adds, any more than the duality of the "now" (*ʿattah*) as the end of the past and the beginning of the future detracts from its simple basic unity (*DE*, 4d).[28] It was the failure to understand that one God could perform opposite actions which led to the ancient heresies of dualism and polytheism, because some evidently believed that opposite effects must be produced by different powers or deities (*DE*, 4d, 18c).

A second argument used by Bibago to show that God is not an agent by necessity is related to the first argument about opposite actions. An agent by necessity, Bibago says, performs only one action constantly without change and in accordance with the necessity of its essence, but the divine actions change from time to time (*DE*, 4b). Change such as this is of the essence of

28. On the "now," cf. Aristotle, *Physics*, IV:10–11, 13; Gersonides, *Milhamot ha-Shem*, VI.i.21; and S. Pines, "Scholasticism after Thomas Aquinas and the Teachings of Hasdai Crescas and His Predecessors," *Proceedings of the Israel Academy of Sciences and Humanities*, I, no. 10 (Jerusalem, 1967), 9–12. Bibago returns to the concept of the "now" in *DE*, 10a–b, 61b, and 87b, d.

will and without it there would be no will. Despite such change in the divine actions and will, however, there is no change in the deity, although Bibago admits that we are ignorant of how this is possible (*DE*, 6b, 7b). God can do whatever He wants whenever He wants without any change occurring in Him, but because the divine will is not like the human will, we don't know how this is possible (*DE*, 4c).

This problem of the change implied in willing as against the divine immutability is the primary issue raised by Joseph Albo in his discussion of the divine will,[29] a discussion that includes many of the elements found in Bibago's treatment of the subject. Albo's solution of the problem, somewhat like that of Bibago, is to restate our ignorance of the divine will.[30] Bibago, however, unlike Albo, says that the divine will does indeed change, although, because the term "will" is used of the divine and human wills only equivocally, this does not result in any change in God (*DE*, 6b, 7b). Albo does not speak of change in the divine will, which is identical with the divine essence. Also Maimonides, to whom Bibago refers for support in this matter (*DE*, 4c), says that the divine will does not change.[31]

Both Joseph ibn Zaddik and al-Ghazali speak at length about change and the divine will when discussing creation.[32] The apparent shift in the focus of the discussion from the problem of change and the divine will to the related concept of will as the ability to perform opposite actions as in Bibago may be connected with a shift from the issue of creation to the issue of the divine providence and miracles.[33]

The third major argument used by Bibago against God being an agent by necessity is based on the dissimilarity between God and the world and is in fact the argument that Bibago discusses first, although we have listed it here third. The argument is that something generated by necessity from another thing must be similar to and related to that other thing somehow, and everyone agrees that nothing is similar and related to God (*DE*, 3b). In the earlier Neoplatonic and Arabic philosophy, a basic dissimilarity between God and the world was the unity of God and the multiplicity of the world.

29. *Sefer ha-ᶜIqqarim*, II:2–3, esp. pp. 13–17 (ed. I. Husik [Philadelphia, 1930]).
30. Ibid., pp. 19–25.
31. *Guide*, II:18, p. 37b (2nd method); also I:11, p. 29 (on the divine immutability). In describing the Aristotelian view that the world is eternal, Maimonides attributes to Aristotle the opinion that it is impossible that the divine will should change or that a new volition should arise in God (II:13, p. 31a).
32. Joseph ibn Zaddik, *Sefer ha-ᶜOlam ha-Qatan*, ed. S. Horovitz (Breslau, 1903), pp. 44–45, 53–54; and *TAF*, I.
33. B. Netanyahu has argued that divine providence was an important theme in the work of Hasdai Crescas and several other Spanish Jewish philosophers at the beginning and middle of the fifteenth century (*The Marranos of Spain from the Late XIVth to the Early XVIth Century According to Contemporary Hebrew Sources* [New York, 1966], pp. 113–16).

The fundamental problem was how to derive the multiplicity of the world from the unity of God by necessity, given the above principle of the similarity of necessarily related beings.[34] When Bibago sets out to demonstrate rationally the lack of similarity and relation between the Creator and His universe, the distinction he uses is not unity and multiplicity but the infinity of God and the finite dimensions of the world. If God is infinite, then by the above principle of the similarity of necessarily related beings, the world generated from God by necessity would also have to be infinite. If the dimensions of the world are finite, it is because the world derives from God not by necessity but by will (DE, 3b–3c).

Although the separation between God and the world in Bibago is distinguished from that found in Maimonides by the element of infinity, the concept of a gulf between God and the world is common to Bibago and Maimonides[35] and the fourteenth-century Christian scholastics who in this regard opposed the Arabic necessitarian philosophies with their gradations and analogies of being between God and the world.[36] Whereas the more Neoplatonic philosophies of necessity derived the world from God only indirectly through intermediaries, many Jewish and Christian thinkers insisted that the gulf between God and the world could be bridged directly as well by the divine will.[37]

Thus Bibago's fourth and last argument against God being an agent by necessity is related to his third argument based on the dissimilarity between God and the world, much as his second argument is closely related to his first. This fourth argument is that an agent by necessity operates only through intermediaries and only upon properly prepared objects, whereas God, Bibago insists, operates either with or without intermediaries and upon whomever He so desires, whether they are prepared or not (DE, 78a–c), although most of the time He does in fact act through intermediaries (DE, 96a). The sin of the twelve spies in the biblical story, Bibago says, was in thinking that God is restricted by these two limitations of agents that operate by necessity (DE, 78a–c). One might add that the requirement of interme-

34. H. A. Wolfson, Philo, I, 282–83; S. Munk, Le Guide des Egarés, II, 172, n. 1; and H. A. Davidson, The Philosophy of Abraham Shalom (Berkeley, 1964), p. 47.

35. See Guide, II:21, p. 47a; A. Altmann, "Essence and Existence in Maimonides," reprinted in his Studies in Religious Philosophy and Mysticism (Ithaca, N.Y., 1969), pp. 126–27; and E. Fackenheim, "The Possibility of the Universe in al-Farabi, Ibn Sina and Maimonides," PAAJR, XVI (1946–47), 68.

36. Heiko A. Oberman, Archbishop Thomas Bradwardine: A Fourteenth-Century Augustinian (Utrecht, 1957), pp. 46, 52; and Gordon Leff, Bradwardine and the Pelagians (Cambridge, 1957), p. 12.

37. Wolfson, Philo, I, 282–83. Cf. Saadya Gaon, Sefer 'Emunot we-De'ot, I.iii, 7th theory; and Judah Halevi, Sefer ha-Kuzari, V.20 (ed. Zifroni, pp. 315–18).

diaries between God and the world was, according to Bibago, a basis for idolatry (*DE*, 18c).

In addition to these four rational arguments against God being an agent by necessity, Bibago also argues that this doctrine would conflict with such basic articles of faith as creation and miracles and the divine providence and retribution (*DE*, 3a–b, 4c–d). Since, therefore, the belief in the generation of the world by necessity negates doctrines basic to the faith of Judaism, and since it has also been shown by four arguments to be philosophically and rationally untenable, Bibago rejects the notion that God is an agent that acts by necessity (*DE*, 4c). Since he also rejects the possibility of God being a natural agent as obviously wrong, he concludes that God is an agent by will (*DE*, 5b). This divine will, Bibago immediately adds, is of course absolutely different from ours, and the term is used of God and man only equivocally (*DE*, 4c, 7b). For we have no concept of the divine will (*DE*, 6b, 7b).

ii. *God Is a Voluntary Agent*

Bibago's classification of agents into natural and voluntary ones has ample precedent.[38] This twofold classification, however, seems to be a distillation of more complete lists of causes which often include chance as well.[39] Although it did not suit Bibago's purpose and scheme in this first chapter to mention chance at the beginning of it, he somewhat later in the chapter notes four types of actions in this world, those by nature, by choice, by chance, and through the stars (*DE*, 6d, 7a). This classification, as Bibago himself says, is based on Maimonides' threefold division of the proximate or intermediate

38. For instance, Clement of Alexandria says that will distinguishes God's action from that of fire (*Stromata*, VII.vii.42). Al-Nazzam and his contemporary Muʿammar ibn Abbad (ninth century) said that agents operate either naturally, as in the case of inanimate things like fire, or voluntarily, as in the case of animate beings like man (Shahrastani, *Kitâb al-Milal wa-l-Nihal*, ed. W. Cureton [London, 1846], p. 46). Both al-Ghazali and Ibn Rushd attributed such a classification of agents to the philosophers (*TAT*, III, p. 153), and Isaac Albalag also said that agents either operate by nature or by will (Vajda, *Isaac Albalag*, p. 68). Thomas Aquinas said that every mover is either natural or voluntary (*ST*, I.xlvi.1, obj. 6) and Duns Scotus divides all active powers into either nature or will (*Quaestiones subtilissimae in Metaphysicam Aristotelis*, IX.5, n. 4). Cf. Albo, *Sefer ha-ʿIqqarim*, II:2, p. 12.

39. For instance, Aristotle says that nature, necessity, and chance are thought to be causes, and also reason and everything that depends on man (*Nicomachean Ethics*, III:3, 1112ᵃ31–32). Judah Halevi usually mentions the divine will, nature, and chance as causes (*Sefer ha-Kuzari*, II.50 [ed. Zifroni, p. 109]), sometimes adding to this list human choice (V.20 [p. 316]) or will (I.97 [p. 51]) or the stars (I.83 [p. 39]). Isaac Polqar (flourished in Spain in the fourteenth century) divides the causes of actions into natural, voluntary, and accidental ones (*Sefer ʿEzer ha-Dat*, ed. G. Belasco [London, 1904], LXVIII, p. 60a).

worldly causes into natural, voluntary, and accidental ones.[40] In good Aristotelian fashion,[41] however, Maimonides says that chance is only an excess of what is natural and that most causes are either natural or voluntary,[42] thus reducing the list to the basic twofold classification of natural and voluntary causes. Bibago also eliminates chance by saying that it occurs on a minority of occasions (DE, 8b)[43] and that it is really our name for our ignorance of the true cause (DE, 6d).

Of the two characteristics by which Bibago distinguishes the voluntary from the natural agent, namely knowledge and the ability to perform opposite actions, knowledge had long been agreed upon as a basic requirement for a voluntary agent. Both Plato and Aristotle had said that a voluntary action could not be done from ignorance.[44] Al-Ghazali also said that will necessarily

40. In Guide, II:48, Maimonides has four lists of intermediate causes. The first list (p. 96b [Arabic: p. 292]) enumerates the three basic types of causes: "essential and natural, or voluntary, or accidental and fortuitous" (Pines's translation, p. 410). Maimonides immediately explains that "choice" includes the choice of man as well as the will of other animals, thus adopting Aristotle's extension of voluntary action to animals and his limitation of rational choice to man (Nicomachean Ethics, III:2, 1111^{b}7-9, 1112^{a}16-17). The second list will be described below, n. 42. In analyzing some biblical verses in terms of these intermediate causes, Maimonides forms a third list of causes with four members: nature, human choice, will, and chance. In this third list (pp. 97a-b [Arabic: pp. 293-94]), the "essential and natural" cause of the first list is called simply "natural," and the "choice" of the first list is here broken up into human choice and animal will, as Maimonides had specified immediately following the first list. Maimonides' fourth and last list also has four members and is almost exactly like the third list. The exception is that the "essential and natural" cause of the first list, which had become the "natural" cause of the third list, is here simply the "essential" cause (p. 97b [Arabic: p. 294]). Although the third and fourth lists each have four members, we can follow Maimonides' procedure in the first list of collapsing human choice and animal will into one voluntary cause, so that we can say that Maimonides basically divides these intermediate causes into natural, voluntary, and accidental ones. "Natural" and "essential" seem to be used interchangeably in these lists.

Bibago's addition of the constellation of stars as a fourth cause to the three mentioned by Maimonides does not indicate any inclination toward astrology on Bibago's part. Bibago in fact devotes a long section of DE, I.3 (pp. 18c-21b), to refuting the claims of astrology. He remarks there at the end of that discussion (p. 21b) that he spent so much time on astrology because so many in his day believed in its claims. Although he attributes his classification to Maimonides, it should be noted that the four types of actions mentioned by Bibago, along with the divine will over them all, are exactly the five types of actions mentioned by Judah Halevi in his various lists in his Sefer ha-Kuzari.

41. See Aristotle, Physics, II:5-6, esp. 198^{a}2-10.

42. In his second list of intermediate causes in Guide, II:48 (pp. 96b-97a [Arabic: p. 293]), Maimonides mentions animal will, human choice, and nature, three of the four members of the third and fourth lists. He then adds that chance is what is left after things are accounted for by nature, and most things are accounted for by either nature or will or choice. Since therefore chance can be eliminated and human choice and animal will can be combined into one voluntary cause, as in Maimonides' first list in this chapter, we are left with most causes being either natural or voluntary.

43. Cf. Saadya Gaon, Sefer 'Emunot we-De^{c}ot, I.3 (the first and second objections to the ninth theory about the beginning of the world, the theory of chance).

44. Plato, Republic, VII, 535E; Aristotle, Nicomachean Ethics, III:1, 1109^{b}35-36, 1111^{a}23. Cf. Wolfson, Philo, I, 434-35.

implies knowledge and Ibn Rushd agreed that knowledge is included in the definition of will.[45] Although Maimonides calls both the celestial intellects and spheres and the corporeal forces angels, he differentiates the corporeal forces as things of nature because they do not apprehend their acts, whereas the celestial intellects and spheres apprehend their acts and have will and free choice.[46] Isaac Albalag says that a voluntary agent is distinguished from a natural one by not being separated from knowledge,[47] a phrase almost exactly duplicated by Bibago (*DE*, 2d), and Menahem ben Abraham Bonafos[48] defines a natural agent as one that acts without knowledge and a voluntary one as the opposite.[49] Shem Tov ben Joseph, in his commentary on the *Guide*, even speaks not of natural and voluntary agents but of natural agents and conscious agents, or agents by knowledge.[50] Bonafos and Shem Tov, like Bibago, use fire and man as examples of the opposing types of agents.

That it is through knowledge alone, however, that the First Cause necessarily generates the universe seems to go back at least to Ibn Sina.[51] Al-Ghazali says that the philosophers' opinion is that the world proceeds necessarily from the divine essence as light does from the sun or as heat does from fire, except that in regard to God this emanation is caused by God's knowledge of the universe, which is identical with His knowledge of His essence.[52] Judah Halevi similarly attributes to the philosophers the opinion that the divine knowledge alone is sufficient to determine any particular time or one of a pair of opposites without the addition of will or power.[53] Maimonides also seems to be referring to Ibn Sina when he describes Aristotle's derivation of the universe from the First Cause by necessity as being not like the procession of a shadow from a body, heat from fire or light from the sun, but rather like the derivation of an intellectum from an intellect.[54]

Like al-Ghazali and Maimonides in the passages referred to, Bibago also

45. *TAT*, III, p. 156.
46. *Guide*, II:7, p. 24b.
47. Vajda, *Isaac Albalag*, p. 68.
48. Flourished in southern France at the end of the fourteenth and the beginning of the fifteenth centuries; *EJ*, IV, 1198.
49. *Sefer ha-Gedarim* (Salonica, 1567).
50. Cf. his commentary on *Guide*, II:22, p. 48a, and on III:13, pp. 16b–17a.
51. Ibn Sina, *Kitāb al-Shifā': Ilāhiyāt*, VIII.7, pp. 366–67; IX.4, pp. 402–3. A view similar to that of Ibn Sina appears in al-Farabi's ʿ*Uyūn al-Masāʾil* [The Main Questions]. Cf. *Alfarabi's Philosophische Abhandlungen*, ed. F. Dieterici (Leiden, 1892), p. 96. The authorship of this essay has been questioned, however, and it is not certain whether the generation of the world, according to al-Farabi, is necessary and eternal or voluntaristic and in time. Cf. A. Hyman and J. J. Walsh, eds., *Philosophy in the Middle Ages* (New York, 1967), pp. 212, 214.
52. *TAF*, V, pp. 155–56; XI, pp. 214–15.
53. *Sefer ha-Kuzari*, V.18, ninth axiom (ed. Zifroni, p. 314).
54. Guide, II:20, p. 46a.

uses the simile of the sun to describe the agent by necessity, adding of course that the deity differs in operating through knowledge (*DE*, 3a–b). The simile of the sun goes back at least to Plotinus,[55] in whose thought, however, the distinction of the One from the sun is not knowledge, for the One is above knowledge and intellect.[56] Thus Ibn Sina's system, in which the world emanates necessarily from God because of His knowledge, seems to combine the Neoplatonic emanation with the Aristotelian God of intellect.[57] Ibn Sina does not deny a divine will but rather identifies it with this divine knowledge. He does deny, however, that the divine actions have a final end.[58]

One of Bibago's main arguments, however, against God's being an agent by necessity, as Ibn Sina contended, was that such an agent lacked the other characteristic of a voluntary agent in addition to knowledge, namely the ability to do either of two opposite actions essentially. This characteristic of the will seems to go back to Philo's interpretation of the biblical tradition.[59] For Philo, a voluntary action was not, as it was for Plato and Aristotle, an action done with knowledge and without external compulsion. This has been called a relative concept of freedom.[60] Philo's concept of absolute freedom of the will meant in God the power to intervene miraculously in nature and in man the similarly miraculous and divinely derived power to choose freely between alternatives.[61]

According to Judah Halevi, the Kalam view of the divine will is that God can do the opposite of everything that He does. His omnipotence inclines equally to either of two opposites and must be directed to one or the other by the will.[62] This is very similar to al-Ghazali's statement that God could have willed the opposite of every work that exists through His will and that, since His power encompasses the opposites, there must be a will that directs the power to one or the other.[63] Maimonides also said that the true reality and quiddity of will is to will and not to will,[64] and that every agent acting by purpose and will and not by nature accomplishes many different acts.[65]

---

55. For instance, *Enneads*, V.iii.12.
56. Ibid., V.vi.l; VI.ix.3, 6.
57. On the divine thought in Aristotle, see *Metaphysics*, XII:7, 9. Cf. also *Guide* I:68.
58. *Kitâb al-Shifa': Ilâhiyât*, VIII.7, pp. 366–67.
59. Cf. Deuteronomy 11:26–29.
60. Wolfson, "St. Augustine and the Pelagian Controversy," pp. 158–59.
61. Wolfson, *Philo*, I, 436–37, 456–57; or idem, "Philo on Free Will," 150, 163–64.
62. *Sefer ha-Kuzari*, V.18, ninth axiom (ed. Zifroni, p. 314).
63. Al-Ghazali, *Al-Risâlah al-Qudsiyyah* [Tract on Dogmatic Theology], ed. and trans. A. L. Tibawi (London, 1965), p. 21 (p. 41 in the English translation). On al-Ghazali's defense of the Kalam concept of the will and its influence on Maimonides, see Pines, "Introduction," pp. cxxvii–cxxviii.
64. *Guide*, II:18, p. 37a (Arabic: p. 210).
65. Ibid., II:22, p. 48a, third proposition (Arabic: p. 221).

Earlier he had pointed out that precisely this was the issue of dispute between the adherents of the Law and the philosophers, namely, that what exists is made by will and is not a necessary consequence and that it could have been made differently from what it is.[66]

Among the Christian scholastics it was especially Duns Scotus, and William of Ockham after him, who said that will in its primary act is free with regard to opposite acts.[67] It has been contended, in fact, that the reputed "voluntarism" of Duns Scotus, instead of being some sort of irrationalism, consists precisely in his insistence that the free will is capable of choosing other than it does.[68] Abner of Burgos, who had converted from Judaism to Christianity, said that the distinction between a voluntary and a natural agent was that the latter could perform only one of two opposing actions in accordance with its nature, whereas a voluntary agent could perform according to its nature either one.[69] Joseph Albo also distinguished natural agents, which could do only one thing essentially, from voluntary agents, who can perform opposite actions at will.[70]

Al-Ghazali, in arguing against the philosophers' view of God as an agent acting necessarily through knowledge, had insisted upon only a twofold classification of agents into natural and voluntary ones. He then concluded that the philosophers who derived the world from God by necessity were in effect reducing God to a natural agent. If it is objected that the world is derived necessarily from God through His knowledge, which is not the case with natural agents such as the sun,[71] al-Ghazali answers that as long as the divine will is denied, the additional factor of knowledge seems to make little difference.[72]

In response to al-Ghazali's criticism of the philosophers, Ibn Rushd used an Aristotelian analysis to show that God operates by both knowledge and

66. Ibid., I:73, p. 124a (Arabic: pp. 147–48).
67. Duns Scotus, *Opus Oxoniense*, ed. L. Wadding (Paris, 1893), Bk. I, Dist. 39; Bk. II, Dist. 25. Cf. also William of Ockham, *Super 4 libros sententiarum* (London, 1962), I.38b, and *Quodlibeta septem*, IV.1. In regard to what God does not will necessarily, Thomas Aquinas says that God can choose one of two opposites because He can will a thing to be or not to be (*ST*, I.xix.10). The general thrust of Aquinas's discussion of the divine will, however, reflects Aristotle's analysis of the will as a combination of appetency and reason (*ST*, I.xix.1). Cf. also Aristotle, *De Anima*, III:10, 433ª23–25.
68. Hyman and Walsh, *Philosophy in the Middle Ages*, p. 556.
69. Y. Baer, "Sefer Minhat Qena'ot shel 'Avner mi-Burgos we-hashpaʿato ʿal Hasdai Crescas," *Tarbiz*, XI (1940), 191–92. After his conversion Abner was known as Alfonso of Valladolid.
70. *Sefer ha-ʿIqqarim*, II:2 (ed. Husik, pp. 12, 16).
71. Since the sun had been used as an example of an agent operating by natural necessity, al-Ghazali here notes that the knowledge that the sun has is not the cause of its light and that the divine knowledge may similarly not be causal. Shem Tov ben Joseph and Efodi, in their commentaries on *Guide*, II:20, p. 46a, reproduce this opinion that the sun has knowledge which is not causal.
72. *TAF*, XI, pp. 214–15.

will. In Aristotle's philosophy, it was because of a rational formula that a potency associated with that rational formula could be capable of contrary effects, whereas a nonrational potency produces only one effect.[73] Thus the ability to produce contrary effects that in the Philonic-biblical framework was a function of the free will is in Aristotle's thought a function of reason. It is appetency or will which then decides which of the opposites is to be done, for without this both would be done at the same time, which is impossible.[74]

Ibn Rushd similarly says that if God operated only by knowledge, in knowing two opposites He would necessarily perform them both at the same time, which is impossible. He therefore has an additional attribute of will or choice through which He performs one of the two opposite acts that He knows.[75] Thus Ibn Rushd, who said that al-Farabi and Ibn Sina introduced into philosophy some of the theological notions of the Kalam,[76] seems himself here to be utilizing an Aristotelian concept to effect somewhat of a compromise between Ibn Sina and the Kalam on the issue of the divine will. For in this response to al-Ghazali's criticism of the philosophers, Ibn Rushd, unlike Ibn Sina, implies that the divine will is not identical with the divine knowledge and that the world is not generated by the divine knowledge alone.

This agency through the divine will, Ibn Rushd adds, of course does not have the deficiencies of agency through the human will, such as the need to better oneself through the desired object.[77] The divine agency is even farther from natural agency, for a natural agent acts without knowledge and final ends.[78] Therefore the division of agents into natural and voluntary ones is not exhaustive, for God is neither one nor the other and possesses instead an agency superior to both. He can thus be said to will only equivocally, for only He can understand how His will is not subject to the deficiencies of human wills.[79] Further, Ibn Rushd insists that, although each of the opposites is possible for the deity, He always performs the better of the two.[80]

73. Aristotle, *Metaphysics*, IX:2, 1046[b]4–24.
74. Ibid., IX:5, 1048[a]8–11.
75. *TAT*, XI, pp. 438–39; XII, p. 450. Cf. Moses Narboni, *Commentary on the Moreh Nevukhim*, ed. J. Goldenthal (Vienna, 1852), on *Guide*, III:25, p. 61a; cf. also the commentary of Shem Tov ben Joseph on *Guide*, III:25, p. 39a, and on II:22, p. 48a.
76. *TAT*, I, p. 54; IV, p. 276.
77. Ibid., III, p. 148; XI, pp. 426, 438, 444; XII, p. 450. Isaac Polqar describes the deficiency of the human will, in contrast to the divine will, in *Sefer ʿEzer ha-Dat*, 47–48, p. 43a.
78. *TAT*, III, pp. 148–49. This interpretation of the passage is based on a somewhat similar passage dealing with natural and voluntary agents in the Church Father Athanasius, referred to by H. A. Wolfson in his *Philosophy of the Church Fathers* (Cambridge, Mass., 1956), pp. 228–29.
79. *TAT*, I, p. 6; III, p. 148; XI, p. 439; XII, pp. 449–50.
80. Ibid., III, p. 160; XI, p. 427.

It should be noted that the Aristotelian analysis of choice that Ibn Rushd used to modify Ibn Sina's theory of necessary emanation differs also from the biblical-Philonic free will in the following manner. In Aristotle's philosophy, both man and animals can act voluntarily.[81] Both are moved by the same motive force, *orexis* or appetency,[82] so that human will and animal impulse are not really different in kind.[83] What distinguishes man from animals, according to Aristotle, is not his free will but his reason, so that choice is characteristic of man's volitions because choice involves a rational principle.[84] In the biblical-Philonic tradition, man is distinguished by the divine gift of free will.[85] In spite of this distinction, however, Ibn Rushd may have been playing upon the similarity between the two concepts in his use of the Aristotelian concept of choice in his answer to al-Ghazali.

In his first chapter Bibago interprets Maimonides' concept of the divine will in terms of the biblical-Philonic tradition found also in the Kalam and in scholastics like Duns Scotus, namely, as the ability to perform either of two opposite acts. Bibago may conceivably have been interpreting Ibn Rushd in this way as well on the basis of Ibn Rushd's application to the divine will of Aristotle's doctrine of rational choice. Thus, when Bibago says that action by knowledge is no added advantage unless the opposite action is also possible (*DE*, 4c), he may not be eliminating the middle type of action by necessity as al-Ghazali had done. He may be saying instead that, given Ibn Rushd's application of the Aristotelian doctrine of rational choice to the divine actions, action by knowledge implies choice between opposites.

Further, although the principal object of Bibago's arguments concerning the divine will are the philosophers like Ibn Sina who derive the world by necessity from the divine knowledge, Bibago would also disagree over this issue of the will with those more voluntaristic philosophers such as Crescas who derive the world from God by both will and necessity. Maimonides had explicitly denied the possibility of a combination of will and necessity in a theory of the eternal emanation of the world from the divine will,[86] and Don Isaac Abravanel said that Crescas's opinion was identical with this theory here described as unsatisfactory by Maimonides.[87] For Crescas said that the will is nothing but the necessary procession of existences from the rational

---

81. Aristotle, *Nicomachean Ethics*, III:2, 1111^{b}6–10.
82. Aristotle, *De Anima*, III:10, 433^{a}9–13, ^{b}28–31.
83. Cf. D. J. Allen, *The Philosophy of Aristotle* (Oxford, 1952), pp. 75, 95, 181.
84. Aristotle, *Nicomachean Ethics*, III:2, 1111^{b}6–15, 1112^{a}13–18.
85. Cf. Wolfson, "St. Augustine and the Pelagian Controversy," pp. 159–60.
86. *Guide*, II:21.
87. In his *Shamayyim Hadashim*, printed as a commentary to *Guide*, II:19, p. 38b.

forms because of a superabundance of goodness.[88] This possibility of a union of free will and necessity is based, as we saw, on the Greek conception of relative free will and goes back most notably to Augustine who, it is interesting to note, describes the will as a delight much as the later philosophers of necessity did.[89]

In addition to insisting that God is a voluntary agent who can perform either of two opposite actions, Bibago says that either action can also be performed essentially, whereas a natural agent can perform only one of two opposite actions essentially and the other, if at all, only accidentally (DE, 2d, 3a). Opposite actions, in other words, can come from the one God whether the actions are in the category of essence or whether they are in the category of accidents (DE, 18c). Like Maimonides,[90] Bibago says that an essential action is the opposite of an action by chance since an essential action completes its goal and so relates its end to its beginning. It has, that is, a certain constancy for the duration required to achieve its end (DE, 8b–c).[91]

Bibago discusses two other characteristics that distinguish an essential agent from an agent that acts accidentally. First, an agent that acts essentially knows its action. Secondly, an essential agent remains in existence as long as its product does, and its product goes out of existence when the agent does, as is the case with essential causes and effects. Thus, according to these two criteria, a human father is not the essential agent of his son's existence, first, because he does not know the exact moment of his son's conception and so is not aware of his action, and secondly, because his son may endure after him. God, on the other hand, is our true Father, for as a voluntary and essential agent He is aware of His action as He performs it and He endures for the duration of His effect (DE, 9d).

Bibago thus says that a voluntary agent also can (and in the case of God must) be an essential agent. Bibago's contemporary Shem Tov ben Joseph, on the other hand, restricted essential agency to what Bibago calls the necessary

88. OH, III.i.5, p. 69a. On the opposition of Crescas's concept of the divine will to that of Maimonides, see Y. Guttmann, Ha-Filosofiyah shel ha-Yahadut (Jerusalem, 1951), p. 211; also Isidore Epstein, "Das Problem des göttlichen Willens in der Schöpfung nach Maimonides, Gersonides und Crescas," MGWJ, LXXV (1931), 335–47. In his arguments against the theory of chance, in the beginning of the next chapter, Bibago says that the essential agency of the divine will has a greater duration than chance occurrences do (DE, 8b–c). As we shall shortly see, however, this does not refer to a voluntary and eternal divine agency but to the completion and perfection of the action.

89. Contra duas epistolas Pelagianorum, I.iii.5. Cf. Wolfson, "St. Augustine and the Pelagian Controversy," pp. 170–74.

90. Guide, II:20, p. 46a (Arabic: p. 218).

91. Cf. Aristotle, Physics, II:8, 199b15–18: "For those things are natural which, by a continuous movement originated from an internal principle, arrive at some completion: the same completion is not reached from every principle, nor any chance completion . . ." (from the Oxford translation of R. P. Hardie and R. K. Gaye).

agent and so denies that a voluntary agent can act essentially. Essential agency for Shem Tov is the distinguishing characteristic of that agent which operates through knowledge like a voluntary agent and yet is not a voluntary agent.[92] Initially, an agent acting essentially was one of the meanings of a natural agent. A natural agent, that is, was one that moved according to its nature or essence. Maimonides evidently used "naturally" and "essentially" interchangeably in his discussion of intermediate causes.[93] Aristotle had said that the primary sense of "nature" is the essence of things that have in themselves, as such, a source of movement.[94] Similarly Judah Halevi defined "nature," according to the philosopher, as the principle and cause in a thing by which it moves and rests essentially, not accidentally, adding that this is how we distinguish natural agents from accidental ones.[95] Since "nature" as well as "necessity" was also initially a term used in opposition to "will,"[96] this association of "natural" and "essential" agency may explain the opposition of essential and voluntary agency in Shem Tov ben Joseph.

On the other hand, the association of "natural" and "essential" also meant that what was "naturally" produced was produced from the essence of God but need not have been produced by necessity. Thus "naturally" and "essentially" came eventually to be used also not in opposition to will.[97] Isaac Albalag notes that the problem of whether one or more actions can come from an agent essentially is the result of a confusion between essential and accidental agents. It is in accidental agents that the number of actions equals the number of accidents, but the agent who operates essentially through reason can perform many different actions equally.[98] Essential actions were

92. Commentary on *Guide*, III:13, p. 17a.
93. *Guide*, II:48; see above, n. 40.
94. *Metaphysics*, V:4, 1015ª13–15; also 1014ᵇ18–20: "'Nature' means . . . the source from which the primary movement in each natural object is present in it in virtue of its own essence"; 1014ᵇ36: "'Nature' means the essence (*ousia*) of natural objects"; 1015ª12–13: "Every essence (*ousia*) in general has come to be called a 'nature,' because the nature of a thing is one kind of essence" (Oxford translation of W. D. Ross).
95. *Sefer ha-Kuzari*, I.70–75. Cf. Aristotle, *Physics*, II:1, 192ᵇ22–23: "Nature is a source or cause of being moved and of being at rest in that to which it belongs primarily, in virtue of itself and not in virtue of a concomitant attribute."
96. Wolfson, *Philosophy of the Church Fathers*, I, 228–29.
97. Ibid., I, 228–29, 232.
98. *Sefer Tiqqun ha-De῾ot*, in Y. H. Schorr, "R. Yitzhaq Albalag," *He-Halutz*, VII (1865), 161. As has already been noted, Abner of Burgos said that a voluntary agent could perform either of two opposite actions in accordance with its nature (see above, n. 69). In view of the preceding discussion, it is likely that Abner's phrase "in accordance with its nature (*mi-tiv῾o*)" is equivalent to Bibago's "essentially (*be῾etzem*)." Since Baer's text is his Hebrew translation of a Spanish translation from the original Hebrew, one wonders if the original text may have spoken of essential actions.
    Although Joseph Albo describes a voluntary agent as Bibago does, as one that can perform opposite actions, Albo does not specify, as Bibago does, that these actions are performed essentially. He does say that a natural agent can perform only one action essentially, as the heat of fire only heats (*Sefer ha-῾Iqqarim*, II:2 [ed. Husik, p. 12]).

in this manner attributed to voluntary agents, as in Bibago, and were also opposed to voluntary agency, as in Shem Tov ben Joseph.

III. *The Divine Will as a Coefficient Cause*: *Providence*

Having thus established that God is a voluntary agent who can perform either of two opposite actions essentially, Bibago turns to a second major theme of his first chapter and insists and reiterates in various ways that God not only created the world by the divine will but also constantly maintains the world in existence by means of the divine will (*DE*, 5b–6b, 6d–7b). God is not like the architect of a house who first builds it and then leaves it to endure solely by its own nature and essence, so that it would not go out of existence if its architect went out of existence. According to both the philosophers and the theologians, the opposite is the case in regard to God and the world. The world, unlike the house, would disappear were it not for its maintenance by the divine will, whereas God endures forever, even after the destruction of His creatures (*DE*, 5d, 91b–c).

For the divine will is the direct coefficient in all events in nature, these events thus becoming vehicles and instruments for the divine will (*DE*, 6a–b, 7b, 8b). Even according to the philosopher, nature is unintelligent, but the philosopher says it is the Active Intellect that guides it towards its final end, whereas we, says Bibago, attribute this guidance to the divine will (*DE*, 5d).[99] This divine coefficiency, for example, is why man cannot live on bread alone,[100] for the essence of bread cannot nourish without the divine will. This also is the lesson of the manna (*DE*, 6a). Consequently, from this point of view there is no longer a distinction between natural and artificial deeds, since natural events are artificial insofar as they are the result of the divine will (*DE*, 23c).

The proof for the divine will as a coefficient cause comes from miracles. Because miracles obviously stem from the divine will, they indicate to us the less obvious element of divine will in natural events (*DE*, 5b). As an example, Bibago supposes a man born suddenly with fully developed faculties. This man would, says Bibago, think that the colors he saw were their own cause

99. On the philosopher's view that nature lacks intelligence and is guided by a higher intellectual principle, see Judah Halevi, *Sefer ha-Kuzari*, I.76–77; *Guide*, III:13, p. 17b; and H. A. Wolfson, "Hallevi and Maimonides on Design, Chance and Necessity," *PAAJR*, XI (1941), 135, 138, 141–42, 148–49, 154–58.
100. Deuteronomy 8:3.

until, failing to see them after sunset, he would realize that they require sunlight as well to be seen. In a similar way, miracles show us that natural causes by themselves are insufficient (*DE*, 5d–6a).[101]

On the other hand, since Bibago believes that God generally acts through intermediaries (*DE*, 96a), he carefully insists that this coefficiency of the divine will does not negate the existence of natural and voluntary intermediate causes in this world (*DE*, 7b).[102] As to how man's free will can be maintained along with this divine coefficiency, Bibago simply draws an analogy and says that, as the divine knowledge does not compromise the realm of possibility, so the divine will does not compromise man's free choice, although in both cases we are ignorant of how this comes about (*DE*, 7a–b).

This emphasis upon the direct agency of the divine will, which evidently goes back at least to Philo[103] and the Muslim Kalam, did not in all systems of thought allow for natural and voluntary intermediate causes as well. Maimonides says that the Muslim Ashʿariyya ascribed each atom in this world directly to the divine will and so denied natural and voluntary intermediate causes.[104] The neo-Augustinian Christian scholastics of the fourteenth century usually emphasized the divine coefficiency in all worldly events at the cost of man's absolute free will.[105] Judah Halevi, however, as Bibago was to do later, insists upon the direct agency of the divine will in this world as well as upon natural and voluntary intermediate causes. Although he emphasizes God's continuing maintenance of the universe through His will, he also

101. Bibago's example, which he says he took from the sage (*hakham*), is somewhat reminiscent of the stories in *Guide*, II:17, p. 35b, and in Ibn Sina's and Ibn Tufayl's *Hayy ibn Yaqzân*. In these latter instances, boys growing up on deserted islands acquire philosophy naturally on their own. In Maimonides' example, the boy's restricted experience leads him to make a gross error which helps Maimonides illustrate his point. Bibago's example differs in that a man is born with fully developed physical and mental powers, but as in Maimonides' example, his restricted experience leads him to make an error that illustrates Bibago's point.

102. Abraham Shalom feels that the inability to perpetuate themselves would indicate an imperfection in the things divinely created. He concludes, in agreement with Gersonides (*Sefer Milhamot ha-Shem*, VI.i.7), that it is not necessary for God to emanate the world constantly anew and that God's maintenance of the world in existence (evidently such as Bibago is speaking of) should be therefore distinguished from His constant reemanation of the world (*Sefer Neweh Shalom*, I.9–10, pp. 11a–12b). Cf. Davidson, *The Philosophy of Abraham Shalom*, p. 46. Shalom's remarks against the theory of the constant emanation of the world are directed, it should be noted, against Hasdai Crescas.

103. It has in fact been called Neophilonism. See H. A. Wolfson, "Causality and Freedom in Descartes, Leibniz and Hume," in his *Religious Philosophy*, pp. 196–98.

104. *Guide*, I:73 (sixth premise).

105. Cf. Oberman, *Archbishop Thomas Bradwardine*, pp. 57, 78–79; and Leff, *Bradwardine and the Pelagians*, p. 50. In this discussion I have borrowed the term "divine coefficiency" from Oberman. Leff uses the term "divine participation" to describe this concept.

says that God implanted in things the power of self-preservation and that this divine maintenance does not impair man's free choice.[106] Bibago followed Halevi in this respect.

The issue of the divine will seems to have been associated usually with the problem of the creation or eternity of the world. Al-Ghazali, for example, devoted so much of his defense of the doctrine of creation to a discussion of the divine will that Ibn Rushd accused him of changing the subject.[107] Also Maimonides, as we have seen, felt that the question of the eternity or creation of the world hinged upon its generation by necessity or by will.[108] Judah Moscato, the sixteenth-century commentator on the *Kuzari*, quotes a passage from Bibago's discussion of the divine will and adds that it comes from Bibago's discussion of creation.[109] Now Bibago certainly considered creation an axiom of the Torah (*DE*, 78d, 86d).[110] It would seem, however, that his protracted emphasis upon the maintenance of the universe by the divine will instead of upon its creation indicates that his basic theme in this discussion of the divine will and in the first third of his book is the divine providence, not creation.[111]

Bibago finally returns to the question that he had raised at the beginning of this first chapter, namely the final end of the divine actions. Final ends, says Bibago, are either the end served by the action or the end that the agent has in mind, for the two are not necessarily the same. For example, the garments made by a tailor will serve to clothe someone, but the end that the tailor has in mind is to make a profit. Since all natural works, not to speak of artificial ones, have a final end, the divine actions certainly serve a final end insofar as the actions themselves are concerned (*DE*, 7b–c). That all natural as well as artificial works have a final end was the view of Aristotle.[112] Aristotle him-

---

106. *Sefer ha-Kuzari*, IV.26, V.20. Most medieval Jewish philosophers maintained man's freedom of the will, but Hasdai Crescas, while admitting that the essence of the human will is its ability to do either of two opposites, followed Ibn Sina in regarding the human will as determined by external causes (*OH*, II.v.3). Don Isaac Abravanel and Abraham Shalom, Bibago's contemporaries, had already noted Crescas's dependence upon the Islamic philosophers in this regard. See Y. Guttmann, "Baᶜayat ha-Behirah ha-Hofshit be-Mishnatam shel Hasdai Crescas we-ha-'Aristotel'ayim ha-Muslemin," in his *Dat u-Maddaᶜ* (Jerusalem, 1956), pp. 149–50, 157–61. Crescas has often been classed with al-Ghazali and Judah Halevi because of his critique of Aristotelian philosophy. On the differences between them, however, see Guttmann, *Ha-Filosofiyah shel ha-Yahadut*, p. 207; and H. A. Wolfson, *Crescas' Critique of Aristotle* (Cambridge, Mass., 1929), pp. 11–18, on the question of whether or not Crescas was acquainted with al-Ghazali's *Tahâfut al-Falâsifah*. In regard to the divine will, however, as we have already seen, and now in regard to the human will, it seems that Crescas has certain affinities with Ibn Sina.

107. *TAT*, I, p. 36.

108. *Guide*, II:18–25.

109. *Qol Yehudah* on *Sefer ha-Kuzari*, II.5.

110. Bibago's discussion of creation is in *DE*, III.3, pp. 86b–89c.

111. Cf. above, n. 33.

112. *Physics*, II:8.

self did not associate this purely natural teleology with the conscious purpose of a higher being,[113] but it is usually assumed that later religious thought did associate this teleology with the conscious purpose of God.[114] Bibago's clear distinction between the final ends of natural works or the divine actions on the one hand and the final ends of the divine agent on the other seems to indicate that such an association between natural teleology and the divine purpose was not automatically and necessarily made even in the Middle Ages.

Having decided that the divine actions are for a final end, Bibago turns to the question of whether or not the divine agent acts for a final end. Either assumption would seem to imply a deficiency in God. If He does act for a final end, He would seem to lack that end, as we saw at the beginning of this chapter. If He does not act for a final end, His actions would be like those of an unintelligent being, which is absurd. The resolution of the problem depends upon the distinction between external and internal ends. It is only if an agent acts for an end external to himself that one can imply that the agent lacks that end. If, however, God acts for the sake of His own essence, this does not imply any deficiency in Him (*DE*, 7c).

This, Bibago concludes, solves our initial problem about the thirteenth chapter in the third part of the *Moreh Nevukhim*. Maimonides' intention there was to deny that the universe as a whole has a final end external to the essence of God. This denial is correct, for God's final end is His essence. Maimonides himself says in that chapter that the only final end of existence as a whole is the divine will or wisdom, which are identical with the divine essence.[115] Thomas Aquinas and Hasdai Crescas had also said that God's final end for this existence is His essence.[116]

In summary, we have seen that Bibago, in his first chapter, interprets Maimonides' concept of the divine will in an orthodox and conservative way in terms of the biblical-Philonic concept of a free divine will. Bibago's particular formulation of this concept, that the will can perform either of two

113. Wolfson, "Hallevi and Maimonides on Design, Chance and Necessity," p. 141. For a forceful statement of the view that Aristotle's teleology is purely natural and immanent and divorced from the conscious purpose of a divine artisan, see John H. Randall, Jr., *Aristotle*, 2nd ed. (New York, 1965), pp. 228–29.

114. Ibid. Maimonides says that final ends in nature are proof of a purposive being (*Guide*, III:13, p. 17b [Arabic: p. 324]). For an interpretation of this proof based on a meaning that differs from the meaning the passage appears to have, see Wolfson, "Hallevi and Maimonides on Design, Chance and Necessity," p. 154. Abraham Shalom had interpreted this passage in Maimonides according to its apparent meaning and said that final ends indicate an agent that acts by will, not necessity (*Sefer Neweh Shalom*, I.9, p. 9b).

115. *Guide*, III:13, p. 18b (Arabic: pp. 326–27).

116. *ST*, I.xix.1, obj. 1 and reply; *OH*, II.vi.5, p. 60b; and III, introduction, p. 61b. Spinoza, in the appendix to Part I of his *Ethics*, rejects this solution of the problem.

opposite actions, can be found in the Muslim Kalam and was emphasized among the scholastics by Duns Scotus. On the basis of four rational proofs and on the basis of tradition as well, Bibago specifically denies that God acts necessarily through knowledge alone, as Ibn Sina contended. Later Averroists had interpreted Ibn Rushd in this manner and had said that the divine agency acting necessarily through knowledge was intermediate between a natural and a voluntary agency.

In addition, Bibago may have been arguing against those more voluntarist philosophers such as Crescas who, utilizing the Greek concept of a relatively free will, had followed Augustine in combining both will and necessity. Bibago further emphasized that the divine will had a purpose and final end, and we have seen that this interpretation of Maimonides opposes not only the philosophers but also the Muslim Ashʿariyya, according to whom the divine will has no final end. Finally, although Maimonides' primary discussion of will and necessity is in relation to the problem of the creation or eternity of the world, Bibago's long discussion of the coefficiency of the divine will in all worldly events, even man's free choice, indicates that Bibago's primary concern is with the divine providence. Divine providence was of major concern to Bibago's contemporaries and to the succeeding generations that endured the expulsion from Spain. Bibago's defense of the absolute freedom of the divine will laid the groundwork for his philosophy of comfort and faith.

Maggidic Revelation in the Teachings of Isaac Luria

Lawrence Fine

Isaac Luria (1534–72) ranks among the most extraordinary and influential personalities that Judaism has produced. Besides being regarded as the greatest Kabbalist of sixteenth-century Safed, Luria's original mystical doctrines and practices were of fundamental importance to virtually all Jewish mystical creativity after him. Lurianism spread throughout the Jewish world and by 1650 had established its supremacy. Lurianic Kabbalah contributed vitally to the Sabbatian and Hasidic movements—neither of which can be adequately understood outside of its relationship to Luria. The immense role of Lurianic Kabbalah is particularly remarkable in light of Luria's short life of thirty-eight years—only two of which were spent in Safed.

Though born in Jerusalem, Luria moved to Egypt after the death of his father. In Egypt, Luria studied with David b. Solomon Zimra and Besalel Ashkenazi. Together with Ashkenazi, Luria wrote several halachic works such as the *Shitah Mequbbetzet* on the talmudic tractate *Zevahim* and annotations to some of Isaac Alfasi's works. While still in Egypt, Isaac Luria undertook the study of Kabbalah, secluding himself on the island Jazirat al-Rawda on the Nile. During this period he apparently studied *Zohar* and other early Kabbalistic texts. In 1569, or early 1570, Luria emigrated to Safed and began to study Kabbalah with Moses Cordovero (1522–70), the community's leading mystical teacher.

It is possible that even before Cordovero's death in the fall of 1570, Luria may have begun teaching on his own to a small group of disciples. In any case, following Cordovero's death Luria attracted a circle of students which included Hayyim Vital (1543–1620), who became his most important follower. Luria's circle, approximately thirty-five of whose members' names we know, was an elite group which engaged in both exoteric and Kabbalistic studies. Luria was a mystical master in the strict sense. He imparted esoteric wisdom to a select group of persons, vouchsafing to each of them mystical knowledge pertinent to their particular soul. Luria was able to inform them of such important matters as the ancestry of their souls and the specific meditations appropriate to their soul-status. They engaged in mystical practices and liturgical exercises unique to their group, the secrets of which they carefully guarded. As indicated, Luria's activities in Safed were exceedingly brief as he died in an epidemic on July 15, 1572.

I

The phenomenon of maggidism which developed within Kabbalistic communities in the sixteenth century constitutes an extremely interesting example of mystical experience. This study seeks to elucidate the theory of maggidic revelation in the teachings of Isaac Luria. The sources for our knowledge of Luria's doctrine of maggidism are *Sha'ar Ruah ha-Qodesh* and *Sha'ar ha-Yihudim*,[1] versions of his teachings formulated by Hayyim Vital.

Luria's doctrine of the *maggid* is associated from the start with the attainment of the holy spirit and prophecy. *Sha'ar Ruah ha-Qodesh* begins with a promise to explain the matter of the holy spirit and prophecy and their various aspects.[2] Likewise, Vital in his own Kabbalistic treatise, *Sha'are Qedushah*, deals with maggidism within a discussion of how to achieve inspiration.[3] Thus, an analysis of the maggidic doctrine will lead at the same time to an understanding of the Lurianic notion of prophetic illumination.

Earlier Kabbalists tended to identify the path leading to *devequt* (cleaving to God) with that of prophecy. No clear distinction is drawn between the prophet and the mystic. The goals of each are the same. Perhaps the finest example of this view is set forth by the thirteenth-century Kabbalist, Azriel of Gerona. According to Azriel in his *Perush ha-'Aggadot*, the contemplative mystic who cleaves with his mind to the "nothingness of thought" in the divine world above, is likened to the prophet who receives unique revelation and mystical knowledge.[4] Just as the levels of mystical ascension vary, likewise the degrees of prophetic inspiration. In his *Sha'ar ha-Kawwanah la-Mequbbalim ha-Rishonim*, Azriel claims that just as the hasidim of an earlier time, described in *Berakhot* 5a, were capable of achieving prophecy through contemplative practice, so too prophecy is possible in our time. The ultimate effect of contemplative practice is the attainment of prophetic qualities.[5]

1. All references to *Sha'ar Ruah ha-Qodesh* (hereafter *SRQ*) are to the Yehuda Ashlag edition of the *Shemonah She'arim* (Tel Aviv, 1962). All references to *Sha'ar ha-Yihudim* (hereafter *SY*) are to the edition by Meqor Hayyim (Jerusalem, 1970).
2. *SRQ*, p. 9a.
3. *Sha'are Qedushah* (Jerusalem, 1926), Part 3, gate VII.
4. I. Tishby, ed., *Perush ha-'Aggadot* (Jerusalem, 1945), p. 40.
5. This text is found in G. Scholem, *Reshit ha-Qabbalah* (Tel Aviv, 1948), pp. 143–44; German translation and commentary in his *Ursprung und Anfänge der Kabbala* (Berlin, 1962), pp. 369–73.

Nahmanides in his commentary on Deuteronomy 11:22 defines *devequt* as remembering God and His love constantly. In his *Sha'ar ha-Gemul* he confirms that those who cleave to God in this way are rewarded as Moses and the other prophets with the holy spirit.[6] Similarly, Isaac of Acre delineates a detailed process of contemplative ascent in which the adept achieves prophetic inspiration by passing through the stages of "cleaving," "equanimity," and "solitude."[7] Clearly, Luria's equation of certain kinds of mystical experience with the attainment of prophetic inspiration has deep roots in Kabbalistic tradition.

For Isaac Luria one of the means of achieving the holy spirit or the state of prophecy was by meriting angelic revelations in the form of a *maggid*. A *maggid*, according to Hayyim Vital, is the progeny of a man's actions. It is dissimilar to other forms of divine revelation in that its creation is the direct result of a person's spiritual activities. Specifically, a *maggid* is a product of study of Torah, and of piety and prayer accompanied by mystical intentions. Thus, we read the following in *Sha'ar ha-Yihudim*: ". . . when a man is righteous and pious, studies Torah, and prays with [Kabbalistic] intention, from those sounds which emerge from his mouth, angels and holy spirits are created. . . . And these angels created from that which a man utters are the secret of *maggidim*."[8] *Maggidim*, then, are angelic creations whose existence is brought about by the sounds of a man's voice uttered in the course of religious devotion such as prayer or study. Intrinsic to Kabbalistic ontology is the belief that everything below is connected to everything above and that everything below *acts upon* everything above. It is this fundamental assertion which endows Kabbalistic devotion, whether it be prayer, ritual, or ethical deeds, with sacred and cosmic significance. In applying this microcosmic-macrocosmic rule to the creation of angelic beings, its quasi-magical implications are laid bare. This alone, however, does not explain how a man's speech issues in celestial beings—a matter whose mythical basis is more complex and to which we shall return shortly.

Vital asserts that angels of varying sorts are brought about depending upon the *nature* of a man's speech and deeds: "As they [the Rabbis] said: He that performs one *mitzwah* obtains for himself one advocate etc. (*Avot* 4:11.) For from man's speech good or evil angels are created, according to [the quality of] his speech."[9] Vital cites *Mishnah Avot* 4:11, the second part of which is a

6. *Sha'ar ha-Gemul*, end of chap. 8.
7. On Isaac of Acre's theory of contemplation, see E. Gottlieb, "Communion with God and Prophecy in *'Otzar Hayyim* by Isaac ben Samuel of Acre" [Hebrew], in *Fourth World Congress of Jewish Studies* (Jerusalem, 1968), II, 327–39.
8. *SY*, p. 2a.
9. *SRQ*, p. 9a.

key to understanding the influence a man's deeds exert upon the character of the maggidic creation. It reads: "But he that commits one transgression obtains for himself one accuser." Thus, the quality of the *maggid* depends directly on the quality of a man's actions. Evil or inadequate deeds are just as powerful as righteous ones. Their enactment produces *maggidim* whose composition is fused with good and evil elements. Consequently, nothing that emerges from a man's mouth is without potential significance:

> Indeed, everything is according to the action of a man, for if that Torah which a man studies is read for the sake of heaven, the angel created thereby will be extremely pure and supernal, and all its words can be believed as utter truth. And thus, if he reads it without error or mistakes, this angel will be without error, and all its words will be trustworthy. And thus the *mitzwah* [commandment] a man performs, if it is properly done, a very pure angel will be produced. . . . And indeed, it is certain that the power of an angel produced from the study of Torah is greater than the power of an angel produced by means of a *mitzwah*.[10]

There are some persons who are not privileged to receive maggidic communications at all: "There are men to whom these *maggidim* are not revealed at all, and there are those to whom they are revealed. Everything depends on the nature of their soul, or their deeds. . . ."[11]

The supernal world from which the *maggidim* derive is also related to the nature of the deeds a man performs. *Maggidim* created from good deeds performed without appropriate *kawwanah* (lit., "intention") have their source in the world of ʿAsiyyah, whereas those brought about through study of Torah are from the higher world of *Yetzirah*. The most exalted *maggidim* originate in the world of Beriʾah and are created by means of study of Torah or the performance of a *mitzwah* accompanied by *kawwanah*.[12] Vital reports that Isaac Luria told him how to determine the truthfulness or reliability of a *maggid*:

> And the criterion that my teacher, may his memory be blessed, gave me [consists in this:] if we see that all his [the Kabbalist's] words are truthful; if all his words are for the sake of heaven, and if he does not nullify a single letter of his words; also, if he is able to explain the mysteries of the

10. Ibid., pp. 9a–b. Cf. *Sefer ha-Gilgulim* (Frankfurt, 1684), p. 32b.
11. *SRQ*, p. 9b. Cf. *SY*, pp. 2a–b.
12. *SRQ*, p. 10a. Based on earlier Kabbalistic sources the Kabbalists of Safed adopted the doctrine of four worlds placed between the 'En-Sof and the earthly cosmos. They are: 'Atzilut, the world of emanation and the highest realms of divinity; Beriʾah, and world of creation, i.e., of the Throne, the Merkavah, and the highest angels; Yetzirah, the world of formation, the chief dwelling place of the angels; and ʿAssiyah, the world of making, the terrestrial world.

Torah and its secrets—certainly such [a man's *maggid*] we can believe in. And according to his words we can determine and recognize his greatness and according to his knowledge [we can recognize] his rank.[13]

In other words, a man must be truthful and able to explain esoteric secrets if his *maggid* is to be considered trustworthy. Moreover, the status of a man's *maggid* can be determined by the wondrous and hidden nature of the Kabbalistic secrets he can reveal.[14]

Exactly how does a *maggid* manifest himself and what are the dynamics of his operation? The angelic communicator which Luria propounded makes himself known through vocalization. The process consists of two parts, each of which requires the adept's own vocal functions. First, the voice that a man utters while engaged in study of Torah or mystical prayer ascends above, thereby creating a *maggid*. At a later point in time this created spiritual voice descends below by "clothing" itself in the mystic's current voice— again, during the course of his speaking while in prayer or study. This second moment constitutes a state of prophetic inspiration in which the *maggid* speaks through the adept's own voice, enabling him to perceive the revelation:

> And here is the secret of prophecy and the holy spirit. It is assuredly a voice sent from above to speak with this prophet, or with this man endowed with the holy spirit. But this same supernal spiritual voice cannot by itself materialize and enter the ears of this prophet unless it first clothes itself in his physical voice which emerges from this man's mouth when, at a given moment [*ʿatah*], he studies Torah or prays and the like. And then it [i.e., the supernal voice] clothes itself in it, [i.e., the physical voice] joining it and comes to the ear of this prophet who [then] hears it. And without the man's own present physical voice it cannot achieve existence.[15]

Vital's description stresses the necessity of vocalization through the actual speaking voice of the adept. The celestial voice requires material incarnation by means of the mystic's own physical utterance during the moment of prophetic inspiration. There is a distinction here in time between the act creating the *maggid*, and the reincarnation of the voice at a later moment in time. This is clearly an experience of automatic speech, a form of motor automatism, in which words begin to issue from the Kabbalist's voice with-

---

13. Ibid. Cf. *SY*, p. 2b.
14. *SY*, p. 2b.
15. *SRQ*, p. 10a.

out prior reflection. A passage in *Shaʿar Ruah ha-Qodesh* explicitly attests to this:

> This is the secret [explanation] of the verse in II Samuel 23:2: "The spirit of the Lord speaks by me and His word is upon my tongue." For the spirit and the word which is the first speech [i.e., the supernal speech], already created through study of Torah and performance of a *mitzwah* as described above, rests at this moment on him upon his tongue. And voice and speech actually issue from his mouth, and truly speak through his mouth. And the man then hears it.[16]

There is a second way in which the celestial voice that a man creates can function. It is possible for the maggidic voice to join with the voice of a departed Zaddik (righteous person) in the world above. These two voices, having merged, then descend and speak through the voice of the adept. The Zaddik whose voice joins the celestial voice can also be "of our time." This refers to a contemporary who has recently departed rather than an actual living person. Vital describes the second process in this way:

> It [the maggidic communication] is also possible another way: That celestial voice will clothe itself in the voice of other early Zaddikim who preceded him, either from the period of the early Rabbis or those of our present time. And the two will unite and will come and speak with him. . . . But know that it is impossible for the voice or speech or breath of another Zaddik to speak with him unless that Zaddik is from the [same] soul-root of this present man. Or unless the *mitzwah* performed by this man is in accordance with this Zaddik's character. And by means of one of these two conditions [the voice of the *maggid*] will come and rest upon him in the manner described.[17]

The idea that some persons have common soul-roots or that certain *mitzwot* correspond to particular souls, is based on Lurianic teachings concerning man's psychic structure. According to Luria, Adam's soul contained within it, as the *Midrash* records, all of the souls of mankind.[18] Each of the 613 "limbs" of Adam's soul, corresponding to the same number of *mitzwot*,[19]

---

16. Ibid., pp. 10a–b. Cf. *SY*, pp. 2b–c.

17. *SRQ*, p. 10b. Cf. *SY*, p. 2c.

18. This motif goes back to *Midrash Tanhuma, Ki Tissa*, 12, and *Pequde*, 3, and *Exodus Rabbah*, 40. Cf. L. Ginzberg, *The Legends of the Jews*, 7 vols. (Philadelphia, 1909–38), V, 75. See the discussion on this Lurianic motif in G. Scholem, *Von der mystischen Gestalt der Gottheit* (Zurich, 1962), pp. 226 ff.

19. The parallelism of *mitzwot* and limbs of the body goes back to the Talmud. *Makkot* 23b records that the 365 negative *mitzwot* correspond to the number of days in the year and the 248 positive *mitzwot* correspond to the number of man's limbs. Similarly, *Targum Jonathan ben Uziel* on

formed a complete *partzuf* (sefirotic configuration) known as a *shoresh gadol* ("great root"). Each of these contained, in turn, 613, or as some versions have it, 600,000 "small roots." The pertinent point for our consideration is that souls descending from a single "small root" comprise "families" having special relations of attraction and affinity for one another. Because of this, souls having a common root are capable of uplifting one another from the realm of material existence. Knowledge of one's soul-root is of extreme importance as it enables a man to restore his soul to its supernal source through communion with a fellow soul who has departed this world. Such sympathy of souls makes possible the joining of a man's *maggid* with the angelic voice of a departed Zaddik. Similarly, it explains why the performance of a particular *mitzwah*, which has its source in an individual "limb," can facilitate the communion of two celestial voices. Every soul has its source in a particular root which, in turn, is the place of special *mitzwot*.

Vital distinguishes three aspects of vocal utterance and their corresponding celestial creations: *qol* (voice), *dibbur* (speech), and *hevel* (breath). Depending upon the status of his soul and the quality of his actions, a person's utterance can manifest itself in any of these aspects.[20] While a supernal *qol* that a person has originally aroused can garb itself, at a later point in time, in the *qol* of his current physical voice, a supernal *dibbur* in the current *dibbur* and so on, a variety of other combinations are also possible. Thus, for example, a supernal *qol* can descend and clothe itself in the current *dibbur* of an individual, or a supernal *hevel* can invest itself in a current *dibbur*. In addition, Vital introduces the notion that a *qol*, *dibbur*, or *hevel* "of the past" can descend at a *later* moment of prophetic inspiration.[21] Inasmuch as every previously created *maggid* manifests itself at some later point in time, the term "of the past" must refer to a celestial *maggid* which materializes at a point *long* after it was originally created.

Based on these distinctions our sources delineate a hierarchy of prophecy and the holy spirit. *Hevel* is the lowest grade of revelation and has its source in the *Sefirah Malkhut*. *Dibbur* is the next highest grade, its source being a

---

Gen. 1:27 draws a parallel between the 613 *mitzwot* and the supposed 613 parts of the human body. This theme is also taken up by the author of the *Zohar*, I, 170b. This correspondence is pronounced in *Sefer Ta'ame ha-Mitzwot* (ca. 1290–1300), a work on the reasons for the commandments erroneously ascribed to Isaac ibn Farhi, which A. Altmann has shown to have been written by Joseph of Hamadan (*KS*, XL, nos. 2–3 [1965] 256–76, 405–12). Cf. in particular the motif expressed in the phrase "limb supports limb" (*'ever mahaziq 'ever*) (ibid., p. 275). The full text has been edited by Menahem Meier, "A Critical Edition of the *Sefer Ta'ame ha-Mitzwot* [A 'Book of Reasons for the Commandments'] Attributed to Isaac ibn Farhi/Section I—Positive Commandments/with Notes and Introduction" (Ph.D. diss., Brandeis University, 1974).

20. *SRQ*, p. 10b.
21. Ibid., p. 11a.

combination of *Tif'eret* and *Malkhut*. The most exalted type of celestial communication is through the utterance of *qol* whose origin is in *Tif'eret* alone. Whereas prophecy has its origin in the male aspect of the Godhead, that of the holy spirit derives from the female aspect. Inasmuch as *qol* is related to *Tif'eret* (male) and *dibbur* to *Tif'eret* and *Malkhut* (male and female), Luria defines prophecy as consisting in the descent of the *qol* or *dibbur* which invests itself in any of the three aspects of man's current physical voice.[22] The holy spirit, on the other hand, manifests itself when a supernal *hevel* clothes itself in any of the other three aspects. In either the attainment of prophecy or the holy spirit, one whose celestial *maggid* descends directly, without first uniting with the *qol, dibbur,* or *hevel* of a departed Zaddik, is of a superior grade.

Our texts do not shed much light on the substantive distinction between prophecy and the holy spirit.[23] They are two degrees of the inspired state of which prophecy is the greater achievement. Prophecy, as we have seen, is tied here to the male side of the Godhead. This is exemplified in the case of Moses who achieved the level of *qol*. This, according to Vital, means that he prophesied through the "luminous mirror" (*aspeqlariah ha-me'irah*). All the other prophets gained their inspiration from the "non-luminous mirror" (*aspeqlariah she-'eyna me'irah*). These two terms refer respectively to the *Sefirot Tif'eret* and *Malkhut*.[24] This view is in accord with that of earlier Kabbalists who, basing themselves on rabbinic passages in which Moses is said to have prophesied by virtue of *aspeqlariah ha-me'irah*, identified this term with the *Sefirah Tif'eret*.[25] Bahya b. Asher, apparently following Ezra of Gerona, records such a tradition.[26] Similarly, Azriel of Gerona, in his *Perush ha-'Aggadot*, indicates that Moses prophesied through *Tif'eret* as well as lower *Sefirot*.[27] The

---

22. Ibid.

23. Dunash ibn Tamim, in his commentary to the *Sefer Yetzirah*, distinguishes among three types of prophecy, reflecting the theory of his teacher, Isaac Israeli (tenth century). Whereas Luria applies the term *qol* to the highest form of inspiration, Ibn Tamim uses it to refer to the lowest form which is "a voice which God creates in the air and which He directs to the ear of him who merits to hear it." Similarly, Israeli's contemporary, Saadya Gaon, interprets the biblical phrase "God spoke" as meaning that God "created a speech, which, through the medium of the air, reached the ear of the prophet or people." A second type of prophecy, according to Ibn Tamim, is *ruah*, while the highest type is *dibbur*. This level of inspiration was attained by Moses, as seen in the biblical passage, "God spoke unto him face to face" (Ex. 33:11; Num. 12:8). Ibn Tamim views *dibbur* as a reference to the "union" of Moses' soul with the supernal light. See A. Altmann and S. M. Stern, *Isaac Israeli* (Oxford, 1958), pp. 209 ff. On Saadya's theory of "created voice," see A. Altmann, "Saadya's Theory of Revelation," in his *Studies in Religious Philosophy and Mysticism* (Ithaca, N.Y., 1969), pp. 155 ff.

24. *SRQ*, p. 12a.

25. See *Yevamot* 49b, and *Leviticus Rabbah*, 1:14. Cf. *Sanhedrin* 97b, and *Sukkah* 45b.

26. E. Gottlieb, *Ha-Qabbalah be-Kitve Rabbenu Bahya ben Asher* (Jerusalem, 1970), pp. 38–39.

27. Tishby, ed., *Perush ha-'Aggadot*, p. 7.

Zohar reports that Moses prophesied through *aspeqlariah ha-me'irah* which is *Tif'eret*, as opposed to all other prophets whose divine source was the *aspeqlariah she-'eyna me'irah*, that is, *Shekhinah* or *Malkhut* which has no light of Her own.[28]

The various prophets of Israel can be ranked by means of these criteria. The greatest prophet of all, of course, was Moses. According to Luria, his preeminence derives from the fact that his own celestial *qol*, without uniting itself with that of another Zaddik, clothed itself in his physical *qol*. That is, his prophecy was of the highest possible type and was the result of direct communication. Moses did, however, prophesy from lower levels of inspiration as well.[29] Following Moses on the ladder of prophetic exaltedness is Samuel whose actions produced a *qol* which invested itself in his physical *dibbur*. No other prophets, according to Luria, achieved such supreme levels of prophetic illumination. Of all those to have attained the inspiration of the holy spirit, King David stands above the rest. His deeds created a *hevel* which at a later point in time manifested itself in his physical *hevel*. As with Moses, David's maggidic communication was achieved without the assistance of another Zaddik.[30]

II

Isaac Luria's primary literary source for the development of his theory of maggidic revelation is the *Zohar*. Both *Sha'ar Ruah ha-Qodesh* and *Sha'ar ha-Yihudim* allude to several Zoharic texts in the context of discussing the maggidic phenomenon. An examination of some of these sources will elucidate the mystical background of the Lurianic doctrine. In describing the relationship between a man's deeds and the creation of a *maggid*, Vital refers to a passage in *Zohar Beshallah* 59a.[31] R. Jose is discoursing on the question of how King Solomon, in Ecclesiastes 1:2, could possibly have asserted that all human actions are vanity (*hevel*). He explains the meaning of *hevel* as a 'breath' that produces a voice on high:

> And these *havalim* are the basis of the world above and below. . . . It has been explained in the following way, and it is truly so. At the moment that proper actions are done, and a man seeks to serve the Holy King,

28. *Zohar*, II, 23b. Cf. Moses de Leon, *Sheqel ha-Qodesh*, ed. A. W. Greenup (London, 1911), pp. 123–24.
29. *SRQ*, p. 11a.
30. Ibid., p. 11b.
31. Ibid., p. 9a.

from that word [that is spoken below] a breath is produced in the world above. And there is no breath which has no voice; and this voice ascends and crowns itself in the supernal world and becomes an intercessor before the Holy One, blessed be He. [Contrariwise,] every action which is not done with this purpose becomes a breath which floats about in the world, and when the soul of the doer leaves his body, this breath rolls about like a stone in a sling. . . . But the act done and the word spoken in the service of the Holy One, ascends high above the sun and becomes a holy breath. . . .[32]

In this passage the *Zohar* asserts the principle which forms the basis for Luria's own conception. Every human action produces a supernal voice which, depending upon the deed and the intention with which it is performed, benefits a man or functions destructively. In the Zoharic schema, however, the holy breath becomes an advocate before God on behalf of the individual. Rather than return to man for the purpose of communication, as in the Lurianic doctrine, this breath guides the soul of the departed to the region of supernal glory. Other Zoharic texts, however, come even closer to Luria's conception.

In *Zohar Lekh Lekha* we learn that it is angels who hover above prepared to grasp any voice they hear and are ready to carry it away to be judged.[33] But it is in *Tiqqune Zohar* that an actual identification between angels and voices is established.[34] Here we find the notion of heavenly voices manifesting themselves as angels. A rabbinic passage in *Hagigah* states that every speech of the Holy One, blessed be He, creates an angel.[35] In *Shaʿar ha-Pesuqim* of the *Shemonah Sheʿarim*, Vital quotes this passage while alluding to *Tiqqune Zohar* where Exodus 20:15 is interpreted in relation to the *Hagigah* text:

And this is the secret meaning of the sages' statement "there is no speech which emerges from God's mouth which does not create an angel" (*Hagigah* 14a). And this is the matter of the breath and the voice which issue from His mouth at the moment of the supernal union of kissing as mentioned above.[36] This is what Scripture said ["By the word of the Lord were the heavens made] and all the host of them by the breath of His mouth" (Psalms 33:6). And these are the angels which are called voices as mentioned in the book of *Tiqqunim* on the verse "and all the people

32. *Zohar*, II, 59a. Cf. *Zohar*, II, 10b; I, 146b (*Sitre Torah*).
33. Ibid., I, 92a.
34. *Tiqqune Zohar* (ed. Livorno, 1795), 79a.
35. *Hagigah* 14a.
36. Luria explains that angels are incorporeal inasmuch as they result from supernal coupling which is purely spiritual. This coupling is known as "kissing" (*Shaʿar ha-Pesuqim*, 54a–b).

perceived the thunderings" [lit. voices] (Ex. 20:15). And more important, we know that even from man's speech other angels are created, both good and evil.[37]

Based on the *Hagigah* text, the author of *Tiqqune Zohar* identifies the voices of Exodus 20:15 with angels which are heard by the Israelites. God's breath or voice is actually an angelic revelation. Drawing upon this motif, Luria carries the idea a significant step forward. According to him, man's *own* utterance is similarly capable of creating angels. Just as God's speech creates angels, so a man's speech likewise brings about angels which communicate with him. Herein lies Luria's innovative conception. Combining two Zoharic themes— to wit, that man's actions produce holy voices and that God's speech creates angels—Luria fashions a theory whereby each action below generates a holy voice, i.e., an angelic *maggid*, whose purpose is to reveal Kabbalistic mysteries to its progenitor.

The germ of the notion that the angelic voice returns in order to communicate with man is also found in the Zoharic literature. Vital cites *Tiqqun 22* of *Tiqqune Zohar* which states that the voices and breaths of man while engaged in study of Torah become chariots to the souls of the righteous.[38] These voices descend in order to teach this man Torah. In *Zohar Shelah Lekha* explicit reference is made to a celestial voice which a man's utterance has produced. Rav Metivta (the fictitious "head of the Academy") is asked by Rabbi Simeon b. Yohai a question regarding new mystical secrets of which he may be ignorant:

> He [R. Simeon] said to him: "Do you know something new of which I am unaware?" He said to him: "Speak." He [R. Simeon] said to him: "I want to know [about] the voice that returns. A man speaks out aloud in a field or another place, and a voice returns [to him] and he does not know [where it comes from.] He replied: "If he is a holy saint, by virtue of this [speaking out aloud] a number of voices are aroused.[39]

In light of the other Zoharic texts we have discussed, it appears likely that "the voice that returns" in this passage refers to the heavenly voices and breaths aroused by a man's righteous activities. The nature of the communication is left undefined.

Thus, there is a variety of themes in the literature of the *Zohar* upon which the Lurianic theory of maggidism draws. Utilizing these motifs, Luria expounds a specific magico-mystical process whose purpose is the revelation of

37. Ibid., 54b.
38. *Tiqqune Zohar*, 64b.
39. *Zohar*, III, 168b.

esoteric Kabbalistic knowledge. Entirely innovative, however, is the notion that the maggidic voice speaks through the Kabbalist's own voice by means of automatic speech. To shed light on this extraordinary phenomenon we shall have to take into account the occurrences of maggidism prior to Isaac Luria.

III

Maggidism was already a known occurrence by the time Luria arrived in Safed. Both the term[40] and the experience were sufficiently commonplace for Vital to speak of it as a well-known matter: "This is the matter of the angels which reveal themselves to man, telling them of the future and [Kabbalistic] secrets, and are called in books *maggidim*."[41]

The first instance of an experience akin to maggidism of which we are aware is that of R. Joseph Taitatzak. Taitatzak stands out as a renowned scholar and a central personality among the Kabbalists of Salonika.[42] A recently discovered manuscript contains maggidic-type revelations received by Taitatzak.[43] The revelations were possibly recorded in Spain shortly before 1492. The text, entitled *Sefer ha-Meshiv*, discloses that the communications received by Taitatzak were related to him, not by an angel or other celestial intermediary, but by God himself. Furthermore, the experiences involved the highly unusual occurrence of automatic writing.[44]

The best known experience of maggidism is that of R. Joseph Karo (1488–1575). There is evidence that Karo knew and was influenced by Taitatzak while he was still in Turkey.[45] It is also clear that Karo was acquainted with Taitatzak's maggidic experiences.[46] Karo met Taitatzak most probably in Salonika where he also entered into the acquaintance of Solomon Alkabetz (1505–76). It is in an account of an experience during a *Shavuʿot* vigil in about

---

40. The earliest use of the noun *maggid* as a technical term may be in Rashi's (1040–1105) commentary to *Pesahim* 105b, on the word "*hozaʾah*." In this context the use of the word *maggid* means the visionary himself, not the angelic communicator as in our texts. According to R. J. Z. Werblowsky, Rashi's use of it in this way seems to suggest that the origin of the term might be found in the literature of the German Hasidim (*Joseph Karo: Lawyer and Mystic* [Oxford, 1962], p. 265, n. 2). It is interesting that Vital mentions in *SY*, p. 2a, that it is these angels (i.e., the *maggidim*) which are spoken of in the *Sefer Hasidim*. The word *maggid* does not appear, however, in any of the extant texts of the work.

41. *SRQ*, p. 9b.

42. Concerning Joseph Taitatzak, see Werblowsky, *Karo*, passim.

43. *Sefer ha-Meshiv*. G. Scholem has described this text in *Sefunot*, XI (1973), 67–112.

44. For other examples of automatic writing, see G. Scholem, *EJ*, X, 637.

45. Werblowsky, *Karo*, pp. 90, 118–19.

46. Ibid., p. 118.

1530 that we learn from Alkabetz of Karo's visitations by a *maggid*-angel.[47] The revelations appear to have consisted in exhortations, spiritual advice, flattering praise of Karo, and the communication of Kabbalistic explanations on biblical passages. The *maggid*, speaking through Karo's mouth and enabling others who were present to hear it, manifested itself following the study of *mishnayyot*. Such maggidic visitations continued throughout Joseph Karo's life. Instructed by his *maggid* to record the communications, Karo composed a diary called *Sefer ha-Maggid*, of which a large portion has survived under the title *Maggid Mesharim*.[48] The *maggid* would come to Karo at different hours of the day and night, although the most propitious time was after midnight, in the early morning, especially on Sabbath mornings. The diligent and continuous study and repetition of the *mishnayyot*, as well as ascetic exercises and austere practices, induced the revelations. The following words of Karo's *maggid* suggest the conditions under which he made his appearance:

> "Yet by the merits of the six orders of the *Mishnah* which thou knowest by heart and by the merit of the mortifications and austerities which thou has practised in former days and also now, it has been decided in the Celestial Academy that I return to speak unto thee as before, not to leave thee and not to forsake thee. . . . Therefore, my son, hearken unto my voice whatever I command thee and devote thyself always, day and night without interruption, to my *Torah*; think of no worldly thing but only of *Torah*, of the fear of me, and of my *Mishnayoth*." Then I slept again for about half an hour and awoke with grief saying, "Now the speech has been interrupted because I fell asleep," and I recited [more] *Mishnayyoth*. [Then] the voice of my beloved [again] knocketh in my mouth, saying, "Thou shouldst know that God and the whole Celestial Academy send thee [the greeting of] peace and have sent me unto thee to reveal unto thee the works of God."[49]

A comparison of Karo's experiences and the Lurianic theory we have delineated is instructive. Whereas according to the Lurianic doctrine maggidic revelation results from the study of Torah, prayer and the mystical performance of *mitzwot*, Karo's messenger is induced specifically by the study

47. Alkabetz's account of this event is recorded in Isaiah Horowitz's *Shne Luhot ha-Berit, Massekhet Shavu'ot* (Feurth, 1764), pp. 180–81. This account was primarily responsible for the widespread knowledge of Karo's *maggid* in later times.

48. The first edition of this book was published in Lublin, 1646. Concerning the history of the work's circulation and publication, see Werblowsky, *Karo*, chap. 3.

49. *Maggid Mersharim*, p. 2a. We have used the translation of this passage by Werblowsky in *Karo*, pp. 257–58. For another example of the use of *Mishnah* for contemplative purposes, see my article, "Recitation of Mishnah as a Vehicle for Mystical Inspiration: A Contemplative Technique Taught by Hayyim Vital," *REJ*, forthcoming.

of *mishnayyot* and acts of mortification. In both instances the *maggid* manifests himself by means of automatic speech. Karo's *maggid* is, however, at least during his Safed period, also the *Mishnah* personified, speaking through Karo's mouth. In both situations the function of the *maggid* is to expound upon and reveal Kabbalistic mysteries, as well as foretell the future. In Karo's case there is a significant additional set of functions. His *maggid* acts as a superego who praises him for his proper behavior, purity of thought, ascetic practices, and study of *mishnayyot*, while admonishing him when he fails to meet these high standards. He is often reprimanded for having overslept and not studied, or for having relaxed his austere life-style.[50] Finally, just as the quality of one's *maggid*, according to Luria, depends on the quality of the mystic's actions, similarly the fluency of Karo's involuntary speech was contingent upon his behavior. Karo is told that stammering or mistakes made by the *maggid* are due to his worldly thoughts during prayer.[51]

There is ample evidence that Hayyim Vital, and no doubt Luria himself knew of Karo's *maggid*. In *Sefer ha-Gilgulim* Vital writes that the *maggid* has led Karo astray with regard to the former incarnations of Karo's son's soul.[52] Vital records in his mystical diary called *Sefer ha-Hezyonot*,[53] in the year 1557, that Karo's *maggid* had declared that half of the world existed because of the merits of Vital's father, a famous scribe who wrote "*tefillin* in holiness," and the other half existed through Vital's own merits.[54] We also learn from *Sefer ha-Hezyonot* that Moses Alsheikh, Karo's disciple and Vital's teacher in exoteric studies, was told by the *maggid* to teach his pupil (Vital) well, as he would someday assume Joseph Karo's place.[55] This passage instructs us not only in Vital's ambitions and his conviction that Alsheikh received a communication from Karo's *maggid*, but also in the faith that Vital had in the prophetic character of Karo's mentor.

Another important source for knowledge of Kabbalistic Safed is the hagiographical work of Solomon Schlomel Dresnitz, published under the title *Shivhe ha-'Ari* (*Praise of the Lion*).[56] Dresnitz preserves the following tradition

50. Ibid., pp. 278–79.
51. Ibid., pp. 262–63.
52. *Sefer ha-Gilgulim* (Przsemysl, 1876), p. 87b.
53. See Werblowsky, *Karo*, p. 15, n. 4. Vital gathered autobiographical notes and diary material including dreams and stories testifying to his greatness and the superiority of his soul. It was compiled while he was in Damascus, primarily between the years 1609 and 1612. The edition by A. Z. Aeschcoly is based on an autograph manuscript of Vital's.
54. *Sefer ha-Hezyonot*, p. 2.
55. Ibid.
56. Dresnitz arrived in Safed in the year 1602 and met many of Luria's and Vital's associates. Vital had by this time settled in Damascus. His work is composed of both fact and legend, making use of what must have been common knowledge in Safed during the Lurianic period. It

which suggests that Karo's *maggid* was well-known in Safed, as was the title of Karo's manuscript diary, *Sefer ha-Maggid*. Dresnitz writes: "Every time Rabbi Joseph Karo—may he rest in peace—recited the *mishnayyot* by heart, the *Maggid* appeared to him . . . and all the things that the *Maggid* revealed to him he recorded in a book which he called *Sefer ha-Maggid*."[57] It is reasonable to conclude that the Kabbalists of the circle around Isaac Luria were familiar, not only with the existence of Karo's *maggid*, but with the nature of his communications as well.

We find in the writings of Moses Cordovero, the most important Kabbalist in Safed before the appearance of Luria, a theory of maggidism which bears some remarkable similarities to that of *Sha'ar Ruah ha-Qodesh* and *Sha'ar ha-Yihudim*. Cordovero composed as part of his commentary on the *Zohar*, known as *'Or Yaqar*, a commentary on *Zohar Song of Songs*.[58] The first part of this commentary is called "Enquiries Concerning Angels" in which Cordovero discusses the nature and function of angels.[59] Among the different kinds of celestial angels which can enter the human soul is a type known as a *maggid*: "And thus we have seen that an angel can invest himself in him and speak within him words of knowledge and this is what men call a *maggid*."[60] According to Cordovero, the angelic messenger can enter a man's *nefesh* (soul), *ruah* (spirit), or *neshamah* (intellectual soul). The angel speaks the words of knowledge through a man's own voice who recalls them only after the angel has departed.[61] Though Cordovero's treatment of the *maggid* is brief and unsystematic, there are several points of similarity with Luria's theory. While Cordovero does not advance the idea that the revelations are man's creation, he does, as in the Lurianic concept, suggest a relationship between receiving communications and the study of Torah and performance of *mitzwot*. He also asserts that the grade of exaltedness of the divine powers that rest upon a man is contingent upon his actions.[62] Moreover, in both cases the *maggid* materializes as automatic speech. Beyond this, Cordovero affirms his

was originally printed in *Ta'alumot Hokhmah* (Basle, 1629). A second version, *Toledot ha-'Ari*, appears in many manuscripts from the seventeenth century and was generally believed to be based on *Shivhe ha-'Ari*. M. Benayahu has published a complete edition of this second recension (*Sefer Toledot ha-'Ari* [Jerusalem, 1967]) and has argued that it served as the source of Dresnitz's letters.

57. Benayahu, ed., *Sefer Toledot ha-'Ari*, p. 217.
58. This commentary is preserved in ms. 4°74 of the Hebrew University. See G. Scholem, *Kitve Yad be-Qabbalah* (Jerusalem, 1930), pp. 94–99.
59. Printed as an appendix in R. Margolioth, *Mal'akhe Elyon* (Jerusalem, 1945).
60. Ibid., p. 64.
61. Ibid.
62. Ibid., p. 70.

belief that some books were composed under the inspiration of the holy spirit in the guise of a *maggid*. He testifies that *Berit Menuhah*[63] was written in such a manner: "And all the words of this book [*Berit Menuhah*] are words of the holy spirit transmitted from mouth to mouth or through the mouth of a genuine *maggid* to the pious and holy person."[64] Although Cordovero's discussion of the *maggid* reveals nothing about any personal experience, his well-known mystical peregrinations with his brother-in-law, Solomon Alkabetz, suggest a type of experience quite akin to maggidism.[65] Cordovero recorded their experiences of wandering about the environs of Safed in which they visited the traditional gravesites of rabbinic teachers. They understood these peregrinations (lit. "exiles") as symbolically imitating the exiled *Shekhinah*. By wandering from tomb to tomb they participated, as it were, in the suffering and homelessness of the female aspect of the Godhead.[66] A corollary purpose of these peregrinations was to receive mystical revelations. The process involved asking a question based on a biblical verse and having an explanation revealed without requiring prior reflection. The communication manifested itself spontaneously by means of involuntary speech inasmuch as the words were "spoken of themselves" or "were shining forth of themselves." Cordovero writes of the experience in the following way in *'Or Ne'erav*:

> . . . what I and others have experienced in connection with *gerushin*, when we wandered in the fields with the Kabbalist Rabbi Solomon Alkabetz, discussing verses from the Torah, suddenly without previous reflection. On these occasions new ideas would come to us in a manner that cannot be believed unless one has experienced it many times. The gifts which I received during [these] *gerushin*, and which came to me by the mercy of God, I will set down in a special treatise.[67]

It is thus evident that Isaac Luria had a considerable tradition of maggidic theories, and experiences of earlier Kabbalists, upon which to draw in the development of his own conceptions. That he in fact did so is apparent from

63. This anonymous work, printed in 1648 in Amsterdam, dates from the second half of the fourteenth century and was incorrectly attributed to Abraham b. Isaac of Granada. It discusses meditations on the inner lights sparkling from the various vocalizations of the Tetragrammaton. *Berit Menuhah* is one of the very few texts dealing with mystical meditations to have been published by the Kabbalists.

64. Cordovero, *Berit Menuhah*, pp. 9–10. Cf. idem, *Pardes Rimmonim* (Munkacs, 1906), pp. 89b, 97a, 99a.

65. These experiences are recorded in Cordovero's *Sefer ha-Gerushin* (Jerusalem, 1962). See Werblowsky, *Karo*, pp. 51 ff.

66. Cordovero, *Tomer Devorah*, beginning of chap. 9. See Werblowsky, *Karo*, pp. 51 ff.

67. Cordovero, *'Or Ne'erav* (Venice, 1587), Part V, chap. 2.

the close similarities of his own theory of maggidic revelation with those of his predecessors. Pre-Lurianic Safed abounded in experiences involving various forms of divine communications and celestial auditions. Techniques designed to encourage and induce such revelations constituted an important dimension of mystical spirituality for these Kabbalists.

It remains to be noted that the occurrence of maggidic experiences became quite frequent following the sixteenth century. The outstanding Polish Kabbalist R. Samson b. Pesah of Ostropol was reported to have had a *maggid* who appeared daily to teach him Kabbalistic mysteries.[68] Sabbatians of no less importance than R. Abraham Rovigo and Nathan of Gaza are known to have had *maggidim* whose influence upon their actions were decisive.[69] Finally, mention ought to be made of the *maggid* of R. Moses Hayyim Luzzato (1707–46), which played such an important role in this scholar's life.[70]

---

68. See G. Scholem, *Sabbatai Sevi*, trans. R. J. Z. Werblowsky (Princeton, 1973), p. 82.

69. Concerning Rovigo's *maggid*, see Scholem, *Sabbatai Sevi*, p. 919; I. Tishby, *Zion*, XXII (1957), 21–55; I. Sonne, "Visitors at the House of R. Abraham Rovigo," *Sefunot*, V (1961), 277–95. On the *maggid* of Nathan of Gaza, see Scholem, *Sabbatai Sevi*, passim.

70. Concerning Luzzatto's *maggid*, see M. Benayahu, "The *Maggid* of R. Moses Hayyim Luzzatto" [Hebrew], *Sefunot*, V (1961), 297–336.

"How Profitable the Nation of the Jewes Are": The Humble Addresses of Menasseh ben Israel and the Discorso of Simone Luzzatto

Benjamin Ravid

I

In the Hellenistic period, the Jews constituted an integral part of the population of the Roman Empire and their economic activities did not assume any patterns different from those of other peoples.[1] However, with the breakup of the Roman Empire, the Christianization of Europe and the emergence and consolidation of feudalism, the Jews came increasingly to assume a significant role in international and regional trade. Important for this development were the widespread dispersal of the Jews in the Islamic lands as well as in Christian western and central Europe, Jewish group solidarity, facility of linguistic communication, and a uniform system of law based on the Talmud which had the additional advantage of often reflecting the relatively advanced commercial practices of the Hellenistic-Roman and Babylonian worlds. Additionally, the increasing exclusion of the Jews from landowning, especially in northern Europe, as a result of clerical opposition to the utilization of Christian labor by Jews, and the frequent danger of confiscation of property and expulsion served to encourage their participation in trade.[2]

The authorities, at first primarily in France and the Rhineland, recognized the value of the Jews and gave them charters granting them protection and

1. See the pointed comments of Victor Tcherikover, *Hellenistic Civilization and the Jews* (Philadelphia, 1959), pp. 333–43; and Harry J. Leon, *The Jews of Ancient Rome* (Philadelphia, 1960), pp. 233–38.

2. An economic history of the Jews, considering both the element of continuity and change in Jewish economic pursuits and the specific influence of local conditions, is a major desideratum. Although more attention is nowadays paid to the role of the Jews in the European economy, specialized monographic research still constitutes a necessary prerequisite for a major synthesis. In the interim, see the comprehensive treatments of Salo W. Baron in *A Social and Religious History of the Jews*, 2nd ed. rev., 16 vols. to date (Philadelphia, 1952–), esp. IV, 150–227, and all of Vol. XII; much additional information on economic matters is to be found in the chapters devoted to specific countries. See also the article by Salo W. Baron and Arcadius Kahan, "Economic History," in *EJ*, XVI, 1266–1324; reprinted in book form, with other articles from *EJ*, in Nachum Gross, ed., *An Economic History of the Jews* (New York, 1975), pp. 3–104.

special commercial privileges. In fact, the presence of Jewish merchants was so desired in the Germanic lands in the eleventh century that, as Bernard Blumenkranz has noted, "It is no exaggeration to say that there was a kind of rival bidding among the various towns whereby they tried to entice them [the Jews] by offering the most attractive concessions."[3]

Later, as a consequence of the increasing difficulties for Jews in international and regional commerce, caused by the rise of the medieval towns, the emergence of a native Christian merchant group, and the exclusive policy of the guilds, the preeminence of the Jews in commerce declined. In the interim, as a result of clerical opposition to Christians lending money at interest to fellow Christians, the Jews came to assume a predominant, although not monopolistic, position in the credit field. Forced into the role of outsiders, the Jews, in order to be tolerated, had of necessity always to turn to those occupational areas open to them, and had to be very successful so as to be able to meet the financial burdens that were imposed upon them.

This reality was most bluntly expressed by the thirteenth-century Rabbi Asher ben Yehiel who observed that "all kinds of taxes are in the category of defense, for they guard us among the nations. What other benefit do the nations derive from defending us and allowing us to live among them, unless it be to their advantage to collect from us taxes and imposts?"[4] For this reason ". . . according to Asher's teacher, Meir b. Baruch of Rothenburg, many communities did not list their poverty-stricken families, for 'it is a matter of common knowledge that if the prince learned that the poor do not pay [taxes] he would expel them.' "[5] On a slightly more general level, " 'God be truly blessed,' wrote the thirteenth-century apologist, Jacob b. Elijah of Valencia (or Venice), 'who has increased our fortune by means of which we can save our lives and those of our families and reduce to naught the evil designs of our enemies.' Similarly, Solomon ibn Adret emphasized that 'it is necessary for us to go on constantly spending money in order to maintain the [governmental] privileges. This factor has been manifest in every grant the Jew has ever obtained from the royal power.' "[6]

---

3. B. Blumenkranz, "Germany, 843–1096," in *The World History of the Jewish People*, 2nd series, Medieval Period, Vol. II, *The Dark Ages: Jews in Christian Europe 711–1096*, ed. Cecil Roth (Tel Aviv, 1966), p. 163.

4. Baron, *Social and Religious History*, XII, 198.

5. Ibid., p. 199. Baron adds the following confirmation of Meir's fears. "In 1473 Margrave John of Brandenburg reported to his father that he located in the entire March only forty Jews able to pay taxes. He asked whether his father wished 'to chase and expel from the country all other Jews' and to replace them by capable taxpayers" (ibid.).

6. Ibid., p. 198.

II

Despite the emergence of moneylending as a widespread form of Jewish economic activity, the older phenomenon of the Jewish trader did not disappear. Indeed, the competition for the presence of the Jewish merchants which had existed in eleventh-century Germany recurred in the sixteenth and seventeenth centuries as a result of a different commercial background. Then the Italian city-states of Tuscany, Savoy, and Venice, and also the Papal States, issued charters to attract Jewish and Marrano merchants to their ports of Livorno, Nice, Venice, and Ancona in order to establish, maintain, or augment their trade with the Ottoman Empire and prevent its loss to the more powerful western nation-states of Spain, France, Holland, and England.[7]

In 1638, apparently in a successful attempt to avert a threatened expulsion of the Jews from Venice, the Venetian Rabbi, Simone Luzzatto, one of the seven members of the Yeshivah Klalit of Venice and its head after the passing of Leone Modena in 1648, published a book entitled *Discorso circa il stato de gl'Hebrei et in particolar dimoranti nell'inclita città di Venezia.* In this book, a pioneering work in its justification of the toleration of the residence of the Jews for reasons of economic utility,[8] Luzzatto pointed out the general utility of commerce and specifically the many benefits accruing to the Venetian republic from the presence of the Jews, emphasizing their role in international trade. In addition, he proceeded to defend the Jews against many of the charges raised by their adversaries in his seventeenth-century Venice. The tone of his book was affected by the general position and status of the Jews in counterreformation Venice, although many of the issues he dealt with were of much wider interest and relevance.[9]

Slightly over a decade after the publication of the *Discorso*, Menasseh ben Israel, the prominent Rabbi in Amsterdam, began to concern himself with the readmission of the Jews to England.[10] In September 1655, he came to London,

7. For an excellent synthesis of the published material, see ibid., XIV, 32–43, 75–76, 85–114. See also Cecil Roth, *The History of the Jews of Italy* (Philadelphia, 1946), pp. 177–93, 294–353 passim; Attilio Milano, *Storia degli Ebrei in Italia* (Turin, 1963), pp. 250–85. On developments in sixteenth-century Venice, see my article, "The First Charter of the Jewish Merchants of Venice, 1589," *AJSreview*, I (1976), 187–222.

8. See Yitzhak F. Baer, *Galut* (New York, 1947), p. 83; Salo W. Baron's review of the 1950 Hebrew translation of the *Discorso* by D. Lattes, ed. A. Z. Aescoly, in *JSS*, XV (1963), 313.

9. For further details, see my *Economics and Toleration in Seventeenth-Century Venice: The Background and Context of the "Discorso" of Simone Luzzatto* (Jerusalem, 1978).

10. On Menasseh ben Israel and the readmission of the Jews to England, see Cecil Roth, *A Life of Menasseh ben Israel: Rabbi, Printer, and Diplomat* (Philadelphia, 1934), esp. pp. 176–287; and the

bringing with him a pamphlet, apparently written originally in Latin and entitled *De fidelitate et utilitate Judaicae gentis, libellus anglicus* but translated for his trip to England into English, with a title page reading *To His Highnesse the Lord Protector of the Common-wealth of England, Scotland and Ireland. The Humble Addresses of Menasseh ben Israel, a Divine and Doctor of Physick, in Behalfe of the Jewish Nation.*[11] The first part of this pamphlet entitled "How Profitable the Nation of the Jewes Are" sought to justify the readmission of the Jews to England on the basis of commercial considerations, while the second part, "How Faithfull the Nation of the Jewes Are" belongs to the more traditional genre of seventeenth-century Jewish apologetica.

The *Discorso* and the *Humble Addresses* differed fundamentally in their purposes and their authors differed greatly in their outlook. First, regarding the purpose of the books, while Luzzatto basically wrote the *Discorso* as a "defense attorney," seeking to retain the residential rights of the Jews of Venice and the unique commercial privileges enjoyed by the Jewish merchants residing in the city, Menasseh ben Israel in the *Humble Addresses* sought a major innovation: the readmission of the Jews to England after an absence of over 350 years since their expulsion by Edward I in 1290. Second, regarding the outlook of their authors, while Menasseh ben Israel was motivated by messianic speculation and sought to hasten the redemption (as he explicitly stated in the declaratory opening to the *Humble Addresses*), Luzzatto had no such considerations in mind. He undertook his role as "defense attorney" of the Jews as a result of a chance event in the history of the Jews of Venice, and hence his *Discorso* can be considered a *pièce de circonstance*. It cannot be ascertained whether Luzzatto really believed all of his arguments, or whether he tended to select arguments that he believed would strengthen his case with his patrician readers. Nevertheless, he was probably expressing his true thoughts when he asserted that the dispersion of the Jews had a positive value in that it facilitated their physical survival and also served as a defense against innovation.[12] Despite these major differences, the two au-

---

later, but briefer account in Cecil Roth, *A History of the Jews in England*, 3rd ed. (Oxford, 1964), pp. 154–72.

11. The text of the *Humble Addresses* is available in M. Kayserling, "The Life and Labours of Manasseh ben Israel," *Miscellany of Hebrew Literature*, 2nd series, II (1877), 35–63; and Lucien Wolf, ed., *Menasseh ben Israel's Mission to Oliver Cromwell* (London, 1901), pp. 73–103.

12. Simone Luzzatto, *Discorso circa il stato de gl' Hebrei et in particolar dimoranti nell'inclita Città di Venetia* (Venice, 1638), consideration 18, pp. 89^{r-v}; Hebrew translation: *Ma'amar 'al Yehude Veneziah*, ed. A. Z. Aescoly, trans. D. Lattes, and introd. R. B. Bachi and M. A. Shulvass (Jerusalem, 1950), pp. 151–52. For the views of Luzzatto and Menasseh ben Israel on the nature of the Diaspora, see Baer, *Galut*, pp. 83–92, 97–100; Bachi's introduction to the Hebrew translation of the *Discorso*, pp. 27–73 (bearing in mind the reservations expressed in the opening editorial note on p. 27); and the final paragraph of n. 15, below.

thors did share a common immediate aim: both sought to demonstrate to a Christian government the desirability of the presence of the Jews on account of the benefits resulting from their activities in international trade.

In view of the similarity between some of the arguments employed first by Luzzatto and then also utilized by Menasseh ben Israel, modern scholars have asserted that Menasseh had read the *Discorso*, had been influenced by it, and had taken some of his arguments from it.[13] However, it is remarkable that Menasseh ben Israel nowhere mentions Luzzatto or the *Discorso*, a book that contains arguments so similar to his own. It might be suggested that this omission is to be accounted for by the fact that the *Humble Addresses* was written for a specific and practical purpose: to influence the head of the English government, the Lord Protector Oliver Cromwell, favorably on the question of readmitting the Jews to England. Concerned with maximizing the impact of his own work and its influence rather than engaging in a display of wide learning so characteristic of his day, Menasseh did not wish to allude to other writers. However, it must be pointed out, against this suggestion, that although in the first part of the *Humble Addresses*, "How Profitable the Nation of the Jewes Are," Menasseh does not refer to any other texts or authors, in the second part, "How Faithfull the Nation of the Jewes Are," he does so, mentioning in addition to the Bible, Talmud, and prayerbook, both Jewish and gentile writers: Simon ben Yochai (as the author of the *Zohar*), Isaac Abravanel, Samuel Usque, St. Augustine, Marcus Antonius Sabellicus, Hieronimus Osorius, Andrea Alciato, Juan de Mariana, Cardinal Parisius, the

13. Kayserling drew attention to some, but not all, parallels to the *Discorso* in his notes to the text of the *Humble Addresses* incorporated into his "Life and Labours"; see nn. 176, 184, 189, 198, 200, 207, 216. These references were, however, not included in the index (ibid., pp. 95–96). Very surprisingly, Wolf made no reference to Luzzatto either when mentioning the sources of Menasseh ben Israel (*Menasseh ben Israel's Mission*, p. 162) or in the notes to his edition of the *Humble Addresses* (ibid., pp. 162–64). On p. 162, Wolf merely wrote that "a very large number of the historical references in this tract are taken without acknowledgment from Imanuel Aboab's *Nomologia* (Amsterdam, 1629) and Daniel Levy de Barrios's *Historia Universal Judayca*. Kayserling has given many of the original passages in his notes to his 'Life of Menasseh ben Israel' (*Misc. Heb. Lit.*, Series II)." Aboab, like Luzzatto, is never mentioned in the *Humble Addresses*. And regarding Menasseh's borrowing from De Barrios, Cecil Roth already observed: "It is impossible to believe (as Kayserling . . . seems to suggest, and Lucien Wolf . . . definitely states) that Menasseh derived from De Barrios, who began to write only after the former's death" ("Imanuel Aboab's Proselytization of the Marranos," *JQR*, XXIII [1932], 128; reprinted in his *Gleanings* [New York, 1967], p. 159). A thorough investigation of the sources of the *Humble Addresses* and an analysis of Menasseh's utilization of them would be desirable. Extensive references and quotations are to be found in the notes of Kayserling, "Life and Labours," pp. 84–92. See also ibid., p. 16; and nn. 14 and 16, below.

Parallels between themes in the *Discorso* and the *Humble Addresses* were noted by M. Wilensky in his *The Return of the Jews to England in the Seventeenth Century* [Hebrew] (Jerusalem, 1943), pp. 93–102, 184–87. See also Bachi's introduction to the Hebrew translation of the *Discorso*, p. 71; S. Ettinger, "The Beginnings of the Change in the Attitude of European Society towards the Jews," *Scripta Hierosolymitana*, VII (1961), pp. 210, 212–13; and I. Barzilay, "John Toland's Borrowings from Simone Luzzatto," *JSS*, XXXI (1969), p. 77, n. 10.

chronicle of the Xarifes, "one famous lawyer in Rome," and two English contemporaries, Henry Jessey and Edward Nicholas.[14] The passage mentioning Abravanel parallels the *Discorso* very closely. Furthermore, it should be noted that in his *Vindiciae Judaeorum*, published in 1656, one year after the *Humble Addresses*, Menasseh ben Israel specifically mentions his lack of knowledge of mercantile affairs;[15] this confession, if indeed taken at face value, increases the probability that Menasseh ben Israel utilized the *Discorso* and makes the question as to why he did not refer his readers to that work even more pertinent.

Menasseh ben Israel's treatment of the Jews of Venice is also noteworthy. In "How Profitable the Nation of the Jewes Are," he mentions several copies of privileges granted by the "great Duke of Tuscany" which he has in his

14. According to Kayserling, "Menasseh did not consult Osorius, but translated literally from Aboab" ("'Life and Labours'" p. 89, n. 227); cf. Wolf, *Menasseh ben Israel's Mission*, p. 163, notes to p. 93, line 26, and p. 100, line 5. It is also probable that Menasseh did not consult Sabellicus, Alciato, or Cardinal Parisius first hand; see n. 16, below.

15. See *Vindiciae Judaeorum*, section 6, in Wolf, *Menasseh ben Israel's Mission*, pp. 139–40: "Having thus discussed the main exceptions, I will now proceed to smaller matters, though lesse pertaining to my faculty, that is to businesse of *Merchandise*. . . . Farther, there may be companies made of the natives, and strangers (where they are more acquainted) or else Factors. All which, if I be not deceived, will amount to the profit of the natives. For which, many reasons may be brought, though I cannot comprehend them, having alwayes lived a sedentary life, applying my self to my studies which are farre remote from things of that nature." In the *Vindiciae* there is also no reference to Luzzatto. Menasseh's disclaimer of a knowledge of commercial matters, however, cannot be taken at face value, since he himself engaged extensively in mercantile activities, ranging in scope from Brazil to Poland. At one point, "strangers who met him casually . . . were impressed by the business man rather than by the rabbi" and, "in 1646–47, he was reckoned one of twenty-two outstanding members of the Amsterdam community engaged in trade" (Roth, *Life of Menasseh ben Israel*, pp. 51–53, 57–58, 67–69).

It should be observed that Menasseh employed one sound argument in the *Vindiciae* which Luzzatto did not utilize in his *Discorso*: "Moreover, they would alwayes bring profit to the people of the land, as well in buying of commodities, which they would transport to other places, as in those they would trade in here. And if by accident, any particular person should lose by it, by bringing down the price of such a commodity, being dispersed into many hands; yet by that means the Commonwealth would gain in buying cheaper, and procuring it at a lesser rate" (Wolf, *Menasseh ben Israel's Mission*, p. 139). Possibly Luzzatto chose not to present this argument, assuming that the Senators and patricians of Venice were more concerned with the profits of individual traders, many of whom came from their ranks, than with keeping down the price of commodities.

Interestingly, despite his emphasis on the commercial utility of the Jews, Menasseh does not appear to have had a particularly favorable attitude towards commerce. Luzzatto, either out of conviction or in order to strengthen his argument in favor of the Jewish merchants of Venice, praised the positive role of trade in human society (see esp. *Discorso*, consideration 1, pp. 8ʳ–10ʳ; Hebrew translation, pp. 81–82). While Menasseh repeated some of these arguments, he nevertheless conceived of Jewish commercial activity as constituting merely a divine compensation for the exile, enabling the Jews to survive until their return to their country, at which time, in the words of Zechariah (quoted by Menasseh), "their [sic] shall be found no more any marchant amongst them in the House of the Lord" (Wolf, *Menasseh ben Israel's Mission*, p. 82). This "temporary dispensation" approach is completely absent from the *Discorso*. See also Baer, *Galut*, pp. 99–100.

possession, and he also relates that "His Majesty, the Illustrious King of Denmark, invited them with speciall Priviledges into Geluckstadt: the Duke of Savoy into Nisa of Provence; and the Duke of Modina in Retio, allowing them such conditions and benefices, as like never were presented unto them by any other Prince, as appeareth by the copy of those Priviledges, which I have in my hands." Additionally, in "How Faithfull the Nation of the Jewes Are," he refers to the privileges granted by Cosimo the Great of Florence, Ercole of Ferara, and Emanuel Filibert of Savoy. Nevertheless, while Menasseh in passing praises the Senate of Venice because it "never deliberats or puts into execution any thing, without great judgement: having the advantage of all Republiqs in their Government and leaving behind them the Romans, Carthagenians, Athenians, and most learned Lacedemonians, and that Parliament of Paris, which in the Government of affaires was alwayes most prudent," he makes no reference whatsoever to the privileges issued by the Venetian Senate for the Levantine and Ponentine Jewish merchants of Venice, which were in effect in his time. Although those privileges did impose many restrictions, nevertheless they granted the Jewish merchants the right of residence, freedom of religion, and permission to engage in overseas trade. Menasseh's only reference to the Jews of Venice consists of a few general remarks in the context of his survey of the tribes of Judah and Benjamin. Specifically, he relates that "in Italy they are generally protected by all the Princes; their principall residence is in the most famous City of Venice; so that in that same City alone they possesse about 1400 Houses; and are used there with much courtesy and clemency."[16]

16. Wolf, *Menasseh ben Israel's Mission*, p. 87. For a discussion of the available data on the Jewish population of seventeenth-century Venice, see my *Economics and Toleration*, n. 70.

The information assembled in the above paragraph of this study requires investigation in two respects: first, ascertaining the sources of Menasseh, and second, indicating what he omitted to relate (i.e., his failure to update or augment his sources).

As far as Menasseh's sources are concerned, the references to the privileges granted by Cosimo of Florence, Ercole of Ferrara, and Emanuel Filibert of Savoy were taken from the "speech" (thus Kayserling) of a "famous lawyer in Rome" preserved in the *Nomologia* of Immanuel Aboab (Amsterdam, 1629); see Kayserling, "Life and Labours," p. 89, nn. 221, 223, 224, 226. It should be noted, in passing, that the text of Aboab as quoted by Kayserling (n. 221) reads ". . . tengo en mi poder una alegacion y discurso muy docto sobre esta materia, que hizo en Roma en lengua Italiana un Jurisconsulto." The word "discurso" may indicate not a speech, but rather a written work never presented orally. This usage of the word is frequently encountered in the titles of sixteenth- and seventeenth-century Italian books; e.g., the *Discorsi* of Machiavelli and the *Discorso* of Luzzatto. The references to Sabellicus, Alciato, and Cardinal Parisius, and also the passage quoted above dealing with the Senate of Venice are contained in that "speech." Accordingly, Menasseh may never have read their works, and the evaluation of the Venetian Senate is not his own formulation.

Menasseh apparently made no attempt to bring the information taken from that "speech," which also contained references to papal privileges given to Marranos in Ancona, up to date. He does not mention the papal reversal of policy in 1555, nor the subsequent privileges given by

A comparison of the first section of the *Humble Addresses*, "How Profitable the Nation of the Jewes Are" with corresponding passages from the *Discorso* (see below) leads to the conclusion that in a few places Menasseh translated verbatim from the *Discorso*. But it is also evident that Menasseh neither repeated all the arguments of the *Discorso*, nor followed its structure. Menasseh's presentation is far more brief, direct and to the point. In those passages where the wording of the *Humble Addresses* corresponds virtually verbatim to that of the *Discorso* (e.g., the five important benefits of trade, and with slight reorganization of the material, the characterization of Spalato and the comments on Livorno), Menasseh has obviously taken his material from the *Discorso*. However, in other cases where no exact textual correspondence can be established, the question of influence becomes more dubious, since similar commercial considerations could lead to the formulation of similar arguments. Luzzatto's uniqueness lay not in his formulating a new approach or outlook. Rather it was in being the first to present a systematic descriptive account of the economic role of the Jews, with emphasis on their activity in international commerce in general and in that of the republic of Venice specifically, within the framework of an ideology stressing the positive function of commerce in human society. Luzzatto articulated basically the status quo, and it would not have been impossible for other observers of the contemporary scene to arrive at similar conclusions, especially for others living in the port city of Amsterdam. However, since Menasseh ben Israel was obviously acquainted with the *Discorso* and had virtually translated passages from it for inclusion in his *Humble Addresses*, it is possible and indeed

popes to Levantine merchants in 1594; see Baron, *Social and Religious History*, XIV, 36–37, 57, 108. Furthermore, the privileges granted by Cosimo of Florence—from the context, the reference must be to Cosimo I (1537–74) and not his grandson, Cosimo II (1609–21)—apparently did not achieve any substantial results; see U. Cassuto, *Gli Ebrei a Firenze nell'età del Rinascimento* (Florence, 1918), pp. 89–90, 171–80; Hebrew translation (Jerusalem, 1967), pp. 71–72, 132–38; Baron, *Social and Religious History*, XIV, 75–76, 91. It was only with the issuance of "La Livornina" in 1593 by Ferdinand I that the Jews came to settle in Livorno; see Attilio Milano, "Gli antecedenti della 'Livornina' del 1593," *RMI*, XXXVII (1971), 343–60; idem, "La costituzione 'Livornina' del 1593," *RMI*, XXXIV (1968), 394–410; Baron, *Social and Religious History*, XIV, 91–92, 108. The liberal provisions issued by Emanuel Filibert of Savoy for Marrano merchants were soon rescinded under the combined pressure of Spain and the Papacy; see H. Beinart, "The Settlement of the Jews in Savoy and the Privileges of 1572" [Hebrew], *Scritti in memoria di Leone Carpi* (Jerusalem, 1967), pp. 72–118. Nevertheless, Jewish moneylenders continued to reside in Savoy; see S. Foa, "The Conflict between the Princes of Savoy and the Pope Concerning the Jewish Bankers from Portugal, 1573–81" [Hebrew], *Eretz-Israel, Archaeological, Historical and Geographical Studies*, III (1954), 240–43; idem, "Banchi e banchieri ebrei nel Piemonte dei secoli scorsi," *RMI*, XXVI (1955), 38–50, 85–97, 127–36, 190–201, 284–97, 325–36, 471–85, 520–35; idem, *La politica economica della casa savoia verso gli Ebrei dal secolo XVI fino alla rivoluzione francese* (Rome, 1962). I hope to deal with these charters at greater length in a future study on the Jewish merchants of Venice.

even most likely that in cases where the general commercial arguments are similar, Menasseh ben Israel had been influenced by Luzzatto.

The question of influence becomes even thornier when one confronts the parallels not in the realm of economic and commercial considerations, in which the *Discorso* was, as stated, a pioneering work, but rather in the sphere of general religious apologetics, presented in the second part of the *Humble Addresses*, "How Faithfull the Nation of the Jewes Are," and also in Menasseh ben Israel's *Vindiciae Judaeorum.* Here in many cases Menasseh may be utilizing arguments encountered in the *Discorso* without being directly indebted to Luzzatto, since these arguments had not been presented for the first time in the *Discorso*, but rather constituted standard arguments of Jewish apologetica, which were doubtlessly familiar to the very widely read Menasseh ben Israel.[17]

The question, to the best of my knowledge not previously asked, arises as to why Menasseh ben Israel did not acknowledge his indebtedness to Luzzatto, or at least refer to Luzzatto or his *Discorso*.[18] As yet, I have not been able to establish the existence of any personal relationship between the two contemporaries. The closest connection so far encountered is that Luzzatto contributed an opening approbation (*haskamah*) to the *Sepher Elim* of Joseph Solomon Delmedigo, published by Menasseh ben Israel in Amsterdam in 1629. Although probably not accounting for Menasseh's silence, it is known that the two rabbis differed on one point of great interest at that time, the whereabouts of the ten lost tribes. In the *Discorso*, Luzzatto stated that "regarding the ten lost tribes which were exiled by Shalmanesser before the destruction of the first temple, we possess no definite knowledge, even though the whole world has been investigated and discovered."[19] Menasseh

---

17. For a brief discussion of this problem, which requires further clarification, see my *Economics and Toleration*, section II. See also the literature cited in n. 13, above. For certain points of contact and contrast among the *Discorso*, the *Humble Addresses*, and Isaac Cardoso's *Las Excelencias de los Hebreos*, see Yosef H. Yerushalmi, *From Spanish Court to Italian Ghetto: Isaac Cardoso, A Study in Seventeenth-Century Marranism and Jewish Apologetics* (New York-London, 1971), esp. pp. 438, 439 n. 63, 443, 448, 450, 468–69. Luzzatto's defense of the political loyalty and obedience of the Jews was criticized in passing by Melchiore Palontrotti in his *Breve risposta a Simone Luzzatto* (Rome, 1641) and much more extensively by Giulio Morosini in his *Via della fede* (Rome, 1683). These two critiques will be discussed in my forthcoming study "Antisemitism in Seventeenth-Century Italy: Two Neglected Responses to the *Discorso* of Simone Luzzatto by Melchiore Palontrotti and Giulio Morosini."

18. Compare this omission on the part of Menasseh ben Israel with the enthusiastic attitude of John Toland towards Luzzatto and his *Discorso* which, Toland stated, he will "in convenient time publish in English translation," a project he did not carry out; see John Toland, *Reasons for Naturalizing the Jews in Great Britain and Ireland* (London, 1714), pp. 48–58; Barzilay, "John Toland's Borrowings," pp. 75–81.

19. *Discorso*, consideration 18, p. 89ᵛ; Hebrew translation, p. 152.

ben Israel, probably not polemicizing directly against Luzzatto, but rather refuting a general sense of scepticism regarding the ten lost tribes, wrote in his *Spes Israelis* (*Hope of Israel*) (1650): "Neither is there weight in the Argument, which some have brought to me, if they be in the world, why doe we not know them better? There are many things which we know, and yet know not their original; are we not to this day ignorant of the heads of the four Rivers *Nilus, Ganges, Euphrates*, and *Tegris*? also there are many unknown Countryes. Besides, though some live in knowne and neighbor Countrys, yet they are unknown by being behind Mountains; so it happened under the reign of *Ferdinand* and *Isabel*, that some Spaniards were found out by accident, at *Batueca*, belonging to the Duke of *Alva*, which place is distant but ten miles from *Salamanca*, and near to *Placentia*, whither some Spaniards fled, when the *Moors* possessed *Spaine*, and dwelled there 800 years. If therefore a people could lie hid so long in the middle of *Spaine*, why may we not say that those are hid, whom God will not have any perfectly to know, before the end of days."[20]

Aside from undocumentable speculation as to any personal or ideological antagonism between Menasseh ben Israel and Luzzatto, there is one plausible explanation for the omission of the name of Luzzatto in the *Humble Addresses*, an explanation which derives from the differences in living conditions between the Jews of Venice and those of Amsterdam. Menasseh had submitted with his *Humble Addresses* a petition in which he specifically requested that "our Hebrew nation be received and admitted into this mighty republic under the protection and care of your Highness like the citizens themselves . . . and that it be allowed us to trade freely in all sorts of merchandise just like every one else."[21] Yet at this time, in most of continental Europe, and

20. Wolf, *Menasseh ben Israel's Mission*, pp. 38–39. Kayserling ("Life and Labours," p. 16) wrote that "Simon Luzzato [sic] strongly blamed Manasseh for this production [*The Hope of Israel*]" without giving any source for his statement. To date, I must concur with Roth's comment that "I cannot, however, find any authority for this [statement]" (*A Life of Menasseh ben Israel*, p. 331 n. 5).

Jacques Basnage, in his *Histoire des Juifs depuis Jesus-Christ jusqu'à présent*, reproduced, with a French translation, parts of the eighteenth consideration of the *Discorso*, including the above-quoted passage questioning the survival of the ten lost tribes, and also a summary of the views of Menasseh ben Israel who believed that the tribes were scattered all over the world and would soon be redeemed (1707 edition: Bk. VII, chap. 33, pp. 2119 ff.; 1716 edition: Bk. IX, chap. 38, pp. 1061 ff.). Basnage commented: "Nous ne prétendons pas concilier ces deux Rabbins, ni les suivre pas à pas: cependant, l'Idée générale qu'ils nous donnent de la Condition présente des Juifs mérite qu'on s'y arrête: ils ne s'accordent pas sur le Sort des dix Tribus. . . ."

21. The original French text is reprinted in Wolf, *Menasseh ben Israel's Mission*, pp. lxxxii–lxxxiv; English translation in Jacob R. Marcus, *The Jew in the Medieval World* (Philadelphia, 1938), pp. 66–68. The extent to which Menasseh's proposals reflect the actual status of the Jews of Holland has, to the best of my knowledge, never been examined; see text below, and n. 25. For some suggestive parallels, see J. Meijer, "Hugo Grotius' *Remonstrantie*," *JSS*, XVII (1955), pp. 97–104, with references to the charters of Haarlem and Rotterdam. (Re: n. 30, perhaps Grotius meant the Hebrew word *memunim*.)

especially in the Germanic lands and in Italy, in those places where the Jews were authorized to live, they were subject to restrictions which were often severe. Specifically, in 1655–56, as Menasseh was seeking the readmission of the Jews into England, the Jews of Venice, for whose sake the *Discorso* had been written, from the legal point of view of the Venetian government, fell into one of two groups. The first and longer settled group, the Tedeschi moneylenders, resided on the suffrance of a five-year charter, subject to renewal, authorizing them only to engage, under clearly stipulated terms, in moneylending (in reality, pawnbroking) at the unprofitable rate of 5 percent, and in the sale of secondhand goods. The second group, the Levantine and Ponentine Jewish merchants, resided since 1589 on the suffrance of a ten-year charter, subject to cancellation on eighteen months' notice, allowing them only to engage in overseas trade. Both groups of Jews were required to wear a special yellow hat and to reside in a compulsory ghetto. While the Venetian government appears to have treated the Jews fairly within the stipulated legal framework and guaranteed them the rights granted in their charters (including freedom of religious observance, thereby establishing the basis for the emergence of Venice as one of the major centers of Jewish cultural and religious life in the sixteenth and seventeenth centuries, a veritable and venerable *ir we-'em be-yisra'el*), the above restrictions did not remain dead-letter enactments on the books, but were strictly enforced, along with many other restrictions. Basically, anything not specifically permitted to the Jews was forbidden to them.[22]

In contrast to this legally circumscribed situation existing in Venice, in Amsterdam, where Menasseh ben Israel lived, a city ordinance of 1619 had specifically forbidden compelling the Jews to wear any distinguishing marks and no compulsory Jewish quarters were ever instituted. The Jews were Dutch subjects, and could purchase burghership, which, however, could not be inherited. Also, many owned the houses in which they lived. Although they could not hold civil or military office, even if they had bought burghership, and were excluded from almost all of the guilds and subjected to

22. On the Tedeschi moneylenders, see Brian Pullan, *Rich and Poor in Renaissance Venice* (Cambridge, 1971), pp. 476–578; and my article, "The Socio-Economic Background of the Expulsion of the Jews from Venice in 1571 and Their Readmission in 1573," to appear in *Essays in Modern Jewish History: A Tribute to Ben Halpern*, ed. Ph. Cohen Albert and F. Malino. On the Levantine and Ponentine merchants, see my article, "The Establishment of the Ghetto Vecchio of Venice, 1541: Background and Reappraisal," *Proceedings of the Sixth World Congress for Jewish Studies, 1973* (Jerusalem, 1975), II, 153–67; idem, "The First Charter"; idem, *Economics and Toleration*, sections III and V. The last charter of the merchants prior to the publication of the *Humble Addresses* was published by Cecil Roth, "La ricondotta degli ebrei ponentini, Venezia, 1647," *Studi in onore di Gino Luzzatto*, 4 vols. (Milan, 1950), II, 237–44. Certain points in Roth's introduction to the text, however, require modification.

varying restrictions, including exclusion from retail trade, at different times, it is apparent that these legal restrictions, especially those involving retail trade, were very often evaded. In practice, the condition of the Jews was far better than would appear from an examination of the legislative enactments. Above all, the Jews of Amsterdam specifically, and those of Holland in general, were not subject to the insecurity of charters valid for specific limited periods, charters that always required renegotiation and renewal.[23]

The English had extensive connections with nearby Amsterdam, and doubtlessly were familiar with the relatively favorable conditions the Jews enjoyed there. Quite probably, Menasseh ben Israel was not anxious to draw attention to the specific conditions of the Jews of Venice with their ghetto segregation, compulsory unprofitable state-controlled pawn shops, and far more extensively enforced civic disabilities, including the prohibition against owning real estate, engaging in domestic trade and the mechanical arts, and being active in the courts, all mentioned by Luzzatto in his *Discorso*, and many additional discriminatory provisions such as the yellow Jewish hat, not mentioned in the *Discorso*, but specified in the charters.[24] It may be assumed that Menasseh wished to emphasize rather the positive side of the *Discorso*, the clear presentation of the contribution of the Jews to international commerce, and hoped that the specific conditions under which the Jews would be allowed to live in England would be similar to those enjoyed by Amsterdam Jewry, rather than the more restrictive ones imposed on Venetian Jewry.[25] Accordingly, he selected from the *Discorso* some general arguments and

23. Herbert I. Bloom, *The Economic Activities of the Jews of Amsterdam in the Seventeenth and Eighteenth Centuries* (Williamsport, Pa., 1937), pp. xvi–xvii, 18–24, 30–31, 34–36, 38, 44, 63, 64–71; Baron, *Social and Religious History*, XV, 30–32. See also n. 26, below. The rivalry between cities to attract Jews in eleventh-century Germany and sixteenth-century Italy also occurred in seventeenth-century Holland and northwestern Germany; see Baron, *Social and Religious History*, XV, 37–38, 396 (conclusion of n. 47).

24. See my *Economics and Toleration*, sections III and V.

25. Roth seems to have believed that Menasseh had a different model in mind: "It is obvious that what Menasseh had in mind was one of the closely controlled, semiautonomous communities of the sort tolerated in a few places abroad, such as Hamburg or Leghorn" (*Life of Menasseh ben Israel*, p. 232). It seems more likely, however, that Menasseh had his home town of Amsterdam in mind. In general, Roth appears to stress excessively the "essentially medieval character" of Menasseh's proposals, which he sees as being "at the bottom . . . removed only in degree from the repressive system which obtained in the less enlightened parts of the Continent" (ibid., pp. 282–84); or "Menasseh ben Israel had of course envisaged something in the nature of a Ghetto system when he laid his proposals before Cromwell . . ." (*History of the Jews in England*, p. 182, n. 1; cf. also, pp. 171–72). In reality, the liberal nature of Menasseh's petition becomes apparent when contrasted with the terms worked out at the Whitehall Conference; see Roth, *Menasseh ben Israel*, pp. 243–45; and idem, *History of the Jews in England*, p. 163. Also, the text of the petition submitted by Menasseh does not seem to imply that he sought the issuance of a "special Jewish charter," as stated by Roth (*Menasseh ben Israel*, p. 283; not repeated in *History of the Jews*). Cf. Marcus, *Jew in the Medieval World*, p. 66: "Menasseh's petition . . . asking for the unconditional readmission of the Jews. . . ."

specific passages, but rejected its deprecatory tone, which reflected the circumstances under which it was written and the status of Venetian Jewry. Menasseh did not want to establish in England a Jewish community similar to that existing in Venice, but rather one similar to that which he knew in Amsterdam or even one with more favorable conditions. What was impossible in counterreformation Catholic Venice was possible in Calvinist Amsterdam and Puritan England.

III

Similar considerations of commercial and fiscal *raison d'état* may have secured the toleration of the Jewish merchants in Venice and in England (as well as in other places in Italy, Western Europe, and the Baltic Germanic lands). However, similar commercial circumstances and rational economic considerations did not exert a uniform effect on the condition of the Jews. The specific conditions of the Jews in every country, once they were admitted to it, depended upon noneconomic factors, reflecting a complex religious, social, and political heritage which differed from one country to the next. Thus it is impossible to posit a simplistic economic determinism.

A detailed comparison of the legal status of the Jews of Venice, Holland—especially Amsterdam—and England is beyond the scope of this paper. Such a comparison should differentiate clearly between two types of legislation: specific prohibitions stipulating that no Jews engage in a given activity, and conversely, other authorization allowing specific activities. Attention must be paid also to the various sources of legislation, and additionally to the guild regulations. However, since legal provisions do not necessarily reflect the actual situation, an attempt must be made to determine the extent to which restrictions were enforced and to ascertain the reasons for any demonstrated laxity. Much can be learned also from an examination of Jewish activities in areas neither specifically prohibited nor authorized by law. Finally, the rights of the Jews must always be viewed in the context of the rights of the various groups of the native Christian population, which could be based on either law or custom.[26]

26. Whatever the legal stipulations, *in actuality*, the Jews of Amsterdam engaged in a wide variety of activities, especially in the retail trades and profession (see Bloom, *Economic Activities*, pp. 33–71). It remains, however, to ascertain the specific position of the Jews in 1655. One point, significant for Jewish cultural life, is that the Jews of Amsterdam were allowed to engage in printing, something legally forbidden to the Jews of Venice since 1548 (not 1571 as usually assumed). See Bloom, *Economic Activities*, pp. 44–60; and Roth, *Venice*, pp. 260–61. B. Pullan in his *Rich and Poor in Renaissance Venice*, p. 521, has noted in passing that the prohibition against Jewish

The situation of the Jews in Venice in the 1650s resulted from a chain of previous historical events. In 1394, the Venetian government had required that all Jews wear a special distinguishing yellow badge, which in 1496 was changed to a yellow hat to make evasion more difficult. Upon the expiration of their charter in 1397, the Jews—with the exception of a few specially privileged individuals—were not allowed to remain in the city for longer than fifteen days at a time. Finally, in 1509 they were permitted, because of special wartime conditions, to return to the city from the neighboring towns for their own safety and the safety of the pledges belonging to Christians which were in the Jewish moneylenders' possession. Soon afterwards, in 1516, they were compelled to live in compulsory segregated quarters known as the ghetto. They were again subjected to charters, eventually issued regularly for five-year periods, which, while granting them the right of residence and guaranteeing their freedom of religion, nevertheless carefully controlled and restricted their economic activities to moneylending and the sale of secondhand goods, as stated above. Visiting Jewish merchants coming to Venice were similarly required to live in a ghetto and wear the badge. When, later on, special attempts were made to attract them to the city on a longer term basis out of considerations of commercial utilitarianism and *raison d'état*, they too were subjected to charters, which also restricted their residence in the city to a limited period (albeit ten years, twice as long as the five years allotted to the moneylenders), specifically required them to live in the ghetto and wear the yellow badge, and permitted them to engage only in overseas commerce.[27]

The Jews of Venice continued to live under this restrictive charter system introduced in the sixteenth century for over 200 years, until in 1797 the Venetian government capitulated to Napoleon Bonaparte. The new revolutionary government proclaimed the equality of all inhabitants, and decreed the removal of the ghetto gates, which were hacked to pieces and burned in the courtyard of the *ghetto nuovo* as Jews and Christians danced together around the flames. However, later in 1797, by the terms of the treaty of Campo-Formo, most of the mainland holdings of the Venetian republic, including the city of Venice itself, were given to Austria. Although the ghetto was not restored, the Jews lost some of their recently acquired rights, and

---

participation in printing activities in Venice was introduced in 1548. For further details, see my "The Prohibition against Jewish Printing and Publishing in Venice and the Difficulties of Leone Modena," in I. Twersky, ed., *Studies in Medieval Jewish History and Literature* (Cambridge, Mass., 1979), pp. 135–53. It can only be noted here that this prohibition was not rigidly enforced in Venice.

27. For an elaboration of this brief account, see the literature cited above, n. 22.

certain old restrictions were reintroduced. After Napoleon's victory over Austria at Austerlitz in 1806, Venice was incorporated into the Kingdom of Italy and from 1806 to 1814, the Jews once more enjoyed complete equality. After the fall of Napoleon, Venice was restored to Austria and the Jews lost their civic equality. They again briefly enjoyed it in 1848 when the ill-fated Republic of Venice was proclaimed and then finally received civic equality in 1866 when Venice joined the newly formed Kingdom of Italy.[28]

In England, on the other hand, the situation was different. In 1655 there was no preexisting Jewish community subject to "medieval" restrictions, and the settlement of the Jewish merchants could take place under "tabula rasa" conditions with no enforced restrictions with a continuity of observance for generations.

Although it is unclear whether the petition of Menasseh ben Israel was accepted by the Council of State in June 1656,[29] in December of that year the Jews of London rented a house for use as a synagogue and early in 1657 acquired burial grounds. Henceforth, the Jews were allowed to reside in England without being subject to any specific anti-Jewish provisions enacted by the central government. Their main restriction was their exclusion, along with Catholics and Protestant nonconformists, from political and public life, including especially any office under the crown and participation in municipal government. This was a result of the requirement to take the sacraments in accordance with the rites of the Church of England, and to take an oath of abjuration to the claims of the deposed Catholic House of Stuart "on the faith of a true Christian," measures which had been enacted because of religious and political struggles within English society, without any reference to the Jews. Their most bothersome disability in everyday life was the inability to acquire the freedom of the City of London, since it was necessary to take an oath administered on the New Testament. This meant that they could not open retail stores in the City of London, a restriction that became less serious as the metropolitan area expanded, and in any case was circumvented by selling retail from supposedly wholesale warehouses. Only as the restrictions on Christians who were not members of the Church of England were gradually eliminated, culminating in the "Catholic emancipation" of 1829, did the Jews become the only group denied participation in public life on

28. Roth, *Venice*, pp. 354–69.

29. The possibility that there was a formal readmission of the Jews to England has been suggested by C. Roth in his "The Resettlement of the Jews in England in 1656," in V. D. Lipman, ed., *Three Centuries of Anglo-Jewish History* (London, 1961), pp. 1–25 (reprinted in his *Essays and Portraits in Anglo-Jewish History* [Philadelphia, 1962], pp. 86–107). The suggestion was incorporated into the third edition of his *History of the Jews in England*, p. 166.

religious grounds. Henceforth, laws originally not intentionally enacted against the Jews were deliberately retained, and the "emancipation" of the Jews became a special issue to be resolved piecemeal in the following decades.[30]

The relatively favorable status of the Jews in Amsterdam in the 1650s and in England in the seventeenth and eighteenth centuries was to be of special significance. When in 1654 a boatload of Jews coming from Dutch Brazil, which had just been retaken by the Portuguese, arrived in New Amsterdam, Peter Stuyvesant, the Dutch governor of the colony, did not wish to allow them to stay. As a result, in January 1655, the merchants of the "Portuguese nation" in Amsterdam petitioned the Dutch West India Company to permit the Jews to settle in the Dutch New World. Among other reasons, they advanced commercial considerations very similar to those of Simone Luzzatto, which were repeated by Menasseh ben Israel: "Yonder land is extensive and spacious. The more loyal people that go to live there, the better it is in regard to the population of the country as in regard to the payment of various excises and taxes which may be imposed there, and in regard to the increase of trade, and also to the importation of all the necessities that may be sent there."[31]

A few years later, the English took over the Dutch colony of New Amsterdam. The "medieval" restrictive policies, which did not exist in either Amsterdam or London, were not introduced into their colonies by the Dutch or English, even though it must be noted that the Jews did not have complete equality. Thus the favorable conditions under which the Jews resided in Amsterdam and England, as compared with their unfavorable circumstances in central Europe, Italy (with the exception of Livorno), and Poland helped to assure that from the very beginning the condition of the Jews in what was to become the United States would be different.[32]

30. For the details, see Roth, *History of the Jews in England*, pp. 173–270, esp. 203–7, 247–70; V. D. Lipman, "The Age of Emancipation, 1815–1880," in Lipman, ed., *Three Centuries*, pp. 69–106; and the older but more detailed H. S. Q. Henriques, *The Jews and English Law* (London, 1908). From a comparison of the presentation of Roth (see esp. pp. 203–4, 248–49, 256) with that of H. Bloom ("Felix Libertate and the Emancipation of Dutch Jewry," in *Essays on Jewish Life and Thought Presented in Honor of Salo Wittmayer Baron* [New York, 1959], pp. 105–22), it appears that in the seventeenth and eighteenth centuries the Jews of England were, on the whole, better off than their coreligionists in Holland. After the revolution of 1795 and the deposition of the House of Orange, however, the National Assembly of the Batavian Republic, in 1796, gave the Jews complete equality; an equality incorporated into the National Constitution of 1798 and maintained under French rule and also after the restoration of the House of Orange in 1813 (Bloom, "Felix Libertate," pp. 120–21).

31. Marcus, *Jew in the Medieval World*, p. 71.

32. For an elaboration of this theme, see B. Halpern, "America Is Different," in M. Sklare, ed., *The Jews: Social Patterns of an American Group* (New York–London, 1958), pp. 23–39.

APPENDIX. *Parallel passages in the* Discorso *of Simone Luzzatto and the* Humble Addresses *of Menasseh ben Israel*

Luzzatto	*Menasseh ben Israel*
... dico, che frà li giovamenti, & utili, che la natione Hebrea apporta alla Città di Venetia, principalissimo è il profitto, che dall'essercitio mercantile ne rissulta, professione quasi di lei propria.... (consideration 1, p. 8ᵛ; Hebrew, p. 81)	It is a thing confirmed, that merchandizing is, as it were, the proper profession of the Nation of the Jews. ("How Profitable," Wolf, p. 81)
... ne meno in alcun loco, hanno facoltà & habilità di acquistare beni stabili, e se l'havessero, non complirebbe à loro interessi il farlo, per non Impegnare, & incarcerare li loro haveri mentre che le persone sono soggette a tante varietà, stantiando in ogni loco con salvi condotti, & indulti de Prencipi.... (consideration 3, p. 15ᵛ; Hebrew, p. 87)	Besides, seeing it is no wisedome for them to endeavour the gaining of Lands and other immovable goods, and so to imprison their possessions here, where their persons are subject to so many casualities, banishments and peregrinations.... ("How Profitable," Wolf, p. 82)
Circa al viaggiare, e formare nuove pratiche, l'Hebreo ad alcun altro non cede, non havendo occasione di trattenersi nella propria patria per coltivare terreni, over'altri esercitij urbani che l'impediscono.... (consideration 4, p. 19ᵛ; Hebrew, p. 90)	The Jews, have no oportunity to live in their own Country, to till the Lands or other like employments, give themselves wholly unto merchandizing, and for contriving new Inventions, no Nation almost going beyond them. ("How Profitable," Wolf, p. 82)
... per il che si osserva che ove sono dimorati gl'Hebrei vi fiorì il traffico & il negotio, come Livorno ne può fare attestatione, & la Città di Venetia giamai porrà in oblio la memoria del primo Inventore della Scala di Spalatro, che fù Hebreo di Natione, che con suoi raccordi transportò il negotio di gran parte di Levante in la Città, giudicata hora detta Scala il più fermo, e solido fondamento di traffico ch'habbia la Città. (consideration 4, pp. 18ᵛ–19ʳ; Hebrew, pp. 89–90)	And so't is observed, that wheresoever they go to dwell, there presently the Traficq begins to flourish. Which may be seen in divers places, especially in Ligorne, which having been but a very ignoble and inconsiderable City, is at this time, by the great concourse of people, one of the most famous places of Trafique of whole Italy. Furthermore, the Inventor of the famous *Scala de Spalatro* (the most firme and solid Traficq of Venice) was a Jew, who by this his Invention transported the Negotiation from a great part of the Levant into that City. ("How Profitable," Wolf, p. 82)
Livorno fù picciol, & ignobil Borgo, ma dall'industria delli Gran Duchi divvene famoso Mercato dell'Italia.... (consideration 4, p. 21ʳ; Hebrew, p. 92)	

. . . dal qual essercitio ne derrivano alla Città cinque importanti benefitij. Primo l'accrescimento de publici datij d'entrata, & uscita. Secondo il transporto di diverse mercantie da paesi remoti, non solo per necessità delli huomini, ma per ornamento della vita civile. Terzo somministrando materie in gran copia a lavoranti, & artigiani come, Lana, Seta, Gottoni, & simili, circa le quali si trattiene l'industria d'operarij mantenendosi in pace, & quiete senza alcuna tumultuaria comotione per penuria del vitto. Quarto, il smaltimento di tante manifatture fabricate, & elaborate nella Città con quali si sostengono tante migliara di persone. Quinto, il commercio, & la reciproca negotiatione, ch'è il fondamento della pace, & quiete frà popoli confinanti. . . .
(consideration 1, pp. 8ᵛ–9ʳ;Hebrew, p. 81)

. . . not onely with what is requisite and necessary for the life of man; but also what may serve for ornament to his civill condition. Of which *Traficq*, there ariseth ordinarily *Five* important benefits.
1. The augmentation of the Publiq Tolls and Customes, at their coming and going out of the place.
2. The transporting and bringing in of marchandises from remote Countries.
3. The affording of Materials in great plenty for all Mechaniqs; as Wooll, Leather, Wines; Jewels, as Diamants, Pearles and such like Merchandize.
4. The venting and exportation of so many kinds of Manifactures.
5. The Commerce and reciprocall Negotiation at Sea, which is the ground of Peace between neighbour Nations, and of great profit to their own Fellow-cittizens.
("How Profitable," Wolf, p. 83)

. . . ma quello è notabile, circa li capitali d'altri Hebrei, che sotto Dominij alieni si ricoverono (che come hò accenato nella precedente consideratione) che in gran somma si rimmettono alli Hebrei della Città li padroni de quali si sodisfano d'ogni poco d'utile, & emolumento che ne traggono, poiche non li ricapitano a Venetia per vantaggio di utili che più in questa piazza, ch'in altra ne sperano, ma solamente per evitare quelli pericoli che ritenendoli appresso di loro agevolmente li potrebbero occorrere. . . .
(consideration 4, p. 19ʳ; Hebrew, p. 90)

. . . ne si deve stimare lieve la negotiatione de detti Hebrei poi che molti di loro che si ritrovano in altri paesi rimettono gran parte de loro haveri in mano delli habitanti della Città non potendosi transferire con le loro persone per varie cause, bastandoli d'haver posto le loro facoltà in loco sicuro. . . .
(consideration 3, p. 17ʳ; Hebrew, p. 88)

This reason is the more strengthened, when we see, that not onely the Jewish Nation dwelling in Holland and Italy, trafficqs with their own stock, but also with the riches of many others of their own Nation, friends, kinds-men and acquaintance, which notwithstanding live in Spaine, and send unto them their moneys and goods, which they hold in their hands, and content themselves with a very small portion of their estate, to the end they may be secure and free from danger that might happen unto them, in case they should fall under the yoke of the Inquisition; whence not onely their goods, but oftentimes also their lives are endangered.
("How Profitable," Wolf, p. 83)

Primieramente s'oppone a ciò l'instinto naturale, e l'affetto indelebile ch'ogn'uno tiene alla sua Patria, e desiderio di terminare la vita ove n'hebbe il principio. . . .
(consideration 3, p. 14ᵛ; Hebrew, p. 86)

Subintrano poi in loro vece li Forastieri nell'animo de quali insurge ancora l'istesso desiderio di quiete e riposo, e dopo l'essere satolli de guadagni, li conducono nelle loro Patrie, & a questi parimente succedano altri Esteri con l'istesso talento, di modo che sempre continua il transporto del danaro ammassato dalla Città, senz'alcun augumento di ricchezze in essa, ma più tosto ne segue evidente detrimento. . . .
(consideration 3, pp. 12ᵛ–13ʳ; Hebrew, pp. 84–85)

. . . ma al sopradetto inconveniente pare che mirabilmente sovenga, e rimedia il traffico maneggiato da gl'Hebrei, non havendo essi propria Patria alla quale aspirano di transportare li loro haveri ammassati nella Città . . . tanto meno aspirano a dignità, Titoli & Dominij, per il ch'ove una volta sono con benignità ricevuti fanno ferma risolutione di non più partirsi. . . .
(consideration 3, p. 15ᵛ; Hebrew, p. 87)

Terza, che li mercanti hanno per costume dopò haver raddunato ricchezze non contentarsi del loro semplice possesso, ma son'assaliti da pensieri di conseguire prerogative, e dignità straordinarie, & insieme con terreni procurare Titoli, Dominij, & Iurisditioni per rendere più Illustre la loro conditione per inanzi ignota. . . .
(consideration 3, p. 15ʳ; Hebrew pp. 86–87)

. . . onde si può arditamente concludere che . . . più giovevole a gl'interessi del Prencipe, e de gl'istessi Cittadini, è . . . il ritrovarsi il traffico in potere della natione Hebrea stabilite nella Città le persone, e fermate le facoltà, ch'in mano di Forastieri. . . .
(consideration 3, p. 16ʳ; Hebrew p. 87)

The love that men ordinarily beare to their own Country and the desire they have to end their lives, where they had their begining, is the cause, that most strangers having gotten riches where they are in a forain land, are commonly taken in a desire to returne to their native soil, and there peaceably to enjoy their estate; so that as they were a help to the places where they lived, and negotiated while they remained there; so when they depart from thence, they carry all away, and spoile them of their wealth: transporting all into their own native Country: But with the Jews the case is farre different; for where the Jews are once kindly receaved, they make a firm resolution never to depart from thence, seeing they have no proper place of their own: and so they are always with their goods in the Cities where they live, a perpetuall benefit to all payments. Which reasons do clearly proove, that it being the property of Citizens in populous and rich countries, to seeke their rest and ease with buying lands and faire possession of which they live; many of them hating commerce, aspire to Titles and Dignities: therefore of all strangers, in whose hands ordinarily Trafique is found, there are none so profitable and beneficiall to the place where they trade and live, as is the Nation of the Jews.
("How Profitable," Wolf, pp. 83–84).

. . . sapiamo che sotto il Re di Persia se ne ricovra quantità grande, e con mediocre libertà. . . .
(consideration 18, p. 89ᵛ; Hebrew, p. 152)

In Persia there is a great number of Jews, and they live indifferent freely.
("How Profitable," Wolf, p. 85)

. . . nel stato del Sig. Turcho è la principale stanza della Natione. . . .
(consideration 18, p. 89ᵛ; Hebrew p. 152)

But the chiefest place where the Jews life, is the Turkish empire. . . .
("How Profitable," Wolf, p. 85)

In Costantinopoli, e Salonichi, vi ne è maggior numero, che in altre Città, e si giudica in queste due solamente esserne più di 80 mila, e si stima che sotto l'Imperio Turchesco passano li miglioni.
(consideration 18, p. 90ʳ; Hebrew, p. 152)

The number of the Jews living in this kingdome of the Great Turke, is very great, and amounts to many Millions. In Constantinople alone there are 48 Synagogues, and in Salaminque 36, and more then fourescore thousand soules in these two Cities alone.
("How Profitable," Wolf, p. 86)

In la Germania sotto l'Imperatore, vi ne sono gran quantità. . . .
(consideration 18, p. 90ᵛ; Hebrew, p. 152)

In Germany, there lives also a great multitude of Jews. . . .
("How Profitable," Wolf, p. 86)

. . . ma molto più in Polonia, Russia, e Lituania, ove vi sono Accademie, & Università di migliaia di Gioveni, e s'esercitano nelle Leggi Civili, e canoniche de Hebrei, havendo in quelle Regioni libera Potestà di giudicare qualunque differenza e controversia si civile come criminale, che accade frà la Natione. . . .
(consideration 18, p. 90ᵛ; Hebrew, p. 152)

But yet a greater number of Jews are found in the Kingdome of Poland, Prussia and Lethuania, under which Monarchy they have the Jurisdiction to judge amongst themselves all causes, both Criminal and Civil; and also great and famous Academies of their own.
("How Profitable," Wolf, p. 87)

In quanto all'Italia sono universalmente da Prencipi che li ricettono protetti, e favoriti, & osservati li loro indulti, e Privileggi, senza alcuna alteratione, che per esser ciò sotto l'occhio d'ogni uno non occorre ch'io vi allungo, e credo arrivare al numero di venticinque mila.
(consideration 18, p. 91ʳ; Hebrew, p. 153)

In Italy, they are generally protected by all the Princes: their principall residence is in the most famous City of Venice; so that in that same City alone they possesse about 1400 Houses; and are used there with much courtesy and clemency. Many also live in Padoa and Verona; others in Mantua, and also many in Rome itself. Finally they are scattered here and there in the chief places of Italy, and do live there with many speciall priviledges.
("How Profitable," Wolf, p. 87)

. . . tutta via ne Paesi Bassi sono con grandissima carità, & amorevolezza trattati, come in Amstradamo, Retrodamo & Amburgo di Olssatia. . . .
(consideration 18, p. 91ʳ; Hebrew, p. 153)

In the Low-Countries also, the Jews are received with great Charity and Benevolency, and especially in this most renowned City of Amsterdam. . . .
("How Profitable," Wolf, p. 88)

... & doppo haver ammassato ricchezze convenevoli procura di godere l'acquistato in quiete, & tranquilità, investendole in beni stabili, & entrate Cittadinesche lontane dall'insulti della fortuna. ...
(consideration 2, p. 10ʳ; Hebrew, p. 82)

... dal che procede, che le Città divenute grandi, & potenti per il traffico de proprij Cittadini, per cause dell'investite di beni stabili, fabriche di sontuosi edifitij, acquisti di pretiosi supeletili, & occupationi urbane, alla fine la negotiatione perviene in mano di Forastieri, & stranieri. ...
(consideration 2, p. 10ᵛ; Hebrew, p. 83)

For the Natives, and those especially that are most rich, they build themselves houses and Palaces, buy Lands and firme goods, aime at Titles and Dignities, and so seek their rest and contentment that way.
("How Profitable," Wolf, p. 89)

Nell'esilio di Castiglia, & altri Regni a lei adgiacenti a tempi del Re Ferdinando, e Regina Isabella si trovarono uniti insieme, vicino al numero di mezzo milione d'anime, che gli esclusi, che non si volsero convertire alla Religione Christiana, furono trecento mila (come narra Isach Abravanello dottissimo Autore, chi vi si trovò come Capo) fra quali vi furno huomini di gran spirito, e Conseglieri di Stato, come fu l'istesso Abravanello; ma non si trovò in tanto numero, alcuno che ardì di proponere partito rissoluto per sollevarsi da quel miserabile esilio; ma si dispersero, e distrassero per tutto il mondo; segno evidente, che gli hodierni instituti de gl'Hebrei, e loro rimmessi costumi gl'inclinano alla soggettione, & ossequio de loro Prencipi.
(consideration 14, p. 57ʳ; Hebrew, pp. 122–23)

This may be seen more clearly yet in their being banished out of Castile in the dayes of Ferdinand & Isabella. Their number at that time was supposed to have been half a Million of men, amongst whom were many of great valour, & courage (as Don Isaac Abarbanel, a Counsellor of State, doth relate) & yet amongst so great a number, there was not found any one man, that undertook to raise a party to free themselves from that most miserable banishment. An evident sign of the proper and naturall resolution of this Nation, and their constant obedience to their Princes.
("How Faithfull," Wolf, p. 91)

It should be apparent from the above juxtaposition of passages that Menasseh ben Israel reworked and adapted material found in the *Discorso*. For example, Luzzatto had pointed out that the native Venetian merchants were retiring from commerce, and in order to preserve their assets and enjoy a life of peace and quiet, invested them in real estate, *palazzi*, and luxury goods. In their place, foreign merchants were coming to the city, and as soon as they became wealthy, leaving it and taking their profits with them, and thus in the long run, they did not enrich the city. It was difficult to induce them to stay in the city for three reasons: first, out of natural and patriotic sentiments they wanted to return to die in their homeland, and also they were reluctant to acquire Venetian citizenship since it could require renouncing citizenship in their place of birth where they enjoyed political privileges; second, they wished to acquire real estate, which was in short supply in the city of Venice; third, in addition to their wealth, they wanted to obtain prerogatives and special honors, and along with land they aspired to titles, power, and jurisdiction. Therefore, Luzzatto claimed that it was desirable to let the Jews engage in trade, since they had no homeland to which they could take their profits, could not invest in real estate and would not do so even if they could because of their insecure legal status, and certainly did not aspire to dignities, titles, and power (considerations two and three). Menasseh ben Israel utilized some of these points. However, he did not follow exactly the argument of Luzzatto, which reflected the closed social system of Venice in which the native Venetian *cittadini* merchants could not rise to the nobility. It was to foreign merchants that Luzzatto ascribed the desire for titles, dominion, and jurisdiction. Menasseh, in adapting the argument of Luzzatto, disregarded this distinction, and applied that desire for honor and power to the native merchants.

Also, Menasseh added to his paraphrase of Luzzatto's reference to Livorno (in the context of showing the role of the Jews in promoting trade, [consideration 4, 18^v] a characterization of Livorno taken from a passage towards the end of the same consideration (21^r). There, in order to justify the contribution of the Jews to the commerce of Venice, Luzzatto made the point that human initiative played a major role in attracting commerce to a city. In support, he gave the example of the grand dukes of Tuscany, through whose commercial policy Livorno, once a small and ignoble "borgo," became a famous emporium. Menasseh took this characterization of Livorno, but worked it into the previous passage, which mentioned the specific role of the Jews in Livorno.

Furthermore, when enumerating the five important benefits derived from trade, in the third benefit Menasseh changed the specific commodities mentioned as imported for the Venetian workers ("wool, silk, cotton, and similar items") to those required, presumably, in England: "Wool, Leather, Wines: Jewels as Diamants, Pearles and such like Merchandize."

Finally, it should be noted that in the passage explaining that the presence of the Jews was desirable because they not only brought their own money with them but also attracted that of their coreligionists elsewhere who wished to put it in a safer place, Menasseh, writing in Protestant Holland for the ruler of Protestant England, could refer to the "nation" living in Spain, and to the danger of the Inquisition. On the other hand, in the very similar passage in the *Discorso* which Menasseh apparently used, Luzzatto, writing in Catholic Venice, had probably not considered it prudent to be so explicit, and therefore merely referred to Jews living under other jurisdictions who desired to avoid dangers which could easily befall them.

As stated above, a further investigation of the sources of Menasseh ben Israel and his utilization of them is desirable.

Rabbi Nahman Bratslaver's Journey to the Land of Israel

Arthur Green

I

The journey of Rabbi Nahman of Bratslav to the Land of Israel in 1798–99 has long been seen as a turning point in the life of that incredibly complex and baffling figure. No wonder; it was Nahman himself, both in direct statements and through various half-hidden references, who first revealed the centrality of this event to any understanding of his life and career. Though he had already, with great reluctance, taken on the role of Zaddik for a small band of followers before his journey, it was only upon his return from Eretz Israel that the twenty-seven-year-old Nahman really allowed himself to become a public figure. He ordered any teachings of his which dated from before that journey be deleted from his collected works, claiming that they were now of little worth.[1] In later periods of spiritual dryness Nahman was to proclaim that it was only the fact of his journey to the Holy Land that kept him "alive" and allowed him to continue in his role as Zaddik.[2]

The account of Nahman's journey has survived in two versions, both of them composed by his leading disciple and secretary Nathan of Nemirov. One of these versions, the one comprising the second part of Nathan's *Shivhe ha-RaN* (also published separately under the title *Mas'ot ha-Yam*), was written with considerable literary flourish, and indeed with just a touch of that mythic imagination which so characterizes Nahman's own *Sippure Ma'asiyyot*. The second version, forming a chapter of the fuller biographical memoir entitled *Hayye MoHaRaN*, is highly fragmentary and unpolished but contains a wealth of materials, particularly with regard to explanations of the journey. The dating of these two accounts and the relationship between them has been the subject of a thoroughgoing study by Ada Rapoport.[3]

---

1. *Hayye MoHaRaN* (henceforth: *Hayye*), *sihot ha-shayyakhim la-torot* 55; *Hayye* II, *Ma'alat torato* 18, 43; *'avodat ha-shem* 33. The two major sources on Nahman's journey will be designated as follows: *Shivhe ha-RaN*, Part II (*Mas'ot ha-Yam*) = *Shiv*; and *Hayye MoHaRaN*, *nesi'ato le-'eretz yisra'el* = EY.

2. *Sihot ha-RaN* (henceforth: *Sihot*) 153.

3. "Two Sources on R. Nahman's Journey to the Holy Land" [Hebrew], *KS*, XLVI (1971), 147–53. Rapoport has shown that the version of *Shivhe ha-RaN* is the earlier of the two accounts.

Nathan's memoirs in general are impressive and unique within Hasidism for their full and highly accurate recording of detail, offered without the supernaturalistic embellishments so characteristic of other Hasidic tales of the masters. In seeking to explain this phenomenon, Joseph Dan has referred to the Bratslav corpus as hagiography that has transcended itself; the events of the master's life are so crucial and holy in themselves that one dare not tamper with them.[4] The accuracy of Nathan as a reporter (with minor exceptions) is also accepted in the studies of Joseph Weiss and Mendel Piekarz, the basic critical writers on the history of Bratslav. Elsewhere we hope to show that this regard for biographical detail, on the face of it so nearly modern, is deeply tied to the Bratslav image of Nahman as the last of the great Zaddikim in world history, and is modeled on what the Hasidim took to be the "historical" descriptions of Rabbi Simeon ben Yohai and his circle in the Zohar.

This high regard for detail does not, however, keep the chronicler in *Shivhe ha-RaN* from filling his account with an exciting aura of mysterious moments of seemingly great but hidden significance: Nahman's nocturnal visit to Kamenets-Podolsk, the childish games he played in Istanbul, his readiness to leave the Land almost as soon as he had set foot on its soil, his strange encounter with a young Arab in Haifa, his visits with the Hasidic community of Tiberias and at the graves of the saints—all of these lend to the account a sense of some secret and divine mission, the precise nature of which remains as hidden as the mysterious nature of Nahman himself. One cannot help but feel, in reading this account, that here Nahman in life has appeared as a character out of one of his own later stories.

The story of Nahman's journey to the Holy Land has fired the imaginations of modern writers on Hasidism no less than it has served as a source of inspiration to the Bratslav Hasidim themselves.[5] Several writers have tried to

---

This version, first published in 1815 as an addendum to the first edition of Nahman's *Sippure Maʿasiyyot*, was probably composed sometime shortly after Nahman's death in 1810. The account in *Hayye MoHaRaN* must have been composed sometime after Nathan's own visit to the Holy Land in 1822, to which he makes reference (#10). Rapoport's conclusions, with which I am in full agreement, are disputed by Joseph Dan (*Ha-Sippur ha-Hasidi* [Jerusalem, 1975], p. 185) who seems to claim that the *Shivhe* version was written by someone other than Nathan. Nahman's sayings with regard to the sanctity of the Holy Land have been collected by Nahman of Cheryn in his *Zimrat he-'Aretz* (Lvov, 1876).

4. Dan, *Sippur*, pp. 183 ff.

5. The chief modern discussions of the journey are to be found in S. A. Horodezky, *Ha-Hasidut we-ha-Hasidim* (Tel Aviv, 1953), III, 23 ff.; IV, 57 ff.; idem, *ʿOle Tziyyon* (Tel Aviv, 1947), pp. 160 ff.; H. Zeitlin, *Reb Nakhman Braslaver* (New York, 1952), pp. 82 ff.; S. M. Dubnov, *Toledot ha-Hasidut* (Tel Aviv, 1960), pp. 292 ff.; M. Buber, *The Tales of Rabbi Nachman* (New York, 1956), pp. 179 ff.; and J. K. Miklishansky in *Ha-Hasidut we-Tziyyon* (Jerusalem, 1963), pp. 246 ff.

describe the journey in proto-Zionist terms, as the example *par excellence* of the great attachment of Hasidism to the Land of Israel. Others have been baffled by it, and like nearly everything else in the life of the much misunderstood Nahman, it has even been the source of calumny.[6] The most interesting explanation of the journey is that undertaken several years ago by Neal Rose, who tried to apply to Nahman the insights of Mircea Eliade concerning rites of passage and the journey to the center, as described in Eliade's many writings on the phenomenology of religion.[7] The present study agrees with Rose in the evocation of Eliade's categories for an understanding of Nahman's voyage, but with some serious shifts of focus. The fact is that despite the many treatments of the subject, no one has yet carefully examined the sources in Nathan's writings, including several very important and revealing statements by Nahman himself, in order to understand the true motivation for the journey and its meaning in Nahman's life.

The fact that Nahman should choose to embark upon a journey to the Land of Israel is on the face of it no cause for surprise. The eighteenth century had seen a great increase in travel and emigration of Eastern European Jews to the Holy Land. At first these journeys took place in circles closely connected to the Sabbatian movement,[8] but the voyagers later came to include key figures of early Hasidism. The meaning and possible messianic implications of these journeys have been much discussed by modern historians of the Hasidic movement.[9]

6. S. M. Dubnov sees the journey as a result of Nahman's quarrel with his uncle Barukh, who could not tolerate Nahman as a competitor for power among Ukrainian Hasidim. Since Nahman had no major support in this battle, "a new idea arose in his mind: to journey to the Land of Israel and to receive a sort of authorization from the holiness of the Land and the group of Zaddikim there" (*Toledot*, p. 292). Following Dubnov's argument is Solomon Zeitlin, who used the occasion of a review of Jacob Minkin's *The Romance of Hasidism* to propose a shockingly vituperative attack on Nahman (*JQR*, n.s. XXVII [1937], 251). Only because such a view has been propounded by otherwise respectable scholars is it worthy of refutation. Nahman's argument with his uncle did not occur until some time after his return from Eretz Israel. In the winter of 1802–3 "there was still peace between them" (*Yeme MaHaRNaT* [Bene Berak, 1956], pp. 12 ff.), and this was four years after Nahman's return in 1799. Further, Nahman was on good terms with any number of Zaddikim in the Ukraine in this early period. Surely Levi Yizhaq of Berdichev, who stood by Nahman through all his later difficulties, would gladly have supported him had he been in any difficulty in 1798. Less pernicious than this view of the journey but no more accurate was that of Horodezky (*Hasidut*, III, 25), who claimed that Nahman's plan was to settle in the Holy Land. There is no evidence to support the contention that anything more than a short visit was intended.

7. "Eretz Israel in the Theology and Experience of Rabbi Nahman of Bratzlav," *Journal of Hebraic Studies*, I (1970), 63 ff.

8. Best known of these is the pilgrimage led by Judah Hasid and Hayyim Mal'akh in 1700. For a full discussion of that journey, see M. Benayahu, "The Holy Brotherhood of R. Judah Hasid," in *Shneur Zalman Shazar Jubilee Volume* (Jerusalem, 1960), pp. 131 ff.

9. Cf. I. Heilpern, *Ha-ʿAliyyot ha-Rishonot shel ha-Hasidim le-'Eretz Yisra'el* (Jerusalem, 1947). These journeys have been discussed within the context of the place of messianism in the Hasidic

The first of these journeys within circles close to Hasidism was that of Gershon of Kutow (Kitov), the brother-in-law of the Ba⁽al Shem Tov and a member of the Klaus in Brody, who arrived in Eretz Israel in 1747.[10] R. Gershon first settled in Hebron and later in Jerusalem, where he joined the already established Kabbalistic community of Beth-El. Nahman's own paternal grandfather, Nahman of Gorodenka, who was also a member of the Ba⁽al Shem Tov's circle, settled in the Galilee in 1764, along with Menahem Mendel of Premyshlyany.[11] The Ba⁽al Shem Tov himself had set out on such a journey, as did his disciple Jacob Joseph of Polonnoye. The BeSHT interrupted his journey at Istanbul and returned to Podolia, a fact which has led to much speculation on the part of historians.[12] In some way he must have felt that it was not right for him to proceed further. Whether this had to do with a sense that his leadership was needed at home or with a feeling of some other spiritual "obstacle" cannot be determined from the available sources, highly shrouded as they are in legendary embellishments. In his famous letter to Gershon of Kutow, written around 1750, the BeSHT admitted that he had given up on his plans to visit the Holy Land.[13] In the case of Jacob Joseph, who was to serve as courier for that letter, it was apparently the BeSHT himself who advised him to stay at home.[14] Years later Pinhas of Korzec also attempted a journey to the Holy Land, but he died shortly after he had set out on his way in 1791.[15] Of the Miedzyrzec circle, Menahem Mendel of Vitebsk and Abraham of Kalisk arrived in Eretz Israel in 1777, settling first in Safed and

---

movement. Those who tend to place a greater emphasis on the role of messianism in Hasidism (Dinur, Tishby) will look for significance in the journeys of early Hasidic figures to the Holy Land (especially Ben Zion Dinur, Be-Mifneh ha-Dorot [Jerusalem, 1955], pp. 192 ff.), while their opponents in this larger controversy (Buber, Scholem, Schatz) will tend to see such pilgrimages as lacking in larger significance.

10. Cf. A. J. Heschel, "R. Gershon Kutover," HUCA, XXIII (1950–51), Part I, Hebrew section, 46 ff. This article contains a wealth of valuable information on the earliest Hasidic journeys to Eretz Israel.

11. Their journey and settlement were described by Simhah ben Joshua of Zalozhty in Sippure 'Eretz ha-Galil, published as a section of his 'Ahavat Tziyyon (Grodno, 1790), and reprinted by A. Ya⁽ari in Mas⁽ot 'Eretz Yisra'el (Tel Aviv, 1946).

12. The BeSHT's aborted journey is briefly mentioned in Shivhe ha-BeSHT, ed. S. A. Horodezky (Berlin, 1922), pp. 48, 111 f. A. Ya⁽ari has pointed out that the Yiddish version of Shivhe ha-BeSHT treats the journey more explicitly than does the better-known Hebrew version (KS, XXXIX [1964], 559 ff.). Dinur (Be-Mifneh) makes much of this journey, seeing its failure as the crucial turning point in the early history of the Hasidic movement.

13. "If God wills it, I shall be with you—but this is not the proper time for it." The letter was published by Jacob Joseph of Polonnoye at the end of his Ben Porat Yosef (Korzec, 1781), and has been frequently reprinted.

14. Shivhe ha-BeSHT, p. 50.

15. M. Biber, Mazkeret li-Gedole Ostrog (Berdichev, 1907), p. 212; Horodezky, Hasidut, I, 152 f.

later in Tiberias. They became the effective leaders of the Hasidic community in the Holy Land.[16]

Among Nahman's stated purposes in journeying to the Land of Israel was his desire to commune with his grandfather, who lay buried in the graveyard of Tiberias. Given the young Nahman's penchant for visiting the grave of the Baʿal Shem Tov (his maternal great-grandfather),[17] it is hardly surprising that he should have wanted to be at the burial place of his paternal grandfather as well, "so that he always have access to that which he is to know through him."[18] A visit to the grave of his saintly forebearer was not merely a matter of respect, but might be a source of some revealed "knowledge" from the upper world.[19] He sought the same sort of instruction at the graveside of the elder Nahman that he felt himself to have received at the grave of the BeSHT. In a larger sense, in seeking to undertake the dangerous but sacred journey to the Holy Land, Nahman was following the example of his two revered ancestral heroes. We must hasten to add, however, that communion with the spirit of his late grandfather was perhaps the least of the highly complicated purposes that moved Nahman toward this voyage. As we shall see, he nearly missed visiting Tiberias altogether, and it seems to have required both the pleas of the living and the attraction of the gravesite to get him there.

Before seeking to understand Nahman's complex motives for journeying to the Holy Land, it is appropriate that we recount the details of the journey itself, as recorded in the writings of Nathan of Nemirov. It should be emphasized that none of this account is first-hand; Nathan met Nahman only several years after the latter's return from Eretz Israel. The account must thus be seen as one based entirely on recollections shared with Nathan by Nahman's friend and earliest disciple, Simeon, who accompanied his master on

16. Heilpern, ʿAliyyot, and further details in Gershon Hundert, "Toward a Biography of R. Abraham Kalisker" (M.A. thesis, Ohio State University).

17. *Shivhe ha-RaN*, I, 19.

18. EY 5. This account contains a typical example of the self-censorship found in many Bratslav sources. When Nahman was living in Medvedevka and was unable to make the journey to Medzhibozh, where the BeSHT was buried, he would send messages to the BeSHT through the Zaddik Isaiah of Yanev, who lay buried in the nearby Smela graveyard. For a while he communed with Nahman of Gorodenka in the same way, but at some point he was prevented from doing so. Nathan's account reads: "He also said that he was going to Eretz Israel for this reason. Previously, when he had needed something from his grandfather R. Nahman, who lay buried in Eretz Israel, he would send the Zaddik R. Isaiah, who lay in Smela. But now, etc., and he could not send him." It would be interesting to know what lies behind that "etc." of censorship.

19. Communion with the spirits of the saintly dead as a means toward mystical enlightenment was well known among the Safed Kabbalists of the sixteenth century. The best example of such mystical visits to sacred gravesites is to be found in Moses Cordovero's mystical diary *Sefer Gerushin*. This phenomenon has been discussed by R. J. Z. Werblowsky in his *Joseph Karo, Lawyer and Mystic* (Oxford, 1962), pp. 51 ff. Cf. especially the passage by R. Hayyim Vital quoted on p. 76.

the journey, and to a lesser extent by Nahman himself. In retelling the tale, we have omitted certain repeated accounts of the great dangers and trials, as well as the constant side remarks in praise of the master's heroism, seeking to glean from Nathan's rather elaborate rendition what is more or less a simple and factual account of Nahman's journey.

II

Nahman's announcement of his decision to travel to Eretz Israel was preceded by another mysterious journey, a visit to Kamenets-Podolsk, which he undertook in the early spring of 1798. This journey set the pattern for a number of such visits to various locales in the Ukraine, which Nahman would visit incognito and where he was reputed to have performed the unfathomable acts of a hidden Zaddik. On his journey to Kamenets he was accompanied by his friend Simeon and by another disciple whose name is not given. When they set out from Medvedevka, their destination was not yet known to them; it was only after a stop at Medzhibozh and a visit with his parents that Nahman was "informed by heaven"[20] as to the destination of this journey.

The city of Kamenets-Podolsk is well known in Jewish history and in Hasidic lore for one reason: it was here that the famous debate with the followers of Jacob Frank had taken place in 1757, and the city—which had no Jews—was thus seen as a locus of the much-hated Frankist movement. According to Hasidic legend, both the Ba'al Shem Tov and Nahman of Gorodenka had debated the Frankists (though some sources connect this legend to the Lvov debate);[21] it is no wonder that Kamenets should have held some fascination for Nahman.

This fact has led Hillel Zeitlin to the highly interesting conclusion[22] that Nahman visited with Frankists in Kamenets, perhaps trying to win back their souls for Judaism. This theory, however, misses the mark in one crucial way: we know of no community of Frankists that survived in Kamenets as late as 1798, and it seems highly unlikely that there was one. The Jews were driven out of that and other cities of Podolia following the death of their protector Bishop Dembowski a few months after that first debate. After the Lvov

20. *Shiv.* 15–16; parallel in *EY* 1.
21. A. D. Twerski, *Sefer ha-Yahas mi-Chernobyl we-Ruzhin* (Lublin, 1938), p. 100. M. Balaban denies the historicity of these traditions (*Toledot ha-Tenu'ah ha-Frankit* [Tel Aviv, 1934], pp. 295 ff., esp. p. 316).
22. Zeitlin, *Reb Nakhman Braslaver*, pp. 84 f.

debate and the conversions of 1759–60 we do not hear of Frankists settling in Kamenets, where as Jews they would not formerly have been permitted to dwell. By the end of the eighteenth century the center of Frankism had moved westward to Moravia and Germany, and those Polish Frankists who had converted were centered in Warsaw. While there may have been isolated crypto-Sabbatians in the Ukraine as late as the turn of the nineteenth century, it is clear that forty years after the debates the association of Kamenets-Podolsk with Frankism was a matter of memory, not of living fact.[23]

Nevertheless, it is quite clear that Nahman's visit to Kamenets had something to do with the *former* presence of Frankists in that city. After violating the local ordinance which forbade any Jew to spend a night within the city limits,[24] Nahman and his anonymous disciple (Simeon had remained behind at Medzhibozh) went calling at certain houses in the city. Once inside the house, Nahman would recite the proper blessing and have a drink of liquor. It would seem that during the night Nahman had inquired or by some means divined which had been the houses occupied by Frankists during the Kamenets debate. He then gained entry to those houses, and by means of his blessing and the glass of *schnapps* sought to perform some mysterious rite of purification. The custom of having a drink for the *tiqqun* (restoration) of a soul is well known in Hasidism; here, however, it seems to be the dwellings rather than the souls which Nahman had in mind. These houses had to be purified of the Frankist stain so that Jews might dwell in them again. Indeed, Nathan tells us, shortly after Nahman's visit the residence ban on Jews in Kamenets was lifted.[25]

That the visit to Kamenets had something to do with the heretical past of that city is confirmed by Nahman's own words concerning the meaning of his visit there: "Our master said that he who understands why the Land of Israel was first ruled by Canaanites and only afterwards by Israel will understand why he was first in Kamenets and only afterwards in Eretz Israel."[26]

The analogy clearly points to a version of the "descent of the Zaddik" into the realm of impurity before he could attain to a higher rung of perfection.

23. Balaban, *Ha-Tenuᶜah ha-Frankit*, pp. 192 ff.

24. There were frequent expulsions of Jews from that city in the seventeenth and eighteenth centuries. The most effective of these bans seems to have been that of 1750, which may in fact have kept Jews out of Kamenets for as long as fifty years. These expulsions are discussed by R. Mahler in *Di Yidn in Poiln* (New York, 1946), p. 234.

25. The ban was lifted, according to Mahler (*A History of Modern Jewry* [New York, 1971], p. 381), in 1797, a year before Nahman's visit. There was, however, a meeting of Podolian notables at Kamenets in June of 1798 (ibid., p. 383) which may have, among other things, ratified this edict.

26. *Shiv.* 2. *Shiv.* 3 contains a censored reference to the fact that the journey to Kamenets caused a good deal of controversy. "Everyone offered some interpretation of it, some praising it while others etc."

This idea, itself deeply rooted in Sabbatian thinking,[27] was generally referred in Hasidism to the work of the Zaddik in redeeming the souls of others. It plays a major role, as is known, in Nahman's own later thinking.[28] To reach the great heights which Nahman sought on his journey to the Holy Land, he would have to stoop to the greatest depths. He who seeks to rise to that most sacred of places must first descend and seek to purify the most defiled of human space.

Shortly afterwards, on the eve of Passover in 1798, Nahman announced his plans to depart for Eretz Israel. At the gathering of Hasidim on that holiday he offered an interpretation of the verse: "When your way led through the sea, your path through mighty water, and no one saw your footprints . . ." (Psalm 77:20), making reference, we should note, to a journey across the seas rather than to a visit to Eretz Israel.[29] He evinced no regard for family or property in the planning of his journey. When his daughter asked what would become of the family while he was away, he replied: "You will go to your in-laws. Someone will take your older sister as a household servant. Your younger sister will be taken into someone's home out of pity. Your mother can find work as a cook, and I shall sell everything in the house to cover expenses for the journey."[30]

Nahman saw the expected opposition of his family to the journey as a meni'ah, an obstacle in the path which had to be overcome. This accounts for the harshness of his retort. In much the same way did Nathan view the violent anti-Hasidic feelings of his own family when he first set out to become Nahman's disciple.[31]

It was about a month after Passover, on the eighteenth of Iyyar—May 4, 1798—that Nahman and Simeon[32] set out on their way. From Medvedevka

27. This idea is discussed at length by J. Weiss in his "Reshit Tzemihatah shel ha-Derekh ha-Hasidit," Zion, XVI (1951).

28. Cf. for example Liqqute MoHaRaN (henceforth: Liqqute), 64:3, which describes the necessary descent of the true Zaddik into the abyss in order to redeem those souls which are lost there.

29. Shiv. 5. For the parallel in EY 19, see below.

30. Shiv. 6.

31. Yeme MaHaRNaT, p. 12, and passim.

32. While in the earlier account Nathan took care not to mention the name of the single Hasid who accompanied Nahman on his journey, it does slip out in EY 8. A. Rapoport ("Two Sources," pp. 147 ff.) claims that most of Nathan's information on the journey came from Simeon rather than from Nahman himself. Simeon returned to the Holy Land to settle there permanently in 1820. It is for this reason, Rapoport claims, that in the account written after 1822 Nathan is more willing to mention him by name. As Piekarz has shown (Hasidut Braslav [Jerusalem, 1972], pp. 203 ff.), there was a struggle for leadership in the community in the early years following Nahman's death, and Simeon at that point may have been a threat to Nathan's position. Mentioning a rival as the one who accompanied the master on his sacred journey, and thus reminding the reader of his own latecomer status within the community, would not have served Nathan's ends at the time of the earlier version; hence the silence.

they traveled overland to Nikolayev, where they found a barge carrying wheat down the Dnieper to Odessa. Departure from Odessa was contrary to the usual route of Jewish travelers, who generally preferred to embark on the Black Sea voyage from Galati (Galatz), at the mouth of the Danube. Nahman of course saved time by choosing Odessa; it may also be that he had gotten word of the particularly severe pogrom that had nearly wiped out the Galati Jewish community in 1797.[33]

From Odessa they found a ship which took them, after a dangerous and stormy four-day journey, to Istanbul. Nahman spent his time on board ship writing down his teachings, but even his friend Simeon was not permitted to see what it was that he had written. This is the earliest reference we have to Nahman's habit of composing "secret" writings, which parallelled his exoteric literary production until his final illness set in; most of these writings were destroyed, on Nahman's orders, by his closest disciples.[34]

On his arrival at Istanbul, where he was forced to stay for some time while awaiting a ship bound for Eretz Israel, Nahman began to behave in a strange manner.

> He acted in all sorts of childish[35] ways, going about barefoot, without a belt, or without a top hat. He would go about [in the street] in his indoor clothing, running around the market like a child. There he would play war games, as children do. They [the players] would call one side "France" and the other something else, and they would war with one another, using real battle tactics. He did very many childish things in Istanbul.[36]

While in the Turkish capital, Nahman and Simeon came across a Hasidic emissary from the Holy Land who was on his way to Russia to collect funds for the Hasidic community of Tiberias, which was then headed by Abraham Kalisker. Nahman refused to reveal his true identity to the emissary, who, beset by the troubles of his own community, assumed that Nahman was an enemy of the Tiberias Hasidim who was being sent to the Holy Land to create some mischief.[37] Nahman compounded the difficulty by applying his "childish" behavior to this man and his companions as well. Each time they would

33. *Shiv.* 8. On the pogrom in Galati, see *Jewish Encyclopedia*, X, pp. 513 f.
34. *Shiv.* 8–9. Nahman's secret writings are discussed by J. Weiss in *Mehqarim be-Hasidut Braslav* (Jerusalem, 1974), pp. 181 ff.
35. Hebrew: ʿoseh kol mine qatnut. The Hebrew term has the *double entendre* of "childishness" or "lower spiritual state."
36. *EY* 11–12.
37. *Shiv.* 10. It is not clear whether they took him to be a *mitnagged* or a Hasid of Shneur Zalman of Liadi, whose controversy with Abraham Kalisker of Tiberias had broken out a year earlier.

ask him his name he would offer a different reply. Once he said that he was a *kohen*, then he denied it; he pretended for a while that he was the son of the Komarno Zaddik,[38] but once the other was convinced of this he turned around and heaped curses upon his alleged father. They became frustrated and angry and began to insult him. Nahman seemed to enjoy their degradations and insults, and once awakened them for no reason in the middle of the night, just to annoy them further. Although one of the emissary's companions was a ritual slaughterer and they thus had kosher meat available to them (pious Ashkenazim would not rely upon the somewhat different rules of kosher slaughter practiced by the Sephardic Jews of Istanbul), they would not share their food with the pestering young man, who was in this matter separated from his more docile, if tight-lipped, companion.[39]

What was the meaning of all this strange behavior? Nahman himself later explained it as having been an essential part of his journey to the Holy Land:

> The fact is that he did all this intentionally. He allowed himself to be reviled in all sorts of ways. He told the one who accompanied him that this degradation would be of great help, both on the forward journey and on their return. For the power of the great obstacles (*meni'ot*) which he had to overcome in going to Eretz Israel cannot be imagined, measured, or told. As he later explicitly said, it would have been impossible for him to get to Eretz Israel without this *qatnut*. He said that had he not undergone these degradations and this *qatnut* it would have been utterly impossible for him to have gotten there. He saw that he would be forced to remain in Istanbul and to die there. The *qatnut* and degradations saved him. . . .[40]

The point is again that of the dialectic of spiritual ascent and descent in the life of the Zaddik, though here in a somewhat less dramatic sense. Just as one who reaches for greater purification must do so by means of prior descent into the realm of defilement, so must one who reaches for *gadlut*, a state of higher spiritual consciousness, begin from an exaggerated position of *qatnut*. Here, as frequently in Hasidism, the Sabbatian sting has been removed from this dialectic, and it is portrayed in almost moralistic terms. The issue has now become one of humility, of seeking to avoid the accusations of the *meqatregim*, negative or "accusing" forces, who would claim that one is seek-

38. The specific person to whom he was referring, who had a son named Isaiah and was involved in some sort of controversy, is unknown to me.
39. *Shiv.* 10, and *EY* 11.
40. *Shiv.* 9.

ing to rise beyond that place which is proper for a human being. Such accusations may be avoided by beginning the ascent through the disguise of self-humiliation.[41]

It is clear that Nahman's choice of Istanbul as the scene for this *qatnut* was in part a reaction to the Ba'al Shem Tov's unsuccessful journey to Eretz Israel some fifty years earlier. Hasidic legend recounts, we will recall, that the BeSHT had terminated his journey in Istanbul. It was in Istanbul that he saw that "heaven was not allowing him to go on to the Holy Land."[42] Another version of the legend has it that the BeSHT saw the fiery sword of Eden warning him of danger unless he returned home without completing his mission.[43] Given this association with Istanbul, Nahman must have considered this to be the crucial point in his journey. If only he could pass through this city in safety, he would be able to reach the Land of Israel.

Once the emissary and his men had left Istanbul, Nahman began to return to his adult self.[44] He admitted his true identity to a Jewish ship-agent, who set out to arrange his passage. Meanwhile, a group of Hasidim from the Ukraine arrived in Istanbul on their way to Eretz Israel. The group included Rabbi Ze'ev Wolf of Charny-Ostrog, a disciple of the Maggid of Miedzyrzec who was later to become a leader of the Hasidic community in the Galilee. The elder Zaddik, informed of Nahman's identity, treated him with the respect due to a descendent of the BeSHT, despite some degree of continued erratic behavior on Nahman's part.[45]

As Nahman and Simeon planned to sail from Istanbul, another type of obstacle threatened to hold them back. By the beginning of 1798, the Napoleonic navy was fighting in the Eastern Mediterranean; Napoleon had by then begun the invasion of Egypt. Due to the dangers of battle, the Jewish community of Istanbul announced a ban on any further Jewish pilgrimages to the Holy Land. Having traditionally assumed primary responsibility for the victims of maritime disasters and piracy in the area, the community did not want to take on unnecessary risks. Nahman's reaction to this ban is highly instructive, and lends credence to the interpretation of the journey which we shall propose:

41. In *EY* 12 the matter is explained specifically with regard to the sanctity of the Holy Land. Because Eretz Israel is *gadlut de-gadlut*, one may only reach it through *qatnut de-qatnut*.

42. In the passages referred to in the preceding note, Nahman is quoted as saying that the BeSHT's journey had failed because he was not able to descend sufficiently into *qatnut*. The quotation from the BeSHT is taken by Dinur, *Be-Mifneh*, p. 192, from *'Adat Tzaddiqim*, p. 4a.

43. *Shivhe ha-BeSHT*, p. 48.

44. *Shiv.* 12.

45. *Shiv.* 13.

Our master did not pay any attention to this [ban] and *wanted to risk his life.*[46] He said to the one who accompanied him: "Know that *I want to place myself in danger, even great and terrible danger.* But I do not want to risk your life. Therefore, if you want, take money for expenses and go home in peace. I shall travel on alone, unbeknown to the people of Istanbul. *For I risk my life, come what may*" and so forth. His companion declined, saying "where my master is, whether for life or death, there will your servant be. 'Whither thou goest, I shall go.'"[47]

As it turned out, Nahman's refusal to change his plans was shared by an elderly and respected Sephardic sage from Jerusalem, who felt that as one already close to death he did not mind the risk. Under pressure from this *hakham*, the community allowed one last ship to sail for Jaffa, and Nahman and Simeon were given passage. Interestingly, Nahman asked the *hakham* to take him directly to Jerusalem, "for he said that he did not want to be in either Safed or Tiberias."[48] Since almost the entire Hasidic community of the Holy Land lived in those two towns of the Galilee, it might seem that Nahman wanted to avoid contact with them. It would also seem from here that a visit to his grandfather's grave was less than essential to his journey. It may be suspected, however, from the fact that Nahman never did go to Jerusalem, that this was but another ruse to fool those demonic powers who might hold him back if he were to reveal his true destination.

The voyage was not an easy one. The ship encountered a terrible storm on the high seas, and the rising waves threatened to engulf them all. Again, Nahman's attitude is instructive as to the meaning this journey had for him:

Nobody thought that they would be saved from death. Everyone cried out to God, and there was a night which was just like Yom Kippur, with everyone crying, confessing his sins, and seeking atonement for his soul. They recited *selihot* as well as other prayers and supplications. But our master sat in silence. When asked why he was silent in such a time of woe, he refused to reply. But then the wife of the rabbi of Khatin, herself a learned woman, who had been crying and screaming all night, asked him the same. It would seem that he cursed her and said "If only you too would be quiet, it would be good. *By this you will be tested.* If you are still, the waters of the sea will become still as well."[49]

The group, we are told, then followed Nahman's counsel, and soon the seas were still again. Having weathered the storm, however, the passengers

46. Hebrew: *le-hafqir 'et ʿatzmo.*
47. *Shiv.* 14. Emphasis mine.
48. *Shiv.* 13.
49. *Shiv.* 14. Emphasis mine.

were confronted with the new danger of a shortage in the supply of drinking water. When these and other tribulations were finally overcome, a fortuitous wind blew them into the port of Jaffa, the point of disembarkment for Jerusalem. Nahman sought to accompany the elder *hakham* to Jerusalem, but the port officials, especially cautious in times of war, were suspicious of his foreign dress and his ignorance of the local languages. They feared he might be a French spy in some outlandish disguise (!) and refused to allow him off the ship. He thus remained on board, proceeding northward along the coast to Haifa, and disembarked on Monday, September tenth—the eve of Rosh Hashanah.

Nahman's feeling as he first set foot on the Holy Land was one of great elation. He promptly informed his faithful companion that he should consider himself to be especially blessed to have been witness to such a momentous event.[50] On his arrival in the Holy Land, Nahman conducted himself as a *rebbe*, accepting petitions for prayer and conducting a public festive meal on the eve of Rosh Hashanah. Here he showed none of the reluctance which had characterized his earlier forays into the public arena. By the end of prayers on the following morning, however, he had become depressed. "Tremendous worry and brokenheartedness were aroused in him, and he did not speak to anyone at all."[51] Immediately after the holiday, he announced that he wanted to depart at once, without traveling to Tiberias or visiting any of the other holy places. It was only the pleas of Simeon and of the Hasidim in Safed and Tiberias, who had meanwhile heard of his arrival, which convinced him to remain awhile in the Holy Land.

While Nahman was in Haifa, another strange incident occured to which he attributed great significance. It seems that a young Arab "discovered" Nahman and began to visit his quarters regularly. The young man took a great liking to Nahman, but in vain did he seek to transcend the language barrier which existed between them. Failing to make his affection for Nahman understood, he at one point became angry and challenged the Zaddik to a duel. Frightened by the prospect, Nahman hid himself in the home of his friend the rabbi of Charny-Ostrog, who had arrived in Haifa with him. The "Ishmaelite," however, was soon appeased, and again showed great affection for Nahman. This too Nahman found disquieting, and said that he "suffered more from the love of this Ishmaelite than from his hate or anger." He felt that some great danger might await him in this person, and he may have claimed[52] that the young man was none other than Samael himself.[53]

50. *Shiv.* 15.
51. Ibid.
52. Hebrew: *ki-medummeh she-nisha* mi-piw.
53. *Shiv.* 17.

Exactly what it was about this man that the already depressed Nahman found so alarming is impossible to reconstruct from the single source which speaks of their encounter. The fact that a Zaddik should find himself the object of affection on the part of a non-Jew was not in itself any cause for wonder; in Eastern Europe it was very common for non-Jews, peasants and nobles alike, to pay homage to certain of the Zaddikim. The relationship here, however, gives no indication of such veneration. The Arab seems to have seen himself as a peer, rather than as a would-be disciple, of Nahman. Perhaps this thought in itself was upsetting to the Zaddik, who was unaccustomed to anyone relating to him outside the traditional canons of his role. His own inability to respond to this offer of friendship may be the reason why the other's offer of love caused Nahman more pain than his hate. We should further note that the word 'ahavah when used in these sources may refer to almost any degree of affection, love, or friendly feeling; it is also within the realm of possibility that Nahman feared sexual advances on the part of the young man. Nahman, ever tormented by his own conflicts with regard to sexuality, would have been particularly terrified by such an advance, a much more common and accepted happening in the Near East than in Eastern Europe. This would account for Nahman's sharp designation of this Arab as the demonic power incarnate.

The depression which had begun to set in on Rosh Hashanah remained with Nahman through the holiday season. Even on Simhat Torah, when a great spirit of celebration engulfed the newly arrived Hasidim in Haifa, Nahman refused to join in the festivities. At the conclusion of the holidays, a month after his arrival, Nahman once again sought to embark on the journey homeward, and it was again only Simeon's insistence that moved him to travel to Tiberias.[54] While the sources offer no particular explanation of this depression, it seems understandable as a kind of postclimactic let-down after the conclusion of what had become to Nahman's mind (as we shall see) the great and transforming journey. Realizing as he did, a day after his arrival, that the burdens which had always weighed down upon his soul had not been lifted from him as he set foot on the holy soil, and that his initial elation had in fact been transitory, he fell into a depression which remained with him until he left Haifa.

At Tiberias the two were greeted with great affection by Abraham Kalisker and his Hasidim. Nahman showed great respect for the leader of the Tiberias Hasidic community, and refused to 'say Torah' in the presence of one he deemed greater than himself. Though Abraham's teachings were presented

54. *Shiv.* 18.

in such a manner that "not a word could be heard amid all the ecstasy and shouting," Nahman praised them lavishly. He was later to confide to Nathan that of all his contemporaries in the Hasidic world, he would attribute the quality of wholeness only to this Zaddik. Indeed, the small and elite community of the Tiberias Hasidim seems to have served as an important model for Nahman, both in the creation of the Bratslav community and in his fantasy of an ideal Hasidic brotherhood with which he opened his tale of *The Master of Prayer*. His respect for Kalisker went so far that when he became ill for a few days while in Tiberias Nahman treated Kalisker as his master, sending him a gift (*pidyon*) accompanied by a petition for prayerful intercession. The local master in turn showed great deference for Nahman (in part, no doubt, because of his lineage), and when the latter on one occasion bowed his head to receive a blessing, Kalisker deferred as a sign of their equality.[55]

Cheered by the warm welcome they received, and perhaps attracted by the pleasant climate of Tiberias in the winter months, Nahman and Simeon remained there until February or March of 1799. From Tiberias they journeyed to several of the holy places in the Galilee. Of particular interest is the account of Nahman's visit to the cave of Simeon ben Yohai:

> When they arrived at the cave of Rabbi Simeon, the young people recited prayers and studied the *Zohar*, as he had instructed them to do. They did not see him do anything, however. He was very elated, and would constantly go back to the one who accompanied him and say: "Blessed are you," etc. At night he went from chamber to chamber, encouraging them to keep reciting passages from the *Zohar*, etc. He himself said nothing, but went about singing to himself, in great happiness, until the light of dawn. When day broke, he donned his *tallit* and *tefillin* and prayed for several hours.[56]

This passage, like so many others in the Bratslav corpus, has undergone the heavy hand of inner censorship. Nahman, at least later in life, having seen himself as R. Simeon reincarnate, clearly was depicted in an original version as viewing this "return" as a highlight of his journey. The words which are blocked by the etceteras of this passage most likely gave some clear indication, later considered too dangerous for publication, of his identification with the hero of the *Zohar*.[57]

55. Ibid.
56. *Shiv.* 19.
57. This notion, while quietly hinted at in Nahman's own statements, is quite clearly stated in later Bratslav literature. Cf. Abraham Hazan, *Sihot we-Sippurim* (Jerusalem, 1961), p. 166; as well as the sources quoted by Piekarz, *Hasidut Braslav*, pp. 15 ff.

Sometime during that winter Nahman made yet another attempt to leave for home. He sent Simeon ahead to Haifa to book passage for them. In Haifa, however, Simeon met Jacob Samson of Shepetovka,[58] who had just returned from a mission abroad[59] to collect funds for the Hasidim of the Holy Land. At that time, however, a certain Jewish informer had told the local Turkish pasha in Tiberias that large sums of money were about to arrive from abroad, and there was a danger that the entire amount would be confiscated by the authorities. Jacob Samson, who was well-known as an emissary, was therefore afraid to deliver the funds in person, and Simeon offered his services as an intermediary. He thus returned safely to Tiberias, bearing the funds but without having arranged a return journey.[60] Seeing that his plans to leave had been thwarted once again, Nahman finally decided that it was indeed meant that he remain in the Holy Land for a longer period of time. He actually made plans for a journey to Jerusalem, but was discouraged by Abraham Kalisker, apparently due to the dangers thought to await Jerusalem from the invading Napoleonic army.

Whatever his resolve was at that point, it was the Napoleonic conquest of the Palestinean coastline, and specifically the threat to the port of Acre, that forced Nahman's hand and finally convinced him to set out for home at once. When he heard that Acre was about to be laid under siege (Haifa having already fallen), he set out for the port immediately, hoping to still find a ship flying the flag of neutral Ragusa.[61] They arrived at Acre on Friday, March 15, and were straightaway caught up in the great rush of civilians leaving the city. The siege actually began on March 19,[62] but the Turks had already warned all civilians to leave the city by Sunday, on pain of death. Passage on a neutral ship became impossible to find, and on the last possible day (March 17) the two passengers were fortunate even to find passage on a Turkish merchant vessel.

In the tumult of the evacuation, however, things went from bad to worse. Not speaking the local languages and not knowing one ship from another, Nahman and Simeon wound up on a Turkish warship which, as soon as it

58. Jacob Samson was a disciple of Jacob Joseph of Polonnoye and of Pinhas of Korzec. He had settled in the Holy Land in 1794. See A. Yaʿari, *Sheluhe 'Eretz Yisra'el* (Jerusalem, 1951), p. 623.

59. There is some question as to where he had been on this journey. Yaʿari (*Sheluhe*, p. 623) speaks of it as a journey to Egypt and North Africa, but Horodezky (*Hasidut*, II, 132 f.) notes that he wrote an approbation to the Slavuta, 1798 edition of *Me'or ʿEnayim* by Menahem Nahum of Chernobyl. This approbation, reprinted in later editions, begins: "On my way the Lord led me here to the holy congregation of Slavuta."

60. *Shiv.* 19.

61. The city-state of Ragusa remained neutral in the Napoleonic wars until 1805. See Francis W. Carter, *Dubrovnik (Ragusa): A Classic City-State* (London, 1972), pp. 524 f.

62. M. Gihon, "Napoleon's Siege of Acco," in *Western Galilee and the Coast of Galilee* (Jerusalem, 1965), pp. 165 ff.

had left the harbor, became entangled in battle with the French navy. Unable to make themselves understood, the pleas of the two to be put ashore went unheeded, and they found themselves in the midst of a raging battle at sea. The Turkish captain and sailors, as can be imagined, were none too happy to discover their two accidental passengers, and Nahman and Simeon hid in a small cabin, fearing to show themselves on deck lest they be killed by the sailors. They were kept alive only by the ship's cook, who took pity on them and brought them a bit of coffee twice a day.[63]

The dangers of battle gave way, after a while, to the even greater dangers of storm. Blown back and forth between one coastline and another, the ship, perhaps already damaged in battle, began to fill up with water. All cargo was thrown overboard to lighten the vessel, but still the ship was sinking. The two passengers feared to leave their cabin, yet the cabin was so filled with water that they had to climb to the top of some tall piece of furniture to escape drowning within the ship. They thought little of their chances for survival, and even if they should survive they were quite convinced that the sailors would sell them as slaves. At this point Nahman resolved that even if he were to be enslaved and thus prevented from living the ritual life of a Jew, he would still be able to fulfill the *mitzwot* in spirit:

> He had reached the understanding of how to serve God even if he were, God forbid, not able to observe the commandments. He had attained the service of the patriarchs who had served God before the Torah was given, fulfilling all the *mitzwot* even though they did not observe them in their ordinary form (*ki-feshutan*). Just as Jacob fulfilled the commandment of *tefillin* by stripping the sticks[64] and so forth—until he understood how he would fulfill all the *mitzwot* in this way if forced to do so in the place where he might be sold, God forbid.[65]

As the ship's pumps were reported to fail, the fear that had overcome the two men worsened. Here the bravado Nahman had borne previously on his journey seems to have fled him. Simeon was so paralyzed by terror that he could not even open his mouth in prayer. Nahman, too, now faced with a truly desperate situation, found that his personal fears were coming between himself and God. Finally he called out in the name of his ancestors, depending on the collective merits of the BeSHT, his daughter Odel, and Nahman of Gorodenka to save him. While the seas did not grow calmer,

---

63. *Shiv.* 20-21.
64. The reference is to Genesis 30:37. We find the interpretation of this mysterious action of the patriarch was a kind of proto-observance of the *mitzwot* already in the writings of Dov Baer of Miedzyrzec. See the sources quoted by R. Schatz, *Ha-Hasidut ke-Mistiqah* (Jerusalem, 1968), p. 56.
65. *Shiv.* 22. The meaning of this rather startling pronouncement will be discussed below.

somehow the sailors managed to repair the leaks in the vessel and they survived the storm.

After a month of terror, the ship sailed into the harbor of Rhodes on the eve of Passover. Nahman and Simeon, having nearly despaired of life itself, now found themselves within near reach of a Jewish community that would save them from the sailors as well as the sea, and would even enable them to celebrate the festival of deliverance. Negotiations ensued between the ship's captain and Jewish communal leaders, and for an adequate price the two captives were released to the Rhodes Jewish community on the third day of Passover. As it turned out, the captain of this ship was well known to the local Jews, and the dangers of murder or enslavement had in fact been quite real.[66] The rabbis of Rhodes, knowing the writings of Jacob Joseph of Polonnoye, were honored to have a descendent of the Baʿal Shem Tov among them. After much rejoicing through the remainder of the holiday, they were put on a safe and fast vessel which got them to Istanbul after only three days' journey. In Istanbul their adventures resumed when they were told that their passports were out of order, and it was only through the helpful hand of bribery that they were permitted to depart for Galati. Once again their ship was caught in a storm and most of the passengers drowned. After various other encounters with ransom, storm, and plague, they arrived home, having traveled overland from Galati via Jassy, sometime in early summer of 1799.[67]

III

In Nathan's first account of his master's journey, from which most of the above rendition has been culled, Nathan paid little attention to the reasons for the voyage or the meaning it had in his master's life. Only when he returned to this aspect of his biographical writings, after an interval of at least a decade, did he begin to set forth the traditions with regard to the journey's meaning. Though this second of Nathan's accounts is, as we have said, more fragmentary, it may also be said to reflect the concerns of a more mature biographer. The relevant chapter in *Hayye MoHaRaN* offers four explanations of the journey, all of them offered in Nahman's own name. This multiplicity of explanations provides no problem for Nathan, we should

66. Piracy was indeed a major danger in the eastern Mediterranean at that time. Cf. the comments by the Crimean Karaite traveler Benjamin Yerushalmi who sailed to Eretz Israel (J. D. Eisenstein (ed.), *'Otzar Masaʿot* [Tel Aviv, 1969], p. 214). For an account of Jews captured for ransom in the Aegean Sea as late as 1880, see *Jewish Encyclopedia*, X, 40.

67. *Shiv.* 24–26.

note, a biographer who will never be found guilty of underestimating the complexity of his subject's mind:

It was thus heard that there were several reasons for his voyage to the Land of Israel, in addition to those hidden reasons which he never revealed at all. Indeed, for all the things he did he never had only a single reason, but rather thousands and tens of thousands of deep and elevated motivations—most especially so for this great journey to Eretz Israel, for which he risked his life so very greatly.[68]

One of Nahman's stated motives for the journey has been discussed above: the hope of receiving some revealed knowledge at the grave of his grandfather. The three other reasons given for the journey also all have to do with some higher form of religious knowledge or illumination accessible only through a journey to the Holy Land. Our task is now to examine each of these in some detail, hoping to see whether they can be integrated into any overarching explanation of the journey which will avoid reductionism while at the same time not veer too closely toward Nathan's recourse to esotericism in explaining his master's actions. We shall quote each of the three explanations directly from Nathan's account.

1. I heard in his name that he said before his journey to Eretz Israel that he wanted to go in order to attain *hokhmah 'ila'ah*. There exist higher and lower forms of *hokhmah*; the lower he had already acquired, but he was yet to attain the higher. For this he had to go to the Land of Israel.[69]

The motif of the two aspects of *hokhmah* has a long history in Kabbalistic literature.[70] While the term may have been employed by Kabbalists in varying ways,[71] it may generally be said that *hokhmah 'ila'ah* is associated with

68. *EY* 5.
69. *EY* 6.
70. The two aspects of *hokhmah* are often mentioned in the Zohar. The upper *hokhmah* is the *sefirah hokhmah*, a hidden entity which cannot be known by man (I, 141b). The lower *hokhmah*, sometimes known as the lesser (*ze'irah*), is more accessible and is identified with the wisdom of Solomon (II, 223a R.M.), an appellative of the *shekhinah*. *Hokhmah* as a name for the tenth *sefirah* is already found in *Sefer ha-Bahir*. Thus it may be said that the earliest Kabbalistic sources contain, at least by implication, a notion of upper and lower *hokhmah*. See G. Scholem, *Ursprung und Anfänge der Kabbala* (Berlin, 1962), index s.v. *Hokhma*. The parallels between this series of symbols and the world of ancient (particularly Valentinean) Gnosticism are known and have been discussed by Scholem there and in his *Von der mystischen Gestalt der Gottheit* (Zurich, 1962), pp. 138 ff.
71. Following the breakdown of each of the ten *sefirot* into a further ten, a move first popularized through the works of Moses Cordovero, Kabbalists variously assigned the term *hokhmah tata'ah* or *hokhmah ze'irah* either to the element of *malkhut* within the upper *hokhmah* or alternatively to *hokhmah* within *malkhut*. The former view is espoused by Hayyim Vital in his (pre-Lurianic) notes to the Zohar included in A. Azulai, *'Or ha-Hamah* to *Zohar*, I, 141b. For the latter view,

the second of the ten *sefirot* (or the first, according to some reckonings), and *hokhmah tata'ah* is associated with *malkhut*, the lowest of the ten sefirotic rungs within divinity. In Nahman's own later writings, the lower *hokhmah* is taken to be the immediate source of all worldly wisdom, while the higher *hokhmah* is the source of the primordial Torah, the "holy of holies" in the sefirotic world, the primal root of all existence.[72] More significantly, *hokhmah 'ila'ah* is identified with the esoteric aspect of each of the *mitzwot*, always higher than the 'revealed' aspect which is embodied in the performance of the act. In Nahman's dialectic of spiritual ascent, the upper *hokhmah* is to be pursued to the point of complete self-transcendence and absorption in the divine *nihil*.[73] Thus our passage would mean that Nahman had already mastered all that could be attained by one who still held on to this-worldly existence and wisdom; only by journeying to the Holy Land could he achieve that total transcendence of self which was the goal of much of early Hasidic piety.

> 2. It was heard from his holy mouth during the Passover season that preceded his journey from Medvedevka to the Land of Israel that he wanted to go to Eretz Israel in order there to fulfill all of the six hundred and thirteen commandments, including those which are dependent upon the land together with those which may be fulfilled outside it, fulfilling them all spiritually so that afterward he would be able to fulfill them all physically.[74]

Once again, now more clearly, the notion of an esoteric aspect of the *mitzwot* makes its appearance. Even the most pious of Jews, living after the destruction of the Temple and outside the Land of Israel, observes far fewer than the originally prescribed 613 commandments of the Torah. Many of the *mitzwot* are completely in abeyance since the Temple's destruction and the suspension of the sacrificial cult; others, particularly those relating to the agricultural cycle, apply only to Jews living in or eating the produce of the Land of Israel. Based upon older mystical speculations propounding an organismic view of Torah, according to which each of the commandments

---

see the commentary to the liturgy by Nahman's contemporary Shneur Zalman of Liadi (New York, 1965), p. 112c. In devotional terms, Shneur Zalman identifies the lower *hokhmah* with *bittul ha-yesh*, a semiintellectual awareness that the world has no existence independent of God, while the higher *hokhmah* is identified with *bittul ha-ʿetzem*, an experience of envelopment in the all-pervasive oneness of God (p. 108d). These terms seem roughly equivalent to the use of the terms *qatnut* and *gadlut* elsewhere in the school of Miedzyrzec, and are quite parallel also to Nahman's later usage of these terms.

72. *Liqqute*, 61:6, and II, 91.

73. *Liqqute*, 22.

74. *EY* 5.

was seen as a particular 'limb' of the Torah's 'body,' in turn both reflecting the 'limbs' of the divine 'body' of *Adam Qadmon* and corresponding to the limbs of the human body, these unobservable *mitzwot* became a problem in Hasidic thought.[75] If the Torah is a single whole, and if its 613 commandments bespeak the fulfillment of the 613 limbs of man's spiritual body which is the image of God in him, how can one possibly achieve that fulfillment if not all the commandments may be followed?[76] Even he who does all he can to live in accordance with the Torah would of necessity leave whole areas untouched, thus not allowing for the completion of the system of correspondences that leads to fulfillment. In response to this and similar problems, Hasidic teachers propounded the rather dangerous doctrine of purely spiritual fulfillment of these divine commandments. While certain of the Torah's precepts still required a bodily act, others could be fulfilled by means of *kawwanah* alone, thus allowing the worshipper to feel that these were not 'dead letters' in his spiritual life. Combined with ancient and well-known speculations concerning the abrogation of certain or all of the *mitzwot* in messianic times, Hasidism here reaches near the border of antinomian thinking. The distinction between the Hasidic view mentioned here and the antinomian view that the *true* fulfillment of all the commandments is purely spiritual is a fine one.[77]

Examining the passage at hand more closely, we will note that the text as it stands does not quite make sense. In order to *spiritually* fulfill the *mitzwot ha-teluyyot ba-'aretz* one would not have to travel to the Holy Land. The order of the final line should probably be reversed to read: "Fulfilling all of them physically so that afterward he should be able to fulfill them all spiritually". One who had never experienced the actual observance of a particular *mitzwah* would not know how to properly spiritualize it. Thus Nahman's journey is seen as an attempt to gain access to those areas of the Torah which apply in the land alone, so that afterwards he might include them in his 'spiritual observance' of the *mitzwot*.

75. On the view of Torah as an organism, see G. Scholem, *On the Kabbalah and Its Symbolism* (New York, 1965), pp. 44 ff. On the problem of the *mitzwot* in Hasidism, see Schatz, *Hasidut*, chap. 5.

76. This notion of Torah as organism also comes to be related to the image of *haluqa de-rabbanan*, the mystical garment the soul is to wear in the afterlife, woven of the *mitzwot* one has fulfilled in this world. According to N. Shapira (*Megalleh ʿAmuqot*, 113), Moses wanted to enter Eretz Israel so that he could perform the *mitzwot ha-teluyot ba-'aretz*, without which his garment would be incomplete. Cf. also Levi Yizhaq of Berdichev, *Qedushat Levi* (Jerusalem, 1958), p. 247.

77. In addition to the Hasidic sources quoted by Schatz (in *Hasidut*), see the views of Cordovero, A. Azulai, and Nathan of Gaza in G. Scholem, *Sabbatai Sevi* (Princeton, N.J., 1973), pp. 319 ff. The progression from the radical insights of the two "orthodox" Kabbalists to the open antinomianism of the Sabbatian prophet leaves one somewhat in doubt as to where the actual cut-off point of heresy is to be found. Schatz demonstrates that the same is true with regard to much of early Hasidic thought with regard to the *mitzwot*.

This reading of the passage is confirmed by that most curious and rather shocking statement Nahman made during the return voyage, to the effect that he could now continue to observe all the *mitzwot* in spirit even if he were to be impressed into slavery and thus unable to keep them in the flesh. It now seems that this statement was not merely a rationalization born of his dire situation on the sea; the realization of the spiritual Torah was in fact an essential and planned part of his journey from the outset. Such an intent, of course, in no way means that Nahman sought to abandon the *mitzwot* in their ordinary sense.

In that statement on the seas Nahman claimed that he had attained the rung of the patriarchs and their spiritual fulfillment of the commandments. The idea that the patriarchs had fulfilled the divine will before Sinai by means of acts other than the accepted *mitzwot*, or even by *kawwanah* alone, is well known in early Hasidic writings. Scholars have seen in this theme the projection of a certain ambivalence the Hasidic authors felt about the need for the actual corporeal fulfillment of the *mitzwot*, given a world-view in which pure spirituality was the ultimate religious value.[78] Here we see that Nahman as a young man was also strongly attracted to such thinking, and that while such antinomian tendencies were not acted out in his life they did occupy a significant place in his speculations.[79] From this perspective, the journey to Eretz Israel may be seen as an attempt to reach new heights of spiritualization with regard to the *mitzwot* by including the commandments relating to the land in his repertoire of contemplation.[80]

> 3. He then told R. Yudel that he wanted to go to the Land of Israel. R. Yudel offered him his blessing and said to him: "Our master! Surely you want to perform some great thing there. May it be God's will to help you do that which you intend." Our master nodded in response

78. Schatz, *Hasidut*, chap. 5; and G. Scholem, *The Messianic Idea in Judaism* (New York, 1971), pp. 203 ff.

79. This comes out most clearly in the interpretation of *Liqqute*, II, 78, which we hope to offer elsewhere. In this connection notice should be taken of another startling statement made by Nahman during his return voyage. He and Simeon were studying Mishnah to occupy themselves during their travels. When they reached *Sotah* V:2 and read "A generation will arise that will proclaim the purity of the third degree [of ritual impurity, those taboos not based upon scriptural injunction]," Nahman became ecstatic, clapped his hands, and proclaimed: "Who sees as I do!" (*EY* 13). The implication seems to be that his is the generation that will find a way to purify this category of the defiled. This in itself cannot be called "antinomian," as it follows the Law's own prediction, but it again is clearly reminiscent of well-known motifs in Sabbatian thought.

80. Levi Yizhaq of Berdichev, in a most daring homily (*Qedushat Levi, lekh lekha*, pp. 15 f.), employs a motif similar to that used here. In noting that Abraham came to know the commandments only after he entered Eretz Israel, he says that until entering the land Abraham served by means of *mesirut nefesh* alone. He could not enter into the world of *mitzwot* until he was in that land where he could observe them in their totality, or else he would have remained unwhole. Only after Sinai do *any* of the commandments become binding outside the land.

to his blessing and afterwards said: "I could fulfill that which I seek and desire to do in Eretz Israel right here by means of prayer and supplication alone. Then I would not have to travel to Eretz Israel. The difference is that if I merit to be in Eretz Israel I will receive my understanding in 'garments', whereas if I stay here I will receive it without the 'garments'. This is also the difference between the holiness of the Sabbath and that of the festival." He opened the prayerbook of the ARI of blessed memory for R. Yudel and showed him in the *kawwanot* that this was the difference between Sabbath and festival: that on Sabbath the light is clothed in garments, while on festivals it does not have this garb, as is known.[81]

Here once again Nahman's journey is depicted as an attempt to achieve some higher degree of spirituality, speaking here in somewhat different and more paradoxical Kabbalistic language. Before Nahman was in the Holy Land, according to this source, he had received his spiritual understanding (*hassagah*) directly, without the "garb" in which such understanding should be clothed. Contrary to what one might expect, "garbed" understanding is here presented as a higher rung of attainment than that which comes to man without such "garb"; the need for covering the understanding indicates that it is derived from a higher source, one which could not be attained by man without such a protective *levush* (garb).

While Nahman did not explain this rather cryptic statement to his disciples, he did make reference to *Siddur ha-'ARI*, the prayerbook edition of Isaac Luria, as the source of his thoughts. While the phrase *Siddur ha-'ARI* in the mouth of a late eighteenth-century Eastern European Jew could well have been applied to any one of several Kabbalistic compendia on the liturgy,[82] all of them based on the Lurianic system, we are here in the fortunate position of being able to identify the precise text which Nahman had been reading. This turns out to be nòne other than the famous *Siddur Qol Yaʿaqov* by Jacob Koppel Lipschütz of Miedzyrzec, whom Tishby has shown to have been a secret Sabbatian but whose *Siddur* was highly prized by the Baʿal Shem Tov and others.[83] In his introduction to the *kawwanot* of the festivals, which

81. EY 7.

82. Two versions of the Lurianic liturgy which were available in print in Nahman's day were those of Sabbatai of Raszkow (Korzec, 1794) and Asher Margulies of Brody (Lvov, 1788). Other versions are discussed by G. Scholem in *Kitve Yad ba-Qabbalah* (Jerusalem, 1930), pp. 129 ff.

83. I. Tishby, *Netive 'Emunah u-Minut* (Israel, 1964), pp. 204 ff. This *Siddur* was first published in Slavuta, 1804. Tishby denies the existence of a Korzec, 1794 edition. Nevertheless, as Tishby notes, the work was widely circulated in manuscript, and exercised an influence on those works mentioned in n. 82, even though they preceded it in print. *Qol Yaʿaqov* is quoted by Simhah of Zalozhtsy as early as 1757.

immediately precedes his discussion of Passover, Jacob Koppel discusses the difference in holiness between Sabbath and festival. Because the Sabbath day is possessed of an inherent holiness, he says, deriving from the blessing of Genesis 2:3, its spiritual status is higher than that of the festivals, the sanctity of which is derivative from the holiness of Israel.[84] For this reason, he continues, the light of *hokhmah* shines more brightly on the Sabbath than it does on other holy days of the sacred calendar. The Sabbath light is so bright that *binah*, the next lower divine emanation, could not receive it unless it were partially veiled in some *levush*. If the much dimmer festival light, on the other hand, were to be transmitted in the same *levush*, it would be totally imperceptible.[85] On the following page the author connects all of this with the difference between the Holy Land and the rest of Creation. That higher "garbed" consciousness, available outside the land only on the Sabbath, is present also on weekdays in the Land of Israel. Here he may be basing himself on older sources which relate the Land of Israel to another sort of garb: the garment of the soul which the righteous are to wear in the world to come.[86]

It was on the eve of Passover in 1798 that Nahman first announced to those around him his plans for a journey to the Holy Land. In preparing for the holiday, he had been reading the appropriate passages in the Kabbalistic liturgy that was revered by his esteemed great-grandfather and had been passed on to him. In it he found confirmation of an idea that had already taken hold of him previously: to achieve a higher rung of enlightenment he would have to journey to Eretz Israel. The image of a veiled revelation emanating from a higher divine rung than an unveiled truth, so typical of the paradoxical dialectic of the Kabbalah, would have been precisely the sort of formula that would have had greatest appeal to Nahman's ever paradoxical turn of mind.

These explanations, all of them recorded in succession in Nathan's memoir, all generally point in the same direction. The purpose of the journey was a search for some higher form of spiritual illumination than that accessible to Nahman outside the land. Though the young ascetic had, through his countless earlier struggles, attained a very high rung of personal development and religious understanding, he now stood before an impasse: further growth now required a major breakthrough, one that was possible only by means of such a journey. In the Holy Land he could receive the garbed or higher wisdom, apprehend the secret of the commandments, and commune

84. Cf. *Betzah* 17a, and RaSHI's commentary thereon.
85. *Qol Yaʿaqov* (Lvov, 1858), pp. 170b, 171b.
86. Cf. Shapira, *Megalleh ʿAmuqot*, 62 (Lvov, 1858), p. 10b.

with the spirit of his grandfather in pursuit of direct knowledge from above. In contrast to a certain tendency toward spiritual glorification of life in the diaspora to be found elsewhere in early Hasidism,[87] at this point in our reading it would seem that Nahman is in his own way echoing the well-known rabbinic dicta to the effect that prophecy or the holy spirit could not easily be attained outside the Land of Israel.[88]

IV

Our thorough biographer could not, however, resist passing on to us one further account of Nahman's announcement of his journey, one that throws all of the above into new relief. Included in a later section of his second account of the voyage, the passage has about it a ring of almost startling authenticity, conveyed not least by the broken bits of language it records.

Shortly before he departed for the Land of Israel, someone asked him why he did not draw them [the disciples] near and speak with them. He said that he now had no words, but he said that "by means of the verse 'When you pass through water I shall be with you' (Isaiah 43:2) it has become known to me *how one may see the patriarchs Abraham, Isaac, and Jacob whenever one wants.* I wondered why it should be through that particular verse, but now I think it is because I have to cross the sea. But why [should I tell] you this? What need have you for it? Even were I to dress it in some moral teaching that would be appropriate to everyone —but I have no words now." Afterwards he walked to and fro in the house saying: "I am poorer and more destitute than any of the great ones. One has money, another has towns [dominated by his hasidim] —and I have nothing. My only comfort comes when I recall that in the world of truth they will all need me and will long to hear my teachings [*hiddushim*] which I create in every moment. What is this 'I'? Rather 'which my soul creates'."[89]

In this fragment, reported to Nathan by one of Nahman's early disciples, we are given a rare glimpse of the young master in a terrible state of agitation. Before he decided on his trip to Eretz Israel, he was undergoing one of his

87. Cf. *No͑am Elimelekh, wa-yeshev*; and the sources listed by Dinur, *Be-Mifneh*, p. 192, n. 4.
88. *Mekhilta, Bo* (ed. Horovitz, p. 2); Mo͑ed Qatan 25a; *Zohar*, I, 141a.
89. *EY* 19. The concluding line reads as follows in the Hebrew: *mahu 'ani? raq mah she-ha-neshamah shelli mehaddesh* (!). Emphasis here and in the following source is mine. The context of the Isaiah passage refers to the return of Israel's exiles to the Holy Land.

famous "dry" periods, which continued to evidence themselves throughout
his later life and which had so great an effect upon his teachings.[90] He had
distanced himself from his students, saying that he "had no words," that he
was not able to teach them anything. His problem was a purely personal one,
knowledge of which would not be of any help to others. True, he retained a
faith in his ultimate vindication, but his present crisis could be resolved only
by a journey over the seas. Here we have an explanation of the journey which
is of a much more dramatic and immediate sort: it was not in order only to
increase his knowledge or illumination that Nahman set out, but rather in
response to a deep personal crisis. Standing behind Nahman's decision for
the journey is no longer an ordered pattern of ascent but rather a precipitous
fall. The depths to which he was shaken by this crisis are poignantly reflected
by his pacing through the house and by the confusion recorded in his closing
lines. Nahman hastens to correct the impression it is his 'I' that constantly
speaks *hiddushe Torah*; it is rather his soul that continues to create, even in
those times when his 'I' is afflicted by spiritual dryness and cannot speak. I *as
a person*, he is saying to his disciples, have nothing to offer you at this time. If
my soul continues to create, do not assume this to mean that *I* have anything
to give you.[91] We should also note that in this text, as well as in the brief
reference to this moment in *Shivhe ha-RaN* (quoted earlier) where a different
scriptural verse is adduced, the reference is to a voyage across the seas, rather
than to Eretz Israel.

What was the nature of this crisis in Nahman's life? And how was it that a
sea journey was seen as its proper resolution? The most direct goal of his
voyage, and the resolution of his personal crisis, seems to be sought in a
vision of the patriarchs. This same motif of a vision of the patriarchs is
reported from an earlier period in Nahman's life, in a dream Nahman had as
an adolescent. The text describing this event is highly revealing.

> He was once sitting at his father-in-law's table during the third Sabbath
> meal. He was seated in a corner and it began to grow dark in the house.
> He as usual went his own way, and he began to ask God *to show him the
> patriarchs Abraham, Isaac, and Jacob.* He promised God that "when You
> show me this, I will cast aside this desire [eating] as well." He did what

90. Cf. Weiss, "Reshit," passim; and my "R. Nahman Bratslaver's Conflict Regarding Leadership," in M. A. Fishbane and P. R. Flohr, eds., *Texts and Responses: Studies Presented to Nahum N.
Glatzer* . . . (Leiden, 1975), pp. 141 ff.

91. The distinction Nahman is making here between "self" and "soul" is quite surprising.
Jewish literature generally does not know of such a distinction. Note, however, the unusual
formulation *ha-neshamah 'amerah le-ha-rav*, "the master's soul said to him" in *Tzawa'at RIVaSH*
(Cracow, 1896), p. 4b. Nahman's novellae are seen by him as a sort of inner revelation, rather
than as a creation of his own mind. See below, n. 95.

he did in this matter, entering into the thoughts very deeply, until he fell asleep. His forebearer the BeSHT came to him in a dream and recited to him the verse 'I shall put grass in the field for your animals' (Deut. 11:14). He awoke wondering what possible connection there could be between this verse and that which he had sought. He then recalled a passage in the *Tiqqune Zohar*[92] which interprets the word *'esev* ['grass', consonantally *'sb*] as referring to the pupil of the eye [abbreviation for *bat 'ayin*, the locus of vision] and the patriarchs, the three of them alluded to by the three-pronged *shin*. This is its meaning: it is impossible to see the patriarchs unless you have first destroyed your animal nature, namely the desire for food. Then he overcame this desire.[93]

The relationship between these two texts has not heretofore been recognized. The desire to obtain a vision of the patriarchs was not new to Nahman in 1798. On the contrary, it had been with him at least since adolescence, the period of his hardest struggles against the desires of the flesh. That this early dream remained crucial to him is witnessed by the fact that it was one of those few events in his life which he specifically instructed his disciples to retell among themselves.[94] The vision of the patriarchs was to be his reward for ultimate victory in the battle against his own animal nature, symbolized here by his desire for food, but elsewhere by his sexual struggles. It appears that now, at the age of twenty-six, he had still not achieved that final victory, for the vision of the patriarchs, or at least constant access to that vision, was still a goal to be sought. Given the violent ups and downs in Nahman's self-esteem, we may well assume that there were points in his life when he felt this goal to be well within his reach—but that these were only to be followed by further falls, during which times the patriarchs once again seemed to distance themselves from him. *The patriarchs, who fulfilled the mitzwot in purely spiritual ways, are, in Nahman's imagination, symbols of complete transcendence of the bodily self.*

It is now clear that Nahman's announcement of his journey has to do with his ongoing struggle and its promised rewards. In his earlier days he had suffered periods of emptiness and awareness of God's distance from him, due to his failure to achieve mastery over his "animal" self and its base desires. As he ambivalently accepted the role of Zaddik, these periods manifested

92. I have not been able to find such a reference in the *Tiqqune Zohar*. The references suggested in the editions of *Liqqute* 47 to Tiqquna 51 and to *Zohar*, I, 25b, lead one to what in fact is an entirely different interpretation of the word *'esev*, containing no exegesis of Deut. 11:15.

93. *Hayye, sippurim hadashim* 12. The pun cannot be fully translated. One reaches the vision (*bat 'ayin*) of the patriarchs (the letter *shin*) by upsetting (*shaded*, here related to *sadekha*) one's animal nature.

94. Ibid.

themselves as times when he "had no words," when he felt himself unworthy to address his disciples. In a world where the teaching of Torah was seen as a pneumatic act rather than as an intellectual exercise, this transition is perfectly clear. If the teaching of Torah is an event in which "the *shekhinah* speaks through his mouth,"[95] the Zaddik who feels himself to be far from God can only be embarrassed by the demands of his disciples.

But what has all this to do with a journey to the Holy Land? The fact is that there is no intrinsic connection between Nahman's struggle to overcome his desires and a visit to the Land of Israel. Our passage speaks only of a sea voyage, and it is the voyage itself which is crucial in this connection. Eretz Israel itself was of great importance for Nahman; he *did* believe that there were higher forms of religious knowing which were accessible only there. But in this passage *it is the voyage rather than the destination which seems to occupy his thoughts.*

This view of the journey is sustained by a number of other interesting references in the writings of both Nahman and Nathan. Only two months before his death in 1810, Nahman underwent the best-known of his depressions. During that time he spoke to his disciples about the Zaddik (the reference is clearly to himself) as one who at times is like the most simple of men. At such moments he knows nothing and has no access to Torah. His only sustenance at such times is through *derekh 'eretz*[96] here taken to refer to *derekh 'eretz yisra'el*, the way to the Land of Israel. "He sustained himself in times of simplicity only by the way to Eretz Israel."[97] In other words, the fact that he had made the journey to the Holy Land, and the memory of that journey, were sufficient to sustain him through even the most bitter periods of dryness and self-doubt.

95. Thus the act of preaching was discussed in the circle of Miedzyrzec. Cf. *'Or ha-Me'ir* by Ze'ev Wolf of Zhitomir (New York, 1954), p. 95c; and the discussion by J. Weiss in *JJS*, XI (1960), p. 150. This phrase and similar ones were first employed to describe the prophetic experience of Moses. Cf. the sources quoted by A. J. Heschel, *Torah min ha-Shamayyim*, II (London, 1965), 215 f., 335 f. Beginning in the sixteenth century, such phrases appear in the description of personal mystical experiences: revelations of *maggidim*, automatic speech, etc. Cf. Werblowsky, *Joseph Karo*, p. 269, and passim. In Hasidism these phrases describe not only the act of preaching by the Zaddik but the act of prayer as well. For one of many examples, see Dov Baer of Miedzyrzec, *'Or ha-'Emet* (Brooklyn, 1960), p. 1b; and the discussions by Weiss and by Schatz, *Hasidut*, pp. 95 ff. This is one of the most striking examples of the popularization of mystical phenomena in Hasidism. For the use of the phrase within a Hasidic context to describe actual prophetic experiences, see Kalonymos Kalman of Cracow, *Ma'or wa-Shemesh* (New York, 1958), p. 51b. A full account of *shekhinah medabberet mi-tokh piw (gerono)* would prove most rewarding. The dependence of the Jewish development upon those Islamic sources discussed by A. Altmann in his *Studies in Religious Philosophy and Mysticism* (Ithaca, N.Y., 1969), pp. 150 ff., might be the proper starting point of such an account.

96. Here Nahman is playing on the well-known rabbinic dictum *derekh 'eretz qademah la-torah* (*Leviticus Rabbah* IX:3).

97. *Sihot* 153.

In order to further understand why the journey itself, as distinct from the destination, should play so central a role in Nahman's thinking, we must touch upon another central motif of his thought to which we have made occasional reference above. This is the motif of "obstacles" (*meni^cot*) which the man of faith has to overcome in his search for a path to God. These *meni^cot* are best described in Nahman's tale of *The Rabbi and His Son*,[98] where the obstacles are at once the result of the doubts which the rabbi entertains about the true Zaddik and the work of the demonic forces themselves. This dual understanding of the *meni^cah*, as psychological block to faith and as the work of demonic powers, is crucial to Nahman's self-understanding. Man's task is ever to do battle with the *meni^cot*, whether they take the form of mental or physical barriers; the search for God requires the strength of a Samson.[99] And the great example in Bratslav literature of the battle to overcome *meni^cot* is none other than the journey of Nahman to the Land of Israel!

> He said that he was very happy to have merited to be in Eretz Israel. For on the way to Eretz Israel he had undergone many obstacles, confusing thoughts, delays, and struggles, including financial obstacles. But he had overcome them all and had brought the matter to completion by reaching Eretz Israel. He further said this: I believe, and indeed I know well, that of all the movements, thoughts, and deeds that one undertakes in order to perform some holy act, not a single one is ever lost. For after all the obstacles have been broken through and the act has been completed, all those confusing thoughts and movements which had taken place while one was still weighing the act . . . are elevated to the highest state of holiness. Everything is recorded above for good, including every move one had to make along the way. Blessed are those who manage to overcome all the obstacles and to complete some good deed.[100]

The lesson to be learned from Nahman's journey to the Holy Land is not that "the atmosphere of Eretz Israel makes one wise" or gives one access to visions, indeed it is not that one should follow in the master's footsteps by making such a pilgrimage, but rather that one should struggle constantly to overcome *meni^cot*! Given this use of the journey, it is no wonder that the voyage itself rather than the destination takes a central place here.

The journey from the Ukraine to the Holy Land was in fact a dangerous one. As we have seen, the frail ships upon which Nahman and his disciple finally did sail were subject to all sorts of natural disasters, and shipwrecks

---

98. *Sippure Ma^casiyyot*, no. 8 (New York, 1949), pp. 18b ff.
99. *Liqqute* 74, 115, 249; II, 43, 46; *Sihot* 146.
100. *Sihot* 11; cf. also *Shiv.* 28.

were fairly common. Added to these were the dangers of shipboard disease, piracy, and the battles of the Napoleonic wars in which Nahman became embroiled. The journey was an act of *mesirut nefesh*, of willingness to endanger one's life to achieve some sacred purpose. As we look back over the account of the journey, we see that Nahman repeatedly sought to stand in the face of the greatest dangers. What greater act of overcoming *meni͑ah* and of transcending the bodily self than the willingness to risk one's very life for God? Despite the rabbinic injunctions against testing the Lord,[101] it apparently became clear to Nahman in the twenty-sixth year of his life that only by such a radical act of self-sacrifice could he overcome those "base" desires continuing to torment him and thus prove his faith in God. When later he spoke of the relationship between purity in the act of eating and the sanctity of Eretz Israel,[102] he clearly had his own journey in mind, a journey undertaken for the purpose of self-purification by ordeal, the ordeal of "when you pass through water." Indeed, this is not the first trial by water that we hear of in his life. Of the adolescent Nahman we are told "he would take a boat out into the river, even though he did not know how to operate it, and when the boat was in the midst of the river, far from land . . . and he was about to drown, he would call out to God."[103] Is it any wonder that this same person, now a young adult, should test his faith by a dangerous voyage across the seas? The journey to Eretz Israel is a repetition on a much grander scale of a "trial by water" that Nahman had already undertaken—repeatedly, it would seem —as an adolescent.

V

The legitimacy of using such terms as "rite of passage" or "voyage of initiation" with regard to Nahman's journey has now been clearly demonstrated. The would-be initiate, whether in primitive tribal culture or in the rich myth-making imagination of a religious figure at the edge of modernity, seeks to undertake the death-defying voyage to the center in order to receive that knowledge which only the initiate may possess. Nahman, in confronting the real possibility of death and disappearance in a watery grave, tests his trust in God and his transcendence of his lower self once and for all. If he survives the great ordeal, he will reach the Holy Land, at once the source of renewed life through Creation (for it was here that Creation had begun)

101. For a clear statement of such prohibition, see Nahmanides' commentary to Deut. 16:6.
102. *Liqqute* 47.
103. *Sihot* 117.

and the locus of prophetic inspiration. Indeed, his voyage is homologous with that journey of which Eliade has written:

> The road is arduous, frought with perils, because it is, in fact, a rite of the passage from the profane to the sacred, from the ephemeral and illusory to reality and eternity, from death to life, from man to the divinity. Attaining the center is equivalent to a consecration, an initiation; yesterday's profane and illusory existence gives place to a new, to a life that is real, enduring, and effective.[104]

Elsewhere Eliade has described the particular forms of initiation which must be undertaken by one who seeks to assert himself as a shaman,[105] a type of religious figure who in his combination of personal ecstasy, communal centrality, and his reputed power to bless and heal, is not altogether lacking in parallels to the Hasidic Zaddik. Nahman feels a call that he can no longer seek to escape: he is to become the leader of a Hasidic community. Later, indeed, he is to see himself as the single leader of his entire generation. The dialectic of descent and ascent, of death and rebirth, must assert itself. If ambivalence and hesitation are ever to be overcome, they are overcome only by means of the ultimate journey.

Our explanation of Nahman's journey as a death-defying *rite de passage* does not necessarily contradict·any of the interpretations that Nahman himself offered and that have been mentioned above. On the contrary, it provides them with that clarity of focus they had previously lacked. The granting of higher wisdom, *hokhmah 'ila'ah* or "garbed" wisdom, as a result of such initiation, corresponds directly to that claimed for rites of initiation in the most varied religious cultures. The account in which Nahman claims his goal was attainment of the spiritualized commandments is also made transparent through this explanation. Whatever ambiguity may be found elsewhere in Hasidism with regard to the enjoyment or transcendence of this-worldly goods is lacking in Nahman. For him it was quite clear that only he who achieves *hitpashtut ha-gashmiyyut*, total transcendence of the bodily self,[106] can

104. M. Eliade, *The Myth of the Eternal Return* [= *Cosmos and History*] (Princeton, 1971), p. 18.
105. M. Eliade, *Rites and Symbols of Initiation* (New York, 1965), pp. 81 ff.
106. The "stripping off" of corporeality is a central term for self-transcendence in Hasidic sources. This medieval term was popularized, if not created, by its inclusion in both the *Tur* and the *Shulhan Arukh* ('*Orah Hayyim* 98:1) as part of the prescription for proper prayer. See the discussion by Werblowsky, *Joseph Karo*, pp. 61 f. Scholem (*Von der mystischen Gestalt*, p. 288, n. 84) claims that the term originates in the *Tur*. It has not been traced to earlier philosophical or Kabbalistic literature. It would seem, however, that various parallel phrases were first employed to describe the prophetic state. See, for example, the use of *shelilat ha-homriyyut* in Bahya ben Asher's commentary to Ex. 3:5, or the somewhat later *nitpashet·gufo mi-malbush ha-homri* in Yehiel of Pisa's *Minhat Qena'ot* (ed. Kaufmann, p. 25). In both of these casès the reference is to Moses. Here too it would seem that we have a description of the prophetic state which later becomes

reach the spiritual Torah. Yet, though it was the higher Torah of Eretz Israel that he sought, that Torah could only be obtained by the ordeal of *derekh 'eretz yisra'el*, the transforming journey. It would seem that he chose varying ways in which to account for his imminent journey, varying in accord with whomever he was addressing or whatever degree of self-revelation he felt prepared to offer in a particular moment. All of the explanations, however, point to the same basic meaning: the journey as an attempt to transcend his own lower self.[107]

This understanding of the voyage also helps to explain the most curious fact of all in Nahman's visit to the Holy Land: as soon as he set foot on the soil of Eretz Israel, on the eve of Rosh Hashanah in 1798, he announced that "when he had walked four ells in the Land of Israel he had already achieved all that he had sought"[108] and he was ready to return home immediately after the festival. Had his goal in fact been a pilgrimage to the Holy Land, including prayers at the holy places, a visit to the grave of his grandfather, or contact with the local Hasidic community, such a readiness to depart after only two days in the port of Haifa makes no sense whatever. If, however, his real goal was the adventurous journey itself, and if *arrival* in Eretz Israel signified the attainment of his goal and the completion of the ordeal, then his willingness to return home at once is rendered completely understandable.

It was indeed through the strength gained on his journey to Eretz Israel that Nahman returned to establish his place as a major figure in the Ukrainian Hasidic community. This strength was not, however, a matter of external "authorization" or prestige; it was rather a sense that he had, in some way that seemed absolute, achieved mastery over his own inner self. He had "passed through water" for the sake of God, and had seen his faith withstand the trial of imminent death. He was now one who could deserve the vision of the patriarchs, having followed their example by the utter denial of his corporeal self. Having survived his great encounter with danger on the seas, he was now ready to return to his people and become the leader they had sought in him.

---

prescriptive for every man in the life of prayer. A parallel development in medieval Islam, where a description first applied to Mohammed's prophecy is taken over to describe mystical experience in general, is traced by A. Altmann in "The Ladder of Ascension," in *Studies in Mysticism and Religion Presented to Gershom G. Scholem* (Jerusalem, 1967), pp. 1–32 (reprinted in his *Studies*, pp. 41 ff.).

107. Another curious passage (*Shiv.* 31) reveals how secretive Nahman himself was with regard to the true meaning of his Eretz Israel journey. When a certain scholar in the Holy Land pleaded with him to reveal the nature of his visit there, Nahman explained that he was sworn to secrecy on this matter. When pressed, he began to discourse on it indirectly. "But as he began to speak, blood came forth from his throat, and he said to the scholar: 'Now you see that God does not agree that I should reveal this to you.'"

108. *Shiv.* 15.

From Patriot to Israelite: Abraham Furtado in Revolutionary France

Frances Malino

Paris will become for us what Jerusalem was for our ancestors in the beautiful days of its glory. . . . Israelites in our Temples, French among our fellow citizens, this is who we are.[1]

These words were written by Abraham Furtado in a private letter to Napoleon on the eve of the dissolution of the Assembly of Notables. Furtado was not merely expressing what he knew to be Napoleon's plan for the Jews of France; he was also describing what he believed to be the appropriate response of French Jews as they strove to make their faith and traditions compatible with their citizenship in an emerging nation-state.

Abraham Furtado was not a great man. Neither as a statesman and philosopher nor as a political activist did he demonstrate the brilliance and creativity associated with original thinkers. Furtado's importance and enduring attraction lie rather in his role as spokesman for the Jews of France during the crucial years of the Revolution and Napoleonic period. During this time he helped both to legitimize and institutionalize the inescapable bifurcation of modern Jewish life. In the following pages we shall examine his political activities and ideological struggles, from his youthful and enthusiastic embrace of the revolutionary dream to his participation in the governmental regulation and control of the Jews of France. Though not a great man, he was an architect of French Jewry and an example of one of the first modern and assimilated Jews.

He was born in London on July 30, 1756, a few months after the escape of his parents, Elie Furtado and Hana Vega, from the destructive earthquake in Lisbon.[2] After a short stay in England (where Elie Furtado and his wife appear to have remarried according to Jewish law),[3] the family arrived in Bayonne.

---

1. This letter is in the possession of Pascal Thémanlys, direct descendant of Emile Furtado, the only surviving child of Abraham.
2. Inaccurate accounts have stated that Furtado was born in 1759 and that his father had died while still in Lisbon. Many archival sources as well as Furtado's own words reveal the accurate biographical details. See, for example, Abraham Furtado, "Lettre à un ami, 12 octobre, 1784," Pascal Thémanlys, Jerusalem.
3. In a letter to Pascal Thémanlys, Cecil Roth writes: "I find that here on the eve of Shabuoth 1756, Eleau Furtado Ferro was married to Hana Pinto Vega; it is not stated specifically that they

There Furtado spent his early years until his marriage to Sara Rodrigues Alvares in 1775.[4]

After his marriage, Furtado and his wife, who had been saved by her father during the same earthquake in Lisbon, settled in Bordeaux where Furtado followed the traditional vocations of the wealthy Bordelais Jews and occupied himself with business affairs and, for a short time, maritime insurance. Subsequently, however, he abandoned business and relied almost exclusively on the income from his properties.[5]

Although never approximating the fortunes of the Gradis or Raba families, Furtado was successful enough to join the cadre of wealthy Sephardim. His influence in the community, however, while dependent upon a certain economic status, was primarily the result of a penetrating intellect and a flowing eloquence. Recognized by the Bordelais Jews as an able spokesman, he was elected syndic of their *nation* in March 1787 and subsequently was chosen along with Lopes-Dubec to journey to Paris on April 8, 1788, to present the Sephardic position to the French Minister, Chrétien-Guillaume de Lamoignon de Malesherbes.[6]

The Bordelais Sephardim (formerly *nouveaux Chrétiens* who had publicly embraced Catholicism) had successfully established during the eighteenth century a secularized and privileged Jewish community whose structure and religious commitments reflected the economic concerns and priorities of its leaders. The goals of the Sephardim were threefold: they hoped to retain the privileged status of their community, to maintain the legal distinctions between themselves and the less assimilated Ashkenazim of the northeast and to acquire the additional rights which the government had recently granted the Protestants.[7] As a representative of the *nation*, and thus despite

came from Portugal, but the fact that the parents' names are not mentioned indicates that they were both of Marrano birth" (letter in the private possession of Thémanlys).

4. Bordeaux, "Furtado-Rodrigues marriage document before Rauzan, notary in Bordeaux, May 8, 1775," Archives départementales de la Gironde, (henceforth: ADG), 3E21702. The illuminated *ketuba* is in the private possession of Thémanlys.

5. By 1798, Furtado owned enough property to provide a surety of 25,000 francs (about the same in dollars), for his friend's daughters, Mathurine and Alexandrine Deleyre, who were involved in the administration of the national lottery. According to the notarized contract, Furtado's wealth consisted of a warehouse in Bordeaux valued at 10,000 francs, two one-storey buildings at 6,000 francs, and a large residence at 16,000 francs. This was exclusive of his personal residential property. ADG, 3E24109, 13th Frimaire An 7 (December 3, 1798).

6. For a documented account of this journey, see Zosa Szajkowski, "The Delegation of the Jews of Bordeaux to the Malesherbes Commission (1788) and to the Assemblée Nationale (1790)," *Zion*, XVIII (1953), 31–79.

7. In 1787 an edict was promulgated concerning the status of non-Catholics. The edict was the direct result of a concern on the part of the king and his ministers with the plight of the French

his perception that the broadening of the rights and responsibilities of French Jewry augured the abandonment of corporative distinctions between Sephardim and Ashkenazim, Furtado presented this Sephardic position to the French ministers in Paris.[8] He obtained from them the promise that the privileges of the Bordelais *nation* would remain unaltered while the rights of all French Jews would be extended.[9]

Malesherbes undoubtedly intended to redefine and ameliorate the condition of French Jewry.[10] His plans, however, were never realized. On January 24, 1789, Louis XVI issued the definitive call for the convening of the Estates General. From the first meeting on May 5, 1789, the discontented among the three estates began the struggle which quickly and somewhat unintentionally led to the emergence of a French citizenry and the declaration of the nationhood of France.

For Furtado, as for most Frenchmen, the question of the Jews was overshadowed by the more immediate question of the fate of France. Having already immersed himself in eighteenth-century political thought, Furtado became an active participant in the revolutionary vanguard of Bordeaux. In both word and deed, he expressed the attitudes of a Frenchman devoted to his country, a bourgeois devoted to his code of ethics, and an aristocratic intellectual devoted to the carefully defined principles of liberty, equality, and fraternity.

By 1784, Bordeaux had begun to emerge as far more than a commercially productive port, and despite its provincial character reflected many of the social and intellectual currents evident in Paris. In 1783, under the patronage

---

Calvinists. Primarily the work of Chrétien Guillaume de Lamoignon de Malesherbes, the edict reflected the significant ideological changes which had occurred in eighteenth-century France. For the first time a non-Catholic minority group was to enjoy civil rights.

8. "Mémoire présenté par MM Lopes-Dubec père et Furtado aîné, députés des Juifs de Bordeaux, à M. de Malesherbes ministre d'Etat, en Juin 1788," ADG, Série I, pp. 80–81.

9. After Furtado and Lopes-Dubec met with Malesherbes, they immediately wrote a letter to Bordeaux (May 2, 1788) in which they recounted both the minister's warm reception and his promise to retain the privileges of the *nation* while simultaneously granting all Jews extended rights and liberties. "Journal of the Bordeaux Jewish Commission in Paris, 1788," Jewish Historical General Archives, Jerusalem, Zf l. This journal appears to have been written by Furtado.

10. Historians have concluded that Malesherbes's desires for reform were mainly means to lead to the conversion of the Jews. Arthur Hertzberg, *The French Enlightenment and the Jews* (New York, 1968), p. 323; and Zosa Szajkowski, "Protestants and Jews of France in Fight for Emancipation," *PAAJR*, XXV (1956), 120. That Malesherbes sought to destroy the *imperium* of the Jews is indisputable. That he saw this accomplished, however, only by converting the Jews to Catholicism is questionable, especially since he had laid the groundwork in the 1787 edict for a secularization of certain basic human rights. Although there was not yet a secular nation-state to which the Jews and Protestants could belong as citizens, the process of secularization had begun and with it was developing an alternative to conversion—assimilation.

of St. Maur, *intendant* of Bordeaux, the Musée was formed. Composed of a cross-section of the intellectual and financial bourgeoisie of Bordeaux, including Catholics, Protestants, and Jews, this group adopted the insignia of the Freemasons, liberty, equality, and fraternity, and pledged itself to pursue social and political questions as well as philanthropy.[11]

The young of Bordeaux had become increasingly more aware of the possibilities for change and reform and were actively shunning the older and more established institutions, such as the university. Furtado, along with the lawyers Vergniaud and Gensonné, future Girondist leaders, could be found among this group of ardent and articulate bourgeois.

The events in Bordeaux, however, did not await the results of the debates held in the Musée or in private gatherings around the Comédie. Elections for the Estates General had taken place, the *cahiers* had been synthesized and organized, and the 90 electors from the Third Estate to the Sénéchaussé of Guyenne held regular private meetings to keep in touch with the Bordelais delegates to the National Assembly.[12] Politics pervaded all and the people were ready to accept a change in the old order. This change came peacefully when the 90 electors, composed of doctors, lawyers, and many merchants, declared themselves a permanent council, raised the tricolored *cocarde*, and on July 19, 1789, addressed themselves to the people of Bordeaux. July 20, 1789, found the 90, all belonging to the bourgeoisie, the accepted governing body of Bordeaux. The areas around Bordeaux quickly followed suit and looked to Bordeaux for formulas. Throughout Guyenne, spontaneous federations of free municipalities sprang up and a patriotic army was successfully formed.[13]

Although Furtado identified himself with the young lawyers and merchants, he was older enough to participate in what was to be the first step in the Bordeaux revolution. As one of the 90 electors, he began to translate the peaceful dreams and generous passions of his peers into political action and to remind the people of Bordeaux that they were free men with the right to govern themselves.

Events continued to move quickly and by March 1790 the 90 electors were replaced by a new municipality. Early in the same year, the Gironde department, with a well-defined departmental administration, was formed. The physiognomy of Bordeaux was changing as well and new political clubs, such as the Club du Café National, the Société des Amis de la Constitution, and Surveillants des Ennemies de la Constitution, were springing up around the

11. Michel Lheritier, *La Révolution à Bordeaux dans l'histoire de la Révolution française* (Paris, 1942), p. 43.

12. Camille Jullian, *Histoire de Bordeaux depuis les origines jusqu'en 1895* (Bordeaux, 1895), p. 639.

13. Ibid., pp. 639–41.

city. In addition, the sections, although still closed to non–tax-paying citizens, began to take a more active role in making themselves heard.

Furtado, along with other Sephardim such as Lopes-Dubec, Pereyre, Azevedo, and Lopes-Dias, was among the founders of the Société des Amis de la Constitution which was the least demagogic of the three clubs. On April 16, 1790, these young Jews united with future Girondist leaders and pledged their support both of the decisions of the National Assembly and the constitution.[14]

Furtado's activities and beliefs accurately reflected the early revolutionary climate in Bordeaux. He was not of the people but rather for the people. In line with the *philosophes*, he was committed to far-reaching reforms which, however, were compatible with keeping the people excluded from the clubs, sections, and municipal government. Forming a closed body which did not at all correspond to the new regime of individual liberty, Furtado, along with the other Bordelais revolutionaires, chose nevertheless to defend that liberty. Illustrative of this paradoxical position is Furtado's letter to the editor which appeared in the June 16 issue of the *Journal de Bordeaux*, the literary organ of the Société des Amis de la Constitution. Furtado was outraged at the electoral assembly's decision to pay its members a small sum during the time they participated in the sessions. Afraid that the honor and commitment to service would be replaced by desire for financial gain, Furtado sought to prevent the poor from participating in the assemblies.[15]

The decision by the electoral assembly was evidence of a beginning schism, which later was to ripen into open revolt, between the people of the Gironde and their bourgeois spokesmen. For the time being, however, Furtado, along with Vergniaud, Ducos fils and Fonfrede aîné, were creating a political furor by resigning on January 15, 1791, from the Musée because of the aristocratic leanings of the society. The Comité des Quatre, as the four were called, publicized their resignations with letters and pamphlets and soon succeeded in attracting almost all the future Girondists to their cause.

Granié, *commissaire* of the Musée, quickly answered the four rebels with a personal letter which was followed by a pamphlet written by the members of the Musée and addressed to the citizens of Bordeaux. "I have been," Granié declared, "I am and I will always be submissive to the decrees of the National Assembly sanctioned by the King."[16] The pamphlet prepared by the Musée

14. Michel Lheritier, *Liberté (1789–1790). Bordeaux et la Révolution française* (Paris, 1947), pp. 253–54.

15. Abraham Furtado, "Lettre au Redacteur," *Journal de Bordeaux et du Département de la Gironde,* June 16, 1790, p. 343, Archives municipales de Bordeaux (henceforth: AMB).

16. *Documents de la période révolutionnaire,* L 8/22, tomb IV, D. 229, p. 98, AMB.

did not rest with an oath of loyalty to the assembly, but rather took its defense to the people. Is it honest and just, the Musée asked, that a whole society be condemned because one finds four out of many journals which are aristocratic? Rather than retarding the progress of the spirit, moreover, we are actively engaged in free discussion which of necessity includes all sides and allows for error.[17]

Changing its tone from one of defense to one of accusation, the Musée asked how Furtado, a Jew, who was accepted by the Musée while his people still lived in a state of debasement and degradation, could now evidence such ingratitude?[18] Apparently Furtado felt no reciprocal obligation for his early recognition and acceptance by the Musée.

Although the Musée was in fact less revolutionary than Furtado and the others would have wished, we cannot disallow the possibility that political recognition also motivated these men. Whether as a result of this controversy or merely by coincidence, shortly thereafter Furtado and Lopes-Dubec were elected notables of the Bordeaux municipality.[19] Furtado's activities during the following year were not at all extraordinary, and the minutes of the municipality contain reports given by him on such benign matters as deciding what type inscription, if any, should be placed on the frontispiece of the large ballroom.

The following year, however, on January 12, 1793, Furtado was elected municipal officer of the General Council of the Commune of Bordeaux.[20] His activities became more numerous and often one finds his name in the minutes of the municipality.[21] As a municipal officer Furtado also became involved with the sections of Bordeaux, and on April 8, 1793, headed a delegation from the 23rd section to search out and disarm suspect persons.[22]

Intellectually, Furtado was no less committed to the Revolution. "Enlighten mankind," he had written in a treatise entitled Folie de Jeunesse.[23] "Banish from its midst error and superstition and those whose interest it is

17. Le Musée aux citoyens de Bordeaux, 1791, p. 13, AMB, R6.
18. Ibid., p. 14.
19. "Registre des déliberations du Bureau municipal," Documents de la période révolutionnaire, L 8/19, no. 93.
20. Ibid., L 8/20, D102.
21. Ibid., L 8/19, no. 97; L 8/20, D123; L 8/20, D102. Among Furtado's activities were the overseeing and verifying of pharmaceutical patents.
22. Ibid., L 8/22, 165. This is a report in Furtado's own handwriting of the details of the search.
23. Abraham Furtado, "Folie de jeunesse." This manuscript, which is incomplete (120 pages), is in the private possession of Pascal Thémanlys. The title which Furtado has given this manuscript is interesting. Perhaps he decided to call it Folie de jeunesse only after rereading it a few years later and realizing the inadequacy of his thinking. Another possibility, however, is that the "folie" is not the author's but rather that of society, for according to Furtado, religion had prolonged "l'enfance du genre humain."

to propagate them and let us see thereafter if man is less unfortunate and better."[24]

Although the *Folie* is undated, Furtado's mood, assumptions, intellectual companions, and direct references indicate that it was written sometime during 1791. Proscription and Robespierre are unimaginable; the same revolutionary speaks who chose to quit the Musée in 1791 and join with three others to accuse former associates of reactionary tendencies. Rousseau, who became a villain in 1793, was still a great man whose ideals and perceptions were worthy of political translation. More a *philosophe* than a politician, Furtado's vision is untainted by practical considerations, political realities, or psychological complexities. France was in need of revolutionary changes and her people of relief from oppressive fetters.

Much of what Furtado wrote in this small treatise was neither original nor uncommon, though for a French Jew it was certainly the latter. The expansion of enlightenment and public education based on enlightened principles, the struggle against ignorance and credulity, the destruction of repressive religious institutions—these are his main concerns. In harmony with his educated peers, who viewed the masses as duped and degraded by traditional religious beliefs and institutions, Furtado believed that the light of reason would soon shine on the oppressed and lead them to accept a more humane and just society.

Of all the *philosophes*, Furtado saw Rousseau as the one who had most inspired the taste for "Justice," "Patrie," and "Liberté." Under his brilliant pen, these virtues had become irresistible. Reason alone could produce good effects, but when joined with an even greater power, "le sentiment," triumph was surer and more durable. Although he appreciated the complexity of Montesquieu and believed that by his victories over the priests Voltaire had severely impaired the power of despotism, it was nevertheless with Rousseau and his social contract that Furtado placed his greatest hope.[25]

This was only the beginning, however, for ignorance and error were everywhere. Enlightenment must be spread, errors destroyed, and among them the most rooted of all, religion. Believing along with Voltaire and Diderot that there was a clear connection between the unenlightened condition of man and the existence of traditional religious beliefs and institutions, but proceeding one step beyond what these *philosophes* would have advocated, Furtado sought to demonstrate that the Revolution could finally destroy the power of the church, to facilitate the spread of rational and just

24. Ibid., p. 90.
25. Ibid., p. 11.

laws, and ultimately to free mankind from his self-estrangement. With this threefold attack, Furtado would have to defend the Revolution against an indignant church, a vociferous aristocracy, and a vacillating royalty.

It is impossible, Furtado reasoned, that laws which solemnly sanctify the rights of man and citizen, rights which almost all preceding institutions had violated or failed to recognize, would not ameliorate the condition of man and make him at the same time better and less unhappy.[26]

Laws alone, however, were not enough to eradicate superstitions and erroneous doctrines. As with diseases that had been neglected since their onset and that had acquired a potency one could control only at great pain, so it was with religious opinions. They were always the first to introduce themselves into man's spirits, and always the last to leave.[27]

Furtado's desire to combat the influence of religion was not motivated specifically by any anti-Jewish feelings. On the contrary, it was invariably the Catholic church, its priests, and its doctrines that bore the brunt of his biting criticism.[28] There were nevertheless in his words a general distrust of all religions (which of necessity included his own) and a belief that progress implied an abandonment of specific religious practices.

I see almost everywhere, Furtado declared as he began his long discussion of the abuses committed if not by religion then in its name, religious beliefs, cults, ceremonies, and priests perpetuating the most monstrous opinions and lies. Rather than accept the inevitability of these lies Furtado chose instead to prove their basic incompatibility with the progressive development of society and to demonstrate, using a phrase undoubtedly coined by himself, that because of them, mankind had become a stranger to itself, socially divided, morally corrupt, politically vicious, and intellectually stagnant.[29] To be convinced, Furtado continued, one need only consider the plights of, for instance, the Protestants and Jews among the Catholics or the Christians among the Turks.

Religious opinions also markedly influenced particular transactions among men. The legislator of the Hebrews, Furtado continued, permitted taking profits from those who were not of his sect while he prohibited it among his own.[30] Jesus Christ sent to eternal damnation in the next life all those who did not practice his dogmas in this.[31] No less powerful were the

26. Ibid., p. 17.
27. Ibid., p. 18.
28. Ibid., p. 57.
29. Ibid., pp. 24–26.
30. This law would be severely challenged by Napoleon. Furtado, along with the rest of the Assembly of Notables, would be required to prove that it was neither directed towards members of a particular religious group nor that it justified usurious rates.
31. Furtado, "Folie de jeunesse," p. 28.

intellectual prejudices perpetuated in the name of religion. Witness Galileo's imprisonment or Descartes's persecution by the priests.

In fact, Furtado could find no area of life immune from the pernicious influence of religion. The glory of Christianity, he declared, had been marked by disasters. In Spain and Portugal, the existing decadence of values, morals, and customs was directly related to the power of the church. The priests, those guardians of religious beliefs, laughed in silence at the credulity that nourished them.[32] On the other hand, during the intervals when tolerance prevailed—Furtado probably had in mind eighteenth-century Bordeaux where Protestants and Jews alike were tolerated by a relaxed church policy —the arts and commerce flourished, sure signs of happiness and public felicity.[33]

Essentially Furtado believed that reason and traditional religious faith were mutually exclusive.

> To the extent that belief in a Supreme Being is beneficial to both the Prince and the people he governs, to that extent is superstition fatal to both. One is unable to be devout without being foolish and one is only able to be an inferior King when one is a bad logician. Reason banishes piety and piety, according to its most general definition, cannot exist without an absolute abnegation of Reason.[34]

Here as well as in his descriptions of the abuses committed in the name of religion, Furtado was influenced by Deism—its denial of the validity of revealed religion, and its accusations that revealed religion fostered false divisions among mankind and ignored the natural laws at work.

Furtado was less critical of Judaism than were many English Deists—for whom Judaism was particularly reprehensible in its emphasis on the concept of the chosen people and in its numerous commandments—and directed his major attacks (as did the French Deists) against the Catholic church.[35] Nevertheless, in sharing the Deists' evaluation of the traditional Jewish community and in supporting their attempts to replace all revealed religion with natural law and natural religion, Furtado would find himself open to criticism by both the church and his fellow Jews. He anticipated his critics' remarks,

32. Ibid., p. 94.
33. Ibid., p. 89.
34. Ibid., p. 49.
35. To English Deists such as Shaftesbury, Collins, Tindal, Morgan, and Bolingbroke, Judaism was neither original, being an inferior imitation of Egyptian and Chaldean traditions, nor representative of any lofty ideals, and the Jews themselves were an "ignorant, barbarous and cruel people." Through the Deists, the anti-Jewish traditions of the Middle Ages were carried forward to the Age of Rationalism, albeit subtly and in a new form consistent with the emergent attitudes. S. Ettinger, "Jews and Judaism as seen by the English Deists of the eighteenth century," *Zion*, XXIX (1964), 182–207.

however, and in the last pages of the *Folie* sought, with phrases common to Deism, to destroy any arguments postulating the necessity of religion.

One might say with some appearance of reason, Furtado's defense began, that religious opinions have at least contributed to softening the gross and savage manners of the peoples of Europe. But even this is not so, for religion has impeded rather than helped the progress of morals by merely substituting corrupt and depraved customs. "Religion is necessary, they tell us. Yes, for tyrants of nations, for artisans of fraud and lies, for hypocrites. . . ."[36]

There are also those who maintain that the people need religion to comfort them in this life of suffering—that it gives them hope for a better future life. These same supporters of religion maintain, moreover, that the laws of society are not enough, that man is in need of religious or divine laws, for without them he would act unscrupulously, in a word that there is only the fear of invisible powers which prevents man from expressing his criminal instincts.[37] Let no one, Furtado maintained, tell us any more that morality alone aided by civil laws is incapable of producing the happiness of societies and of perpetuating order and harmony, for accepting this notion is to misunderstand the force of virtue and to reduce man to being led only by the grossest errors.[38]

Furtado concluded his treatise with a final defense of the Revolution. Civil war might be a great evil, he reasoned, but there were times when it was necessary, justifiable, and even preferable to the despotism that it opposed.[39]

Furtado would soon have cause to regret the enthusiasm and optimism with which he embraced the Revolution. By the spring of 1793, Bordeaux was involved in more than a peaceful and orderly bourgeois revolution. In August 1792, the sections, of which there were 28, had declared themselves in permanent session and opened their doors to everyone, including non–tax-paying citizens. The municipality was finding its authority challenged, not only by the sections and the clubs, but also more seriously by the union of dissident city leaders with those in the countryside who were antagonistic to the Bordelais government. The ideological seeds that Furtado and his peers, along with their counterparts in the national and legislative assemblies, had sown were rapidly producing a growth that would overwhelm not only Bordeaux but also the whole of France.

36. Furtado, "Folie de jeunesse," p. 98.
37. Ibid., p. 102.
38. Ibid., p. 109. Deists had not only concluded that revelation was superfluous and reason the touchstone to religious validity, but also that religion and ethics were natural phenomena. Thus the traditional God need hardly be appealed to since man could find in nature the necessary guides for moral and religious living.
39. Ibid., p. 118.

Bordeaux had been following the events in Paris with great interest and no less anxiety. On August 9, 1792, the revolutionary Paris Commune, composed of delegates from all the sections, ejected the legal commune, took control of the national guard and the next day attacked the Tuileries. The king fled to the assembly for asylum, the palace was ransacked, and the guard, now swollen in numbers, attacked all suspects of the revolutionary cause.

The assembly, shown to be as impotent as feared, immediately set up a provisional executive and ordered elections by universal manhood suffrage. When the new assembly (the National Convention) finally convened on September 22, 1792, Paris had already witnessed a series of massacres and pillaging which caused consternation among many deputies and dramatized the inevitable power conflict between the commune, its radical supporters, and the leaders of the convention.

France was declared a republic, the king condemned, and on January 21, 1793, after a series of heated debates, which continued the rivalry over leadership of the convention, the king was executed. Calm was not restored to Paris, and on February 25 and March 9–10, riots broke out anew. News of the desertion of Dumouriez, the hero of the battle of Valmy, further lowered the esteem of the now conflict ridden convention, and on April 15 the sections of Paris demanded a purge of their national government. By May 4, however, the first *maximum* had been enacted and with it the beginning of a legislative expression of the wishes of the Parisian populace.

The deputies from the Gironde, among whom were Gensonné, Gaudet, Vergniaud, and Grangeneuve, along with Brissot, Condorcet, Isnard, and Lasource, had played a significant role in determining the actions of both the legislative assembly and the National Convention. Their distrust of Paris and subsequently of Robespierre and his Jacobin followers had ripened, however, into deep mutual hatred and now they rightly feared for their own survival as well as that of the convention.

On May 4 and 5, 1793, Vergniaud wrote two letters appealing for support to the Société des Amis de la Constitution in Bordeaux.[40] Bordeaux did not tarry in coming to the aid of her deputies. On May 9, the sections declared themselves in a state of insurrection against the anarchists of Paris and invited the different authorities of the department to unite and to determine effective means of restoring liberty of opinion to the convention.[41] On June 9 the Commission Populaire de Salut Public of Bordeaux was formed, seven days after a crowd, organized by the Parisian sections, surrounded the Tuil-

40. A. Vivie, *La Terreur à Bordeaux* (Bordeaux, 1877), pp. 215–16.
41. M. Bernadau, *Histoire de Bordeaux depuis l'année 1675 jusqu'à 1836* (Bordeaux, 1837), p. 204.

leries and demanded the proscription of 29 deputies, among whom were Gensonné, Grangeneuve, Gaudet, and Vergniaud.[42] Furtado, as one of the nine commissioners of the General Council of the Commune of Bordeaux and Lopes-Dubec, one of two members of the Tribunal of Commerce of Bordeaux were among those Bordelais who united to save France from the "tyranny" of Paris.

On June 10, the Commission Populaire decided on the actions which it would take. A departmental army of about 1,200 men would be equipped and kept in reserve to obey orders. Emissaries would be sent to other departments to propose that they take similar measures and finally the various detachments would march on Paris where they would protect the liberty of discussion of the convention and the persons of its members.[43] "It is in this way," Furtado wrote a few months later in his *Mémoires d'un Patriote Proscrit*, "that Bordeaux saw itself caught up without having calculated the consequences in what has since been called the system of federalism."[44]

On June 17, two commissioners, Treilhard and Mathieu, were sent by the convention, now under the control of the *Montagnards*, to Bordeaux with the message that the welfare of France demanded forgiveness. The Commission Populaire received them and invited them to leave the city, which they did on June 27.[45] Furtado recalled, "One spoke only of the advantages which the city had had over the commissioners. The President of the Commission, bolstered by this pretended success and the applauds of the people, decided to form an army able to restore independence to the Convention."[46]

Shortly thereafter, on June 30, the commission sent a letter—written by Grangeneuve jeune, brother of the *conventionnel* and secretary of the commission—to General Custine, asking him to quit his post at the northern army and to take over the command of the departmental force. Rather than answer the Bordelais directly, Custine sent the letter to the convention where it was read publicly.[47]

Despite the original enthusiasm on the part of the Bordelais to come to the aid of their deputies in the convention, the commission was unable to organize an army. The people began to feel that their government was *avocatisé*

42. M. J. Sydenham, *The Girondins* (London, 1961), p. 179.
43. Bernadau, *Histoire de Bordeaux*, p. 204.
44. Abraham Furtado, "Mémoires d'un patriote proscrit," Bibliothèque de la ville de Bordeaux, ms 1946. Furtado's diary was originally in the possession of the bibliophile Euryate (Félix) Solar, a grandson of Furtado. Subsequently the diary was sold to Labadie, a Bordeaux historian and bibliophile, who made a copy of the original. The original has been lost, and the city library of Bordeaux has only what appears to be Labadie's copy. E. Labadie, in his *La Presse bordelaise pendant la Révolution* (Bordeaux, 1910), p. 116, n. 2 mentions the diary.
45. Jullian, *Histoire de Bordeaux*, p. 673.
46. Furtado, *Mémoires d'un patriote proscrit*.
47. E. Labadie, *La Presse bordelaise*, p. 116.

and *aristocratisé* and were unwilling to sacrifice their lives to what had become a questionable cause directed by the most prosperous bourgeois of Bordeaux.[48]

The commission, finding itself in the position of a general staff without an army (they could boast a detachment of 300 men) and a government without a people, decided on August 2 to end its less than two months' existence.[49] "Delayed by an unfortunate fate which would clothe Bordeaux in mourning and cover her with tears," Furtado wrote somewhat apologetically, "this dissolution was finally deliberated, too late to be sure, but early enough to precede by 4 days the decree of August 6 which proscribed those who had provoked, seconded or accepted this commission. A terrible decree whose full force was only felt two months later."[50]

The decree of which Furtado wrote was a declaration by the National Convention which stated that all those who had participated in the ephemeral attempt, though disastrous in its consequences, to rise to the defense of the Girondist representatives were to be treated as traitors.[51] Furtado and Lopes-Dubec, having actively supported the revolutionary cause for four years, were now required, along with most of the Bordelais bourgeoisie, to save their lives if not their property.[52]

Proscription removed Furtado from the political, intellectual, bourgeois world he knew; his refuge became introspection, observation, and fantasy as he awaited the time when he too would be marched to the guillotine. The Jacobin world which invaded Bordeaux, which sought to redress the economic and ideological wrongs of a bourgeois monopoly by giving to the *sans cullotes* nourishment and dignity, was alien to Furtado. First in hiding with friends, then in a *grenier* of poor relatives, finally on the road traveling to Bayonne, Furtado recorded in his *Mémoires d'un Patriote Proscrit* what he saw, felt, regretted, anticipated.[53]

48. Jullian, *Histoire de Bordeaux*, p. 673.
49. Bernadau, *Histoire de Bordeaux*, pp. 206–7.
50. Furtado, *Mémoires d'un patriote proscrit.*
51. Labadie, *La Presse bordelaise*, p. 116.
52. Furtado and Lopes-Dubec were not the only Sephardi Jews involved in this phase of the Revolution. Jews could be found in many offices of the Commission Populaire and in the departmental army. Zosa Szajkowski, "The Sephardi Jews of France during the Revolution of 1789," *PAAJR*, XXIV (1955), 137–64.
53. Shortly after the proscription decree of August 6, two commissioners from the convention, Baudot and Ysabeau, arrived in Bordeaux. Maltreated by the Bordelais population, the two retreated to La Reole, known for its Jacobin spirit. On September 11, however, the Jacobins peacefully gained control of Bordeaux, set up a Comité de Surveillance, and by October 16, Ysabeau and Baudot, along with Tallien and Chaudron-Rousseau, were able to return as "représentants du people en séance à Bordeaux." Jullian, *Histoire de Bordeaux*, pp. 675–76. These representatives, devoting themselves to bettering the condition of the poor, established clinics, hospitals, and schools, made sure that there was bread available to everyone, and freely distributed the money from the wealthy merchants, lawyers, priests, and nobles who were tried by the

To enter these *Mémoires* is to view one of the most formative experiences of Furtado's life. For it was during this significant transitional period that he abandoned the intellectual friends of his youth (Rousseau and Voltaire), renounced his faith in a revolutionary idealism, and began the painful struggle of reconstructing for himself a meaningful approach to the philosophical, psychological, and political complexities which his youthful arrogance had so easily dismissed. For guidance Furtado now turned to the writings of Montesquieu and Locke. As little interested in exploring Jewish sources as he was in discovering Jewish solutions, Furtado was led, nevertheless, through the influence of these men, to appreciate the role of historic experience, to reevaluate the essential bulwarks of society and ultimately to reconsider the legitimacy of traditional institutions including those of religion.

To enter Furtado's *Mémoires* is also to view the terror in Bordeaux through the eyes of a sensitive bourgeois committed to the principle that all men were entitled to liberty but only men of property possessed the education necessary to defend and implement that liberty. In his repulsion from what he described to be the uncontrolled frenzy of the populace, Furtado reflected the inevitable, although generally unforeseen, ideological conflict between eighteenth-century enlightened utilitarianism and the Rousseauist-inspired belief that all Frenchmen could share equally in the creation of a new moral order.

To seek in the *Mémoires* the existential struggles of a Heine or Boerne, a quest for identity, a challenge to Judaism, is to seek in vain. Furtado's anguish is not that of a Jew proscribed from a country to which he was only tenuously attached, but rather of a Frenchman proscribed from his country and his people. As a Jew, Furtado felt no more and no less.

Furtado had turned his attention to the Jews of the present only once, when he questioned whether his head would satisfy those who were asking for a Jewish victim. "The people, who have now become accustomed to blood and

---

Military Commission. Bertrand was chosen temporary mayor of Bordeaux, and Lacombe, president of the Revolutionary Tribunal (subsequently called the Military Commission). During the year of Jacobin rule, those Bordelais who had the good fortune to be poor were rarely harassed. The bourgeois, on the other hand, accused of having sold out to the English and having wished to isolate Bordeaux from the rest of France and to make her the capital of a federated republic, were sought out and judged by the Military Commission. Their chief crime in the eyes of the revolutionaries, however, was their wealth which was always confiscated during trials. Bernadau, *Histoire de Bordeaux*, pp. 221–22. With the fall of Robespierre, Lacombe himself was brought to trial and subsequently guillotined. Far less idealistic and committed than the Paris representatives, Lacombe was accused, among other things, of having sent innocent men to the gallows. Jullian, *Histoire de Bordeaux*, pp. 692–93.

for whom executions are merely a spectacle, have remarked that members of all classes and of both sexes have perished while no individual of the Jewish faith has yet mounted the scaffold."[54] At a time when all differences of religion have been suppressed, ridiculed and trampled underfoot, at the moment when the cult of reason has been established, it is surprising, Furtado mused in a tone which belied his own Jewishness, how one holds so tenaciously to this idea of killing someone who belonged to this ancient cult.[55]

Furtado's most immediate thoughts, however, were neither on the future of the Jews nor on their past. "I spent most of my time," he confessed, "considering the misfortunes of my unhappy country."

Unable to disengage himself completely from the events around him, Furtado had begun to seek a way of safely ending his proscription. He did not view his possible release with equanimity, however, for he alternated between hope and fear, feelings of disgust for the obtainment of liberty and the desire, nevertheless, to obtain it.

With the help of his friend, Robles, Furtado decided to prepare a petition to send to Emmerth, a Bordeaux councilman and deputy to the convention, who had promised to intervene on his behalf.[56] After writing a second letter to Emmerth, Furtado also wrote to his old friend Alexandre Déleyre.[57] Déleyre responded by sending many letters of recommendation to the representatives of the convention in Bordeaux, including Hérault de Sechelles and Phillippeaux.[58] The combination of letters, petitions, and the unrelenting

54. Furtado, *Mémoires d'un patriote proscrit.*
55. Ibid.
56. Lopes-Dubec had also gone into hiding during the Terror and subsequently had requested from his section, number 19, a proof of his patriotism. The section of *Bon Accord* agreed to give Lopes-Dubec an extract of the *procès verbal* of the session in which his loyalty and patriotism were confirmed. "Registres de la Section du Bon Accord, n° 19, séance du 25 du premier mois de la deuxiéme année de la République Française, une et indivisible," Jewish Theological Seminary, New York. Furtado felt that he could receive no help from his section since his municipal activities had prevented him from attending their meetings.
57. "Ancien élève des Jèsuits, il voulut d'abord entrer dans cette société et débuta dans le monde par une dévotion outrée; mais étant parti pour Paris, il se lia avec les encyclopédistes, fit profession d'incrédulité et se mêla au mouvement philosophique. . . . Envoyé au Convention Nationale par le département de la Gironde, Déleyre vota la mort du roi avec l'appel au peuple; passa au Consistoire des Anciens, et devint membre de l'Institut, dans la classe des sciences morales et politiques." E. Feret, *Statistique générale du département de la Gironde* (Bordeaux, 1889), p. 178.
58. We have found a letter which, although not in Déleyre's handwriting, appears to be a copy of the letter he sent to Philippeaux. The letter begins: "Le citoyen Philippeaux est prié de vouloir écrire lui-même, ou d'engager le citoyen Chaudron Rousseau à écrire au citoyen Isabeau Représentant Commissaire à Bordeaux, en faveur d'Abraham Furtado qui fût officier municipal dans cette commune. C'est un bon Israelite d'origine et de caractère dans le sens que la Bible donne à ce mot. Il s'est montré dès la révolution, constant et fidele Patriote, ami d'une liberté qui relevoit l'homme et surtout sa nation persécutée et flétrie depuis dix huit siècles" (ADG, 13L23).

interest of men such as Déleyre, Emmerth, and Dassas, finally won Furtado his freedom, not before, however, he had consented to work with the agency delegated to deal with neutral countries.[59]

As Furtado returned to political life, M. A. Jullien, a radical young representative from Paris, arrived in Bordeaux and succeeded in spurring a renewal of proscriptions and trials. Fearing his safety once again, Furtado left Bordeaux and made his way to Bayonne passing through Dax and Pau where he observed the guillotines erected in the central squares. After five weeks in seclusion in his home in Bayonne, Furtado returned to Bordeaux to find his enemy, J. B. M. Lacombe, president of the Military Commission, under arrest and awaiting trial. "It appears that the department of Bec d'Ambés (the Jacobin name for the Gironde) has been delivered of a plague capable of destroying all humanity."[60] And Furtado was relieved of the stigma of proscription and finally permitted in the summer of 1794 to reenter, this time unconditionally, the political life of Bordeaux.

Furtado wrote as he reflected on the recent past and its effects on the future:

One may view France today as a ship which after having made a long voyage in seas threatened by storms, after having endured 1000 tempests, fought against wild elements, lost its mast, its sails, its rich cargo, seen perish its best sailors, arrives nevertheless at port, pouring forth water on all sides and in a state of ruin which elicits both surprise and pity from those who view it.

The unfortunates who descend, pale, worn from fatigue and hunger, bemoan, but too late, their imprudence and their errors in this long voyage; inexperienced navigators, they were not at all well supplied; without a determined goal, they have traversed the savage and dangerous shores; without a compass and without a telescope, they were unable, nor did they know how to avoid the dangers.[61]

Furtado's disillusion with the events of 1793–94 is certainly understandable when one realizes with what enthusiasm he had approached the Revolution. Man was finally to be given the opportunity to create a just and harmonious society in which all unnatural divisions would cease to exist.

59. On March 31, 1794, the Comité de Salut public established in Bordeaux a commercial agency whose task was to stimulate the citizens to take part in exporting goods, to make known to the Commission des Subsistances the obstacles and difficulties that were retarding commerce and also to renounce those who by lack of patriotism and indifference were impeding commercial success. Pierre Bécamps, "Les relations avec les neutres au temps de la Révolution: l'agence commerciale de Bordeaux," *Revue historique de Bordeaux*, IV (1955), 314.
60. Furtado, *Mémoires d'un patriote proscrit.*
61. Ibid.

Instead of greater freedom, greater security, and more widespread enlightenment, however, Furtado had witnessed a society at war with its neighbors and a people led to unimagined cruelties, not by pernicious religious beliefs but rather by an excess and distortion of the very principles in which he had placed such confidence.

Thus we find Furtado compelled to explore, reconsider, and reevaluate the foundations on which his political hopes and philosophical beliefs had been based. While in his *Mémoires d'un Patriote Proscrit* he concentrated on capturing the circumstances surrounding his proscription and the atmosphere in which the Terror throve, in two small works each entitled *Pensées* and probably written also in 1793–94, Furtado began the outline of a lifetime's task.[62] He sought now not to destroy the evils of religion, prejudice, and credulity, but rather to understand why revolutions fail, where the causes of civil dissension lie, and how, if at all, men can achieve greater happiness.

The *philosophes*, Furtado wrote with a hindsight tinged with regret and self-criticism, who would appear to be the best guides in matters of political institutions, are not always the most reliable.[63] Furtado now concluded that man's happiness and tranquility often depended on precisely those opinions and prejudices which he and his fellow *philosophes* had dismissed as reprehensible. Experiencing the chaos produced by what he considered sane and just ideas, moreover, led Furtado to acknowledge (as did Burke who saw the Revolution causing a devaluation of tradition and inherited values and a thoughtless destruction of the material and spiritual resources of society) the role experience played in his own as well as in society's development.

But the *philosophes* were not alone in their misjudgment. A far more sophisticated Furtado was now able to perceive the hidden motivations underlying man's political actions. "Our desire for innovation, our distaste for that which already exists, while sometimes the result of a regime too oppressive to bear, can be caused also by fickleness, hidden ambition, vindictive rivalry or some other such passion. It then becomes only a source of calamity. And if man finally succeeds in freeing himself, he is often unable to protect and preserve his new found freedom."[64]

In his second notebook of *Pensées*, Furtado outlined the structure for a comprehensive study on the nature of civil dissensions.[65] Here too, however,

62. Gabrielle Moyse, "Les Pensées inédites de Furtado," *La Revue Littéraire Juive*, VI (1931), 456–69. Abraham Furtado, "Pensées," Pascal Thémanlys, Jerusalem.

63. Moyse, "Les Pensées inédites," p. 464.

64. Ibid., p. 467.

65. Furtado, "Pensées." Furtado's outline is the following: "Livre 1—des dissensions civiles dans les premières sociétés du première époque de genre humain. Livre 2—des dissensions civiles dans les premiers établissements de l'ordre politique ou seconde époque du genre humain. Livre 3—des dissensions civiles dont les causes appartiennent aux Révolutions de la

he was unable to refrain from dwelling in greater detail on the antecedents of the recent revolution. To aid him in his understanding, Furtado now turned to Montesquieu and Locke whose political theories he had read with delight during his forced retreat.

Furtado had both matured and become more conservative. His spirit, tempered by the "atrocities" of 1793-94, no longer sought immediate and irrevocable solutions. For, as he had observed, these solutions often created graver problems than those one sought to solve. Nor were the problems as simple as his youthful confidence had imagined them to be. More aware of the complexity of injustice and more convinced of society's need for stability and historic continuity, Furtado could no longer justify the civil war which only a few years earlier he had viewed as a necessary revolution.[66]

In spite of his disillusion, despair, and his increased desire to devote himself to his writings, Furtado soon returned to the political scene.[67] Unlike Bayonne, where the end of Jacobin rule signaled the exclusion of the Jews from the newly formed municipality, Bordeaux saw no recrudescence of anti-Jewish feelings.[68] After his extended vacation, however, Furtado needed an "introduction" to political life. This he received on April 27, 1797, in a letter to the prefect of the Gironde from the "chef de la Division des Fonds et Comptabilité."[69] On May 3, 1797, Furtado was elected one of the administrators of the Bordeaux municipality.[70]

---

propriété et de la Sureté—ou 3ème époque du genre humain. Livre 4—de la diversité des Gouvernements et de la Nature et du caractère particulier des dissensions qui appartiennent à chacun ou 4ème époque du genre humain. Livre 5—Débuts des moyens des artisans des discordes civiles aux différentes époques de sociétés—5ème époque du genre humain. Livre 6—Du résultat des dissensions civiles sur le bonheur des hommes en Société dans la décadence des Empires—6ème époque du genre humain." The larger work, which we have also obtained, remained unfinished at the time of Furtado's death. It is our hope someday to examine in detail this "Traité des dissensions civiles."

66. Ibid. "Il faut rendre au plus grand nombre la justice de croire, que s'ils avoient eu quelqu'expérience en Révolutions ils auroient moins osé; que s'ils avoient prevu la centième partie des maux que leur doctrine et leurs écrits ont attirés sur leur Pays, ils auroient renoncé à l'idée de le régénérer.

67. Unfortunately, we have little information concerning Furtado's political activities during these years.

68. Henry Léon, *Histoire des Juifs de Bayonne* (Paris, 1893), p. 170. In Bayonne, the Jews had formed the majority in the Jacobin clubs and thus were the first to be persecuted when the defeat of Robespierre and his followers was complete. Since there was less anti-Jewish feeling in Bordeaux than Bayonne, and since the Jews were not exclusively committed to one political group, the defeat of the Jacobins did not alter radically the position of the Jews in the community.

69. "Lettre d'introduction pour A. Furtado, du Chef de la Division des Fonds et Comptabilité, 8 Floreal, an 5 (?)," Pascal Thémanlys, Jerusalem.

70. "Registre des délibérations de l'Administration municipale du second arrondissement de Bordeaux, dit du Sud, 10 Prairal, an IV," *Documents de la période révolutionnaire*, L8/21, D193. "Installation de la Municipalité; les citoyens Lortique, Lagrifouille, Lamarque, Furtado et Nairac sont proclamés administrateurs."

Furtado's activities during the next two years remain unclear, as do the reasons for his departure for Paris in the beginning of 1799.[71] Apparently finding little reason to return to Bordeaux or else finding more reason to remain in Paris, Furtado settled in the capital where for approximately four years he frequented the homes of Mme Condorcet and Mme Helvetius, involved himself in the Parisian Sociétés, and sadly observed the political scene.

The Thermidorian Convention, despised by both the right and left, had succeeded in granting a general amnesty to the Girondists and a grudging toleration to the Catholic church, as well as in delivering a severe blow to the starving Parisian crowds attempting insurrection before it made way for a new government in November 1795.

Under the new government there was now to be a Directory of five men, one of whom retired annually, and two representative bodies, the five-hundred and the Ancients, both elected on the basis of a suffrage severely restricted by property qualifications. The assemblies wielded the legislative power and the Directory, elected by the five-hundred and the Ancients, the executive power, with no provision for avoiding deadlocks between them. Composed mainly of middle-class republicans of wealth and position, the Directory, like the convention before, was required to hold at bay, often illegally, their royalist opponents on the right and their Jacobin opponents on the left. In domestic affairs the rule of the Directory was marked by corruption. Public life was demoralized by profiteering in business, graft in politics and administration, and a vulgarity in morals and manners. All this Furtado was to observe and record in his *Journal à Paris*.[72]

"I dined today with Madame de Condorcet," Furtado wrote on July 3, 1799. Among the invited guests was Madame de Staël, a woman who simultaneously amazed and repelled Furtado.[73] Politically Madame de Staël and Furtado did not agree. When she proposed the possibility that man might soon surpass the need for any particular form of political administration, Furtado could hardly refrain from stating what he felt to be the absurdity of

71. In the same entry (but dated May 4) that records his election to the municipality is the following note: "Nomination, comme administrateurs temporaires, des citoyens Graves, Martinfils, Gemet et Rouquette, en remplacement des citoyens Dormaignac, Chicori-Bourbon, Nairac et Furtado." It is possible that the May 4 entry was for 1798 (the reference covers An IV and V) and that Furtado held a one-year appointment. It is also possible, however, that Furtado, along with Nairac who was both installed and replaced at the same time as Furtado, chose to resign a day later or was required to do so. In the event that the latter was the case, the reasons escape us entirely. If Furtado remained as a municipal officer for a year, however, his subsequent departure may be explained by his decision—again a matter for speculation but perhaps related to the life annuity he was to receive in Paris in August 1799—to leave Bordeaux.
72. Abraham Furtado, "Journal à Paris," Pascal Thémanlys, Jerusalem.
73. Ibid.

this notion. Far from conceptualizing the future irrelevance of government, Furtado was fearing rather the despotism that he viewed as inevitable when republics were given more liberty than they could support.

Nor for that matter could Furtado accept this infamous woman's manner of living. It was not Madame de Staël's affair with Benjamin Constant which repelled Furtado—he too had been involved with at least one mistress[74]—but rather the indiscreet way in which she conducted herself and her blatant disrespect and lack of concern for bourgeois propriety and morals. Her advertisement of her affair with Constant and their willingness to advance socially and politically through any available channels, moreover, not only offended Furtado's ethical code, but also epitomized the present degradation and abuse of political life.

Turning from Madame de Staël to the recent losses in Italy, Furtado described the French General Staff as being motivated only by a love of money. Unable to view with optimism any of the events around him, Furtado expressed his doubts as to whether a true republic could ever be established in France. We may become more enlightened, Furtado added with an insight missing from his writing of ten years earlier, but will that make us any more virtuous?

Talk of a republic, however, was to be short lived, because Napoleon Bonaparte, allying himself with one of the five directors, the Abbé Sieyés, staged a *coup d'état* on November 9, 1799 (the 18th Brumaire). The Directory had nothing left, Furtado wrote on December 3. They had neither money nor the justice of their cause and the respect of the people.[75]

Furtado had lived through another revolution, though far less violent than the first. The result was to sensitize him even more to the hypocrisy of those around him and to destroy what little remained of his political naiveté of ten years before. Having first believed that the *ancien régime* was too oppressive to bear and that the enemies of enlightenment, progress, and happiness were the protectors of religious institutions, Furtado had committed himself to the bourgeois revolution. He saw the revolution transform itself, however, into the Reign of Terror and himself into a disillusioned young man. The failures and intrigues of the Directory, moreover, confirmed his conclusion that it was neither religion nor her ministers but personal interest, disguised in the costume of public interest, which was the invincible enemy of mankind. Disillusioned and disgusted, Furtado saw the France he still loved unable to

74. "Fonds de Cardozo de Bethencourt," no. 2, p. 1490. "Le philosophe israelite Furtado est battu par Montesinos, ex-amant de la femme Cazares, maîtresse de Furtado" (April 16, 1788).
75. Furtado, "Journal à Paris."

provide the type of government in which honesty, justice, and stability could thrive.

For a lover of beaux-arts, Furtado wrote sadly, a *séjour* in Paris is more enchanting than any other in the world. But if one views Paris from a different perspective, one finds the receptacle of all that is perverse and wicked. Paris then becomes "a *séjour* of egotism, intrigue, and all types of ambition."[76]

Burdened by the atmosphere in Paris and finding no solace in the past, Furtado left Paris and returned to Bordeaux. Renewing his interest in the Bordelais societies, he was soon invited to become a member of the Société Médicale d'Emulation, founded in 1797.[77]

In addition to being chosen as a member of the electoral college of the Gironde,[78] Furtado also contributed to literary journals. On December 6, 1804, he wrote a review of the book "Essai sur la décomposition de la Pensée," which appeared in the Bordelais journal *L'Indicateur*.[79] After praising the author, C^xxx, for his new principles, development of ideas, and simplicity and clarity of style, Furtado then described what he felt the study of metaphysics had thus far achieved. With this as his intention, however, he succeeded also in revealing the effects of his intellectual marriage and divorce first with Rousseau, and then with Montesquieu and Locke. After having felt at different periods in life that he had found the key answers in the writings of these "geniuses," Furtado was left ultimately with the realization that there was neither one system which could explain all phenomena successfully nor one man who had uncovered the truths of metaphysics or morality.

Shortly after his return to Bordeaux, Furtado received the following letter from the prefect of the Gironde, M. Fouche.

> Monsieur. I have the honor of informing you that in accordance with the Imperial Decree of May 31 which summons to Paris on the 15 of July an Assembly of individuals professing the Jewish religion and residing on French territory, I have designated you to participate in this assembly.

76. Ibid.
77. We have been able to locate the following two references to this *société*: (1) "24 brumaire an VI: arrêté de la municipalité de Bordeaux autorisant la SOCIÉTÉ D'ÉMULATION EN L'ART DE GUERIR à recevoir de la commission administrative des hôpitaux les cadavres nécessaires pour les cours d'anatomie, de chirurgie et d'accouchement." AMB, D 156. (2) "L'école du droit ou collège des Lois ayant été vendus comme bien national, un arrêté de M. de Préfet Charles Delacroix, daté du 19 Prairial An XI (1803), transfera l'Ecole élémentaire de médecine et la société médicale d'émulation au Collège de chirurgie, rue Lalande." G. Pery, *Histoire de la Faculté de Médecine de Bordeaux, et de l'enseignement médical dans cette ville* (Paris, 1888), p. 254.
78. According to an anonymous biography of Furtado (*Archives Israélites*, II [1841], 363) "les votes des assemblées cantonnales portèrent M. Furtado au collège électoral de la Gironde."
79. C^xxx, Review of "Essai sur la décomposition de la Pensée," by Abraham Furtado, *L'Indicateur*, December 6, 1804, p. 3.

In choosing you, Monsieur, I have fulfilled Article 3 of the decree which intended that the prefects choose among those proprietors distinguished both for their honesty and enlightenment.[80]

Furtado accepted this nomination and left immediately for Paris where he would soon be chosen by the other deputies as the president of the Assembly of Notables.

Furtado's return to the Jewish community was not that of a prodigal son; on the contrary, representatives of the French community had drafted him. His primary allegiance was still to France. More politically conservative and less optimistic than in 1789, however, he now acknowledged that communal participation and institutional guarantees were necessary to transform the Jews into French citizens. For more than two years he undertook to inspire that participation and to elicit those guarantees.

As the assembly was to become involved with the details of making the Jews "useful citizens," Furtado's secular attitudes would cause suspicion among those deputies for whom Judaism was at least as essential as the demands made by the government.[81] Notwithstanding the lessened respect felt for him by the more traditional deputies, there is little doubt that as spokesman for both emperor and Jew, Furtado played a significant role in directing the discussions of the assembly and in influencing the answers which were subsequently sanctioned by the Sanhedrin.

Napoleon is often viewed as the popular general who brought the French internal peace (and for a short time international peace) while simultaneously preserving for them the accomplishments of their revolution. Paradoxically Napoleon must also be viewed as the first consul and emperor who abandoned the republic along with the ideal of equality and who thus laid the foundations for the July monarchy. "We do not have a Republic and we will not have one unless we sow some blocks of granite on the soil of France," Napoleon had said to his Council of State.[82] His blocks of granite, however,

80. "Nomination de Furtado comme délégué à l'Assemblée par le Préfet de la Gironde, 1er Juillet, 1806," Pascal Thémanlys, Jerusalem.
81. "Il fut bientôt avéré que les Juifs portugais étaient suspects à tous leurs coreligionnaires, qui les considéraient comme des apostats. Le président Furtado était plus qu'un autre en butte aux soupçons. On semblait croire qu'il ne tenait à sa religion que par ce sentiment de respect humain qui ne permet d'abandoner celle où l'on est né que dans le cas où l'on serait entraîné par la plus forte des convictions. Or, telle n'était pas la disposition d'esprit de M. Furtado, l'indifférence philosophique faisait le fondement de ses opinions. Les rabbins d'Alsace et ceux de l'ancien comtat d'Avignon, aux quels appartenait le premier rang pour la science, disaient de leur président qu'on voyait bien qu'il n'avait appris la Bible que dans Voltaire." Israel Lévi, "Napoléon 1er et la réunion du Grand Sanhédrin," REJ, XXVIII (1894), 273-74 (extrait des mémoires du Chancelier Pasquier).
82. Louis Madelin, "Napoleon," in The European Past, Vol. I (New York, 1970), 432.

were comparable to the corporate bodies of the *ancien régime*, revived not to compete with a monarchy but to be subjected to a modern state and to be used to assure the obedience of the masses. The assemblies, the Legion of Honor, the electoral colleges and even eventually the Jews were so many blocks set in the "grains of sand" Napoleon called his nation.

Although the Sephardim of southwestern France had made an easy transition from their status under the *ancien régime* to their citizenship under the republic, emancipation had dealt a severe blow to the discipline and organization of the Ashkenazic communities, whose leaders, unable to control the threatening anarchy and seeking a reenforcement of their authority, appealed to the government to intervene on their behalf. Specifically, they wished to see the Jews organized officially and included along with the Protestants in the decree of 1802.[83]

At the same time that Berr Isaac Berr and others were petitioning the government to recognize an official Jewish leadership, the non-Jews were increasing both their verbal and physical attacks upon the Jews. The residents of Alsace and Lorraine accused the Ashkenazim of usury and feared that soon all their property would be mortgaged to these "enemies" of the church. Municipal councils began to suggest measures which would reduce the credits owed the Jews, and the debtors began to take the situation into their own hands.[84]

Continuous complaints by the general councils of Haut- and Bas-Rhin, along with the increase in violent outbreaks in the summer and fall of 1805, finally prompted the minister of justice to examine the problem. Although specifically denouncing the usury of the Jews, he advised, nevertheless, a general remedy which would no longer permit the rate of interest to be established by the parties involved.[85]

Neither the projects of Portalis, the minister of cults, nor those of the minister of justice were realized; not until Napoleon addressed himself to the

83. Intent upon reuniting the clergy of France, making peace with the Holy See, and obtaining papal recognition for the Revolution, Napoleon signed a concordat with the Vatican on 26 Messidor, An IX (1801). The pope received the right to depose French bishops and agreed to raise no question over the former tithes and church lands. Publicity of Catholic worship was again allowed, Napoleon stated that Catholicism was the religion of the majority of the Frenchmen and the state was henceforth required to pay the salaries of the clergy. Napoleon had not agreed, however, to establish Catholicism as the religion of the state. In order to make this clear, he issued a decree on 18 Germinal, An X (1802), according to which Protestant ministers of all denominations were also to be paid by the state.

84. Robert Anchel, *Napoléon et les Juifs* (Paris, 1928), pp. 66–67.

85. Ibid., p. 76. The civil code had not established any legal rate of interest, but rather relied on the acceptable and going rate. Not until September 3, 1807 (fifteen months after the May 30 decree) was the legal rate of interest set at no more than 5 percent in private credit and 6 percent in commercial credit. Penalties were provided for not observing the legal rate.

Jewish problem were the dual issues of internal organization and usurious practices joined together. The results—an arbitrary infringement of the economic freedom of the northeastern Jews, a resolution of all questions concerning the relation of Jewish and French law and the union of all the Jews of France in one centrally controlled organization—were consistent with Napoleon's decision both to consolidate the accomplishments of the Revolution and to reconstruct subservient intermediary bodies. In obtaining these results, however, Napoleon was to reverse the process by which the Revolution had emancipated the Jews. The issue of citizenship and the worthiness of the Jews were again questioned and doctrinal as well as concrete economic proof of their intentions were demanded.

On Saturday, July 26, 1806, after having assembled for prayers in the Parisian synagogues of the "rue Sainte Avoye" and the "rue du Chaume," the deputies from France and Italy gathered together at the Hôtel de Ville to name their officers. Abraham Furtado, receiving 62 votes against 32 for Berr Isaac Berr, was elected president.

The assembly met a second time on July 29. The imperial commissioners were present and Molé, speaking on behalf of the government, addressed the assembled Jews. Reminding them that they had been called together from different parts of the empire because of the "justifiable" complaints against many of them, he revealed that they would be presented with twelve questions.[86] Your task, he warned in a tone which revealed his lack of respect and sympathy, is to answer each question honestly, for to do otherwise is to render yourselves both guilty and blind to your true interests.[87]

Molé followed his unconcealed threat with a list of the twelve questions, which dealt with marriage and divorce, the commitments of the Jews to France and the Frenchmen, and the internal regulations of the Jewish community in regard to their organization and their economic transactions.[88] Despite the "unanimous" feeling on the part of the deputies that the questions implied a lack of attachment on the part of the Jews to France and their fellow Frenchmen (a response which was justified merely by the fact that such questions were asked), Furtado replied to Molé's presentation by

86. Although the authorship of the questions is unknown, Napoleon probably gave this task to Molé.

87. *Procès-Verbal des séances de l'Assemblée des Députés français professant la religion juive; imprimé d'après le manuscrit communiqué par M. le Président* (Paris, 1806). Curiously this volume, found in the private possession of Pascal Thémanlys, Jerusalem, includes the minutes of the Sanhedrin. Thus the publication date must be inaccurate. What is most probable is that the edition of 1806 was republished to include the decisions of the Sanhedrin. Other editions include: Diogène Tama, *Collections des écrits et des actes relatifs au dernier état des individus professant la religion hébraïque* (Paris, 1806); Id., *L'organization civile et religieuse des Israélites* (Treultel et Wurtz, 1808); S. Romanelli, *Raccolta de inni ed ode de parechi Rannini dell'Assemblea degli Ebrei e del Gran Sinedrio* (Mantua, 1807).

88. *Procès-Verbal.*

praising the genius who had finally put an end to the anarchy within France, the ambitious enemies outside of France, and who now had taken upon himself the immediate regeneration of the Jews.[89]

The answers to the twelve questions, which had been formulated by a commission of twelve headed by Furtado and often challenged by the assembly before their adoption, indicate the differences of approach and intention between the Sephardic and Ashkenazic deputies. Biblical quotes, always more acceptable to the enlightened, are interwoven with Talmudic precepts; common denominators of religious morality are reinforced by common geographic boundaries, political institutions, and a common humanity. Both the secular and the sacred are intermingled and compromises between the two are often the result.

Despite the confusion within the assembly and the disagreement among the deputies, there was no group for whom emancipation was undesirable or French citizenship deniable. The deputies were united in their attempts to make Judaism and the Jews completely compatible with France and the Frenchmen. They were deeply divided, however, over the significance of the preservation of Jewry and Judaism, as the controversy concerning intermarriage and the never unanimous votes on the functions of the rabbis indicate. These conflicts, made more complex by the differing attitudes towards the essence of Judaism, were the most profound and the most enduring divisions within the assembly.

On September 18, Molé appeared again before the assembly. The Jews, he stated, have continuously born the brunt of their sovereign's avarice. Their customs and practices have isolated them from society which, in its turn, has pushed them away. Even today they explain the antipathy on the part of some to agriculture and the professions by a lack of confidence in a future whose existence has always depended on the spirit of the moment.[90] From now on, he declared, unable to complain, you will thus be unable to justify yourselves. And to be sure that no excuse remains, His Majesty asks from you a religious guarantee of the principles announced in your answers.[91]

The religious guarantee was to be the formation of the Sanhedrin whose responses would acquire in the eyes of the Jews of all the countries and for all the centuries "the greatest authority possible." Molé concluded by asking the deputies to form a committee of three Portuguese, three Italian, and three German deputies, and to announce to all the synagogues of Europe the advent of the Sanhedrin.

89. Ibid.
90. This is probably a reference to Furtado's defense of the northeastern Jews.
91. *Procès-Verbal.*

Furtado, who had been aware of the government's plans since at least September 11, applauded Napoleon's decision and promised that this great and beneficent ruler would live to see, millions of useful citizens.[92] The deputies then prepared a resolution in which they expressed their loyalty to Napoleon, their decision to invite 25 members of the assembly to participate in the Sanhedrin, their acceptance of the government's intention to include 29 rabbis from France and Italy, and finally their willingness to remain in existence until the Great Sanhedrin had terminated its sittings.[93]

The deputies never suspected that they would remain in Paris until the spring. In a personal letter written on September 11 to his friend Pery in Bordeaux, Furtado predicted hopefully that he would stay only another two months.[94] Feeling himself free to describe to Pery how he viewed the events around him, Furtado complained of his committee (the commission of twelve) whose noise and gossip were deafening and of the assembly, none of whose members were more worthy than he. One is able to say of us, Furtado admits, what we say of so many others: from afar it is something and from within it is nothing.[95]

Despite his position as president of the assembly, Furtado continued to feel little identification with and respect for his fellow deputies. "Oh how I have need of you and your excellent Ferrère," he wrote Pery.[96] Tell me, he asked, what both of you think of the responses to the first questions?[97] It appears,

92. In Furtado's letter to Pery on September 11, he was already aware of the plans to convene the Sanhedrin. On September 8, 1806, however, we find the following letter sent to Furtado from Molé. Obviously Furtado was informed of Napoleon's plans after September 8. "Je reçois Monsieur, la lettre que vous avez adressé à mes collegues et à moi et je m'empresse d'y répondre. Nous pensons que le désir que manifeste une partie de l'Assemblée que vous presidez pour voir renouveller son comité, ne doit vous engager à aucune démarche; et que sur cet objet comme sur tous autres vous devez attendre les nouvelles communications que nous irons faire à l'assemblée très prochainement." Pascal Thémanlys, Jerusalem.

93. *Procès-Verbal.*

94. ADG, Série IV, J209. Pery was obviously the son of Constantin Pery who was condemned to death by the Military Commission of Bordeaux, and executed 16 Frimaire, An II. Constantin had been a member of the *Société de Musée*, the *Société de la Jeunesse bordelaise*, and an administrator and "procureur syndic" of Bordeaux. Feret, *Statistique*, p. 496. From the tone of the letter, Pery was a young man with whom Furtado had developed a warm friendship. See my book, *The Sephardic Jews of Bordeaux: Assimilation and Emancipation in Revolutionary and Napoleonic France* (University, Ala., 1978), p. 142, n. 75.

95. ADG, Série IV, J209.

96. Philippe Ferrère was a Bordelais lawyer (1767–1815) who was highly regarded by his peers.

97. Furtado had obviously sent the responses to all twelve questions to the Bordelais Jewish community. On September 10, 1806, about sixty prominent Bordelais Jews wrote to Paris to express their satisfaction and agreement with the answers adopted by the assembly. "Les français soussignez professant la religion de Moïse, à Bordeaux, déclarant qu'ayant eu connais-sance des douze questions proposées par Messieurs les Commissaires du Gouvernement à l'assemblée des Juifs à Paris, et des réponses qu'elle y a faites, ils n'ont rien trouvé dans ces réponses qui ne fut entièrement conforme aux opinions généralement reçues et suivies. C'est pourquoi ils approuvent en tant que besoin serait les dites réponses." Microfilm from Zosa Szajkowski.

he confided, that the emperor has great plans for us. No longer is it a question of revealing in what ways our religion accords with and differs from the French and Italian code of laws, but rather how we can give to the decisions of our assembly the solemnity and force of the decisions of a synode or an ecumenical council.[98]

Wary of this new and even more demanding task, Furtado asked Pery to comment on the speech he planned to deliver when the assembly was presented to Napoleon.[99] With his usual eloquence, Furtado intended to use this opportunity to praise the emperor, to explain the causes (while discrediting the results) of the present situation of the northeastern Jews as distinct from those of the southwest, and finally to assure Napoleon that the distinctions between the Jews and those of other religions would soon disappear.[100]

Napoleon had explained in his August 23 instructions sent to Champagny, the minister of the interior, that the Sanhedrin was to translate the responses of the assembly into articles of faith and principles of religious legislation. The recreation of a legislative body of a supposedly defunct nation may have appealed to Napoleon in yet another way. The Jews, dispersed throughout all of Europe, might find themselves sympathetic to such a beneficent ruler; this sympathy could then be used to Napoleon's advantage in his battles against both Germany and Poland.[101] That the Jews would be as committed to the Sanhedrin of 1807 as to that of the past appears to have been a naive hope on the part of Napoleon; nevertheless, the convening of the Sanhedrin after the Assembly of Notables had dutifully answered in their eighth response that the rabbis had no judicial powers and after the deputies had insisted that the Jews no longer formed a nation indicates the extent to which the Jews of France were willing to comply with the contradictory demands of their emperor.

Napoleon's ulterior political motives and inconsistent expectations

98. ADG, Série IV, J209.
99. As early as July 31, the assembly had made known its desire to meet with Napoleon. We have located three letters addressed to Furtado from Champagny and dated July 31, September 3, and September 29. Pascal Thémanlys, Jerusalem. (See my book, *The Sephardic Jews of Bordeaux*, pp. 142–43, n. 80.) The deputies, however, were never presented to the emperor. "Son [Napoleon] départ précipité pour une guerre dont le but est d'éloigner pour long-temps ce fleau de l'Europe civilisée, d'y assurer et d'y garantir l'empire de la justice et de la raison, nous a privés de l'honneur d'être présentés à notre illustre bienfaiteur." *Procès-Verbal*, March 25 session.
100. ADG, Série IV, J209.
101. Pasquier, in his mémoires, states that Napoleon probably had precisely this in mind when he called for a Sanhedrin. "Il [Napoleon] s'était dit probablement qu'un tel bienfait attacherait à jamais cette race à sa fortune et que partout où elle était répandue, il trouverait des auxilliaires disposés à seconder ses projets. Il allait entreprendre une nouvelle invasion en Allemagne qui devait le conduire à travers la Pologne et dans les pays voisins, où les affaires alors se traitaient presque exclusivement par l'intermédiare des Juifs; il était donc naturel de penser que nuls auxilliaires ne pouvaient être plus utiles que ceux-là et par conséquent plus nécessaires à acquérir." Lévi, "Napoléon 1er," pp. 272–73 (extrait des mémoires du Chancelier Pasquier).

notwithstanding, Furtado and a commission of nine immediately began to direct their energies towards insuring the smooth adoption and sanction of the assembly's decisions. On January 21, 1807, Furtado wrote a memorandum to the imperial commissioners in which he discussed the arrangements which remained to be made. A leader and two advisors have yet to be named, he wrote, and it would be more convenient if the government proposed these nominations in order to avoid the inevitable "intrigues and factions."[102] In essence, Furtado wished to avoid giving the Sanhedrin any chance for independent expression.[103]

If Furtado and the imperial commissioners were sure of the position in which they wished to place the Sanhedrin, they were unsure of the way to present the decisions and the additional tasks, if any, that Napoleon had in mind for that body. Champagny decided, in the absence of any detailed instructions from the emperor and with the hope that some such help would come soon, to begin the sessions and if necessary to prolong them indefinitely.

The first meeting of the Sanhedrin took place on February 9. The format followed was to be the same for all eight sessions; the deputies, arranged in the fashion of the original Sanhedrin, heard reports delivered primarily by Furtado and subsequently adopted each decision unanimously. As decided in advance, discussions and debates, so common in the assembly, were nonexistent.[104]

At the February 9 meeting, Furtado delivered a report introducing the first three decisions (polygamy, divorce, and marriage). Rather than discuss the details of these decisions, Furtado chose instead to emphasize the *liaison intime* between the duties prescribed by religion and the dictates established by society. After proclaiming that man's wisdom came from God whose law was the fundamental principle of all order and morality, Furtado then indicated the dangers inherent in an excess and distortion of religiosity. Although less rigid than the young man who had once advocated abolishing all religious institutions, Furtado appears no more sympathetic to the cultural and moral atmosphere of the Jewish communities. Although persecution may revive religious sentiments, he admitted, more often it leads to fanaticism, in the same way that continual and daily contempt leads to superstition. Na-

102. Furtado, "Letter to the Imperial Commissioners," January 21, 1807, Thémanlys, Jerusalem.

103. Ibid. Not even purely theological issues were to be discussed. The Sanhedrin was to delegate to the central consistory the task of revising the daily prayers of the Italians, Portuguese and Germans, which Furtado described as being neither uniform nor in perfect harmony with the doctrinal decisions.

104. Because of the lack of discussion in the Sanhedrin, we have no way to determine what, if any, changes were made as a result of the deputies' written remarks.

poleon, in finally freeing the Jews from persecution and contempt, had made possible the emergence of productive and respected citizens. The Sanhedrin, by its sanction of the doctrinal decisions, would confirm that Judaism, rather than impeding this emergence, demanded it.[105]

In his second report of February 12, which introduced the fourth doctrinal point (fraternity), Furtado made specific what he had only implied in the previous session. When the people of Israel formed a nation, he recalled, there was a religious obligation to follow all the laws (whether political and civil or religious) of the "divine legislator." Israel ceased to be a nation, however, and from that moment on the Jews were obliged "by necessity" to follow the political and civil laws of the states in which they lived. They were to retain "in all their vigor" only those laws which pertained to their religious society.

When this distinction is understood, Furtado continued, and when it is equally understood that there is perfect conformity between our religious laws and the civil code, then we can no longer be accused of living differently from those around us. The Sanhedrin, by adopting these first four decisions, will be declaring publicly and unequivocally that the Jews, in fulfilling their duties as citizens and in expressing their sentiments of fraternity towards their fellow countrymen, are simultaneously fulfilling their duties as Jews.[106]

The Sanhedrin adopted the first decision on February 16, the second and third on February 19 and the fourth on February 23, all of them unanimously.[107]

Furtado addressed the deputies again on February 23 when he introduced the eighth and ninth decisions (usury). Two advantages, he explained, will result from an exposition of the true doctrine of Moses; the first will show that this doctrine accords with the most severe principles of justice; the second will establish that the habit of lending on interest, a reproach directed at the Israelites of some parts of France and unhappily with too much reason, is not at all the effect of their religious dogmas but rather an abuse resulting from their civil and political situation.[108] Furtado concluded with an admonition to the rabbis. Do not confuse appearance with reality, he warned them, or false zeal with true piety; know that all too often the man who wishes to appear the most religious is not always the most honest.

With these words as well as with his previous descriptions of the degenerative expressions of religion, Furtado revealed his deep criticism of and estrangement from traditional Jewish life. His unveiled disdain, however, did

105. *Procès-Verbal.*
106. Ibid.
107. Ibid.
108. Ibid.

not prevent the Sanhedrin from adopting unanimously the fifth, sixth, and seventh decisions (morality, civil and political relations, and useful professions).[109]

The deputies, well on their way to completing the adoption of the assembly's decisions, were finally informed of their tasks in a letter written by Napoleon sometime in January and received by the impatient Champagny around February 16.[110] In order to proceed in an orderly fashion, Napoleon wrote, "it is necessary to begin by declaring that there are in the laws of Moses both religious and political dispositions."[111] While the former are immutable, the latter are susceptible to modification, and it is only the Sanhedrin which can establish this distinction. Once this principle is declared, the Sanhedrin must apply it to prohibiting polygamy in the West, extending fraternity to all men without exception (providing the Jews enjoy the same rights as they), defending the country, requiring mixed marriages, and finally, obeying the laws pertaining to lending on interest. In addition, the Sanhedrin must proclaim that divorce and marriage be subject to the observance of the formalities prescribed by the civil code.[112]

On February 25, the imperial commissioners informed Champagny that the decisions of the Sanhedrin would receive the modifications contained in the last instructions, after which its mission would be terminated.[113] Either Furtado had already anticipated these instructions in his speech of February 12, or he revised the speech before publishing it. In either event, except for the obligation of mixed marriages, he assured their inclusion in the preamble and doctrinal decisions.

On March 2, the Sanhedrin completed its task by adopting the eighth and ninth decisions as well as a preamble to all the preceding decisions. The imperial commissioners had not been mistaken when they promised Champagny compliance with Napoleon's instructions. The preamble, which was probably written by Furtado, was virtually a repetition of Napoleon's distinction between religious and political dispositions.

The deputies were not to be left with any doubts concerning the conformity of the decisions and preamble to Jewish law. "Doctors and Notables," Rabbi David Sintzheim proclaimed, "your religious, civil, and political

---

109. These decisions were adopted on February 26.

110. Historians had always believed that these instructions were attached to Napoleon's letter dated November 29, 1806. Anchel has been able to prove on the basis of Champagny's reports, Napoleon's whereabouts and archival sources, that the instructions only arrived on February 16 or at most a few days earlier. Robert Anchel, *Napoléon*, p. 210.

111. Archives Nationales, F[19] 11005.

112. Ibid.

113. Ibid.

principles are known to me; I am pleased to find that they conform to the spirit of the law and I thank God."[114] Furtado also assured the deputies of the wisdom of their decisions. He was less concerned, however, with theological justifications. On the contrary, his satisfaction was derived primarily from the Sanhedrin's acceptance of a universal basis for the union of mankind and a secular standard for the evaluation of contemporary Jewish practices.[115]

On March 9, Rabbi Sintzheim delivered the final address to the Sanhedrin. He reminded the deputies of the distinctions they had made between civil and religious acts and their condemnation of antisocial opinions. On behalf of all Jews, he then addressed a prayer to the God of Jacob. We shall no longer offer you sacrifices, nor sanctify you with imposing ceremonies, he declared, but at least our hearts will be free from fear and our voices will be raised to proclaim the glory of your name.[116] With the conclusion of this apologetic prayer and the recognition of gratitude to emperor and "chef," the Sanhedrin was terminated.

The responses which the Sanhedrin had sanctioned differed from those provided by the Assembly of Notables both in their form and emphasis. While the assembly had answered specific questions, the Sanhedrin provided what were to be considered definitive statements on all issues which concerned Jew and non-Jew. These statements, moreover, were not at all explanatory, as were those of the assembly, but rather declared, often very concisely, the official Jewish position. Despite its more emphatic and conciliatory resolutions, however, the Sanhedrin did not comply with Napoleon's views on intermarriage. The Grand Sanhedrin declares, Article III stated, "that marriage between Israelites and Christians, contracted in conformity with the laws of the civil code, are binding and civilly valid, and although not to be invested with religious forms, will entail no anathemas."[117]

The Sanhedrin did declare, nevertheless, that all Jews called to military service were freed during the duration of their service from any observances which conflicted with military life. Every Jew, moreover, born and raised in France and Italy, was religiously obligated to view that country as his own, to serve and defend it, obey all laws, and conform in every transaction to the dispositions of the civil code.[118] In essence, as the preamble had stated, the Jews were to cease to regulate their civil and political lives in accordance with Jewish law or tradition.

114. *Procès-Verbal.*
115. Furtado's speech, quoted in full in the minutes, was also published separately. *Discours prononcé par M. Furtado à la séance du Grand Sanhédrin du 2 Mars, 1807,* Thémanlys, Jerusalem.
116. *Procès-Verbal.*
117. Ibid.
118. Ibid.

There is no doubt that Napoleon's instructions provided the stimulus for this clean-cut distinction between purely religious obligations and social and political duties. Nevertheless, this did not represent a significant departure either from principles debated by the revolutionaries or those acknowledged by the Sephardim and their leading spokesman, Furtado. In setting forth the separation of belief and ritual from daily life, the dissolution of nationhood and the reinterpretation of the messianic dream, however, the doctrinal decisions provided a definitive formula and an enduring rationale for a profound break with Jewish tradition. Herein lies both the real significance of the Sanhedrin and the influence exerted by Furtado.

In addition to his notes on the Sanhedrin, Napoleon had included in his February instructions the tasks remaining to be accomplished by the Assembly of Notables and sanctioned by the Council of State. Among these tasks was the establishment of an organization to supervise and represent French Jewry.

In fact, the Assembly of Notables, amidst anger and despair on the part of the deputies and pressure on the part of Furtado, had already passed on December 9 a consistorial plan for the organization of the synagogues and rabbis of France. In essence the plan established the consistories of France and outlined the functions of the departmental consistories, the central consistory, and the rabbis. A synagogue and consistory were to be established in every department which contained two-thousand individuals professing the religion of Moses. Under no circumstances, however, was there to be more than one consistory for each department. The consistorial synagogue, moreover, had to sanction any additional synagogues established in the department. For each consistory, 25 notables would be selected by a competent authority and these notables, all of whom were to be men of means, would in turn choose the grand rabbi and the three other "Israelites" who would head the consistorial organization.

The functions of the consistories were four-fold: to oversee that the rabbis acted in accordance with the decisions of the assembly and the Sanhedrin, to maintain order within the synagogues, to encourage Jews to engage in useful occupations and to report those without any means of existence, and to inform the authorities of the number of Jewish conscripts each year. The central consistory of Paris was to correspond with the local consistories, oversee compliance with consistorial regulations, denounce any infractions of those regulations to the competent authority, and finally to confirm the nomination of rabbis and propose, when necessary, the removal of any member of the consistory. The rabbis were to teach religion, inculcate the doctrines contained in the decisions of the Sanhedrin, preach obedience to the laws and especially those relating to the defense of the country, and to celebrate marriages and pronounce divorces, after their sanction by the civil authority. The consistories were to be responsible for paying, with sums levied on each district, the expenses of the rabbis as well as other expenses of worship.[119]

Although the minutes of the assembly only allude to the atmosphere in which the consistorial plan was adopted, Furtado's personal reflections reveal the extent of disagreement among the deputies and mounting frustration on the part of their president.

> But what is at the height of imprudence and dishonesty is that after nine meetings of the full committee, where everything had been examined, discussed, and reconciled, where everything had been settled ahead of time to adopt the project, four or five disturbers come and repeat all that had been said and refuted and make a truly revolting public scandal. . . . Finally four individuals, with no knowledge whatsoever dare to want to preach the law to the assembly, questioning what had already been decided, and the assembly had the inconceivable feebleness to tolerate this outrage and to condescend to decide a second time what had been decided a first time. An excess of outrage from one side, of unqualified apathy and cowardice on the other. This is what the assembly of the Jews at Paris is like. . . .[120]

On March 17, 1808, Napoleon approved a series of three decrees. Imposing the duties and responsibilities of Frenchmen on all Jews, these decrees simultaneously legitimized an inequality characteristic of the *ancien régime*. The first two, concerned with the organization of the Jewish communities, merely confirmed the consistorial plan adopted by the Assembly of Notables in December 1807 and clarified certain of its articles. The third decree, against which the Jews of France and Furtado in particular had battled since the passage of the infamous moratorium on Jewish debts in 1806, successfully annulled or reduced all past loans made by the Jews and established new and repressive restrictions on commercial transactions, conscription, and residence.[121] Significantly, the Jews of Bordeaux and those of the depart-

---

119. Ibid.
120. Manuscript, two pages, December 11, 1806, Thémanlys, Jerusalem.
121. Archives Nationales, AF[IV] p1 2151, n° 136. Although the moratorium was now officially terminated, all loans made by Jews to minors, women, unauthorized military, husbands or military and naval officers, were annulled. In addition the decree permitted a reduction of those credits whose capital exceeded 5 percent by the accumulation of interests and annulled those debts whose capital exceeded 10 percent. Finally, the courts could decide upon a delay for all legitimate and nonusurious credits.
No less restrictive were those measures which regulated future commercial transactions. After

ments of the Gironde and Landes, having given no cause for complaint, were exempted from all the provisions of the third decree.

Furtado had written to his friend Pery during the fall of 1806 that the work of the assembly might seem great from afar, but from a close perspective it was little. This might equally well be said of all the accomplishments of both the assembly and Sanhedrin. For what became most obvious immediately following the convocation of these bodies was that the majority of the Jews of France had been reduced to second class citizens, emasculated economically and discriminated against socially and politically.

Furtado failed to secure for the Jews of France the just and equal treatment he demanded for them. He had convinced them (and not without some bitter struggle) to place their faith in Napoleon and to declare their willingness to fulfill all the obligations of French citizens. As with the terrorist events during the Revolution, Furtado was both angered and disillusioned by what he quickly understood to be the government's deception. The Israelites of France were to be treated as Jews. Not only did Furtado undertake almost single-handedly the struggle to prevent the enactment of any discriminatory legislation,[122] but also he publicly refused the position of deputy major offered to him by the "victorious" Napoleon upon his return from Elba.[123]

July 1, every Jew wishing to engage in any form of commerce was required to obtain a special license issued annually and revocable when warranted. The prefect was to issue the licenses after he had received the necessary information provided by the municipal council and the consistory. Thus the special licenses, reserved by Champagny and the commissioners for certain restricted categories, had been made mandatory for all Jews engaged in commerce, without distinction or exception.

The articles concerning residence and conscription were equally rigorous. No Jew could henceforth establish residence in the departments of the Haut- and Bas-Rhin, and no Jew would be allowed to reside in the other departments unless he acquired a rural property and devoted himself to agriculture. Lastly, no Jew could supply replacements for military duty; every Jewish conscript was to be subject to personal service.

Only in the last two articles was there an attempt to soften these measures. The decree was to last for ten years with the hope that at its expiration there would be no difference between the Jews and the other citizens of France. If, however, this was not the case, the decree would then be extended.

122. In addition to three letters written to Napoleon, one of which was a *reclamation* by the Portuguese, Spanish, and Avignonese Jews, Furtado's activities included a journey with Maurice Lévy (from Nancy) to Prussia and possibly also to Poland to see Napoleon in person and the publication of a detailed mémoire in which he passionately rejected any legislation which threatened to treat the Jews differently from other French citizens. Cf. "Letter to Napoleon," Thémanlys; "Letter to Napoleon," ADG, Série I; "Reclamation des Juifs Portugais, Espagnols, et Avignonais de Paris, de Bordeaux, de Bayonne et du Midi de la France," Archives Nationales, F[19] 1108; *Mémoire sur les projets de décrets présentés au Conseil d'État concernant les Israélites*, Bibliothèque Nationale, Ld[184]82.

123. "Les feuilles publiques annoncèrent son refus, et il vécut retiré à la campagne pendant la durée de l'interegne." Michel Berr, *Éloge de M. Abraham Furtado*, Bibliothèque Nationale, Ln[27] 8099A.

The revolutionary who had accused the Musée of aristocratic leanings now accepted the Legion of Honor of Royalty from the duc d'Angoulème, nephew of Louis XVIII.[124]

Furtado did not fail, however, to lay the blueprint for the assimilation of the French Jews. His solution no longer lay in the utopian panacea of revolution; instead he supported the institutionalization of a Jewish community whose primary dedication was to France and whose members were committed as French citizens to the regulation of their civil and political lives in accordance with French law. His solution was predicated on an axiomatic relationship between the Jews' perfectibility (defined in accordance with enlightened standards) and Europe's lack of prejudice.[125]

On January 29, 1817, at the age of sixty-one, Abraham Furtado died. The central consistory declared on February 9, 1817:

> The entire life of Abraham Furtado is one of the most convincing proofs that one can acquire profound knowledge in literature, administration and politics, fill important functions, undertake delicate missions, enjoy the esteem of both government and one's fellow citizens, and yet die in the religion in which one is born as the honorable coreligionist whose death we mourn was born and died in the religion of Israel.[126]

Furtado was one of the first Jews to confront the demands of a modern nation-state. He was typical neither of the Jews of France—the process leading to his acceptability was unique to the privileged Sephardic community—nor was he representative of other European Jews—his citizenship in a titularly secular state entailed no spiritual or intellectual crisis. Thus in his political and intellectual struggles, Furtado resembles less his contemporaries of Western Europe than their children whose discomfort lay not with their breach with tradition but rather with their retention of any religious particularity.

If Furtado himself, however, is in many respects atypical, the position he

124. "Son Altesse Royale Monseigneur le Duc d'Angoulème par decision du 12 Juillet 1814 autorise M. Furtado, membre du Conseil Municipal de la Ville de Bordeaux à porter la décoration du Lis." This citation is in the possession of Pascal Thémanlys.

125. In answer to a letter from Jacques Neumann, in which this Viennese Jew described his attempt to awaken his fellow Jews to a consciousness of their dignified origin, Furtado wrote the following: "Ce n'est qu'à force de vertu que nous forçerons les nations à renoncer à leurs préjugés à notre égard, et à nous rendre justice; ... l'Europe, dans quelques années décidera cette question mais c'est notre conduite qui dictera son jugement." Both Neumann's letter written on February 27, 1807, and Furtado's answer of April 12, 1807, are in the private possession of Pascal Thémanlys.

126. "Minutes of the February 9, 1817, meeting of the central consistory," Jewish Theological Seminary, New York.

achieved, articulated, and defended bears striking similarities to that advocated by Western Jewry and later by the Jews of America. Partly as a result of his own position within the bourgeois Bordelais community (for which he provides an excellent barometer), and partly as a result of his political education during the tumultuous years of the Revolution, Furtado came to understand the nature and character of modern statehood. Both the Judaism he encouraged—denationalized, shorn of its ethnic, legal, and cultural particularity—and the Jews he envisioned—bourgeois gentlemen of the Mosaic persuasion—form a pervasive theme in modern Jewish history.

Ethnicity and Jewish Solidarity in Nineteenth-Century France

Phyllis Cohen Albert

I

Although nineteenth-century French Jews were under pressure to preserve the gains of the Emancipation through integration into French social, cultural, political, and economic life, they displayed a remarkable sense of ethnic identification and Jewish solidarity. Yet this aspect of their social life has been neglected and often denied as a result of the common argument that gives undue weight to their assimilatory tendencies.

It is a well-known fact that in 1791 France became the first modern nation to grant full civil and political emancipation to its Jewish population, and thereby to raise the Jews to full and equal citizenship. The story of the Napoleonic "Sanhedrin" has often been told: the government's carefully chosen representatives of the Jews made the historic declaration that French Jews are, first and foremost, citizens of France who recognize France as their *patrie* and Frenchmen as their brothers. There were to be no religious obstacles to their full identification with, and integration into the French community; even intermarriage was possible, although it was not blessed by the rabbinate.[1]

The Emancipation spurred the political, social, cultural, and economic advancement of the Jewish population at a rate that had been impossible previously, and that would be achieved by European Jews outside of France only at a later date. Because the Emancipation was ultimately responsible for geographic and demographic changes in the Jewish population, and because it brought about a significant slackening in religious observance, scholars have claimed that the French Jews of the post-Revolutionary period were assimilationists, displaying optimism and confidence in France, and identifying more with France and Frenchmen than with Judaism and Jews. Such

1. The Sanhedrin has been discussed in detail by Robert Anchel in his *Napoléon et les Juifs* (Paris, 1928). Several editions of the minutes exist. For a list of them, see Zosa Szajkowski, "Judaica Napoleonica: A Bibliography of Books, Pamphlets and Printed Documents, 1801–1815," *Studies in Bibliography and Booklore*, II (1956), 107–52; reprinted in his *Jews and the French Revolutions of 1789, 1830, and 1848* (New York, 1970).

theorists claim that French Jews eschewed all notions of transnational Jewish solidarity and identity.[2]

The reality, however, was otherwise. Jews, in fact, *failed* to merge with the French population at any time in the history of French Jewry, until and including the present time. This reality became obvious to everyone only during and after the Second World War and the Six Day War, but it was equally true during times when it was not so brutally brought to the attention of the public.[3] Jews failed to merge politically, geographically, occupationally, ethnically, with the French population.[4] Antisemitism, although not in its most virulent or political form until the end of the century, was a constant factor that maintained the Jews' sense of insecurity and their fear that the gains of the Emancipation could easily, and almost without warning, be revoked. Each change of regime during the politically unstable century, brought the question: "What will this mean to the Jews?" Deputations were sent offering felicitations to the new government, and not incidentally, to receive reassurances that the Emancipation would not be abrogated. This need for reassurance was not the result of Jewish paranoia. Rather, it was a realistic appraisal of the political situation. After all, the Emancipation had been granted, not because of French philo-Semitism, but because of logical imperatives implicit in the political meaning of the Revolution.[5] Anti-Jewish sentiment had been maintained institutionally in the post-Revolutionary

2. This is the case, most notably, in Michael Marrus, *The Politics of Assimilation: A Study of the French Jewish Community at the Time of the Dreyfus Affair* (Oxford, 1971).

3. Although Zionism was late in implanting itself in France, it became obvious in the wake of the Six Day War that it had succeeded in commanding the loyalty of most French Jews. Since then, French Jewish students have been particularly active in the combatting of anti-Zionist campus activity. The once very inward-looking *consistoire* now devotes considerable space to the news from Israel in its community journal.

4. In my book, *The Modernization of French Jewry: Consistory and Community in the Nineteenth Century* (Hanover, N.H., 1977), these points are developed individually. For example, the geographic spread of the Jewish population, long anticipated as a beneficial result of the Emancipation, was of very minor significance. The 38 departments of France which held no Jews in 1808 had a total Jewish population of only 1034 (or 1.08 percent of the total French Jewish population) in 1861. Of this small number, most were further concentrated in only 15 of the departments. Urbanization of the French Jewish population occurred at a rate far higher than that of the general population. Although there was an increasing diversification of Jewish occupations, throughout the nineteenth century, trade remained the dominant Jewish occupation, while some careers such as agricultural and military ones were chosen by Jews much less frequently than by the general population.

5. On September 27, 1791, Duport, deputy of Paris, observed that the constitution which had just been adopted guaranteed equality of rights for all, and that therefore all discrimination had to be abolished. Consequently the assembly revoked all exceptional provisions referring to the Jews; see François Delpech, "La Révolution et l'Empire," in Bernhard Blumenkranz, ed., *Histoire des Juifs en France* (Toulouse, 1972), p. 281.

period during the three generations following the Emancipation.[6] Social prejudices remained strong, and translated themselves into economic and occupational inequalities.

Insecurity and fear, then, rather than optimism and confidence in the France of 1789, determined the mood of nineteenth-century French Jewry. This insecurity, combined with past habits and associations, family ties and the religious needs of the always significant number of traditionally obser-vant Jews, was responsible for the retention of ethnic institutions and ties (even "ethnic politics") and Jewish solidarity. This is not to deny the accul-turation of Jews that took place in France, but to deny the supposed equation between acculturation and all forms of assimilation.

The difference between the concepts of acculturation and assimilation has been stated by modern sociologists in varying ways.[7] For our purposes we use Milton Gordon's distinction between two kinds of assimilation: behav-ioral assimilation and structural assimilation. Acculturation is interchange-able with Gordon's behavioral assimilation—that state in which the ethnic group has acquired the language, social ritual, and cultural pattern of the host community. It takes place at the level of secondary group associations.[8] This definition of assimilation is not incompatible with Jewish nationalism, cul-tural pluralism, ethnicity, or solidarity. According to it, Herzl, Weizmann, and every Zionist leader and member was assimilated, because it implies only the taking on of the language and values, and identifying with the history of the host country, without the loss of separate identity.[9] The second

6. Government funding of the Christian churches was instituted by Napoleon, but Judaism was not a beneficiary of such funding until after the July Revolution and the institution of the Orleanist monarchy in 1830. The discriminatory special Jewish oath was abolished by the courts only in 1846, and after that year there were some provincial courts which sought to reinstitute it. The Jews were obligated to pay off their pre-Revolutionary communal debts, which unlike those of other religious communities had not been nationalized by the Revolution. This state contin-ued in Alsace until the loss of that region in 1871 as a consequence of the Franco-Prussian War.

7. Arnold Rose, in his *Sociology: The Study of Human Relations* (New York, 1956), pp. 557–58, defines them this way. Acculturation is "the adoption by a person or group of the culture of another social group. Or, the process leading to this adoption." Assimilation is "the adoption by a person or group of the culture of another social group to such a complete extent that the person or group no longer has any particular loyalties to his former culture. Or, the process leading to this adoption."

8. Milton Gordon, *Assimilation in American Life: The Role of Race, Religion, and National Origins* (New York, 1964), pp. 65–71.

9. Marcus Hansen has spoken of the third generation effect: that the third generation wants to remember what the second generation wanted to forget; see his *The Problem of the Third Generation Immigrant* (Rock Island, Ill., 1938), pp. 9–10. Gordon elaborates the example of this which has taken place in America: "My point is not that Negroes, Jews, and Catholics in the United States do not think of themselves as Americans. They do. It is that they also have an 'inner layer' sense of peoplehood which is Negro, Jewish, or Catholic . . ." (Gordon, *Assimilation*, p. 77 n. 27).

kind of assimilation, structural assimilation, takes place at the primary group level, and involves large-scale entry into cliques, clubs, and other institutions of the host society. It implies the ultimate disappearance of all particularism.[10]

Integration is a corollary of acculturation. With the taking on of the values and culture of the dominant society, the ethnic group finds a place for itself in the structure of the society. Such acculturated individuals are, however, still closely associated with the subgroup culture.

Prior to Gordon's distinction between behavioral and structural assimilation, sociologists wavered between the two meanings of assimilation,[11] and it is no surprise, then, that when historians speak of assimilation in regard to the Jews they do not always take the trouble to define the kind of assimilation they mean. At its most extreme, assimilation would mean the complete disappearance of the Jews, or the process leading toward that state. It could, however, also mean simple acculturation and integration. Although the term does not consistently imply a single attitude toward group survival and ethnic identity, it is generally used to indicate a state which is indifferent, or even antagonistic, to ethnicity and solidarity. When the French Jews are labeled "assimilationist," it is usually with such connotations that the term is used.[12]

Yet indications of ethnicity and examples of solidarity can be clearly enumerated for the entire period of the nineteenth century. There are three kinds of solidarity: local, national, and international. Local solidarity is evidenced by Jews' readiness to help other Jews and to act in concert with them at the local community level. National solidarity is demonstrated by the nationwide institutional and political ties within French Jewry. Finally, we can point to international connections and a sense of mutual responsibility

10. Ibid., pp. 62–67 passim.

11. Park and Burgess, in 1921, defined assimilation in a way that corresponds to Gordon's structural assimilation, while a few years later, in 1930, Park's definition of assimilation was modified by a behavioral perspective to read more like Gordon's definition of behavioral assimilation. For him an immigrant to America is "considered assimilated as soon as he has acquired the language and the social ritual of the native community and can participate, without encountering prejudice, in the common life, economic and political" (ibid., pp. 62–64).

12. Thus Marrus says that the Emancipation, in conferring citizenship, demanded assimilation. "Jewishness might be preserved, but only in a sphere which did not affect the Jew's relationship with the nation" (Marrus, *Politics*, p. 87). But Marrus does not analyze fully the type of assimilation that would be required to fulfill this demand. Clearly, structural assimilation would fulfill it, and, indeed, many Frenchmen, in the words of one contemporary, "confuse[d] assimilation and uniformity" (Yves Guyot, quoted by Marrus, *Politics*, p. 86). But would behavioral assimilation (acculturation) also fulfill the requirement that the retention of Jewishness not affect the Jew's relationship with the nation? In fact, within the French Jewish community, as within France in general, there was a range of opinion as to what constituted a threat to the Jew's relationship with the nation, and therefore there existed a range of opinion as to what kind of assimilation was sought.

that transcends national limits. At the end of the century the French Jewish historian Theodore Reinach felt constrained to explain the obvious solidarity of the Jews as legitimate and even morally necessary. Members of all religious groups, he argued, feel a special kinship for their coreligionists. But in the case of the Jews there is not only identity of belief; there are also common origins and historical experiences ("le souvenir de maux glorieusement souffert en commun"). These factors reinforce fraternal sentiments and impose even greater mutual obligations than are felt by members of other religious groupings. Admitting that Israel constitutes a family, Reinach predicted that it will cease to be one only when all of humanity becomes one large family.[13] He was, in short, hinting at the concept of ethnicity.

Like assimilation, the term ethnicity has been used in various ways. In order to define it, Gordon reminds us that the Greek word "ethnos" means "people" or "nation." The modern concept of an ethnic group is, therefore, a "group with a shared feeling of peoplehood," and this sense of peoplehood is called "ethnicity." The elements in such peoplehood are racial, historical, territorial, religious, and cultural, or any combination of these categories.[14] Clearly the ethnicity of the nineteenth-century French Jews drew on such elements. Jews were those whose ancestors had not been considered French, but Jewish. They had enjoyed a well-developed life in France throughout the Middle Ages, and were distinguished by civil, political, social, and religious factors. After their partial expulsions, enacted between the end of the fourteenth century and the beginning of the sixteenth century, two very different groups began arriving in France. During the sixteenth century, Marranos, or New Christians, arrived in the south, and Jews appeared in the east as a consequence of the annexation of Germanic lands. Until the Revolution this Jewry in Alsace-Lorraine and southwest France (and some made its way to Paris) had a clearly defined separate national existence. Even after the Emancipation and throughout the nineteenth century, French Jews frequently used the term "race" in regard to their own common origins and continued sense of kinship.[15]

A good indication of ethnicity is resistance to intermarriage. When Napoleon sought to effect structural assimilation through the requirement that a

13. Theodore Reinach, *Histoire des israélites depuis l'époque de leur dispersion jusqu'à nos jours* (Paris, 1884), pp. 388–90.

14. Milton Gordon (basing himself on Robert Redfield and E. K. Francis) *Assimilation*, pp. 23–27. Cf. Nathan Glazer's definition of an ethnic group: "A social group which consciously shares some aspects of a common culture and is defined primarily by descent" ("The Universality of Ethnicity," *Encounter*, XLIV, no. 2 [February 1975], p. 8).

15. Marrus, *Politics*, pp. 10–27. For the earlier part of the century, I observed both this usage and the use of the word *nation* consistently in the Jewish periodical press and in the books of the period.

certain percentage of Jewish marriages be intermarriages, the Jews, although fearful for the security of the Emancipation, rejected the suggestion. Subsequently, when Napoleon requested that the Sanhedrin at least proclaim the religious legitimacy of intermarriages, that generally docile and acquiescent body adamantly refused. Throughout the nineteenth century, French Jews displayed a very low incidence of intermarriage.[16]

The vast majority of the Jews retained their own primary group associations. Persistence of ethnicity was not caused by discrimination alone, but was due to the preferences of the members of the groups for such ethnic ties as special schools, charitable institutions, and neighborhoods which served their special needs.

Recently scholars have been revising the earlier notion that there was a tendency within multinational states for the disappearance of ethnic identity. This is now considered *not* to be the case in diverse instances, both in repressive and in democratic regimes, such as Russia, France, and America.[17] Writing about America, Gordon says:

> My essential thesis here is that the sense of ethnicity has proved to be hardy. As though with a wily cunning of its own, as though there were some essential element in man's nature that demanded it—something that compelled him to merge his lonely individual identity in some ancestral troup of fellows smaller by far than the whole human race, smaller often than the nation—the sense of ethnic belonging has survived. It has survived in various forms and with various names, but it has not perished, and twentieth-century urban man is closer to his stone-age ancestors than he knows."[18]

16. Ibid., p. 63.

17. The literature on this topic is abundant and growing. Some trace the beginning of the awareness to the second edition of Nathan Glazer and Daniel P. Moynihan, *Beyond the Melting Pot: The Negroes, Puerto Ricans, Jews, Italians, and Irish of New York City* (Cambridge, Mass., 1970). Although the first edition of 1963 had already pointed out the importance of ethnicity, it had also ascribed great weight to the religious factor. By 1970 the authors decided that religion was not as significant, and ethnicity was more significant than they had previously suspected; see the introduction to the second edition. In 1963, Milton Gordon had already written that "ethnicity has proved to be hardy" (*Assimilation*, pp. 24-25). In 1967, Michael Parenti showed that the extent of ethnic assimilation in the United States had been exaggerated ("Ethnic Politics and the Persistence of Ethnic Identification," *American Political Science Review*, LXI, no. 3 [September 1967]). In the same year Walker Connor argued that the problem of ethnic consciousness and aspirations in authoritarian states "must . . . be considered still another testament to the increasing power of ethnic aspirations, for it indicates that the immunity believed to be enjoyed by authoritarian governments four decades ago is no longer effective" ("Self-Determination: The New Phase," *World Politics*, XX, no. 1 [October 1967], quoted in Zvi Y. Gitelman, *Jewish Nationality and Soviet Politics: The Jewish Sections of the CPSU, 1917-1930* [Princeton, 1972], p. 506). Zvi Gitelman, in 1972, pointed out that "in the Communist states, growing ethnic consciousness often implies heightened ethnic dissatisfaction, though it is difficult to determine which is cause and which is effect" (ibid.). The literature on this topic continues to grow. Most recently Nathan Glazer has developed the theme of "The Universality of Ethnicity."

18. Gordon, *Assimilation*, pp. 24-25.

A reappraisal of Jewish ethnic identification during the nineteenth century is called for in light of current perceptions of the ethnic reality of the twentieth. My hypothesis is that previous generations either failed to perceive ethnicity or consciously denied it for political purposes.

II

The social and institutional history of nineteenth-century French Jewry demonstrates a sense of ethnicity and solidarity. Jewish geographical distribution was not the same as that of the general French population, and Jews tended to live in areas of Jewish density many times greater than the 0.26 percent that the Jews comprised in the 1861 general French population. In Toul (Meurthe), for example, 8 percent of the 1861 population were Jews. In three other cities in the east they comprised more than 5 percent of the population. In another three cities they comprised close to, or more than, 3 percent.[19] Thus, they were numerous enough to maintain their own communities and neighborhoods. A historian of the Dreyfus period who believes that the Jewish community was in a state of dissolution at the end of the nineteenth century admits, nonetheless, that there existed a sense of community.[20]

The 1860 *Manifesto* of the Alliance Israélite Universelle seems to address itself to a class of Jews who were neither religious nor completely assimilated. Today we would say that they exhibited feelings of ethnicity, but the word did not exist at the time and the concept was described with some difficulty. Thus, the document appeals to the Jews who "remain attached to the ancient religion of their ancestors, regardless of how weak is this attachment."[21] This wording suggests the existence of Jews who found expression for their sense of peoplehood, for their attachment to the Jewish community, in the only terms that were available, those of religion.

There is a curious parallel between our findings in this regard and those of Will Herberg, who studied the growth spurt of religious institutions in post-World War II America. Although Americans were becoming increasingly secular in outlook, the only forms available for expressing group identity and a feeling of belonging were religious institutions. But the cate-

19. Albert, *Modernization*, p. 25.

20. Marrus, *Politics*, p. 83: ". . . it is apparent that at the end of the nineteenth century Jews in France were not so closely identified with French society that they had broken entirely with an older pattern of identification. This pattern persisted, though in a weakened form; it was a reality. . . ." Cf. ibid., p. 3.

21. *Manifeste de juillet 1860*, reprinted in Andre Chouraqui, *L'Alliance Israélite Universelle et la renaissance juive contemporaine* (Paris, 1965), pp. 407–12.

gories into which men were classified were "based less on theological than on social distinctions." This was accentuated in the case of the Jews by the overlapping of religion and ethnicity for that group.[22]

The analogous phenomenon in nineteenth-century French Jewry is manifested by the advocates of Reform. Extreme reformers, such as Olry Terquem, proposed ritual changes of a far-reaching nature, including the transfer of the Sabbath to Sunday in order to bring Jewish behavior into line with general French behavior. His underlying religious assumptions were deistic, and designed to be identical with enlightened Christianity. When Terquem talks, therefore, of the need to reform Judaism in order to retain the Jewish elite and to bring it back to a Jewish existence, we may legitimately ask what is Jewish about the existence he envisages? Certainly not the religion; it would seem that Terquem's religious language hides an ethnic reality.[23]

Additional aspects of the religious behavior of French Jews indicate communal cohesion. We know that there were individuals whose attachment to their Jewish historical origins found expression only through the traditional ritual observance in which they no longer believed.[24] The notably low rates of conversion and intermarriage in nineteenth-century France are further testimony to the sense of peoplehood.[25]

The use of religious terminology and religious institutional expression delayed awareness of the ethnic reality that underlay these phenomena. But the use of the concept of religious union and of assisting one's coreligionists was, of course, useful in a nineteenth-century France that was actively claiming the right to protect Catholics and Christian holy places in the East. The same year that the Alliance Israélite Universelle announced its organization and aims, France landed an expeditionary force in Syria to protect the Christian population.

Jewish historians of the period evince a pride in what is clearly for them a national-religious heritage. L. M. Lambert, in his 1840 publication, *Précis de l'histoire des Hébreux, depuis le Patriarche Abraham, jusqu'en 1840*, wrote that Jewish history is not like ordinary history, because it teaches peace and virtue. In it we can point to great heroes, "noble and sublime characters," such as Judah Maccabee, who fought "for religion and the fatherland." In

22. Hansen, *Third Generation Immigrant*; and Will Herberg, *Protestant-Catholic-Jew: An Essay in American Religious Sociology*, rev. ed. (New York, 1960), pp. 31, 257.

23. Writing under the penname Tsarphati ("a Frenchman"), Olry Terquem published nine numbered "Letter[s] from a French Israelite to his Coreligionists" between 1821 and 1837. He also wrote articles in the Jewish press, and after the deathbed conversion of his brother by the Jewish convert, Ratisbonne, in 1845 Terquem published a pamphlet protesting missionary activity.

24. Marrus, *Politics*, pp. 62–63.

25. Ibid., pp. 60–64.

both Lambert's work and in *Histoire des Israélites depuis l'époque de leur dispersion jusqu'à nos jours* by Theodore Reinach (published in 1884), there is concern about Jewish status abroad and the battle for emancipation. Lambert writes of the ongoing struggle and reports the successes country by country. Reinach writes all of his modern Jewish history as a history of the Emancipation. The Jewish periodical press, which developed after 1840, was always full of news about Jewish status elsewhere and the struggles, successes, and difficulties of the Jews abroad.

III

The impression that Jews felt a sense of ethnicity is further supported by a linguistic analysis of contemporary documents. For example, in 1858 the Strasbourg consistory sent a letter of thanks to Lionel de Rothschild of England for his efforts to have Jews admitted into the Chamber of Deputies. That they chose to *thank* him, rather than to congratulate him, reveals their ethnic identification. Similarly, the wording of the 1860 *Manifesto* of the fledgling Alliance Israélite Universelle also shows that the writers identified with suffering Jews abroad. In proposing a program of aid and assistance, it speaks of the "prejudice which *we* still suffer" (emphasis mine). The *Manifesto* refers to the long-felt need for creating an organization of "union."[26] In fact, many voices had been raised during the previous fifteen years, calling for an organization to give expression to existent Jewish solidarity.[27]

Ethnic identity is expressed by nineteenth-century French Jews in the repeated use of certain words and expressions. For example, the Jews often used the word "race" to describe their sense of peoplehood. "Only the biological terminology of race provided a semantic framework within which all Jews could express their feelings of Jewish identity," says one recent student of French Jewry.[28] However, there were in fact additional terms which served the same function. Thus we repeatedly encounter *nation, people, our brothers, family, Israel,* and even *solidarity.*

Throughout the nineteenth century the French Jews continued to use the pre-Revolutionary concept *nation* in referring to themselves. Often the term is

26. *Manifeste*, pp. 407–12.
27. For example, Simon Bloch, editor of the *Univers Israélite*, had written: "Tous les esprits sérieux dans le judaïsme, tous les vrais et sincères israélites, ont depuis longtemps reconnu la nécessité d'un rapprochement, d'une union plus étroite entre nos coreligionnaires habitant les diverses contrées de la terre" (*Univers Israélite*, February 1860; reprinted in Chouraqui, *Alliance*, p. 406).
28. Marrus, *Politics*, p. 26.

used in referring to the past, but with the implicit, or even explicit, extension to the present. Thus, in his 1801 *Appel à la justice des nations et des rois,* Michel Berr regrets the fall of the "Jewish nation." If the Emancipation should fail to obtain for all of European Jewry the benefits the French Jews have been granted, Berr suggests that the Jews should arm themselves and reconquer their ancient homeland. Within the framework of the Emancipation, he imagines the Jews learning both the local language and their ancient Hebrew language. He suggests that the Jews will then regard the two languages "as being almost equally national for them."[29]

Forty years later, in 1840, Grand Rabbi L. M. Lambert, chief rabbi of Metz, wrote that he expected the Jews to one day reestablish their national existence. He objected to the notion that they, more than Poles, Italians, or Greeks in exile in France, should be expected to promise never to intend to return to their old homeland. The Jews, he declared, "merit nationality as much as the Greeks and the Poles."[30]

Sometimes the idea that there is a national aspect to Jewry was expressed without actually using the term *nation.* For example, the word *Israel* was also used to refer to the totality of the Jews, understood in a tribal sense—a clearly ethnic notion.[31] Occasionally writers noted the lack of institutional expression for the national element in Judaism and proposed ways of filling the gap. Thus the Alliance Israélite Universelle, in its 1860 *Manifesto,* suggests that it will substitute for the nonexistent Jewish nation, by defending the interests of the Jews, as existing nations defend the interests of their nationals or of religious minorities whose protection they assure.[32]

It is clear that had the Jews been understood as a religious grouping, rather than a national one, there would have been more histories of Judaism and fewer of "the Jewish people" or "the Israelites." In fact, the repeated use of these terms, and similar ones, amply demonstrates the widespread conception that the Jews were a national group. One of the earliest examples is the title proposed in 1813 for a journal which never appeared: *Annales Historiques*

29. Michel Berr, *Appel à la justice des nations et des rois* (Strasbourg, 1801), passim, esp. pp. 54–55, 66–67.

30. L. M. Lambert, *Précis de l'histoire des Hébreux, depuis le patriarche Abraham, jusqu'en 1840* (Paris, 1840), p. 414: ". . . ceux, qui ont répandu la morale et la civilisation sur toute la terre, méritent sans doute la nationalité aussi bien que les grecs et les polonais." If we are tempted to speculate about Lambert's proto-Zionism, we are especially startled by his observation that there was a serious threat to the physical existence of world Jewry in 1840. Referring to the many false accusations of the period, he concludes: ". . . il ne s'agissait de rien moins que d'exterminer tous les Hébreux de la surface du globe" (ibid., p. 421).

31. For example, S. Bloch wrote: ". . . quand Israel et son culte seront admis partout, et mieux connus des peuples, la lumière, la vérité, la conscience du monde fera le reste" (quoted in Chouraqui, *Alliance,* p. 407).

32. *Manifeste,* p. 411.

et Littéraires du Peuple Juif (Historical and Literary Annals of the Jewish People).[33] Toward the middle of the century, Eugène Manuel, professor of literature and language in Paris, employed a similar notion when he claimed that he had been influenced by three classical sources: Greece, Rome, and "mon peuple hébreu" (my Hebrew people).[34] During the period of severe political antisemitism at the end of the century, Hippolyte Prague, reviewing a book entitled *La Désolation du peuple juif,* by Abbé Soullier, condemned the religious antisemitism of the book, but did not choose to dispute the author's use of the term *peuple juif.*[35]

The term *Israélite français* (French Israelite), in use from the very early days of the Emancipation,[36] and also the title of the earliest French Jewish periodical (1817–18), emphasizes Jewish identity, modified by the qualification "French." Later in the century, it was suggested that the order of this familiar phrase be reversed to "Français israélite" (Jewish Frenchman), thereby emphasizing the French nationality.

Our brothers ("nos frères") is often used to refer to other Jews, whether in France, Europe, Asia, or Africa. Examples of such usage include the 1844 call of Samuel Cahen to help the Jews in the east: "It is urgent that western Israelites raise up their eastern brothers."[37] Similarly, an 1860 article by S. Bloch recommends the establishment of an Alliance Israélite Universelle to protect the "interests, the social position, often the life of our brothers." It points out the need to be strong "in view of the persecutions of which our brothers in many countries are still the victims."[38] In 1865 the officers of the Alliance called upon their "dear brothers" of Europe, America, and Australia, to contribute financially to the Alliance schools which were helping to "regenerate" their "brothers in Asia and Africa."[39]

Underlying the usage of the term *brothers* is the concept of family, frequently used to explain and to justify Jewish ethnicity. It was often argued that coreligionists have a tight natural bond that unites them, analogous to that found among members of a single family. Although this observation was considered true of all religious groups, it is clear that the factor of descent—the ethnic factor—was assumed to characterize Jewish unity, far beyond any possible analogy in Christianity. The sense of family is evident,

33. L. Setier, Paris, November 1813, 12 pp. The journal itself never appeared.
34. Chouraqui, *Alliance,* p. 33.
35. *Archives Israélites,* March 12, 1891, pp. 81–83.
36. The earliest known use of this term occurs (in the Hebrew language) in a prospectus for a prayer book that was to be published in Paris about 1798 or 1799. My thanks to Dr. Simon Schwarzfuchs of Jerusalem who called my attention to this observation.
37. Quoted in Chouraqui, *Alliance,* p. 22.
38. *Univers Israélite,* February 1860; quoted in Chouraqui, *Alliance,* pp. 406–7.
39. *Appel du 1ᵉʳ mars 1865,* reprinted in Chouraqui, *Alliance,* p. 447.

for example, in the title of a Jewish periodical published in Avignon from 1859 to 1891, *La Famille de Jacob* (The Family of Jacob).

Even the term *solidarity* was used and the concept openly acknowledged. The Alliance may have been the first Jewish organization to advocate such solidarity and to claim that free regimes had nothing to fear from it. In the *Manifesto*, which launched the Alliance, this is expressed unequivocally: ". . . a bond must be created, a solidarity established from country to country. . ."[40]

IV

Several factors were responsible for the retention of ethnicity among the French Jews. The international aspect of Jewish existence sharply clashed with attempts to deny any conflicts with local loyalties. In the face of this reality all arguments concerning Jewish patriotism had an unavoidable tone of apologetics. Related to this was the continual migration of the Jewish population during the nineteenth century. Not only did large numbers of Jews switch countries, and therefore loyalties, but they constituted a noticeable poor and nonacculturated mass, at least in the early years of their arrival in new places. The continual arrival in France of Jews from the east, as well as the internal migrations from areas of higher Jewish density in Alsace-Lorraine to the center of the country, contributed to the maintenance of a distinctly Jewish subgroup.[41]

Judaism itself, as a religion, in any of its denominational forms, is not easily differentiable from Jewish ethnicity, as has been well demonstrated by Will Herberg in his classic study, *Protestant-Catholic-Jew*.[42] Speaking of post-World War II American Jewry's "return" to the form and institutions of Judaism, Herberg notes: "The dual meaning of 'Jewishness' as covering both ethnic group and religion made the 'return' movement of the third generation into a source of renewed strength and vigor for the American Jewish community."[43]

In addition to the difficulty of sharply differentiating between the ethnic

40. *Manifeste*, p. 411.

41. Jews from eastern Europe began immigrating into France in the 1850s, and arrived in large numbers after 1880. Throughout the entire nineteenth century an internal migration, especially from Alsace-Lorraine to Paris, took place, such that the relative percentages of Jewish population in Alsace-Lorraine and Paris, respectively, were 79 percent and 6 percent, in 1808, and 56.5 percent and 26 percent, in 1861 (Albert, *Modernization*, p. 19). Poverty levels were high. In 1870, 60 percent of the Parisian Jewish burials were at public expense. The poor shied away from official (consistorial) weddings, because of the expense, and tended to retain old communal customs which had a strong ethnic aspect (ibid., p. 304).

42. Herberg, *Protestant-Catholic-Jew*.

43. Ibid., p. 187.

and religious aspects, the same third generation effect is to be observed in France. The third generation, as third generation Americans were to do later, wanted to remember what its parents wanted to forget.[44] This was the generation born between 1820 and 1840, and which became adult between 1840 and 1860. It is the generation, understandably, which established the French Jewish press, and which founded the Alliance Israélite Universelle.

Observant Jews realized there was a national component to their religion, and refused to give it up. They refused to deny the traditional hope for ultimate national restoration. They refused to do without traditional communal institutions, especially the *minyanim* (prayer meetings) and mutual aid societies, which predated the official consistory, had no legal status under the new regime, and were as much social-ethnic societies as they were religious ones.[45]

The conservative leader, S. Bloch, editor of the *Univers Israélite*, pleaded for the continued observance of Jewish ritual law. The civil laws, he argued, "do not separate us from the Jewish community" ("ne nous séparent point de la communauté israélite").[46] Further indication that Bloch was conscious of the social-national aspect of Judaism is to be found in the choice of words he used to denounce the Frankfurt Reformers, who sought, he said, a Judaism without Jews ("judaïsme idéal, spirituel, qui n'aurait ni révélation, ni histoire, ni tradition, ni fêtes, ni cérémonies, . . . un judaïsme sans Juifs.")[47] The word *Juif*, used here by Bloch, was the word used by the nineteenth-century French Jews to indicate the old national type of unemancipated, ethnic Jew, as opposed to the modern "Israelite," the Jew by "faith" alone.

Another reason that religion tended to foster the retention of communal consciousness and identity is that the truly secular state did not exist. The government was not blind to religion; rather, it recognized the major religious groupings and gave them certain legal status and financial assistance in their religious as well as social activities. The consistory's recognized charitable and administrative work thus betrayed an acceptance by all parties of a de-facto and not unimportant vestige of the pre-Revolutionary corporate organization.[48]

44. Ibid., p. 267.
45. In *Modernization*, pp. 197–221, I develop fully the story of the stubborn maintenance of these nonconsistorial institutions in the face of continuous legal prosecution.
46. *Univers Israélite*, I (1844).
47. Ibid.
48. Separate schools and hospitals were maintained. Financial aid was provided for separate social welfare organizations. The various clergy were represented on certain public committees such as the education committee. Chaplaincies were maintained in the army, schools, and hospitals. Furthermore, the consistory was responsible, until 1870, for the collection of the outstanding pre-Revolutionary Jewish community debts. Early in their existence, during the Napoleonic regime, the consistories also registered Jews, provided lists of conscripts, and denounced those without a living (Albert, *Modernization*, p. 308).

The official Jewish institutions were involved in various "regeneration" projects for the improvement of the educational and socioeconomic level of the Jewish population. Such activities existed primarily on a national and local level, but to some extent also on the international level. With the founding of the Alliance Israélite Universelle in 1860, international solidarity increased. Ben Halpern has aptly noted that "the actual nature of the work done—political intercession, aid to emigrants, vocational retraining, colonization—did not fall short of the scope of activities later undertaken by secular Zionists as an open program of ethnic politics."[49]

The civil-ethnic quality of the consistorial institutions was not lost on contemporaries, both Jewish and non-Jewish, who discussed the nature of the institutions and the division of powers between the consistory and the rabbinate. It was often stated that the rabbinate was in charge of religious affairs, and the consistory was responsible for "civil" affairs.[50]

The consistorial institutions served the function of retaining the Jewish elite by providing them with leadership positions within the Jewish community, positions that were grounded ultimately in the French governmental authority. Thus, ethnicity in France was served by the very institutions that were designed to promote assimilation. Had they not existed, it is possible that assimilation would have been more rapid.

Post-Emancipation France provided acceptable, and even official, outlets for talents that were related to the backgrounds of Jews, thus creating no need among the intellectual classes for denial of their origins. Jews became librarians and professors, specializing in Oriental languages, and especially in Hebrew and ancient and medieval Hebrew studies.[51]

Antisemitism is a pressure that has sometimes led towards renewed efforts at assimilation, and sometimes to an acceptance of, and even an assertion of, ethnic identity. Antisemitism was a constant factor during the nineteenth century, and social and even legal prejudice had to be recognized as part of the Jew's world. Although it is true that antisemitism became most virulent only in the post-1880 period with the European-wide development of political antisemitism, the assumption that pre-Third Republic France, and especially the Second Empire, was relatively free of anti-Jewish prejudice, is

49. Ben Halpern, *Jews and Blacks: The Classic American Minorities* (New York, 1971), p. 110.

50. Albert, *Modernization*, p. 436 n. 3; and p. 309. In a personal letter to the German orthodox leader Rabbi Ezriel Hildesheimer, Grand Rabbi S. Klein wrote (5623, 1862–63) that the consistory had no interest in religion. Speaking of the degradation of Judaism at the hands of the consistory, he says: "Ses pieds sont entravés, ses mains liées, et elle est livrée comme prisonnière aux mains du Consistoire." Speaking of the central consistory members, he says that less than three of the nine men observed Kashrut and Shabbat. Some did not even have their sons circumcised (Simon Schwarzfuchs, *Les Juifs de France* [Paris, 1975] , p. 256).

51. A few examples are Salomon Munk, Arsène and James Darmesteter, Hartwig and Joseph Derenbourg, Adolphe Franck, and Joseph Salvador.

incorrect.[52] Full documentation of the antisemitism of the period would itself constitute the material for an essay, and here we can only make brief reference to representative instances. Jewish status experienced its "ups and downs" with the various regimes. It made the most tangible gains during the July Monarchy, achieving public funding in 1831, and permission to send chaplains to the military hospitals in 1839. But even this beneficent government was not uniform in its attitude. An 1832 court decision required Jewish "usurers" to prove that the debts they tried to collect were legal according to the law of March 17, 1808 (which was supposed to have expired in 1818). In 1840 the press reported the accusations against the Jews of Damascus, without any reservations. The French Jewish population was shocked by this act of hostility of many of the leading newspapers.[53] In 1845 the French Jews had been complaining that their rights of trade and domicile in Switzerland, according to the French-Swiss trade agreement, were not being honored because of Swiss anti-Jewish regulations. The Orleanist government replied that it could do nothing about this situation because it had been agreed upon by a secret 1820 clause between the two countries.

A worsening of the Jewish position took place after the ascension of Louis Napoleon to power. In 1849, I. Weill, a Jewish teacher of mathematics, was refused a post in the public "college" (secondary school) of Haguenau.[54] Later in the same year Isidore Cahen wrote to the central consistory, asking its assistance in his own case. Cahen had achieved third place in the competitive examination (*concours*) in philosophy, and had been named to a chair in the Lycée de Napoléon in Luçon (Vendée). The bishop of Luçon had refused to allow Cahen to assume his post because of his religion. The government, despite Cahen's appeals, had not offered him another post at the appropriate level, but, rather, had insulted him by offering him a lower position. Cahen urged the consistory to act in the interest of all Jews to prevent the establishment of a precedent whereby being an "Israelite" would be incompatible with the holding of a post as a professor of philosophy in the public secondary schools.[55] Despite consistory efforts, however, Cahen was never reinstated in his post, nor did he receive an appropriate alternative one. This experience launched him in a career in Jewish journalism and with the Alliance Israélite Universelle, of which he was one of the founders. Antisemitism had led to a reassertion of ethnicity and Jewish solidarity.

The campaign against Jews in the public schools continued. In 1850 Jérôme

52. For example, Michael Marrus argues that before 1880 antisemitism had "little mass following" (*Politics*, p. 124).

53. A particularly strong example of this kind of reporting appeared in *La Gazette du Languedoc*, June 14, 1840.

54. Archives, central consistory, 1B5, October 22, 1849.

55. Isidore Cahen to the central consistory, December 11, 1849.

Aron, a history teacher at the *Lycée* in Strasbourg, was fired.[56] The following year Jews (and Protestants) were barred from the competitive entrance examination for the prestigious teacher-training school, the Ecole Normale.[57]

In 1851 there occurred several instances in which the government slighted the official representatives of the Jews by excluding them from public ceremonies. At least three occasions arose during 1851 and 1852, at which Jewish representatives were not invited to celebrations attended by representatives of other faiths. The central consistory complained about the discrimination, citing the "great principles of equality."[58] To the anxious inquiry of the chief rabbi of Bordeaux, Prince Louis Napoleon promised to maintain the principles of 1789 in regard to the Jewish population.[59] But antisemitism was deeply engrained in France. In 1853 the Strasbourg consistory was advised by the central consistory that it was useless to expect governmental assistance in regard to the repeated threats menacing the Jews of Alsace.[60]

The campaign against Jews in the lycées took new turns. In 1853 two Jewish children of Mâcon were refused admission to the *Lycée*. After the central consistory complained to the government, the children were admitted, but for a while they were forced to participate in Christian religious worship.[61]

The problem spread to the courts. In 1853, a certain Weill, a Jewish lawyer of Colmar, was refused the right to practice at the bar of Colmar because of his religion.[62] In 1856 a Jew was refused a judgeship in Alsace on the grounds that the local population was prejudiced against Jews.[63]

The 1860 anti-Christian riots in Damascus threatened a repetition of the 1840 Damascus Affair. The French press printed unfounded charges against the Syrian Jews, claiming that they had participated in the massacres of Christians; French Jews took up pens in defense of their maligned brethren. But French anti-Jewish sentiment was prevalent. Throughout the 1850s journals all over the country had printed false accusations against the Jewish population and anti-Jewish pamphlets had appeared. The Jews had discovered that the law did not protect them.[64] Afraid of defeat in a court battle against such publications, the consistory had abstained from any public action. But a young rabbi, Elie-Aristide Astruc, was bolder. In 1859 he

56. Archives, central consistory, 1B5, November 10, 1850.
57. Ibid., July 29, 1852. Cf. Archives, Paris consistory, AA4, August 11, 1852.
58. Archives, central consistory, 1B5, January 27, 1851; January 11, 1852; May 3, 1852.
59. Archives, Bordeaux consistory, 2A6, October 20, 1852.
60. Archives, Strasbourg consistory, Minutes, March 14, 1853.
61. Archives, central consistory, 1B5, October 5, November 10, November 19, 1853.
62. Ibid., May 17, July 11, 1853.
63. Archives, Strasbourg consistory, Minutes, December 18, 1856; and March 25, 1857.
64. Albert, *Modernization*, pp. 160–65.

published a reply to one of the persistent antisemitic writers, Louis Veuillot, *Les Juifs et Louis Veuillot*. The following year Astruc was one of the founders of the Alliance Israélite Universelle. Again, antisemitism had led to ethnicity and Jewish solidarity. In addition to Cahen and Astruc, at least one other founder of the Alliance, Jules Carvallo, had personally experienced anti-Jewish prejudice.[65]

Antisemitic feelings and expressions continued to be manifested after the Alliance took up the battle against them. In 1862 Protestants in Nancy complained that a military service had been held in a Catholic church. Writing about the complainants, in order to dismiss their charge, the Marquis de la Rochejaquelin wrote, "Ce sont des juifs!"

V

Solidarity among French Jews is demonstrated by the many examples of concerted action undertaken to solve Jewish material and physical problems, both within France and on an international level. Initiatives in this direction were taken by individuals, local community institutions, and consistories. The consistory was the official administrative unit of the French Jewish community. There were seven to nine branches located throughout metropolitan France, and they were hierarchically administered by a central consistory located in Paris. Each consistory was responsible for the entire region it governed, and for the local affairs of all the communities included in that region.

Because of a tendency to conservative political action at the central consistory level, the battles for Jewish rights and for protection against antisemitism and discriminatory practices were often waged at the regional level. For example, the attempt of courts in Alsace-Lorraine to enforce the special Jewish oath (moré judaïco) was a problem that the central consistory defined as a regional one. Ceding the initiative in the battle for the elimination of the oath to the eastern consistories, the central consistory nevertheless announced that it viewed the problem with sympathetic interest. The traditional solidarity of the eastern communities was strong; the battle against the Jewish oath was fought at their initiative, and won.[66] Another example of the strength of traditional group loyalties is the maintenance of the old Sephardi-Ashkenazi distinctions. The failure of the central and Paris consistories

65. Chouraqui, *Alliance*, p. 23.
66. The Supreme Court, in 1846, ruled that imposition of the moré judaïco oath was illegal.

to achieve a *rite français* through the fusion of Sephardi and Ashkenazi ceremonies, is testimony to the deep ethnic loyalties of the separate groups, more
than to their religious differences of opinion.

Charitable institutions at a local community level are indications of spontaneous Jewish solidarity. One historian has noted

> . . . the critical role which charity played in providing cohesion for a
> Jewish community divided by both class and interests. Jews of whatever
> background, of whatever Jewish consciousness, had sufficient memory
> of the time of persecutions to take pity on those who suffer. . . . This
> benevolence, commonly referred to as "Jewish solidarity," flowed from
> all elements of the Jewish community. Charitable associations, particu-
> larly in Paris, were the meeting-places for Frenchmen who had nothing
> in common but their Jewishness.[67]

It was a practice in the larger communities to build a Jewish hospital where,
it was said, Jewish patients could be fed kosher food and would not have to
fear the visits of Christian clergymen. But these two problems could have
been solved in less drastic ways, within the institutional framework of the
public hospitals. The Jewish hospitals were a historical outgrowth of the
functions of traditional mutual aid societies, which assured sick-care as part
of their services to members. Other charitable activities included the running
of orphanages; charitable grants for maintenance of poor families; grants for
special needs, such as clothing, weddings, childbirth, "religious initiation";
loans to businessmen; vocational training; general education; even the
bringing of Oriental Jews to Paris for a French education to prepare them for
leadership and educational roles in their home communities.

Not all charity was a product of official institutions. Traditional Jewish
solidarity, expressed in the form of private personal charity, was a firmly
entrenched custom in the eastern communities, and even under the threat of
consistorial reprisals for allegedly interfering with regeneration attempts,
personal charity continued. During the 1850s three Parisian Jews, Manuel
and Narcisse Leven and Eugene Manuel, took the initiative in organizing
evening classes for young Jewish apprentices of the capital. These men had
been inspired by the principles of 1848, but it is notable that they chose to
express their liberal ideals through activity within their own ethnic group.
The same three men were later among the founders of the Alliance Israélite
Universelle.

At all levels (regional, national, and international) consistories sponta-

67. Marrus, *Politics*, pp. 77–78.

neously began to take initiatives—not required by law—to protect Jews and Jewish interests. It should not be assumed, however, that all of the instances which involved foreign Jewries were indeed examples of international solidarity. In many cases the real issue was ultimately French Jewish status within France and vis-à-vis the French authorities. Thus, the Damascus Affair of 1840, the accusations against Damascus Jews in 1860, the problem of Jewish rights in Switzerland, Jewish rights in Russia—all may appear at first glance to be indications of French Jewish mobilization for the assistance of foreign Jews. But there is a pattern in these cases. In all of them the French government and/or the press and public opinion in France had been aroused against Jewry, and French Jews had reason to fear a worsening of their position *within* France. It became extremely important to establish Jewish rights to equal consular and passport protection as French citizens abroad, and to see that the French government not take any active public position—as it did take in the 1840 Damascus Affair—which was openly hostile to Jewish interests. While the governments of England and Austria were actively intervening to obtain the release of the Damascus prisoners, France's consul was encouraging their persecution as part of the French Middle East policy of supporting Mehmet Ali against the Ottoman regime.

Similarly, at least part of the French Jewish concern for Russian and Swiss policies regarding Jews was provoked by the fact that the French government was not affording equal protection to its Jewish citizens in regard to the honoring abroad of the French passport and the rights granted to French citizens by international treaties. Thus, the main thrust of the complaints about Russian and Swiss policies concerned the rights refused to *French* Jews in these countries, not to the local Jewish population, although a secondary benefit of the campaign in Switzerland was the eventual emancipation of the Swiss Jews. From the 1830s, for more than thirty years, French Jewish citizens and official representatives repeatedly appealed for French government assistance in obtaining equality for the French Alsatian Jews who had traditionally done business in Switzerland. The initiative was divided among the local consistories, the central consistory, and an especially active and devoted local leader, Rabbi Nordmann of Hegenheim.[68]

As an instrument for the expression of Jewish solidarity, the periodical press also operated on several levels. Some Jewish journals were concerned with local issues; others had a broader circulation and were engaged in exchanges with the foreign Jewish press. All of them were by Jews, about Jews, for Jews. The Jewish press is an ethnic institution *par excellence*; it was

---

68. Nordmann deserves credit for keeping the issue alive and achieving ultimate victory.

used to encourage Jewish achievement and socioeconomic advance, to maintain Jewish solidarity by informing French Jews of the status and problems of their coreligionists abroad. Thus, it became an instrument for combatting anti-Jewish prejudice by adopting the developing nineteenth-century liberal view that knowledge creates freedom. It was this growing liberal outlook, grounded ultimately in faith in public opinion, that spawned the Alliance Israélite Universelle. The founders of the Alliance were not unaware of this, and in their *Manifesto* made reference to the salutory effect the press had had in "overturning mountains of prejudice. . . ." They added that "at every moment there are facts to reveal, accusations to refute, truths to disseminate."[69]

During the two decades preceding the founding of the Alliance, the press was, in fact, the instrument most responsible for spreading the idea of uniting to give practical expression to Jewish solidarity and to achieve material gains for Jews living under oppressive conditions. Thus, in 1844, at a time when the Jews of Russia and Poland experienced a worsening of their condition, Samuel Cahen, editor of the *Archives Israélites*, proposed the creation of a European Committee for Jewish Colonization (comité européen de colonisation israélite) to improve the condition of persecuted Jewry by giving them land to work.[70] The following year another journalist recommended the creation of a world society for the defense of Jewish rights,[71] and in 1846 Jean Jacques Altaras of Marseille proposed colonizing Russian Jews in Algeria. In 1851 and 1853 Jules Carvallo used the medium of the press to suggest the convening of a Jewish congress (un congrès israélite).[72] In 1858, in the columns of the *Archives Israélites*, Isidore Cahen suggested that the Jews imitate the model of the Protestant organization, the Alliance Évangélique Universelle.[73] Early in 1860, Simon Bloch, in the *Univers Israélite*, endorsed the idea and even proposed the name that was subsequently used: Alliance Israélite Universelle.[74]

Even before the establishment of the Jewish press in 1840 there had been attempts by French Jews to use international diplomacy for the benefit of nonemancipated Jewry. The first French Jew to attempt to implement this idea was the eccentric lawyer Michel Berr. In 1801, on the eve of the anticipated international peace conference in Luneville, Berr published an appeal

69. *Manifeste*, p. 409.
70. Chouraqui, *Alliance*, p. 22.
71. Ibid., p. 20.
72. *Manifeste*, p. 408.
73. *Archives Israélites*, XIX (1859), pp. 623 ff.
74. Quoted in Chouraqui, *Alliance*, p. 406.

to the statesmen who were to participate in the conference. He urged them to support the cause of Jewish emancipation in their own countries.[75]

In 1833 James de Rothschild and Adolphe Crémieux secretly worked with "The Philanthropic Society for the Acceleration of Jewish Emancipation throughout the World" (known as the Lafayette Committee). This committee had been organized by Polish non-Jewish émigrés in Paris, whose political motivations had interested them in the Jews of Poland and the Middle East. The Jewish members of the committee were involved purely because of their concern for Jews abroad, although they preferred not to release news of the society's establishment until a later date because "at present it will be considered by the despotic government as merely political propaganda and thus might make worse the situation of the Jews who are scattered throughout the world instead of aiding them."[76]

In 1836 a converted French Jew and former adherent of the Saint-Simon movement (until its demise in 1832), Gustave d'Eichthal, undertook a private project to obtain the emancipation of the Austrian Jews. Eichthal envisaged the emancipation of world Jewry as a necessary step in the eventual achievement of the Saint-Simonian ideal of the unity of mankind through the union of East and West. Deriving his thought largely from the writings of the French Jewish scholar, Joseph Salvador, Eichthal displayed a strong appreciation of the continual significance of the Jewish people's contribution to world civilization. Furthermore, his conception of Judaism was not a narrow "confessional" view, but a larger racial view, which embodied biological and cultural elements. He spoke of the "indelible character" of one's Jewish origins. He, himself, although converted, associated mainly with Jews. Eichthal traveled to Vienna where he obtained an interview with Metternich, but failed to convince the chancellor of the need and value of emancipating the Jews. Although his mission failed, it is of historic note that Eichthal "extended the battle for emancipation beyond the frontiers of a single country and thereby solicited Jewish solidarity."[77]

Consistorial activity on behalf of Jewry in other parts of the world was entangled with, and not always well distinguished from, the history of Rothschild family initiative. It frequently happened that the Rothschilds preferred to work through the consistory or its charity committee, in order to

75. Michel Berr, *Appel*, p. 52.

76. Abraham Duker, "The Lafayette Committee for Jewish Emancipation," *Essays in Jewish Life and Thought, Presented in Honor of Salo Baron* (New York, 1959), pp. 169–76.

77. Michael Graetz, "Une Initiative Saint-Simonienne pour l'émancipation des Juifs," *REJ*, CXXIX (1970), 167–84. Graetz errs in assuming that the Eichthal mission was the first example of enlarging the Emancipation struggle beyond the borders of a single country.

make their private activities appear to be official acts of the French Jewish community. For a long time Albert Cohn was the link between the Rothschilds and the Paris consistory's charity board, working in the employ of both. In 1854 when the Rothschilds sent Cohn to Jerusalem to create charitable institutions, they suggested that he be officially named to survey the status of Jerusalem Jewry on behalf of the central consistory. The Rothschilds provided the money to found a school for which the consistory agreed to raise maintenance funds.[78]

The Rothschilds frequently undertook to represent Jewish interests to the government, although they were not always given a sympathetic ear. Sometimes the consistory asked them to bring a case to the attention of the government; sometimes the Rothschilds took the initiative before the consistory even met to consider what action to take.

By around 1840 the third generation effect that we have described above began to be manifested by an increased interest in Jewish affairs abroad. In 1841 the Paris consistory asked the central consistory to organize financial aid for Smyrna Jews. In 1843 a private individual, Eugène de Dalmeyda, acting independently, published an appeal to the pope, in which he argued that the edict of inquisition that had just been promulgated would ruin the Jews of the papal lands. In 1846 the consistory itself was involved in obtaining from the pope a statement of benevolence regarding the Jews in the papal lands, as we know from an 1847 consistory letter thanking the pope for his reassurances. Official influence in this case was possible because it coincided with French foreign policy; France was supporting the pope against nationalist revolutionary forces. In 1849, when France sent an expeditionary army to suppress the Revolution and the 1848 constitution, the central consistory asked the government to maintain the Jewish liberties accorded by the pope.

French governmental interests continued to coincide with Jewish interests in Poland. France had long been supporting the Polish national struggle against Russia (as part of her Middle East policy and her competition with Russia over the anticipated succession to the Ottoman Empire). Just as this kind of consideration had explained the policy of the Lafayette Committee, it also underlay France's policy in 1844, when Russia increased its persecution

78. The Rothschilds carried out philanthropic activities in Jerusalem because they believed in the special role of Jerusalem in Jewish history. This is clear from an 1854 discussion in the central consistory, during which two opposite views emerged—that of Adolphe Franck, who favored extending financial and educational aid to all the Jews of the Ottoman Empire, and Rothschild, who insisted that Jerusalem was a special case. It is worth remembering in this context that Rabbi Zvi Hirsch Kalischer had contacted Albert Cohn around 1836 with his views that settlement in Palestine will be the first step toward the messianic era.

of Polish Jewry, and the French government spoke out, earning the praise of both the Paris and central consistories.

For twenty years before the establishment of the Alliance and its widespread network of schools for Oriental Jews, French Jewry had a tradition of building schools in the Middle East. Crémieux had opened schools in Egypt, on his way home from Damascus in 1840. The Rothschild family built schools in Jerusalem, Smyrna, Alexandria, and Constantinople. They influenced the development of additional schools in Trieste, Cairo, and Damascus.[79] In 1856 Salonican Jewry asked the central consistory to supply them with a teacher. The consistory endorsed the proposal made by Ludwig Philippson in 1854 that young Jews from the Ottoman Empire be brought to Europe to study and prepare themselves for leadership and educational activities at home.[80] Arrangements were made—but did not materialize—for the students to live and study at the Strasbourg consistory's École de Travail. (The same idea later found expression in the Alliance's École Normale Israélite Orientale, opened in Paris in 1867.)[81]

French Jewry's interest in Oriental Jews was not confined to pedagogy. In 1854 the central consistory asked the emperor to try to obtain the same rights for the Ottoman Jews as were enjoyed by the Christians under the capitulations agreements with the Ottoman Empire. But French Jewry went further than requesting the assistance of their own government. In the same year Albert Cohn, on behalf of both the Rothschilds and the central consistory, obtained the following statement from the sultan in Constantinople: "All the rights, privileges and immunities which have been or will be accorded to any Christian group will be accorded automatically to the Jews, because His Imperial Majesty's heart will never permit the establishment of the slightest difference among the non-Muslim subjects (*raias*) of his Empire."[82]

In 1859 the central consistory, through the intermediary of James de Rothschild, influenced the French government to intervene on behalf of two Rumanian Jews imprisoned in Galantz. The two were released. In 1860 the central consistory appealed to French Jews for financial contributions to aid Moroccan Jews who had escaped to Oran in Algeria.

The consistory's consistent policy of aiding Ottoman Jewry fit well into France's Middle East policy; not all suggestions to help foreign Jews were

79. Isidore Loeb, *Biographie d'Albert Cohn* (Paris, 1878), pp. 67, 75, 77, 80, 82, 90, 108.
80. Ibid., pp. 52–55. On this occasion the central consistory designated Cohn to survey the needs of the Turkish Jews and Loeb reports the incident without mentioning that Cohn was really sent by the Rothschilds.
81. On the Ecole Normale Israélite, see Chouraqui, *Alliance*, pp. 177–81.
82. Loeb, *Albert Cohn*, p. 80.

embraced by the consistory, if the French government could not be expected to exert a salutary influence. The choice of causes was thus based entirely on the practical evaluation of the likelihood of obtaining results by working through the French government. The central consistory considered that it did not have the right or freedom to act independently of the government.[83]

This constituted an essential difference between the consistory and the Alliance Israélite Universelle. The new organization, under the leadership of younger and less cautious men, was more solidly committed to the active public defense of Jewish interests, regardless of French government policy. Thus, in addition to continuing the tradition of support for Ottoman Jewry, one of the early acts of the Alliance was to intervene directly with Cavour in regard to the Mortara Affair, whereas the consistory had refused to take such bold action. The Alliance took up the battle of the Algerian Jews who were being discriminated against in taxation matters by the French military government and it raised a public cry against the missionary activities of Notre Dame de Sion—both unpopular causes with the consistory. This kind of vigorous approach earned the Alliance Israélite Universelle the suspicion and hostility of some consistory members—especially those in Paris.[84] However, within a few years of its establishment the Alliance had the support of—and in some cases even shared leaders with—the consistories, and by the end of the century it was more cautious to harmonize its activities with French public policy.[85]

VI

It has long been the consensus of Jewish historians that nineteenth-century French Jewry was assimilationist in ideology and assimilated in practice.

83. Thus, the consistory turned down Montefiore's 1854 proposal that French Jews join British Jews in asking the Spanish Cortes, then about to meet, to revoke the expulsion of the Jews from Spain. The reason is that the central consistory was willing to act only when it could have the support of the French government in assuring a successful intervention. In the case of Spain, France was supporting the conservative monarchist interests; the queen had just fled to exile in Paris; and it would be dangerous for the consistory to intervene with the Spanish liberal revolutionaries who were in a position to legalize the status of the Jews in Spain.

84. A member of the central consistory declared at the meeting of October 18, 1860: "Cette société agit avec peu de prudence et pourrait quelque fois, par ses démarches inconsiderées, nuire au veritable intérêt du judaïsme" (quoted in Chouraqui, Alliance, p. 42). Cf. the reaction of even Ludwig Philippson, who was always active in organizing international Jewish pressure: "La fondation de l'Alliance Israélite Universelle vaudra aux juifs un surcroît de discrédit, en renforçant la légende de la solidarité juive, du complot maçonnique dirigé secrètement par le judaïsme international . . ." (quoted in ibid., p. 43).

85. Marrus, Politics, pp. 238–39. In 1861 the Strasbourg, Nancy, Bayonne, Bordeaux, and Marseille consistories offered their support to the Alliance. The journals Archives Israélites, Univers Israélite, and Le Lien d'Israel quickly offered the Alliance an enthusiastic welcome.

Historians, writing of the Jews of France, tend to present the single schema: Sanhedrin—assimilation—Dreyfus.[86] Scholars continue to repeat previous conclusions to the effect that nineteenth-century French Jews "were totally absorbed in their non-Jewish surroundings"; that "Judaism for this generation was no longer a religious, social, or political concept"; that Jewish history and tradition had no meaning for many French Jews.[87]

The latest to argue this point is Michael Marrus, whose *Politics of Assimilation* contends that until the Dreyfus Affair, there was a single view within Judaism which saw Jewish loyalty as primarily directed toward France.[88] In my view this monolithic view of an assimilationist pre-Zionist French Jewry ignores the many shades of opinion that existed within the community and ignores the numerous examples of language and action which contradict the theory.

One of the reasons that the error has been made and repeated so often is that statements by nineteenth-century writers urging "fusion" have been exaggerated, misinterpreted, and taken out of context. For example, L. M. Lambert wrote in 1840 of the need for civil, and even religious, fusion of Jews with the French population. The only differences that need remain, he said, are "the obligations to our creator according to the Bible and the tradition."[89] This is an impressive statement which could appear to be very strong evidence of assimilationism, if the reader is not familiar with the full range of Lambert's thought. Lambert, in fact, argued in the very same publication that the Jews deserve nationality as much as the Poles, the Greeks, and the Italians.[90]

If by "assimilated" one refers to behavioral assimilation, or acculturation, then French Jews of the nineteenth century were assimilated.[91] But since this

86. See, for example, Cecil Roth, *A History of the Jews from Earliest Times through the Six-Day War*, rev. ed. (New York, 1970), p. 323. Speaking of the Sanhedrin, Roth says: ". . . it is frequently regarded with good reason as having set the footsteps of French Jewry upon the pathway of assimilation. . . ." Roth's next statements on French Jewry are the reporting of the founding of the Alliance (p. 346) and the Dreyfus Affair (p. 349). The same program is followed by Howard Morley Sachar in his *The Course of Modern Jewish History* (New York, 1958). On pp. 62–65 Sachar discusses the Sanhedrin; on pp. 98–99 he describes the increasing assimilation of the French Jews into such institutions as the army, the universities, and politics; on p. 227 he begins a discussion of the rise of antisemitism in France. An exception to the general pattern is Simon Dubnov, whose discussion of French Jewry during the Second Republic and the Second Empire is more sensitive to the reality, especially the problem of continual antisemitism in France. He too, however, judges "the process of assimilation with the surrounding milieu . . . went on apace" (Simon Dubnov, *History of the Jews*, 5 vols. [London, 1967–73], V, 362–63).

87. Walter Laqueur, *A History of Zionism* (New York, 1972), pp. 34–35.

88. Marrus, *Politics*, pp. 120–21.

89. Lambert, *Précis*, p. 413.

90. Ibid., pp. 413–14.

91. The Jewish leadership was "mildly liberal in regard to religion and integrationist socially and economically . . . generally non-observant, although not assimilated" (Albert, *Modernization*, pp. 305–6).

would be a trivial statement, encompassing even Jewish nationalists and Zionists, it is clear that the charge of assimilation generally made in regard to French Jewry implies a moving in the direction of total disappearance of all differences, and an eventual merging with the French population.

However, this claim is contradicted by much of the evidence; the low incidence of intermarriage, the low rate of conversion, the numerous ethnic institutions, the tendency among Jews to maintain primary group associations among other Jews, the many examples of language use which betray ethnic feeling, the repeated instances of international Jewish solidarity, and the attempts to use international diplomacy to improve the status of Jews abroad. Recognition of the ethnicity and solidarity of nineteenth-century French Jewry helps to explain the genesis of the twentieth-century ethnic reality.

Leadership and Charisma: The Case of Theodor Herzl

Jehuda Reinharz *and*
Shulamit Reinharz

The emergence of a revolutionary leader can be viewed from various perspectives. One can examine his ideological program within a broader historical context, elucidate the sociological differences between his constituents and opponents, or portray the psychological characteristics of his leadership, among others. The particular leader can be seen as one case within the vast array of revolutionary figures in order to test or expand relevant theory. On the other hand, previously derived theory might be temporarily suspended, leaving room for new generalizations based on the case in question. This chapter treats a revolutionary movement within the limited time span of the birth of the revolutionary idea to the first major sign of its achievement. It investigates the problems of the formation, emergence, and confirmation of revolutionary power within the framework of sociological theory,[1] specifically Weber's study of *charismatic legitimacy* in his *The Sociology of Religion* and *The Theory of Social and Economic Organization*.[2]

1. For a psychoanalytic interpretation of Herzl, see Peter Loewenberg, "Theodore Herzl: A Psychoanalytic Study in Charismatic Political Leadership," in Benjamin B. Wolman, ed., *The Psychoanalytic Interpretation of History* (New York, 1971), pp. 150–91. For a general and comparative assessment of Herzl, see J. L. Talmon, "Types of Jewish Self-Awareness: Herzl's 'Jewish State' after Seventy Years (1896–1966)," in his *Israel among the Nations* (London, 1970), pp. 88–129. For some interesting observations on Herzl, see David Vital, "Zionism Revisited: Herzl," *Commentary* (May 1973), 69–74. For biographies, see Alex Bein, *Theodore Herzl* (New York-Philadelphia, 1962); and Amos Elon, *Herzl* (New York, 1975). For a reassessment of Herzl, see Jacques Kornberg, "Theodore Herzl: A Reevaluation," *Journal of Modern History*, LII (June 1980), 226–52.

2. The most pertinent interpretations and examinations of Weber's theory for our study are: *Max Weber on the Methodology of the Social Sciences*, trans. and ed. Edward A. Shils and Henry A. Finch (Glencoe, Ill., 1949); Talcott Parsons, "Introduction" to Weber's *The Theory of Social and Economic Organization* (London-New York, 1947), pp. 1–70; A. Solomon, "Max Weber's Sociology," *Social Research*, II (1935), 60–73; Edward A. Shils, "Some Remarks on the Theory of Social and Economic Organization," *Economica*, XV (1948), 36–50; and idem, "Charisma, Order and Status," *American Sociological Review*, XXX (1965), 199–213. See in particular the excellent introduction by S. N. Eisenstadt, "Charisma and Institution Building: Max Weber and Modern Sociology," in Eisenstadt, ed., *Max Weber on Charisma and Institution Building* (Chicago, 1968), pp. ix–lvi. See also Ann Ruth and Dorothy Willner, "The Rise and Role of Charismatic Leaders," *Annals of the American Academy of Political and Social Studies*, CCCLVIII (1965); Karl Lowenstein, *Max Weber's Political Ideas in the Perspective of Our Time* (Amherst, Mass., 1966); Reinhard Bendix and Guenther Roth, *Scholarship and Partisanship: Essays on Max Weber* (Berkeley, 1971), esp. pp. 170–87; Claude Ake, "Charismatic Legitimation and Political Integration," *Comparative Studies in History and Society*, IX (1966), 1–13; and Bryan Wilson, *The Noble Savages: The Primitive Origins of Charisma and Its Contemporary Survival* (Berkeley, 1975).

The term *charisma* has been popularized to mean a special quality of leadership that inspires enthusiasm. This diluted, vague definition has led to its indiscriminate application to numerous merely popular leaders. The reader should suspend this loose meaning and substitute for mere popularity a form of leadership with at least the following specifications: (1) charisma is a revolutionary power; (2) it neglects economic efficiency and rationality; (3) the charismatic leader inspires followers who become personal disciples; (4) the charismatic leader is a leader only by virtue of the recognition of those who put themselves under his authority, and the followers follow because they perceive it as their duty to do so.

As used by Weber, charisma is a form of authority or legitimacy which can be contrasted with two other forms, traditional and rational. People obey a charismatic leader because he is extraordinary in some way and is seen as having special powers. In traditional authority, one believes in the authority of precedents and the natural succession of power from one generation or group to another. Within the rational form, authority is gained through regularized, orderly appointments and legal mechanisms based on universal principles, and the particular leader is interchangeable with another who fulfills the appropriate rational qualifications. No surrogate is imaginable for the seemingly unique charismatic leader.[3] Charisma should be contrasted with the other two forms by virtue of the fact that the former implies change and the latter implies order. In charisma there is a rejection of the routine, a disruption of the status quo and an innovation of new forms of authority into society; in tradition and rationality the authority preserves continuity and routine.[4] Demanding new obligations, the charismatic leader disrupts existing forms of authority such as law and religion, and similarly these forms mitigate against the emergence of charismatic leadership.

These are only a few of the specific qualities Weber discussed, and one must keep in mind that Weber spoke in terms of ideal types, of which reality is only an approximation. Charisma is presented in its purest possible form against which Weber uses examples to highlight his points. The leader who embodies everything Weber has to say about charisma does not exist. Therefore, a discussion of a particular case helps to illustrate the points of lack of fit between the ideal type and the real case. Moreover, in his formulation of established charismatic leadership, Weber himself included systematic examination of individual empirical cases, from which he generated concepts and a theoretical framework. His theory of charisma clarified the general process by which social movements develop, but the particular

3. See Paul Honigsheim, *On Max Weber* (New York, 1968), p. 117.
4. See Shils, "Charisma, Order and Status," pp. 199–213.

case extends and modifies the theory with its specific facts. This method of mutual refinement enhances the meaningful interpretation of cases as well as the proper grounding of theory.

In such a way Weber's theory of charisma can be refined by examining the specific case of Theodor Herzl (1860–1904). Similarly, Herzl's acquisition of legitimate authority can be elucidated by utilizing the analytic framework of Weber's theory. To accomplish these mutual goals, this study begins with a brief survey of the historical context of Herzl's ideology—political Zionism—stressing both its continuity with traditional Jewish strivings and its uniqueness as a solution to contemporary antisemitism. An account of the evolution of Herzl's ideology follows in the form of a description of his pre-Zionist years. The emergence of his revolutionary fervor is traced through an initial sensitizing period, dormancy, maturation, and dedication. Once the ideology had crystallized, Herzl became a man possessed by "the word" and compelled to amass adherents. We discuss his search for recognition and believers, the birth of his charismatic leadership. Through the use of his diaries and the memoirs of other people we are able to find confirming examples of Weber's characterizations of charismatic leaders, e.g., being considered insane and adherents' focus on a leader's physical appearance. Herzl's eventual reception by others as the messenger he knew himself to be resulted in his formation of a movement. We suggest that it was partially the lack of other forms of authority binding the world-wide Jewish community that permitted him to ascend to leadership. Charisma as a disruptive force is fragile and quickly disintegrates into the stable forms. This too will be seen in Herzl's case, for he concurrently set out to institutionalize his leadership as he sought to accomplish and spread his message. Although we trace his development only to his launching of the movement and not through its establishment and eventual success, we include a discussion of two concepts which Weber treated in conjunction with established charismatic leadership: its relation to economy and to bureaucracy.

There is one additional feature which makes the discussion of charisma within the context of Jewish history rather special. Within the Jewish religion and culture, although people are understood as having been created in the image of the supernatural being, there is also a sharp cleavage between God and Man with customs designed to demonstrate that difference. The force behind events is supposed to be God's or his personification in the Messiah, but not our own. Some unusual men and women are prophets, perhaps, vehicles of God's will, but not gods themselves. In other words, a sanction prevails within Judaism against the formation of cults surrounding an individual, against hero worship. Even great figures are cut down to size by cynicism and criticism, so that unlike Jesus, Stalin, or Mao Tse-tung, for example, Weizmann or Ben Gurion could never become idols or personifications of God's will. Herzl's attainment of charismatic leadership overcame even the resistance of this deeply rooted cultural tendency. As such it was an extraordinary achievement. But his ambivalence to being admired and hailed as a savior, rooted as it was in his own culture, was one of the psychological components of the rapid institutionalization of his personal power through the establishment of a bureaucracy. With the creation of this organization, other men and women were able to challenge his ideas, denying therefore that his power transcended criticism. He so successfully displaced his personal charisma onto the ideology itself that when his aspirations were posthumously fulfilled with the creation of the State of Israel, a personality cult did not arise even while recognition of his contributions did.

I. *Historical Context*

The revolutionary movement under consideration is political Zionism. The term "revolutionary" refers to three conditions: (1) the group membership itself was never before assembled or organized as a movement; (2) the ideology is original; and (3) the aims demand a disruption of the status quo and an ushering in of a new age. Examination of political Zionism's historical context clearly demonstrates that the movement was indeed revolutionary.

Since the exile and dispersion of the Jews from Palestine in 70 c.e., they had never lived as a united people in one territory, and instead were scattered throughout the world. Jewish life persisted as a function of the community rather than as part of a world-wide organization such as the bureaucratic hierarchy of the Catholic church. The political Zionists at the turn of the century ended this 1800-year era by creating a world parliament for Jews in which all Jews would be represented. The political Zionist movement must be considered revolutionary, therefore, as the reunifier of the Jewish people.

The group's goals were to become the internationally recognized spokesman of the Jewish people (in the status of an extraterritorial political entity), and to secure a territory in which the reunified people would establish a national home. This politicization of the Jewish people was an entirely original idea because the Jews had been considered (primarily by Gentiles and often by themselves as well) a religious-ethnic group which clearly had national characteristics, but was nevertheless apolitical in the modern sense of the word.

The nationalist movements and the efforts of Western European nation-states to unify the segments of society that resided in a certain territory brought to an end the autonomous status of the medieval Jew. As part of the liberal nationalist trend, culminating in the French Revolution and spreading over Europe with the armies of Napoleon, the Jews came to be considered equal citizens of a different religion—at least as far as the law was concerned. Their social and legal autonomy ended as they integrated themselves into their respective national units. This policy, known as the "Emancipation of the Jews," was successful to the extent that it destroyed the corporate powers of the Jewish communities and created an assimilationist trend among Jews who strove to "deserve" the rights bestowed on them by the Gentile community. The Jews were unsuccessful, however, in becoming mere citizens of a different religion, and a reactionary movement developed in response to the Emancipation: political antisemitism.

Traditional antisemitism took the form of an anti-Judaism sentiment, which accused the Jews of blasphemy, paganism, and the killing of Christ. The modern form of antisemitism was an anti-Jewish-people spirit, which included allegations of an international Jewish conspiracy designed to undermine national governments. This brand of antisemitism denied the Jews the privilege of sincere patriotism. Theodor Herzl recognized that this antisemitic attitude complemented the yearning of the Jews to return to Zion as expressed in traditional prayers. He combatted political antisemitism by fulfilling its allegations: he created an international organization and thereby created an alternative nationalism.

Jews, especially assimilationists, actively participated in the European nationalist movements. Political antisemitism, however, demonstrated that no degree of nationalist sentiment would ensure the rights in practice which had been granted on paper; Herzl recognized that this antisemitism was not a fleeting phenomenon to be remedied by increased patriotic fervor.

During the period of the Western European nationalist upheavals, the Jews of Eastern Europe, especially Poland and Russia, continued to live in isolated communities. They had not been emancipated at the time of the Western European emancipations, and they therefore remained politically naive as well as less voluntarily committed to their governments than were their western counterparts. The Eastern Jews were harrassed by the traditional type of Jew-baiting (pogroms, blood libels, economic oppression). Since the mid-nineteenth century, small groups of Jewish intellectuals escaped Russian persecution by emigrating to Western Europe and later to Palestine. These groups, however, did not form an ideologically nationalist Jewish movement, but they did respond enthusiastically to the movement once it was created on their behalf in Vienna, Berlin, Paris, and London.

The political Zionists revolutionized the Jewish as well as the Gentile definition of Jews by introducing the idea of political nationhood. They argued that a people is defined not only by itself but by those with whom it is in contact. If the outside world erroneously considered the Jews a politically unified people, then antisemitism could be turned on its head—Jews could indeed become unified! If the non-Jewish world considered them a nation as well as a distinctive religious group, then bonds must be created to supplement the religious-ethnic ones. And finally, if the world considered the Jews a nation, then the Jews should demand the logical consequences of that definition, i.e., they should be granted a territory in which they would be sovereign.

Theodor Herzl and the revolutionary political Zionists aimed for an upheaval within Jewish history as well as in international affairs. They hoped to add a new nation to the world of nations, a new sense of identity to the Jewish people, and a new solution to the old problem of Jew-baiting which had become the modern problem of antisemitism. For these reasons it is proper to consider the movement revolutionary. The political Zionists applied to the Jews the same goals and principles which they had learned as enthusiastic participants in other nationalist upheavals.

Frequently when "the time is ripe" for the emergence of an idea, that idea appears in various places simultaneously (especially evident in the history of science). A little more than a decade before Herzl developed his concept of political Zionism, a Russian, Leo Pinsker (1821–91), published the pamphlet "Autoemancipation" which advocated a similar solution to the problems which antisemitism posed. He had been an assimilated Jew and an ardent Russian patriot who believed that a constitutional monarchy would eventually bring to Russia equal rights for Jews and Gentiles. The horrendous pogroms of 1881, however, shattered his faith in the gradual liberalization of the Russian people, and he turned instead to the Jews themselves to provide a remedy for the intolerable persecutions which they suffered. He argued that the Jews could no longer live anywhere in a minority position, and that in order to form a majority, they would have to concentrate themselves in a Jewish national state.

Leo Pinsker and Moshe Lilienblum (1843–1910)—among others—were successful in establishing the *Hibbat Zion* organization which sponsored the colonization of Palestine. They seized upon the idea of a nationalist solution to the "Jewish Question" almost simultaneously with Herzl, yet the Russian attempt did not result in a viable movement toward the fulfillment of their goals, while Herzl's did. Similar ideas were expressed in the West by Moses Hess (1812-75), a German revolutionary, closely associated with Marx and Engels. In his book *Rome and Jerusalem* (1862), he urged Jews to recognize their nationality and work for its regeneration by keeping alive the hope of a political rebirth. Moses Hess, however, did not start a political movement toward this end.[5] Granted that these ideas are the logical consequence of historical developments, why was Herzl able to seize them and contribute substantially to their translation into reality? The particular convergence of historical, sociological, and psychological characteristics in Herzl's case can offer an explanation.

II. *Development of Sensitivities and Abilities*

Theodor Herzl was born in Budapest, the son of a rich merchant and a cultured mother. His parents early inspired confidence in him, encouraging him in his studies in the Jewish Elementary School and in the technical high school (*Realschule*). At thirteen he organized a group of friends in a "Wir" society dedicated "to enrich our knowledge, to make progress in the use of the language, and to perfect the style."[6] As president, Herzl was responsible for the club's rules and regulations as well as for the majority of its literary contributions. In these early experiences he experimented with his inclination toward leadership and literature.

The essays which Herzl presented to "Wir" concerned the relations of members of different religions to each other, the relation between church and state, and the importance of faith in noble ideas. Although his moral heroes came from Gentile rather than Jewish history, he was extremely sensitive to derogation of his religion. When his *Realschule* teacher defined Jews and Moslems as heathens, Herzl decided to transfer schools. He wrote:

5. For an analysis of the precursors of Zionism, especially Moses Hess, Jehuda Alkalay, and Zvi H. Kalischer, see Jacob Katz, "The Jewish National Movement: A Sociological Analysis," in H. H. Ben Sasson and S. Ettinger (eds.), *Jewish Society through the Ages* (New York, 1971), pp. 267-83. For some general assessments of the forerunners of Zionism in the East and West, see Nathan Birnbaum, *Ausgewählte Schriften zur jüdischen Frage* (Czernowitz, 1910); Max Bodenheimer, *So Wurde Israel* (Frankfurt, 1958); R. Brainin, *Peretz Smolenskin* (Warsaw, 1896); S. L. Citron, *Toledot Hibbat Tziyyon* (Odessa, 1914); B. Dinaburg, *Hibbat Tziyyon* (Tel Aviv, 1922-24); N. M. Gelber, *Vorgeschichte des Zionismus* (Vienna, 1927); Israel Klausner, *Hibbat Tziyyon be-Rumania* (Jerusalem, 1948); idem, *Ha-Tenuᶜah le-Tziyyon be-Russia* (Jerusalem, 1962); Richard Lichtheim, *Die Geschichte des deutschen Zionismus* (Jerusalem, 1954); Edmund Silberner, *Moses Hess. Geschichte seines Lebens* (Leiden, 1966); Nahum Sokolow, *Hibbat Tziyyon* (Jerusalem, 1935); and David Vital, *The Origins of Zionism* (Oxford, 1975).

6. Joseph Patai, "Herzl's School Years," *Herzl Year Book*, III (New York, 1960), 59.

After this peculiar definition, I had quite enough of the Realschule and wanted to become a classical scholar. My good father never constrained me into a narrow groove for my studies and I became a pupil of the gymnasium. At the gymnasium which was called the Evangelisches Gymnasium, the Jewish boys formed the majority, and therefore we had not to complain of any *Judenhetze*.[7]

Even as a boy Herzl understood the relation between minority status and security, demonstrated sensitivity to his position as a Jew in a supposedly liberal society, and displayed great energy which he channeled into prolific writing. He showed the propensity to act on that which disturbed him and to organize around him that which interested him.

After the death of his sister, the Herzl family moved to Vienna where Herzl entered the university to study law. Student organizations in Vienna of the 1800s were undergoing major changes in the directions of radical nationalism and antisemitism, chiefly under the influence of Deputy Ritter von Schoenerer. The single exclusively Jewish club was strictly assimilationist. Despite the fact that the Jewish members of the other clubs enthusiastically espoused assimilationism and German nationalism, often admitting to antisemitism themselves, they were gradually expelled. The liberal "corporations" were the only ones that retained a few Jewish members, and that only temporarily. These academic clubs assumed much importance in the lives of university students—as an arena for the highly significant activities of dueling, drinking, and debating.

At first Herzl participated energetically in the "Albia" club, where he was one of three Jewish members. But gradually even this liberal group became too nationalist for him. Antisemitism became the primary topic of literature and discussion. Eager to understand this phenomenon, Herzl read Eugen Dühring's *The Jewish Problem as a Problem of Race, Morals, and Culture* (1881).[8]

In January 1882 Herzl began a diary which records the struggle of the young law student-litterateur. Early entries in the diary comment on the antisemitic books he read and thereby reveal his attitudes toward Jewish-Gentile relations:

An infamous book. . . . If Dühring, who unites so much undeniable intelligence with so much universality of knowledge, can write like this, what are we to expect from the ignorant masses? The hunger for loot is the base, stinking motive of all movements against the Jews; the cen-

7. Ibid., p. 73.
8. Joseph Fraenkel, *Theodore Herzl* (New York, 1949), p. 26.

turies have brought no change into this Christian morality. . . . But even these nursery tales of the Jewish people will disappear, and a new age will follow, in which a passionless and clear-headed humanity will look back upon our errors even as the enlightened men of our time look back upon the Middle Ages.[9]

Herzl's initial repugnance to even subtle antisemitism gave rise during his student days to a complete personal alignment with the Jewish people and a fascination with the intricacies of the Jewish question. His disgust with his antisemitic environment culminated in his resignation from "Albia" in response to its approval of a passionately antisemitic speech delivered by Hermann Bahr at the memorial to Richard Wagner. A fellow Jewish member in the "Albia" reacted to the change in events by committing suicide rather than face expulsion.

These experiences afforded Herzl the opportunity of speaking in public, of undergoing the wrenching alienation of a psychologically tormented Jew, and of examining closely the attitudes and behaviors of the liberals and reactionaries. Clearly Herzl was torn between acknowledging the upsurgence of antisemitism and retaining his faith in the "enlightened era." The dissonance depressed him and contributed to his turning inward to find comfort in profuse reading, writing, and introspection. He seems to have been less angered by insults to his pride as a Jew than disappointed by the degradation of enlightened men of his time.

III. *The Dormant Period*

After being admitted to the bar, Herzl spent only one year in law service to the state. His drive for fame, fortune, and prestige, unrealizable as a Jew in the legal profession, led to his renunciation of law and his turning to full-time writing. He experienced both the sobering impact of legal procedures and the liberating, if insecure, life-style of a litterateur. His feuilletons from his extensive travels won him considerable success, leading to the enviable position of feuilleton editor of the Viennese *Neue Freie Presse*, one of the most influential papers in Europe.

Herzl's concern with antisemitism receded as he delighted in being admitted to fashionable society, in traveling widely, and in having his plays produced in European theaters. He grew detached from those people with

9. Bein, *Theodore Herzl*, pp. 37–38.

whom brotherhood was a source of pain. "Yesterday there was a grande soirée at Treitel's," he wrote, "thirty or forty ugly little Jews and Jewesses. Not a very refreshing sight."[10] On his journeys he glimpsed the impoverished Jewish masses of Italian ghettos and felt sincere, but detached, sympathy. "What a steaming in the air, what a street! Countless open doors and windows thronged with innumerable pallid and worn-out faces. The ghetto! With what base and persistent hatred these unfortunates have been persecuted for the sole crime of faithfulness to their religion. We've travelled a long way since those times: nowadays the Jew is despised only for having a crooked nose, or for being a plutocrat even when he happens to be a pauper."[11]

His faith in modern man blurred the conditions before his eyes. A further illustration of Herzl's retreat into dormancy or self-deception during this period is given in an incident which occurred in Belgium. "I dropped in one evening at a cheap concert hall, drank my glass of beer and began to make my way out. As I was moving through the noisy room a young lad shouted 'Hep! Hep!' after me, and a tumult rose around him."[12] This scene was not recorded soon after it occurred, probably because it was too dissonant with Herzl's humanistic faith. Instead, the repressed experience returned to consciousness after Herzl later relinquished this faith in the liberal tradition.

Before receiving the post on the *Neue Freie Presse*, Herzl married Julie Naschauer with whom he had an unsuccessful relationship, resulting in a series of separations. Although legally married, Herzl lived a life quite free of daily familial obligations which might have distracted him from complete dedication to the movement he founded soon after his marriage.[13]

IV. *Maturation of an Idea*

After considerable literary success Herzl earned the position of Paris correspondent for his newspaper and thereby became deeply involved in the

10. Ibid., p. 49.
11. Ibid., p. 57.
12. Ibid., p. 60.
13. An interesting examination of the relation between "singleness" and leadership (esp. charismatic) is found in an essay of the psychiatrist Raymond Headlee: "At this stage of our knowledge about charisma, the dangers inherent in the charismatic position extend over a number of areas. The amount of energy required to maintain even the appearance of charisma is considerable, as any clinician who has treated exhausted persons of this sort must know. A corollary of this is the absorption into charisma to the neglect of all other areas of personal life. Such absorption may suit those who have some fear of more ordinary relationships, like marriage, or those who simply fear women" ("The Nature and Nurture of Charisma," mimeo [1968], p. 6). Herzl always remained the loving son of his parents rather than the loving husband of his wife.

reporting of French domestic and foreign political developments. In Paris his light-hearted, literary period ended with his serious reconsideration of the problems that had previously bothered him. At that time French Jews were under attack by Eduard Drumont whose *La France Juive* (1885) became a nineteenth-century bestseller. The antisemitism that Herzl had encountered vividly in Vienna had its parallel in turn-of-the-century France, and as a journalist Herzl was committed to studying it closely. His reports on the infamous scandals and incidents falsely denouncing Jews led to his lengthy newspaper report entitled "French Anti-Semitism."[14] His articles revealed an increasing preoccupation with social problems almost to the exclusion of his literary interests. He developed the ability to concentrate his energies around one theme, shedding the extraneous aspects of his life.

As Herzl focused sharply on the problem of antisemitism, he experimented with the possibility of several different solutions. Romantically he considered challenging von Schoenerer or Karl Lueger, the antisemitic mayor of Vienna, to a duel and then having a posthumous letter published informing the world that he had sacrificed himself "to the most unjust movement in the world."

> If, however, it had been my lot to kill my opponent and be brought to trial, then I would have delivered a brilliant speech which would have begun with my regrets for the death of a man of honor—after the fashion of Môrès, who killed Captain Mayer. Then I would have turned to the Jewish question and delivered an oration worthy of Lassalle. I would have sent a shudder of admiration through the jury. I would have compelled the respect of the judges, and the case against me would have been dismissed. Thereupon the Jews would have me as one of their representatives and I would have declined because I would refuse to achieve such a position by the killing of a man.[15]

His theatrical background informed his magical conception of vanquishing his enemies. The "Jewish Problem" would allow him to be the leader he wanted to be. Herzl, the dreamer and moralist, was prepared to act, but he lacked a realistic plan.

> To remedy this situation, two possibilities suggest themselves to me. 1. The fight with brutal force against the symptoms. Half a dozen duels would considerably elevate the social position of the Jews. 2. The curative process of the evil. The Jews must rid themselves of characteristics for which they are justly rebuked. Because one is inclined to consider

14. Bein, *Theodore Herzl*, p. 85.
15. Ibid., p. 88.

them as worse than they actually are, they are compelled to turn the prejudice into the reverse.[16]

As late as 1893 Herzl's only answer to the "Jewish Question" was complete assimilation by baptism or intermarriage. The Jew should not merely change his religion but rather "submerge in the people" to put an end to his "living perpetually in enemy territory."[17] The "Jewish Question" would disappear only with the disappearance of the Jew. Toward this end he even planned to address the pope: "Help us against anti-Semitism, and I in return will lead a great movement amongst the Jews for voluntary and honorable conversion to Christianity."[18]

The bizarre plans which Herzl developed represent an imagination desperately seeking a program to alleviate the oppressive psychological and social conditions under which Jews lived. He was so seriously involved with the problem, so overwhelmed by it, that he considered solutions which bordered on the absurd. Neither cautious nor timid in his thinking, he was not yet ready to share his dreams but confided them to his diary alone.

Another solution of his pre-Zionist period encouraged Jewish espousal of the socialist movement to reduce persecution by those accusing Jews of abetting revolutionary parties. "If one cannot suppress a movement [anti-semitism], one reacts with another movement. By that I simply mean Socialism. It is my conviction that the Jews, pressed against the wall, will have nothing other than Socialism."[19] "There is a Jewish question, there can be no doubt about it. Those who deny it are wrong."[20] The solution of the Jewish question in Germany was available in the Jewish conversion to Socialism. As Herzl struggled for logical alternatives to the status quo, the Dreyfus trial erupted in Paris, revealing the extent to which antisemitism was rooted in France.

v. *Revelation*

On January 5, 1895, Herzl observed the public degradation ceremonies of Captain Dreyfus, which served as a traumatic experience compelling Herzl to a full recognition of popular sentiment. The crowd watching with Herzl

16. Chaim Bloch, "Herzl's First Years of Struggle: Unknown Episodes and Personal Recollections," *Herzl Year Book*, III (1960), 78.

17. Ibid.

18. Bein, *Theodore Herzl*, p. 94.

19. Bloch, "Herzl's First Years," p. 79.

20. Bein, *Theodore Herzl*, p. 94.

yelled "A mort! A mort les juifs!" because they believed one Jew had committed a crime. Herzl felt that

> the Dreyfus case embodies more than a judicial error; it embodies the desire of the vast majority of the French to condemn a Jew, and to condemn all Jews in this one Jew. Death to the Jews! howled the mob, as the decorations were being ripped from the captain's coat. . . . Where? In France. In republican, modern civilized France, a hundred years after the Declaration of the Rights of Man. The French people, or at any rate the greater part of the French people, does not want to extend the rights of man to Jews. The edict of the great Revolution has been revoked.[21]

This occasion led Herzl to a final choice between the two ideas which he had alternately upheld: he rejected faith in the ultimate good will of man as the solution of the problem of antisemitism; and he accepted the fact that the Jews must themselves create a new solution. In retrospect he said:

> Until that time most of us believed that the solution of the Jewish question was to be patiently waited for as part of the general development of mankind. But when a people which in every other respect is so progressive and so highly civilized can take such a turn, what are we to expect from other peoples, which have not even attained the level which France attained a hundred years ago?[22]

Watching the crowds, he abandoned hope in the French people. His turmoil expressed itself in anger, frustration, and ultimately action. Abandoning emancipation, assimilation, conversion, and socialism as solutions to the problem of antisemitism, he energetically advocated the reunification and return of the Jewish nation to a territory of its own.

In the course of Herzl's short life, and especially after his death, a legend arose about the manner in which he dedicated himself to Zionism. He was attributed with undergoing a radical conversion similar to Moses, Paul, Buddha, and Mohammed, from a state of complete lack of concern to utter dedication. Many of Herzl's biographers[23] claim that he became aware of his life's mission fortuitously and spontaneously, although it is obvious from an examination of his diaries that the concern was deep-rooted and its development gradual. The Dreyfus trial was not the impetus for Herzl's desire to help the Jews; instead it was the culmination of years of discomfort which triggered his specific plan. The "Affaire" was one of many experiences that

21. Ibid., p. 116.
22. Ibid.
23. Fraenkel, *Theodore Herzl*, p. 44; and Bloch, "Herzl's First Years," p. 77.

contributed to the maturation of Herzl's sensitivities and ideas. It produced his final disillusionment and revived long-buried memories of unpleasant antisemitic incidents and significant feelings of closeness to the Jews as a people. The Dreyfus Affair was a traumatic event for Herzl in the sense that its impact led to a reshuffling of his values and a reorientation of his thought. This "crisis of disillusionment"[24] redirected his energies from his work in the mundane world to work carried on as part of a mission.

Four months after the degradation scene, Herzl began recording his Zionist activities—from the first crystallization of the idea until a few days before his death. The opening paragraphs demonstrate the process of change which his personality underwent. He began to dissociate himself from his former journalist and litterateur selves in the process of forming an identity which would devote itself to a new idea. He hoped to divorce himself from the life of the written word and embark instead on a new life of action. No longer would he report others' activities, rather he would be engaged in activities which others would report: "But what are the experiences of a newspaper correspondent compared with what I am now working on! What dreams, thoughts, letters, meetings, actions I shall have to live through—disappointments if nothing comes of it, terrible struggles if things work out."[25] In characteristically introspective manner,[26] he searched immediately for the origins of his new commitment.

> When did I actually begin to concern myself with the Jewish question? Probably ever since it arose; certainly from the time that I read Dühring's book. In one of my old notebooks, now packed away somewhere in Vienna, are my first observations on Dühring's book and on the Question. At that time I still had no newspaper as an outlet for my writings. . . . As the years went on, the Jewish question bored into me and gnawed at me, tormented me and made me very miserable. In fact, I kept coming back to it whenever my own personal experiences—joys and sorrows—permitted me to rise to broader considerations.[27]

This first diary entry represents Herzl's self-affirmation as "possessor of the word." He formulated his prophecy in a moment of supreme excitement and intoxication. This formulation was a combination of insight and revela-

24. Ben Halpern, *The Idea of the Jewish State*, 2nd ed. (Cambridge, Mass., 1969), p. 63.

25. All quotes from Herzl's diaries rely on *The Complete Diaries of Theodor Herzl*, ed. Raphael Patai, trans. Harry Zohn, 5 vols. (New York, 1960). Hereafter cited as *Complete Diaries*. Here: *Complete Diaries*, I:3–4.

26. Ben Halpern, "Herzl's Historic Gift: The Sense of Sovereignty," *Herzl Year Book*, III (1960), 28: "Herzl was a true charismatic leader in this, too, that he was fascinated by the unfolding of his own legend; which in a way was for him a revelation of the true self he had sought in mounting frustration in years past."

27. *Complete Diaries*, I:4.

tion; he acknowledged that he was immersed in an atmosphere of mystery. It is important to note that the process of discovery is separate from the substantive content of the discovery. Whereas the content is a rational resolution of the problems carefully considered during his nearly thirty-five years, the manner in which the ideas were grasped is not through the process of logical argument, but through insight or revelation. Like most prophets, the origins of Herzl's teaching are shrouded in mystery:

> For some time past I have been occupied with a work of infinite grandeur. At the moment I do not know whether I shall carry it through. It looks like a mighty dream. But for days and weeks it has possessed me beyond the limits of consciousness; it accompanies me wherever I go, hovers behind my ordinary talk, looks over my shoulder at my comically trivial journalistic work, disturbs me and intoxicates me. It is still too early to surmise what will come of it. But my experience tells me that even as a dream it is something remarkable, and that I ought to write it down—if not as a reminder to mankind, then at least for my own delight or reflection in later years. And perhaps as something between these two possibilities—that is, as literature. If my conception is not translated into reality, at least out of my activity can come a novel.[28]

vi. *Searching for a Format*

Herzl understood that when he spoke or wrote, he represented himself alone. As an editor of the *Neue Freie Presse* he attempted to exercise power and influence policy. But the two publishers, Benedikt and Bacher, assimilated Jews who feared Herzl's converting their paper into a "Judenblatt," rejected his ideas and even denied him the right to mention his Zionist work in his articles. As he abandoned hope of using the newspaper as an instrument of power, he simultaneously abandoned the idea for which he had proposed to use the paper: papal intervention against antisemitism.

He returned to his own resources and decided to write a play which would help clarify his thoughts and would become a means of communicating with the vast audience he needed. The physical act of writing was intended as relief from the psychological torment and excitement that accompanied his attempts to express his radical plans.

> I became quite heated as I talked, and when I left, my excitement still glowed in me. With the swiftness of that dream involving a pitcher of

28. Ibid., I:3.

water in the Arabian fairy-tale, the outline of the play came into being. I believe I hadn't gone from the Rue Descombes to the Place Péreire when the whole thing was already finished in my mind.

The next day I set to work. Three blessed weeks of ardor and labor. I had thought that through this eruption of playwriting I had written myself free of the matter. On the contrary; I got more and more deeply involved with it. The thought grew stronger in me that I must do something for the Jews. During these days I was more than once afraid that I was going out of my mind. So furiously did the cataract of thoughts race through my soul. A lifetime will not suffice to put everything down. But I am leaving behind me a spiritual legacy. For whom? For all men. I believe that I shall be among the great benefactors of mankind. Or is this feeling of mine the beginning of delusions of grandeur?[29]

The idea seemed to exist outside him and to gradually take possession of him. The plan for the play was replaced by a novel, which was discarded for a political pamphlet, "The Jews' State." The atmosphere of mystery still clung to him: "How I proceeded from the idea of writing a novel to a practical program is already a mystery to me, although it happened within the last few weeks. It is in the realm of the Unconscious. Perhaps these ideas are not practical ones at all and I am only making myself the laughing-stock of the people to whom I talk about it seriously. Could I be only a figure in my novel?"[30]

Herzl considered the best forms of government to be those in which there is a contrast with the form of state: aristocratic republic and democratic monarchy.[31] Observation of the mass hysteria connected with the "Affaire Dreyfus" had made him wary of popular governmental control and uncontrolled mass power. On the other hand, he understood that the driving force behind the creation of the Jewish state would not be rational, legal, or economic. Rather it would be the driving force of despair, as he called it, "the Jewish tragedy, the crying need of the Jewish people."[32] He planned therefore to channel this need into careful diplomatic action before allowing himself to lead a mass movement. He presented his position in *The Jews' State: An Attempt at a Modern Solution of the Jewish Question:* "The Jewish question exists. It would be stupid to deny it. I think the Jewish question is no more a social than a religious one, notwithstanding that it takes these and other forms. It is a national question, which can only be solved by making it a political-world question to be discussed and settled by the civilized nations of the world in

29. Ibid., I:11.
30. Ibid., I:13.
31. Bein, *Theodore Herzl*, p. 147.
32. Ibid., p. 151.

council."[33] Because of Herzl's fame as staff member of the *Neue Freie Presse*, the publication of his pamphlet in Vienna (February 14, 1896) made a great impact.

Herzl emerged from this crisis of confusion and rebirth as a man who considered himself to have a personal mission but was unsure of the means with which he should act. The problem is to discover how Herzl was able to progress from the moment when he formulated the idea and the mission, to the moment when he was recognized by a following as the carrier of the idea, as their leader-prophet.

The psychological and cognitive processes which Herzl underwent correspond to Weber's formulation of the development of the potentially charismatic leader. Weber analyzed this concept in the framework of the contrast between the emergence of revolutionary forces by way of reason and by way of charismatic leadership. In the case of the revolutionary force of reason, an individual is intellectually stimulated to change his attitudes toward specific problems. In the case of charisma, the emergence of the revolutionary idea occurs through a subjective process of "internal reorientation born out of suffering, conflicts, or enthusiasm. It may then result in a radical alteration of the central system of attitudes and directions of action with a completely new orientation of all attitudes toward the different problems and structures of the 'world.'"[34] In other words, the rethinking that occurs is typically not limited to a specific problem but is generalized to include a reorientation of the entire value system. The charismatic leader seeks to change the moral order, the social structure, or the entire political system, for example, instead of a limited problem within these systems. This process functions to loosen the former authority which was vested in the world's structures and arrangements and provides the charismatic leader with the intellectual freedom and flexibility to experiment with new arrangements. The new solution to old problems in the revolutionary idea carries the authority of enthusiastic, subjective conviction born of personal distress. In this way, the charismatic leader is the instrument of extensive change.

VII. *Herzl's Qualities of Leadership*

A revolutionary leader is an agent of change: he is one of the dynamics of history. There are two ways, however, in which such a person effects the "breakthrough." He can recognize a movement that is beginning or has

---

33. Herzl, *Der Judenstaat*, in *Theodor Herzls Zionistische Schriften*, ed. Leon Kellner (Berlin, 1920), p. 47.
34. Weber, *Social and Economic Organization*, p. 363.

developed substantially, seize its leadership, and thereby give it added force and a new, personal direction. Such a person responds to the process of change and then vitalizes it by creating a focus in his own leadership. In this situation, the movement, loosely organized in a typical instance, already exists and the followers wait for a leader to appear. When he does appear, he occupies the position that has been prepared; the expectant followers rally to their awaited leader.

The second type of leader has an even more prodigious task. He actually creates the new idea and then draws adherents. Such an individual does not assume the leadership of an already interested group but rather rejects the status quo, develops (or "receives") a new idea, and by virtue of this possession of the idea, spontaneously becomes the leader of those who acknowledge him and find salvation in the message. Herzl seems to personify this second mode of leadership. True, the idea of the return of the Jews had existed since the dispersion, but the plan to establish a world body to represent the Jews and to establish a political Jewish state had not been voiced before. Nor was there any positive sentiment towards these political goals at the time Herzl first advocated them (with the exception of a few individuals such as Leo Pinsker).[35] Herzl did not step into a preexisting position of leadership; there was no group waiting for him to engage in diplomatic maneuvers with the world powers or to organize the various kinds of Jews (although the *Hibbat Zion* movement did exist and formed the nucleus of the Zionist movement in Eastern Europe which later supported him). There was no institution to which he could appeal for assistance, present his ideas for consideration, or offer his alliance. Psychologically, he was compelled to communicate his ideas. He craved authority, but the typical source, the bureaucratic institution, was unavailable. He would have to make a personal appeal and create an institution of his own. To his advantage was the fact that he had developed a personal reputation; he was well-known and respected in the cultural circles of Western Europe. In addition, he possessed qualities which would assist him in public work. Stefan Zweig writes, "The man was strikingly handsome—courteous, obliging, entertaining; indeed, none was more beloved, better known or more celebrated than he among the entire bourgeoisie—and also the aristocracy—of old Austria.[36]

35. Walter Laqueur sums up well why Pinsker was not able to achieve what Herzl did: "When Pinsker wrote *Autoemanzipation*, he was past sixty, and much as Zionism became the centre of his life, he lacked the dynamism of youth, and also the ambition and vanity which were so characteristic of Herzl. The time was ripe, but he could not and would not be the new Moses. 'History,' he once wrote, 'does not grant a people such guides repeatedly.' Pinsker's name figures larger in the history of ideas than in the history of Jewish politics. The immediate political impact of his work was limited; not many were converted to Zionism as the result of reading *Autoemanzipation*" (*A History of Zionism* [New York, 1972] , p. 74).

36. Stefan Zweig, "King of the Jews," *Herzl Year Book*, III (1960), 110.

Herzl spoke clearly and simply, demonstrating his ability to present an uncomplicated and concise interpretation of the problem and the solution. He grasped the myriad complexities of the issues that he had reviewed for years, and he discovered the unifying theme that provided the solution. His lucidity is apparent in these opening sentences of the conversation with Baron de Hirsch whom he approached for support:

Throughout our two thousand years of dispersion, we have been without unified political leadership. I regard this as our chief misfortune. It has done us more harm than all the persecutions. . . .

If we had such leadership, we could tackle the solution of the Jewish question. . . .

The aim that we will pursue once we have a center, a head, will determine the means.

There are two possible aims: either we stay where we are or we emigrate somewhere else.

For either course we need certain identical measures for the education of our people. For even if we emigrate, it will be a long time before we arrive in the Promised Land. It took Moses forty years. We may require twenty or thirty. At any rate, in the meantime new generations will arise whom we must educate for our purposes. . . .

Whether the Jews stay put or whether they emigrate, the race must first be improved right on the spot. It must be made strong as for war, eager to work, and virtuous. Afterwards, let them emigrate—if necessary.[37]

The leader of a social movement who presents his ideas in a clear, simple fashion has an advantage in attracting and binding followers over one whose ideology is complex or vague. Simple sentences and concise thoughts often resemble slogans, and slogans are easily remembered, preserved, and glorified. This lucid style, achieved through years of literary work, characterized all of Herzl's speeches and writings. The unsophisticated masses of Eastern European Jewry as well as the intellectual circles of Vienna were fascinated by the self-confidence which Herzl exuded through his straightforward (and sometimes objectionable) ideas. Herzl was a man who believed in the power of ideas. These ideas never lacked an element of glorification, or what Herzl called, the visionary, reflecting himself as the prophet, the disrupter of the oppressive status quo, the creator of a new order. Herzl had no qualms about displaying this vision of grandeur. His confidence sprang from his sense of personal mission. The force of his experiences, observations, and the grow-

37. *Complete Diaries*, I:19–22.

ing pressure of antisemitism were his only credentials to perform his work in the face of opposition.

Herzl began early to recognize himself as the prophet, missionary, and revolutionary leader of the oppressed. This characteristic is not unique in Herzl's case. Great self-assurance is required to initiate and perpetuate a revolutionary movement. The leader must be certain of the true and imperative quality of his ideas. He must have supreme faith in himself. His judgment must then be confirmed by the response of followers who espouse him and his mission, but the initial conviction is personal. Self-recognition, then, is a component of the qualities that combine to create a charismatic leader. And this recognition must be accompanied by a relatively high degree of self-assurance. Robert Tucker recognized this quality in his study of charisma: "Although charismatic leaders may vary in type, there appear to be certain qualities common to them as a class. Notable among these is a peculiar sense of mission, comprising a belief both in the movement and in themselves as the chosen instrument to lead the movement to its destination."[38]

Another typical phenomenon connected with charismatic leadership is the need to prove a sincere commitment to oneself and one's followers by either a great sacrifice or a great risk of sacrifice. This proof can occur on the unconscious level or it may be specifically designed so that it may be demonstrated. In this context Herzl's relation to his newspaper, the *Neue Freie Presse*, is understandable. Herzl had informed its publishers of his new commitments and had read the manuscript to them, but as staunch assimilationists they would neither take up his cause nor permit him to mention Zionism in the paper. Herzl felt a deep allegiance to this paper, the epitome of his previous aspirations. He had even declined the position of head publisher of the official newspaper of Prime Minister Badini in favor of retaining his old post. While Herzl awaited publication of *The Jews' State*, he feared dismissal from the *Neue Freie Presse*. This risk-taking reaffirmed his role as prophet. Ten days before *The Jews' State* appeared he wrote in his diary: "Lay awake for hours during the night, reflecting about the situation at the "Neue Freie Presse" . . . I am staking a lot, my entire position."[39] The publishers of the paper pointed to Herzl's personal risks in an effort to dissuade him, but the thought of sacrifice encouraged him all the more: "He [Benedikt] said there was a personal danger for myself in that I was risking my established pres-

38. Robert C. Tucker, "The Theory of Charismatic Leadership," *Daedalus* (Summer 1968), p. 749.
39. *Complete Diaries*, I:291–92.

tige. By doing this I was also harming the paper, for among its assets was my literary reputation. Furthermore, I was in direct opposition to several principles of the "Neue Freie Presse." He wants me to refrain from publication. I answered: 'My honor is pledged. I have already published the idea in the "Jewish Chronicle." It no longer belongs to me, but to the Jews. If I kept silent now, I would endanger my reputation all the more.'"[40] Once established, the risk cannot be revoked without demonstrating that the leader is no leader at all, but a fraud and a coward. The confrontation inspired him with new courage which he expressed in very vigorous language: "Hanc veniam damus petimusque vicissim. Whoever slashes me I will slash. Je ne me laisserai pas faire. I'll fight hard. Those, however, who go with me will leave a name in history."[41]

VIII. *Reception: Positive and Negative*

Although Herzl did not claim to be "called" in a religious sense, he believed that his grasp of the connection between the Jewish problem and the political solution made him responsible for carrying out all the activities that the new solution implied. He acknowledged this duty in a personal sense: his powers of reason and his membership in the Jewish people had "called" him, had singled him out to become the spokesman for the new word. As Weber described pure charisma: "Whenever it appears, it constitutes a 'call' in the most emphatic sense of the word, a 'mission' or 'spiritual duty.'"[42] This sense of obligation combined with the enthralling prospects of "what the world would look like" should he succeed, obsessed Herzl to such a degree that his friends thought him mad, as most charismatic leaders appear: "Am I working it out? No! It is working itself out in me. It would be an obsession if it were not so rational from beginning to end. An earlier term for such a condition was 'inspiration.'"[43]

The special qualities of the charismatic leader are often misinterpreted, so that instead of being considered extraordinary, the person is thought abnormal. After having been discouraged in his appeal to the philanthropist Baron de Hirsch, Herzl turned to a friend, Friedrich Schiff, and revealed the manuscript containing his ideas. Herzl recorded the scene: "In the midst of the

40. Ibid., I:292.
41. Ibid., I:299.
42. Weber, *Social and Economic Organization*, p. 362.
43. *Complete Diaries*, I:95–96.

reading he suddenly burst into tears. . . . He thought that I had lost my mind."[44] Two years later Herzl wrote:

> And just like this man [Schiff], who once thought me insane, all the others who called me crazy will come round.[45] I must be prepared for this sort of thing [mockery]. The grown-up street urchins will be on my heels. But a man who is to carry the day in thirty years has to be considered crazy for the first two weeks.[46]

> I have the solution to the Jewish question, I know it sounds mad; and at the beginning I shall be called mad more than once—until the truth of what I am saying is recognized in all its shattering force.[47]

Schiff suggested that Herzl speak with Max Nordau, an eminent psychiatrist. Herzl introduced himself with the words: "Schiff says that I'm insane." Then he spent three days reading his manuscript to Nordau and discussing it with him. Nordau was "overcome and impressed. At last he rose and opened his arms to his trembling friend: 'If you are insane, we are insane together. Count on me!'"[48] Nordau virtually swore personal allegiance to Herzl and his ideas, so overcome was he by both Herzl's personality and the vision of salvation presented in the manuscript. Nordau thereby became the great disciple and follower of a man who represented no other authority than the force of his personality and ideas. To Nordau, Herzl became "the great prophet, the harbinger of a new age."[49] It must be remembered that those who encounter the charismatic leader believe him to have extraordinary qualities and capacities. This separateness enables the leader to stand apart from the conventional authority which informs people's behavior. Because the leader is "different" and preaches a new moral order, there is a disruption of the old forms of authority, i.e., revolutionary innovations. Weber wrote that "the 'natural' leaders in distress have been holders of specific gifts of the body and spirit; these gifts have been believed to be supernatural, not accessible to everybody."[50]

In Herzl's case much was made of his "extraordinary" physical appearance. In a recent biography, Amos Elon writes:

> So dignified were his personality and bearing, that together they often induced an almost religious awe. Many spoke to him with reverence

44. Ibid., I:113.
45. Ibid., II:649.
46. Ibid., I:300.
47. Bein, *Theodore Herzl*, pp. 139–40.
48. Anna and Maxa Nordau, *Max Nordau: A Biography* (New York, 1943), p. 120.
49. *Complete Diaries*, I:284.
50. Eisenstadt, ed., *Weber on Charisma and Institution Building*, p. 19.

even while they disagreed with him. His physical appearance seemed to take on unusual attributes in the minds of his beholders. Thus he was invariably described by his admirers as 'majestically tall,' towering over everyone. In his army medical examination papers, however, he is described as being of medium height; the French Prefecture de Police listed his height at five feet eight inches. And yet there cannot be any doubt that in the eyes of those who met him he appeared much taller.[51]

The following are some examples illustrating the fascination with his physical being as expressed by those who met him.

The first view of his face, seen from one side, made a deep impression upon me. It was a faultlessly handsome face. The soft, well-kept black beard gave it a clear, almost rectangular outline, into which the clean-cut nose, set exactly in the middle, fitted well, as did also the high, slightly rounded forehead. But this beauty—perhaps almost too regular, too much like a work of art—was deepened by the gentle almond-shaped eyes with their heavy black, melancholy lashes—ancient Oriental eyes in this somewhat French face in the style of Alphonse Daudet, in this face which would have seemed slightly artificial or effeminate, or suggestive of the beau, had not the thousand-year-old melancholy of his soul shone through it.[52]

A majestic Oriental figure, not so tall as it appears when he draws himself up and stands dominating the assembly with eyes that brood and glow—you would say one of the Assyrian Kings, whose sculptured heads adorn our museums, the very profile of Tiglath Pileser. . . . In a congress of impassioned rhetoricians he remains serene, moderate; his voice is for the most part subdued; in its most emotional abandonments there is a dry undertone, almost harsh. . . . And yet beneath all this statesmanlike prose, touched with the special dryness of a jurist, lurk the romance of the poet and the purposeful vagueness of the modern evolutionist; the fantasy of the Hungarian, the dramatic self-consciousness of the literary artist, the heart of the Jew.[53]

In his description of Herzl, Raoul Auernheimer, a member of the "young Vienna" circle of writers wrote from personal acquaintance:

He displayed a blend of ambitious romanticism, diplomatic realism, worldly wisdom, and fiery idealism. Herzl had the princely demeanor of

51. Elon, *Herzl*, p. 9.
52. Zweig, "King of the Jews," p. 112.
53. Israel Zangwill quoted in Marvin Lowenthal, *The Diaries of Theodor Herzl* (New York, 1962), pp. 215–16.

an instantly captivating personality. His blue-black beard, his dark, dreamy eyes, his full glance, his well-proportioned tall figure, his face with its noble pallor and the expressive features as though engraved in wax impressed themselves upon all those who met him as the most beautiful portrait in an art gallery does. I have never encountered a person of greater magic, nor anyone whose magic was embellished with so much grace.[54]

Similar statements come from Count (later Prince) Phillipp zu Eulenburg (1847–1921), Prussian courtier, diplomat, and literary dilettante, who was the intimate friend and advisor of Wilhelm II. Eulenburg recommended Herzl and Zionism to the Kaiser after being impressed by Herzl's extraordinary personality.

Undeniably, one of the most interesting personalities I ever met was Dr. Theodor Herzl, the leader of the Zionist movement. Herzl was not only an extraordinarily gifted man but he also made a great impression by his outward appearance: he is a tall man with a head resembling King David's, the prototype of a militant Jewish leader from the age of the Jewish kings, with no particle of the type we call 'trading Jew.' My association with this high-minded, selfless, distinguished man will remain in my memory forever.[55]

Kaiser Wilhelm II had this to say about Herzl: "A clever, very intelligent man with expressive eyes. Dr. Theodor Herzl decidedly was an enthusiastic idealist with an aristocratic mentality."[56] Herzl, therefore, was an imposing figure physically, intellectually, and spiritually.

Herzl's tasks were manifold: he had to communicate with, persuade, and unify the Jews from every country, every class, and every religious or ideological division. He had to convince or bargain with the national powers to support his efforts to secure land for the resettlement. He could not ask the Jews to throw the foreigners out, as is the case with many nationalist movements; instead he had to ask the Jews to throw themselves out, and to recognize that they were perpetual foreigners in enemy territory. In other words, Herzl's two goals—organization of the Jews and acquisition of a

---

54. Raoul Auernheimer, "Beard of the Prophet," *Herzl Year Book*, VI (1965), 75–76.

55. Alex Bein, "Memoirs and Documents about Herzl's Meetings with the Kaiser," *Herzl Year Book*, VI (1965), 59–61.

56. Ibid., p. 61. There are hundreds of accounts by contemporaries similarly expressing admiration and even veneration for Herzl. See in particular Meyer W. Weisgal, ed., *Theodor Herzl: A Memorial* (New York, 1929).

political homeland for them—required two different sets of skills, the skills of the revolutionary leader and those of a genteel diplomat.

In order to assemble delegates from Russia, Germany, Austria-Hungary, Rumania, Bulgaria, Holland, Belgium, France, Switzerland, Sweden, England, the United States, Algeria, and Palestine in a First Congress of Jews, he needed the extraordinary powers of charismatic leadership. He had the requisite energy for the task, self-confidence in himself as a leader, the ability to manipulate people, and a strikingly handsome physical appearance.

According to Weber, the term *charisma* applies to "a certain quality of an individual personality by virtue of which he is set apart from ordinary men and treated as endowed with supernatural, superhuman, or at least specifically exceptional powers or qualities. These are such as are not accessible to the ordinary person, but are regarded as of divine origin or as exemplary, and on the basis of them the individual concerned is treated as a leader."[57] The application of this definition to a specific historical case requires testimony from individuals alive at the time of the charismatic leader in order to determine whether or not the leader is "treated as endowed with exceptional qualities" or not. The cautious analyst would achieve a higher degree of objectivity from persons who were not part of the following, since they would be less influenced by the leader, and probably more critical. Objectivity would also be increased by selecting testimony from someone generally familiar with powerful personalities. In addition to these two methodological stipulations, it is advisable, as Robert C. Tucker mentions, "to study his impact upon those around him *before* he achieves office," because when a "leader-personality is genuinely charismatic, his charisma will begin to manifest itself before he becomes politically powerful."[58] The testimony of Georges Clemenceau as presented in an interview with Pierre van Paassen fulfills these three qualifications.

> There was a breath of eternity in that man Herzl. The Burning Bush and Revolutionary Sinai took shape in his appearance. He was a man of genius, not to be confounded with a man of talent. There are plenty of men of talent in the world. Men of genius are rare. . . . Men of genius are recognized by their gigantic proportions, often enclosed in a cadre of an ordinary existence. Their evolution is accomplished according to an unseizable process. Their way of acting, of understanding, or discovering the real substance of things and being is manifested in an altogether

57. Weber, *Social and Economic Organization*, pp. 358–59.
58. Tucker, "Charismatic Leadership," p. 740.

personal and original manner. They are beyond ordinary logic, they surpass the level of their contemporaries and are therefore often misunderstood—or, rather, not understood at all. Such a man was Herzl. Amid all the defection of character which marked his day, the weakness of thought, the furor of clashing interests, he dared to give himself. All the ancestral disquietude of Israel expressed itself in him.[59]

A second testimony is taken from Ahad Ha'am, four years older than Herzl and an ardent Zionist. One of Herzl's greatest critics, Ahad Ha'am, opposed with open hostility Herzl's political Zionism in contrast to his own cultural Zionism. He became especially bitter when his friends and former adherents flocked to Herzl's side.[60] Yet even this lifelong opponent could not deny that Herzl evoked a charismatic response:

... the ideal figure of Herzl, which is being created before our eyes in the popular mind—what a splendid vision, how potent its influence to cleanse that very mind of the taint of galuth, to awaken it to a sense of national self-respect, and to wet the desire for a real national life! As time goes on and the ideal picture of the national hero attains its perfect form, he will perhaps become for our day what the old national heroes were for our ancestors in days gone by: the people will make him the embodiment of its own national ideal, in all its radiance and purity, and will derive from him strength and courage to struggle onward indefatigably along the hard road of its history.

But one thing Herzl gave us involuntarily, which is perhaps greater than all that he did of set purpose. He gave us *himself*, to be the theme of our Hymn of Revival, a theme which imagination can take and adorn with all the attributes needed to make him a Hebrew national hero, embodying our national aspirations in their true form.[61]

The reaction of others was strikingly different. The popularity which Herzl had enjoyed among the bourgeoise was shattered immediately.

59. "Clemenceau Remembers Herzl," by Georges Clemenceau as told to Pierre van Paassen, *Herzl Year Book*, III (1960), 122.

60. Adolf Böhm considered Ahad Ha'am the most accurate observer of Herzl's personality: "No one recognized the significance of Theodor Herzl's personality as clearly as his great antipode, the most consequential opponent of his Zionist ideology and politics: Ahad Ha'am. In the memorial address dedicated to him in the introduction to the second volume of his writings' Hebraic collection, he calls him one of those great central personalities that arise from time to time in a people to perform the miracle 'of strengthening in many hearts the faith in things which surpass nature and understanding' so that the masses will follow such figures with closed eyes. The Jewish people have transferred their belief in the Messiah to Herzl" (*Die Zionistische Bewegung* [Tel Aviv, 1935], p. 281).

61. Sir Leon Simon, "Herzl and Ahad Ha'am," *Herzl Year Book*, III (1960), 148–49.

There gradually penetrated a rumor (for no one ever dreamed of reading his pamphlet) that this graceful, aristocratic, master causeur had, without warning, written an abstruse treatise which demanded nothing more nor less than that the Jews should leave their Ringstrasse homes and their villas, their businesses and their offices—in short, that they should emigrate, bag and baggage, to Palestine, there to establish a nation. The first reaction of his friends was regretful irritation at this 'indiscretion' on the part of an extraordinarily clever and highly gifted author, who, for that matter, held an excellent position, and surely had no cause for complaint.[62]

Herzl failed to move these people because they were too comfortable: "We have not yet reached the right degree of despair. That is why the savior is greeted with laughter."[63] The assimilationists thought it bizarre that the eminent correspondent would want to ally himself with the Jews and have them settle in an ancient, foreign, uncivilized land.

If the personality of the burgeoning leader is truly charismatic, then all who come in contact with him will be affected by him. He usually evokes a positive response in those who are distressed. He encounters blind devotion, derision, and scorn, but he is not ignored. Tucker remarks upon this aspect of charismatic leadership: "Here is probably a universal feature of the charismatic leader: his capacity to inspire hatred as well as loyalty and love."[64] The charismatic leader demands notice and response, and that reaction is usually as emotional as the appeal he makes. Even when he is scorned, his scoffers give testimony to his charismatic powers. Witness a booklet by L. Neumann, "The New Messiah" issued soon after the appearance of *The Jews' State*: "After the best-known of these, Sabbathai Zevi in the East and Josef Frank in the West, there now comes a third of the same species, Theodor Herzl, in Vienna . . . they know how to infatuate the masses through the charm of their personalities, their persuasiveness and their style. . . quite a new mental disease, called 'Zionism.'"[65] The negative reaction demonstrates the power of the revolutionary spirit to evoke a reaction of similar force.

The charismatic leader is the innovator. His primary battle is with the status quo. The tests of his impact are the quantity and quality of his responses, both positive and negative. What brings hope and salvation to some, brings downfall and ruination to others: "Extravagant praise and blame are heaped on my book. I knew it would leave no one indifferent."[66]

62. Zweig, "King of the Jews," p. 110.
63. Bein, *Theodore Herzl*, p. 141.
64. Tucker, "Charismatic Leadership," p. 746.
65. Fraenkel, *Theodore Herzl*, p. 65.
66. *Complete Diaries*, I:306.

The charismatic leader, appealing to one group, impinges on the other, and a negative reaction of "counter-charisma" develops. The man of genius in the eyes of one is the mentally ill in the eyes of another. The most striking example of the counter-charisma which developed in response to Herzl's publication was Karl Kraus's pamphlet "Der König von Zion" whose title became the epithet which was sarcastically applied to Herzl by the rich, and admiringly bestowed on him by the poor Jews.

This ironic title peered at him through every conversation, through every glance. The papers vied with one another in ridiculing the new idea—that is, those in which it was not prohibited, as it was in Herzl's own "Neue Freie Presse," to mention the word Zionismus altogether. At the beginning of the new century this sarcastic city perhaps derided no one more than Theodor Herzl, unless it was that other man who, at the same time, alone and unaided, set up another great universal concept: his fellow Jew, Sigmund Freud, whom the University faculty even now, on his seventieth birthday, did not deign to greet with a congratulatory word.[67]

After being discouraged by Hirsch, the "Moneyed Jew," Herzl turned to the "Religious Jew," the learned and influential chief rabbi of Vienna, Dr. Moritz Güdemann. In a little Jewish hotel room in Munich the two men met to read the manuscript. Güdemann was not receptive at first, but when the reading was nearing completion he said, "You remind me of Moses. . . . Remain as you are! Perhaps you are the one called of God."[68] Herzl contacted high-ranking French, German, and British Jews. In some he awoke great interest and devotion, and in others, he faced doubt and suspicion. He understood clearly that he was addressing these notables for their assistance, not to test the value or validity of his plan. When told that a committee of the English group of notables would study the ideas and then decide whether or not they would participate, Herzl replied: "Of course this committee would take up the matter, but I am not submitting it to them. You can't make me yield to majorities. Whoever goes along with me is welcome. I am first turning to notable Jews who have made a name for themselves by their past efforts, but I do not need them. It will only please me if respected people join with me. But I am not dependent on them.[69]

Herzl as prophet was utterly convinced that he understood the problem and the solution. He had the message, he knew the way, although others

67. Zweig, "King of the Jews," pp. 110–11.
68. *Complete Diaries*, I:233.
69. Ibid., I:279.

disagreed by retaining faith in the ways of the past or clinging to their delusion that things were better than they actually were. Those who believed in him and those who scorned him responded to his publication: "The first manifestation of support, from a London book dealer, P. Michaelis, who places at my disposal his 'devotion and energy.' . . . The second is from Rabbi A. Kaminka in Prague, who calls on me to form a national Jewish party in Austria. . . . Levysohn's letter arrived today in which he announces that he will fight me vigorously."[70] He is called "The Jewish Jules Verne" by mocking journalists but he recognized in them "the street scoffer who laughs at the prophet or the people's spokesman."[71]

IX. *The Binding of Leader and Following*

Herzl's charisma was intertwined with the legend[72] that assured the dispersed Jews of the coming of the Messiah to lead them to the Promised Land. For the desperate masses of oppressed Eastern European Jewry, Herzl filled this role of the Messiah.

> It was as an improbable and legendary figure that Herzl dawned upon the eastern masses of Jewry. His book, kept out of the country by the Russian censorship, was hardly known; only the name passed over the heads of the masses, and the stories that accompanied it gripped the hearts and stirred the imagination of thousands. The masses saw the new Moses in him, the leader, who had returned "like Moses from Midian" to liberate the Jews from their wretchedness.[73]

Letters containing similar expressions of faith came from Bulgaria, Germany, Russia, and Palestine, pleading with Herzl to assume the leadership of all the Jews. They told him that they were ready to leave with him, that all East European Jewry had been waiting for him now and would follow him anywhere.

> March 3, 1896. A fashion-goods dealer at Semlin, S. Waikenkorn, wrote me that all the Semlin Jews are ready to emigrate, bag and baggage, as soon as the "Jewish Company" is founded.

70. Ibid., I:286, 289.
71. Ibid., I:287.
72. Halpern, *The Idea of the Jewish State*, p. 82: "The adulation of Herzl in the crowded towns of Eastern Europe was certainly shared by many a Jew who had only a slight idea of his views, or who opposed them, but was moved by the legendary figure of this 'King of the Jews.'"
73. Letter from the Society "Ahavat Zion," Borislav, Galicia; quoted in Bein, *Theodore Herzl*, p. 184.

March 10, 1896. An enthusiastic letter from Dr. Bierer, Sofia. The Chief Rabbi there considers me the Messiah. This Passover, a lecture on my publication will be given in Bulgarian and Spanish before a large audience.

March 26, 1896. The "Sion" society of Sofia sends me an enthusiastic resolution in which I am proclaimed the Leader.[74]

Jewish students of the associations "Kadimah," "Ivria," "Libanonia," "Hasmonaea," "Gamala," etc., sent him in May 1896 an "Address of Austria Students" asking him to take over the leadership of the movement for the erection of a Jewish state and promising him the active collaboration of the Jewish intellectuals in the holy cause of the Jewish people.[75]

The most amazing acclamation came from a Protestant chaplain, Rev. Hechler, who "burst into Herzl's room and stammered 'Here I am! I brought the great tidings to the Grand Duke of Baden, and now I want to help you.'" Hechler proclaimed Herzl the Messiah and became his liaison to the German Kaiser and devoted diplomatic lieutenant. In characteristic fashion his devotion was spontaneous and sprang from the need to follow Herzl's call. He received no payment for his services other than travel expenses. Hechler fulfills Weber's description exactly: "Psychologically this 'recognition' is a matter of complete personal devotion to the possessor of the quality, arising out of enthusiasm, or of despair and hope."[76] The Jews regarded Herzl's audiences with the Grand Duke of Baden and the Kaiser, which Hechler arranged, as signs or proofs of Herzl's messianic qualities.

On his travels to Constantinople, Jerusalem, Vienna, Paris, London, and elsewhere, Herzl had the opportunity to see for himself the effect that he had created in the Jewish masses.

> In Sofia a touching scene awaited me. Beside the track on which our train pulled there was a crowd of people—who had come on my account. . . .
> There were men, women and children, Sephardim, Ashkenazim, mere boys and old men with white beards. At their head stood Dr. Ruben Bierer. A boy handed me a wreath of roses and carnations—Bierer made a speech in German. Then Caleb read off a French speech, and in conclusion he kissed my hand, despite my resistance. In this and subsequent addresses I was hailed in extravagant terms as Leader, as the Heart of Israel, etc., I think I stood there completely dumbfounded. . . . I kissed Bierer farewell. They all pressed about me to shake my hand.

74. *Complete Diaries*, I:308, 310, 317.
75. Fraenkel, *Theodore Herzl*, p. 64.
76. Weber, *Social and Economic Organization*, p. 359.

People cried "Next Year in Jerusalem!" The train started moving. Hat-waving, emotion. I myself was quite touched. . . . [77] At the Zionist society, speeches. Afterwards I had to go to the synagogue, where hundreds were awaiting me. . . . I stood on the altar platform. When I was not quite sure how to face the congregation without turning my back to the Holy of Holies, someone shouted: "It's all right for you to turn your back to the Ark, you are holier than the Torah." Several wanted to kiss my hand.[78]

One of the reasons that the message of the charismatic leader evokes such a fervent response among his followers is that the message is not a minor one, dealing with a slight alteration in the followers' lives, a minor modification of an isolated problem. Rather the charismatic leader addresses life itself; he deals with the whole moral and social order under which the followers experience their hopelessness and then gives them hope. The charismatic leader introduces radical change in the followers' very perception of life, meaning, value, etc. Only those in distress are able to accept this reordering since they have nothing to lose but their hopelessness. The charismatic leader deals with the nonroutine in a nonroutine manner. In Isaiah Berlin's words:

Herzl appealed to, indeed he did much to create, their vision of them-selves as restored to full human dignity, and it was this that moved them to follow him to new paths of freedom. What inspired them was not a further development of the old religious and cultural tradition which they had heroically preserved amid oppression and squalor, but the beckoning goal of a new moral and social life, above all a life of their own in dignity and freedom, that had been denied them as a people, in Russia, Poland, Rumania and even Berlin, Vienna and Prague.[79]

Herzl empathized with the poor without being condescending; he ac-knowledged the power of the rich without being subservient. Although the revolutionary leader is the extremist vis-à-vis the rest of society, he can usually maintain maximum support within his own group by taking the moderate stance—not as extreme as the most radical followers nor as hesitant as the most cautious. Herzl fulfilled this type of position with regard to the religious composition of his following. In accordance with his upbringing he was neither an observant Jew nor was he as removed from his religious heritage as were most of the assimilationists. He insisted on the position of

77. *Complete Diaries*, I:368.
78. Ibid., I:402.
79. Isaiah Berlin, *Chaim Weizmann* (London, 1958), p. 18.

the freethinkers that each man choose for himself which religious grouping is best-suited to him, and he warned against creating a theocracy in the future Jewish state. He argued moderation when the enthusiastic crowds urged mass demonstrations, and he argued moderation when inflamed students suggested an attack on the land they hoped to claim.

Herzl initiated his practical work by seeking the approval and assistance of wealthy Jews and heads of state. He reasoned that this approach would expedite the acquisition of land and impress the Jews sufficiently to encourage them to unite for work in the Zionist effort. He was hesitant to agitate the masses that were already responding enthusiastically to his compelling personality. He constantly "warned against manifestations and advised a calm demeanor lest popular passions be aroused against the Jews."[80] Time and again he advocated moderation so that the Jews would not suffer added persecutions as their "patriotic loyalty" became doubted. When the rich Jews and heads of state proved to be overly cautious, Herzl wrote: "Flectere si nequeo superos, Acheronta movebo (If I cannot sway the powers on high, I will move those of the nether world). I said that I did not want a demagogic movement, but if worst came to worst—if the gentry should prove too genteel—I was willing to set even the masses in motion."[81]

His work during the year since the publication of *The Jews' State* had aroused the devotion of a large segment of Jewry to such a degree that they denied him the right of relinquishing his leadership or his dedication. As Weber wrote, "It is recognition on the part of those subject to authority which is decisive for the validity of charisma."[82] The masses not only imbue a man with charismatic leadership (by virtue of their response), they modify and sustain it as well. The following creates the leader as much as the leader creates the following. Once the relation is established between leader and follower, each continues to mold the other. Herzl became aware of this process when he addressed a mass-meeting in London.

> As I sat on the platform of the workingmen's stage on Sunday I experienced strange sensations. I saw and heard my legend being born. The people are sentimental; the masses do not see clearly. I believe that even now they no longer have a clear image of me. A light fog is beginning to rise around me, and it may perhaps become the cloud in which I shall walk. But even if they no longer see my features distinctly, still they divine that I mean very well by them, and that I am the man of the little

80. *Complete Diaries,* I:402.
81. Ibid., I:412–13.
82. Weber, *Social and Economic Organization,* p. 359.

people. . . . This is perhaps the most interesting thing I am recording in these notebooks—the way my legend is being born.

And while I was listening, on that people's tribunal, to the emphatic words and the cheering of my adherents, I inwardly resolved quite firmly to become even worthier of their trust and their affection.[83]

Usually charismatic leaders are recognized and followed, but Herzl also sought specific help outside the masses. His hesitancy to become an agitator led him to make one final request for an endorsement to a powerful Jew, the Baron Edmond de Rothschild. If he would adhere to Herzl's proposals, the baron would be granted leadership of the movement in Herzl's stead. If not, Herzl would create a demagogic movement. The baron, however, advocated the policy of gradual infiltration of Jews in Palestine without negotiating with the major powers for an autonomous state. This policy was incompatible with Herzl's mission and the important decision was reached. On July 20, 1896, Herzl noted in his diary: "I am writing De Haas in London that they should begin to organize the masses.[84] Talked with Nordau and Beer yesterday and told them the answer I had found to Rothschild's objection: the organization of our masses, without delay. Our people will be organized before their departure, and not merely upon their arrival. . . . In the afternoon I spoke in the club rooms of the Russian Jewish students. . . . I called on them to start organizing the cadres."[85] He did not hide his decision from Rothschild: "I am recommending to my friends in all countries that they should create the cadres for a possible migration. I believe that within a few months, say by spring, the nationalist Jews will be firmly organized. The movement will be continued and it will spread like wild fire."[86]

The masses were to be organized so that a "General Zionist Conference" could be held, at which the movement could assess its strength and determine its direction. The world-wide propaganda was to begin with the congress where "at long last, there will meet again a Jewish National Assembly. The Jewish question must be taken away from the control of the benevolent individual. There must be created a forum, before which everyone acting for the Jewish people must appear and to which he must be responsible."[87] Herzl knew that he had the power to convene such a meeting, because before he had resolved to turn from the wealthy to the people, from the benefactors to

83. *Complete Diaries*, I:421–22.
84. Ibid., I:430.
85. Ibid., I:430–31.
86. Ibid., II:533.
87. Bein, *Theodore Herzl*, p. 218.

the beneficiaries, the people had already decided to turn to Herzl.[88] The supreme test of his charismatic powers was the actualization of this aspect of his mission. The culmination of two years' work since his initial self-dedication was captured in two short sentences: "The congress will take place. That is all that matters."[89]

On August 29, 1897, the First Zionist Congress met at Basel, Switzerland, and began the work which eventually led to the fulfillment of Herzl's mission 50 years later, the creation of the State of Israel. The devotion which certain powerful individuals as well as the desperate masses had granted Herzl by virtue of his charisma alone, was reinforced by his demonstration in the congress of this ultimate "proof," the mark of the first major success. The prophet's partial realization of his prophecy firmly cemented his following to him. The dynamic force of the charismatic leader reached its summit as the convention began, but simultaneously the movement began to lose its general charismatic quality as a stable organization was established. As the charisma reached its peak, it began its decline. As Weber wrote: "If this is not to remain a purely transitory phenomenon, but to take on the character of a permanent relationship forming a stable community of disciples or a band of followers or a party organization or any sort of political or herocratic organization, it is necessary for the character of charismatic authority to become radically changed. Indeed, in its pure form charismatic authority may be said to exist only in the process of originating."[90]

It is not within the scope of this paper to discuss the development of the Zionist organization, and the transformation of charismatic leadership into other forms of organization. It is important, however, to note that as the movement realizes its goals, gains new adherents, and increases its authority, it loses the character that marked its inception. The special dynamism necessary for bringing something into being is not needed to perpetuate it. The leadership is less concerned with creation than with maintenance and goal-fulfillment. The charismatic rapport that was necessary for the movement's formation is transformed as the movement becomes institutionalized.

x. *Charisma and Economy*

Weber emphasized that a major difference between charismatic and bureaucratic leadership is their economic substructure. In some cases the char-

88. Halpern, *The Idea of the Jewish State*, p. 129: "The result was that in a surprisingly short time the Zionist Congress now took place."

89. Bein, *Theodore Herzl*, p. 219.

90. Weber, *Social and Economic Organization*, p. 364.

ismatic leader rejects possessions altogether and in most cases there is no personal monetary benefit from his labors. Pure charisma, divorced from anything mundane, typical or ordinary, is incompatible with the economic considerations of bureaucracy, which is firmly rooted in the regularized everyday routine. Charisma rejects "as undignified any pecuniary gain that is methodical and rational . . . all rational economic conduct."[91] In its revolutionary dynamism it makes a break with the economic world. Typically, the charismatic leader is supported by gifts. In true charismatic fashion, Herzl never earned money for his Zionist activities; the very notion of earning implying the existence of bureaucratic routinization. Instead he exhausted his personal fortune to meet the movement's expenses.

There is some ambiguity, however, in Weber's formulation concerning the relationship between charisma and economic activities. For although personal gain is anathema to the supernatural-like charismatic leader, he does require the material means of power. What is despised ". . . is traditional or rational everyday economizing, the attainment of a regular income by continuous economic activity devoted to this end. . . ." Since charismatic leadership is an ideal type, we can see that real exemplars such as Herzl were unable to divorce themselves entirely from the need for an income to survive. It is interesting to note that whereas Herzl could have siphoned a small fraction of the gifts that were sent him for his personal use, he unhesitatingly diverted all of these funds to further his mission. Specifically, he founded the "Jewish Company" or "Jewish Colonial Bank" for the purposes of bargaining and of buying land. Both the unsolicited financial gifts, which are one means of the followers' expression of their devotion, and the painstakingly gathered funds were rejected as a means of private gain. Since self-support was a routine but real economic consideration separate from his visionary concerns, Herzl maintained one component of his precharismatic identity for the purpose of earning a living. This journalist self, split off from his Zionist self, continued to work for the *Neue Freie Presse*, albeit in a sporadic and not a routine manner. His ability and decision to continue a salaried job has been explained by Herzl's puzzled biographers by his need to provide for his estranged wife and children and by his unbroken loyalty to the publishers who had given him his initial start in life. The real, in contrast with the ideal, charismatic leader does not always make a total break with his past or present extramissionary lives. To do so would be to completely realize the supernatural image, i.e. a complete estrangement with every claim past and present except the vision itself.

In support of Weber's theory we see entries in Herzl's diaries which reveal

91. Eisenstadt, ed., *Weber on Charisma and Institution Building*, p. 21.

the real leader's anguish at being unable to make the complete break and having to continue working for a salary:

> Too bad that I am a wage slave of the "Neue Freie Presse." Everything would be different if the tramps with whom I have so often struggled for my existence were different.[92]
>
> I miss everywhere the more than 50,000 guilders [$24,000] which I have put into [the Zionist movement], and that makes me even more restricted in my relations with the "Neue Freie Presse" than I was before. I have to tremble lest I be dismissed; I cannot dare to take the leave my health requires, for I have already been away for six weeks, although I spent all that time in the service of Zionism.
>
> Today then, I return to the office once more, after having been a free man and a great lord at Basle, and have to enter the room of Big Boss Bacher like a meek little office boy. Cruel![93]

The anguish reflects his awareness that earning wages from others implies being accountable to them, therefore not free. It means being part of a system rather than creating a new world order. It means being subject to the authority of others' position rather than subject only to the overwhelming, natural authority of the idea. But he was also pained because he knew that "in order to do justice to his mission, the holder of charisma, the master as well as his disciples and followers, must stand outside the ties of this world, outside of routine occupations, as well as outside the routine obligations of family life."[94] He was frustrated by guilt lest his working for the newspaper diminish his single-minded devotion to the cause. All energy and time spent on the newspaper was stolen from the movement. But although painful, Herzl shows that it is possible and sometimes necessary for a charismatic leader to maintain contact with the economic world to support himself.

Another refinement of Weber's discussion of economy and charisma is possible by examining the case of Herzl: "Charisma rejects rational economic conduct . . . it does not involve an orderly taxation for the material requirements of its mission. . . . It is the opposite of all ordered economy. It is the very force that disregards economy."[95] Here again we must examine the real case in contrast with the ideal type. For Herzl, economics and his movement had to be compatible partners. He needed vast sums to achieve his goals. At

92. *Complete Diaries*, II:677.
93. Ibid., III:864.
94. Weber, *Social and Economic Organization*, p. 362.
95. Eisenstadt, ed., *Weber on Charisma and Institution Building*, p. 21.

first he approached the major philanthropists as an expedient means to accomplish his purposes and to obtain a "sign" that he was indeed the leader of a movement about to be launched. With utmost confidence Herzl initiated his Zionist activities by addressing a letter to the multimillionaire Baron Maurice de Hirsch, who had already demonstrated his interest in alleviating the misery of East European Jewry by financing experimental Jewish agricultural colonies in Argentina. Calling himself the "Spiritual Jew," Herzl hoped to demonstrate to Hirsch, the "Moneyed Jew," that since philanthropy perpetuates poverty, the Argentina scheme was doomed to failure. Therefore, he should use those funds to support Herzl's plans. Winning the help of the influential Hirsch was to be a personal psychological boost for Herzl and a sign that he was the "carrier of the message." His ideas would then have had the borrowed patriarchal authority of one of the great men of Europe. The "Jewish-political conversation" between the two men did not yield these results and Herzl sought confirmation of his calling elsewhere. He knew he needed money but he was already convinced of the authority of the idea to such an extent that lack of funding or response could not affect its validity. Rather the other's failure to acknowledge Herzl's authority revealed a shortcoming in the other's ability to comprehend. The leader in search of a following and funds explained to Hirsch how detached he was from Hirsch's validation: "I shall go to the German Kaiser; he will understand me, for he has been brought up to be a judge of great things. . . . To the Kaiser I shall say: Let our people go! We are strangers here; we are not permitted to assimilate with the people, nor are we able to do so. Let us go! I will tell you the ways and the means which I want to use for our exodus, so that no economic crisis or vacuum may follow our departure."[96]

This detachment was not always affordable. Herzl needed money to accomplish his goals and he worked hard to obtain it, but never did he allow his financial success or lack of it to determine the truth value of his idea. This independence of economy and charisma, rather than Weber's discussion in terms of the incompatibility of charisma and routine, seems more fitting an explanation for Herzl's continuous attention to monetary issues in the service of his cause. His desire to establish a Jewish bank implies deep involvement in economic matters. Herzl combined the qualities of a visionary prophet with those of a practical realist. Although planning a future world, he had to build it in this one. Not only would the transportation of the Jews to Palestine and the acquisition of land require large funds, but so would every minor aspect of organization, communication, and transportation. In order to en-

96. *Complete Diaries*, I:23.

gage in an exchange with the sultan of Turkey for the land of Palestine, he would need financial power and skill. Herzl's proposal to obtain the land in exchange for rectifying the financial chaos known as the Turkish Debt required real financial acumen.

Charisma is not foreign to economic considerations per se, but rather to personal economic reward as an end in itself. Economic knowledge can be useful to a charismatic leader as a means of fulfilling the revolutionary goal. In his relations with his following, the leader is not granted a salary. He acts because he has been called, because he is utterly obligated to act. If his following does support him, it is gratuitous although contingent upon some signs of success. He attempts to be set apart from the mundane world in which wages hinge on specific work hours or completed tasks. But the leader does not become blind to the mundane world when he receives his mission. He deals with the economic world to render his scheme feasible rather than only true and utopian. His mission might demand major involvement in the world of affairs, which he chooses to enter in order to communicate and be efficacious.

Charisma, it must be remembered, is defined as a certain set of qualities recognized by a following in a leader which causes them to dedicate themselves to him. The definition can be applied to movements of widely diverse substantive missions, which is what Weber intended when he emphasized that these terms are value-neutral. But the qualification "repudiation of any sort of involvement in the everyday routine world" refers to the substantive goal, rather than the formal function of the group. This criterion dismisses the charismatic potential of those leaders whose mission requires their dealing with the economic world and amassing funds. We are suggesting instead that "what is despised so long as the genuinely charismatic type is adhered to" is not rational everyday economizing as such, but rather rational everyday economizing for personal gains. Economic activity may persist as a means for the achievement of the mission. In this way a revolutionary leader may find himself involved in the everyday routine world, without detracting from his charismatic relations with his following.

xi. *Charisma and Bureaucracy*

This same line of criticism can be applied to Weber's remarks on the relation between charisma and bureaucracy. The charismatic leader, by definition, is set apart from the kind of leader who achieves his position by virtue of a slow and steady climb within a bureaucratic organization and who derives his authority by virtue of his possession of an institutional position. The charismatic leader does not assume a position that has inherent power, rather he is a source of power himself.

The authority of the charismatic leader is considered special, magical, even supernatural. He does not earn authority, he demands and inspires it. Nevertheless, once the authority is enjoyed, and a cohesive bond is established between the followers and their leader, the group may decide to establish some sort of bureaucratic organization as a goal in itself. Frequently a party organization is formed. Such is the case with Herzl whose major goal was the establishment of a world congress in which all Jews would be represented. The group of loyal followers that surrounded him, plus the masses that were devoted to him by the legends that were created, were bound to him, not by the rules and regulations of a bureaucratic organization, but by a sense of dedication to their savior. They set up a giant bureaucratic organization, however, known as the "Society of Jews" which theoretically formalized these relationships and preserved the unity of the following after Herzl's death. Herzl's powers were only slightly curtailed by the creation of the organization since his special nature lifted him beyond the rules. The charismatic leader is outside the limits of a democratic organization, because he is elite. He can use his extraordinary qualities to organize, but his charisma is not devoured in the organization. The Herzl case leads to another hypothesis which merits lengthy consideration elsewhere. Not only was Herzl's leadership unconnected to acquisition of a position in a preexisting bureaucracy, it was precisely that lack of bureaucracy that created a vacuum which an ascendant charismatic leader could fill. Before Herzl's efforts there was no World Zionist Organization to legitimize leaders and compete with individualistic outsiders. The organizational vacuum allowed Herzl to step in and assume leadership, which he then institutionalized into a bureaucracy to resolve the problem of succession and maintenance, i.e., to provide the mechanism for the continuation of his work after him.

Rosenzweig and Kant: Two Views of Ritual and Religion

Paul R. Mendes-Flohr

I

In his now famous open-letter to Martin Buber, "The Builders" (1924),[1] Franz Rosenzweig praises Buber for having "removed us from the imminent danger of making our spiritual Judaism depend on whether or not it was possible for us to be followers of Kant."[2] Rosenzweig is referring to Buber's essay "Herut" (1919),[3] in which he urged a rejection of the then regnant tendency amongst Jews to catechise the "essentials" of Jewish belief according to principles external to Judaism—principles that were recurrently sought in the thought of Immanuel Kant. In that essay, Buber calls upon the contemporary Jew to suspend all such preordained views of Judaism, and to base his understanding of Jewish "teachings" on "reverent and unbiased knowledge."[4] Such knowledge, Buber insists, emerges only from an intimate exploration of "the [Jewish] people's literature and . . . the depths of its life."[5] Indeed, only through an immersion in the ramified spiritual process of Judaism will its primal forces "dwell" within the Jew, permitting him genuinely to determine what aspects of Jewish teachings are personally relevant or not.

Rosenzweig observes in "The Builders," however, that Buber is curiously inconsistent: regarding the Law—the *mitzwot* or the ritual precepts of Judaism—he fails to adopt the open-ended attitude he urged anent the teachings of Judaism. Buber, as Rosenzweig notes, summarily rejects the Law, which he deems to be a narrow legal corpus, as a meaningful option for the modern Jew. In sponsoring this view of the Law, according to Rosenzweig, Buber retains "the shackels put on [the Law] . . . by the nineteenth century."[6]

1. "The Builders: Concerning the Law," trans. W. Wolf, in Franz Rosenzweig, *On Jewish Learning*, ed. N. N. Glatzer (New York, 1965), pp. 72–92.
2. Ibid., p. 77.
3. "Herut: On Jewish Youth and Religion," trans. E. Jospe, in Martin Buber, *On Judaism*, ed. N. N. Glatzer (New York, 1967), pp. 149–74. Rosenzweig referred to the 1923 edition of this essay ("Cheruth"), published in Buber, *Reden über das Judentum* (Frankfurt a/M, 1923).
4. "Herut," p. 171.
5. Ibid., p. 173.
6. "The Builders," p. 77.

The immediate reference here is to the "legalistic" conception of the Law held by Western neo-Orthodox Jewry. By implication Rosenzweig also seems to suggest that although Buber may have freed Jewish teachings from their enslavement to Kantian principles, he, paradoxically, remains beholden to those principles in his approach to the Law. Specifically, Rosenzweig seems to accuse Buber of holding fast to a Kantian view of the Law. This impression is reinforced by the terms of the philosophic argument that follows: Rosenzweig challenges Buber's view that the precepts of Judaism are merely heteronomous laws (*Gesetze*); these precepts, Rosenzweig argues, may also be understood as divine commandments (*Gebote*) which are refracted through man's autonomous will. This argument is already adumbrated in *The Star of Redemption* (1921). In "The Builders" and the subsequent exchange with Buber, Rosenzweig extends it, concluding what may be construed as a critique of the Kantian view of Jewish religious practice—a view that dominated modern thought. In our exegesis of this critique we will focus on Kant's and Rosenzweig's reading of the terms *Gesetz* and *Gebot*. Implicit in our discussion of their respective positions will be two varying views—illuminating in their contrast—of religion and ritual.

II

For Kant the Enlightenment was a period that witnessed the maturation of the human personality. Through his increasing courage to use Reason, man was freeing himself from the spiritual and intellectual enslavement to external authority (heteronomy). Recognizing his inalienable right to an independent access to Reason, the man of the Enlightenment rejected the claims of the traditional purveyors of truth. Man will now be his own "autonomous" authority regarding Truth—both metaphysical and ethical. Kant's own writings constitute perhaps the Enlightenment's most sustained exercise of such autonomy.[7]

In the moral sphere, Kant held, man has an autonomous sense (or spontaneous knowledge) of what, in a particular situation, is objectively right or wrong. This sense, "practical reason," implores one to act in accord with moral judgment despite all personal inclinations. Thus, practical reason is said to issue a categorical imperative, indicating our moral duty.[8] In paying heed to our duty, Kant avers, we naturally assume that (a) respect for moral

7. Cf. Y. Yovel, "The God of Kant," *Scripta Hierosolymitana*, XX (1968), 91–97.
8. Ibid., p. 103.

duty renders us "worthy" (*würdig*) of true happiness; and that (b) the world, despite empirical evidence to the contrary, is ultimately amenable to moral action. These assumptions, designated by Kant as the *summum bonum*, logically compel the postulate of an agent or principle, independent of man and nature, guaranteeing their realization. Logically this principle assures the "ontological possibility" of the realization of the *summum bonum*. Now because of admittedly cultural and subjective factors,[9] we draw a "second inference" (*ein zweiter Schluss*) and "imagine" this principle to be the supreme personal God of traditional religion.[10]

Kant uses the term "God" to explain the dynamic aspect between the postulated principle supporting the *summum bonum* of morality and the moral consciousness of the individual it serves. The God of the *summum bonum* inspires faith and hope in the efficacy of morality. It is only in this capacity that we "know" God—pure reason and empirical cognition do not furnish such knowledge. Kant's God is strictly an inferred feature of the transcendental knowledge apprehended by practical reason. By asserting that this is the extent of our knowledge of God, Kant is denying the traditional understanding of the deity as a transcendent being who miraculously and graciously reveals his will. Surely the God of Kant is not identical with the God of creation, revelation, and redemption.[11]

Subjectively, however, God may be understood, according to Kant, to be the author of the categorical imperative; although, he emphasizes, objectively "the idea [of God] . . . is not the ground of morality."[12] "Religion is (subjectively regarded) the recognition of all duties as divine commands (*Gebote*)."[13] Responding to moral duty *qua* God's commands is the very substance of religion for Kant. The moral act stemming from God's command is the only

9. "Kant even adds that, from a purely objective (or logical) point of view, it makes no difference how we represent this factor [guaranteeing the *summum bonum*] to ourselves, and makes it 'subject to our own choice'" (Yovel, "The God of Kant," p. 98). On one occasion Kant expressly referred to the God idea as symbolic (*Kritik der Urteilskraft*, 2. Auf., p. 257).

10. *Kritik der Urteilskraft*, p. 455; referred to in Yovel, "The God of Kant," p. 98 n. 11.

11. ". . . in spite of the traditional terminology of the discussion, [the God of Kant] has no theological meaning. He is neither the author of moral precepts nor an object of love, of awe or of any religious experience. He cannot intervene in nature or break its laws, nor does he have any superior value to that of an individual man or to that of historical humanity. God is a 'moral author of the world' whom neither the world nor morality needs in itself, and both speculative and practical reason cannot and should not presuppose. . . . The postulate of 'the existence of God' tells nothing of God, only of Man and the world, and the Kantian theory of the deity remains strictly humanistic" (Yovel, "The God of Kant," pp. 101, 123). Indeed, as John R. Silber observes, Kant refused to acknowledge "the religious experience [as] a genuine, autonomous aspect of human experience" ("The Ethical Significance of Kant's *Religion*," in Kant, *Religion Within the Limits of Reason Alone*, trans. T. M. Greene and H. H. Hudson [New York, 1960], pp. cii f., n. 60).

12. *Religion*, p. 5.

13. Ibid., p. 142; German: Cassirer ed., VI, 302.

possible religious act that Kant would acknowledge as genuinely religious. All other religious practices, remaining outside the pale of morality, can never be autonomous acts. Hence, they can never receive the sanction of Kant's moral God. The religious practices (e.g., liturgy, ritual) prescribed by a church are for Kant all historical products of man's creation. Even if one should assume that they are revealed, ecclesiastical practices are nonetheless historical and particularistic, that is, they are not universal.[14] Lacking universality, they cannot of course be acceded to by practical reason. (Had these practices not been revealed they would not be known; proof that they are contingent and historic.)[15] To accept ecclesiastical practices is to enslave oneself to heteronomous laws or *Gesetze*. Kant thus juxtaposes divine commandments (*Gebote*)—refracted, as they are, through man's autonomous will—to the heteronomous laws (*Gesetze*) of ecclesiastical religion.[16]

Hence for Kant the prescribed religious practices of ecclesiastical religion are irrelevant to genuine, "rational" faith. Prayer and ritual are deemed meaningless, utterly irrelevant.[17] They induce at most "a dizzying *illusion of virtue.*"[18] Ceremony is an insipid, superstitious way of ingratiating oneself to God.[19] Any substitute for the moral service of God is deemed by Kant as a "pseudo-service."[20] "Kant sees," according to one commentator, "religion as neither an enlargement of our speculative knowledge, nor yet a collection of special duties toward God distinct from those to our neighbor, but a peculiar way of regarding the latter."[21]

Although encrusted by ecclesiasticism, Christianity has at its core, in Kant's view, the pure moral faith of Jesus. "The Teacher of the Gospel announced himself to be an ambassador from heaven. As one worthy of such a mission, he declared that servile belief (taking the forms of confessions and practices on days of divine worship) is essentially vain and that moral faith, which

14. *Religion*, p. 95.
15. Ibid.
16. Cf. "Denn bei dem [reinen Religionsglauben] kömmt es bloss auf das, was die Materie der Verehrung Gottes ausmacht, nämlich die moralischer Gesinnung geschehende Beobachtung aller Pflichten, als seiner *Gebote*, an; eine Kirche aber . . . bedarf einer öffentlichen Verpflichtung, einer gewissen auf Erfahrungsbedingungen beruhenden kirchlichen Form [staturarische Gesetze]. . . ." (*Religion innerhalb der Grenzen der blossen Vernunft*, Cassirer ed., VI, 250 [italics added]). Cf. also "Die staturarischen bürgerlichen Gesetze kann man zwar nicht göttliche Gebote nennen" (ibid., p. 244 n. 1). Already in his first treatise on ethics, *Grundlegung zur Metaphysik der Sitten*, Kant reserved the term "*Gebot*" for the moral imperative. Cf. "Die Vorstellung eines objektiven Princips, sofern es für einen Willen nöthigend ist, heisst ein Gobot (der Vernunft), und die Formel des Gebots heisst Imperativ"; and "Gebote sind Gesetze, denen gehorcht, d.i. auch wider Neigung Folge geleistet, werden muss" (Akademie Textausgabe, IV, 413, 416).
17. Cf. Kant, "Vom Gebet," *Werke*, ed. K. Vorländer, VIII, 169 f.
18. *Religion*, p. 161 (italics in original).
19. Ibid., pp. 160 ff.
20. Ibid., p. 156.
21. C. J. Webb, *Kant's Philosophy of Religion* (Oxford, 1926), p. 135.

alone renders man holy 'as their Father in Heaven is holy' [Matt. 5:48] and which proves its genuineness by a good course of life, is the only saving faith."[22] Jesus forcefully taught that not ritual piety but "pure moral disposition of the heart alone can make man well-pleasing to God."[23] His teachings are fundamentally "a universal religion of reason";[24] they constitute "a pure and searching religion comprehensible to the whole world (and thus natural)."[25] And thus as long as Jesus' moral faith remains at the core of the church, Christianity has the power gradually to develop from an ecclesiastical faith to a pure, universal religion, establishing the kingdom of God—"an ethical commonwealth" in which rational morality will reign supreme.[26] Christianity should be inspired to this goal if it recalls that "all [Jesus] did was done . . . in the face of a dominant ecclesiastical faith which was onerous and not conducive to moral ends."[27] This ecclesiastical faith that Jesus fought was, of course, Judaism. Indeed, according to Kant, Judaism does not know the pure moral faith of Jesus. Israel knows divine service but as a complex of exacting rituals. In that these ecclesiastical prescriptions are knowable only through historical revelation, Judaism manifestly lacks the capacity to become "a pure religious faith equally obvious to the whole world."[28] In this respect, Kant implicitly doubts the divine origins of Judaism and suggests Judaism is "a collection of mere statutory laws upon which was established a political organization."[29] In consonance with their political origin, the laws of Judaism have a coercive force, demanding external obedience. Conformity to these laws then involves legality; inner rational acknowledgment of their value is neither required nor relevant. Whatever moral addenda that may be found in Judaism are not essential to its faith. Even the Ten Commandments, affirmed universally as rational ethical commands, are in the legislation of the Jews "not so prescribed as to induce obedience by laying requirements upon the *moral disposition* (Christianity later placed its main emphasis here); they are directed to absolutely nothing but outer observance."[30] Clearly Israel's God is not the God of practical reason, "for a

---

22. *Religion*, p. 119.
23. Ibid., p. 147.
24. Ibid., p. 146.
25. Ibid.
26. Ibid., p. 140.
27. Ibid., p. 146.
28. Ibid., p. 126. Various aspects of Kant's attitude toward Judaism are discussed in: E. L. Fackenheim, "Kant and Judaism," *Commentary*, XXXVI (December 1963), 460–67; H. M. Graupe, "Kant und das Judentum," *Zeitschrift für Religions- und Geistesgeschichte*, XIII (1961), 308–33; idem, *Die Entstehung des modernen Judentums* (Hamburg, 1969), pp. 144–54; J. Guttmann, *Kant und das Judentum* (Leipzig, 1908); J. Katz, "Kant and Judaism: The Historical Context" [Hebrew], *Tarbiz*, XLI, no. 2 (1970), 219–37; and N. Rotenstreich, *The Recurring Pattern* (New York, 1963), pp. 23–47.
29. *Religion*, p. 116.
30. Ibid.

God who desires merely obedience to commands for which absolutely no improved moral disposition is requisite is, after all, not really the moral Being the conception of whom we need for a religion."[31] *In nuce*, for Kant, Judaism, not knowing pure moral faith, is but a pseudo-religion. The ecclesiastical rules of Judaism—the *mitzwot*—are not the commandments of the moral God, but merely a collection of heteronomous laws.

In Kant's conception of Judaism resonate the views of Spinoza and Mendelssohn.[32] The former, in his *Tractatus theologico-politicus*, held that the ceremonial law of Moses "served to establish and preserve the Jewish kingdom," and that Scripture itself testifies that these laws are not identical with the universal moral law of God.[33] Mendelssohn, while not agreeing with Spinoza that the Law of Moses was merely temporal and that its validity was limited to the life of the Jewish commonwealth, likewise characterized the "revealed legislation" promulgated *through* Moses, viz., the prescribed ceremonies and rituals, as the essence of Judaism.[34] The picture of traditional Judaism portrayed by Solomon Maimon may have also informed Kant's image of Judaism.[35] It should be borne in mind, however, that Kant's view of Judaism conforms with the Pauline rejection of the Torah (= *Gesetz*, in the Luther Bible translation).[36] Undoubtedly this view was prominent in the Pietism of Kant's youth. In any event, because of his prestige, Kant gave, as the perspicacious Saul Ascher (1769–1822) already in 1794 noted, "an a priori status" to the view that Judaism was a spiritually and morally vacuous ritualism.[37]

A leading response of those Jews affected by the Enlightenment was to accept Kant's definition of true religion, but to claim that it was, contrary to

31. Ibid., pp. 117 f.

32. Cf. Guttmann, *Kant und das Judentum*, pp. 50–51, 61, n. 3. See also J. Guttmann, "Mendelssohns Jerusalem und Spinozas Theologisch-politischer Traktat," 48. *Bericht der Hochschule für die Wissenschaft des Judentums* (Berlin, 1931), 31–67.

33. Spinoza, *Theologico-Political Treatise*, trans. R. H. W. Elwes, in *The Chief Works of Benedict de Spinoza*, 2 vols. (New York, 1951), I, 69. Cf. ". . . diese Polemik Spinozas ist die Quelle geworden zu einem fundamentalen Missverständnis der jüdischen Religion. Als solche hat sie die edelsten Zeiten der deutschen Literatur hindurch gewirkt. . . . Aus Spinoza hat Kant seine Kenntnis und sein Urteil über das Judentum geschöpft" (Hermann Cohen, *Religion der Vernunft*, 2. Auf. [Frankfurt a/M, 1929], p. 385).

34. Moses Mendelssohn, *Jerusalem*, trans. A. Jospe (New York, 1969), pp. 99–102. For a comparative discussion of Mendelssohn and Spinoza on the Law, see A. Altmann, *Moses Mendelssohn: A Biographical Study* (University, Ala., 1973), pp. 536–37.

35. Maimon endorsed Spinoza's protrayal of Judaism as a legalistic theocracy (*Lebensgeschichte*, 2 vols. [Berlin, 1792–93], II, 180–83). His autobiography "was avidly read by German intellectuals who developed their concepts of orthodox Judaism from it" (M. A. Meyer, *The Origins of the Modern Jew* [Detroit, 1967], p. 67).

36. Cf., e.g., Rom. 3:20.

37. S. Ascher, *Eisenmenger der Zweite* (Berlin, 1794), pp. 78–79; cited in Katz, "Kant and Judaism," p. 237.

the master's opinion, also applicable to Judaism.[38] Mendelssohn had erred, they claimed: the ceremonial law is not central to Judaism. The abiding core of Judaism, they averred, is a set of principles that indicate a marked affinity to the precepts of universal morality. These apologists were not just seeking to adjust Judaism to suit Kant, but also to pay heed to the fact that Jews were increasingly abandoning traditional practice. Saul Ascher, in a work written prior to the publication of Kant's critical comments on Judaism, calls attention to the urgent need to redefine Judaism in light of the fact that numerous Jews now find the performance of the *mitzwot* incompatible with modern life.[39] Mendelssohn's designation of the *mitzwot* as the essence of Judaism, Ascher avers, does a disservice to Judaism and those Jews estranged from the Law who nonetheless wish to maintain their affiliation with the House of Israel. Significantly, Ascher later uses Kant to strengthen his case against defining Judaism exclusively in terms of the *mitzwot*.[40] Throughout the nineteenth century, Reform[41] and even neo-Orthodox circles[42] in Germany endeavored to demonstrate the compatibility of Judaism with Kantianism. As a result Jewish religious thought tended to be what may be called a "theology of morality."

Paul Tillich has observed that nineteenth-century Protestant theology was similarly affected by Kant, in at least that it sought to transcend him.[43] That it was unable to do so is testified to be the "back to Kant" movement led by ·August Ritschl (1822–89) in the wake of the impasse arrived at by the theology inspired by Schleiermacher and Hegel. Ritschlians,[44] who dominated German theology during the last decades of the past century, resiled to Kant's *Religion within the Limits of Reason Alone*, and reiterated that God is manifest in the moral imperative.[45] Unlike Kant, however, Ritschlians identified this manifestation of God's will as "revelation"—a concept, which after all is the axis of positive religion, that was radically questioned since the Enlightenment.

Indeed, at the bottom of the perplexities of both nineteenth-century Prot-

38. Cf. Graupe, *Entstehung*, pp. 144–54.

39. *Leviathan oder über Religion in Rücksicht des Judentums* (Berlin, 1792), p. 227.

40. Ibid., pp. 230–34. Cf. M. Weiner, *Jüdische Religion im Zeitalter der Emanzipation* (Berlin, 1933), p. 41.

41. Cf., e.g., A. Geiger, "Die Rabbinerzusammenkunft," *Wissenschaftliche Zeitschrift für jüdische Theologie*, III (1837), 313–32; and idem, "Die Formglaube in seinem Umwerth und seinen Folgen," ibid., IV (1839), 1–22.

42. Cf. I. Grunfeld, "Introduction," in S. R. Hirsch, *Horeb*, trans. I. Grunfeld (London, 1962), pp. lxxiii–lxxxiv.

43. P. Tillich, *Perspectives on 19th and 20th Century Protestant Theology* (New York, 1967), pp. 70, 216.

44. H. R. Mackintosh, *Types of Modern Theology* (London, 1964), pp. 136–74.

45. Ibid., pp. 168 ff.; and Tillich, *Perspectives*, p. 217.

estant and Jewish theology is the Enlightenment's ambiguous view of divine revelation. This view, Deism, held that man through the free exercise of his reason is capable of apprehending all truths said to be communicated by revelation. While rejecting this proposition, known as natural theology, Kant's critical philosophy also deepened the scepticism regarding revelation. Kant's theology, we recall, also discards revelation. The conception of revelation attacked by the Enlightenment and Kant was very specific, however. In consonance with medieval tradition, revelation was understood as God's communication at discrete moments in history of information regarding His will and the nature of Being. This notion of revelation may be called the propositional conception of revelation, since the revealed information can be formulated as propositions.[46] The difficulties faced by nineteenth-century theology could in a large part be ascribed to the inability to overcome the Enlightenment's and Kant's critical view of (propositional) revelation. Even Schleiermacher, who did so much to further our understanding of religious consciousness, was embarrassed by the notion of revelation. In his systematic presentation of Christian doctrine, *Der christliche Glaube*, he relegated the discussion of revelation to a "footnote" in which he admits his difficulty in reconciling the notion with the rest of his thinking.[47] The iconoclastic Jewish theologian, S. L. Steinheim (1789–1866), felt he had overcome Kant's scepticism regarding revelation with his elaborate argument that there was compelling epistemological ground for upholding revelation as a cognitive supplement to reason. For Steinheim too revelation was a communication of information, namely of vital cosmological and ontological knowledge not otherwise available; incidentally he expressly excludes ceremonial laws from such communication.[48] Steinheim was a lone voice in his affirmation of revelation.

For the most part, nineteenth-century theology, especially in Jewish circles, retains Kant's critical attitude, generally treating the question of God's revelation of truth and law metaphorically or with embarrassed silence. Gradually, however, a conception of revelation began to take shape that would suggest that God does not disclose propositional truths, but rather Himself, His providential love and Presence. Moreover, His self-revelation is not confined to specific historical moments, but is recurrent in both the collective and personal realm. This view, now known as the *heilsgeschichtliche*

46. J. Hick, "Revelation," *The Encyclopaedia of Philosophy*, VII, 189–91.
47. *Der christliche Glaube* (Berlin, 1884), I, Zusatz, Par. 10, pp. 57–63.
48. H. J. Schoeps, "S. L. Steinheim. Lebenslauf—Werk—Einordnung," in H. J. Schoeps, ed., *Salomon Ludwig Steinheim zum Gedanken* (Leiden, 1966), pp. 33 f.; and H. M. Graupe, "Die philosophischen Motive der Theologie S. L. Steinheims," in ibid., pp. 40–76.

conception of revelation,[49] is advanced by such early twentieth-century theologians as Barth, Paul Tillich, Martin Buber, Eugen Rosenstock-Huessy, and Franz Rosenzweig. Although not at all necessarily challenging the Kantian critique of ecclesiastical religion, the *heilsgeschichtliche* understanding of revelation provides the basis for revaluating ritual as divine service, viz., as an occasion peculiarly suited for God to reveal His Presence. Rosenzweig was to lead Jewish thought in this direction.

III

Philosophy, especially since the Enlightenment, according to Rosenzweig, reified the world-view of the pagan. To the pagan, Rosenzweig observes in *The Star of Redemption*, the world we live in is a self-contained fact which is fundamentally indifferent to its human inhabitants. Even the most sophisticated pagan, who ascribes the advent of the world and man to a creative act of God, does not see the Creator's continued providential relationship with his creation; the God of the pagans slips back into his primordial concealment. Creation *qua* God's self-revelation remains a fact of the past, God being at most the distant, hidden principle of existence. Biblical faith, on the other hand, recognizes creation as prophecy, as an event marking "the revelation of divine providence . . . , as a 'plan of salvation' (*Heilsplan*).[50] To biblical man creation bespeaks God's decisive and continuous relationship to his creatures; indeed the Hebrew liturgy celebrates God's daily renewal of "the work of creation."[51]

But this awareness of God's abiding presence in creation flows from an experience, testified to by biblical faith, that God acknowledges each of His creatures in their particularity. Without such acknowledgment, God's presence in the immediacy of life would be concealed by the infinite magnitude of creation.[52] God thus "supplements"[53] the revelation of creation by turning to each individual and whispering "Thou" in his ear. This "Thou" affirms man in his "presentness"; it signifies the total acceptance of his existential

49. Cf. W. Pannenberg, "Introduction," in Pannenberg, ed., *Revelation as History* (London, 1968), pp. 3–21; and J. Baille, *The Idea of Revelation in Recent Thought* (New York, 1956), pp. 19–40, 62–82.

50. *The Star of Redemption*, trans. W. W. Hallo (New York, 1970), p. 116; *Der Stern der Erlösung*, 3. Auf. (Heidelberg, 1954), 2. Teil, p. 37.

51. *Star*, p. 122.

52. Ibid., p. 206.

53. Ibid., p. 160. Cf. "He who has not yet been reached by the voice of revelation has no right to accept the idea of creation as if it were a scientific hypothesis" (ibid., p. 135).

self. Affirmed, indeed loved by God, man now recognizes the providential hand of God in creation.[54]

Man experiences divine love as a commandment (*Gebot*): "Love me."[55] But in order to obviate a solipsistic withdrawal of the beloved from the world— creation—God couples this command with a second: "Love thy neighbor."[56] Indeed, the love of God is to be expressed in the love of one's neighbor. By enjoining His beloved to turn with love to his fellow man, God beckons him to assist in the act of redemption; graced by God's love one serves Providence—directed by God one fills the world with divine, agapeic love, crowning the *moment* in which he says Thou to his neighbor with Eternity. "For what is redemption other than that the I learns to say Thou to the He?"[57]

God reveals Himself to man, beholds his countenance with love and commands him to love. God chooses to address man in the form of the commandment for only it captures the presentness of the revelatory moment. God's address is "the imperative commandment, immediate, born of the moment and, what is more, becoming audible at the instant of birth, for emerging and finding voice are one and the same thing in the case of the imperative."[58] Any other form of address but the imperative commandment would fail to express the dialogical presentness of revelation. "Only [the imperative] does not abandon the ambit of I and Thou."[59] The present tense, the indicative, is informed by the past rationalizations of experience. Past and future tense would be similarly inappropriate. Indeed, the imperative makes no provision for the future: "It can only conceive the immediacy of obedience."[60] Moreover, "if it were to think of a future or an Eve, it would be, not commandment (*Gebot*) nor order (*Befehl*), but law (*Gesetz*)."[61] Law, locked in the matrix of past and future, is void of the revelatory voice of God. Law cannot comprehend the presence of revelation, for "the sole commandment of love is simply incapable of being law; it can only be commandment."[62] Any particular commandment that detaches itself from the "Urgebot"[63] of love and becomes simply law loses the "immediate presentness and unity of consciousness, expression, and expectation of fulfillment" that distinguishes

54. Ibid., pp. 158–64.
55. Ibid., p. 177.
56. Ibid., p. 205.
57. Ibid., p. 274.
58. Ibid., p. 177. Cf. ". . . Gotteserfahrungen sind ja allermeist imperativische" (Rosenzweig, *Briefe*, ed. E. Rosenzweig [Berlin, 1935], p. 611).
59. *Star*, p. 186.
60. Ibid., p. 177.
61. Ibid.; *Stern*, 2. Teil, p. 114.
62. *Star*, p. 177.
63. *Stern*, 2. Teil, p. 114.

commandment.[64] Further, law which cannot refer back to the *Urgebot*, law which is incapable of being retransformed into the immediacy of commandment is bereft of the divine.

The distinction that Rosenzweig makes between law and commandment clearly has a Kantian quality.[65] But he uses this distinction in a manner that constitutes a radical critique of Kant. Interestingly, prior to his 1913 conversion to a "faith based on revelation" (*Offenbarungsglaube*),[66] Rosenzweig seems to have upheld a Kantian moral theology. In a letter to Hans Ehrenberg dated October 1910,[67] he emphatically endorses Kant's understanding of "the practical [i.e., ethical] moment of religion." Schleiermacher and Hegel, he continues, lacked this understanding and neglected "praxis." Their error derives from the ontological status they ascribed to history. History, Ro-

64. *Star*, p. 177.
65. Rosenzweig concludes the letter designated by him as the "germ-cell" of the *Star* with an afterthought that amongst those who have influenced him he should mention especially "Christoph Schrempf (do you at all know him?)—who in his early, probably his first work on Kant and Christ sought to correct the opposition of autonomy and heteronomy through that of law (*Gesetz*) and order (*Befehl*)" ("'Urzelle' des Sterns der Erlösung," *Kleinere Schriften* [Berlin, 1937], p. 372). Rosenzweig is apparently referring to Schrempf's *Grundlage der Ethik* (Tübingen, 1884), a study of Kant and Jesus. Until 1930 this volume was available only in a handwritten edition. It marks the beginning of Schrempf's early Kantian period (1884–99). O. Engel gives a brief description of the first part of the *Grundlage*, which deals with Kant's ethics: "Diese 391 Seiten . . . geben in tiefdringenden Analysen eine Rechtfertigung und Verteidigung der imperativischen Ethik Kants gegenüber jeder materialen, zweckbestimmten wie jeder deskriptiven Ethik. Aber freilich bleibt Schrempf trotz aller Verehrung bei Kant nich stehen. Er vermisst bei Kant die strenge, konsequente Durchführung seiner Grundposition. Die Kantische Fragestellung, die Schrempf in eigenen Worten so formuliert: 'Wo finde ich den ausweichlichen, nezessitierenden Bestimmungsgrund für mein Handeln?' drängt den, der sie konsequent durchdenkt und durchlebt und der sich vor allem dabei selbst nicht schont, über Kant hinaus. . . . Kant begnügte sich mit der Kritik von vermeintlichen Bestimmungsgründen und rang nicht konsequent, nicht spröde genug um die Unabweisbarkeit des echten Bestimmungsgrundes, der 'einen den Tod herbeiwünschenden und ihn suchenden Menschen zu leben nötigt.' Kant vermag also zur Kritik von Pseudobestimmungsgründen anzuleiten, vermag aber keine echten, positiven Bestimmungsgründe zu geben. . . . Wäre Kant selber dies zum Bewusstsein gekommen, so hätte.er erkannt, dass es eine strenge Wissenschaft des Sittlichen nicht gibt. . . .[Schrempf] kommt in unerbittlicher Analyse zu einem wenig erquicklichen Resultat: er endet bei der Suche nach unausweichlichen sittlichen Halt in der absoluten ethischen Skepsis, in der völligen sittlichen Rat-, ja Haltlosigkeit. . . . In dieser Ratlosigkeit sieht sich Schrempf nun 'in der Geschichte nach einem Herrn, dem der Mensch mit unbedingter Wahrung seiner Würde seine spröde sittliche Selbständigkeit opfern, in dessen Willen er den gesuchten, unbedingten Bestimmungsgrund seines Willens anerkennen könnte.' Und so klopft er denn bei Jesus an" (O. Engel, "Vom Verhältnis Christoph Schrempfs zu Immanuel Kant," *Kantstudien*, XXXV, no. 4 [1930], pp. 513–14). There is much here that is suggestive regarding Rosenzweig's thought. Unfortunately, neither Schrempf's *Grundlage* nor any other works from his Kantian period are available to us. From what we are able to gather from Engel's brief article, a comparative study of Schrempf and Rosenzweig is a *desideratum*.
66. *Briefe*, p. 639; English translation by D. Emmet is cited in A. Altmann, "Franz Rosenzweig and Eugen Rosenstock-Huessy: An Introduction to Their Letters on Judaism and Christianity," in E. Rosenstock-Huessy, ed., *Judaism Despite Christianity* (New York, 1971), p. 31 n. 10.
67. *Briefe*, no. 46, pp. 54 f.

senzweig noted in his diary, is not the unfolding of Being, rather it is but the discrete acts of men (*Tat der Täters*). "We see God in every ethical event (*Geschehen*), but not in one complete Whole, not in history." Indeed, history which takes shape in the phenomenal world cannot serve as a vessel for divinity. "Every human act becomes sinful as it enters history"—although the actors intend otherwise, the morality of an act is neutralized in the material world of necessity. In contrast, "Hegel summarily dismissed the discrete act—being a-historical, moral, subjective—as undivine." For Hegel "passion," "the individual," "good intention," "the knight of virtue" are irrelevant to history *qua* theodicy. For Rosenzweig, however, "religion is the only true theodicy." By religion Rosenzweig here seems to mean moral religion,[68] with its singular emphasis on intentionality.

Rosenzweig would later criticize the moral law of Kant precisely because of its emphasis on intentionality and its consequent failure to indicate the

---

68. Early twentieth-century religious thought was influenced by the moral theology of the Ritschlian school. This school of theology, profoundly critical of Schleiermacher and Hegel, appealed to Kant in their claim that "the divine appears through the moral imperative and nowhere else" (Tillich, *Perspectives*, p. 217). Cf. also A. Altmann, "Leo Baeck and the Jewish Mystical Tradition," *The Leo Baeck Memorial Lecture* No. 17 (1973), p. 9. True, Rosenzweig approvingly records in his diary Ellen Key's criticism of Adolf Harnack, the leading representative of the Ritschlian school at the time. In a diary entry from March 1906 Rosenzweig echoes Key's doubts whether "pure ethics" has anything to do with religion (N. N. Glatzer, *Franz Rosenzweig: His Life and Thought* [New York, 1953], p. 8). But this was before Rosenzweig registered in Professor Jonas Cohn's Kant seminar—autumn 1906—and became an enthusiast of the critical method; see the argument in the text, below. Although in the *Star* Rosenzweig explicitly criticizes Ritschl and his school, strong traces of their theology may be discerned in that work. The Ritschlian equation of acts of love with the content of ethics and the proposition that these acts constitute the human counterpart to redemption present a suggestive parallel, *mutatis mutandis*, to the *Star*'s thesis regarding the redemptive character of divinely directed love of one's neighbor. In light of this interpretation, one sentence in the diary entry cited in the October 1910 letter to H. Ehrenberg is problematic: ". . . God must redeem man not through history, but really (*wirklich*)—there is no other alternative—as 'the God of religion.'" This sentence suggests an anticipation of Rosenzweig's later theology. First, however, it must be noted that this is the single reference to "redemption" in his pre-1913 letters and the few diary excerpts published from that period. Moreover, "redemption" is not in this context associated with the notion of revelation as it later is. Also, in the present context "redemption" is introduced as a logical inference: "es bleibt nicht anders übrig"; "redemption" here is not an affirmation of religious conviction. One may possibly understand the sentence "God must redeem man . . ." as quasi-metaphorical, much in the vein of Ritschlian theological discourse. Apropos, in his first essay testifying to his *Offenbarungsglaube*, Rosenzweig observed that the prevailing tendencies in contemporary theology implicitly reject the reality of revelation, yet devise various techniques to preserve "religious values." "Hier nun hilft sich die atheistische Theologie mit einem eigentümlichen Schema, durch das sie das Hereinbrechen des tätigen Göttlichen über das ruhende Menschliche umbildet zu einer wunderbar unvermittelten oder nur durch ihre eigene Spannung vermittelten Gegensätzlichkeit im Menschlichen selbst. Statt der Menschwerdung behauptete man so das Menschsein Gottes, statt seines Niedersteigens zum Berge der Gesetzgebung die Autonomie des Sittengesetzes, überhaupt statt der Offenbarungsgeschichte bestehendes menschliches Wesen, worin Geschichte mehr abrollte, als dass es selber Geschichte erlitt" ("Atheistische Theologie" [1914], *Kleinere Schriften*, pp. 285 f.).

desirable content of moral action.[69] These limitations Rosenzweig traces to Kant's uncertainty about the ontological status of the phenomenal world—an uncertainty which derives from his agnosticism regarding noumenal knowledge. In his youth, Rosenzweig himself was for a period an enthusiastic student of Kant's critical epistemology. In the autumn of 1906, Rosenzweig began his philosophical studies, registering in Professor Jonas Cohen's seminar on Kant's *Critique of Pure Reason*.[70] After the first session of the seminar he wrote his parents that he felt "like a wild-man who had been brought to Europe; I understood nothing."[71] A year later he wrote his mother with the air of a man who had mastered the First Critique. He advises his mother not to take up the study of Kant if she could only devote to such study but a few weeks.[72] A cursory reading of Kant would surely lead to many gross misconceptions. Moreover, "Kant's philosophy is not at all what one usually imagines philosophy to be; on the contrary, it is a critique of all philosophers prior to himself. Now, I believe that you are not familiar with these philosophers. You thus will read Kant as if you heard a man grumble and not know what he was complaining about." Kant actually wishes to obtain the goal of no longer philosophizing, "to cease to prattle about unprovable matters." The study of Kant, however, is unnecessary for practical-minded individuals, such as ordinary physicians, businessmen, historians or women—"these individuals already know what [Kant] has to teach them." Rosenzweig then sarcastically notes that his mother seeks inspiration regarding "inner-being," the "true essence" of existence—"*in nuce*, precisely that which Kant fights: metaphysics, philosophical poetry." And then he quickly adds, "I know very well that Kant can be so construed that he will appear to be a [metaphysician]." Yes, he warns his mother, with a few weeks study this is about all one could get out of him.

It may also be assumed from this letter to his mother that the young Rosenzweig adopted Kant's critique of dogmatic metaphysics and his skepticism regarding transcendent knowledge.[73] It may be further inferred that it

69. This theme is developed by Schrempf. Cf. n. 65, above.
70. *Briefe*, no. 20, p. 30.
71. Ibid.
72. Ibid., no. 24 (November 18, 1907), pp. 33–35.
73. To be sure, this agnosticism was but methodological. Rosenzweig seems to have been personally or 'existentially' dissatisfied with it. Prior to his adoption of religious faith, he seems to have recurrently sought some intellectually adequate affirmation of the subjective aspect of experience. Thus perhaps his interest in Meinecke's historicism and in *Geistesgeschichte* in general. Here his involvement in the Baden-Baden conference (1909) of intellectuals who met under the slogan "durch Objektivität zur Subjektivität" is of note; cf. *Briefe*, p. 48. His study of Hegel also points in this direction. But his 'subjectivism,' although engaging, ultimately did not prove methodologically persuasive. This is the dilemma that Rosenzweig brought with him in his

was this position, also known as critical relativism,[74] that Eugen Rosen-stock-Huessy challenged in that "memorable"[75] conversation of July 1913 when he converted Rosenzweig to a faith in revelation. Rosenzweig himself observed that in that conversation Rosenstock-Huessy effectively challenged his "philosophical relativism," which he characterized as "a dualism between revelation and the world," transcendent and phenomenal knowledge.[76] Had he been able, Rosenzweig further observed, "to buttress this dualism . . . with a metaphysical dualism between God and the devil my position would have been unassailable."[77] Had Rosenzweig's relativism indeed been, as sug-gested, a Kantian critical relativism, then we may assume that the dualism between God and the devil refers to a radical separation between God and the world *qua* the sovereign realm of evil. Rosenzweig was, however, ultimately prevented from endorsing such a dualism "because," as he says, "of the first sentence of the Bible."[78] God created the world and beheld it was good. An abiding, naive faith did not permit him to deny the possibility of God's relationship to creation. In the conversation of July 1913 Rosenstock-Huessy apparently convinced Rosenzweig that God may speak to man, that "faith based on revelation" was a tenable position for a man of critical awareness.[79]

At that time Rosenstock-Huessy's conception of revelation, as Professor Altmann has observed, probably already contained adumbrations of his view of divine love as a form of dialogue—a view that was to characterize both his and Rosenzweig's mature theology.[80] But it seems Rosenzweig's own under-standing of revelation remained inchoate for some time. In a letter dated 18 September 1917 to his cousin Rudolf Ehrenberg (the third participant in the conversation of July 1913), Rosenzweig recalls a discussion the two had during a hike through the Harz forest in 1914.[81] In that discussion they sought unsuccessfully to clarify the distinction between revelation and ordinary cognition (*eigenmenschliche Erkenntniss*).[82] Now, in the letter of September 1917,

---

confrontation with Rosenstock-Huessy; cf. *Briefe*, nos. 7, 23, 25, 41, 42, 124. I should like to thank Mr. Noam Sachs for encouraging and assisting me to clarify this issue.

74. In German academic circles this term was used to characterize Kant's attitude toward metaphysical knowledge; cf. R. Eisler, *Handwörterbuch der Philosophie*, 2. Auf. (Berlin, 1922), p. 547.

75. Altmann, "Franz Rosenzweig and Eugen Rosenstock-Huessy," p. 31.

76. *Briefe*, p. 71; trans. in Altmann, "Franz Rosenzweig and Eugen Rosenstock-Huessy," pp. 32–33.

77. Ibid., p. 32.

78. Ibid.

79. Glatzer, *Franz Rosenzweig*, 2nd rev. ed. (New York, 1961), p. xiv.

80. Altmann, "Franz Rosenzweig and Eugen Rosenstock-Huessy," pp. 30–31.

81. This letter, deemed by Rosenzweig to be the "germ-cell" of the *Star*, is included in his *Kleinere Schriften*, pp. 357–72, under the title "'Urzelle' des Sterns der Erlösung."

82. Ibid., p. 357.

he informs his cousin with great enthusiasm that he feels he understands that distinction. The conception of revelation which he presents in this letter—now viewed as the "Urzelle" of *The Star of Redemption*—is similar to Rosen-stock-Huessy's: revelation is a dialogical relationship of love.

> [Man] may demand, indeed he must, that God return his love. Yes, he must demand that God even love him first. For his I is dull and mute and awaits the redeeming word of God's own mouth: "Adam, where art thou?," so that the first Thou that distinctly asks for him be answered by the first I, half audibly and hesitantly in its shame. . . .[83]

In contradistinction to the logical, a-temporal structure of cognition, revelation takes shape in time, respecting the contingencies of each unique situation. God enters time, speaks to man, transforming his consciousness and thereby enables him to surmount his finitude, reaching out to God and his fellow creatures.

In *The Star of Redemption*, this liberating effect of revelation is further explored. In a state untouched by God's revelatory love, Rosenzweig contends, the inner self of man expresses itself through erratic "defiance"[84] of the external order of the world. But the self could never be truly expressed through such defiance, for such expressions cannot be integrated in a harmonious and balanced pattern of relationships with the world. Hence, bereft of God's love, the *daimon* of man, his innermost character, is often viewed as an element or passion deeply disturbing him. Instead of "being something 'affirmed' once and for all, [the *daimon*] has to become something struggling to the fore. . . ."[85] But after one has "heard the call of God and found bliss in His love," his defiance is transformed into "trust" and his *daimon* emerges in serene fulness.[86] This emergence is quickened by God's agapeic love, but the beloved's daimonic or "essential will"[87] is directed by God's commandment to love one's neighbor. The self, affirmed by God, expresses itself in the act of love. "It is only, after all, in the love of God that the flower of the soul begins to grow out of the rock of the self. Previously man had been a senseless and speechless introvert; only now is he—beloved soul."[88]

"The wholly disclosed man"[89] is then the beloved soul who is integrated in

83. Ibid., p. 364; cited and trans. by J. O. Haberman, "Franz Rosenzweig's Doctrine of Revelation," *Judaism*, XVIII, no. 3 (Summer 1969), p. 320.
84. *Star*, pp. 167 f.
85. Ibid., p. 212. Cf. "What I call daimon is destiny become man, character incarnate" (from Rosenzweig's diary [September 2, 1906], cited in Glatzer, *Franz Rosenzweig*, p. 12).
86. *Star*, p. 212.
87. Ibid., p. 213.
88. Ibid., p. 169.
89. Ibid., p. 209.

the peace of God's love. He is the saint. And "every saintly figure has its own traits: the figure of the saint is inseparable from the legend of the saint."[90] True acts of love, which Rosenzweig equates with true moral acts, bear the particular imprint of the lover's character; it must be so, for love is borne only by the inner-being of man come manifest through the agapeic love of God. Unlike the fulfillment of a law, each expression of love is unique and its essence cannot be comprehended by philosophical parameters that ignore and fail to give primacy to its ever unique, existential dimension. Hence, it is not surprising that all formalism, such as "the ethics of Kant and his followers," with its exclusive emphasis on universal forms fails to appreciate "the uncannily incalculable rapture of the saint," the moral man *par excellence*.[91]

Because it ignores the question of content, Rosenzweig argues, Kant's ethical law is ambiguous.[92] From a Kantian perspective, individual acts, which obviously must be filled with a specific content, always court the danger that they will be betrayed by their content. "In [Kantian] ethics everything is uncertain. Everything, after all, can be moral, but nothing is moral with certainty. The moral law is necessarily purely formal and therefore not only ambiguous, but open to an unlimited number of interpretations."[93] Kant insisted on *a priori* formalism, for all content derived as it is from the sensible world of experience is contingent and determined, thus violating the *conditio sine qua non* of ethics, viz., freedom and universality. In contrast to Kant, Rosenzweig holds that there is a basis to accept content without endangering these conditions. This position is based on belief in revelation and the attendant trust in the world: the material world is God's creation and His gentle hand guides both creation and our actions.[94]

Without such trust the world does indeed seem to resist man's well-intentioned actions. Yet it has been suggested—Rosenzweig observes in a letter from May 1917—that despite its ontological resistance the world would "become good only through good actions [of men]."[95] There is a contradic-

90. Ibid., p. 217.
91. Ibid.
92. Cf. n. 65, above.
93. *Star*, p. 214.
94. Cf. "Schon für den morgigen Tag braucht man die ganze Kraft des Vertrauens, um nicht zu verzweifeln" (*Briefe*, p. 213). In a private discussion Prof. Michael Fishbane of Brandeis University has observed that in a subtle way Rosenzweig retains Kant's formalism. In a dialectical fashion the "trust" that is obtained in God's love permits one to relate to the concrete, contingent content of experience, and yet in doing so one is animated by a proleptic assurance that this act has universal redemptive import. This assurance seems to parallel Kant's requirement of the universability of moral motives. We might add that Rosenzweig's concept of "trust" also seems to echo the postulate—which Kant holds to be logically demanded by practical reason—regarding the ultimate amenability of the world to the moral act.
95. *Briefe*, no. 169 (May 30/31, 1917), p. 213.

tion in this proposition, Rosenzweig says, in that the beginning, doing good, presupposes the goal, the amenability of the world to our actions. In this oblique reference to Kant's *summum bonum*, Rosenzweig argues that "the contradiction points out that just as the 'categorical imperative' is clear to the individual, so the image of the *Endzustand* and the path thereto is beyond the purview of reason."[96] Kant's ethical formalism cripples action. In a letter from 1928,[97] Rosenzweig notes that Kant's inability to indicate the specifics or the content of ethical action leads to an undesirable "quietism": "precisely when the principle of morality is purely formal, the content of the given situation rushes into the empty space. The general law which Kant employs in the formulation of the categorical imperative [sanctions] the present situation of the universe."[98]

We need not know, however, the shape of the future in order to act. The "demand of the day" is sufficient, Rosenzweig says in a letter of 1917, to enjoin our ethical response.[99] The present calls upon us to effect social reforms, and more pertinently to approach he whom "I meet" with love. We are certain of this step because we have reconciled ourselves to "the tragic aspect of *human action (Handeln)*; that enmity between humanity and the speechlessness of Nature cannot be overcome by the strength of human action [alone]. . . ."[100] This reconciliation is made possible by faith and the attendant preparedness to accept the facticity of the external world without any crippling doubt regarding its ontological status.[101] In the aforementioned letter from 1928, Rosenzweig records his faith in that "truly transformative acts always spring from the actual, experiential (*erfahrende*) address"— i.e., from an apprehension of a voice found in the phenomenal world, "be it the voice of God, of conscience, or of a crying stone."[102] Here Rosenzweig opposes "the experiential (*erfahrende*) imperative" to Kant's "categorical imperative"; the former is more compelling "precisely because it is not categorical in Kant's sense," it has a specific content, it has direction.[103] God commands us, as Rosenzweig observes in *The Star of Redemption*, through concrete situations. "By contrast [to Kant's moral law], the commandment to love one's neighbor is clear and unambiguous in content."[104]

96. Ibid.
97. Ibid., no. 516 (April 13, 1928), pp. 610–11.
98. In ibid. Rosenzweig also remarks: "Der Weg von Kant zu Hegel ist kein zufälliger."
99. Ibid., p. 213.
100. Ibid., pp. 213 f.
101. Ibid., p. 212.
102. Ibid., p. 611.
103. Ibid.
104. *Star*, p. 214. Cf. "Gottes Gebot ist ein Befehl, eindeutig an diesen Menschen und in diese Lage dieses Menschen hineingerufen. . . . So ist dem Frommen kein 'Gesetz' gegeben, denn er steht unter einem 'Befehl'" ("'Urzelle,'" p. 367); cf. n. 65, above.

The act of love, as we have seen, related exclusively to the present. Thus without reference to past or future it does not enmesh itself in the determinant network of the sensible world. Independent of this network, love —although it grasps its content from the sensible world—remains a free, autonomous act. But love is not a purely volitional turning to our dear ones and circle of friends—it is not an arbitrary matter of personal affinity. If it were, it would, of course, be devoid of the ethical criterion of justice. He who heeds the commandment to love also includes in his orbit of love the stranger, indeed, whomever God leads into his arms. God directs our love to the next one, the "abstract" next one.[105]

> In reality . . . it is not up to love [whom] it seizes with its power and delivers out of the context of life into its eternity. Not only is this not up to love; rather the law of growth is instituted in the world by its Creator just as much as the overflowing drive of its love is instituted in love itself by the Revealer, and this law determines, without man himself being conscious of it, the way and object of love.[106]

In summary, Rosenzweig holds that sheer obedience to a formal moral law does not assure a meaningful ethical life, a life that truly transforms the community of men into a fellowship. Only the actions originating in divine love are ethically efficacious. "Only the soul beloved of God can receive the commandment to love its neighbor and fulfill it. Ere man can turn himself over to God's will, God must first have turned to him."[107]

Judaism knows the paradoxical freedom of divinely directed volition. Jewish piety is only apparently heteronomous, its positive laws are but signs of the primal commandment to love. In The Star of Redemption, Rosenzweig is clearly exercised by Kant's characterization of Judaism as heteronomous.[108]

---

105. For a discussion of the philosophical significance of this thesis, see J. Agus, *Modern Philosophies of Judaism* (New York, 1941), pp. 177–79.

106. *Star*, p. 241.

107. Ibid., p. 215 (italics added).

108. This charge is by innuendo recurrent throughout Rosenzweig's famous correspondence with Rosenstock-Huessy. Cf. the latter's statement: the Jew "ist ein Paragraph des Gesetzes; c'est tout" (*Briefe*, p. 682 [October 30, 1916]). Rosenzweig read Kant's *Religion Within the Limits of Reason Alone* in February 1916 (*Briefe*, p. 674). In October 1916 he read Harnack's *What Is Christianity?* Harnack also echoes Kant's evaluation of Judaism: "By being bound up with religious worship and petrified in ritual observance, the morality [of the Pharisees] had indeed been transformed into something that was the clean opposite of it. . . . Jesus severed the connexion existing in his day between ethics and the external forms of religious worship and technical observance. . . . In all questions of morality he goes straight to the root, that is , to the disposition and intention. . . . What he freed from its connexion with self-seeking and ritual elements, and recognized as the moral principle, he reduced to *one* root and to one motive—love" (A. Harnack, *What Is Christianity?*, trans. T. B. Saunders [New York, 1957], pp. 70–71).

Significant is Rosenzweig's patent transfer of the charge of heteronomy to Islam.

> The piety of the Moslem finds its way into the world by obediently walking [the way of Islam], . . . by adhering to the laws prescribed for it. . . . It is a way of subservience. This more than its content distinguishes it from the love of neighbor. . . . The difference, then, does not lie in the content, but solely the inner-form. In the way of Allah, this form is subservience by volition to the prescription established once and for all; in love of neighbor it is the ever-new disruption of the permanent mold of character by ever-unexpected eruption of the act of love. . . . The world act [attendant to the commandment to love] . . . is therefore incalculable love, wholly free, while in Islam it is obedience to the law once promulgated. It follows that Islamic law everywhere strives to go back to direct pronouncements of the founder, thus veritably developing a strictly historical method, while both Talmudic and canon law seek to make their points by means, not of historical fact-finding, but of logical deduction. For deduction is subconsciously determined by the goal of the deduction, that is to say the present, and therefore it gives the contemporary power over the past. Investigation, on the other hand, makes the present dependent on the past. Even in this seemingly pure world of law, then, one can still recognize the difference between the commandment to love and the obedience to law.[109]

Heteronomy is certainly not the stuff that morality and true religion are made of. But it would, according to Rosenzweig, be grossly erroneous to view Judaism as rote obedience to prescribed laws. This may be true of Islam.[110] Judaism, however, is a religion of agapeic love; Jewish piety is characterized by the passion of spontaneous love. Thus the inner being of the Jew is always relevant to the fulfillment of the commandment. The Jew's piety "finds an exact counterpart, strangely enough, in the secular piety of more recent times which freely conforms to universal law. The ethics of Kant and his followers, for instance, as well as the general consciousness, [in vain] sought to evolve such a piety. . . ."[111] In contrast to the commandment to love with its profound respect for the "essential will," Kant's moral law, which ignores

109. *Star*, pp. 215–217.
110. It has been noted that Rosenzweig is unjudicious in his treatment of Islam. Cf., e.g., I. Maybaum, *Trialogue Between Jew Christian and Muslim* (London, 1973), pp. 43–55; and J. Taubes, "The Issue Between Judaism and Christianity," in A. Cohen, ed., *Arguments and Doctrines* (New York, 1970), p. 410.
111. *Star*, p. 217.

this will, is paradoxically more akin to heteronomy. Judaism being rooted in the commandment to love knows authentic autonomy.

Rosenzweig acknowledges that to the world Judaism appears as a system of spiritually and morally jejune laws. "Though as content of revelation and claim on the individual [the Torah] is commandment, seen as world it is law."[112] Rosenzweig explains this paradox by attributing to Israel a unique task in the scheme of redemption. The legal structure of Judaism creates a life detached from the process of history, the incessant struggle of peoples for power and possession. The Jews' metahistorical position serves to propel them to the goal of history: proleptically they live in eternity, messianic fellowship graced by God's enduring presence.[113] Judaism anticipates this eternity as a community of prayer. The house of Israel gathers at prescribed times to pray in common and know themselves as an eternal "We."[114] In the "cultic prayer" of Judaism the particular time of each individual is super-seded by a common time that foreshadows messianic togetherness. "For the time which the cult prepares for the visit of eternity is not the time of an individual; it is not mine, nor thine, nor his secret time. It is the time of All. Day, week, and year are the common property of all."[115] The consciousness that accompanies cultic prayer "is common to all, beyond all individual points of view and beyond differences of perspective . . . , and so it can be but one thing: the end of all things, the ultimate things."[116] Personal prayer, in contrast to cultic prayer, comes at the height of revelation, when the blessed individual cries out to God to sustain His love.[117] But cultic prayer *precedes* revelation. The congregation knows itself as an "eternal we," and God is obliged to descend into the community and say Amen.[118] The cultic prayer of the Jews then "mediates between revelation and redemption."[119] In united prayer the Jews bear witness to past manifestations of God's love and record their faith in future revelations of that love, in such they release upon themselves "the irresistible force of the love of neighbor."[120] Israel thus anticipates the redemptive advent of the ethical messianic kingdom and

112. Ibid., p. 405.
113. On Rosenzweig's understanding of Judaism's role in history, see A. Altmann, "Franz Rosenzweig on History," in A. Altmann, ed., *Between East and West: Essays Dedicated to the Memory of Bela Horovitz* (London, 1958), pp. 194–214, esp. pp. 200–05.
114. *Star*, pp. 292 f. Cf. "The We are eternal; death plunges into the Nought in the face of this triumphal shout of eternity. Life becomes immortal in redemption's eternal hymn of praise" (ibid., p. 253).
115. Ibid., p. 292.
116. Ibid., pp. 292 f.
117. Ibid., pp. 184 f.
118. Ibid., p. 293.
119. Ibid., p. 294.
120. Ibid., p. 293.

God's presence graces their community of prayer: He "can do no other; he must accept the invitation."[121] Paradoxically, although despised for their separateness, Israel is looked upon by the peoples of the world as a source of hope, as an "Eternal light," reminding mankind of the final goal.[122] To be sure, Jewish piety is hardly a matter of ceremonialism, of acts that Kant and his followers would have deemed heteronomous. In *The Star of Redemption*, however, Rosenzweig focuses exclusively on the liturgy of the Jew. Aside for one brief suggestion that the ritual laws "are the sign language of the love of God,"[123] he neglects a discussion of the numerous extraliturgical rituals of Judaism. Such a discussion would have to wait his debate with Buber.

IV

For Rosenzweig the affirmation of Judaism meant his reappropriation into the religion of his forefathers. As a "hymnical"[124] presentation of the piety of the Jews, the third book of *The Star of Redemption* is an eloquent testimony to this desire. Only subsequent to writing *The Star of Redemption*, however, did Rosenzweig include in his purview of Jewish piety those *mitzwot* that extend beyond the precincts of communal prayer. Upon marrying and establishing a Jewish home, and joining his fellow Jews in the study of the tradition, especially the Talmud, Rosenzweig resolved to embrace the Law.[125] The "task of returning home,"[126] as he put it, was now preeminently a matter of the Law, in the fullest sense. To be sure, as he wrote Rudolf Hallo, this resolution did not imply a summary adoption of all "the 613 *mitzwot*." The "all or nothing approach" to Jewish law was certainly not a reasonable expectation of most modern Jews seeking to return to the tradition.[127] For these Jews the question was rather of approaching the Law with "good will" and an "open-ended" attitude, committed to accept as many *mitzwot* as personally possible.[128]

What Rosenzweig meant by "personally possible" was elaborated in "The Builders," his open-letter to Buber, and in the ensuing exchange between

121. Ibid.
122. Ibid., p. 413.
123. Ibid., p. 216.
124. In his theological "disputation" with Rosenstock-Huessy, Rosenzweig noted that ultimately he "would have to show you Judaism from within, that is, to be able to show it . . . in a hymn" (Rosenstock-Huessy, ed., *Judaism Despite Christianity*, p. 133).
125. Glatzer, "Introduction," in Rosenzweig, *On Jewish Learning*, p. 20.
126. "The Builders," p. 91.
127. *Briefe*, p. 425.
128. Ibid.

them; and in correspondence between Rosenzweig and a number of his disciples. In "The Builders" Rosenzweig takes Buber to task for precisely not adopting an open-ended attitude to the Law (das Gesetz = Torah). In his early addresses on Judaism, Buber had categorically dismissed the Law as an option for the modern Jew.[129] In doing such, Buber had characterized the Law as a spiritually desiccated legal code. Rosenzweig protested, charging Buber with an uncritical rehearsal of nineteenth-century prejudices. Specifically, Buber had been misled by the apologists for Jewish tradition Moses Mendelssohn and especially S. R. Hirsch, who held that Israel remained obedient to the Law because God imposed it upon them.[130] Rosenzweig admits that the Law so presented is indeed a dogmatic legalism. However, he asks Buber:

> ... is it really Jewish law with which you try to come to terms? ... Is that really Jewish law, the law of millennia, studied and lived, analyzed and rhapsodized, the law of everyday and of the day of death, petty and yet sublime, sober and yet woven in legend; a law which knows both the fire of the Sabbath candle and that of the martyr's stake? ... [T]he law that always rises beyond itself, that can never be reached—and yet has always the possibility of becoming Jewish life, of being expressed in Jewish faces?[131]

Had Buber maintained an open attitude to the inner power of the Law, as he does regarding the teachings of Israel, he would cease to view the mitzwot as merely Gesetze, heteronomous laws, and acknowledge that the Law can in the living reality (Heutigkeit) of Jewish piety be Gebote, divine commandments that speak to the deepest core of an individual.[132]

It is essential to suspend all preconceptions regarding the Law, for its "inner power" (Kraft)[133] can only be known from within, from "doing."[134] "An outsider," Rosenzweig wrote to a group of his disciples, "no matter how willing and sympathetic, can never be made to accept a single commandment as a 'religious' demand."[135] The commanding voice of God can only be heard from wtihin, from performing the mitzwot. Thus, what in regard to the Law "is do-able and even what is not do-able ... cannot be known like [objective]

129. See "Jewish Religiosity" (1916), in On Judaism, pp. 80, 88, 91 f.; and "The Holy Way" (1919), in ibid., pp. 120, 136–39.
130. "The Builders," p. 78.
131. Ibid., p. 77.
132. Ibid., p. 85. "Heutigkeit" is apparently Rosenzweig's coinage. Cf. "dies imperativische Heute des Gebots" and "Die ganze Offenbarung tritt unter das grosse Heute" (Stern, 2. Teil, 115).
133. "The Builders," p. 85.
134. Ibid.
135. On Jewish Learning, p. 121. Cf. also Briefe, no. 413 (November 1924).

knowledge, but can only be done."[136] In the performance of a *mitzwah* we obtain the possibility of quickening its inner power. This inner power is that which transforms the *mitzwah* from a law to a commandment. As commandment the *mitzwah* becomes "our inner power," giving the performance of the *mitzwah* a fullness of spontaneous deed. The commandment we hear from *within* the *mitzwah* addresses "not our will but our ability to act."[137] Hearing the commanding voice of God, the question of appropriating His commandment to our will is irrelevant, for His commandment has already been transformed into "our inner power"; His will already animates our actions. Unlike "a general law (*ein allgemeines Gesetz*) [which] can address itself with its demands to the will"—the reference seems clearly to be to the universal ethical law of the Kantian variety—"ability carries in itself its own law; there is only my, your, his ability, and built on them, ours; not everybody's. . . . The deed is created at the boundary of the merely do-able, where the voice of commandment causes the spark to leap from 'I must' to 'I can.' The Law is built on such commandments, and only on them."[138] In that a *mitzwah* becomes a question of *my* "inner ability," of *my* "inner must,"[139] as he wrote Hallo, it is not a coercive, but a free act. Indeed, only as a free act enjoined by the commanding voice of God does the performance of a *mitzwah* obtain its religious fulness.

It is the Law's *Heutigkeit*, its living, contemporary reality that grants it religious validity. This *Heutigkeit* more than the fact that God gave it to six hundred thousand Israelites at the foot of Mt. Sinai authenticates the Law. The historicity of the Sinaitic Revelation "certainly does play a part, but no greater part than all we have mentioned before, and all that our ancestors perceived in every 'today' of the Torah: that all the souls of all generations to come stood on Sinai along with those six hundred thousand, and heard what they heard."[140] Rosenzweig even admits that he is not certain whether the traditional content of the Law is truly divine,[141] for after all Revelation is but

136. *On Jewish Learning*, pp. 81 f.
137. Ibid., p. 86.
138. Ibid.
139. *Briefe*, p. 427.
140. *On Jewish Learning*, p. 79. Cf. "Hat wohl je ein Jude früher, wenn er nicht gefragt wurde, gemeint, er hielte das Gesetz—und das Gesetz ihn—nur deswegen, weil es von Gott Israel unterm Sinai auferlegt sei? Gewiss, wenn man ihn fragte, so mochte vielleicht dieser Grund sich in seinem Bewusstsein nach vorne drangen. . . . Aber den fraglos Lebenden war dieser Rechtsgrund des Gesetzes nur einer neben andern gewesen und kaum der stärkste" (*Kleinere Schriften*, pp. 110 f.). For Rosenzweig the Sinaitic revelation is not primarily a historical concept. I. Heinemann suggests that Rosenzweig's thinking on this matter was encouraged by the views of an Orthodox Jew, Saul Kaatz, *Die mündliche Lehre und ihr Dogma*, vol. I (Frankfurt a/M, 1922–23); see Heinemann, *Ta'ame ha-Mitzwot be-Sifrut Yisra'el* (Jerusalem, 1956), II, 293 n. 110.
141. Letter to Buber, June 5, 1925; included in *On Jewish Learning*, p. 117.

the disclosure of God's love.[142] (He does, however, believe "in the right of the Law to prove its character as an exception against all other types of law.")[143] What is significant is that the *mitzwot* are heard as divine commandments; this experience is akin to that "of the theo-human reality of the commandment that permits us to pray. . . ."[144] That is to say, *mitzwot qua* divine commandments mark a revelatory experience of God's love. Rosenzweig seems to be suggesting then that the *mitzwot qua* religious rite have a sacramental power, that is, as a recent student of Rosenzweig comments, the *mitzwot* may become "vehicles for further Revelation,"[145] an opportunity to behold God's presence. Thus we can understand the somewhat enigmatic statement he made to Rudolf Hallo: "Judaism is not law, but it creates law."[146] *Ab initio* and ideally the *mitzwot* are performed not as heteronomous obligations, but as God's commandments, as such they are a locus for the theo-human encounter. The *mitzwot* are then recorded, so to speak, as a testimony to their revelatory power, serving as an invitation to all Jews in every generation. This invitation is not a guarantee but it points in faith to the *mitzwot*'s revelatory possibility.[147] The corpus of these invitations, the Law of Moses, provide individual Jews with a "common landscape."[148] Within this landscape traditional Jews tread upon a single path encompassing all the *mitzwot*. The *ba-al teshuvah*, the modern Jew seeking to return to the Tradition, finds within this landscape his own path—those sets of *mitzwot*—in which he *personally* hears the commanding voice of God.[149]

V

Buber's response was succinct: "God is not a law-giver."[150] *Ergo*, the *mitzwot*—as all ritual precepts—do not stem from God. "I do not believe that

---

142. Ibid., p. 118. Cf. "Gott offenbart in der Offenbarung eben nur immer—die Offenbarung. Anders gesagt: er offenbart immer nur sich selbst dem Menschen, dem Menschen sich selber. Dieser Akkusativ und Dativ in seiner Verbindung ist der einzige Inhalt der Offenbarung" (Rosenzweig, *Jehuda Halevi*, 2. Auf. [Berlin, s.d.], p. 174).

143. *On Jewish Learning*, p. 118.

144. Ibid., p. 122.

145. Haberman, "Rosenzweig's Doctrine of Revelation," p. 335.

146. "Das Judentum *ist nicht* Gesetz. Es schafft Gesetz" (*Briefe*, p. 425 [italics in original]).

147. Cf. "Not that doing [the *mitzwot*] necessarily results in hearing and understanding [the voice of God]. But one hears differently in doing" (*On Jewish Learning*, p. 122).

148. *Briefe*, p. 426.

149. Ibid., pp. 426 f.

150. *On Jewish Learning*, p. 115. Buber actually refused to engage Rosenzweig in debate on this issue. He confined his reply to a few brief letters, publishing them reluctantly in 1935 in the *Schocken Almanach (auf das Jahr 5697)*, "Offenbarung und Gesetz," pp. 147–54. For an analysis of

revelation is ever a formulation of law."[151] God's commandments are issued ever anew according to the unique exigencies of each situation; these commandments demand a dialogical (*qua* ethical)[152] response. "I cannot [accept formalized laws] if I am to hold myself ready as well for the unmediated word of God directed to a specific hour of life."[153] Recurrent throughout Buber's writings is an antagonism toward rituals as a proper form of divine-human encounter.[154] In "Herut," the essay that prompted Rosenzweig's open-letter, Buber refers to rituals as "unholy conditionalities."[155] Specifically, "religion is detrimental to an unfolding of the people's energies only where it concentrates . . . on the enlargement of *the thou shalt not,* on the minute differentiation between the permitted and the forbidden. When this is the case, it neglects its true task, which is and remains: man's response to the Divine, the response of the total human being . . . the sanctification of the relationship to all things; that is *freedom in God.*"[156] Here Buber sponsors a typical Kant-informed attitude toward ritual, insisting that ethics (i.e., dialogue) is true

---

the "debate" from various perspectives, see D. Bruisin, "Rosenzweig's Approach to Jewish Law," *Reconstructionist,* XL, no. 5 (June 1974), 7–12; Heinemann, *Taʿame ha-Mitzvot,* II, 212, 220 f.; B. Kraut, "The Approach to Jewish Law of Martin Buber and Franz Rosenzweig," *Tradition,* XII, nos. 3–4 (Winter/Spring 1972), 49–71; B. Kruzweil, "Three Views on Revelation and Law," *Judaism,* IX, no. 4 (Fall 1960), 292–98; I. Maybaum, "Das Gesetz. Franz Rosenzweigs Ringen mit den jüdischen Traditionen," *Emuna. Horizonte zur Diskussion über Israel und das Judentum,* V, no. 2 (March 1970), 86 ff.; and H. J. Schoeps, "Franz Rosenzweig und seine Stellung zum jüdischen Gesetz," *Theologische Literaturzeitung,* LXXX (Berlin, 1955), 119–24.

151. *On Jewish Learning,* p. 111.

152. Cf. "[Buber locates] the source of the moral 'ought' in dialogue" (M. Friedman, "The Bases of Buber's Ethics'" in P. S. Schilpp and M. Friedman, eds., *The Philosophy of Martin Buber* [LaSalle, 1967], p. 177).

153. *On Jewish Learning,* p. 111.

154. For references to Buber's attitude toward ritual prior to his exchange with Rosenzweig, see n. 129, above. This attitude was not altered through the exchange; if anything, Buber became more adamant in his opinion. A passage not included in the letters Buber published in the *Schocken Almanach* (and thus not in the English translation of those letters in *On Jewish Learning*) reads: "Offenbarung ist nicht Gesetzgebung. Für diesen Satz würde ich in einer jüdischen Weltkirche mit Inquisitionsgewalt hoffentlich zu sterben bereit sein" (Buber, *Briefwechsel aus sieben Jahrzehnten,* 3 vols. [Heidelberg, 1973], II, 222 [Letter to Rosenzweig: June 3, 1925]). For a typical expression of his attitude in his later period, see "The Silent Question" (1952), in *On Judaism,* p. 203. Ernst Simon interprets a passage in Buber's novel, *For the Sake of Heaven* [Hebrew] (1941), as his final reply to Rosenzweig. In the novel, Yeshaja, the Hasidic rabbi, who (Simon believes) represents Rosenzweig, warns the 'Yehudi' (Buber) that his teaching does not provide sufficient guidance for the community. "Buber gives the 'Yehudi' the last word but it is not the expression of victorious triumph: 'Maybe it will come about as you say, Yeshaja. But we dare not spare ourselves. God marches to His victory along the path of our defeats.' Here ends the dialogue in which Buber castigates himself more severely than any critic could have done. 'They parted from each other with their friendship unimpaired but in a sadness which knew no comfort'" (Simon, "Martin Buber and German Jewry," *LBIYB,* III [1958], pp. 35 f.).

155. "Herut," p. 152.

156. Ibid., p. 158 (italics added).

devotio.[157] Buber, of course, radically parts from Kant in his affirmation of divine revelation. Like Rosenzweig, he believes God speaks to man in time.[158] That the Sinaitic Revelation had a special status in God's continuous self-revelation, however, he refused to accept. "[I cannot endorse] the belief in a one-time revelation, transmitted in its entirety and binding for all time."[159] Rosenzweig also affirms that God continually discloses Himself to man, but he does so to the Jew preeminently through the ritual "laws" (qua commandments) associated with the Sinaitic Revelation: "For me, too, God is not a Law-giver. But He commands. It is only by the manner of his observance that man in his inertia changes the commandments into Law, a legal system with paragraphs, without the realization that 'I am the Lord,' without 'fear and trembling,' without the awareness that the man stands under God's commandment."[160] Buber did not share this faith. Ritual as "human law" (Menschengesetz) could not 'generate' God's revelatory Presence.[161] Buber was a religious anarchist, suspicious of all formal structures of devotio.[162] The difference between Buber and Rosenzweig perhaps ultimately lies in their varying conceptions of a renewed Judiasm. For Buber, this renewal would come with the restoration of the "primal" Jewish awareness of the truth of dialogue and the quest to realize that truth in communal life; traditional Jewish modalities of community, based as they are on the Law, are not at all essential to this vision.[163] For Rosenzweig, on the other hand, the restoration of the Law to the center of Jewish life was the very focus of his vision of a renewed Judaism. Thus in adumbrating this vision to his contemporaries, he

157. Fritz Kaufman observes: "The meditative movement toward God . . . [Buber] consciously pushes into the background in favor of an evocative movement that emphasizes the 'primacy of practical reason.' I use this expression purposely in order to call attention to the affinity (in spite of all differences) between Buber's thinking and Kant's" (Kaufman, "Buber's Philosophy of Religion," in Schilpp and Friedman, eds., The Philosophy of Martin Buber, pp. 213 ff.). Note the language in this passage from Buber: "Judaism knows that true autonomy is one with true theonomy: God wants man to fulfill his commands as a human being, and with the quality peculiar to human beings. The law is not thrust upon man; it rests deep within him, to waken when the call comes" (Buber, "Teaching and Deed" [1934], in Buber, Israel and the World [New York, 1948], p. 142). Buber's metanomian attitude, however, was more consciously influenced by Nietzsche; see my Von der Mystik zum Dialog: Martin Bubers geistige Entwicklung bis hin "Ich und Du" (Königstein/Ts., 1978), passim.

158. On Buber's understanding of revelation, see A. A. Cohen, "Revelation and Law: Reflections on Martin Buber's View of Halakhah," Judaism, I, no. 3 (July 1956), 250–56; and E. L. Fackenheim, "Martin Buber's Concept of Revelation," in Schilpp and Friedman, eds., The Philosophy of Martin Buber, pp. 273–96.

159. "Herut," p. 166.

160. On Jewish Learning, p. 116.

161. Briefwechsel, II, 201.

162. Cf. G. Scholem, "Martin Buber and Hasidism: A Critique," Commentary, XXXII (October 1961), p. 315.

163. Cf. "True community is the Sinai of the future" (Buber, "The Holy Way," in On Judaism, p. 139).

sought to indicate that traditional forms of Jewish piety need not offend their Kantian sensibilities; and moreover, Jewish prayer and ritual as channels of God's love could serve as a powerful supplement to ethics.

Rosenzweig's words on the matter of the Law were relatively brief and remained incomplete. His hope to write an extended study of the *mitzwot* was never realized.[164] This is sad for we know that in his later years he sought to adopt and explore the spiritual interior of an increasing number of *mitzwot*. All who visited Rosenzweig during these years gave witness to an observant, deeply pious Jew, who "beheld the presence of God."[165]

164. *Briefe*, pp. 496 f.
165. Glatzer, *Franz Rosenzweig*, p. xxxiv.

Bibliography of Alexander Altmann's Writings

1927–39

1. "Zum Wesen der jüdischen Aesthetik." *Jeschurun,* ed. Joseph Wohlgemuth, XIV (1927), 209–26.

2. "Metaphysik und Religion." *Jeschurun,* XVII (1930), 321–47.

3. *Metaphysik und Religion: Das Problem der absoluten Transzendenz.* Berlin:
   Reuther & Reichard Verlag, 1931. 27 pp. *Identical with 2.*

4. *Die Grundlagen der Wertethik: Wesen, Wert, Person. Max Schelers Erkenntnis-
   und Seinslehre in kritischer Analyse.* Berlin: Reuther & Reichard Verlag,
   1931 (= Berlin, inaugural dissertation, 1931). 113 pp.

5. *Was ist jüdische Thelogie? Beitrage zur jüdischen Neuorientierung.* Frankfurt
   am Main: Verlag des Israelit und Hermon, 1933. 38 pp.

6. "Zwischen Philosophie und Theologie. Drei Buchbesprechungen: Erich
   Przywara, *Analogia Entis* (1932); J. C. Franken, *Kritische Philosophie und
   dialektische Theologie* (1932); Ernst Bergmann, *Entsinkung ins Weiselose*
   (1932)." *Der Israelit* (April 7, 1933).

7. "Religion und Wirklichkeit. Zur Problematik der Gegenwart." *Bayerische
   Israelitische Gemeindezeitung,* IX (April 15, 1933), 113–18.

8. "Bilanz der Emanzipation. Zwei Buchbesprechungen: Max Wiener,
   Judentum im Zeitalter der Emanzipation (1933); Joachim Prinz, *Wir Juden*
   (1934)." *Der Israelit* (December 21, 1933).

9. "Die religiöse Welt des Mittelalters." *Der Morgen,* X, no. 9 (December
   1934), 390–96.

10. "Erneuerung des Sanhedrin." *Israelitisches Familienblatt,* Hamburg, Feb-
    ruary 7, 1935.

11. *Des Rabbi Mosche ben Maimon More Newuchim (Führer der Verirrten) im
    Grundriss.* Auswahl, Übertragung und Nachwort. Berlin: Schocken
    Verlag, 1935. 88 pp.

12. "Rambam und die Halacha." *Mose ben Maimon 1135–1935. Festbeilage der
    C. -V. -Zeitung,* March 30, 1935.

13. "Der Sinn der Offenbarung in der Lehre des Rambam." *Gemeindeblatt der
    jüdischen Gemeinde zu Berlin,* XXV (March 31, 1935).

14. "Die jüdische Mystik." *Der Israelit* (July 11, 1935).

15. "Die jüdische Mystik." *Bayerische Israelitische Gemeindezeitung,* XI (August
    1, 1935). *Reprint of 14.*

16. "Zur Auseinandersetzung mit der dialektischen Thelogie." *MGWJ,*
    LXXIX, N.F. XLIII (1935), 345–61.

17. "Grundsätzliches zur Arbeitsmethode der Lehrhäuser." *Zion*, VII (August–October 1935), 46–49.

18. "Das Verhältnis Maimunis zur jüdischen Mystik." *MGWJ*, LXXX, N.F. XLIV (1936), 305–30. *See 136.* English translation in *Studies in Jewish Thought: A Selection from the German*, ed. Alfred Jospe. Detroit: Wayne State University Press, 1981.

19. "Bildautorität und Wortautorität." *Bayerische Israelitische Gemeindezeitung*, XII (June 1, 1936).

20. "Olam und Aion. Zum religionsgeschichtlichen Problem der jüdischen Olam haba-Lehre." *Festschrift zum siebzigsten Geburtstage von Jakob Freimann*. Berlin: 1937, pp. 1–14.

21. "Joseph Wohlgemuth 70 Jahre." *Jüdische Rundschau*, Berlin (June 15, 1937).

22. "Um das Erbe Franz Rosenzweigs. Zu zwei Büchern von Ignaz Maybaum." *Jüdische Rundschau* (September 3, 1937).

23. "Dogmen im Judentum?" *Der Morgen*, XIII, no. 6 (September 1937), 228–35.

24. "Gnostische Motive im rabbinischen Schrifttum." *MGWJ*, LXXXIII, N.F. XLVII (1939), 369–89. *Entire volume reprinted Tübingen (1963).*

1940–59

25. "Gnostic Themes in Rabbinic Cosmology." *Essays in honour of the Very Rev. Dr. J. H. Hertz, Chief Rabbi . . . on the occasion of his Seventieth Birthday . . .* , ed. I. Epstein, E. Levine, and C. Roth. London: n.d., pp. 19–32.

26. "Saadya's Theory of Revelation: Its Origin and Background." *Saadya Studies*, ed. Erwin I. J. Rosenthal. Manchester: Manchester University Press, 1943, pp. 4–25. *Reprinted in 139.*

27. "Haluqat ha-Mitzwot le-Rabbi Seʿadya Gaʾon." *Rav Seʿadya Gaʾon*, ed. Yehuda L. Fishman, Jerusalem: 5703, pp. 659–73.

28. "Saadya's Conception of the Law." *Bulletin of The John Rylands Library*, XXVIII (1944), 320–39.

29. "Torat ha-ʾAqlimim le-Rabbi Yehuda ha-Levi." *Melila*, ed. Edward Robertson and Meir Wallenstein. Manchester: Manchester University Press, 1944, pp. 1–17.

30. "Franz Rosenzweig and Eugen Rosenstock-Huessy: An Introduction to Their 'Letters on Judaism and Christianity.'" *The Journal of Religion*, XXIV (1944), 258–70. *See 141.*

31. "Symbol and Myth." *Philosophy*, XX, ed. Sydney E. Hooper (July 1945), 162–71.

32. "The Gnostic Background of the Rabbinic Adam Legends." *Jewish Quarterly Review*, n.s. XXXV (1945), 371–91.

33. *Saadya Gaon. The Book of Doctrines and Beliefs*. Abridged edition. Translated from the Arabic with an Introduction and Notes. Oxford: East and West Library, 1946. 191 pp. *See 92, 122, 140.*

34. "Shire Qedushah be-Sifrut ha-Hekhalot ha-Qedumah." *Melila*, ed. Edward Robertson and Meir Wallenstein, II (1946), 1–24.

35. "Joseph Herman Hertz Memorial Address." *Essays and Addresses in Memory of J. H. Hertz*, ed. Wolf Gottlieb. London: 1946, pp. 1–6.

36. "William Wollaston (1659–1724); English Deist and Rabbinic Scholar." *The Transactions of the Jewish Historical Society of England*, XVI (1948), 185–211. *Reprinted in 139.*

37. "Leo Baeck: The Thinker." *Supplement to AJR Information: Tribute to Leo Baeck on the Occasion of his 75th Birthday*. London (May 23, 1948).

38. Review of Karl Kerényi, *Die antike Religion* (1941) and four other works of his (1941–1945). *Philosophy*, XXIV (October 1949), 351–55.

39. "Judaism and World Philosophy." *The Jews: Their History, Culture and Religion*, II, ed. Louis Finkelstein, Philadelphia: Jewish Publication Society of America, 1949, pp. 624–79. Further editions: 1955; 1960 (pp. 954–1009). *See 146.*

40. Review of E. O. James, *The Concept of Deity: A Comparative and Historical Study* (1950). *The Jewish Chronicle* (April 14, 1950).

41. Review of Samuel Rosenblatt, *Saadia Gaon. The Book of Beliefs and Opinions Translated from the Arabic and the Hebrew* (1948). *Bibliotheca Orientalis*, VIII (1951), 193–95.

42. Review of John Baillie, *The Belief in Progress* (1950). *The Jewish Chronicle* (January 19, 1951).

43. "The Modern Analysis of Faith." *Addresses Given at the Ninth Conference of Anglo-Jewish Preachers*. London: 1951, pp. 33–38.

44. "Notes on the Kedusha." *Chayenu*, XX (May–June 1952).

45. "Gishot Shonot la-Historiografia ha-Yisra'elit." *Tarbut*, VI, nos. 7–8 (Nisan-Iyyar 5712/1952), 31–34. *Abridged version of 50.*

46. Review of Walther Eichrodt, *Man in the Old Testament*, trans. K. and R. Gregor Smith (1952). *The Jewish Chronicle* (March 28, 1952).

47. "The Composition of the Berakah." *Chayenu*, XXI (July–August 1952).

48. "Jewish Philosophy." *History of Philosophy Eastern and Western*, II, ed. Sarvepalli Radhakrishnan. London: Allen & Unwin, 1953, pp. 76–92. *See 104.*

49. "Essence and Existence in Maimonides." *Bulletin of The John Rylands Library*, XXXV (1953), 294–315. *Reprinted in 139.*

50. "Gishot Shonot la-Historia ha-Yisra'elit." *Yad Sha'ul. Sefer Zikkaron ʿal Shem ha-Rav Dr. Sha'ul Weingort*, ed. J. J. Weinberg and Pinhas Biberfeld. Tel Aviv: 5713/1953, pp. 133–41. *See 45.*

51. Review of Victor White, *God and the Unconscious* (1953). *The Jewish Chronicle* (March 6, 1953).

52. Review of Max Kadushin, *The Rabbinic Mind* (1953). *The Jewish Chronicle* (April 3, 1953).

53. Review of Morris Ginsberg, *The Idea of Progress: A Revaluation* (1953) *The Jewish Chronicle* (July 10, 1953).

54. "Aristo we-ha-Yahadut." *EI*, V (5713/1953), 853–60.

55. "God and the Self in Jewish Mysticism." *Judaism*, III (Spring 1954), 1–5.

56. "The Legacy of Maimonides." *The Jewish Chronicle* (July 2, 1954).

57. "Isaac Israeli." *The Manchester Review* VII (1955), 246–47.

58. Review of *Theologie als Glaubenswagnis: Festschrift Karl Heim*. *JJS*, VI (1955), 253–54.

59–62. (Ed.) *Journal of Jewish Studies*, VI, VII, VIII, IX (1955–59).

63. "What is Judaism?" *The Observer* (July 1, 1956).

64. Review of Arnold Toynbee, *An Historian's Approach to Religion* (1956). *The Jewish Chronicle* (November 30, 1956).

65. "Tribute to Leo Baeck." *AJR Supplement in Memory of Leo Baeck* (December 1956).

66. "Theology in Twentieth Century German Jewry." *LBIYB*, I (1956), 193–216.

67. "In Memoriam Leo Baeck." *JJS*, VI (1956), 1–2.

68. "Isaac Israeli's 'Chapter on the Elements' (Ms Mantua)." *JJS*, VII (1956), 31–57.

69. "A Note on the Rabbinic Doctrine of Creation." *JJS*, VII (1956), 195–206. *Reprinted in 139.*

70. "Isaac Israeli's *Book of Definitions*: Some Fragments of a Second Hebrew Translation." *Journal of Semitic Studies*, II (1957), 232–42.

71. Review of Abraham J. Heschel, *God in Search of Man. A Philosophy of Judaism* (1956). *The Manchester Guardian* (March 6, 1957).

72. Review of Eric Voegelin, *Order and History. Volume I: Israel and Revelation* (1956). *The Manchester Guardian* (March 22, 1957).

73. Review of H. J. Schoeps, *Jüdische Geisteswelt, Zeugnisse aus zwei Jahrtausenden* (1953). *Journal of Semitic Studies*, II (1957), 407.

74. "In Memoriam—Isaak Heinemann." *JJS*, VIII (1957), 1–3.

75. Review of *Evangelium Veritatis Codex Jung*, ed. M. Malinine, H. -C. Puech, G. Quispel (1956). *JJS*, VIII (1957), 228.

76. Review of *Studia Patristica*, I–II, ed. K. Aland and F. L. Cross (1957). *JJS*, VIII (1957), 232–34.

77. Review of Georges Vajda, *L'Amour de Dieu dans la théologie juive du moyen age* (1957). *JJS*, VIII (1957), 236–37.

78. Review of *The Oxford Dictionary of the Christian Church*, ed. F. L. Cross (1957). *JJS*, VIII (1957), 249.

79. "Ma'amar be-Yihud ha-Bore'." *Tarbiz*, XXVII (1958), 301–9. Presented to Gershom G. Scholem in honor of his sixtieth birthday.

80. *Isaac Israeli. A Neoplatonic Philosopher of the Early Tenth Century. His Works Translated with Comments and an Outline of His Philosophy*, jointly with S. M. Stern. London: Oxford University Press, 1958. 226 pp.

81. (Ed.) *Between East and West. Essays Dedicated to the Memory of Bela Horovitz*. London: East and West Library, 1958. 214 pp.

82. "Franz Rosenzweig on History." *Between East and West* (no. 81), pp. 194–214. *Reprinted in 139.*

83. *Tolerance and the Jewish Tradition*. Robert Waley Cohen Memorial Lecture, 1957. London: The Council of Christians and Jews, 1958. 19 pp.

84. *Jewish Studies. Their Scope and Meaning Today*. Hillel Foundation Annual Lecture. London: 1958. 16 pp.

85. *Vorwort* to Siegmund Hurwitz, *Die Gestalt des sterbenden Messias*. Zürich and Stuttgart: Rascher Verlag, 1958, pp. 7–8.

86. "Be'ayot be-Mehqar ha-Neo-Aflatoniut ha-Yehudit." *Tarbiz*, XXVII (1958), 501–7.

87. Review of Leo Schaya, *L'Homme et l'absolu selon la kabbale* (1958). *JJS*, IX (1958), 101–2.

88. "The Motif of the 'Shells' (Qelipoth) in ʿAzriel of Gerona." *JJS*, IX (1958), 73–80. *Reprinted in 139.*

89. Review of Georges Vajda, *L'Amour de Dieu*. . . . *KS*, XXXIV (1959), 52–54. *See 77.*

1960–1976

90. "Chassidism Today." In commemoration of the bicentary of the death of the Baal Shem Tov. *The Jewish Chronicle* (May 20, 1960).

91. "Jewish Studies: Their Scope and Meaning Today." *Reflections, 1960*, ed. Jack Parnes (Toronto, 1960), 5–12. *Reprinted from 84.*

92. "Saadya Gaon: Book of Doctrines and Beliefs." *3 Jewish Philosophers*. Philadelphia: Meridian Books and The Jewish Publication Society of America, 1960. 191 pp. *Reprinted from 33. See 33, 122, 140.*

93. Review of Else Freund, *Die Existenzphilosophie Franz Rosenzweigs*, Second Revised Edition (1959). *Historia Judaica*, XXII (1960), 76–78.

94. "Eleazar of Worms' Hokhmath Ha-'Egoz." *JJS*, XI (1960), 101–12. *Reprinted in 139 under the title: "Eleazar of Worms' Symbol of the Merkava."*

95. Review of Georges Vajda, *Isaac Albalag, averroïste juif, traducteur et annotateur d'Al Ghazali* (1960). *KS*, XXXVII (1961–62), 197–200. Also in *Bulletin of the School of Oriental and African Studies*, XXV (1962), 167–168.

96. "Zur Frühgeschichte der jüdischen Predigt in Deutschland: Leopold Zunz als Prediger." *LBIYB*, VI (1961), 3–59.

97. Review of Max Scheler, *On the Eternal in Man*, trans. Bernard Noble (1960). *Conservative Judaism*, XVII (1962), 87–89.

98. "Hermann Cohens Begriff der Korrelation." *In Zwei Welten: Siegfried Moses zum fünfundsiebzigsten Geburtstag*, ed. Hans Tramer. Tel-Aviv: 1962, pp. 377–99.

99. "Hashgahah ba-Pilosofia ha-Yehudit shel Yeme ha-Beynayim." *EI*, XV (5722/1962), 478–83.

100. "Wolfson, Sebi (Harry Austryn)." *EI*, XV (5722/1962), 919–20.

101. (Ed.) *Biblical and Other Studies*. Philip W. Lown Institute of Advanced Judaic Studies, Brandeis University Studies and Texts, Volume I. Cambridge: Harvard University Press, 1963. 266 pp.

102. "The Delphic Maxim in Medieval Islam and Judaism." *Biblical and Other Studies. See 101.* Pp. 196–232. *Reprinted in 139.*

103. "Nahum N. Glatzer: The Man and His Work." *Judaism*, XII (1963), 195–202.

104. "Jewish Philosophy." *Philosophy A to Z*, ed. James Gutmann. New York: 1963, pp. 89–104. *Reprinted from 48.*

105. "An Unknown Letter by Abraham Geiger." *Living Legacy*, Dedicated to Hugo Hahn on the occasion of his 70th birthday. Ed. Bernhard N. Cohn. New York: 1963, pp. 105–13.

106. "Aristobulus of Paneas." *EB*, II (1963), 387.

107. "Cabala." *EB*, IV (1963), 536–539.

108. (Ed.) *Studies in Nineteenth Century Jewish Intellectual History*. Philip W. Lown Institute of Advanced Judaic Studies, Brandeis University Studies and Texts, Volume II. Cambridge: Harvard University Press, 1964. 215 pp.

109. "The New Style of Preaching in Nineteenth-Century German Jewry." *Studies in Nineteenth Century Jewish Intellectual History*, pp. 65–116. *See 108.*

110. Review of Julius Guttmann, *Philosophies of Judaism*, trans. David. W. Silverman (1964). *Conservative Judaism*, XIX (1964), 73–77.

111. Review of *The Guide of the Perplexed. By Moses Maimonides*. Trans. with an Introduction and Notes by Shlomo Pines. With an introductory essay by Leo Strauss (1963). *The Journal of Religion*, XLIV (1964), 260–61.

112. "Ahad Haam." *EB*, I (1964), 408.

113. "Crescas, Hasdai." *EB*, VI (1964), 726.

114. "Gersonides." *EB*, X (1964), 367.

115. "Ibn Falaquera." *EB*, XII (1964), 34.

116. "Ibn Gabirol." *EB*, XII (1964), 34.

117. "Israeli, Isaac ben Solomon." *EB*, XII (1964), 732.

118. "León, Moses ben Shem-Tob de." *EB*, XIII (1964), 932.

119. "Maimonides." *EB*, XIV (1964), 684–85.

120. "Philo." *EB*, XVII (1964), 739–41.

121. "Li-She'elat Ba'aluto shel Sefer Ta'ame ha-Mitzwot ha-Meyuhas le-Rabbi Yitzhaq ibn Farhi." *KS*, XL (1965), 256–76, 405–12.

122. "Saadya Gaon: Book of Doctrines and Beliefs." *Three Jewish Philosophers*, New York: Harper Torch Books, 1965. *See 33, 92, 140.*

123. "Ibn Bajja on Man's Ultimate Felicity." *Harry Austryn Wolfson Jubilee Volume*, I. Jerusalem, 1965, pp. 47–87. *Reprinted in 139.*

124. "The Divine Attributes. An Historical Survey of the Jewish Discussion." *Judaism*, XV (Winter 1966), 40–60.

125. (Ed.) *Biblical Motifs: Origins and Transformations*. Philip W. Lown Institute of Advanced Judaic Studies, Brandeis University Studies and Texts, Volume III. Cambridge: Harvard University Press, 1966. 251 pp.

126. "Moses Mendelssohn on Leibniz and Spinoza." *Studies in Rationalism, Judaism and Universalism in Memory of Leon Roth*, ed. Raphael Loewe. London: 1966, pp. 13–45. *Reprinted in 139 and 208.*

127. "Midrash 'Allegori 'al pi Derekh 'ha-Qabbalah ha-Penimit' 'al Bereshit kaf-dalet." *Sefer ha-Yovel Tif'eret Yisra'el li-Khevod . . . Yisra'el Brodie*, ed. Z. Y. Zimmels, Y. Rabinovitz, and Y. S. Feinstein. London: 5727/1967. Hebrew part pp. 57–65.

128. (Ed.) *Jewish Medieval and Renaissance Studies*. Philip W. Lown Institute of Advanced Judaic Studies, Brandeis University Studies and Texts, Volume IV. Cambridge: Harvard University Press, 1967. 384 pp.

129. "Moses Narboni's 'Epistle on Shi'ur Qoma': A Critical Edition of the Hebrew Text with an Introduction and an Annotated English Translation." *Jewish Medieval and Renaissance Studies*, pp. 225–64. *See 128. Reprinted in 139.*

130. "An Ode to Professor Tzwi (Harry Austryn) Wolfson on the Occasion of his Eightieth Birthday." (Hebrew.) *Ha-Do'ar*, XLVIII (November 3, 1967).

131. "An Ode to Professor Harry A. Wolfson Octogenarian." *Jewish Advocate.* (November 9, 1967).

132. "The Ladder of Ascension." *Studies in Mysticism and Religion Presented to Gershom G. Scholem on his Seventieth Birthday by Pupils, Colleagues, and Friends.* Jerusalem: 1967, pp. 1–32.

133. "*Homo Imago Dei* in Jewish and Christian Theology." *The Journal of Religion,* XLVIII (1968), 235–59.

134. "Eine neu aufgefundene Moses Mendelssohn-Korrespondenz zur Frage des Selbstmords." *Zeitschrift für Religions- und Geistesgeschichte,* XX (1968), 240–58.

135. "Moses Mendelssohns Kindheit in Dessau." *Bulletin des Leo Baeck Instituts,* X (1967), 237–75.

136. "Das Verhältnis Maimunis zur jüdischen Mysrik. *Wissenschaft des Judentums im deutschen Sprachbereich,* ed. Kurt Wilhelm. Tübingen: 1968, pp. 441–60. *Reprinted from 18.*

137. "'Yerushalayim' shel Mendelssohn be-'Ispaqlaryah Biografit Hadasha." *Zion,* XXXIII (5728/1968), 47–58.

138. "'Moses Mendelssohn's Gesammelte Schriften': Neuerschlossene Briefe zur Geschichte ihrer Herausgabe." *Bulletin des Leo Baeck Instituts,* XI (1968), 73–115.

139. *Studies in Religious Philosophy and Mysticism.* Ithaca: Cornell University Press, 1969. London: Routledge & Kegan Paul, 1969. Plainview, N.Y.: Books for Libraries Press. 1969. *Includes 26, 36, 49, 70, 82, 88, 94, 102, 123, 126, 129, 132.*

140. "Saadya Gaon: Book of Doctrines and Beliefs." *Three Jewish Philosophers.*" New York: Atheneum, 1969. *See 33, 92, 122.*

141. "Franz Rosenzweig and Eugen Rosenstock-Huessy: An Introduction to Their 'Letters on Judaism and Christianity.'" *Judaism Despite Christianity,* ed. Eugen Rosenstock-Huessy. University, Ala.: University of Alabama Press, 1969, pp. 26–48. *Reprinted with minor revision from 30.*

142. *Moses Mendelssohns Frühschriften zur Metaphysik Untersucht und Erläutert.* Tübingen: J. C. B. Mohr (Paul Siebeck), 1969. 396 pp.

143. "Briefe Karl Gotthelf Lessings an Moses Mendelssohn." *Lessing Yearbook,* I. Munich, 1969, pp. 9–59.

144. "Die Entstehung von Moses Mendelssohns Phaedon." *Lessing Yearbook,* I. Munich, 1969, pp. 200–233. *Reprinted in 208.*

145. "Lessing und Jacobi: Das Gespräch über den Spinozismus." *Lessing Yearbook,* III. Munich: 1971, pp. 25–70. *Reprinted in 208.*

146. "Judaism and World Philosophy: From Philo to Spinoza." *The Jews: Their*

Role in Civilization, ed. Louis Finkelstein. New York: Schocken Books, 1971, pp. 65–115. *Reprinted, with the omission of the last section, from 39.*

147. (Ed.) *Moses Mendelssohn. Gesammelte Schriften Jubiläumausgabe*, I. Stuttgart-Bad Cannstatt: Frommann-Holzboog, 1971.

148. *Geleitwort* to 147, pp. v–viii.

149. "Albo, Joseph." *EJ*, II (1971), 535–37.

150. "Angels. In Jewish Philosophy." *EJ*, II (1971), 973–76.

151. "Aristotle. Jewish Aristotelianism." *EJ*, III (1971), 445–48.

152. "Articles of Faith." *EJ*, III (1971), 654–60.

153. "Beatitude." *EJ*, IV (1971), 359–63.

154. "Bible. Allegorical Interpretations." *EJ*, V (1971), 895–99.

155. "Commandments, Reason for." *EJ*, V (1971), 783–89.

156. "God. Attributes of God." *EJ*, VII (1971), 664–69.

157. "Israel, Isaac ben Solomon." *EJ*, IX (1971), 1063–65.

158. "Moses ben Joseph Ha-Levi." *EJ*, XII (1971), 421–22.

159. "Providence. In Medieval Jewish Philosophy." *EJ*, XIII (1971), 1282–84.

160. "Maimonides' 'Four Perfections.'" *Israel Oriental Studies*, II, *In Memoriam* Samuel Miklos Stern. Tel-Aviv University: 1972, pp. 15–24.

161. "Das Menschenbild und die Bildung des Menschen nach Moses Mendelssohn." *Mendelssohn Studien. Beiträgen zur neueren deutschen Kultur- und Wirtschaftsgeschichte*, I, ed. Cécile Lowenthal-Hensel. Berlin: 1972, pp. 11–28. English translation in *Studies in Jewish Thought: A Selection from the German*, ed. Alfred Jospe. Detroit: Wayne State University Press, 1981. *Reprinted in 208.*

162. "Mitzwah ba-Sifrut ha-Yehudit ha-Hellenistit—bi-Yeme ha-Beynayim—ba-Zeman he-Hadash." *EI*, XXIV (5732/1972), 116–19.

163–165. (Ed.) *Moses Mendelssohn. Gesammelte Schriften Jubiläumsausgabe*, II, III(1), XIV. Stuttgart-Bad Cannstatt: Frommann-Holzboog, 1972. 428 pp., 464 pp. cxix, 386 pp.

166. "The Divine Attributes: A Survey of the Jewish Discussion." *Faith and Reason*, ed. Robert Gordis and Ruth B. Waxman. New York: 1973, pp. 9–29. *Reprinted with bibliographical additions from 124.*

167. "Mal'akhba-Sifrut ha-Yehudit ha-Hellenistit u-vi-Yeme ha-Beynayim." *EI*, XXIII (5733/1973), 518–20.

168. "Ishaq b. Sulayman al-Isra'ili." *Encyclopaedia of Islam*, IV (1973), 111.

169. *Neuerschlossene Briefe Moses Mendelssohns an Friedrich Nicolai*. In Gemeinschaft mit Werner Vogel herausgegeben von Alexander Altmann. Stuttgart: 1973. 122 pp.

170. *Moses Mendelssohn: A Biographical Study*. University, Ala.: University of

Alabama Press, 1973. Philadelphia: The Jewish Publication Society of America, 5733/1973. London: Routledge & Kegan Paul, 1973. 900 pp.

171. "Eternality of Punishment: A Theological Controversy within the Amsterdam Rabbinate in the Thirties of the Seventeenth Century." *PAAJR*, XL 1972 (1973), 1–88.

172. "Neuerschlossene Briefe Moses Mendelssohns an Friedrich Nicolai." *Lessing Yearbook*, V (1973, appeared 1974), 13–60. *A selection, with a revised preface, from 169.*

173. *Leo Baeck and the Jewish Mystical Tradition*. Leo Baeck Memorial Lecture 17. New York: Leo Baeck Institute, 1974. 28 pp.

174. (Ed.) *Moses Mendelssohn. Gesammelte Schriften Jubiläumsausgabe*, III(2). Stuttgart-Bad Cannstatt: Frommann-Holzboog, 1974. 342 pp.

175. *Vorbemerkung* to *174*.

176. "Letters from Dohm to Mendelssohn." *Salo Wittmayer Baron Jubilee Volume*, English section, Volume I. Jerusalem: 1974. New York-London: 1974. Pp. 39–62.

177. "The Religion of the Thinkers: Free Will and Predestination in Saadia, Bahya and Maimonides." *Religion in a Religious Age*, ed. S. D. Goitein. Cambridge, Mass.: Association for Jewish Studies, 1974, pp. 25–51.

178. "The Philosophical Roots of Mendelssohn's Plea for Emancipation." *JSS*, XXXVI (1974), 191–202. *Reprinted in 208.*

179. "A Tribute." *A Tribute in Appreciation of Professor Harry Austryn Wolfson*. Brookline, Mass.: Hebrew College, 1974, pp. 3–7.

180. "The German Rabbi: 1910–1939." *LBIYB*, XIX (1974), 31–49.

181. "Moses Mendelssohn's Proofs for the Existence of God." *Mendelssohn Studien*, II, ed Cécile Loewenthal-Hensel. Berlin: 1975, pp. 9–29. *Reprinted in 208.*

182. "Leo Strauss—In Memoriam." *PAAJR*, XLI–XLII (1975), xxxiii–xxxvi.

183. *Moses Mendelssohn. Gesammelte Schriften Jubiläumsausgabe*, XII(1), Briefwechsel II(1). Bearbeitet von Alexander Altmann. Stuttgart-Bad Cannstatt: Frommann-Holzboog, 1976. 332 pp.

184. *Moses Mendelssohn. Gesammelte Schriften Jubiläumsausgabe*, XII(2), Briefwechsel II(2). Bearbeitet von Alexander Altmann (Stuttgart-Bad Cannstatt: Frommann-Holzboog, 1976. 276 pp.

185. "Lessings Glaube an die Seelenwanderung." *Lessing Yearbook*, VIII (1976), 7–41. *Reprinted in 208.*

1977–81

186. *Moses Mendelssohn. Gesammelte Schriften Jubiläumsausbage*, XIII. Brief-

wechsel III. Bearbeitet von Alexander Altmann. Stuttgart-Bad Cannstatt: Frommann-Holzboog, 1977. 436 pp.

187. (Ed.) *Moses Mendelssohn. Gesammelte Schriften Jubiläumsausgabe,* IV. Stuttgart-Bad Cannstatt: Frommann-Holzboog, 1977. 549 pp.

188. "Maimonides and Thomas Aquinas: Natural or Divine Prophecy?" *AJSreview,* IV (1978), 1–19.

189. "Gewissensfreiheit und Toleranz: Eine begriffsgeschichtliche Untersuchung." *Mendelssohn Studien,* IV, ed. Cécile Loewenthal-Hensel and Rudolf Elvers. Berlin: 1979, pp. 9–46. *Reprinted in 208.*

190. Mendelssohn, Moses. Collected Works. 20-Volume Jubilee Edition. *Philosophy and History,* XII(1) (1979), *German Studies,* Section I, 34–37.

191. *Moses Mendelssohn Briefwechsel der letzten Lebensjahre.* Sonderausgabe eingeleitet von Alexander Altmann. Stuttgart-Bad Cannstatt: 1979, 342 pp.

192. "Moses Mendelssohn et les preuves de l'existence de Dieu." *Archives de Philosophie,* XLII (1979), 397–419. *Translation of 181.*

193. *Isaac Israeli* [*see 80*]. Reprint: Westport, Conn.: Greenwood Press, 1979.

194. "Mendelssohn, Lavater und Lessing." *Mitteilungen aus dem Lessingjahr 1979, Heft 2.* Wolfenbüttel: 1979, pp. 10–11.

195. "Aufklärung und Kultur: Zur geistigen Gestalt Moses Mendelssohns." *MB Wochenzeitung des Irgun Olej Merkas Europa,* XLVII (September 21, 1979), nr. 35/36, 5–6, 16.

196. "Isaac Israeli on Creation and Emanation." *Harvard Studies in Jewish Intellectual History,* ed. Isadore Twersky. Cambridge: Harvard University Press, 1979, pp. 1–15.

197. "Sefer 'Or Zaruʿa le-Rabbi Mosheh de Leon, Mavoʾ, Text Qriti we-Heʿarot." *Kobez Al Yad,* IX (XIX), pp. 217–93. Ed. E. E. Urbach. Jerusalem: 1979.

198. "Gersonides' Commentary on Averroes' Epitome of Parva Naturalia, II.3. Annotated Critical Edition." *American Academy for Jewish Research Jubilee Volume.* New York: 1980, pp. 1–31.

199. "Moses Mendelssohn on Miracles." *Hommage à Georges Vajda. Etudes d'histoire et de pensée juives.* Louvain: 1980, pp. 463–77. *Reprinted in 208.*

200. "Moses Mendelssohn on Excommunication: The Ecclesiastical Law Background." *Studies in the History of Jewish Society . . . Presented to Jacob Katz,* English Section. Jerusalem, 1980, pp. 41–61. *Reprinted in 208.*

201. "Festansprache zur Feier des 250. Geburtstages von Moses Mendelssohn am 6. September 1979." *Jahrbuch der Stiftung Preussischer Kulturbesitz.* Berlin: 1980.

202. 'Baqashat ha-Herut ba-Pilosofia ha-Politit shel Mosheh Mendels-sohn." *Da'at*, V (Summer 5740/1980), 13–24. *See 211, 212.*

203. "Aufklärung und Kultur: Zur geistigen Gestalt Moses Mendelssohns." *Ich handle mit Vernunft. Moses Mendelssohn und die deutsche Aufklärung,* ed. Norbert Hinske. Hamburg: Felix Meiner Verlag, 1981. *Combines 195 and parts of 201.*

204. "Moses Mendelssohn über Naturrecht und Naturzustand." *Ich handle mit Vernunft. Moses Mendelssohn und die deutsche Aufklärung,* ed. Norbert Hinske. Hamburg: Felix Meiner Verlag, 1981. *Reprinted in 208.*

205. *Moses Mendelssohn Gesammelte Schriften Jubiläumausgabe,* VI(1). Bearbeitet von Alexander Altmann. Mit einem Beitrag von Fritz Bamberger. Stuttgart-Bad Cannstatt: Frommann-Holzboog, 1981.

206. *Essays in Jewish Intellectual History.* Hanover, N.H.: The University Press of New England, 1981.

207. *Prinzipien politischer Theorie bei Mendelssohn und Kant.* Mit einem Vorwort von Arnd Morkel. Trierer Universitätsreden. Trier, 1981. *Reprinted in 208.*

208. *Die trostvolle Aufklärung. Studien zur Metaphysik und politischer Theorie Moses Mendelssohns.* Stuttgart-Bad Cannstatt: Frommann-Holzboog, 1981. *Includes 126, 144, 145, 161, 178, 181, 185, 189, 199, 200, 204, 207.*

209. "Adolf Altmann (1879–1944). A Filial Memoir." *LBIYB* (1981).

210. "He'arot 'al Hitpattehut Torato ha-Qabbalit shel Rabbi Menahem 'Azaryah mi-Fano." *Sefer Yesha'yah Tishby.* Jerusalem, 1981.

211. "The Quest for Liberty in Moses Mendelssohn's Political Philosophy." *Humanität und Dialog. Proceedings of the Los Angeles International Lessing-Mendelssohn Symposium,* ed. Ehrhard Bahr and Lawrence G. Lyon. Detroit: Wayne State University Press, 1981. *Enlarged version of 202.*

212. "The Quest for Liberty in Moses Mendelssohn's Political Philosophy." *Lessing Yearbook,* XII (1981). *Reprint of 211.*

Index to Subjects and Names

Index to Classical and Medieval References

I. Biblical and Pseudepigraphical texts

II. *Rabbinics*